INTRODUCTION TO ORGANISATION AND MANAGEMENT

PEARSON

At Pearson, we have a simple mission: to help people make more of their lives through learning.

We combine innovative learning technology with trusted content and educational expertise to provide engaging and effective learning experience that serve people wherever and whenever they are learning.

We enable our customers to access a wide and expanding range of market-leading content from world-renowned authors and develop their own tailor-made book. From classroom to boardroom, our curriculum materials, digital learning tools and testing programmes help to educate millions of people worldwide — more than any other private enterprise.

Every day our work helps learning flourish, and wherever learning flourishes, so do people.

To learn more, please visit us at: www.pearsoned.co.uk/personalised

INTRODUCTION TO ORGANISATION AND MANAGEMENT

Fourth Edition

Selected cases and articles from:

Harvard Business Review
Oxford Review of Economic Policy
The American Magazine
Business History Review
Academy of Management Executive
McKinsey Quarterly
Trinity Business School, Trinity College Dublin
Sloan Management Review
Organizational Dynamics
California Management Review
The New York Times Magazine
Academy of Management Perspectives

PEARSON

Harlow, England • London • New York • Boston • San Francisco • Toronto • Sydney • Auckland • Singapore • Hong Kong
Tokyo • Seoul • Taipei • New Delhi • Cape Town • Sao Paulo • Mexico City • Madrid • Amsterdam • Munich • Paris • Milan

Pearson Education Limited
Edinburgh Gate
Harlow
Essex CM20 2JE

And associated companies throughout the world

Visit us on the World Wide Web at:
www.pearson.com/uk

First published 2009
This edition © Pearson Education Limited 2016

ISBN 978-1-78448-468-2

Printed and bound in Great Britain by CPI Group.

Contents

Introduction

Introduction to Organisation and Management is your first course with the Trinity Business School, and is one component of Trinity's unique common first year programme for students in Business, Economic and Social Sciences. The course is designed as a foundation course for students intending to take business as part of their degree and as an overview course for those who do not so intend. The course assumes no prior study of organisation and management.

At a general level, it is intended that students taking this course will come to appreciate the centrality of organisations in modern society, and why the study of their origins, form, management, and performance is so important. Another objective is to introduce students to a new way of learning and studying – by independent inquiry, critical appraisal, debate and discussion. In place of a traditional textbook, the course is designed around a selection of seminal readings, reprinted in this book, representing five themes. These themes are: (i) *the historical context of organisations & management*, (ii) *the competitive environment of organisations*, (iii) *modes of organising*, (iv) *managing people*, and (v) *managing today*.

Each of these themes is structured around a central question – the answers to which are not always clear or perhaps even fully known. The *historical* theme explores the emergence of the modern organisation in the nineteenth century and its development to the present day. The *competitive environment* theme explores how organisations are shaped by the environments in which they operate. The *modes of organising* theme considers how best to design organisations so that they achieve the objectives set for them. The *managing people* theme looks at the task of leading today's organizations. Finally, the *managing today* theme explores an issue of contemporary interest – in this instance, the question of corporate social responsibility and sustainability.

The course does not follow the traditional large lecture method of many first year university courses. Instead, the course is taught through a comprehensive series of *plenary lectures* and a *seminar programme* with business school faculty and doctoral students. Eight two-hour plenary lectures serve to introduce each of the main themes. Twelve small-group seminars allow students to explore themes in greater detail through discussion and debate with Business School faculty.

Those of you who proceed to take Business as part of your degree, will find yourselves returning to these readings in subsequent years, so I advise you to retain the book. Finally, I hope that you enjoy the course and find the reading stimulating and challenging.

John Quilliam

May 2015

Theme 1

The Historical Context of Organisations & Management

The Enduring Logic of Industrial Success

Alfred D. Chandler

In 1881, John D. Rockefeller combined Standard Oil and 39 allied companies to form the Standard Oil Trust. His aim was not monopoly. Linked by financial ties, the companies in the Trust already controlled close to 90% of the kerosene produced in the United States. Rockefeller's goal was the cost advantages that could only be realized by placing the companies' refining facilities under a single management.

Quickly, the Trust's management concentrated close to one-quarter of the world's production into three 6,000 barrel-a-day refineries. Thanks to economies of scale, the unit cost per gallon dropped from 2.5 cents in 1879 to 0.5 cents in 1884 and to 0.4 cents in 1885. With this fivefold reduction in costs, Standard Oil could undersell kerosene made from Russian oil in Europe and kerosene made from Southeast Asian oil in China and still generate profits that created at least three of the world's largest industrial fortunes. Its successor, Exxon, remains the nation's biggest oil company.

At the same time in Germany, Bayer, BASF, and Hoechst—the world's oldest and still largest chemical companies—were driving down the price of dyes and pharmaceuticals by using economies of scope to reduce their production costs. Alizarin, a new, man-made red dye widely used in yarns, fabrics, and leather products, is representative. When the German companies began producing the dye, its price was close to 200 marks per kilo. By 1878, the price per kilo had dropped to 23 marks, and by 1886, it had fallen even further, to 9 marks. By the end of the 1880s, the large German plants were producing more than 500 different dyes and pharmaceuticals at unit costs far below those of smaller competitors.

Over the next century, these stories were repeated in the other industries that have been most critical to the growth of modern economies. Whether we look at chemicals and electrical equipment in the 1880s and 1890s, motor vehicles in the 1920s, or computers today, the same pattern recurs. The dominant companies are those whose founders and senior executives understood what I call the logic of managerial enterprise, that is, the dynamic logic of growth and competition that drives modern industrial capitalism.

By conforming to this logic, entrepreneurs and managers helped to make Germany the most powerful industrial nation in Europe before World War I, the United States the most productive country in the world from the 1920s to the 1960s, and Japan their most successful competitor since that time. Conversely, ignoring the logic—departing from its basic principles—in large part explains why the United States lost its competitive capabilities in such vital

Alfred D. Chandler, Jr. is the Isidor Straus Professor of Business History, Emeritus at the Harvard Business School. Among his best-known books are Strategy and Structure *(MIT Press, 1962) and* The Visible Hand: The Managerial Revolution in American Business *(Harvard University Press, 1977). He also assisted Alfred Sloan in the writing of* My Years with General Motors *(Doubleday, 1963).*

industries as semiconductors, machine tools, and consumer electronics.

The term managerial enterprise refers to large industrial concerns in which operating and investment decisions are made by a hierarchy of salaried managers governed by a board of directors. Recently, such organizations have been roundly attacked for dissipating wealth and stifling innovation. In fact, they have been the engines of economic growth and social transformation in industrial nations for the past 100 years. This lesson emerges clearly from my 10-year study of the 200 largest manufacturing companies in the United States, Britain, and Germany from the 1880s, when the modern industrial corporation first appeared, until World War II. (The insert "The Making of *Scale and Scope*" contains a brief overview of this research.) But we also see it reflected in the pages of the current business press. The logic that drives the creation and growth of large managerial enterprises is as relevant now as it was when John D. Rockefeller put together Standard Oil.

THE LOGIC OF MANAGERIAL ENTERPRISE

The logic of managerial enterprise begins with economics—and the cost advantages that scale and scope provide in technologically advanced, capital-intensive industries. In these industries, large plants can produce products at a much lower cost than small ones because the cost per unit drops as the volume of output rises. (This is what is meant by economies of scale.) In addition, large plants can use many of the same raw and semifinished materials and intermediate production processes to make a variety of different products. (This is what is meant by economies of scope.) But these potential cost advantages can be fully realized only if the flow of materials through the plant can be kept constant to assure capacity utilization. That is why entrepreneurs like Rockefeller did not build giant industrial works until the 1880s, when integration of the railroad, the telegraph, the steamship, and the cable made it possible to speed goods and messages through an entire economy for the first time. It is also why large plants quickly became so common in chemicals, branded packaged foods, steel, agricultural machinery, and all the other "high technology" industries of the late nineteenth century.

But size alone is not enough to fully exploit the cost advantages of scale and scope. To capitalize on their manufacturing investments, the entrepreneurs who built these large plants had to make two related sets of investments. They had to create national—and then international—marketing and distribution organizations. And they had to recruit teams of managers: lower and middle managers to coordinate the flow of products through production and distribution, and top managers to coordinate and monitor current operations and to plan and allocate resources for future activities. Those who first made these large investments—the companies I call first movers—quickly dominated their industries and continued to do so for decades.[1] Those who failed to make these investments rarely became competitive at home or in international markets, nor did the industries in which they operated.

The advantages of being a first mover were immense. To benefit from comparable costs, challengers had to build plants of comparable size—even as the first movers were working out the bugs in the new production processes. Challengers had to create distribution and sales organizations to capture markets where first movers were already established. They also had to recruit management teams to compete with those already well down the learning curve in their specialized activities of production, distribution, and research and development. Challengers did appear. But they were few.

First movers' investments also transformed the structure of the industries in which they competed. These soon came to be dominated by a small number of large companies that vied for market share and profit in new ways. In these competitive battles, innovation and strategy were more powerful weapons than price. As far back as the 1890s, companies like Singer Sewing Machine, Procter & Gamble, and National Cash Register were competing by improving quality and creating new markets as well as by lowering costs. They searched for ways to carry out production and distribution more capably. They engaged in systematic research and development to improve their products and processes. They located better sources of supply and provided more effective marketing services. They differentiated their products (in branded packaged products, primarily through advertising). And they moved rapidly into growing markets and out of declining ones. The test of such competition was market share—and in the new oligopolistic industries, market share and profits changed constantly.

Such competition sharpened the product-specific capabilities of both workers and managers, and these, in turn, became the basis for continuing growth. Companies did grow horizontally (by combining with competitors) and vertically (by moving backward to control materials and forward to control outlets). But such moves were usually responses to specific opportunities. Long term, management's strategy was to grow by moving into related product markets or by moving abroad. In 1913, for instance, the two largest commercial enterprises in Imperial Russia were

The Making of *Scale and Scope*

The historical data in this essay are drawn from *Scale and Scope: Dynamics of Industrial Capitalism* (Harvard University Press, 1990), a comparative study of managerial enterprise in the United States, Great Britain, and Germany from the 1880s through the 1930s. For more than half a century, these three countries accounted for some two-thirds of the world's industrial output. Thus their 200 largest manufacturing companies—the companies whose collective histories *Scale and Scope* reports—constitute a global sample from which the patterns of growth and competitiveness described in this essay clearly emerge.

For information on individual companies I consulted a wide variety of sources: company and industry histories; scholarly monographs; journal articles and other secondary sources; investment directories such as *Moody's Manual* for the United States, *The Stock Exchange Yearbook* for Great Britain, and the *Handbuch der deutschen Aktiengesellschaften* for Germany; published company and governmental reports; and, for those whose histories were most revealing, archival records. These sources provide information on changing product lines, production processes, shifts in markets, and sources of supply. They also indicate how and when companies grew: by direct investment, by merger and acquisition, by expansion overseas, and by expansion into new product lines. Finally, in many cases, they identify the company's senior decision makers as well as the nature of the critical decisions these managers had to face and the decision-making processes they used.

Singer Sewing Machine and International Harvester (and these were not the largest of those companies' European operations).

Geographic expansion was usually based on economies of scale, while moves into related product markets more often rested on economies of scope. In both cases, however, organizational capabilities honed by oligopolistic competition provided the dynamic for continuing growth—of the companies themselves, the industries they dominated, and the national economies in which they operated.

COMPETITIVE DYNAMICS: WHERE BRITAIN WENT WRONG

The dynamics of the new competitive battles—and the costs of disregarding the logic of managerial enterprise—are evident in the history of British industry in the years before the second world war. Chemicals is a case in point. Of all the industries developed in this period (which historians rightly call the Second Industrial Revolution), chemicals was the most technologically advanced and provided the widest range of new industrial and consumer products. Among those products were medicines, fertilizers, textiles, film, and the industry's first major innovation—synthetic dyes.

An Englishman, William Perkin, invented the first man-made dyes in 1856, and in the 1860s and 1870s Britain had almost every comparative advantage in the new industry. Dyes are made from coal, and Britain had the largest supplies of high-quality coal in Europe. Its huge domestic textile industry constituted the world's largest market for the new dyes. All it lacked was experienced chemists, and British entrepreneurs had little trouble hiring trained German chemists for their factories. By any economic criteria, British entrepreneurs should soon have dominated the world in this new industry. Instead, German companies—Bayer, BASF, Hoechst, and three smaller enterprises—took the lead. Why? Because they made the essential investments in production, distribution, and management that the British industrialists failed to make.

Bayer's experience is representative. In the late 1870s, Friedrich Bayer & Co. was a relatively small pioneer. Under the guidance of Carl Duisberg, a chemist still in his twenties, the company began exploiting economies of scope—developing first new dyes and then pharmaceuticals. Then in 1891, it decided to expand by purchasing a dye maker on the Rhine at Leverkusen, near Cologne, a location that was better for receiving raw materials and shipping finished goods than Bayer's original works at Elberfeld. At first, plans called for enlarging the Leverkusen plant. But then Duisberg convinced his colleagues to scrap the existing facilities and build a giant new works that would meet the company's needs for the next half century. (Today, almost 100 years later, Leverkusen is still one of the most efficient chemical plants in the world.)

Duisberg designed the new works to assure a steady flow of material from arrival through production to storage and shipment of the final products. He also made sure that each of the five production departments had its own laboratories and engineering staff and that the offices of the production engineers were close to the chemical laboratories so that "works chemists can at any time get into direct communication with the works engineers." As a result, Leverkusen's laboratories became and remained among the most innovative in the world, producing a stream of new dyes, pharmaceuticals, films, pigments, resins, and other products.

At the same time, Bayer invested heavily in marketing, distribution, and management. By the time the Leverkusen works went into operation, Bayer's global sales force of experienced chemists was contacting and working with more than 20,000 customers, all of whom had to be taught how to apply the new synthetic dyes to their materials. And by the turn of the century, Bayer had created one of the largest and most carefully defined managerial hierarchies the world had yet seen.

The Germans' competitive advantages demolished Britain's economic comparative advantages. In 1913, 160,000 tons of dye were produced. German companies made 140,000 (with the big three accounting for 72% of that output); 10,000 more came from Swiss neighbors up the Rhine. Total British production—4,400 tons. Figures for pharmaceuticals, films, agricultural chemicals, and electrochemicals tell much the same story.

A similar scenario was played out in the electrical equipment industry after 1882, when the first central power station opened in New York City. The industry sparked by Thomas Edison's inventions transformed economic life in myriad ways: by providing sources of light and power that altered urban living and transportation; by changing the ways of the workplace; and by giving rise to new industrial methods such as electrolytic processes for producing copper and other materials. British pioneers were as active in this industry as any in Germany or the United States. Sir William Mather, the senior partner of Mather & Platt, one of the largest British textile machinery manufacturers, obtained the Edison patents at the same time that Emil Rathenau did at AEG. But in the 1880s and 1890s, it was AEG and Siemens—and General Electric and Westinghouse in the United States—that made the essential first-mover investments, not Mather & Platt.

Again, the German story is instructive. In 1903, after merging with a major competitor, Siemens embarked on a ten-year plan to assure its global position, systematizing and rationalizing production by concentrating its operations under a single management. The result was the world's largest industrial complex, a giant set of works covering several square miles that Siemens financed largely from retained earnings. (The municipality of Berlin that the complex dominated soon became officially known as Siemensstadt.) Where Bayer had built a single works, Siemens constructed several in which more than 20,000 workers made telecommunications equipment and instruments, large machinery, small motors, dynamos, electrochemicals, and cables. Its domestic rival AEG built a similar though somewhat less massive set of works only a few miles away during these same years.

By 1913, two-thirds of the electrical equipment machinery made in British factories by British labor came from subsidiaries of GE, Westinghouse, and Siemens. AEG sold more products in Britain than the largest British company. Mather & Platt had become a minor producer of electrical equipment for factories. From the 1890s on, research and development to improve existing products and develop new ones was carried out in Schenectady, Pittsburgh, and Berlin—but not in Britain.

What was true of chemicals and electrical equipment was also true in heavy and light machinery, steel, and copper and other metals. In metals the British pioneered, but Germans and Americans made the essential investments that drove the British out of international markets. In machinery the British did not even try. German companies quickly took the lead in producing heavy processing machines and equipment for the new industries of the second industrial revolution (as well as many of the old). Americans acquired a near-global monopoly in sewing, business, agricultural, and other light machinery produced by fabricating and assembling standardized parts. By the 1880s, this high-volume production process was already known as "the American system of manufacturing."

As these examples suggest, the opportunity to make first-mover investments and create a managerial enterprise is short-lived. And once the opportunity is lost, it is hard for an enterprise and its national industry to regain competitive capabilities, even in its own domestic market. The British did succeed in chemicals through the creation of Imperial Chemical Industries (ICI), as the insert "Regaining Competitive Capabilities" relates. But that was the only major technologically advanced industry in which they ever regained a strong competitive edge.

COMPETITIVE DYNAMICS: WHAT IBM DID RIGHT

The passage of time has not made the logic of managerial enterprise obsolete. On the contrary, its principles were clearly at work in the development of the computer industry after World War II, and they drive competition in the industry today. But there is one striking historical difference: most of the computer industry's pioneers were long-established managerial enterprises in closely related industries, not entrepreneurs.

U.S. business machine companies were the first to see the commercial possibilities of the costly giant computers initially developed for scientific and military purposes. In 1951, Remington Rand, the nation's leading typewriter company, began to develop UNIVAC, the first computer designed for business uses. Other leading business machine companies—IBM,

Regaining Competitive Capabilities

By 1900, the German chemical companies had driven nearly all the pioneering companies in Britain out of business. Earlier, the dye makers had petitioned Parliament for tariff or other protective legislation. But the British textile manufacturers—the most powerful industrial group in England—were delighted with the low price and high quality of the German products, while British scholars and policymakers had come to accept free trade as both an economic theory and an article of faith. (The fact that in the 1890s Britain was still the world's largest exporter of machine-made goods doubtless deepened their commitment.) So the dye makers had little hope of government protection, and their enterprises failed.

Then came World War I. To meet acute shortages, the British producer expanded its output. The government set up another enterprise, British Dyestuffs Corporation, and then, in 1918, acquired the private company. This expansion of capacity plus the greatly enlarged output of the Swiss producers (Ciba, Geigy, and Sandoz) permitted Britain to obtain essential dyes at high cost.

Once the war was over, however, the German companies came back quickly. By 1921, the newly appointed head of British Dyestuffs told the Board of Trade that he saw little hope of making the company competitive unless it acquired technical skills from the Germans. The latter were willing enough to strike a deal, but their proposal would give them de facto control. British Dyestuffs would become little more than their selling agents in Britain. Neither the Conservative nor the Labour party could accept such terms.

In 1925, the government pulled out, but British Dyestuffs did little better in private hands. As 1926 opened, Reginald McKenna, head of the Midland Bank, former Chancellor of the Exchequer, and former chairman of the Board of Trade's committee to supervise British Dyestuffs, began to plead with one and then the other of the two largest British chemical companies, Nobel Industries and Brunner, Mond, to take British Dyestuffs under their wing. His pleas set off a series of complex negotiations that led to the formation of Imperial Chemical Industries (ICI) in the fall of 1926. (By then, both industry and government saw the merger as an essential response to the creation of I.G. Farben, which consolidated Bayer, BASF, Hoechst, and five smaller German chemical companies.)

Nobel Industries and Brunner, Mond were the *only* two chemical companies in Britain that had recruited a substantial set of top and middle managers. And both had strengthened their organizational capabilities after the war. Nobel Industries had acquired several

small explosives producers and then become one of the first companies in Britain to do what had become standard practice in the United States—reorganize and rationalize the merged companies. Explicitly following the example of its American ally, E.I. du Pont de Nemours, Nobel Industries centralized its administrative structure, created functional departments, closed down 44 older factories, sold off obsolete plants and equipment, and invested in up-to-date machines.

Brunner, Mond, the other merger partner, had grown more by direct investment in plant and personnel than by acquisitions. Of these investments, by far the most costly and important was one to produce synthetic nitrates for fertilizers through a process acquired from the Germans as a spoil of war. By 1926, Brunner, Mond had invested £3 million in the project (undertaken at the urging of the British government) and had yet to show a profit. Once fully in operation, however, it assured Britain a strong position in international markets.

More reorganization and rationalization followed the formation of ICI. Eventually, management created a multidivisional structure with autonomous integrated divisions, or "groups," for explosives, synthetic alkalis, dyestuffs, nitrates and fertilizers, and chemicals, among others. By the 1930s, ICI was becoming an effective global competitor in all these products. Agreements struck by international cartels during the depression years reflect its growing strength. In the nitrate agreement of 1932, for example, ICI received a quota of close to 20% and exclusive marketing rights in several large markets. That same year, it obtained close to 10% in comparable agreements on dyes—a far cry from the outcome of the British Dyestuffs negotiations in the early 1920s. As one ICI executive observed, "the only way BDG [ICI's Dyestuff Group] could get into the dye business was to invent its way in. The I.G. [Farben] never took much notice of BDG until they found that BDG could invent."[1]

As this comment indicates, capabilities developed in exploiting economies of scale and scope encouraged process and product innovation. From 1933 through 1935, the dyestuffs laboratory came up with 87 new products including rubber goods, chemicals, synthetic resins and lacquers, detergents, pesticides, and pharmaceuticals.

The moral? Through management's decisions and actions, ICI and its two predecessors were able to achieve what too few British industrial enterprises have ever done: develop the product-specific facilities and skills essential to obtain and maintain a competitive position in world markets.

Burroughs Adding Machine, National Cash Register, and Honeywell (all players in their industry for decades)—quickly followed. Still other pioneers were large, established enterprises with electronics capabilities—Raytheon, General Electric, RCA, and Philco. The only new company to enter the competition was Control Data, founded by William Norris in 1957.

All these pioneering companies made substantial investments in producing and distributing the new machine. But IBM was the first to make the investments that transformed it into the industry's first mover. The strategy of IBM's top managers, particularly Thomas Watson, Jr., was to pursue as wide a commercial market as possible. Several years of intensive investment in research and production led, in 1964, to the introduction of the System 360, a broad line of compatible mainframe computers with peripherals for a wide range of uses. IBM's massive investment in research and production, the swift expansion of its international marketing organization, and an impressive increase in its management ranks gave the company the dominant industry position it retains today.

With the single exception of Control Data, IBM's successful mainframe competitors continued to be business machine companies, all of which acquired electronics companies to improve their production and research competences. In contrast, the electronics companies dropped out of the business. Raytheon and General Electric sold their operations to Honeywell. RCA's computer activities were acquired by Sperry Rand. And Philco dropped its computer operations soon after it was taken over by the Ford Motor Company. These companies had as great a potential for success in computers as the business machine companies did. But by the 1960s, they had become widely diversified. Because computers were only one of many product lines, top management was unwilling to allocate the time and make the large investments necessary to build an effective competitive capability. (Much the same thing has happened more recently in consumer electronics.)

Entrepreneurial companies played a greater role in mini- and microcomputers where opportunities existed to design machines using different technologies for different markets. Nevertheless, the logic holds: the successful companies followed a first-mover strategy. At Digital Equipment, for example, heavy investments in manufacturing for the PDP-8 line of minicomputers were accompanied by the creation of a worldwide marketing network and a sharp rise in the number of managers. Edson de Castro, the engineer who headed the design team for the PDP-8, made a comparable set of investments when he left DEC in 1968 to form Data General. However, the third pioneer, Scientific Data Systems, failed to scale up and quickly disappeared from the scene after it was acquired by Xerox in 1969.

The most successful challengers to DEC and Data General were not entrepreneurial enterprises but managerial companies. By 1980, DEC ranked second and Data General fourth in revenues generated. IBM was first, Burroughs third, and Hewlett-Packard, an established producer of electronic measuring and testing instruments, fifth. The sixth was Wang Laboratories, a first mover with a new product for a different market—word processing and office systems. Together these six accounted for 75% of the revenues generated in the minicomputer branch of the industry.

Much the same pattern appears in personal (micro) computers. By 1980, the first entrepreneurial companies to make extensive three-pronged investments—Apple Computer, Tandy, and Commodore—accounted for 72% of U.S. dollar sales. (The three pioneers that accounted for 50% of sales in 1976 had already dropped by the wayside.) Two years later, however, three established companies—IBM, NEC, and Hewlett-Packard—moved in and captured 35% of the market, driving the entrepreneurial first movers' share down to 48%.

Like American machinery manufacturers in earlier years, these computer companies quickly moved abroad. IBM almost immediately became the leading producer of mainframe computers in Europe. DEC led in microcomputers. By the mid-1980s, Apple and IBM were already world leaders in personal computers. Long-established enterprises created all but one of the successful European or Japanese competitors. True to form, British pioneers failed to make the necessary investments in production, distribution, and management. By 1974, only a little over a quarter of all computer installations in Britain came from British producers.

Major players in the industry have changed little in the past decade. Of the 20 largest hardware producers in 1987, only two were founded in the 1980s. The single successful challenger in existing sectors was Compaq (ranked fourteenth in total revenues), whose management announced in its very first annual report that it thought of itself "as a major company in its formative stage rather than as a small company with big plans" and invested accordingly. The other new company, Sun Microsystems (ranked twentieth), followed the path entrepreneurial companies had traditionally taken and developed a new architecture for a new market, workstations.

Conforming to the logic of industrial growth kept U.S. computer companies competitive—even as they encountered hurdles like the rising cost of capital, the fluctuating dollar, and antitrust and other regulatory legislation that are often cited to explain the decline of other industries. In 1987, U.S. companies still enjoyed just under 60% of the European market in mainframe and minicomputers and just over 20% of the Japanese market. In Europe, IBM's market share was 35%, DEC's 7%, Unisys's (formed by the merger of Burroughs and Sperry Rand in 1986) 5%, and Hewlett-Packard's 3%. In Japan, IBM has 15%, Unisys 3%, and NCR 2%. In microcomputers, Apple and IBM (with Japan's NEC) accounted for 50% of the world market. Foreign competition in the United States remains limited except in some peripherals.

In semiconductors, the story has been very different. This industry, which supplies critical components for computers, telecommunications, factory automation, robotics, aerospace, and production controls, was created in the United States. In the mid-1970s, the pioneering American companies held 60% of the world market, 95% of the domestic market, half the European market, and a quarter of the Japanese market. By 1987, their world market share had fallen to 40%, while the Japanese share had risen to 50%. The United States had become a net importer, with the Japanese supplying 25% of its market. Japanese enterprises controlled over 80% of the world's sales of DRAMs invented by the U.S. company, Intel. IBM, the only world-class producer of semiconductors in the United States, is working with the Defense Department through Sematech to try to save the industry.

What happened? Again, the diversified electronics companies with the greatest capabilities for production and continuing research in semiconductors—RCA and GE—pulled out, while Ford's takeover of Philco destroyed the potential there. More serious, though, was the pioneering companies' failure to invest and grow. If IBM is the prototype of the giant managerial enterprise as first mover, surely the semiconductor companies in Silicon Valley epitomize entrepreneurial enterprise. Instead of making the long-term investments to create organizational capabilities and then continuing to reinvest, they remained small or sold out, often to the Japanese. Repeatedly, groups of engineers left their companies to start new ones. Too many companies—both old and new—ignored the logic of industrial growth. Those few that did not—Texas Instruments, Motorola (both established well before World War II), and Intel—remain significant players, America's major hope (with IBM) of staving off the Japanese challenge.

In Japan, on the other hand, makers of semiconductors followed the logic to its profitable conclusion. Like IBM, all made computers; unlike IBM, they produced semiconductors not only for themselves but also for the larger domestic and international markets. These companies—NEC, Hitachi, Toshiba, Mitsubishi Electric, Oki Electric, Fujitsu, and Matsushita—were long-established producers of electrical and telecommunications equipment. They had diversified but only into closely related product lines. Moreover, all belonged to *keiretsu*—groups of allied, independent enterprises with their own bank and trading companies—and these allies provided further financial, marketing, and research benefits.

By aggressively exploiting the cost advantages of scale and scope, these Japanese companies easily drove entrepreneurial American competitors and the large, more widely diversified electronics companies out of the business or into specialized niches. Efforts by the very few remaining U.S. semiconductor companies may permit them to win back market share. But if the experience of British entrepreneurs in the chemical, electrical, and machinery industries is any indication, such restructuring is difficult and the opportunity to regain competitiveness, fleeting.

WHEN LARGE IS NOT LOGICAL

If size makes sense, as I have been arguing, why have so many large U.S. companies done so poorly in the last few decades? Why is size so often a disadvantage rather than an asset? One answer is that like any human institution, managerial enterprises can stagnate. In the 1920s, Henry Ford destroyed his company's first-mover advantages with a series of wrong-headed decisions, including the firing of his most effective executives. Both GM and Chrysler seized the opportunity to challenge Ford's dominance, first by investing in mid- and high-priced cars and then by moving into the low-price range where Ford had held a worldwide monopoly. Only after Henry Ford died—and his son had hired a group of GM managers to restructure the company—did the automaker begin to regain competitive strength and profits. A similar tale is unfolding today, of course, as the Big Three struggle to regain market share and profitability lost to foreign competitors in the 1970s.

More serious to the long-term health of American companies and industries was the diversification movement of the 1960s—and the chain of events it helped to set off. When senior managers chose to grow through diversification—to acquire businesses in which they had few if any organizational capabilities to give them a competitive edge—they ignored the logic of managerial enterprise. Under these circumstances, bigger was worse, not better.

The catalyst for this diversification was unprecedented competitive pressure. Growth has always been a basic goal of managerial enterprises. And as I have already pointed out, growth came primarily by moving abroad or into new markets in related industries. But until the 1960s, the full impact of this international and interindustry competition was held back by world events.

World War I and the massive inflation and military occupation of the Ruhr and the Rhineland that followed kept German companies out of international markets for almost a decade. They returned with impressive strength between 1925 and 1929, only to be reined in again by the coming of the Great Depression, Hitler's command economy, and the disastrous second world war. Depression, global war, and postwar recovery also dampened or redirected the growth of U.S. enterprises and those in other European nations. As a result, the international competition that had been developing before 1914 only became a full-fledged reality in the 1960s, once the economic health of the European nations was fully restored and Japan (following a massive technology transfer) was rapidly industrializing. At the same time, unprecedented investments in research and development were intensifying interindustry competition in the United States and Europe.

This new competition challenged many American companies as they had not been challenged since their founding decades earlier. The challenge was particularly unexpected because the American economy was so prosperous. Even so, markets became saturated. And with capacity underutilized, costs rose.

Many U.S. managers responded as the business machinery executives did, by reinvesting to improve their capabilities in their own and closely related industries. But others began to grow by moving into industries in which their enterprises had no particular competitive advantage. Because they had had little competition abroad since well before World War II—and because they were being told by academics that management was a general skill—many of these executives had come to believe that if they were successful in their own industries they could be just as successful in others. Moreover, their companies were cash-ladened precisely because the postwar years of American hegemony had been so prosperous. So they sought to invest retained earnings in industries that appeared to show a greater profit potential than their own, even though those industries were only distantly related or even unrelated to their companies' core capabilities. And because they lacked knowledge of their targets' operations, they obtained these plants and personnel not through direct investment as in the past but through acquisitions or, occasionally, mergers.

THE TANGLED LOGIC OF DIVERSIFICATION

By the late 1960s, acquisitions and mergers had become almost a mania. The number rose from just over 2,000 in 1965 to over 6,000 in 1969. From 1963 to 1972, close to three-fourths of the assets acquired were for product diversification, and one-half of these were in unrelated product lines. From 1973 to 1977, one-half of all assets acquired through merger and acquisition came from unrelated industries.

Such unprecedented diversification led to another new phenomenon: the separation of top management at the corporate office from the middle managers who were responsible for running the operating divisions and battling for profits and market share. This separation occurred for two reasons. First, top managers often had little specific knowledge of or experience with the technological processes and markets of the divisions or subsidiaries they had acquired. The second was simply that the large number of acquired businesses created an extraordinary overload in decision making at the corporate office. Before World War II, the corporate executives of large, diversified international enterprises rarely managed more than 10 divisions, and only the largest companies had as many as 25. By 1969, many companies were operating with 40 to 70 divisions, and a few had even more.

Because few senior executives had either the training or the experience to evaluate the proposals and monitor the performance of so many different divisions, they had to rely more and more heavily on financial data. But as H. Thomas Johnson and Robert S. Kaplan point out in *Relevance Lost: The Rise and Fall of Management Accounting,* such data were no longer very helpful for understanding the complexities of competitive battles. The reason was simple: accounting methods developed by Carnegie, Brown of Du Pont and General Motors, and other industrialists to manage costs had been replaced by financial reporting techniques devised by professional independent public accountants (imported from Britain) that focused on defining profits.[2]

Managerial weaknesses arising from the separation of top and operating management quickly led to another new phenomenon—the sale of operating units in unheard-of numbers. Before the mid-1960s, divestitures were rare. By the early 1970s, they had become commonplace. In 1965, there was only one divestiture for every 11 mergers; by 1970, it was 1 to 2.4; and from 1974 to 1977, the ratio was close to or even under 1 to 2.

All these mergers, acquisitions, and divestitures established the buying and selling of corporations as a business—and a lucrative one at that. While the industrialists pioneered in this business, the financial community prospered most from it. Many financial institutions (particularly investment banks) turned away from what had been their basic function for almost a century: providing funds to supplement retained earnings to keep people and plants competitive. (Financial institutions in Japan and continental Europe still perform this function effectively.)

The new business was further encouraged by another unprecedented change—this one in the ownership of U.S. industrial companies. Before World War II, most securities were held by relatively wealthy individuals and families. Even as late as 1952, only 4.2% of the American population held corporate securities (and this includes owners of mutual funds). The major institutional investors were insurance companies and the trust departments of commercial banks, which normally invested for growth and assets rather than for short-term gains in share prices and dividends.

After World War II, however, growing numbers of shares were held by pension and mutual funds. Begun in the 1920s, these funds grew little during the depressed years of the 1930s. But by the 1960s, they had come into their own, and their managers were being measured by how well their portfolios performed against the Standard & Poor's indexes. To succeed they had constantly to buy and sell securities. As time passed, they increasingly traded securities in large blocks of 10,000 shares or more.

As the number of such funds and the volume of the securities traded increased, both block sales and turnover rose rapidly. And this made possible still another new phenomenon—the coming of an institutionalized market for corporate control. For the first time, individuals, groups, and companies could obtain control of well-established companies in industries in which the buyers had no previous connections simply by purchasing their shares on the stock exchange. Large blocks of stock were being traded regularly and such buyers had little trouble raising funds for their purchases from financial institutions and financiers.

By the mid-1970s, widespread restructuring was clearly required. Continuing intense competition made it imperative that senior managers reinvest in reshaping and rationalizing operations to maintain—or regain—competitiveness. The same was true for enterprises that had grown huge and unwieldy through unbridled diversification. But the desire of investment banks and other financial institutions to maintain their new and profitable business and the need of pension and mutual fund managers to maintain the current value of their portfolios clearly affected how managers could proceed.

RESTRUCTURING FOR COMPETITIVENESS

Taken together, these phenomena have greatly facilitated corporate restructuring. Large companies can be bought, sold, split up, and recombined in ways that would have been impossible before the acquisition wave of the 1960s. Such restructuring can be destructive. It contributed greatly to the dissolution of powerful U.S. companies such as International Harvester and Singer Sewing Machine, to the loss of others like B.F. Goodrich and Uniroyal to foreign control, and to the destruction of the U.S. machine tool industry. Nevertheless, this flexibility has not been all bad. On the contrary, it can help enhance competitive capabilities if it is used in the service of a carefully considered long-term strategy. Again, the chemicals industry provides a case in point.

The intensified interindustry and international competition of the 1960s hit chemical companies especially hard. Forced to restructure, the managerial enterprises that had long dominated their national industries—Du Pont, Union Carbide, Dow, and Monsanto in the United States—as well as BASF, Bayer, and Hoechst in Germany, Ciba-Geigy in Switzerland, and ICI in Britain—reshaped their product lines and organizational strategies. In the process, they also restructured the industry.

These companies narrowed their product lines, spinning off many of the commodity products, particularly petrochemicals. (At Dow, for example, commodities dropped from 63% of sales to 35% in five years.) They expanded output in existing higher value-added specialties. And they moved into new areas such as pharmaceuticals, biotechnology, and advanced materials, often through acquisitions of pioneering companies. In other words, they stuck to the same basic strategy they had followed for a century—pursuing growth through economies of scope and developing markets that best fit their distinctive core production and research technologies.

New entrepreneurial companies played almost no role in the restructured industry, although some smaller businesses did appear to operate and occasionally consolidate the petrochemical activities the giants had spun off. Today the United States remains an exporter of chemicals. Japanese companies have yet to become serious competitors in U.S. or international markets.

Other manifestations of the market for corporate control can also build competitiveness. Take conglomerates. As long as their executives concentrate on a relatively small number of divisions (as, for example, those at Tenneco do), they can often provide a more effective and immediate discipline over managerial inertia than the product markets can. Similarly, outside directors representing financial institutions or large stockholders can play an important role in reviving stagnant companies by bringing in outsiders to turn the company around. But the basic task of conglomerate managers, outside directors, and new

CEOs must be to recruit managers with the experience and skills to understand the enterprise's complex technological products and processes, the intricacies of its many markets, and the activities of its competitors.

Individual financiers, managers, and shareholders have often profited from ignoring the dynamics of managerial enterprise in capital-intensive industries. But the consequences of their actions have hurt the long-term health of the enterprises and industries involved. The development, production, and distribution of goods for national and global markets require a wide variety of activities calling for many different facilities and skills. Only when all these activities are carefully coordinated can they be integrated in ways that reduce price, assure quality, and provide essential services. Such cooperative efforts are so profitable that if entrepreneurial enterprises fail to become managerial and managerial enterprises fail to maintain and nourish their competitive capabilities, they will lose markets and profits to those in other nations and other industries that do. At least that has been the experience of the industries that have done most to transform the world since the coming of modern transportation and communication networks more than a century ago.

---

1. It is important to distinguish first movers from the inventors of a product or process and from the pioneers who first commercialize an innovation. In mainframe computers, for example, several pioneers invested in marketing the new machines on a national scale. But it was IBM's massive investments in the production, distribution, and management of the System 360 that made it the industry's first mover. Often there is more than one first mover in an industry: BASF, Hoechst, and Bayer were all first movers in chemicals.

2. Boston: Harvard Business School Press, 1987.

VARIETIES OF CAPITALISM IN THE TWENTIETH CENTURY

RONALD DORE
Centre for Economic Performance, London School of Economics and The European Institute of Business Administration (INSEAD)
WILLIAM LAZONICK
University of Massachusetts Lowell and The European Institute of Business Administration (INSEAD)
MARY O'SULLIVAN
The European Institute of Business Administration (INSEAD)

Of the world's multiple national variations on a basically capitalist system, the paper compares the century's history of four—the British and American, the two 'pioneers' whose institutions and economic behaviour patterns most closely confirm to, and those of Germany and Japan whose institutions most significantly deviate from, the prescriptions of neo-classical textbooks. There is no obvious story of a long and steady process of gradual convergence—capitalist rationality slowly washing out the effects of differing cultural traditions,. All four societies have changed in key respects; finance and corporate control structures were arguably more similar in the 1920s than later. By the end of the post-war golden age, there were signs of convergence on similar forms of managerial capitalism. The crucial, and for us unpredictable, question is how far the transition to shareholder capitalism in Britain and America over the last two decades will be duplicated in Germany and Japan.

I. CONVERGENCE TO A DOMINANT MODE?

France, Italy, the Netherlands, China, Argentina— the history of their capitalist institutions over the last century all have their fascinating particularity. In this article, though, we concentrate on Britain, the USA, Germany, and Japan, the four countries at the core of the 'Rhenish versus Anglo-Saxon capitalism' debate which, for all its simplifications, involves central issues of both welfare and economic efficiency.

What pattern does a backward look over the last century of those countries' evolution suggest? Is it one of gradual convergence as the pressures of globalization relentlessly force abandonment of practices deeply rooted in national cultures? That is not the whole story, since arguably there was a greater similarity among the institutions of Japan, Germany, and the United States in the 1920s than today. Is it, then, the story of the rise and fall (at a differing pace in different countries) of a major twentieth-century heresy—the belief that state interference in the economy could have benign effects (the 'mixed economy' notions of the 1960s being pale reflections of Soviet planning)? Hardly, since many of the distinctive features of the Japanese economy have nothing much to do with the state. So is it a story of the stubborn immutability of deep-rooted cultures? Hardly, since institutional evolution (and, in Japan and Germany, great institutional leaps) have been a feature of all four countries. Ebb and flow, then? Apparent convergence towards patterns of managerial capitalism in the 1960s, followed by renewed divergence in the 1980s as increasingly untrammelled market forces and the rising power of institutional investors have transformative effects chiefly in the Anglo-Saxon countries? And then, again in the 1990s, renewed convergence as both the market forces and the investors become more global and increase their impact on Germany and Japan? A possible interpretation. By reviewing the detailed history of this ebb and flow, might one hope to arrive at a reasoned assessment of how far that convergence will go, which is, after all, a crucial determinant of the history of the next century? We certainly do not arrive at confident predictions. Perhaps the reader will.

II. FROM MANAGERIAL REVOLUTION TO GREAT DEPRESSION

(i) Britain

The USA and Germany were coming up fast, but, as the century began, Britain—the 'workshop of the world'—was still the global leader in GDP per capita and exports. Its manufacturing enterprises were still predominantly under family control, while ample supplies of locally concentrated and highly skilled craft workers enabled Britain to dominate the world economy without systematically educating and training technical specialists and administrative personnel to build managerial organizations (Burgess, 1975; Hobsbawm, 1984; Harrison and Zeitlin,

1985; Lazonick, 1990, chs 3–6). In industrial sectors that were characterized by the separation of share ownership from managerial control in other major capitalist economies, proprietary capitalism persisted in Britain through the first half of the twentieth century; top managers were often substantial shareholders by virtue of family connections (Hannah, 1983; Chandler, 1990, pt 2; Church, 1993). Even within science-based enterprises, technical specialists found little opportunity to become, over the course of their careers, generalist 'leaders of men', and, particularly in machine-based enterprises, control over work organization stayed in the hands of craft workers (Lazonick, 1985; Lewchuk, 1987).

If industry, located in the Midlands and the north of England, was the world's workshop, the City of London was the world's banker, and between workshop and bank, the difference in social status was clear. The skills of the Rothschilds and Barings were married to the social cachet of the landed gentry (only Queen Victoria stopped Gladstone from giving Rothschild a peerage in 1869), and successful middle-class manufacturers sent their sons to the same gentlemanly educational institutions—the 'aristocratic' public schools and Oxbridge—that supplied the future élite to City firms as well as to politics, law, colonial administration, and agriculture/estate management (Cassis, 1985; Daunton, 1992). And it was from those public schools, and from the arts, not science, departments of the élite universities, that growing business enterprises recruited their top managers when sons or sons-in-law were unavailable (Coleman, 1973; Sanderson, 1988). British engineers never acquired the social status that their counterparts enjoyed in the United States, Germany, or Japan, even in chemical and electrical engineering, where companies had, perforce, to recruit university-educated engineers, much less in the machine-based industries (Lazonick, 1985).

The power gap between top management who controlled the allocation of resources, and the technical specialists upon whom businesses relied to improve process and product quality and reduce costs, was also a social gap and a cultural gap. The consequent underdevelopment of modern managerial organization contributed to what the Liberal Industrial Inquiry of 1928 called 'remediable inefficiency'—a mixture of 'individualism instead of cooperation, secretiveness instead of publicity, neglect of marketing, indifference and often hostility to research' (Liberal Industrial Inquiry, 1928, p. 127).

(ii) The United States

It was in the United States that, by the 1920s, a much more powerful form of managerial capitalism evolved. Stock ownership came to be separated from managerial control. The Great Merger Movement at the turn of the century played a pivotal role in effecting this separation. Until then, a market in 'industrial' (as distinct from railroad or government) securities did not exist. Wall Street (led by J. P. Morgan) created the market in industrial securities by floating stocks and bonds to carry out mergers, using the money raised or the (now tradable) securities themselves to buy out, and typically retire, the owner-entrepreneurs (Navin and Sears, 1955). Taking their places at the top were salaried managers who had worked their way up and around the increasingly formalized structures of the growing enterprises (Chandler, 1977). As, during the first three decades of the twentieth century, the stocks of these dominant corporations came to be widely held by the public, the stock market became increasingly liquid, while ever fewer stockholders had any interest in exercising their ownership rights to monitor corporate managers (Means, 1930).

But the stock market played only a minor role, in providing new capital. Retained earnings, not external sources of capital, became the financial foundation for investing in the further growth of the industrial enterprise. The managerial organizations which, as Berle and Means pointed out, thus became increasingly autonomous, melded and integrated both executive generalists and technical specialists (Berle and Means, 1932). Their mass-production technologies vastly reduced the need for operator skills, thereby sharpening the line of division between manager and shop-floor worker.

As American industry made the transition from the machine-based first industrial revolution to the science-based second industrial revolution, higher education became central to supplying technical specialists to industrial corporations (Noble, 1977; Servos, 1980). Given the separation of ownership and control, these specialists could potentially over the course of their careers rise to generalist positions as upper-level managers within their enterprises. These university-educated managers took an ever more active interest in ensuring that, in terms of both teaching and research, the system of higher education served corporate needs. They began to create their own corporate research facilities and developed close links with the leading research universities.

New and more automated processes eliminated the need for many of the skilled craft workers. But, the high fixed costs of developing and installing new technology, and the cost of materials tied up in work-in-progress, meant that managers had to win the cooperation of production workers in maintaining the flow of work. In the 1920s 'welfare capitalism, company unions and corporate efficiency' went hand in hand (Jacoby, 1997, p. 21). In what was called the 'non-union era', the promise of long-term employment, a greater recognition of seniority, employee welfare, and subordination of line management to personnel departments offered a softer approach to countering the threat of independent unions than the more directly repressive American Plan (Jacoby, 1985; Lazonick, 1990, chs 7–8).

(iii) Germany

Of our two late developers, the German variety of capitalism is, like those of its British and US counterparts, more deeply rooted in history than the Japanese. Its educational preparation for industrialization was considerable, for instance. Whereas Japan's pre-Meiji education was primarily classical, moral and Confucian, in Germany state-building ambitions, particularly those of Prussia in the wake of its ignominious defeat by Napoleon, provided early incentives for the promotion of technical education. The diffusion of high-level scientific and technical education in the *technische hochschulen* from mid-century and the network of *ingenieur-schulen* for more practical skills created in the 1890s gave German industry a competitive edge, particularly in chemicals, metals, and electrical and heavy machinery (Gispen, 1989; Konig, 1993). The balance of German exports had already shifted from textiles and consumer goods to these technically based industries by the beginning of the century. Although there was still a greater predominance of family enterprise than in the USA, the inheritors of those enterprises were much more likely to have a thorough technical training than in Britain. And in the enterprises that outgrew family control (even while, in the case of Siemens, Krupp, Thyssen, Wolff, and many more, the family still held a majority share of the capital), the hierarchies of salaried managers allowed many of the technically trained to climb to the top (Kocka, 1981; Pohl, 1982; Brockstedt, 1984; Feldenkirchen, 1991).

The second distinguishing characteristic was the *venture-capital* role played by the leading banks, the *Grossbanken*, founded in the decades before and after unification. A typical sequence was as follows. The bank's own technical department or, later, its associated trustee (*Treuhand*) societies, would evaluate an entrepreneurial project and provided the loan capital to enable the new venture to become a going concern. This 'Hausbank' would then arrange a public share flotation that enabled the enterprise to repay its bank loans, while leaving enterprise managers with control over retentions to finance future expansion. Even after the loans were repaid, the bank continued to hold seats on the supervisory boards (which controlled appointments to, and major financial commitments of, the management board) and, through the system of 'bearer shares', held extensive proxy voting rights. In the larger and stronger firms, links with other banks diluted dependence on the Hausbank, but the relation remained close (Barrett Whale, 1930; Kocka, 1980; Pohl, 1984; Feldenkirchen, 1991).

A third characteristic of German managerial capitalism was a greater mobilization, and further development of, the capacity for collective action. Compulsory membership in local chambers of the artisanal *handwerk* (an inheritance from Napoleon) and of the newer chambers of industry provided a basis for developing a widespread apprenticeship system in which firms were induced to train, not simply for their own needs but for their sector's collective needs. The direct continuity in many trades of traditional guild organization made this easier—a factor wholly lacking in 'new country' United States, and largely destroyed by a century of slow pioneer industrialization in Britain (Sorge and Warner, 1986). And the continuity was not merely a matter of 'cultural lag'. Bismarck consciously fostered these traditions by legally bolstering their licensing system as he sought to preserve socially stable artisanal production to counterbalance the dangerous proletarianization of the factory system.

The Bismarckian establishment sought other means of responding to the growing worker movement and deflecting the dangers of class-conflict observed in the early industrializers, notably the social insurance systems in which Germany was a pioneer (Streeck, 1992, p. 112). Works councils to co-opt the worker movement by giving it a legitimate but limited voice were also promoted in the 1890s, but it was not until 1920 and the Weimar Republic, with a much stronger Social Democratic Party, that they became statutory—along with increased regulation of the employment contract and collective bargaining (Braunthal, 1978; McKitrick, 1994, ch. 6)

The expansion for war production, subsequent military defeat, the loss of international markets, and the victors' demands for reparations had a crippling effect on the German economy. The corporate sector responded to Germany's economic crisis by intensifying its capacity for collective action through the formation of industrial concerns (*Konzerne*), that created a dense web of interlocking shareholdings and directorates among companies. In the meantime the process of rationalization and concentration of industrial production during the Weimar years strengthened the power of industrialists and weakened that of workers and their unions. The *handwerk* sector suffered too, caught between the dynamic industrial enterprise on the one hand and the socialism of the working classes on the other. Its frustrations and fears helped in mobilizing the small business sector in what became the Nazi movement, against a ('red', Moscow-puppet, unGerman) labour movement (McKitrick, 1994).

(iv) Japan

Japan was a later late-developer. In 1900, industrialization was barely a quarter century old. From the outset, the nation pursued a strategy of borrowing and improving upon Western technology. Critical to this development effort was the rapid creation of a high-quality system of higher education, supported by the state and pioneering industrialists (Yonekawa, 1984). At the same time, Japan lacked the supplies of skilled craft labour in metalworking technologies that had accumulated in Britain, the United States, and Germany over the course of the nineteenth century. Gradually, however, through education and training, Japan developed its critical metalworking sectors, and during the First World War was able to capture Asian export markets that the Europeans could no longer supply (Gordon, 1985). Japan subsequently made great progress in the manufacture and export of cotton textiles and textile machinery, industries in which by the 1930s it had taken over world leadership from Britain (Mass and Lazonick, 1990). While a relatively small number of cotton spinning companies integrated forward into weaving cotton textile manufacturing, they coexisted with large numbers of family enterprises that specialized in weaving. The widespread adoption of gas and electric engines increased the viability of these family enterprises in weaving, ceramics, export flatware, and engineering parts supply (Minami, 1976).

In the late nineteenth century, state investments in armouries, shipbuilding, steel, mining, and railways (nationalized in 1906) fostered many of the early large-scale enterprises. But ownership and control over many of these state enterprises were handed to the *zaibatsu*, of which Mitsui, Mitsubishi, Sumitomo, and Yasuda emerged as the most prominent. Meanwhile, groups of entrepreneurs launched successful joint-stock companies in a number of industrial sectors, including textiles, paper, and engineering (mechanical, electrical, and chemical) by investing in the training (often including long foreign sojourns) of key engineering personnel who could improve upon and adapt to local conditions technologies that were borrowed from abroad. During the first decades of the twentieth century, many of these joint-stock companies affiliated with the *zaibatsu*, which by the 1940s had become the biggest conglomerates in the world (Morikawa, 1992).

Ownership of the *zaibatsu* was in the hands of powerful families who ran their empires by building substantial managerial organizations. From the late nineteenth century, they recruited engineers and administrators from the nation's new universities, and created promotion systems that enabled these managers to advance within the enterprise group over the course of their careers. The *zaibatsu* and their constituent enterprises were strategic in making long-term employment commitments to their personnel. As a general rule, they made these commitments only to highly trained technical and administrative employees within the managerial structure (Morikawa, 1997). But, for lack of work-

ers trained in industrial skills, in the decades between the wars, a small number of innovative enterprises began developing formal training and promotion schemes for key blue-collar workers as well (Gordon, 1985). Yet, despite such incipient attempts to extend organizational integration to the shop floor, a distinguishing feature of the inter-war period was the emergence of class-conscious protest movements by those workers on low pay and in unstable employment. The intensified industrial unrest of the 1920s sparked off a brief policy debate between those who favoured the British legitimate conflict approach and those heirs of the Japanese transplant, *Verein für Sozialpolitik*, who favoured the 'harmonize–suppress' approach. The latter won, and founded the influential Harmonization Society (*Kyochokai*) to mediate—often remarkably even-handedly—in industrial disputes.

American 'welfare capitalism' also had some influence on these developments. In fact, in 1930, one might have thought that managerial control and worker co-option was the organizational pattern towards which the whole world was moving.

III. DEPRESSION, WAR, AND DIVERGENT DEVELOPMENT

The Depression changed all that. In the United States, intimations of welfare capitalism gave way to intensifying industrial conflict, which became increasingly institutionalized. In contrast, in both Germany and Japan, a mixture of repression and patriotic mobilization put an end to the class conflict of the early 1930s, only to set up the two nations for a devastating defeat at the hands of the Allies. What emerged in Germany and Japan from the ashes of the Second World War were distinctive capitalist regimes characterized by substantial worker–manager cooperation and less worker–manager inequality of power and reward than in either of the Anglo-Saxon countries.

New Deal labour legislation in America made it possible to force powerful corporations to engage in collective bargaining, but their bargaining power in the recession was greatly limited. Despite a significant increase in government intervention into the economy under the New Deal, it would take US entry into the Second World War to pull the nation out of depression; in 1940 the unemployment rate was still 14.6 per cent. While industrial corporations failed to maintain steady employment for their 'hourly' workers during the 1930s, they made every effort to keep their organizations of salaried managers intact and, indeed, over the course of the 1930s expanded their R&D efforts (Mowery, 1986, pp. 191–2). During the Second World War, government spending vastly increased the research capabilities and production capacity of the major corporations.

The United States dominated the post-war world economy, with over 40 per cent of world GDP in 1950. This dominance was also reflected in the preponderant influence that America subsequently exercised and continues to exercise in post-war international institutions. Wartime expansion continued with the demand generated by European reconstruction, with the overseas spread of American corporations to Latin America and to Europe, and with the Cold War focus on high-technology military spending. Throughout this process, managerial control of enterprises was strengthened. Corporations and the state joined forces through the Taft–Hartley legislation of 1947 and the communist purges of 1949 to keep the growing power of the industrial unions in check. Meanwhile, the institutionalization of collective bargaining and seniority provisions of labour contracts improved the stability of employment and levels of pay for blue-collar workers (Brody, 1980; Harris, 1982; Lichtenstein, 1985). Arms spending deepened technological relations among corporations, research universities, and the military, thus creating the post-war 'military–industrial complex'—a phrase coined by President Eisenhower as he departed from office and a structure described so incisively by John Kenneth Galbraith (1967) in *The New Industrial State*.

The legacy of the Depression in Britain was the victory of the Labour Party in the 1945 election. When combined with the expansion of the welfare system and the commitment to full employment, nationalization of railways, steel, and coal—industries that were all in dire need of modernization—greatly increased the role of the state. But the marginal infusions of new blood into the managerial cadres of the backward industries that were nationalized did little either to change the adversarial pattern of industrial relations or to rationalize management structures. In private industry, large firms

increased their preponderance (the 100 biggest producing 30 per cent of manufacturing output in the early 1950s compared with 16 per cent in 1909), and the takeover movement of the late 1950s finally reduced the scale of family ownership and family control. The salaried managers who now took control of companies still sought to emulate the aristocratic British élite, and thus segmented themselves from interaction with technical specialists, while they remained reliant upon shop-floor workers to manage skill formation and work organization (Lazonick, 1985). At the same time, financial interests in the City of London, which included equity-based pension funds, looked to the publicly traded industrial enterprises as sources of high returns. By the 1960s, a form of managerial capitalism had evolved in Britain, but it was one in which, compared with the managerial capitalisms that had emerged in the other advanced economies, British managers exercised little power over the 'stakeholders' within their enterprises (Wright, 1962; Hannah, 1986; Chandler, 1990, ch. 9).

In Nazi Germany, the highly concentrated industrial sector provided ready foundations for its coordination by the Third Reich to mobilize the economy for war. Preparation for war and the actuality of war led to a strengthening of linkages among companies through the Nazi policy of enforced cartellization followed by their system of main committees and industrial rings. Especially during the early 1940s, the Nazis transformed the economy's traditional sectors by forcing many smaller enterprises to integrate their industrial operations with those of the larger combines. The authoritarian hand of the Nazi state also intervened to shape the skill formation system by integrating the apprenticeship training structures in the *handwerk* sector with industrial needs, thus laying the foundation for the modern German system of apprenticeship (McKitrick, 1994).

With Germany's defeat, the declared intention of the Allied Occupation forces, particularly the Americans, was to break the institutional support for Germany's distinctive variety of capitalism and to replace it with a system of so-called 'free enterprise'. But the onset of the Cold War, and the perceived importance of a strong West German economy as a bulwark against the power of the Soviets, led to a decline in the commitment to this path. What emerged from the war was a curious amalgam of old and new: ordo-liberal ideology, tough competition policy, compulsory *Kammern* membership, still strong and strongly hierarchical sectoral business associations, a reinforcement of a collectively oriented training system (Shonfield, 1965).

The final distinguishing characteristic of German capitalism crystallized fully in the post-war period. Class conflict became contained on the one hand by the institutionalization of the zero-sum elements of the employment relationship in a highly organized wage-bargaining system through industrial-sector union and employers' associations, and on the other by institutionalization of the positive-sum elements in the system of codetermination. The West German movement for industrial democracy may have fallen short of its ambitions, but the post-war institution of codetermination, which ensures employee representation on the supervisory boards of corporate enterprises and on works councils that operate at the plant and enterprise levels, gave West Germany the most extensive formal system of employee representation in the world (Weidemann, 1980).

Japanese wartime mobilization learned a lot from the German—notably in the imperative integration of small-firm supply networks which laid foundations for the modern system of long-term subcontracting. But the wartime changes had more profound consequences for what became established as the 'Japanese management system'. Some powerful strands in the Japanese version of 'fascism' (to accept the term loosely as covering the three Axis regimes) were as strongly anti-capitalist and more overtly socialist than German National Socialism. The Young Officer conspiracies (which paved the way for the army to take effective power out of the hands of all political parties) assassinated leading *zaibatsu* managers as well as bourgeois politicians. The managers were accused of being more interested in extracting revenues from their firms in the forms of dividends and directors' bonuses than committing these financial resources to the further development of the enterprises and, hence, of the nation.

Many younger bureaucrats shared these anti-capitalist sentiments, so that, when the war came, industrial mobilization was in the hands of men who believed passionately in organizational efficiency, but not in shareholders' rights. During the war, the stock exchange was closed, and the bureaucrats directed the allocation of bank loans to particular enterprises. Industry control associations run by experienced managers also rationalized trading relations of parts suppliers and controlled the allocation of raw materials. But the measure that had the most lasting effect on the post-war corporation was a decree that required Ministry approval of board appointments in major firms. Officials used that power to replace shareholder representatives with experienced and competent managers, mostly lifetime employees of their firms (Okazaki, 1994). Until the arrival of foreign firms in the 1980s, Japan had practically no external labour market for executive talent.

The post-war dissolution of the *zaibatsu* under the Allied occupation served to consolidate this wartime shift in control over the allocation of corporate resources. The *zaibatsu* dissolution completely disenfranchised the *zaibatsu* owners and war-guilt purges forced large numbers of top managers to resign from their posts (Hadley, 1970; Morikawa, 1997). Managerial control was left in the hands of 'third-rank executives'—relatively young middle managers committed to catching up with the substantial development of technology in the West during the war, in close touch with the practical manufacturing problems, and with an acute sense of the need to commercialize technology if their firms were to survive. With the reopening of the stock market in 1949, these corporate managers refashioned in a much looser form the inter-firm and firm–bank relationships of the *zaibatsu* system by building a web of cross-shareholdings with other companies. This strategy of acquiring 'stable shareholders' (preferably shareholders one did business with) was greatly strengthened in the 1960s as defence against takeover by American companies that capital liberalization was making a real possibility (Hodder and Tschoegl, 1993). The cross-shareholding system enabled an enterprise to maintain control over its revenues for the sake of developing its organizational and technological capabilities. This control over corporate revenues in turn created the financial foundations for both high levels of debt relative to equity through the 'main bank system' and the long-term employment of enterprise personnel.

The post-war labour compact was the final element in the system. The militant movement of the immediate post-war period was dominated by leaders bent on the replacement of capitalism by socialism (Moore, 1983). But grass-roots unionism and the wartime workers' councils that replaced unions had always been enterprise-based; 'production control'—the union taking over the running of factories and shutting out managers—was a common form of strike in the late 1940s, and managers' attempts to cut back employment to match their reduced output was a major cause of strikes (Gordon, 1985, pt 3). Out of the turbulence there emerged, by the mid-1950s, a settled compromise that recognized the negotiation and consultation rights of enterprise unions (which included white- as well as blue-collar workers and university graduates on management tracks for the first decade of their employment), and an implicit commitment of employers to provide 'lifetime employment' (Cusumano, 1985; Hiwatari, 1996).

Helping to transform that commitment into reality over the course of the 1950s were first the Korean War boom and then strong domestic consumer markets. Japanese household consumption grew on the basis of the ability of lifetime employees to share in the prosperity of their companies and the high level of income equality engendered by taxation and farm-subsidy policies, as well as the conventions of the 'community firm'. Meanwhile, within companies, the development of multiskilled production workers combined with organizational learning in which these workers interacted with engineers made possible the Japanese management practices—among them quality control, just-in-time, and continuous improvement (*kaizen*)—that were later to be adopted around the world.

IV. THE 1960S: THE HEYDAY OF MANAGERIAL CAPITALISM

By the late 1960s, the final years of the Golden Age of post-war growth, managerial capitalism had become what seemed like a global norm. Everywhere, owners, now mainly public shareholders, had come to have less control than managers over the strategic direction as well as the day-to-day administration of the organizational empires they nominally owned. The 'property system' on which theorists considered capitalism to be founded had been subtly modified. In Japan and Germany, juridical patterns of ownership meant, in practice, that the managers of industrial concerns were constrained only by ties of mutual dependence forged with the managers of banks and other enterprises, whose world view, interests, and criteria of judgement coincided basically with their own. In the United States, as in Britain, 'there has been great reluctance to admit of a significant and enduring shift of power from the owners of capital', to quote Galbraith, but that is what had happened. As Galbraith (1967, p. 50) went on to say: 'A small proportion of the stock is represented at stockholders' meetings for a ceremony in which banality is varied chiefly by irrelevance. The rest is voted by proxy for the directors who have been selected by the management.'

Galbraith argued that the technological complexity of the activities in which major corporations were engaged demanded such an array of specialist knowledge that control over decision-making had passed to the 'technostructure'. The *planning*, not just the implementation, of the operations of the company required the contribution and assessment of information not just by top management but a large group of subordinate employees that included, as Galbraith once told one of the authors, 'everyone who wears a tie'. Excluded from the 'technostructure' was the 'outer perimeter' of production and clerical workers who only had to do what they were told (Galbraith did not anticipate the Toyotism—or Saturnism—of the 1980s which brought even the shop-floor stratum in from the cold).

In the modern corporate enterprise, individual entrepreneurship and individual leadership had become more or less irrelevant (Galbraith, 1967, p. 71). The planning habit was spreading: 'shortly after World War II . . . many business corporations began formalizing a systematic means whereby a company seeks to become what it wants to be by the formulation of corporate-wide objectives and systematic performance controls . . . for at least five years ahead' (US Bureau of the Budget, *Goal Setting and Comprehensive Planning*, 1963, quoted in Shonfield, 1965). A McGraw Hill survey found that by the early 1960s a survey of companies responsible for a half of total industrial investment could provide details of their investment plans 3

Table 1
GDP Per Capita
(average annual percentage changes)

	Britain	United States	Germany	Japan
1950–9	2.6	4.0	8.5	8.6
1960–9	3.2	4.0	4.9	10.7
1970–9	2.4	2.8	3.1	5.3
1980–9	2.3	2.9	1.9	4.1

Source: Maddison (1991, pp. 216–19).

Table 2
Unemployment Rates
(annual averages)

	Britain	United States	Germany	Japan
1950–9	2.5	4.4	5.0	2.0
1960–9	2.7	4.7	0.8	1.3
1970–9	4.4	6.1	2.2	1.7
1980–9	10.0	7.2	6.0	2.5

Source: Maddison (1991, pp. 262–5).

years ahead—compared with only 20 per cent in the late 1940s (Shonfield, 1965).

The legitimacy of managerial control could be celebrated because, by and large, it was seen as delivering the goods. Growth rates were high (Table 1), unemployment was contained (Table 2), and in all four societies, the primary distribution of income was at least not becoming more unequal and the secondary distribution somewhat more equal, thanks to income taxes of a considerable, but at the time largely thought inevitable, degree of progressivity (Blinder, 1980).

Largely as a result of the expansion of corporate employment and the strength of union bargaining, private pension plan coverage reached 41 per cent of the US work-force in 1960, more than double the rate of coverage at the end of the war. Lyndon Johnson's Great Society project seemed to promise that the USA, too, would use some of the proceeds of productivity growth to transform itself into a welfare state. With real hourly wages of US manufacturing workers rising on average by over 2 per

cent per annum over these decades, and with blue-collar employees of major corporations becoming more consumption oriented and politically conservative, much was written about the 'end of ideology' and the 'bourgeoisification' of the working class.

Which is far from saying that the distributional conflict had been resolved. Germany and Japan had both settled down into relatively 'orderly' and predictable wage-bargaining systems, but in Britain and the United States, conflict was endemic. Compared with Germany, days lost to strikes per employee between 1966 and 1970 were 38 times higher in Britain and 99 times higher in the United States (Flanagan *et al.*, 1983, p. 225). In Britain, where plant-level shop stewards exercised considerable control over labour relations, the 'unauthorized' strike, or even the threat of one, was a most powerful bargaining weapon. It was this fragmentation of bargaining and the power of the shop stewards—itself reflecting a failure of British industrial managers to take control over shop-floor work organization—that made British manufacturing enterprises so vulnerable to worker actions and that reinforced Britain's lag in productivity growth (Bain, 1983).

But the central topic of the 'whither capitalism' debates of the 1960s—the Cold War decade in which the communist and free-market systems came closest to a nuclear exchange—revolved less around labour versus capital than around the state versus market theme. Although the dichotomy 'developmental state/regulatory state' did not enter into common discourse until the 1980s and the term 'industrial policy' only a little earlier, there was a widespread awareness that in Japan, growing faster in the 1960s than any large economy had ever grown before, the state had by no means abjured all the powers of direction and control that it had acquired during the war. Selective subsidies and tariff policies, preferential credits, 5-year indicative plans to concentrate the thinking and direct the efforts of private business, investment cartels and recession cartels, were all seen as positive ingredients in Japan's growth recipe

In Europe, Andrew Shonfield, in his *Modern Capitalism*, remarked that not even Schumpeter (1942), with his predictions that capitalism would eventually be socialized to eliminate the disruptions of economic crises, had foreseen what had become obvious in Britain, France, Italy, Sweden, and Austria—namely 'the vast importance of the authoritative calculations made by post-war governments, whose activities as entrepreneurs have become much the most important single force of the whole system' (Shonfield, 1965). In Britain, for example, the creation in the 1960s of the tripartite National Economic Development Council and Organization, and its multiple sector sub-committees, was intended to inject a national planning element into the stimulation of investment and productivity improvement in the private sector.

Germany and the USA stood out as having very low levels of public ownership and being dominated by a free-market ideology that rejected state intervention in the economy. Yet, as Shonfield (1965) pointed out, the *ordo* part of the *ordo-liberalism* that Erhardt espoused, as well as the *soziale* part of the *soziale marktwirtschaft*, loomed large in the economy. It helped to make the tax-take 34 per cent of German GNP in 1960, compared with only 28 per cent in Britain. At the *Land* level, public banks

helped to foster and direct the growth of the *Mittelstand*, while the strength of hierarchically organized industry associations, albeit part of civil society rather than the state, played an important coordinating role.

And, as for the United States, given that Boeing and General Dynamics each sold some 65 per cent of their output to the state, Raytheon 70 per cent, and Lockheed 80 per cent, given the post-Sputnik realization of the importance of the state's role in producing trained and educated manpower, given the industrial system's dependence on the state to regulate aggregate demand, given the close fusion of interests and concerns between corporate managers and state bureaucrats (and their frequent swapping of roles), who can doubt, argued Galbraith (1967), that the industrial system will 'evolve into a penumbra of the state', converging eventually with a Soviet Planning system evolving towards a greater concern with liberty and autonomy. That prediction was made, of course, well before the 'end of history' was in sight.

V. THE 1970S: SURGING INFLATION AND CORPORATIST RESPONSES

The transition from the managerial capitalism of the 1960s to the neo-liberal free-market system which became the dominant aspiration of the British and American governments in the 1980s, was mediated by the traumas of the 1970s. The central problem, inflation, was common to all four economies. The resolution of the problem was primarily determined by the pattern of class conflict. Japan and Germany came through the crucible of the 1970s with their existing class compromise more or less intact, their form of capitalism reinforced. America, and to a much more overt degree Britain, came out of the decade with a decisive shift in the balance of power under way.

Most observers of post-war capitalism assumed that full employment would engender inflation, both through the labour-market mechanisms embodied in the Phillips curve and because of an increasing bargaining power of unions combined with the power of corporations to administer prices. In the 1960s, however, Keynesian fine-tuning had kept inflation within acceptable—even benign—limits as long as growth fed both wages and profits. But the tendency through the 1960s for labour to gain a greater share of the proceeds of growth, was most marked in Britain where the profit squeeze was clearly affecting investment by the end of the decade (Glyn and Sutcliffe, 1972, Appx G).

The in-built factors producing inflation were vastly accentuated by the commodity price rise culminating in the great shift in oil prices brought about by OPEC. Both Japan and Britain had inflation rates of over 25 per cent in 1974–5. Yet Japan reduced inflation to single figures in 1 year, while Britain still had double-figure inflation—and much higher unemployment than Japan—at the end of the decade.

How did Japan do it? By a shift in the power balance within the framework of a stable, well-established pay-bargaining system. Its 'spring offensive' (*shunto*) system was a single, decentralized but simultaneous, national bargaining round with clear wage leaders, and months of public pre-negotiation discussions which had the effect of setting 'expectations norms'. These discussions always had assumed some willingness of both employers and unions to think in terms of a common national interest in stable prices and increased productivity (an element conspicuously lacking in Britain). But unions—in part a carry-over from immediate postwar militancy—had, until the runaway inflation of 1975, considerable power to mobilize bargain-period strikes. And used it. But in that year the sense of national crisis and the combined jawboning of government and employer associations reduced the resolve of the unions to secure wage gains, and the initiative shifted—as it turned out, permanently—to managers (Dore, 1987).

Control of inflation was also made far easier by the fact that rapid increases in output (and thereby also of productivity) were possible through exports which contributed a great deal to the 24 per cent growth in real GDP, 1975–80. Japan had reached the optimal stage of development: world levels of technology and product quality, plus wages that were still below those of its competitors.

A final important factor was the willingness (and, with a still highly controlled financial sector, the ability) of the government to sustain demand by

deficit spending. Between 1975 and 1980, bond issues covered never less than 25 per cent and in 1979 as much as 35 per cent of government expenditure.

Germany, too, saw its already well-established, industry-by-industry wage-bargaining system—with an institutionalized pattern of wage leadership by the metal-workers union—reinforced and made more effective by what one might call 'arm's-length corporatism'. Employers and unions cooperated to deliver wage restraint, partly because of their shared knowledge of the independent Bundesbank's relentless determination to control inflation by monetary policy, whatever level of unemployment might result. 'Face-to-face corporatism'—the *Konzertiert Aktion* of 1967–78—also helped to create shared expectations between employers and unions, but a condition of the unions' participation was that there should be no attempt at norm-setting. Nor was the Bundesbank prepared to compromise its capacity for unilateral action (Streeck, 1994, pp. 121–2).

Germany had not been immune to the spill-over effects of France's May 1968 and Italy's 'hot autumn', and the mid-decade crisis was preceded by spells of wildcat strikes, which provided the background to formal legitimate strikes forcing double-digit wage rises in 1974. In agreeing to mildly reflationary measures at the end of the year, however, the Bundesbank made it clear that it expected restraint in the next round in return. And got it. (Kloten *et al.*, 1985). As a sweetener, the unions got a major reinforcement of the system of enterprise codetermination in 1976.

It was the structure of social relations at the levels of the enterprise and the state that made Britain's plight worse than that of the others. The ability of craft unions, represented by their shop stewards, to control work organization and to reinforce their control through 'wildcat' strikes (i.e. strikes that ignored 'constitutional' procedures) reduced managers' power to restructure production processes, while the need to 'buy out' restrictive practices reduced their power to resist wage claims (McKersie *et al.*, 1972). This labour–management conflict mapped, much more closely than in the other three countries, on to the political system—a major workers' party and a major bosses' party, both having enough electoral support to alternate in government as its inability to solve basic conflicts discredited each government in turn.

So industrial and political antagonism multiplied each other by mutual feedback, and each successive UK government was more likely to tear down than build on the 'rationalizing' institutional innovations of the other. This vitiated both the attempts to 'constitutionalize' work-place industrial relations (the Industrial Relations Acts from 1971 onwards) and the attempts at incomes policy. Even during the periods when Labour was in power, 'face-to-face' or 'beer and sandwiches' corporatism was never very effective. Social contracts went little beyond horse-trading bargains: so much in social benefits and worker-protection legislation for so much wage restraint. The sense of a collective overriding interest in controlling inflation and raising productivity that served to modify the interest conflict in the smaller economies of Scandinavia, etc. seemed hard to generate (Crouch and Dore, 1990). Central union negotiators could not deliver the restraint of their constituent unions, and the officials of those unions could not deliver the cooperation of their factory-level bargainers. And at the factory level the 'extra pay for extra productivity' loopholes in the wage-increase norms were exploited by craft unions and complaisant management. Bargaining over the buying out of restrictive practices (which the system encouraged unions to invent for the purpose) became the norm. Despite a decline in real wages, from 1975 to 1977, thereafter—with unemployment also at high levels—wage gains once again began to outpace inflation and work stoppages were endemic. Talk of the country's 'ungovernability', a massive increase in strikes (from an average 3m days lost in strikes in the 1960s to 29m in 1979), particularly in the public services, prepared the way for Mrs Thatcher's electoral victory.

The 1970s were an equally unhappy decade for America, ending with the soon-to-be-ousted President Carter making speeches about the nation's 'crisis of confidence'. America's inflation sprang from the need to print money in the late 1960s to cover the cost of the ever more unpopular war in Vietnam. Nixon tried a wage and price freeze in 1971 and again in 1973, but its effects were overtaken by the impact of the oil crisis, and the experiment was not repeated (Gordon, 1980, p. 141)

Thereafter the government increasingly looked to monetary policy to control inflation, and to financial deregulation to permit capital to maintain its rate of return. One of the seeds of later stock-market developments was planted when the Employment Retirement Income Security Act (ERISA) of 1974, as amended in 1978, enabled pension funds, their real rates of returns decimated by inflation, to seek higher, even if riskier, returns through portfolio investments in corporate equities, high-yield (or 'junk') bonds, and venture-capital funds (Lazonick and O'Sullivan, 2000).

There were concerns about labour problems—the bargaining strength of unions pushing wages ahead of productivity increases, worker alienation giving rise to absenteeism and low productivity (HEW, 1972). But (the AFL–CIO/Democratic Party relation having nothing like the real class-sentiment base of the TUC/Labour Party alliance) it was not central to American politics, and it was not, as in Britain, the key issue triggering the following decades of neo-liberalism. That role was played, rather, by government regulation. The regulatory tide reached its peak in the Nixon years and it was the reactive growth of the anti-regulation, deregulation movement in the late 1970s (in which Chicago economists played a key role) which provided the leitmotif of the early Reagan years (Yergin and Stanislaw, 1998).

VI. THE 1980S AND 1990S

Nevertheless, a drastic reduction of the power of the unions was a crucial element of the new directions taken by the Anglo-Saxon economies. It was accomplished, in both countries, less by legislation (though the whittling down of employment protection and the ban on the closed shop in Britain, and the growth of 'right to work' state legislation in the USA were important) as by recession—the great British manufacturing shake-out of 1980–1 and the concurrent American 'blue-collar' recession—and by spectacular government victories in marathon disputes with public-sector unions—the air-traffic controllers in the USA, the steel workers, the railway workers, and the coal miners in quick succession in Britain.

Top-end income and capital gains tax cuts, deregulation, particularly of the financial sector, tax provisions to stimulate equity investment, along with labour-market 'flexibilization' policies were other supply-side policies which Reaganomics and Thatcherism had in common. Privatization—a clear assertion of belief in the importance of the profit motive which linked directly to 'shareholder value' doctrines—was more a British than an American concern because there was more to privatize. It was acknowledged that competition was an essential ingredient if the profit motive was to lead to efficiency, but, especially where it had to be artificially created in what had hitherto been monopolies (with great difficulty in the case of natural monopolies such as railways and gas), privatization involved the creation of large-scale regulatory agencies.

Another more strikingly British than American phenomenon—because Britain's civil service and universities and health service still had nineteenth-century upper-middle-class traditions of public service suspected by the Thatcherites as hypocrisy—was the shift to individual bottom-lineism in reward structures. The managerial organizations of major firms such as ICI, BP, and Unilever had come to resemble the civil service in their career structures and incremental salary scales. They were transformed by performance pay and recruitment at market price. Notions of loyalty which once had precluded any 'lifelong' employee of one bank from moving to another became memories of a quaint outmoded past. Mobility via the market, rather than commitment to organizations, began increasingly to shape careers and ambitions. Market principles were brought into civil service employment, university teaching, and, to a lesser extent, medicine.

It was mostly in the United States, however, that a central ingredient of the new Anglo-Saxon pattern was developed, namely the ideology of shareholder value, the dominant belief that the business enterprise was making its best social contribution, as well as serving its owners' purposes, if it was run to maximize shareholder value—a concept in which, for quoted companies, the share price played a major role. Shareholder activism, responding to instances of managerial delinquency, the substitution of voice strategies for exit strategies forced on the larger funds with an index-linked portfolio, techniques of mobilizing large funds, and the development of a junk-bond market for leveraged buy-outs,

all contributed to the shift. The Garn–St Germain Act of 1982 gave a great impetus to the last development by permitting savings and loans institutions (S&Ls), to engage in riskier lending activity. But the S& L fiasco did not diminish the pressures of institutional investors on corporate boardrooms.

Managers responded. Efficiency was pursued with relentless cost-cutting, particularly through downsizing, which permitted higher dividends and share buy-backs. (The latter became, by the 1990s, a major component of corporate distributions to shareholders, frequently financed by debt.) The managers were exceedingly well rewarded, thanks to increasing resort to devices to align managerial and shareholder interests, particularly the stock option. The 1980s and 1990s witnessed an explosion in top management income, much of it in the form of stock-based rewards (Lazonick and O'Sullivan, 2000).

Britain was a faithful follower of these trends, which were further fuelled by the growth of pension funds (now over £800 billion and growing at £50 billion a year) with the whittling back of state pension systems, and by tax provisions that privileged those savings channelled into equity funds. Britain's explosion in managerial pay did not come until the 1990s when it was the 'fat cats' in the boardrooms of recently privatized former state enterprises which drew—and continue to draw—media attention (Plender, 1997). As the figures for income distribution shifts during the 1980s became available (OECD, 1993), it became obvious that this was only part of a widening income gap in Britain and the United States, not reproduced in the other two economies.

These institutional trends in the Anglo-Saxon economies were continuing trends throughout the 1980s and 1990s—confirmed in 1997 by the arrival of a Labour government in Britain which quite explicitly endorsed the neo-liberal policies it had once so vociferously denounced and sought to modify them only by marginally more caring welfare services and employee protection.

But the big difference in those economies between the 1980s and the 1990s was in economic performance: a change from stagnation to dynamism—in the United States even exuberant dynamism.

In the 1980s the main problem for American manufacturers of cars, machines, and electronics products had been the emergence of formidable Japanese competitors who took larger shares of the US and world export markets in these products even as Japanese wages rose and the Japanese yen strengthened. America seemed to be losing ground, even in its bastions of high technology strength. IBM started the decade (much aided by Cold War government research funding and procurement) with about 75 per cent of the world's computer market. It launched its personal computer (PC) business in response to a Silicon Valley start-up called Apple and in short order its PC became the industry standard, permitting IBM 'clones' such as Compaq in the 1980s and Dell in the 1990s to capture large shares of the PC market. The IBM strategy also created two new behemoths—Intel and Microsoft—the companies to which IBM had turned in 1980 to supply its PCs with microprocessors and operating system software. But Japanese rivals seemed to be catching up fast, aided, to a degree which will for ever be disputed, by government-coordinated cooperative research programmes. Their success in capturing the semiconductor manufacturing equipment market prompted a parallel American response—the lavishly funded Sematech scheme which began to bear fruit in the early 1990s. By that time, the longest boom in American history—one which produced new jobs all across the skill spectrum and even halted the trend to income inequality—had begun. At its core were the high-tech industries. With its own native intellectual resources greatly supplemented by the brain-drain (via graduate schools) from Asia, Europe, and Latin America, the American lead in electronics and biotechnology seemed, in selected fields at least, to increase (O'Sullivan, 2000, ch. 6).

America, with its ballooning trade deficit, did not, overall, however, eclipse the export performance of Japan and Germany which continued to build on their long-standing strengths—organizational learning in firms whose institutions promoted cooperation across the authority hierarchy, the extension of close cooperation to suppliers, the willingness to make long-term investments (Lazonick, 1990, ch. 10). True, as a careful McKinsey study showed, they seemed to get lower returns on capital (McKinsey Global Institute, 1996). But that hardly affected competitiveness. And capital productivity was not, in any case, their first priority. Japan's problem in the 1990s, in fact, was an excess of capital: the backward-sloping supply curve for savings—more saving as interest rates fell—was a major source of the demand deficiency which not even massive Keynesian spending packages seemed able to cure.

Yet the ability to capture world markets—a source of great national self-confidence in both economies, especially in the bubbling Japan of the late 1980s—began to be eclipsed by other problems—persistent high unemployment in Germany, and post-bubble stagnation in Japan. Confidence ebbed badly, and pressures for convergence to the Anglo-Saxon (that is, the American) model began to receive a hearing.

Germany first. The export performance of the German economy grew stronger throughout the 1980s and the reunification process initially prompted a further upsurge in economic performance. However, unemployment, which, though rising substantially in the early 1980s, had remained at a lower level than in the United States and much, much lower than in most other European countries, through that decade, shot up to double figures in 1992–3 as the economy plunged into its worst recession since the Second World War. Talk of the strengths of German capitalism was replaced by anxious discussion of the viability of *Industriestandort Deutschland* (Germany as an industrial location). Employers became more vociferous in their claims that the high wages, short working hours, tight labour-market regulations, and high taxes that prevail in Germany had undermined the competitive position of German enterprises. They warned that German companies would be forced to relocate production abroad if drastic reforms of corporate structures, and, indeed, the foundations of the social market economy, were not undertaken to ensure closer attention to the bottom line. Senior German managers seemed to be increasingly influenced by what was happening overseas, especially in the US corporate economy, and they displayed a growing propensity to adopt practices that until recently were regarded as anathema in German business circles. Companies such as Daimler–Benz and Deutsche Bank, previously seen as synonymous with the distinctive German post-war system of managerial capitalism, have emerged at the forefront of a shareholder-value movement in Germany in the mid- to late 1990s (O'Sullivan, 2000, ch. 8).

However, corporate resource-allocation processes are only beginning to be overhauled to accord with shareholder-value logic. True believers, moreover, are sceptical that German managers know what they mean and mean what they say, when they speak of the merits of shareholder value for enhancing corporate performance. Their conversion may have more to do with their efforts to maintain control in the wave of mergers and acquisitions in which they are caught up than any serious commitment to the virtues of the Anglo-American management practices for generating superior performance.

It may be a mistake, however, to dismiss the rhetoric of German managers as grandstanding, faddish, and self-serving. One of the most important lessons that can be drawn from the recent history of the American corporate economy is that 'organization men' can be induced to be ardent proponents of shareholder value, given appropriate incentives for self-enrichment.

On the other hand, the institutional defences of the German system are formidable. Codetermination within corporations, and the coordinated wage bargaining system, remain both legally and socially entrenched, and are both staunchly defended by unions which remain powerful in spite of all the structural changes which weaken unions everywhere. Moreover, as export performance picks up at the end of the decade, with little impact on employment figures, it is not obvious that a wave of down-sizing in pursuit of shareholder value will make any contribution to what is recognized as the nation's most serious problem, and increasingly diagnosed—everywhere except in union circles—as an insider/outsider problem, if not a straightforward real wages versus employment trade-off. The Alliance for Jobs which Kohl tried, and Schröder with difficulty succeeded in setting up, is having only limited success. The currency given to shareholder-value rhetoric is one factor contributing to union intransigence.

Labour–management conflict is the least of the problems which seem likely to alter Japan's distinc-

tive form of capitalism. The main factor is the devastating loss of national self-confidence, particularly after a premature burst of fiscal prudence halted the 1995–6 recovery from the post-bubble recession. Today, the dominant consensus as reflected in the pronouncements of politicians, businessmen, bureaucrats, and the mass media, is that the Japanese model was good for catch-up, but is too cumbersome and undynamic for the new global megacompetition among mature economies. Dynamism comes from competition, not from managerial planning: hence the need for wholesale deregulation; more auction markets, fewer customer markets in trading between firms; active and flexible labour markets. Cross-shareholding distorts share prices and should be prevented. Personal morality needs to be overhauled: individuals should take responsibility for their own old age and illness, and for ensuring their employability in the labour market. Returns on equity should be the major measure of firm performance. Japanese society has been too preoccupied with equality of outcomes rather than equality of opportunity, etc., etc.

Much of this current 'philosophy' is being reflected, gradually, in legislation. Laws to permit holding companies, to facilitate share buy-backs, the unwinding of cross-shareholdings, the bringing of shareholder class-action suits against managers, and to legalize stock options as executive compensation, have all been passed in the 1990s (Dore, 2000). Some leading firms such as Sony (45 per cent of its shares held by foreigners) declare their total adherence to shareholder-value objectives. But even in those firms, change in practice is another matter. Downsizing still means primarily protracted natural wastage. The cross-shareholding pattern is still dense. Wages and bonuses are sticky downwards and returns on equity remain low. Loyalties and obligations still count in sub-contracting relations.

And in both Japan and Germany, defenders of their systems seem lately to be speaking up more confidently. Toyota's chairman tells an audience that includes Jack Welch that his firm is not going to abandon lifetime employment, however much Standard and Poor's lowers their credit rating (*Nikkei*, 8 October 1999). The chairman of Altana tells *Der Spiegel* that 'Anglo-Saxon cold capitalism, which exclusively focuses on maximizing profits, will lead to a crisis in our system and to a decline of acceptance for the pillars of the social free market economy' (21 May 1999).

Japan and Germany remain very different. Japan's economic institutions are deeply *socially* embedded, in spite of a legal framework—company law, for instance—hardly different from that of Anglo-Saxon countries. By contrast, Germany's system derives its strength from its firm legal entrenchment. The crucial capital–labour relation is seen in Germany as a clear and conscious class compromise in a situation of structural antagonism. In Japan it is fragmented within community-like corporations, where managers identify more closely with their workers than with the providers of their capital. The systems differ, but they both produce economic behaviour and value priorities that continue to be very different from those of the Anglo-Saxon economies.

VII. VARIETIES OF CAPITALISM IN THE TWENTY-FIRST CENTURY?

Will they remain different? We can only give a bemused answer. Bemused, first, by the fact noted by Albert (1991) when he started the 'varieties of capitalism' debate, namely that it is not just product-market competition and factor mobility that presses for convergence. For all the social and economic-efficiency virtues of their systems, a lot of Germans and Japanese actually *admire* the American way of life, in spite of a widespread recognition that it involves bursting prisons and rapidly widening inequality. Bemused, secondly, by the phenomenon that recently reinforces that admiration—the sustained exuberance of the American economy and the hypnotic Greenspan's ability to persuade the world's fund managers that it has a new growth paradigm which will allow its price–earnings ratios, its outstanding margin loans, its consumer debt, and its trade deficit to go on rising for ever without affecting the value of dollar assets. Bemused, thirdly, by our memory of the days when the business schools now preaching shareholder value were abuzz with talk of planning, the technostructure, and the social responsibility of capital, and of the more recent days when Japanese management (in general—not just production management) was supposed to be everybody's model.

And bemused, fourthly by the impossibility, though we can see clearly some of the potential determinants of convergence or diversity, of assessing their effects. Is the search for a 'new financial architecture' after the Asian, Russian, and Brazilian crises, going to slow down free capital flows? Will the shift in pension systems from publicly regulated fixed obligations to private risk-bearing financial assets proceed further in the Anglo-Saxon economies and become a serious trend in the others? How far will Chinese capitalism turn out to resemble the Japanese version as the weight of China in the world economy increases?

We leave readers to make their own predictions.

REFERENCES

Albert, M. (1991), *Capitalisme contre capitalisme*, Paris, Seuil.

Bain, G. (ed.) (1983), *Industrial Relations in Britain*, Oxford, Basil Blackwell.

Barrett Whale, P. (1930), *Joint Stock Banking in Germany*, London, Macmillan.

Berle, A. A., and Means, G. C. (1932), *The Modern Corporation and Private Property*, New York, Macmillan.

Blinder, A. (1980), 'The Level and Distribution of Economic Well-being,' in M. Feldstein (ed.), *The American Economy in Transition*, Chicago, IL, University of Chicago Press.

Braunthal, G. (1978), *Socialist Labor and Politics in Weimar Germany: The General Federation of German Trade Unions*, Hamden, CT, Archon Books.

Brockstedt, J. (1984), 'Family Enterprise and the Rise of Large-scale Enterprise in Germany, 1871–1914', in A. Okochi and S. Yasuoka (eds), *Family Business in the Era of Industrial Growth: Its Ownership and Management*, Tokyo, University of Tokyo Press.

Brody, D. (1980), *Workers in Industrial America*, New York, Oxford University Press.

Burgess, K. (1975), *The Origins of British Industrial Relations: The Nineteenth Century Experience*, London, Croom Helm.

Cassis, Y. (1985), 'Bankers in English Society in the Late Nineteenth Century', *Economic History Review*, **38**(2), 210–29.

Chandler, A. D. (1977), *The Visible Hand: The Managerial Revolution in American Business*, Cambridge, MA, Harvard University Press.

— (1990), *Scale and Scope: The Dynamics of Industrial Capitalism*, Cambridge, MA, Harvard University Press.

Church, R. (1993), 'The Family Firm in Industrial Capitalism: International Perspectives on Hypotheses and History', *Business History*, **35**.

Coleman, D. C. (1973), 'Gentlemen and Players', *Economic History Review*, **26**(1), 93–116.

Crouch, C., and Dore, R. (1990), *Corporatism and Accountability*, Oxford, Clarendon Press.

Cusumano, M. A. (1985), *The Japanese Automobile Industry: Technology and Management at Nissan and Toyota*, Cambridge, MA, Harvard University Press.

Daunton, M. (1992), 'Financial Elites and British Society, 1880–1950', in Y. Cassis (ed.), *Finance and Financiers in European History, 1880–1960*, Cambridge and New York, Cambridge University Press.

Dore, R. (1987), *Taking Japan Seriously: A Confucian Perspective on Leading Economic Issues*, Stanford, CA, Stanford University Press.

— (2000) *Stockmarket Capitalism, Welfare Capitalism: Japan and Germany versus the Anglo-Saxons*, Oxford, Oxford University Press.

Feldenkirchen, W. (1991), 'Banking and Economic Growth: Banks and Industry in Germany in the Nineteenth Century and Their Changing Relationship During Industrialization', in W. R. Lee (ed.), *German Industry and German Industrialisation*, London, Routledge.

Flanagan, R., Soskice, D., and Ulman, L. (1983), *Unionism, Economic Stabilization and Incomes Policies: European Experience*, Washington, DC, Brookings Institution.

Galbraith, J. K. (1967), *The New Industrial State*, Boston, MA, Houghton Mifflin.

Gispen, K. (1989), *New Profession, Old Order: Engineers and German Society, 1815–1914*, Cambridge, Cambridge University Press.

Glyn, A., and Sutcliffe, B. (1972), *British Capitalism, Workers and the Profit Squeeze*, London, Penguin.

Gordon, A. (1985), *The Evolution of Labor Relations in Japan: Heavy Industry, 1853–1955*, Cambridge, MA, Harvard University Press.

Gordon, R. (1980), 'Postwar Macroeconomics', in M. Feldstein (ed.), *The American Economy in Transition*, Chicago, IL, University of Chicago Press.

Hadley, E. (1970), *Antitrust in Japan*, Princeton, NJ, Princeton University Press.

Hannah, L. (1983), *The Rise of the Corporate Economy*, 2nd edn, Baltimore, MD, Johns Hopkins University Press.

— (1986), *Inventing Retirement: The Development of Occupational Pensions in Britain*, Cambridge, Cambridge University Press.

Harris, H. J. (1982), *The Right to Manage: Industrial Relations Policies of American Business in the 1940s*, Madison, WI, University of Wisconsin Press.

Harrison, R., and Zeitlin, J. (eds) (1985), *Divisions of Labour: Skilled Workers and Technological Change in Nineteenth Century England*, Sussex, Harvester Press.

HEW (1972), *Work in America*, United States Department of Health, Education and Welfare, Cambridge, MA, MIT Press.

Hiwatari, N. (1996), 'Japanese Corporate Governance Reexamined: The Origins and Institutional Foundations of Enterprise Unionism', paper prepared for the Conference on Employees and Corporate Governance, Columbia University Law School, 22 November.

Hobsbawm, E. L. (1984), *Worlds of Labour*, London, Weidenfeld & Nicolson.

Hodder, J., and Tschoegl, A. (1993), 'Corporate Finance in Japan', in S. Takagi (ed.), *Japanese Capital Markets: New Developments in Regulations and Institutions*, Oxford, Blackwell.

Jacoby, S. M. (1985), *Employing Bureaucracy: Managers, Unions, and the Transformation of Work in American Industry, 1900–1945*, New York, Columbia University Press.

— (1997), *Modern Manors*, Princeton, NJ, Princeton University Press.

Kocka, J. (1980), 'The Rise of Modern Industrial Enterprise in Germany', in A. D. Chandler and H. Daems (eds), *Managerial Hierarchies: Comparative Perspectives on the Rise of the Modern Industrial Enterprise*, Cambridge, MA, Harvard University Press.

— (1981), 'The Entrepreneur, the Family, and Capitalism: Some Examples from the Early Phase of Industrialisation in Germany', in *German Yearbook of Business History*, Berlin, Springer.

Kloten, N., Ketterer, K.-H., and Vollmer, R. (1985), 'West Germany's Stabilization Policy', in L. N. Lindberg and C. Maier (eds), *The Politics of Inflation and Economic Stagnation: Theoretical Approaches and International Case Studies*, Washington, DC, Brookings Institution.

Konig, W. (1993), 'Technical Education and Industrial Performance in Germany: A Triumph of Heterogeneity', in R. Fox and A. Guagnini (eds), *Education, Technology and Industrial Performance in Europe, 1850–1939*, Cambridge, Cambridge University Press.

Lazonick, W. (1985), 'Strategy, Structure, and Management Development in the United States and Britain', in K. Kobayashi and H. Morikawa (eds), *Development of Managerial Enterprise*, Tokyo, University of Tokyo Press.

— (1990), *Competitive Advantage on the Shop Floor*, Cambridge, MA, Harvard University Press.

— O'Sullivan, M. (2000), 'Maximising Shareholder Value: A New Ideology for Corporate Governance', *Economy and Society*, **29**(1).

Liberal Industrial Inquiry (1928), *Britain's Industrial Future*, reprinted 1976, London, Ernest Benn.

Lichtenstein, N. (1985), 'UAW Bargaining Strategy and Shop-floor Conflict, 1946–1970', *Industrial Relations*, **24**(3), 360–81.

Lewchuk, W. (1987), *American Technology and the British Vehicle Industry*, Cambridge, Cambridge University Press.

McKersie, R., Hunter, L., and Sengenberger, W. (1972), *Productivity Bargaining: The American and British Experience*, Washington, DC, US Government Printing Office.

McKinsey Global Institute (1996), *Capital Productivity*, Washington, DC.

McKitrick, F. (1994), 'The Stabilization of the Mittelstand: Artisans in Germany from National Socialism to the Federal Republic, 1939–1953', Ph.D. dissertation, Columbia University.

Maddison, A. (1991), *Dynamic Forces in Capitalist Development*, Oxford, Oxford University Press.

Mass, W., and Lazonick, W. (1990), 'The British Cotton Industry and International Competitive Advantage: The State of the Debates', *Business History*, **32**(October), 9–65.

Means, G. C. (1930), 'The Diffusion of Stock Ownership in the United States', *Quarterly Journal of Economics*, **44**(4), 561–600.

Minami, R. (1976) 'The Introduction of Electric Power and its Impact on the Manufacturing Industries', in H. Patrick (ed.), *Japanese Industrialization and its Social Consequences*, Berkeley, CA, University of California Press.

Moore, J. (1983), *Japanese Workers and the Struggle for Power, 1945–1947*, University of Wisconsin Press.

Morikawa, H. (1992), *Zaibatsu: The Rise and Fall of Family Enterprise Groups in Japan*, Tokyo, University of Tokyo Press.

— (1997), 'Japan: Increasing Organizational Capabilities of Large Industrial Enterprises, 1880s–1980s', in A. D. Chandler, F. Amatori, and T. Hikino (eds), *Big Business and the Wealth of Nations*, Cambridge, Cambridge University Press.

Mowery, D. (1986), 'Industrial Research, 1900–1950', in B. Elbaum and W. Lazonick (eds), *The Decline of the British Economy*, Oxford, Oxford University Press.

Navin, T., and Sears, M. (1955), 'Rise of a Market in Industrial Securities, 1887–1902', *Business History Review*, **29**(2), 105–38.

Noble, D. F. (1977), *America by Design: Science, Technology, and the Rise of Corporate Capitalism*, New York, Oxford University Press.

OECD (1993), *Employment Outlook*, Paris.

Okazaki, T. (1994) 'The Japanese Firm under the Wartime Planned Economy', in M. Aoki and R. Dore (eds), *The Japanese Firm*, Oxford, Oxford University Press.

O'Sullivan, M. (2000), *Contests for Corporate Control: Corporate Governance and Economic Performance in the United States and Germany*, Oxford, Oxford University Press.

Pohl, H. (1982), 'On the History of Organisation and Management in Large German Enterprises Since the Nineteenth Century', in *German Yearbook of Business History*, Berlin, Springer.

— (1984), 'Forms and Phases of Industry Finance up to the Second World War', *German Yearbook of Business History*, Berlin, Springer.

Plender, J. (1997) *A Stake in the Future*, London, Nicholas Brealey.

Sanderson, M. (1988), 'The English Civic Universities and the "Industrial Spirit", 1870–1914', *Historical Research*, **61**.

Schumpeter, J. (1942), *Capitalism, Socialism, and Democracy*, New York, Harper & Row.

Servos, J. (1980), 'The Industrial Relations of Science: Chemical Engineering at MIT, 1900–1939', *ISIS*, **71**, 531–49.

Shonfield, A. (1965), *Modern Capitalism: The Changing Balance of Public and Private Power*, Oxford, Oxford University Press.

Sorge, A., and Warner, M. (1986), *Comparative Factory Organisation: An Anglo-German Comparison of Manufacturing, Management and Manpower*, Aldershot, Gower.

Streeck, W. (1992), *Social Institutions and Economic Performance: Studies of Industrial Relations in Advanced Capitalist Economies*, London and Newbury Park, CA, Sage.

— (1994), 'Pay Restraint without Incomes Policy: Institutionalised Monetarism and Industrial Unionism in Germany', in R. Dore, R. Boyer and Z. Mars (eds), *The Return to Incomes Policy*, London, Pinter.

Weidemann, H. (1980), 'Codetermination by Workers in German Enterprises', *American Journal of Comparative Law*, **28**, 79–92.

Wright, J. (1962), 'The Capital Market and the Finance of Industry', in G. Worswick and P. Ady (eds), *The British Economy in the Nineteen-Fifties*, Oxford, Oxford University Press.

Yergin, D., and Stanislaw, J. (1998), *The Commanding Heights*, New York, Simon & Schuster,

Yonekawa, S. (1984), 'University Graduates in Japanese Enterprises before the Second World War', *Business History*, **26**(July), 193–218.

FREDERICK WINSLOW TAYLOR

The results of thirty years of experimentation by Mr. Taylor, who is the originator of Scientific Management, have come suddenly to public view through the recent demand before the Interstate Commerce Commission that the railroads be required to adopt Scientific Management.

THE AMERICAN MAGAZINE

VOL. LXXI   *MARCH, 1911*   *No. 5*

The Gospel of Efficiency

A NEW SCIENCE OF BUSINESS MANAGEMENT

TWO articles appear in the following pages. First: An introductory article by Mr. Ray Stannard Baker, dealing with the remarkable work and service of Mr. Frederick W. Taylor of Philadelphia. Mr. Taylor is a distinguished engineer, former president of the American Society of Mechanical Engineers. His inventions in the art of making tool-steel have revolutionized machine-shop practice, and his system of Scientific Management, now being rapidly introduced in many factories, plants and business enterprises, is proving of equally revolutionary importance. He was awarded at the Paris Exposition a personal gold medal and the Franklin Institute of Philadelphia has conferred upon him the distinguished honor of the Elliott Cresson gold medal.

Second: Mr. Taylor's own account (beginning on page 570) of the "Principles of Scientific Management." This, with two other articles written by Mr. Taylor for the April and May numbers of this magazine, is the first authoritative presentation of the whole subject, the first comprehensive account of the history of the discoveries, with the ripe conclusions of the originator.

Dean E. F. Gay, of the Graduate School of Business Administration of Harvard University, says:

"I regard the development of Scientific Management as promising to be the most important advance in industry since the introduction of the factory system and power machinery."

H. C. H. Carpenter, Professor of Metallurgy of Victoria University, England, says:

"Mr. Taylor's work (on the art of cutting metals) will rank among the most remarkable practical researches ever published."

Professor H. Le Chatelier, member of the French Academy and one of the foremost industrial scientists in the world, says:

"Few discoveries in the arts have been the occasion of so many successive surprises as those of Mr. Taylor."

The *Iron-Trade Review* calls Mr. Taylor's paper "On the Art of Cutting Metals," delivered as his presidential address in 1906 before the American Society of Mechanical Engineers, "the most important contribution ever made to engineering literature." The *Ironmonger* of London says: "Never in the history of any institution has a more important paper been submitted."

Machinery, one of the leading technical papers, says that "this remarkable investigation into the laws of cutting metals . . . almost staggers the mind to comprehend," and that it, with "the parallel work of improving shop management, will mean a great change not only in the metal-working industries, but in all branches of manufacturing as well, and this means that some of the present economic ideas may be turned upside down."

FREDERICK W. TAYLOR—SCIENTIST IN BUSINESS MANAGEMENT

BY

RAY STANNARD BAKER

AUTHOR OF "THE SPIRITUAL UNREST," "ON THE POLITICAL FIRING LINE," ETC.

ILLUSTRATED WITH PHOTOGRAPHS

FOR three days last November I sat in the court room of the Interstate Commerce Commission at Washington, listening to one of the most remarkable cases ever presented before that distinguished body. On one side were ranged the powerful Eastern railroads, present in the persons of some half a hundred attorneys, and pleading permission from the Government to raise their rates; on the other side were the Eastern shippers, disputing the demands of the railroads. Upon the issue hung vast commercial and financial interests.

The railroads pleaded that they must have more money from the people to meet the "increased cost of living," especially the wages of their employees. The shippers responded by boldly attacking the railroads at the point where they have always felt strongest—that of managerial efficiency. The shippers declared that the railroads were not efficiently managed, and that if they would "look within," they could save more money than they now demanded in increased rates.

To support this bold response Mr. Louis D. Brandeis, the shippers' attorney, placed on the stand eleven witnesses who told of a singular new system or method of securing a marvelous degree of efficiency in all manner of industrial operations. This new system, or philosophy, which they said, frankly, was revolutionary in its aims, they called Scientific Management.

Few of those present had ever even heard of Scientific Management or of Mr. Taylor, its originator, and the testimony, at first, awakened a clearly perceptible incredulity. Nor was such incredulity surprising; for it was asserted that Scientific Management would commonly double or treble the producing capacity of every workman in a given industry, it would raise wages, it would increase profits, it would go far toward solving the labor problem. It was even asserted with confidence by one witness, Mr. Emerson, that, if applied to the railroads, Scientific Management could be counted upon to save at least $1,000,000 a day.

To those who heard this testimony there seemed at first something almost magical about the new idea; but as one sober, hard-headed business man after another testified as to what had been actually accomplished in his plant, when it appeared that Scientific Management had been applied with extraordinary results to widely diversified industries, from steel plants to bleacheries and cotton mills, and including railroad repair shops, the spirit of incredulity changed to one of deep interest. Another factor in carrying conviction to the hearers was the extraordinary fervor and enthusiasm expressed by every man who testified. Theirs was the firm faith of apostles: it was a philosophy which worked, and they had the figures to show it.

"This," said Mr. Commissioner Lane to one of the witnesses, "has become a sort of substitute for religion with you."

"Yes, sir," responded Mr. Gilbreth.

Since then I suppose there have been thousands of articles and editorials written for the newspapers regarding Scientific Management, with every view advanced, from that of sarcastic unbelief to that of firm conviction.

Mr. Taylor himself was not present at the hearing, but he was constantly referred to as the originator of the system; and he has since become a man of whom the world wishes to know more. What is this Scientific Management, and who is Mr. Taylor?

With my interest keenly aroused, I went to see Mr. Taylor at his beautiful home at Chestnut Hill, Philadelphia; and I have talked with most of the men who have been prominent in developing the principles of Scientific Management. I have also visited some of the shops and factories where its introduction has produced such extraordinary results.

One day, some thirty-six years ago, a young man named Taylor began work in a Philadelphia machine shop. He swept up the shavings in the morning, handled the materials, and attended the wants of the pattern-makers. He was an apprentice. A boyish-looking young man, small of stature, he was as close-knit and wiry as a steel spring, and he had the peculiar light, quick step which goes with superior physical and intellectual energy. Also, he was equipped with a gray eye and a square chin. He had an air of determination.

Emerson has commented somewhere upon the commotion which arises when the Almighty lets loose a thinker upon this planet. This young man Taylor was a thinker. He had come of one of the old Quaker families of Philadelphia. One of his ancestors came over from England in the *Mayflower*, another followed William Penn to the settlements in Pennsylvania. His father's father was a rich East India merchant and his father a lawyer

EMILY WINSLOW, MR. TAYLOR'S MOTHER

When only twenty years old she was one of the group of remarkable women, including Lucretia Mott, who were appointed delegates to the "World's Anti-Slavery Convention in London"

and a Princeton man of the class of 1840. On his mother's side, his grandfather, Isaac Winslow of New Bedford, was so successful as a whale fisher that he was selected by the French Government to introduce the art of whale fishing in France. After making a large fortune at this employment he returned to America and devoted his remaining years to mechanical inventions, obtaining a patent for a process of canning vegetables upon which is founded the modern canning industry. Mr. Taylor's mother, Emily Winslow, was a woman of extraordinary talent and of unusual beauty. When only twenty years old she was one of the group of remarkable women, including Lucretia Mott, who were appointed delegates to the World's Anti-Slavery Convention in London. She was one of the earliest of the defenders of women's rights, and the Taylor home 'in Church Lane in Philadelphia during young Taylor's boyhood was frequented by the leading spirits in the anti-slavery and reform causes.

The boy was given two years of school in France and Germany and then a year and a half of travel in Italy, Switzerland, Norway, England, France, Germany and Austria— "All of which," he says, "I heartily disapprove of for a young boy." After this he returned to the healthy outdoor life of Germantown, in which sport was the leading idea—"than which there is nothing finer in the world"—then two years of really very hard study, coupled with athletics at Exeter. At that time one half the pupils at Exeter were dropped each year and the discipline was exceedingly severe.

Young Taylor was preparing for Harvard, but after two years at Exeter his eyes failed,

MR TAYLOR AT THE AGE OF TEN

and he went home to Philadelphia and began work as an apprentice in a pattern shop, and afterward in a machine shop.

Here he met workingmen for the first time and made the discovery which some young men of his upbringing never make, that the finest kinds of men and women live in all ranks of society and in the smallest and most out-of-the-way places. He made, in short, that democratic discovery without which a man's life in modern America is not worth much. He regards the early years of his apprenticeship as the best training he ever had and the workman under whom he served, who was a man of extraordinary ability, coupled with fine character, as one of the best teachers. He was instinctively democratic and it was not long before the workmen all called him "Fred," as many of them do to this day. For many years, while he served as a laborer, as a machinist, as a boss, as a foreman, and finally as chief engineer of the great steel works of the Midvale Company, his interests and sympathies were strongly enlisted by the human element in industry.

Serving as a workman, he knew the workman's side, and serving as a boss and foreman, he knew the employer's side. He had also gone through the bitter struggle for more education which so many workmen have to meet. He was told that he could not become chief engineer of the Midvale plant without a college degree; accordingly, he set to work at nights and in two years and a half he had passed all the examinations and won the degree of M.E. from Stevens Institute.

From the very first young Taylor, with

his early home environment in a reform atmosphere and his natural democratic instincts, was impressed with the deplorable conditions of industry, the bitter warfare between capital and labor, the neglect of the employer, the "soldiering" of the employees; the utter wastefulness, inefficiency, and heartlessness which characterized nearly all industrial operations. It was as natural as sunlight for him to inquire:

"How can I change these things?"

No sooner did he reach a position where he had any authority at all than he began the long series of experiments which have resulted in the remarkable new Science of Management. I shall not here go into these experiments in detail: Mr. Taylor tells the whole story much better than I could in his own articles in this magazine. But this point I wish strongly to make: While the attention of most industrial scientists and inventors has been fixed upon the machine—the material aspects of industry—Mr. Taylor's eye has always been fixed upon the man. It has been his chief ambition, as he says, to make every industry, first of all, a "manfactory." He has invented many useful mechanical devices, and his studies in the art of cutting metals have revolutionized machine-shop practice, but whether he studied belting, or experimented with tool steel, or worked on the problem of the storage of materials, it was always with a clear eye to the effect upon the man in the shops. He would make the machines serve the man, not the man the machines.

There are two varieties of the scientific mind—one the mind that with infinite analytical patience studies minute details and produces the data, the raw material, of science; the other and far rarer type, that which combines the infinite patience of the investigator with the imaginative genius of the generalizer. Mr. Taylor belongs to this higher type of the scientist.

When he began he had no idea of a new system of managing industry. He found himself face to face with a practical question which he could not answer:

How can all the forces of industry, the workman on one side and the employer on the other, be made to work harmoniously together?

In seeking to answer that question, he found that he must formulate a vast range of knowledge which had always in the past lain inchoate and unorganized in the brains of workingmen. In short, he had to work out a science of metal-cutting, a science of bricklaying, a science of plastering. His effort was to socialize and render available a vast body of knowledge hitherto possessed only by individuals and passed down from father to son by word of mouth. In doing this he carried on tens of thousands of careful experiments, under the most difficult conditions, for he had to make his work pay as he went along; that is, he had to show results enough to warrant the owners of the plant where he worked in advancing the money for these experiments. Thus he collected a vast amount of data in regard to the human element of industry.

Having this data, he discovered that in

MR. TAYLOR AS A YOUNG MAN OF TWENTY-SEVEN

He won the national tennis championship at Newport in 1881

order to use the cunning human machine with real efficiency the whole system of management must be changed. No army can advance far while two internal factions are bitterly quarreling. Industry cannot advance by war and waste; it must advance by coöperation and efficiency. Employer and employee must work together. Instead of commanding the workman as in the past, requiring him often to make bricks without straw, the management under Mr. Taylor's system is to use its new scientific information as a basis for teaching and serving the workmen, with the end that not only the product but the rewards of both hand-worker and brain-worker may be largely increased. In short, Mr. Taylor would shift the management of industry from the old military basis to an educational and co-operative basis. Under the new system a man who enters a factory as a workman does not find himself driven to his task and exploited, but discovers that he has entered a great educational institution where the management is eager to train him to his utmost ability, pay him according to his product, and advance him as rapidly as his capabilities permit. When scientifically regarded there is no employment that is not skilled, no employment to which brains will not add a vast increment of improvement.

Upon these great fundamental ideas Mr. Taylor's fame will ultimately rest. But it is a significant fact that until recently, even among engineers, his work in developing Scientific Management has not been as highly regarded as his work in inventing high-speed steel and in improving the art of cutting metals. This is easily explainable: high-speed steel is a mechanical device which can be handled and seen, and its adoption results in immediate profit, while the Science of Management is a philosophy, dealing with intangible human and psychological elements, and, like any great step forward, it requires care in its application and time before it begins to show profits in dollars and cents.

Scientific Management was presented in two papers before the American Society of Mechanical Engineers; the first called "A Piece Rate System" in 1895, and the second, "Shop Management," in 1903. "Shop Management" is one of the great books of recent years, and will in time be so regarded. As Harrington Emerson said of it, in the discussion which followed its presentation:

"I regard the paper presented at this meeting by Mr. Taylor as the most important contribution ever presented to the society,

and one of the most important papers ever published in the United States."

It has now been translated into German, French, Russian, Dutch, and Danish, and is known to students all over the world. Dean E. F. Gay, of the Harvard Graduate School of Business Administration, early recognizing the great importance of Mr. Taylor's work, has devoted an entire course to the presentation of the principles of Scientific Management, and Mr. Taylor, Mr. Barth, Mr. Emerson, Mr. Gantt, Mr. Cooke, Mr. Thompson and other leaders of the movement have lectured before the Harvard classes. The system is now being studied and adopted not only in this country, but in England, France and Germany, although this country, so far, has a long start.

The other notable work of Mr. Taylor, an offshoot of his studies in Scientific Management, was his paper "On the Art of Cutting Metals," which he delivered as his presidential address in 1906 before the American Society of Mechanical Engineers. It was the first account of his discovery and invention of high-speed steel and of his studies in the forms and sizes of tools for cutting metals. High-speed steel is now used in every well-equipped machine shop in the world, and Mr. Taylor's paper "On the Art of Cutting Metals" is recognized by the highest authorities as being one of the greatest studies in industrial science ever produced.

Professor H. Le Chatelier, member of the French Academy and the foremost French authority on metallurgy, has said:

"Few discoveries in the arts have been the occasion of so many successive surprises as those of Mr. Taylor. At the time of the exhibition in Paris, nobody quite believed in the prodigious result which was claimed by the Bethlehem Works (for tools made of high-speed steel), but we had to accept the evidence of our eyes when we saw enormous chips of steel cut off from a forging at such high speed that the nose of the tool was heated to a dull red color. . . . We can admire without reserve the scientific method which has controlled this whole work. It is an example unique in the history of the mechanic arts. We have all admired the researches of Sir Lothian Bell on blast furnaces, and those of Sir William Siemens on the regenerative furnace, but in reading their papers neither of them leaves an impression on the mind which can be compared with that of Mr. Taylor's paper."

Other tributes to Mr. Taylor's work are published in the introduction to this article.

MR. TAYLOR'S HOME AT CHESTNUT HILL, PHILADELPHIA
"A stately house, surrounded by wide-stretching gardens and hedges of box"

Mr. Taylor was also rewarded at the Paris Exposition with a personal gold medal, and the Franklin Institute of Philadelphia has conferred upon him the distinguished honor of the Elliott Cresson gold medal.

His inventions have brought him a considerable fortune, and he lives now at Chestnut Hill, Philadelphia, in one of the most beautiful of homes, a stately house, surrounded by wide-stretching gardens and hedges of box. Since 1901 he has devoted practically his entire time, and wholly without pay, to spreading the knowledge of his new philosophy of management.

"I can no longer afford to work for money," he says.

He has drawn around him a notable group of associates and assistants. Essentially he is a great teacher, for he possesses not only the ability to impart knowledge, but the genius to inspire his followers with a sort of passion of enthusiasm. All of his associates, being men of unusual ability, have contributed much to the development of his ideas and have borne the brunt of the practical work of introducing the system into shops and factories. Mr. Taylor has recognized the coöperative accomplishment in the true scientific spirit when, in his "On the Art of Cutting Metals," he gave to Mr. White the credit of being "a much more accomplished metallurgist than any of the rest of us," when he said that Mr. Gantt was "a better all-round manager," and Mr. Barth "the best mathematician of the

group." He has given credit in similar terms to the work of Mr. Cooke, Mr. Emerson, Mr. Thompson, Mr. Day and others. To himself he gives this credit:

"And the writer of this paper has perhaps the faculty of holding on tighter with his teeth than any of the others."

He has coöperated with Mr. Sanford E. Thompson in conducting a series of studies of other industries, such as cement work, plastering, bricklaying, excavating and so on. One book, called "Concrete, Plain and Reinforced," under the joint authorship of Taylor and Thompson, has now been issued and is already regarded as the standard work on the subject, having sold upward of ten thousand copies at $5 each, a remarkable circulation for a technical book. In time other books will be issued, on the various building trades, which are expected to be as thorough studies in those subjects as Mr. Taylor's "Art of Cutting Metals" is in that field.

Outside of these notable scientific accomplishments, Mr. Taylor is a man of wide cultivation, of varied interests and of personal charm. He has a lively and progressive mind, seizing eagerly upon the problems of the day. He has always had a keen interest in sport, having in the year 1881 won the national championship at tennis (doubles) in a tournament played at Newport. His inventions of tennis posts and tennis nets are still widely in use. He is also an enthusiastic golf-player.

At present he is gratifying his love of investigation by a series of truly remarkable experiments in grass-growing. He started with the idea of learning how to grow better grass for putting greens, and he has made a number of notable discoveries. The United States Department of Agriculture, recognizing the importance of his results, is now coöperating with him in his further experiments. A rare, high type of American, a public servant in the best sense, the nation surely is not to be despaired of when it affords an atmosphere in which such a man can be developed. It is to the fine scientific habit of mind, with its catholicity of interest, its reverence for facts, its high sense of the value of human life, that the country must look for its salvation. There have been times in recent years when it seemed as though our civilization were being throttled by things, by property, by the very weight of industrial mechanism, and it is no small matter when a man arises who can show us new ways of commanding our environment.

"The genius of mechanism," says Carlyle, "will not always sit like a choking incubus on our soul; but at length, when by a new Magic Word the old spell is broken, become our slave, and as familiar-spirit do all our bidding."

THE PRINCIPLES OF
SCIENTIFIC MANAGEMENT*

BY

FREDERICK W. TAYLOR

ILLUSTRATED WITH PHOTOGRAPHS

PRESIDENT ROOSEVELT, in his address to the Governors at the White House, prophetically remarked that "the conservation of our national resources is only preliminary to the larger question of national efficiency."

The whole country at once recognized the importance of conserving our material resources, and a large movement has been started which will be effective in accomplishing this object. As yet, however, we have but vaguely appreciated the importance of "the larger question of increasing our national efficiency."

We can see our forests vanishing, our water powers going to waste, our soil being carried by floods into the sea; and the end of our coal and our iron is in sight.

We can see and feel the waste of material things. But we cannot see or feel the larger wastes of human effort going on all around us. Awkward, inefficient, or ill-directed movements of men leave nothing visible or tangible behind them. Their appreciation calls for an act of memory, an effort of the imagination. And for this reason, even though our daily loss from this source is greater than from our waste of material things, the one has stirred us deeply, while the other has moved us but little.

The search for better, for more competent men, from the presidents of our great companies down to our household servants, was never more vigorous than it is now. And more than ever before is the demand for competent men in excess of the supply.

What we are all looking for is the ready-made, competent man; the man whom some one else has trained. It is only when we fully realize that our duty, as well as our opportunity, lies in systematically coöperating to train this competent man that we shall be on the road to national efficiency.

In the past the man has been first; in the future the system must be first. This in no sense, however, implies that great men are not needed. On the contrary, the first object of any good system must be that of developing first-class men; and under Scientific Management the best man rises to the top more certainly and more rapidly than ever before.

This article has been written:

First. To point out the great loss which the whole country is suffering through inefficiency in almost all of our daily acts.

Second. To try to convince the reader that the remedy for this inefficiency lies in systematic management, rather than in searching for some unusual or extraordinary man.

Third. To prove that the best management is a true science, resting upon clearly defined laws, rules, and principles, and that these fundamental principles of Scientific Management are applicable to all kinds of human activities, from our simplest individual acts to the work of our great corporations. And that whenever these principles are correctly applied results follow which are truly astounding.

In order to develop the subject of Scientific Management in a logical and orderly manner, the writer will present the problems of industry in exactly the way in which he himself had to meet them. He encountered the difficulties blindly, and the conclusions at which he has arrived are the results of the hard teachings of actual experience.

The writer came into the machine shop of the Midvale Steel Company of Philadelphia in 1878, after having served an apprenticeship as a patternmaker and as a machinist. This was close to the end of the long period of depression following the panic of 1873 and business was so poor that it was impossible for many mechanics to get work at their trades. For this reason he was obliged to

start to work as an unskilled day laborer, instead of working as a mechanic. Fortunately for him, soon after he came into the shop the clerk was found to be stealing. There was no one else available, and so, having more education than the other laborers (since he had been prepared for college), he was advanced to the position of clerk. Shortly after this he was given work as a machinist in running one of the lathes, and as he turned out rather more work than other machinists were doing on similar lathes, after several months he was made gang boss over the lathes.

Almost all of the work of this shop had been done on piecework for several years. As was usual then, and in fact as is still usual in most shops of the country, the shop was really run by the workmen and not by the bosses. The workmen together had carefully planned just how fast each job should be done, and they had set a pace for each machine, which amounted to about one third of a good day's work. Every new workman who came into the shop was told at once by other workmen exactly how fast he was to work on every job, and unless he obeyed these instructions he was sure before long to find himself out of work.

In short, the writer here made, for the first time, an intimate acquaintance with the fundamental principle upon which industry seems now to be run in this country. This principle is that the employer shall pay just as low wages as he can and that the workman shall retaliate by doing just as little work as

HENRY L. GANTT

One of the leaders in the practical introduction of Scientific Management. His "bonus system" for paying workingmen is widely known. His book, "Work, Ways and Profit," is a lucid explanation of the new ideas

he can. Industry is thus a warfare, in which both sides, instead of giving out the best that is in them, seem determined to give out the worst that is in them.

The English and American people are the greatest sportsmen in the world. Whenever an American workman plays baseball, or an English workman plays cricket, it is safe to say that he strains every nerve to secure victory for his side. He does his very best to make the largest possible number of runs. The universal sentiment is so strong that any man who fails to give out all there is in him in sport is branded as a "quitter" and treated with contempt by those around him.

When the same workman returns to work on the following day, instead of using every effort to turn out the largest possible amount of work, in a majority of cases this man deliberately plans to turn out far less work than he is well able to do—in many instances he does not more than one third or one half of a proper day's work. And in fact if he were to do his best to turn out his largest possible day's work, he would be abused by his fellow-workers for so doing, even more than he would if he had proved himself a "quitter" at sport.

"Soldiering" as it is called in this country, "hanging it out" in England, "ca canny" in Scotland, is thus almost universal in industrial establishments, and prevails also to a large extent in the building trades; and the writer asserts without fear of contradiction that this constitutes the greatest misfortune, one may almost say the greatest evil, with which the working people of both England and America are now afflicted.

When to soldiering is added the natural inefficiency, ignorance, and wastefulness which characterize many if not most of the common operations of industrial establishments, it will be seen in what a deplorable state modern industry finds itself. What other reforms, among those which are being discussed by these two nations, could do more toward promoting prosperity than the introduction of some form of coöperation which should abolish this warfare of industry, which results in so much wastefulness, inefficiency, and soldiering? Is it not the root question of all the questions?

It was not, however, until the writer had been made gang boss over the lathes that he began to see the full iniquity of the system under which he and all his fellow-workmen were making their living. As soon as his appointment was known, one after another of the men came to him and talked somewhat as follows:

"Now, Fred, we're very glad to see that you've been made gang boss. You know the game all right, and we're sure that you're not likely to be a piecework hog. You come along with us and everything will be all right, but if you try breaking any of these rates you can be mighty sure that we'll throw you over the fence."

The writer told them plainly that he was now working on the side of the management, and that he proposed to do whatever he could to get a fair day's work out of the lathes. This immediately started a war; in most cases a friendly war, because the men who were under him were his personal friends, but none the less a war, which as time went on grew more and more bitter, the writer using every expedient to make the men do a fair day's work, such as discharging or lowering the wages of the more stubborn men, lowering the piecework price, hiring green men and personally teaching them how to do the work with the promise from them that when they had learned how they would then do a fair day's work, and later, after they had become skilled, having them forced by the public opinion of the shop to do what all the rest were doing. No one who has not had this experience can have an idea of the bitterness which is gradually developed in such a struggle. In a war of this kind, the workmen have one expedient which is usually effective. They use their ingenuity to contrive various ways in which the machines are broken or damaged—apparently by accident, or in the regular course of work—and this they lay always at the door of the foreman, who, they assert, is forcing them to drive the machine so hard that it is being ruined. And there are few foremen who are able to stand up against the combined pressure of all of the men in the shop.

The writer had certain advantages, however, which are not possessed by the ordinary foreman. *First*, owing to the fact that he happened not to be of working parents, the owners of the company believed that he had the interest of the works more at heart than the other workmen, and they therefore had more confidence in his word. When the machinists reported to the general superintendent that the machines were being smashed up because of an incompetent foreman, the general superintendent accepted the word of the writer when he said that these men were deliberately breaking their machines as a part of the piecework war.

Second, if the writer had been one of the workmen, and had lived where they lived, they would have brought such social pressure to bear upon him that it would have been impossible to have stood out against them. He would have been called "scab" and other foul names every time he appeared on the street; his wife would have been abused and his children would have been stoned. Once or twice he was begged by some of his friends among the workmen not to walk home about two and a half miles along the lonely path by the side of the railway. He was told that if he continued to do this it would be at the risk of his life. In all such cases, however, a display of timidity is apt to increase rather than diminish the risk, so the writer told these men to say to the other men in the shop that he proposed to walk home every

E. F. GAY, OF HARVARD UNIVERSITY

Early recognizing the great importance of Mr. Taylor's work, Professor Gay, who is the Dean of the Graduate School of Business Administration at Harvard, has devoted an entire course to the presentation of the principles of Scientific Management

friends came to him continually and asked him, in a personal, friendly way, whether he would advise them, for their own interest, to turn out more work. And, as a truthful man, he had to tell them that if he were in their place, he would fight against turning out any more work, just as they were doing, because under the piecework system they would be allowed to earn no more wages than they had been earning, and yet they would be made to work harder. That is the meanness of the old system; it is based on hatred and force and greed.

Soon after being made foreman, therefore, he decided to try to change in some way the system of management, so that the interests of the workman and the management would be coöperative instead of antagonistic. He began his experiments gropingly, but with the

night right up that railway track; that he never had carried and never would carry any weapon of any kind, and that they could shoot and be d——.

After about three years of this kind of struggling, the output of the machines had been materially increased, in many cases doubled, and as a result the writer had been promoted from one gang boss-ship to another until he became foreman of the shop. For any right-minded man, however, such a success was in no sense a recompense for the bitter relations which he was forced to maintain with all of those around him. Life which is one continuous struggle with other men is hardly worth living. His workmen

result that three years later he started a new type of management in the Midvale shops which he described later in two papers read before the American Society of Mechanical Engineers and entitled, "A Piece-Rate System," and "Shop Management."

In beginning his studies the writer realized that the greatest obstacle to harmonious coöperation between the workmen and the management lay in the ignorance of the management as to what really constituted a proper day's work for a workman. He therefore obtained the permission of Mr. William Sellers, who was at that time president of the Midvale Steel Company, to spend some money in a careful scientific study of the men and the processes of work in the shops, and particularly the amount of time required to do various kinds of work. Mr. Sellers permitted this more as a reward to the writer for having, to a certain extent, "made good" as foreman of the shop in getting more work out of the men than for any other reason. He stated that he did not believe that any scientific study of this sort would give results of much value.

It was these investigations, however, the minute, painstaking analysis and study of the movements of men to find their quickest and best motions, which were started in 1881 at the Midvale Steel Works, and which have been carried on in increasing volume ever since, that mark the first steps taken toward Scientific Management. Particular illustrations explaining the methods of making this time study will be given later in this paper.

At the same time that this study of men was started, a similar investigation as to the best tools and implements to be used in each trade was begun. In the study of the tools and methods which constitute the art of cutting metals alone, and which lasted through a term of twenty-six years, between 30,000 and 50,000 experiments have been carefully recorded and many experiments have been made of which no record was kept. In studying these laws more than 800,000 pounds of steel and iron have been cut up into chips with experimental tools, and it is estimated that from $150,000 to $200,000 has been spent in the investigation.

These were only two of many lines of inves-

CARL G. BARTH

Whom Mr. Taylor describes as "the best mathematician of the group." Mr. Barth's wonderful development of slide rules for use in the metal-cutting industries have been invaluable and are extensively employed

tigation into which our studies carried us. In addition to this detail study of men and implements, we found that in order to bring about a greater efficiency of the men and better relationship between the management and the men, we had also to study shop arrangement, methods of keeping stores, the routing of materials, the best ways of using belts, etc., and we had to establish standards for all details throughout the works, and finally undertake the scientific planning of the work.

As a result of these studies certain principles of coöperation — which we have called Scientific Management— were discovered. These principles are no mere theories, for they have now been applied practically and profitably for nearly thirty years. During this period the employees of one company after another, including a large range and diversity of industries, have gradually changed from the ordinary to the scientific type of management. At least 50,000 workmen in the United States are now employed under the new system and they are receiving from 33 to 100 % higher wages daily than are paid to workmen of similar caliber with whom they are surrounded, while the companies employing them are more prosperous than ever before. In these companies the output per man per machine has on an average been doubled. Under this type of management there has never been during all these years a single strike. In place of the suspicious watchfulness and the more or less open warfare which characterize the ordinary types of management, there is universally friendly coöperation between the management and the men.

The Finest Type of Ordinary Management

Before starting to illustrate the principles of Scientific Management, it seems desirable to outline what the writer believes will be recognized as the best type of management which is in common use. This is done so that the great difference between the best of the ordinary management and Scientific Management may be fully appreciated.

In an industrial establishment which employs, say, from 500 to 1,000 workmen, there will be found in many cases at least twenty to thirty different trades. The workmen in each of these trades have had their knowledge handed down to them by word of mouth, through the many years in which their trade has been developed from the primitive condition to the present state of great subdivision of labor, in which each man specializes upon some comparatively small class of work.

The methods which are now in use may in a broad sense be said to be an evolution representing the survival of the fittest and best of the ideas which have been developed since the starting of each trade. However, while this is true in a broad sense, only those who are intimately acquainted with each of these trades are fully aware of the fact that in hardly any element of any trade is there uniformity in the methods which are used. Instead of having only one way which is generally accepted as a standard, there are in daily use, say, fifty or a hundred different

HARRINGTON EMERSON

Who has asserted that by the use of efficient management the railroads of the country could save $1,000,000 a day. His book, "Efficiency," is one of the ablest presentations of the philosophy of Scientific Management

ways of doing each element of the work. And a little thought will make it clear that this must inevitably be the case, since our methods have been handed down from man to man by word of mouth, or have, in most cases, been almost unconsciously learned through personal observation. Practically in no instances have they been codified or systematically analyzed or described.

Now, in the best of the ordinary types of management, the managers recognize frankly the fact that the 500 or 1,000 workmen, included in the twenty to thirty trades, who are under them possess this mass of traditional knowledge, a large part of which is not in the possession of the management. The management, of course, including foreman and superintendents, know, better than anyone else, that their own knowledge and personal skill fall far short of the combined knowledge and dexterity of all the workmen under them. The most experienced managers, therefore, frankly place before their workmen the problem of doing the work in the best and most economical way. They recognize the task before them as that of inducing each workman to use his best endeavors, his hardest work, all his traditional knowledge, his skill, his ingenuity and his good will—in a word, his "initiative," so as to yield the largest possible return to his employer. The problem before the management, then, may be briefly said to be that of obtaining the best *initiative* of every workman.

On the other hand, no intelligent manager

would hope to obtain in any full measure the initiative of his workmen unless he felt that he was giving them something more than they usually receive from their employers. Only those among the readers of this article who have been managers or who have worked themselves at a trade realize how far the average workman falls short of giving his employer his full initiative. It is well within the mark to state that in nineteen out of twenty industrial establishments the workmen believe it to be directly against their interests to give their employers their best initiative, and that instead of working hard to do the largest possible amount of work and the best quality of work for their employers, they deliberately work as slowly as they dare while they at the same time try to make those over them believe that they are working fast.

This *special incentive* can be given in several different ways, as, for example, the hope of rapid promotion or advancement; higher wages; shorter hours of labor; better surroundings and working conditions than are ordinarily given, etc.; and above all, that personal consideration for, and friendly contact with the workmen which comes only from a genuine and kindly interest in their welfare and their success. It is only by giving a special inducement or "incentive" of this kind that the employer can hope to even approximately get the "initiative" of his workmen. Under the ordinary type of management, the necessity for offering the workman a special inducement has come to be so

MORRIS LLEWELLYN COOKE

A leading engineer in applying the principles of Scientific Management. His recent inquiry into the efficiency of University work under the auspices of the Carnegie foundation has awakened the widest interest

generally recognized that a large proportion of those most interested in the subject look upon the adoption of some one of the modern schemes for paying men (such as piecework, the premium plan, or the bonus plan, for instance) as practically the whole system of management.*

Broadly speaking, then, the best type of management in ordinary use may be defined as management in which the workmen give their best *initiative* and in return receive some *special incentive* from their employers. This type of management will be referred to as the management of "*initiative and incentive*" in contradistinction to modern scientific management, or task management, with which it is to be compared.

Under the old type of management (the management of "initiative and incentive") success depends almost entirely upon getting the "initiative" of the workmen, and it is indeed a rare case in which this initiative is attained. Under scientific management the "initiative" of the workmen (that is, their hard work, their good will and their ingenuity) is obtained with absolute uniformity and to a greater extent than is possible under the old system. In addition to this improvement on the part of the men the managers assume new burdens, new duties and responsibilities never dreamed of in the past. The managers assume, for instance, the burden of gathering

* Under Scientific Management, the particular pay system which is adopted is merely one of the subordinate elements of management.

together all of the traditional knowledge which in the past has been possessed by the workmen and then of classifying, tabulating and reducing this knowledge to rules and formulæ which are immensely helpful to the workmen in doing their daily work.

These new duties of the management are grouped under four heads:

Four Fundamental Elements

First: They develop a science for each element of a man's work, which replaces the old rule of thumb method.

Second: They scientifically select and train the workman, where in the past he chose his own work and trained himself as best he could.

Third: They heartily coöperate with the men, so as to insure all of the work being done in accordance with the principles of the science which has been developed.

Fourth: There is an almost equal division of the work and the responsibility between the management and the workmen. The management take over all work for which they are better fitted than the workmen, while in the past almost all of the work and the greater part of the responsibility were thrown upon the men.

It is this combination of the initiative of the workmen coupled with the new types of work done by the management that makes Scientific Management so much more efficient than the old plan. Three of these elements exist in many cases under the management of "initiative and incentive," in a small and rudimentary way, but they are, under this management, of minor importance, whereas under Scientific Management they form the very essence of the whole system.

The writer is fully aware that, to perhaps most of the readers of this paper, the four elements which differentiate the new management from the old, will at first appear to be merely high-sounding phrases; and he would again repeat that he has no idea of convincing the reader of their value merely through announcing their existence. His hope of carrying conviction rests upon demonstrating the tremendous force and effect of these four elements through a series of practical illustrations. It will be shown, first, that they can be applied absolutely to all classes of work, from the most elementary to the most intricate, and second, that when they are applied the results must of necessity be overwhelmingly greater than those which it is possible to attain under the management of initiative and incentive.

The first illustration is that of handling pig iron, and this work is chosen because it is typical of perhaps the crudest and most elementary form of labor which is performed by man. This work is done by men with no other implements than their hands. The pig-iron handler stoops down, picks up a pig weighing about 92 pounds, walks for a few feet or yards and then drops it onto the ground or upon a pile. This work is so crude and elementary in its nature that the writer firmly believes that it would be possible to train an intelligent gorilla so as to be a more efficient pig-iron handler than any man can be. Yet it will be shown that the science of handling pig iron is so great and amounts to so much that it is impossible for the man who is best suited to this type of work to understand the principles of this science, or even to work in accordance with these principles, without the aid of a man better educated than he is. And the further illustrations to be given will make it clear that in almost all of the mechanic arts the science which underlies each workman's act is so great and amounts to so much that the workman who is best suited to actually doing the work is incapable (either through lack of education or through insufficient mental capacity) of understanding this science. This is announced as a general principle, the truth of which will become apparent as one illustration after another is given. After showing these three elements in the handling of pig iron, several illustrations will be given of their application to different kinds of work in the field of the mechanic arts, at intervals in a rising scale, beginning with the simplest and ending with the more intricate forms of labor.

One of the first pieces of work undertaken by us, when the writer started to introduce Scientific Management into the Bethlehem Steel Company, was to handle pig iron. The opening of the Spanish war found some 80,000 tons of pig iron piled in small piles in an open field adjoining the works. With the opening of the war, the price rose and the pig iron was sold. This gave us a good opportunity to show the workmen, as well as the owners and managers of the works, on a fairly large scale the advantages of Scientific Management over the old-fashioned day-work and piecework system.

The Bethlehem Steel Company had a pig-iron gang consisting of about 75 men. They were good, average pig-iron handlers, were under an excellent foreman who himself had been a pig-iron handler, and the work was done, on the whole, about as fast and as cheaply as it was anywhere else at that time. A railroad switch was run into the field, right along the edge of the piles of pig iron. An inclined plank was placed against the side of a car, and each man picked up from his pile a pig of iron weighing about 92 pounds, walked up the inclined plant and dropped it on the end of the car.

This gang was loading on the average about 12½ long tons per man per day. We were surprised to find, after a scientific study of the men at work, that a first-class pig-iron handler ought to handle between 47 and 48 long tons per day, instead of 12½ tons. This task seemed to us so very large that we were obliged to go over our work several times before we were absolutely sure that we were right. Once we were sure, however, that 47 tons was a proper day's work for a first-class pig-iron handler, the task which faced us as managers under the modern scientific plan was clearly before us. It was our duty to see that the 80,000 tons of pig iron piled on the open lot was loaded on to the cars at the rate of 47 tons per man per day, in place of 12½ tons. And it was further our duty to see that this work was done without bringing on a strike among the men, without any quarrel with the men, and to see that the men were happier and better contented when loading at the new rate of 47 tons than they were when loading at the old rate of 12½ tons.

The first practical step, therefore, was the scientific selection of the workman.

In dealing with workmen under this type of management, it is an inflexible rule to talk to and deal with only one man at a time, since each workman has his own special abilities and limitations, and men vary to such an extent that it is impossible to educate and improve them in masses. What we are trying to do, then, is to develop each individual man to his highest state of efficiency and prosperity. We therefore carefully watched and studied these 75 men for three or four days. We finally picked out four men, looked up their history as far back as we could, and made thorough inquiries as to the character, habits and the ambition of each of them. Finally we selected one from among the four as the most likely man to start with. He was a little Pennsylvania Dutchman, who would trot back home for a mile or so after his work in the evening, about as fresh as he was when he came trotting down to work in the morning. We found that upon wages of $1.15 a day he had succeeded in buying a small plot of ground, and that he was engaged in putting up the walls of a little house for himself in the morning before starting to work and at

night after leaving. He also had the reputation of being exceedingly "close." As one man whom we talked to about him said, "A penny looks about the size of a cartwheel to him." This man we will call Schmidt.

The task before us, then, narrowed itself down to getting Schmidt to handle 47 tons of pig iron per day and making him glad to do it. Schmidt was called out from among the gang of pig-iron handlers and talked to somewhat in this way:

"Schmidt, are you a high-priced man?"

"Vell, I don't know vat you mean."

"Oh, come now, you answer my questions. What I want to find out is, whether you are a high-priced man or one of these cheap fellows here. What I want to find out is whether you want to earn $1.85 a day or whether you are satisfied with $1.15, just the same as all those cheap fellows are getting."

"Did I vant $1.85 a day? Vas dot a high-priced man? Vell, yes, I vas a high-priced man."

"Oh, you're irritating me. Of course you want $1.85 a day—everyone wants it! You know perfectly well that that has very little to do with your being a high-priced man. Now come over here. You see that pile of pig iron?"

"Yes."

"You see that car?"

"Yes."

"Well, if you are a high-priced man, you will load that pig iron on that car to-morrow for $1.85. Now do wake up and answer my questions. Tell me whether you are a high-priced man or not?"

"Vell—did I get $1.85 for loading dot pig iron on dot car to-morrow?"

"Yes, of course, you do, and you get $1.85 for loading a pile like that every day right through the year."

"Vell, dot's all right. I could load dot pig iron on the car to-morrow for $1.85, and I get it every day, don't I?"

"Certainly you do—certainly you do."

"Vell, den, I vas a high-priced man."

"Now, hold on, hold on. You know just as well as I do that a high-priced man has to do exactly as he's told from morning till night. You have seen this man here before, haven't you?"

"No, I never saw him."

"Well, if you are a high-priced man, you will do exactly as this man tells you to-morrow, from morning till night. When he tells you to pick up a pig and walk, you pick it up and you walk, and when he tells you to sit down and rest, you sit down. You do that right straight through the day. Now you come on to work here to-morrow morning and I'll know before night whether you are really a high-priced man or not."

This seems to be rather rough talk. And indeed it would be if applied to an educated mechanic, or even an intelligent laborer. With a man of the mental type of Schmidt, it is appropriate and not unkind.

What would Schmidt's answer be if he were talked to in the manner which is usual under the old system of management, that of initiative and incentive, say as follows?

"Now, Schmidt, you are a first-class pig-iron handler and know your business well. You have been handling at the rate of 12½ tons per day. I have given considerable study to handling pig iron, and feel sure that you could do a much larger day's work than you have here. Now don't you think that if you really tried you could handle 47 tons of pig iron per day, instead of 12½ tons?"

What do you think Schmidt's answer would be to this?

Schmidt started in to work, and all day long, and at regular intervals, was told by the man who stood over him with a watch, "Now, pick up a pig and walk. Now sit down and rest. Now, walk—now, rest," etc. He worked when he was told to work, and rested when he was told to rest, and at half-past five in the afternoon had his 47½ tons loaded on the car. And he practically never failed to work at this pace and do the task that was set him during the three years that the writer was at Bethlehem. And throughout this time he averaged a little more than $1.85 per day, whereas before he had never received over $1.15 per day, which was the ruling rate of wages at that time in Bethlehem. One man after another was picked out and trained to handle pig iron at the rate of 47½ tons per day, until all of the pig iron was handled at this rate, and all of this gang were receiving 60% more wages than other workmen around them.

If Schmidt had been allowed to attack the pile of 47 tons of pig iron without the guidance or direction of a man who understood the art, or science, of handling pig iron, in his desire to earn his high wages he would probably have tired himself out by 11 or 12 o'clock in the day. He would have kept so steadily at work that his muscles would not have had the proper periods of rest absolutely needed for recuperation, and he would have been completely exhausted. By having a man, however, who understood this law stand over him and direct his work, day after day, until he acquired the habit of resting at

proper intervals, he was able to work at an even gait all day long.

To go into the matter in more detail, however, as to the scientific selection of the men: it is a fact that in this gang of 75 pig-iron handlers, only about 1 man in 8 was physically capable of handling 47½ tons per day. With the very best of intentions, the other 7 out of 8 men were physically unable to work at this pace. Now, the 1 man in 8 who was able to do this work was in no sense superior to the other men who were working on the gang. He merely happened to be a man of the type of the ox—no rare specimen of humanity, difficult to find and therefore very highly prized. On the contrary, he was a man so stupid that he was unfitted to do most kinds of laboring work, even. The selection of the man, then, does not involve the finding of some extraordinary individual, but merely the picking out from among very ordinary men the few who are especially suited to this type of work. Although in this particular gang only 1 man in 8 was suited to doing the work, we had not the slightest difficulty in getting all the men who were needed, some of them from inside of the works and others from the neighboring country.

Can Workmen Select Themselves?

Under the old forms of management, the attitude of the management is that of "putting the work up to the workmen." What likelihood would there be, then, under the old type of management, of these men properly selecting themselves for pig-iron handling? Would they be likely to get rid of seven out of eight from their own gang, and retain only the eighth man? No. And no expedient could be devised which would make these men properly select themselves. Even if they fully realized the necessity of doing so in order to obtain high wages (and they are not sufficiently intelligent to properly grasp this necessity), the fact that their friends or their brothers who were working right alongside of them would temporarily be thrown out of a job because they were not suited to this kind of work, would entirely prevent them from properly selecting themselves.

The writer has given above a brief description of the practical application of three of the four elements which constitute the essence of Scientific Management: first, the careful selection of the workman, and second and third, the method of first inducing and then training and helping the workman to work according to the scientific method.

Nothing has as yet been said about the science of handling pig iron. The writer trusts, however, that before leaving this illustration the reader will be thoroughly convinced that there is a science of handling pig iron, and that this science amounts to so much that the man who is suited to handle pig iron cannot possibly understand it, nor even work in accordance with its laws without the help of those who are over him.

Work a Man Should Do in a Day

This science was developed as the result of experiments started while the writer was foreman in the Midvale works in 1881 to find some rule, or law, which would enable a foreman to know in advance how much of any kind of heavy laboring work a man who was well suited to his job ought to do in a day. That is, to study the tiring effect of heavy labor upon a first-class man. Our first step was to employ a young college graduate to look up all that had been written on the subject in English, German and French. Two classes of experiments had been made; one by physiologists who were studying the endurance of the human animal, and the other by engineers who wished to determine what fraction of a horse-power a man-power was. These experiments had been made largely upon men who were lifting loads by means of turning the crank of a winch from which weights were suspended. Others, to determine the energy expended in walking, running and lifting weights in various ways. However, the records of these experiments were so meager that no law of any value could be deduced from them. We therefore started a series of experiments of our own.

Two first-class laborers were selected, men who had proved themselves to be physically powerful, and who were also good, steady workers. These men were paid double wages during the experiments, and were told that they must work to the best of their ability at all times, and that we should make certain tests with them from time to time to find whether they were "soldiering" or not, and the moment either one of them started to try to deceive us that he would be discharged.

Now, it must be clearly understood that in these experiments we were *not* trying to find the maximum work that any man could do on a short spurt or for a few days, but that our endeavor was to learn what really constituted a full day's work for a first-class man; the best day's work that a man could

properly do, year in and year out, and still thrive under. These men were given all kinds of tasks, which were carried out each day under the close observation of the young college man who was conducting the experiments, and who at the same time noted with a stop watch the proper time for all of the motions that were made by the men. Useless motions were eliminated, and fast motions substituted for awkward, inefficient movements. Every element in any way connected with the work which we believed could have a bearing on the speed and efficiency was carefully studied and recorded. What we hoped ultimately to determine was what fraction of a horse-power a man was able to exert—that is, how many foot pounds of work a man could do in a day.

After making this series of experiments, therefore, each man's work for each day was translated into foot pounds of energy, and to our surprise we found that there was no apparent relation between the foot pounds of energy which the man exerted during a day and the tiring effect of his work. On some kinds of work the man would be tired out when doing perhaps not more than one eighth of a horse-power, while in others he would be tired to no greater extent by doing half a horse-power of work. We failed, therefore, to find any law which was an accurate guide to the maximum day's work for a first-class workman.

Some years later a second series of experiments was made, similar to the first, but somewhat more thorough. This, however, resulted, as the first experiments, in obtaining valuable information, but not in the development of a law. Again, some years later, a third series of experiments was made, and this time no trouble was spared in our endeavor to make the work thorough. After this data was again translated into foot pounds of energy exerted for each man each day, it became perfectly clear that there is no direct relation between the horse-power which a man exerts (that is, his foot pounds of energy per day), and the tiring effect of the work on the man. The writer, however, was quite as firmly convinced as ever that some definite, clear-cut law existed as to what constitutes a full day's work for a first-class laborer, and our data had been so carefully collected and recorded that he felt sure that the necessary information was included somewhere in the records. The problem of developing this law from our accumulated facts was therefore handed over to Mr. Carl G.

Barth, who is a better mathematician than any of the rest of us, and we decided to investigate the problem in a new way, by graphically representing each element of the work through plotting curves, which should give us, as it were, a bird's-eye view of every element. In a comparatively short time Mr. Barth had discovered the law governing the tiring effect of heavy labor on a first-class man. And it is so simple in its nature that it is truly remarkable that it should not have been discovered and clearly understood years before.

The law is confined to that class of work in which the limit of a man's capacity is reached because he is tired out. It is the law of heavy laboring, corresponding to the work of the cart horse, rather than that of the trotter. Practically all such work consists of a heavy pull or a push on the man's arms, that is, the man's strength is exerted by either lifting or pushing something which he grasps in his hands. And the law is, that for each given pull or push on the man's arms it is possible for the workman to be under load for only a definite percentage of the day. For example, when pig iron is being handled (each pig weighing 92 pounds), a first-class workman can be under load only 43% of the day. He must be entirely free from load during 57% of the day. And as the load becomes lighter, the percentage of the day under which the man can remain under load increases. So that, if the workman is handling a half pig, weighing 46 pounds, he can then be under load 58% of the day, and only has to rest during 42%. As the load grows lighter the man can remain under load during a larger and larger percentage of the day, until finally a load is reached which he can carry in his hands all day long without being tired out.

When a laborer is carrying a piece of pig iron weighing 92 pounds in his hands, it tires him about as much to stand still under the load as it does to walk with it, since his arm muscles are under the same severe tension whether he is moving or not. A man, however, who stands still under a load is exerting no horse-power whatever, and this accounts for the fact that no constant relation could be traced in various kinds of heavy laboring work between the foot pounds of energy exerted and the tiring effect of the work on the man. It will also be clear that in all work of this kind, it is necessary for the arms of the workman to be completely free from load—

that is, for the workman to rest—at frequent intervals. Throughout the time that the man is under heavy load, the tissues of his arm muscles are in process of degeneration, and frequent periods of rest are required in order that the blood may have a chance to restore these tissues to their normal condition.

As to the possibility, under the old type of management, of inducing these pig-iron handlers (after they had been properly selected) to work in accordance with the science of doing heavy laboring, namely, having proper scientifically determined periods of rest in close sequence to periods of work. As has been indicated before, the essential idea of the ordinary types of management is that each workman has become more skilled in his own trade than it is possible for anyone in the management to be, and that, therefore, the details of how the work shall best be done must be left to him. The idea, then, of taking one man after another and training him under a competent teacher into new working habits until he continually and habitually works in accordance with scientific laws, which have been developed by some one else, is directly antagonistic to the old idea that each workman can best regulate his own way of doing the work. And besides this, the man suited to handling pig iron is too stupid to properly train himself. Thus it will be seen that with the ordinary types of management, the development of a science to replace rule of thumb, the scientific selection of the men, and inducing the men to work in accordance with these scientific principles, are entirely out of the question. And this because the philosophy of the old management puts the entire responsibility upon the workmen and uses force to secure results, while the philosophy of the new places a great part of it upon the management and seeks coöperation.

With most readers great sympathy will be aroused because seven out of eight of these pig-iron handlers were thrown out of a job. This sympathy is entirely wasted, because almost all of them were immediately given other jobs with the Bethlehem Steel Company. And indeed it should be understood that the removal of these men from pig-iron handling, for which they were unfit, was really a kindness to themselves, because it was the first step toward finding them work for which they were fitted, and at which, after receiving proper training, they could permanently and legitimately earn higher wages.

Next month Mr. Taylor will develop further the principles of Scientific Management and show how they are being applied in other occupations

Harvard Business Review

www.hbr.org

The classical view says that the manager organizes, coordinates, plans, and controls; the facts suggest otherwise.

The Manager's Job
Folklore and Fact

by Henry Mintzberg

The classical view says that the manager organizes, coordinates, plans, and controls; the facts suggest otherwise.

HBR CLASSIC

The Manager's Job
Folklore and Fact

by Henry Mintzberg

If you ask managers what they do, they will most likely tell you that they plan, organize, coordinate, and control. Then watch what they do. Don't be surprised if you can't relate what you see to these words.

When a manager is told that a factory has just burned down and then advises the caller to see whether temporary arrangements can be made to supply customers through a foreign subsidiary, is that manager planning, organizing, coordinating, or controlling? How about when he or she presents a gold watch to a retiring employee? Or attends a conference to meet people in the trade and returns with an interesting new product idea for employees to consider?

These four words, which have dominated management vocabulary since the French industrialist Henri Fayol first introduced them in 1916, tell us little about what managers actually do. At best, they indicate some vague objectives managers have when they work.

The field of management, so devoted to progress and change, has for more than half a century not seriously addressed *the* basic question: What do managers do? Without a proper answer, how can we teach management? How can we design planning or information systems for managers? How can we improve the practice of management at all?

Our ignorance of the nature of managerial work shows up in various ways in the modern organization—in boasts by successful managers who never spent a single day in a management training program; in the turnover of corporate planners who never quite understood what it was the manager wanted; in the computer consoles gathering dust in the back room because the managers never used the fancy online MIS some analyst thought they needed. Perhaps most important, our ignorance shows up in the inability of our large public organizations to come to grips with some of their most serious policy problems.

Somehow, in the rush to automate production, to use management science in the functional areas of marketing and finance, and to apply the skills of the behavioral scientist to the problem of worker motivation, the manager—the person in charge of the organization or one of its subunits—has been forgotten.

I intend to break the reader away from Fayol's words and introduce a more supportable and useful description of managerial work. This description derives from my review and synthesis of research on how various managers have spent their time.

In some studies, managers were observed intensively; in a number of others, they kept detailed diaries; in a few studies, their records were analyzed. All kinds of managers were studied—foremen, factory supervisors, staff managers, field sales managers, hospital administrators, presidents of companies and nations, and even street gang leaders. These "managers" worked in the United States, Canada, Sweden, and Great Britain.

A synthesis of these findings paints an interesting picture, one as different from Fayol's classical view as a cubist abstract is from a Renaissance painting. In a sense, this picture will be obvious to anyone who has ever spent a day in a manager's office, either in front of the desk or behind it. Yet, at the same time, this picture throws into doubt much of the folklore that we have accepted about the manager's work.

Folklore and Facts About Managerial Work

There are four myths about the manager's job that do not bear up under careful scrutiny of the facts.

Folklore: The manager is a reflective, systematic planner. The evidence on this issue is overwhelming, but not a shred of it supports this statement.

Fact: Study after study has shown that managers work at an unrelenting pace, that their activities are characterized by brevity, variety, and discontinuity, and that they are strongly oriented to action and dislike reflective activities. Consider this evidence:

Half the activities engaged in by the five chief executives of my study lasted less than nine minutes, and only 10% exceeded one hour.[1] A study of 56 U.S. foremen found that they averaged 583 activities per eight-hour shift, an average of 1 every 48 seconds.[2] The work pace for both chief executives and foremen was unrelenting. The chief executives met a steady stream of callers and mail from the moment they arrived in the morning until they left in the evening. Coffee breaks and lunches were inevitably work related, and ever-present subordinates seemed to usurp any free moment.

A diary study of 160 British middle and top managers found that they worked without interruption for a half hour or more only about once every two days.[3]

Of the verbal contacts the chief executives in my study engaged in, 93% were arranged on an ad hoc basis. Only 1% of the executives' time was spent in open-ended observational tours. Only 1 out of 368 verbal contacts was unrelated to a specific issue and could therefore be called general planning. Another researcher found that "in *not one single case* did a manager report obtaining important external information from a general conversation or other undirected personal communication."[4]

Is this the planner that the classical view describes? Hardly. The manager is simply responding to the pressures of the job. I found that my chief executives terminated many of their own activities, often leaving meetings before the end, and interrupted their desk work to call in subordinates. One president not only placed his desk so that he could look down a long hallway but also left his door open when he was alone—an invitation for subordinates to come in and interrupt him.

Clearly, these managers wanted to encourage the flow of current information. But more significantly, they seemed to be conditioned by their own work loads. They appreciated the opportunity cost of their own time, and they were continually aware of their ever-present obligations—mail to be answered, callers to attend to, and so on. It seems that a manager is always plagued by the possibilities of what might be done and what must be done.

When managers must plan, they seem to do so implicitly in the context of daily actions, not in some abstract process reserved for two weeks in the organization's mountain retreat. The plans of the chief executives I studied seemed to exist only in their heads—as flexible, but often specific, intentions. The traditional literature notwithstanding, the job of managing does not breed reflective planners; managers respond to stimuli, they are conditioned by their jobs to prefer live to delayed action.

Folklore: The effective manager has no regu-

Henry Mintzberg is the Bronfman Professor of Management at McGill University. His latest book is *Mintzberg on Management: Inside Our Strange World of Organizations* (Free Press, 1989). This article appeared originally in HBR July–August 1975. It won the McKinsey Award for excellence.

lar duties to perform. Managers are constantly being told to spend more time planning and delegating and less time seeing customers and engaging in negotiations. These are not, after all, the true tasks of the manager. To use the popular analogy, the good manager, like the good conductor, carefully orchestrates everything in advance, then sits back, responding occasionally to an unforeseeable exception. But here again the pleasant abstraction just does not seem to hold up.

Fact: Managerial work involves performing a number of regular duties, including ritual and ceremony, negotiations, and processing of soft information that links the organization with its environment. Consider some evidence from the research:

A study of the work of the presidents of small companies found that they engaged in routine activities because their companies could not afford staff specialists and were so thin on operating personnel that a single absence often required the president to substitute.[5]

One study of field sales managers and another of chief executives suggest that it is a natural part of both jobs to see important customers, assuming the managers wish to keep those customers.[6]

Someone, only half in jest, once described the manager as the person who sees visitors so that other people can get their work done. In my study, I found that certain ceremonial duties—meeting visiting dignitaries, giving out gold watches, presiding at Christmas dinners—were an intrinsic part of the chief executive's job.

Studies of managers' information flow suggest that managers play a key role in securing "soft" external information (much of it available only to them because of their status) and in passing it along to their subordinates.

Folklore: The senior manager needs aggregated information, which a formal management information system best provides. Not too long ago, the words *total information system* were everywhere in the management literature. In keeping with the classical view of the manager as that individual perched on the apex of a regulated, hierarchical system, the literature's manager was to receive all important information from a giant, comprehensive MIS.

But lately, these giant MIS systems are not working—managers are simply not using

them. The enthusiasm has waned. A look at how managers actually process information makes it clear why.

Fact: Managers strongly favor verbal media, telephone calls and meetings, over documents. Consider the following:

In two British studies, managers spent an average of 66% and 80% of their time in verbal (oral) communication.[7] In my study of five American chief executives, the figure was 78%.

These five chief executives treated mail processing as a burden to be dispensed with. One came in Saturday morning to process 142 pieces of mail in just over three hours, to "get rid of all the stuff." This same manager looked at the first piece of "hard" mail he had received all week, a standard cost report, and put it aside with the comment, "I never look at this."

These same five chief executives responded immediately to 2 of the 40 routine reports they received during the five weeks of my study and to 4 items in the 104 periodicals. They skimmed most of these periodicals in seconds, almost ritualistically. In all, these chief executives of good-sized organizations initiated on their own—that is, not in response to something else—a grand total of 25 pieces of mail during the 25 days I observed them.

An analysis of the mail the executives received reveals an interesting picture—only 13% was of specific and immediate use. So now we have another piece in the puzzle: not much of the mail provides live, current information—the action of a competitor, the mood of a government legislator, or the rating of last night's television show. Yet this is the information that drove the managers, interrupting their meetings and rescheduling their workdays.

Consider another interesting finding. Managers seem to cherish "soft" information, especially gossip, hearsay, and speculation. Why? The reason is its timeliness; today's gossip may be tomorrow's fact. The manager who misses the telephone call revealing that the company's biggest customer was seen golfing with a main competitor may read about a dramatic drop in sales in the next quarterly report. But then it's too late.

To assess the value of historical, aggregated, "hard" MIS information, consider two of the manager's prime uses for information—to identify problems and opportunities[8] and to

How often can you work for a half an hour without interruption?

build mental models (e.g., how the organization's budget system works, how customers buy products, how changes in the economy affect the organization). The evidence suggests that the manager identifies decision situations and builds models not with the aggregated abstractions an MIS provides but with specific tidbits of data.

Consider the words of Richard Neustadt, who studied the information-collecting habits of Presidents Roosevelt, Truman, and Eisenhower: "It is not information of a general sort that helps a President see personal stakes; not summaries, not surveys, not the *bland amalgams*. Rather…it is the odds and ends of *tangible detail* that pieced together in his mind illuminate the underside of issues put before him. To help himself he must reach out as widely as he can for every scrap of fact, opinion, gossip, bearing on his interests and relationships as President. He must become his own director of his own central intelligence."[9]

The manager's emphasis on this verbal media raises two important points. First, verbal information is stored in the brains of people. Only when people write this information down can it be stored in the files of the organization—whether in metal cabinets or on magnetic tape—and managers apparently do not write down much of what they hear. Thus the strategic data bank of the organization is not in the memory of its computers but in the minds of its managers.

Second, managers' extensive use of verbal media helps to explain why they are reluctant to delegate tasks. It is not as if they can hand a dossier over to subordinates; they must take the time to "dump memory"—to tell subordinates all about the subject. But this could take so long that managers may find it easier to do the task themselves. Thus they are damned by their own information system to a "dilemma of delegation"—to do too much or to delegate to subordinates with inadequate briefing.

Folklore: Management is, or at least is quickly becoming, a science and a profession. By almost any definition of *science* and *profession*, this statement is false. Brief observation of any manager will quickly lay to rest the notion that managers practice a science. A science involves the enaction of systematic, analytically determined procedures or programs. If we do not even know what procedures managers use, how can we prescribe them by scientific analy-

sis? And how can we call management a profession if we cannot specify what managers are to learn? For after all, a profession involves "knowledge of some department of learning or science" *(Random House Dictionary)*.[10]

Fact: The managers' programs—to schedule time, process information, make decisions, and so on—remain locked deep inside their brains. Thus, to describe these programs, we rely on words like *judgment* and *intuition*, seldom stopping to realize that they are merely labels for our ignorance.

I was struck during my study by the fact that the executives I was observing—all very competent—are fundamentally indistinguishable from their counterparts of a hundred years ago (or a thousand years ago). The information they need differs, but they seek it in the same way—by word of mouth. Their decisions concern modern technology, but the procedures they use to make those decisions are the same as the procedures used by nineteenth century managers. Even the computer, so important for the specialized work of the organization, has apparently had no influence on the work procedures of general managers. In fact, the manager is in a kind of loop, with increasingly heavy work pressures but no aid forthcoming from management science.

Considering the facts about managerial work, we can see that the manager's job is enormously complicated and difficult. Managers are overburdened with obligations yet cannot easily delegate their tasks. As a result, they are driven to overwork and forced to do many tasks superficially. Brevity, fragmentation, and verbal communication characterize their work. Yet these are the very characteristics of managerial work that have impeded scientific attempts to improve it. As a result, management scientists have concentrated on the specialized functions of the organization, where it is easier to analyze the procedures and quantify the relevant information.[11]

But the pressures of a manager's job are becoming worse. Where before managers needed to respond only to owners and directors, now they find that subordinates with democratic norms continually reduce their freedom to issue unexplained orders, and a growing number of outside influences (consumer groups, government agencies, and so on) demand attention. Managers have had nowhere to turn for help. The first step in providing such help is

Today's gossip may be tomorrow's fact—that's why managers cherish hearsay.

to find out what the manager's job really is.

Back to a Basic Description of Managerial Work

Earlier, I defined the manager as that person in charge of an organization or subunit. Besides CEOs, this definition would include vice presidents, bishops, foremen, hockey coaches, and prime ministers. All these "managers" are vested with formal authority over an organizational unit. From formal authority comes status, which leads to various interpersonal relations, and from these comes access to information. Information, in turn, enables the manager to make decisions and strategies for the unit.

The manager's job can be described in terms of various "roles," or organized sets of behaviors identified with a position. My description, shown in "The Manager's Roles," comprises ten roles. As we shall see, formal authority gives rise to the three interpersonal

roles, which in turn give rise to the three informational roles; these two sets of roles enable the manager to play the four decisional roles.

Interpersonal Roles

Three of the manager's roles arise directly from formal authority and involve basic interpersonal relationships. First is the *figurehead* role. As the head of an organizational unit, every manager must perform some ceremonial duties. The president greets the touring dignitaries. The foreman attends the wedding of a lathe operator. The sales manager takes an important customer to lunch.

The chief executives of my study spent 12% of their contact time on ceremonial duties; 17% of their incoming mail dealt with acknowledgments and requests related to their status. For example, a letter to a company president requested free merchandise for a crippled schoolchild; diplomas that needed to be signed were put on the desk of the school superinten-

Research on Managerial Work

In seeking to describe managerial work, I conducted my own research and also scanned the literature to integrate the findings of studies from many diverse sources with my own. These studies focused on two different aspects of managerial work. Some were concerned with the characteristics of work—how long managers work, where, at what pace, with what interruptions, with whom they work, and through what media they communicate. Other studies were concerned with the content of work—what activities the managers actually carry out, and why. Thus, after a meeting, one researcher might note that the manager spent 45 minutes with three government officials in their Washington office, while another might record that the manager presented the company's stand on some proposed legislation in order to change a regulation.

A few of the studies of managerial work are widely known, but most have remained buried as single journal articles or isolated books. Among the more important ones I cite are:

- Sune Carlson developed the diary method to study the work characteristics of nine Swedish managing directors. Each kept a

detailed log of his activities. Carlson's results are reported in his book *Executive Behaviour*. A number of British researchers, notably Rosemary Stewart, have subsequently used Carlson's method. In *Managers and Their Jobs*, she describes the study of 160 top and middle managers of British companies.
- Leonard Sayles's book *Managerial Behavior* is another important reference. Using a method he refers to as "anthropological," Sayles studied the work content of middle and lower level managers in a large U.S. corporation. Sayles moved freely in the company, collecting whatever information struck him as important.
- Perhaps the best-known source is *Presidential Power*, in which Richard Neustadt analyzes the power and managerial behavior of Presidents Roosevelt, Truman, and Eisenhower. Neustadt used secondary sources—documents and interviews with other parties.
- Robert H. Guest, in *Personnel*, reports on a study of the foreman's working day. Fifty-six U.S. foremen were observed and each of their activities recorded during

one eight-hour shift.
- Richard C. Hodgson, Daniel J. Levinson, and Abraham Zaleznik studied a team of three top executives of a U.S. hospital. From that study they wrote *The Executive Role Constellation*. They addressed the way in which work and socioemotional roles were divided among the three managers.
- William F. Whyte, from his study of a street gang during the Depression, wrote *Street Corner Society*. His findings about the gang's workings and leadership, which George C. Homans analyzed in *The Human Group*, suggest interesting similarities of job contents between street gang leaders and corporate managers.

My own study involved five American CEOs of middle- to large-sized organizations—a consulting firm, a technology company, a hospital, a consumer goods company, and a school system. Using a method called "structural observation," during one intensive week of observation for each executive, I recorded various aspects of every piece of mail and every verbal contact. In all, I analyzed 890 pieces of incoming and outgoing mail and 368 verbal contacts.

dent.

Duties that involve interpersonal roles may sometimes be routine, involving little serious communication and no important decision making. Nevertheless, they are important to the smooth functioning of an organization and cannot be ignored.

Managers are responsible for the work of the people of their unit. Their actions in this regard constitute the *leader* role. Some of these actions involve leadership directly—for example, in most organizations the managers are normally responsible for hiring and training their own staff.

In addition, there is the indirect exercise of the leader role. For example, every manager must motivate and encourage employees, somehow reconciling their individual needs with the goals of the organization. In virtually every contact with the manager, subordinates seeking leadership clues ask: "Does she approve?" "How would she like the report to turn out?" "Is she more interested in market share than high profits?"

The influence of managers is most clearly seen in the leader role. Formal authority vests them with great potential power; leadership determines in large part how much of it they will realize.

The literature of management has always recognized the leader role, particularly those aspects of it related to motivation. In comparison, until recently it has hardly mentioned the *liaison* role, in which the manager makes contacts outside the vertical chain of command. This is remarkable in light of the finding of virtually every study of managerial work that managers spend as much time with peers and other people outside their units as they do with their own subordinates—and, surprisingly, very little time with their own superiors.

In Rosemary Stewart's diary study, the 160 British middle and top managers spent 47% of their time with peers, 41% of their time with people inside their unit, and only 12% of their time with their superiors. For Robert H. Guest's study of U.S. foremen, the figures were 44%, 46%, and 10%. The chief executives of my study averaged 44% of their contact time with people outside their organizations, 48% with subordinates, and 7% with directors and trustees.

The contacts the five CEOs made were with an incredibly wide range of people: subordinates; clients, business associates, and suppliers; and peers—managers of similar organizations, government and trade organization officials, fellow directors on outside boards, and independents with no relevant organizational affiliations. The chief executives' time with and mail from these groups is shown in "The Chief Executive's Contacts." Guest's study of foremen shows, likewise, that their contacts were numerous and wide-ranging, seldom involving fewer than 25 individuals, and often more than 50.

Informational Roles

By virtue of interpersonal contacts, both with subordinates and with a network of contacts, the manager emerges as the nerve center of the organizational unit. The manager may not know everything but typically knows more than subordinates do.

Studies have shown this relationship to hold for all managers, from street gang leaders to U.S. presidents. In *The Human Group*, George C. Homans explains how, because they were at the center of the information flow in their own gangs and were also in close touch with other gang leaders, street gang leaders were better informed than any of their followers.[12] As for presidents, Richard Neustadt observes: "The essence of {Franklin} Roosevelt's technique for information-gathering was competition. 'He would call you in,' one of his aides once told me, 'and he'd ask you to get the story on some

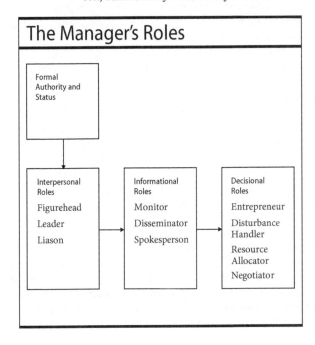

The Manager's Roles

Formal Authority and Status

Interpersonal Roles

Figurehead

Leader

Liason

Informational Roles

Monitor

Disseminator

Spokesperson

Decisional Roles

Entrepreneur

Disturbance Handler

Resource Allocator

Negotiator

complicated business, and you'd come back after a couple of days of hard labor and present the juicy morsel you'd uncovered under a stone somewhere, and *then* you'd find out he knew all about it, along with something else you *didn't* know. Where he got this information from he wouldn't mention, usually, but after he had done this to you once or twice you got damn careful about *your* information.'"[13]

We can see where Roosevelt "got this information" when we consider the relationship between the interpersonal and informational roles. As leader, the manager has formal and easy access to every staff member. In addition, liaison contacts expose the manager to external information to which subordinates often lack access. Many of these contacts are with other managers of equal status, who are themselves nerve centers in their own organization. In this way, the manager develops a powerful database of information.

Processing information is a key part of the manager's job. In my study, the CEOs spent 40% of their contact time on activities devoted exclusively to the transmission of information; 70% of their incoming mail was purely informational (as opposed to requests for action). Managers don't leave meetings or hang up the telephone to get back to work. In large part, communication *is* their work. Three roles describe these informational aspects of managerial work.

As *monitor*, the manager is perpetually scanning the environment for information, interrogating liaison contacts and subordinates, and receiving unsolicited information, much of it as a result of the network of personal contacts. Remember that a good part of the information the manager collects in the monitor role arrives in verbal form, often as gossip, hearsay, and speculation.

In the *disseminator* role, the manager passes some privileged information directly to subordinates, who would otherwise have no access to it. When subordinates lack easy contact with one another, the manager may pass information from one to another.

In the *spokesperson* role, the manager sends some information to people outside the unit—a president makes a speech to lobby for an organization cause, or a foreman suggests a product modification to a supplier. In addition, as a spokesperson, every manager must inform

and satisfy the influential people who control the organizational unit. For the foreman, this may simply involve keeping the plant manager informed about the flow of work through the shop.

The president of a large corporation, however, may spend a great amount of time dealing with a host of influences. Directors and shareholders must be advised about finances; consumer groups must be assured that the organization is fulfilling its social responsibilities; and government officials must be satisfied that the organization is abiding by the law.

Decisional Roles

Information is not, of course, an end in itself; it is the basic input to decision making. One thing is clear in the study of managerial work: the manager plays the major role in the unit's decision-making system. As its formal authority, only the manager can commit the unit to important new courses of action; and as its nerve center, only the manager has full and current information to make the set of decisions that determines the unit's strategy. Four roles describe the manager as decision maker.

As *entrepreneur*, the manager seeks to improve the unit, to adapt it to changing conditions in the environment. In the monitor role, a president is constantly on the lookout for new ideas. When a good one appears, he initiates a development project that he may supervise himself or delegate to an employee

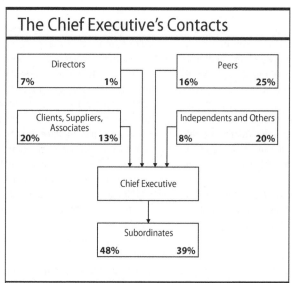

The Chief Executive's Contacts

Directors		Peers	
7%	1%	16%	25%

Clients, Suppliers, Associates		Independents and Others	
20%	13%	8%	20%

Chief Executive

Subordinates	
48%	39%

Note: The first figure indicates the proportion of total contact time spent with each group and the second figure, the proportion of mail from each group.

Retrospective Commentary

Henry Mintzberg

Over the years, one reaction has dominated the comments I have received from managers who read "The Manager's Job: Folklore and Fact": "You make me feel so good. I thought all those other managers were planning, organizing, coordinating, and controlling, while I was busy being interrupted, jumping from one issue to another, and trying to keep the lid on the chaos." Yet everything in this article must have been patently obvious to these people. Why such a reaction to reading what they already knew?

Conversely, how to explain the very different reaction of two media people who called to line up interviews after an article based on this one appeared in the *New York Times*. "Are we glad someone finally let managers have it," both said in passing, a comment that still takes me aback. True, they had read only the account in the *Times*, but that no more let managers have it than did this article. Why that reaction?

One explanation grows out of the way I now see this article—as proposing not so much another view of management as another face of it. I like to call it the insightful face, in contrast to the long-dominant professional or cerebral face. One stresses commitment, the other calculation; one sees the world with integrated perspective, the other figures it as the components of a portfolio. The cerebral face operates with the words and numbers of rationality; the insightful face is rooted in the images and feel of a manager's integrity.

Each of these faces implies a different kind of "knowing," and that, I believe, explains many managers' reaction to this article. Rationally, they "knew" what managers did—planned, organized, coordinated, and controlled. But deep down that did not feel

quite right. The description in this article may have come closer to what they really "knew." As for those media people, they weren't railing against management as such but against the cerebral form of management, so pervasive, that they saw impersonalizing the world around them.

In practice, management has to be two-faced—there has to be a balance between the cerebral and the insightful. So, for example, I realized originally that managerial communication was largely oral and that the advent of the computer had not changed anything fundamental in the executive suite—a conclusion I continue to hold. (The greatest threat the personal computer poses is that managers will take it seriously and come to believe that they can manage by remaining in their offices and looking at displays of digital characters.) But I also thought that the dilemma of delegating could be dealt with by periodic debriefings—disseminating words. Now, however, I believe that managers need more ways to convey the images and impressions they carry inside of them. This explains the renewed interest in strategic vision, in culture, and in the roles of intuition and insight in management.

The ten roles I used to describe the manager's job also reflect management's cerebral face, in that they decompose the job more than capture the integration. Indeed, my effort to show a sequence among these roles now seems more consistent with the traditional face of management work than an insightful one. Might we not just as well say that people throughout the organization take actions that inform managers who, by making sense of those actions, develop images and visions that inspire people to subsequent efforts?

Perhaps my greatest disappointment

about the research reported here is that it did not stimulate new efforts. In a world so concerned with management, much of the popular literature is superficial and the academic research pedestrian. Certainly, many studies have been carried out over the last 15 years, but the vast majority sought to replicate earlier research. In particular, we remain grossly ignorant about the fundamental content of the manager's job and have barely addressed the major issues and dilemmas in its practice.

But superficiality is not only a problem of the literature. It is also an occupational hazard of the manager's job. Originally, I believed this problem could be dealt with; now I see it as inherent in the job. This is because managing insightfully depends on the direct experience and personal knowledge that come from intimate contact. But in organizations grown larger and more diversified, that becomes difficult to achieve. And so managers turn increasingly to the cerebral face, and the delicate balance between the two faces is lost.

Certainly, some organizations manage to sustain their humanity despite their large size—as Tom Peters and Robert Waterman show in their book *In Search of Excellence*. But that book attained its outstanding success precisely because it is about the exceptions, about the organizations so many of us long to be a part of—not the organizations in which we actually work.

Fifteen years ago, I stated that "No job is more vital to our society than that of the manager. It is the manager who determines whether our social institutions serve us well or whether they squander our talents and resources." Now, more than ever, we must strip away the folklore of the manager's job and begin to face its difficult facts.

(perhaps with the stipulation that he must approve the final proposal).

There are two interesting features about these development projects at the CEO level. First, these projects do not involve single decisions or even unified clusters of decisions. Rather, they emerge as a series of small decisions and actions sequenced over time. Apparently, chief executives prolong each project both to fit it into a busy, disjointed schedule, and so that they can comprehend complex issues gradually.

Second, the chief executives I studied supervised as many as 50 of these projects at the same time. Some projects entailed new products or processes; others involved public relations campaigns, improvement of the cash position, reorganization of a weak department, resolution of a morale problem in a foreign division, integration of computer operations, various acquisitions at different stages of development, and so on.

Chief executives appear to maintain a kind of inventory of the development projects in various stages of development. Like jugglers, they keep a number of projects in the air; periodically, one comes down, is given a new burst of energy, and sent back into orbit. At various intervals, they put new projects on-stream and discard old ones.

While the entrepreneur role describes the manager as the voluntary initiator of change, the *disturbance handler* role depicts the manager involuntarily responding to pressures. Here change is beyond the manager's control. The pressures of a situation are too severe to be ignored—a strike looms, a major customer has gone bankrupt, or a supplier reneges on a contract—so the manager must act.

Leonard R. Sayles, who has carried out appropriate research on the manager's job, likens the manager to a symphony orchestra conductor who must "maintain a melodious performance,"[14] while handling musicians' problems and other external disturbances. Indeed, every manager must spend a considerable amount of time responding to high-pressure disturbances. No organization can be so well run, so standardized, that it has considered every contingency in the uncertain environment in advance. Disturbances arise not only because poor managers ignore situations until they reach crisis proportions but also because good managers cannot possibly anticipate all the consequences of the actions they take.

The third decisional role is that of *resource allocator*. The manager is responsible for deciding who will get what. Perhaps the most important resource the manager allocates is his or her own time. Access to the manager constitutes exposure to the unit's nerve center and decision maker. The manager is also charged with designing the unit's structure, that pattern of formal relationships that determines how work is to be divided and coordinated.

Also, as resource allocator, the manager authorizes the important decisions of the unit before they are implemented. By retaining this power, the manager can ensure that decisions are interrelated. To fragment this power encourages discontinuous decision making and a disjointed strategy.

There are a number of interesting features about the manager's authorization of others' decisions. First, despite the widespread use of capital budgeting procedures—a means of authorizing various capital expenditures at one time—executives in my study made a great many authorization decisions on an ad hoc basis. Apparently, many projects cannot wait or simply do not have the quantifiable costs and benefits that capital budgeting requires.

Second, I found that the chief executives faced incredibly complex choices. They had to consider the impact of each decision on other decisions and on the organization's strategy. They had to ensure that the decision would be acceptable to those who influence the organization, as well as ensure that resources would not be overextended. They had to understand the various costs and benefits as well as the feasibility of the proposal. They also had to consider questions of timing. All this was necessary for the simple approval of someone else's proposal. At the same time, however, the delay could lose time, while quick approval could be ill-considered and quick rejection might discourage the subordinate who had spent months developing a pet project.

One common solution to approving projects is to pick the person instead of the proposal. That is, the manager authorizes those projects presented by people whose judgment he or she trusts. But the manager cannot always use this simple dodge.

The final decisional role is that of *negotiator*. Managers spend considerable time in negotiations: the president of the football team

The scarcest resource managers have to allocate is their own time.

works out a contract with the holdout superstar; the corporation president leads the company's contingent to negotiate a new strike issue; the foreman argues a grievance problem to its conclusion with the shop steward.

These negotiations are an integral part of the manager's job, for only he or she has the authority to commit organizational resources in "real time" and the nerve-center information that important negotiations require.

The Integrated Job
It should be clear by now that these ten roles are not easily separable. In the terminology of the psychologist, they form a gestalt, an integrated whole. No role can be pulled out of the framework and the job be left intact. For example, a manager without liaison contacts lacks external information. As a result, that manager can neither disseminate the information that employees need nor make decisions that adequately reflect external conditions. (This is a problem for the new person in a managerial position, since he or she has to build up a network of contacts before making effective decisions.)

Here lies a clue to the problems of team management.[15] Two or three people cannot share a single managerial position unless they can act as one entity. This means that they cannot divide up the ten roles unless they can very carefully reintegrate them. The real difficulty lies with the informational roles. Unless there can be full sharing of managerial information—and, as I pointed out earlier, it is primarily verbal—team management breaks down. A single managerial job cannot be arbitrarily split, for example, into internal and external roles, for information from both sources must be brought to bear on the same decisions.

To say that the ten roles form a gestalt is not to say that all managers give equal attention to each role. In fact, I found in my review of the various research studies that sales managers seem to spend relatively more of their time in the interpersonal roles, presumably a reflection of the extrovert nature of the marketing activity. Production managers, on the other hand, give relatively more attention to the decisional roles, presumably a reflection of their concern with efficient work flow. And staff managers spend the most time in the informational roles, since they are experts who manage departments that advise other parts of the organization. Nevertheless, in all cases, the interpersonal, informational, and decisional roles remain inseparable.

Toward More Effective Management
This description of managerial work should prove more important to managers than any prescription they might derive from it. That is to say, *the managers' effectiveness is significantly influenced by their insight into their own work*. Performance depends on how well a manager understands and responds to the pressures and dilemmas of the job. Thus managers who can be introspective about their work are likely to be effective at their jobs. The questions in "Self-Study Questions for Managers" may sound rhetorical; none is meant to be. Even though the questions cannot be answered simply, the manager should address them.

Let us take a look at three specific areas of concern. For the most part, the managerial logjams—the dilemma of delegation, the database centralized in one brain, the problems of working with the management scientist—revolve around the verbal nature of the manager's information. There are great dangers in centralizing the organization's data bank in the minds of its managers. When they leave, they take their memory with them. And when subordinates are out of convenient verbal reach of the manager, they are at an informational disadvantage.

The manager is challenged to find systematic ways to share privileged information. A regular debriefing session with key subordinates, a weekly memory dump on the dictating machine, maintaining a diary for limited circulation, or other similar methods may ease the logjam of work considerably. The time spent disseminating this information will be more than regained when decisions must be made. Of course, some will undoubtedly raise the question of confidentiality. But managers would be well advised to weigh the risks of exposing privileged information against having subordinates who can make effective decisions.

If there is a single theme that runs through this article, it is that the pressures of the job drive the manager to take on too much work, encourage interruption, respond quickly to every stimulus, seek the tangible and avoid the abstract, make decisions in small increments, and do everything abruptly.

Here again, the manager is challenged to deal consciously with the pressures of superficiality by giving serious attention to the issues that require it, by stepping back in order to see a broad picture, and by making use of analytical inputs. Although effective managers have to be adept at responding quickly to numerous and varying problems, the danger in managerial work is that they will respond to every issue equally (and that means abruptly) and that they will never work the tangible bits and pieces of information into a comprehensive picture of their world.

To create this comprehensive picture, managers can supplement their own models with those of specialists. Economists describe the functioning of markets, operations researchers simulate financial flow processes, and behavioral scientists explain the needs and goals of people. The best of these models can be searched out and learned.

In dealing with complex issues, the senior manager has much to gain from a close relationship with the organization's own management scientists. They have something important that the manager lacks—time to probe complex issues. An effective working relationship hinges on the resolution of what a colleague and I have called "the planning dilemma."[16] Managers have the information and the authority; analysts have the time and the technology. A successful working relationship between the two will be effected when the

Self-Study Questions for Managers

1. Where do I get my information, and how? Can I make greater use of my contacts? Can other people do some of my scanning? In what areas is my knowledge weakest, and how can I get others to provide me with the information I need? Do I have sufficiently powerful mental models of those things I must understand within the organization and in its environment?

2. What information do I disseminate? How important is that information to my subordinates? Do I keep too much information to myself because disseminating it is time consuming or inconvenient? How can I get more information to others so they can make better decisions?

3. Do I tend to act before information is in? Or do I wait so long for all the information that opportunities pass me by?

4. What pace of change am I asking my organization to tolerate? Is this change balanced so that our operations are neither excessively static nor overly disrupted? Have we sufficiently analyzed the impact of this change on the future of our organization?

5. Am I sufficiently well-informed to pass judgment on subordinate's proposals? Can I leave final authorization for more of the proposals with subordinates? Do we have problems of coordination because subordinates already make too many decisions independently?

6. What is my vision for this organization? Are these plans primarily in my own mind in loose form? Should I make them explicit to guide the decisions of others better? Or do I need flexibility to change them at will?

7. How do my subordinates react to my managerial style? Am I sufficiently sensitive to the powerful influence of my actions? Do I fully understand their reactions to my actions? Do I find an appropriate balance between encouragement and pressure? Do I stifle their initiative?

8. What kind of external relationships do I maintain, and how? Do I spend too much of my time maintaining them? Are there certain people whom I should get to know better?

9. Is there any system to my time scheduling, or am I just reacting to the pressures of the moment? Do I find the appropriate mix of activities or concentrate on one particular function or problem just because I find it interesting? Am I more efficient with particular kinds of work, at special times of the day or week? Does my schedule reflect this? Can someone else schedule my time (besides my secretary)?

10. Do I overwork? What effect does my work load have on my efficiency? Should I force myself to take breaks or to reduce the pace of my activity?

11. Am I too superficial in what I do? Can I really shift moods as quickly and frequently as my work requires? Should I decrease the amount of fragmentation and interruption in my work?

12. Do I spend too much time on current, tangible activities? Am I a slave to the action and excitement of my work, so that I am no longer able to concentrate on issues? Do key problems receive the attention they deserve? Should I spend more time reading and probing deeply into certain issues? Could I be more reflective? Should I be?

13. Do I use the different media appropriately? Do I know how to make the most of written communication? Do I rely excessively on face-to-face communication, thereby putting all but a few of my subordinates at an informational disadvantage? Do I schedule enough of my meetings on a regular basis? Do I spend enough time observing activities firsthand, or am I detached from the heart of my organization's activities?

14. How do I blend my personal rights and duties? Do my obligations consume all my time? How can I free myself from obligations to ensure that I am taking this organization where I want it to go? How can I turn my obligations to my advantage?

manager learns to share information and the analyst learns to adapt to the manager's needs. For the analyst, adaptation means worrying less about the elegance of the method and more about its speed and flexibility.

Analysts can help the top manager schedule time, feed in analytical information, monitor projects, develop models to aid in making choices, design contingency plans for disturbances that can be anticipated, and conduct "quick and dirty" analyses for those that cannot. But there can be no cooperation if the analysts are out of the mainstream of the manager's information flow.

The manager is challenged to gain control of his or her own time by turning obligations into advantages and by turning those things he or she wishes to do into obligations. The chief executives of my study initiated only 32% of their own contacts (and another 5% by mutual agreement). And yet to a considerable extent they seemed to control their time. There were two key factors that enabled them to do so.

First, managers have to spend so much time discharging obligations that if they were to view them as just that, they would leave no mark on the organization. Unsuccessful managers blame failure on the obligations. Effective managers turn obligations to advantages. A speech is a chance to lobby for a cause; a meeting is a chance to reorganize a weak department; a visit to an important customer is a chance to extract trade information.

Second, the manager frees some time to do the things that he or she—perhaps no one else—thinks important by turning them into obligations. Free time is made, not found. Hoping to leave some time open for contemplation or general planning is tantamount to hoping that the pressures of the job will go away. Managers who want to innovate initiate projects and obligate others to report back to them. Managers who need certain environmental information establish channels that will automatically keep them informed. Managers who have to tour facilities commit themselves publicly.

The Educator's Job

Finally, a word about the training of managers. Our management schools have done an admirable job of training the organization's specialists—management scientists, marketing researchers, accountants, and organizational development specialists. But for the most part, they have not trained managers.[17]

Management schools will begin the serious training of managers when skill training takes a serious place next to cognitive learning. Cognitive learning is detached and informational, like reading a book or listening to a lecture. No doubt much important cognitive material must be assimilated by the manager-to-be. But cognitive learning no more makes a manager than it does a swimmer. The latter will drown the first time she jumps into the water if her coach never takes her out of the lecture hall, gets her wet, and gives her feedback on her performance.

In other words, we are taught a skill through practice plus feedback, whether in a real or a simulated situation. Our management schools need to identify the skills managers use, select students who show potential in these skills, put the students into situations where these skills can be practiced and developed, and then give them systematic feedback on their performance.

My description of managerial work suggests a number of important managerial skills—developing peer relationships, carrying out negotiations, motivating subordinates, resolving conflicts, establishing information networks and subsequently disseminating information, making decisions in conditions of extreme ambiguity, and allocating resources. Above all, the manager needs to be introspective in order to continue to learn on the job.

No job is more vital to our society than that of the manager. The manager determines whether our social institutions will serve us well or whether they will squander our talents and resources. It is time to strip away the folklore about managerial work and study it realistically so that we can begin the difficult task of making significant improvements in its performance.

References

1. All the data from my study can be found in Henry Mintzberg, *The Nature of Managerial Work* (New York: Harper & Row, 1973).

2. Robert H. Guest, "Of Time and the Foreman," *Personnel*, May 1956, p. 478.

3. Rosemary Stewart, *Managers and Their Jobs* (London: Macmillan, 1967); see also Sune Carlson, *Executive Behavior* (Stockholm: Strombergs, 1951).

4. Francis J. Aguilar, *Scanning the Business Environment* (New York: Macmillan, 1967), p. 102.

5. Unpublished study by Irving Choran, reported in Mintzberg, *The Nature of Managerial Work*.

6. Robert T. Davis, *Performance and Development of Field Sales Managers* (Boston: Division of Research, Harvard Business School, 1957); George H. Copeman, *The Role of the Managing Director* (London: Business Publications, 1963).

7. Stewart, *Managers and Their Jobs*; Tom Burns, "The Directions of Activity and Communication in a Departmental Executive Group," *Human Relations 7*, no. 1 (1954): 73.

8. H. Edward Wrapp, "Good Managers Don't Make Policy Decisions," HBR September-October 1967, p. 91. Wrapp refers to this as spotting opportunities and relationships in the stream of operating problems and decisions; in his article, Wrapp raises a number of excellent points related to this analysis.

9. Richard E. Neustadt, *Presidential Power* (New York: John Wiley, 1960), pp. 153–154; italics added.

10. For a more thorough, though rather different, discussion of this issue, see Kenneth R. Andrews, "Toward Professionalism in Business Management," HBR March–April 1969, p. 49.

11. C. Jackson Grayson, Jr., in "Management Science and Business Practice," HBR July–August 1973, p. 41, explains in similar terms why, as chairman of the Price Commission, he did not use those very techniques that he himself promoted in his earlier career as a management scientist.

12. George C. Homans, *The Human Group* (New York: Harcourt, Brace & World, 1950), based on the study by William F. Whyte entitled *Street Corner Society*, rev. ed. (Chicago: University of Chicago Press, 1955).

13. Neustadt, *Presidential Power*, p. 157.

14. Leonard R. Sayles, *Managerial Behavior* (New York: McGraw-Hill, 1964), p. 162.

15. See Richard C. Hodgson, Daniel J. Levinson, and Abraham Zaleznik, *The Executive Role Constellation* (Boston: Division of Research, Harvard Business School, 1965), for a discussion of the sharing of roles.

16. James S. Hekimian and Henry Mintzberg, "The Planning Dilemma," *The Management Review*, May 1968, p. 4.

17. See J. Sterling Livingston, "Myth of the Well-Educated Manager," HBR January–February 1971, p.79.

Reprint 90210; *Harvard Business Review*
OnPoint 5429
To order, see the next page
or call 800-988-0886 or 617-783-7500
or go to www.hbr.org

Harvard Business Review OnPoint articles enhance the full-text article with a summary of its key points and a selection of its company examples to help you quickly absorb and apply the concepts. *Harvard Business Review* OnPoint collections include three OnPoint articles and an overview comparing the various perspectives on a specific topic.

Further Reading

The Manager's Job is also part of the *Harvard Business Review* OnPoint collection **Your Best Managers Lead and Manage**, Product no. 5402, which includes these additional articles:

Managers and Leaders: Are They Different? (Classic)
Abraham Zaleznik
Harvard Business Review
December 2001
Product no. 8334

The Five Minds of a Manager
Jonathan Gosling and Henry Mintzberg
Harvard Business Review
November 2003
Product no. 5364

To Order

For reprints, *Harvard Business Review* OnPoint orders, and subscriptions to *Harvard Business Review:*
Call 800-988-0886 or 617-783-7500.
Go to www.hbr.org

For customized and quantity orders of reprints and *Harvard Business Review* OnPoint products:
Call Frank Tamoshunas at
617-783-7626,
or e-mail him at
ftamoshunas@hbsp.harvard.edu

Theme 2

The Competitive Environment of Organisations

Pankaj Ghemawat

Competition and Business Strategy in Historical Perspective

A review of theories of competition and business strategy over the last half-century reveals a fairly linear development of early work by academics and consultants into efforts to understand the determinants of industry profitability and competitive position and, more recently, to add a time or historical dimension to the analysis. The possible implications of the emergence of a market for such ideas are also discussed.

"Strategy" is a term that can be traced back to the ancient Greeks, for whom it meant a chief magistrate or a military commander in chief. The use of the term in business, however, dates only to the twentieth century, and its use in a self-consciously competitive context is even more recent.

After providing some historical background, this essay focuses on how the evolution of ideas about business strategy was influenced by competitive thinking in the second half of the twentieth century. The review aims not to be comprehensive but, instead, to focus on some key topical issues in applying competitive thinking to business strategy. Particular attention is paid to the role of three institutions—Harvard Business School and two consulting firms, the Boston Consulting Group and McKinsey & Company—in looking at the historical development and diffusion of theories of business competition and strategy. The essay concludes with some discussion of how the emergence of a market for ideas in this broad domain is likely to affect future developments in this area.

PANKAJ GHEMAWAT is the Jaime and Josefina Chua Tiampo Professor of Business Administration at Harvard Business School.

The author has drawn upon an earlier draft prepared by Dr. Peter Botticelli under his supervision and has also benefited from helpful comments by Walter A. Friedman, Thomas K. McCraw, and three referees.

Historical Background

Until the nineteenth century, the scope for applying (imperfectly) competitive thinking to business situations appeared to be limited: intense competition had emerged in many lines of business, but individual firms apparently often lacked the potential to have much of an influence on competitive outcomes. Instead, in most lines of business — with the exception of a few commodities in which international trade had developed — firms had an incentive to remain small and to employ as little fixed capital as possible. It was in this era that Adam Smith penned his famous description of market forces as an "invisible hand" that was largely beyond the control of individual firms.

The scope for strategy as a way to control market forces and shape the competitive environment started to become clearer in the second half of the nineteenth century. In the United States, the building of the railroads after 1850 led to the development of mass markets for the first time. Along with improved access to capital and credit, mass markets encouraged large-scale investment to exploit economies of scale in production and economies of scope in distribution. In some industries, Adam Smith's "invisible hand" was gradually tamed by what the historian Alfred D. Chandler Jr. has termed the "visible hand" of professional managers. By the late nineteenth century, a new type of firm began to emerge, first in the United States and then in Europe: the vertically integrated, multidivisional (or "M-form") corporation that made large investments in manufacturing and marketing and in management hierarchies to coordinate those functions. Over time, the largest M-form companies managed to alter the competitive environment within their industries and even across industry lines.[1]

The need for a formal approach to corporate strategy was first articulated by top executives of M-form corporations. Alfred Sloan (chief executive of General Motors from 1923 to 1946) devised a strategy that was explicitly based on the perceived strengths and weaknesses of its competitor, Ford.[2] In the 1930s, Chester Barnard, a top executive with AT&T, argued that managers should pay especially close attention to "strategic factors," which depend on "personal or organizational action."[3]

---

[1] Alfred D. Chandler Jr., *Strategy and Structure* (Cambridge, Mass., 1963) and *Scale and Scope* (Cambridge, Mass., 1990).

[2] See Alfred P. Sloan Jr., *My Years with General Motors* (New York, 1963).

[3] Chester I. Barnard, *The Functions of the Executive* (Cambridge, Mass., 1968; first published 1938), 204–5.

The organizational challenges involved in World War II were a vital stimulus to strategic thinking. The problem of allocating scarce resources across the entire economy in wartime led to many innovations in management science. New operations-research techniques (e.g., linear programming) were devised, which paved the way for the use of quantitative analysis in formal strategic planning. In 1944, John von Neumann and Oskar Morgenstern published their classic work, *The Theory of Games and Economic Behavior*. This work essentially solved the problem of zero-sum games (most military ones, from an aggregate perspective) and framed the issues surrounding non-zero-sum games (most business ones). Also, the concept of "learning curves" became an increasingly important tool for planning. The learning curve was first discovered in the military aircraft industry in the 1920s and 1930s, where it was noticed that direct labor costs tended to decrease by a constant percentage as the cumulative quantity of aircraft produced doubled. Learning effects figured prominently in wartime production planning efforts.

World War II also encouraged the mindset of using formal strategic thinking to guide management decisions. Thus, Peter Drucker argued that "management is not just passive, adaptive behavior; it means taking action to make the desired results come to pass." He noted that economic theory had long treated markets as impersonal forces, beyond the control of individual entrepreneurs and organizations. But, in the age of M-form corporations, managing "implies responsibility for attempting to shape the economic environment, for planning, initiating and carrying through changes in that economic environment, for constantly pushing back the limitations of economic circumstances on the enterprise's freedom of action."[4] This insight became the rationale for business strategy—that, by consciously using formal planning, a company could exert some positive control over market forces.

However, these insights on the nature of strategy largely lay fallow for the decade after World War II because wartime destruction led to excess demand, which limited competition as firms rushed to expand capacity. Given the enormous job of rebuilding Europe and much of Asia, it was not until the late 1950s and 1960s that many large multinational corporations were forced to consider global competition as a factor in planning. In addition, the wartime disruption of foreign multinationals enabled U.S. companies to profit from the postwar boom without effective competitors in many industries.

A more direct bridge to the development of strategic concepts for business applications was provided by interservice competition in the

[4] Peter Drucker, *The Practice of Management* (New York, 1954), 11.

U.S. military after World War II. In this period, American military leaders found themselves debating the arrangements that would best protect legitimate competition between military services while maintaining the needed integration of strategic and tactical planning. Many argued that the Army, Navy, Marines, and Air Force would be more efficient if they were unified into a single organization. As the debate raged, Philip Selznick, a sociologist, noted that the Navy Department "emerged as the defender of subtle institutional values and tried many times to formulate the distinctive characteristics of the various services." In essence, the "Navy spokesmen attempted to distinguish between the Army as a 'manpower' organization and the Navy as a finely adjusted system of technical, engineering skills—a 'machine-centered' organization. Faced with what it perceived as a mortal threat, the Navy became highly self-conscious about its distinctive competence."[5] The concept of "distinctive competence" had great resonance for strategic management, as we will see next.

Academic Underpinnings

The Second Industrial Revolution witnessed the founding of many elite business schools in the United States, beginning with the Wharton School in 1881. Harvard Business School, founded in 1908, was one of the first to promote the idea that managers should be trained to think strategically and not just to act as functional administrators. Beginning in 1912, Harvard offered a required second-year course in "business policy," which was designed to integrate the knowledge gained in functional areas like accounting, operations, and finance, thereby giving students a broader perspective on the strategic problems faced by corporate executives. A course description from 1917 claimed that "an analysis of any business problem shows not only its relation to other problems in the same group, but also the intimate connection of groups. Few problems in business are purely intra-departmental." It was also stipulated that the policies of each department must maintain a "balance in accord with the underlying policies of the business as a whole."[6]

In the early 1950s, two professors of business policy at Harvard, George Albert Smith Jr. and C. Roland Christensen, taught students to question whether a firm's strategy matched its competitive environment. In reading cases, students were instructed to ask: do a company's

---

[5] Philip Selznick, *Leadership in Administration* (Evanston, Ill., 1957), 49–50.
[6] Official Register of Harvard University, 29 Mar. 1917, 42–3.

policies "fit together into a program that effectively meets the requirements of the competitive situation"?[7] Students were told to address this problem by asking: "How is the whole industry doing? Is it growing and expanding? Or is it static; or declining?" Then, having "sized up" the competitive environment, the student was to ask: "On what basis must any one company compete with the others in this particular industry? At what kinds of things does it have to be especially competent, in order to compete?"[8]

In the late 1950s, another Harvard business policy professor, Kenneth Andrews, built on this thinking by arguing that "every business organization, every subunit of organization, and even every individual [ought to] have a clearly defined set of purposes or goals which keeps it moving in a *deliberately chosen direction* and prevents its drifting in undesired directions" (emphasis added). As shown in the case of Alfred Sloan at General Motors, "the primary function of the general manager, over time, is supervision of the continuous process of determining the nature of the enterprise and setting, revising and attempting to achieve its goals."[9] The motivation for these conclusions was supplied by an industry note and company cases that Andrews prepared on Swiss watchmakers, which uncovered significant differences in performance associated with their respective strategies for competing in that industry.[10] This format of combining industry notes with company cases, which had been initiated at Harvard Business School by a professor of manufacturing, John MacLean, became the norm in Harvard's business policy course. In practice, an industry note was often followed by multiple cases on one or several companies with the objective, *inter alia*, of economizing on students' preparation time.[11]

By the 1960s, classroom discussions in the business policy course focused on matching a company's "strengths" and "weaknesses"—its distinctive competence—with the "opportunities" and "threats" (or risks) it faced in the marketplace. This framework, which came to be referred to by the acronym SWOT, was a major step forward in bringing explicitly competitive thinking to bear on questions of strategy. Kenneth Andrews put these elements together in a way that became particularly well known. (See Figure 1.) In 1963, a business policy confer-

[7] George Albert Smith Jr. and C. Roland Christensen, *Suggestions to Instructors on Policy Formulation* (Chicago, 1951), 3–4.

[8] George Albert Smith Jr., *Policy Formulation and Administration* (Chicago, 1951), 14.

[9] Kenneth R. Andrews, *The Concept of Corporate Strategy* (Homewood, Ill., 1971), 23.

[10] See Part I of Edmund P. Learned, C. Roland Christensen, and Kenneth Andrews, *Problems of General Management* (Homewood, Ill., 1961).

[11] Interview with Kenneth Andrews, 2 Apr. 1997.

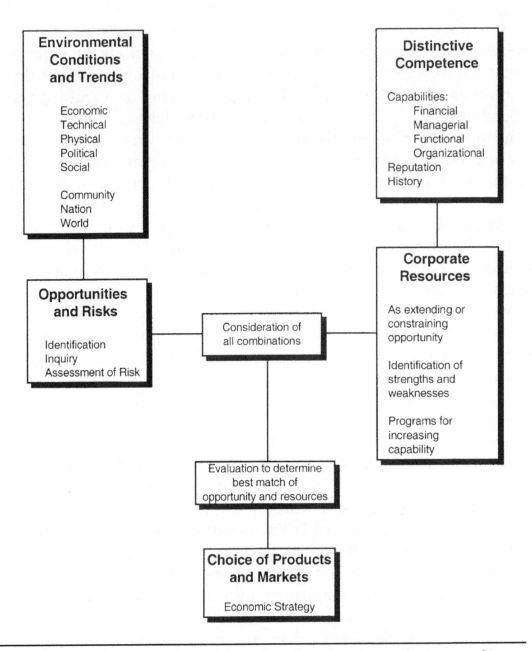

Figure 1. Andrews's Strategy Framework. (Source: Kenneth Andrews, *The Concept of Corporate Strategy*, rev. ed. [Homewood, Ill., 1980], 69.)

ence was held at Harvard that helped diffuse the SWOT concept in academia and in management practice. Attendance was heavy, and yet the popularity of SWOT—which was still used by many firms, including Wal-Mart, in the 1990s—did not bring closure to the problem of actually defining a firm's distinctive competence. To solve this problem, strategists had to decide which aspects of the firm were "enduring and unchanging over relatively long periods of time" and which were "necessarily more responsive to changes in the marketplace and the pressures of other environmental forces." This distinction was crucial because "the *strategic* decision is concerned with the long-term development of the enterprise" (emphasis added).[12] When strategy choices were analyzed from a long-range perspective, the idea of "distinctive competence" took on added importance because of the risks involved in most long-run investments. Thus, if the opportunities a firm was pursuing appeared "to outrun [its] present distinctive competence," then the strategist had to consider a firm's "willingness to gamble that the latter can be built up to the required level."[13]

The debate over a firm's "willingness to gamble" its distinctive competence in pursuit of opportunity continued in the 1960s, fueled by a booming stock market and corporate strategies that were heavily geared toward growth and diversification. In a classic 1960 article, "Marketing Myopia," Theodore Levitt was sharply critical of firms that seemed to focus too much on delivering a product, presumably based on its distinctive competence, rather than consciously serving the customer. Levitt thus argued that when companies fail, "it usually means that the product fails to adapt to the constantly changing patterns of consumer needs and tastes, to new and modified marketing institutions and practices, or to product developments in complementary industries."[14]

However, another leading strategist, Igor Ansoff, argued that Levitt was asking companies to take unnecessary risks by investing in new products that might not fit the firm's distinctive competence. Ansoff argued that a company should first ask whether a new product had a "common thread" with its existing products. He defined the common thread as a firm's "mission" or its commitment to exploit an existing need in the market as a whole.[15] Ansoff noted that "sometimes the customer is erroneously identified as the common thread of a firm's business. In reality, a given type of customer will frequently have a range of unrelated product missions or needs."[16] Thus, for a firm to maintain its strategic focus, Ansoff suggested certain categories for defining the common thread in its business/corporate strategy. (See Figure 2.) Ansoff and others also focused on translating the logic of the SWOT framework into a series of concrete questions that needed to be answered in the development of strategies.[17]

In the 1960s, diversification and technological changes increased the complexity of the strategic situations that many companies faced, and intensified their need for more sophisticated measures that could

---

[12] Andrews, *The Concept of Corporate Strategy*, 29.

[13] Ibid., 100.

[14] Theodore Levitt, "Marketing Myopia," *Harvard Business Review* (July/Aug. 1960): 52.

[15] Igor Ansoff, *Corporate Strategy* (New York, 1965), 106–9.

[16] Ibid., 105–8.

[17] Michael E. Porter, "Industrial Organization and the Evolution of Concepts for Strategic Planning," in T. H. Naylor, ed., *Corporate Strategy* (New York, 1982), 184.

	Present Product	New Product
Present Mission	Market Penetration	Product Development
New Mission	Market Development	Diversification

Figure 2. Ansoff's Product/Mission Matrix as adapted by Henry Mintzberg. (Source: Henry Mintzberg, "Generic Strategies," in *Advances in Strategic Management*, vol. 5 [Greenwich, Conn., 1988], 2. For the original, see Igor Ansoff, *Corporate Strategy* [New York, 1965], 128.)

be used to evaluate and compare many different types of businesses. Since business policy groups at Harvard and elsewhere remained strongly wedded to the idea that strategies could only be analyzed on a case-by-case basis in order to account for the unique characteristics of every business, corporations turned elsewhere to satisfy their craving for standardized approaches to strategy making.[18] A study by the Stanford Research Institute indicated that a majority of large U.S. companies had set up formal planning departments by 1963.[19] Some of these internal efforts were quite elaborate. General Electric (GE) is a bellwether example: it used Harvard faculty extensively in its executive education programs, but it also independently developed an elaborate, computer-based "Profitability Optimization Model" (PROM) in the first half of the 1960s that appeared to explain a significant fraction of the variation in the return on investment afforded by its various businesses.[20] Over time, like many other companies, GE also sought the help of private consulting firms. While consultants made important contributions in many areas, such as planning, forecasting, logistics, and long-range research and development (R&D), the following section traces their early impact on mainstream strategic thinking.

The Rise of Strategy Consultants

The 1960s and early 1970s witnessed the rise of a number of strategy consulting practices. In particular, the Boston Consulting Group

---

[18] Adam M. Brandenburger, Michael E. Porter, and Nicolaj Siggelkow, "Competition and Strategy: The Emergence of a Field," paper presented at McArthur Symposium, Harvard Business School, 9 Oct. 1996, 3–4.

[19] Stanford Research Institute, *Planning in Business* (Menlo Park, 1963).

[20] Sidney E. Schoeffler, Robert D. Buzzell, and Donald F. Heany, "Impact of Strategic Planning on Profit Performance," *Harvard Business Review* (Mar./Apr. 1974): 139.

(BCG), founded in 1963, had a major impact on the field by applying quantitative research to problems of business and corporate strategy. BCG's founder, Bruce Henderson, believed that a consultant's job was to find "meaningful quantitative relationships" between a company and its chosen markets.[21] In his words, "good strategy must be based primarily on logic, not . . . on experience derived from intuition."[22] Indeed, Henderson was utterly convinced that economic theory would someday lead to a set of universal rules for strategy. As he explained, "[I]n most firms strategy tends to be intuitive and based upon traditional patterns of behavior which have been successful in the past. . . . [However,] in growth industries or in a changing environment, this kind of strategy is rarely adequate. The accelerating rate of change is producing a business world in which customary managerial habits and organization are increasingly inadequate."[23]

In order to help executives make effective strategic decisions, BCG drew on the existing knowledge base in academia: one of its first employees, Seymour Tilles, was formerly a lecturer in Harvard's business policy course. However, it also struck off in a new direction that Bruce Henderson is said to have described as "the business of selling powerful oversimplifications."[24] In fact, BCG came to be known as a "strategy boutique" because its business was largely based, directly or indirectly, on a single concept: the experience curve (discussed below). The value of using a single concept came from the fact that "in nearly all problem solving there is a universe of alternative choices, most of which must be discarded without more than cursory attention." Hence, some "frame of reference is needed to screen the . . . relevance of data, methodology, and implicit value judgments" involved in any strategy decision. Given that decision making is necessarily a complex process, the most useful "frame of reference is the concept. Conceptual thinking is the skeleton or the framework on which all other choices are sorted out."[25]

BCG and the Experience Curve. BCG first developed its version of the learning curve—what it labeled the "experience curve"—in 1965–66. According to Bruce Henderson, "it was developed to try to explain price and competitive behavior in the extremely fast growing segments" of industries for clients like Texas Instruments and Black and

---

[21] Interview with Seymour Tilles, 24 Oct. 1996. Tilles credits Henderson for recognizing the competitiveness of Japanese industry at a time, in the late 1960s, when few Americans believed that Japan or any other country could compete successfully against American industry.

[22] Bruce Henderson, *The Logic of Business Strategy* (Cambridge, Mass., 1984), 10.

[23] Bruce D. Henderson, *Henderson on Corporate Strategy* (Cambridge, Mass., 1979), 6–7.

[24] Interview with Seymour Tilles, 24 Oct. 1996.

[25] Henderson, *Henderson on Corporate Strategy*, 41.

Decker.[26] As BCG consultants studied these industries, they naturally asked why "one competitor outperforms another (assuming comparable management skills and resources)? Are there basic rules for success? There, indeed, appear to be rules for success, and they relate to the impact of accumulated experience on competitors' costs, industry prices and the interrelation between the two."[27]

The firm's standard claim for the experience curve was that for each cumulative doubling of experience, *total* costs would decline by roughly 20 to 30 percent due to economies of scale, organizational learning, and technological innovation. The strategic implication of the experience curve, according to BCG, was that for a given product segment, "the producer . . . who has made the most units should have the lowest costs and the highest profits."[28] Bruce Henderson claimed that with the experience curve "the stability of competitive relationships should be predictable, the value of market share change should be calculable, [and] the effects of growth rate should [also] be calculable."[29]

From the Experience Curve to Portfolio Analysis. By the early 1970s, the experience curve had led to another "powerful oversimplification" by BCG: the "Growth-Share Matrix," which was the first use of what came to be known as "portfolio analysis." (See Figure 3.) The idea was that after experience curves were drawn for each of a diversified company's business units, their relative potential as areas for investment could be compared by plotting them on the grid.

BCG's basic strategy recommendation was to maintain a balance between "cash cows" (i.e., mature businesses) and "stars," while allocating some resources to feed "question marks," which were potential stars. "Dogs" were to be sold off. In more sophisticated language, a BCG vice president explained that "since the producer with the largest stable market share eventually has the lowest costs and greatest profits, it becomes vital to have a dominant market share in as many products as possible. However, market share in slowly growing products can be gained only by reducing the share of competitors who are likely to fight back." If a product market is growing rapidly, "a company can gain share by securing most of the *growth*. Thus, while competitors grow,

---

[26] Bruce Henderson explained that, unlike earlier versions of the "learning curve," BCG's experience curve "encompasses all costs (including capital, administrative, research and marketing) and traces them through technological displacement and product evolution. It is also based on cash flow rates, not accounting allocation." Bruce D. Henderson, preface to Boston Consulting Group, *Perspectives on Experience* (Boston, 1972; first published 1968).

[27] Boston Consulting Group, *Perspectives on Experience*, 7.

[28] Patrick Conley, "Experience Curves as a Planning Tool," in Boston Consulting Group pamphlet (1970): 15.

[29] Bruce Henderson, preface, Boston Consulting Group, *Perspectives on Experience*.

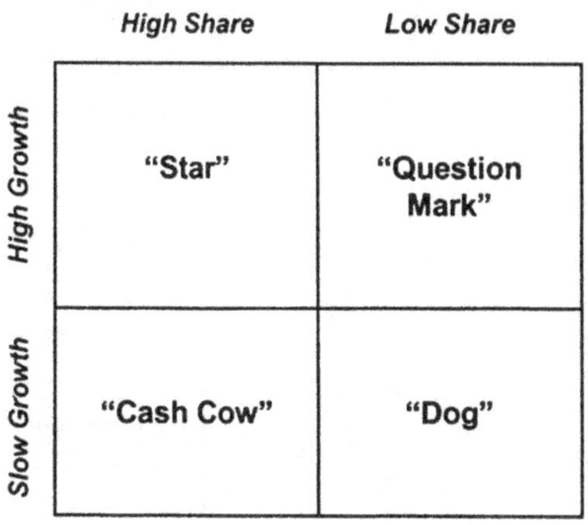

Figure 3. BCG's Growth-Share Matrix. (Source: Adapted from George Stalk Jr. and Thomas M. Hout, *Competing Against Time* [New York, 1990], 12.)

the company can grow even faster and emerge with a dominant share when growth eventually slows."[30]

Strategic Business Units and Portfolio Analysis. Numerous other consulting firms came up with their own matrices for portfolio analysis at roughly the same time as BCG. McKinsey & Company's effort, for instance, began in 1968 when Fred Borch, the CEO of GE, asked McKinsey to examine his company's corporate structure, which consisted of two hundred profit centers and one hundred and forty-five departments arranged around ten groups. The boundaries for these units had been defined according to theories of financial control, which the McKinsey consultants judged to be inadequate. They argued that the firm should be organized on more strategic lines, with greater concern for external conditions than internal controls and a more future-oriented approach than was possible using measures of past financial performance. The study recommended a formal strategic planning system that would divide the company into "natural business units," which Borch later renamed "strategic business units," or SBUs. GE's executives followed this advice, which took two years to put into effect.

However, in 1971, a GE corporate executive asked McKinsey for help in evaluating the strategic plans that were being written by the company's many SBUs. GE had already examined the possibility of using the BCG growth-share matrix to decide the fate of its SBUs, but its top management had decided then that they could not set priorities on the basis of just two performance measures. And so, after studying the problem for three months, a McKinsey team produced what came to be known as the GE/McKinsey nine-block matrix. The nine-block matrix used about a dozen measures to screen for industry attractive-

[30] Conley, "Experience Curves as a Planning Tool," 10–11.

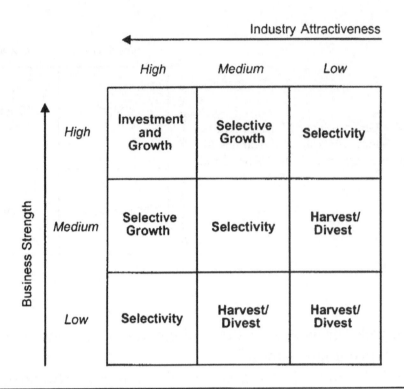

Figure 4. Industry Attractiveness–Business Strength Matrix. (Source: Arnoldo C. Hax and Nicolas S. Majluf, *Strategic Management: An Integrative Perspective* [Englewood Cliffs, N.J., 1984], 156.)

ness, or profitability, and another dozen to screen for competitive position, although the weights to be attached to them were not specified.[31] (See Figure 4.)

Another, more quantitative, approach to portfolio planning was developed at roughly the same time under the aegis of the "Profit Impact of Market Strategies" (PIMS) program, which was the multicompany successor to the PROM program that GE had started a decade earlier. By the mid-1970s, PIMS contained data on six hundred and twenty SBUs drawn from fifty-seven diversified corporations.[32] These data were used, in the first instance, to explore the determinants of returns on investment by regressing historical returns on variables such as market share, product quality, investment intensity, marketing and R&D expenditures, and several dozen others. The regressions established what were supposed to be benchmarks for the *potential* performance of SBUs with particular characteristics against which their *actual* performance might be compared.

[31] Interview with Mike Allen, 4 Apr. 1997.

[32] Sidney E. Schoeffler, Robert D. Buzzell, and Donald F. Heany, "Impact of Strategic Planning on Profit Performance," *Harvard Business Review* (Mar./Apr. 1974): 139–40, 144–5.

In all these applications, segmenting diversified corporations into SBUs became an important precursor to analyses of economic performance.[33] This forced "de-averaging" of cost and performance numbers that had previously been calculated at more aggregated levels. In addition, it was thought that, with such approaches, "strategic thinking was appropriately pushed 'down the line' to managers closer to the particular industry and its competitive conditions."[34]

In the 1970s, virtually every major consulting firm used some type of portfolio analysis to generate strategy recommendations. The concept became especially popular after the oil crisis of 1973 forced many large corporations to rethink, if not discard, their existing long-range plans. A McKinsey consultant noted that "the sudden quadrupling of energy costs [due to the OPEC embargo], followed by a recession and rumors of impending capital crisis, [meant that] setting long-term growth and diversification objectives was suddenly an exercise in irrelevance." Now, strategic planning meant "sorting out winners and losers, setting priorities, and husbanding capital." In a climate where "product and geographic markets were depressed and capital was presumed to be short,"[35] portfolio analysis gave executives a ready excuse to get rid of poorly performing business units while directing most available funds to the "stars." Thus, a survey of the "Fortune 500" industrial companies concluded that, by 1979, 45 percent of them had introduced portfolio planning techniques to some extent.[36]

Emerging Problems. Somewhat ironically, the very macroeconomic conditions that (initially) increased the popularity of portfolio analysis also began to raise questions about the experience curve. The high inflation and excess capacity resulting from downturns in demand induced by the "oil shocks" of 1973 and 1979 disrupted historical experience curves in many industries, suggesting that Bruce Henderson had oversold the concept when he circulated a pamphlet in 1974 entitled "Why Costs Go Down Forever." Another problem with the experience curve was pinpointed in a classic 1974 article by William Abernathy and Kenneth Wayne, which argued that "the consequence of intensively pursuing a cost-minimization strategy [e.g., one based on the experience curve] is a reduced ability to make innovative changes and to re-

---

[33] See Walter Kiechel III, "Corporate Strategists under Fire," *Fortune* (27 Dec. 1982).

[34] Frederick W. Gluck and Stephen P. Kaufman, "Using the Strategic Planning Framework," in McKinsey internal document, "Readings in Strategy" (1979), 3–4.

[35] J. Quincy Hunsicker, "Strategic Planning: A Chinese Dinner?" McKinsey staff paper (Dec. 1978), 3.

[36] Philippe Haspeslagh, "Portfolio Planning: Uses and Limits," *Harvard Business Review* (Jan./Feb. 1982): 59.

spond to those introduced by competitors."[37] Abernathy and Wayne pointed to the case of Henry Ford, whose obsession with lowering costs had left him vulnerable to Alfred Sloan's strategy of product innovation in the car business. The concept of the experience curve was also criticized for treating cost reductions as automatic rather than something to be managed, for assuming that most experience could be kept proprietary instead of spilling over to competitors, for mixing up different sources of cost reduction with very different strategic implications (e.g., learning versus scale versus exogenous technical progress), and for leading to stalemates as more than one competitor pursued the same generic success factor.[38]

In the late 1970s, portfolio analysis came under attack as well. One problem was that, in many cases, the strategic recommendations for an SBU were very sensitive to the specific portfolio-analytic technique employed. For instance, an academic study applied four different portfolio techniques to a group of fifteen SBUs owned by the same Fortune 500 corporation; it found that only one of the fifteen SBUs fell into the same portion of each of the four matrices, and only five of the fifteen were classified similarly in terms of three of the four matrices.[39] This was only a slightly higher level of concordance than would have been expected if the fifteen SBUs had been randomly classified four separate times!

An even more serious problem with portfolio analysis was that even if one could figure out the "right" technique to employ, the mechanical determination of resource allocation patterns on the basis of historical performance data was inherently problematic. Some consultants acknowledged as much. In 1979, Fred Gluck, the head of McKinsey's strategic management practice, ventured the opinion that "the heavy dependence on 'packaged' techniques [has] frequently resulted in nothing more than a tightening up, or fine tuning, of current initiatives within the traditionally configured businesses." Even worse, technique-based strategies "rarely beat existing competition" and often leave businesses "vulnerable to unexpected thrusts from companies not previously considered competitors."[40] Gluck and his colleagues sought to loosen some of the constraints imposed by mechanistic approaches,

[37] William J. Abernathy and Kenneth Wayne, "Limits of the Learning Curve," *Harvard Business Review* (Sept./Oct. 1974): 111.

[38] Pankaj Ghemawat, "Building Strategy on the Experience Curve," *Harvard Business Review* (Mar. /Apr.): 1985.

[39] Yoram Wind, Vijay Mahajan, and Donald J. Swire, "An Empirical Comparison of Standardized Portfolio Models," *Journal of Marketing* 47 (Spring 1983): 89–99. The statistical analysis of their results is based on an unpublished draft by Pankaj Ghemawat.

[40] Gluck and Kaufman, "Using the Strategic Planning Framework," 5–6.

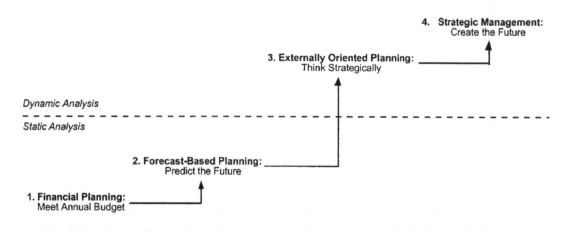

Figure 5. Four Phases of Strategy. (Source: Adapted from Frederick W. Gluck, Stephen P. Kaufman, and A. Steven Walleck, "The Evolution of Strategic Management," McKinsey staff paper [Oct. 1978], 4. Reproduced in modified form in Gluck, Kaufman, and Walleck, "Strategic Management for Competitive Advantage," *Harvard Business Review* [July/Aug. 1980], 157.)

proposing that successful companies devise progressive strategies to take them through four basic stages. Each stage requires these companies to grapple with increasing levels of dynamism, multidimensionality, and uncertainty, and they therefore become less amenable to routine quantitative analysis. (See Figure 5.)

The most stinging attack on the analytical techniques popularized by strategy consultants was offered by two Harvard professors of production, Robert Hayes and William Abernathy, in 1980. They argued that "these new principles [of management], despite their sophistication and widespread usefulness, encourage a preference for (1) analytic detachment rather than the insight that comes from 'hands on experience' and (2) short-term cost reduction rather than long-term development of technological competitiveness."[41] Hayes and Abernathy in particular criticized portfolio analysis as a tool that led managers to focus on minimizing financial risks rather than on investing in new opportunities that require a long-term commitment of resources.[42] They went on to compare U.S. firms unfavorably with Japanese and, especially, European ones.

These and other criticisms gradually diminished the popularity of portfolio analysis. However, its rise and fall did have a lasting influence on subsequent work on competition and business strategy because it highlighted the need for more careful analysis of the two basic dimensions of portfolio-analytic grids: industry attractiveness and competi-

[41] Robert H. Hayes and William J. Abernathy, "Managing Our Way to Economic Decline," *Harvard Business Review* (July/Aug. 1980): 68.
[42] Ibid., 71.

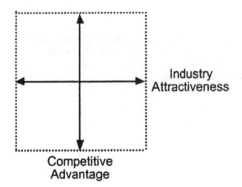

Figure 6. Two Basic Dimensions of Strategy.

tive position. Although these two dimensions had been identified earlier—in the General Survey Outline developed by McKinsey & Company for internal use in 1952, for example—portfolio analysis underscored this particular method of analyzing the effects of competition on business performance. U.S. managers, in particular, proved avid consumers of insights about competition because the exposure of much of U.S. industry to competitive forces increased dramatically during the 1960s and 1970s. One economist roughly calculated that heightened import competition, antitrust actions, and deregulation increased the share of the U.S. economy that was subject to effective competition from 56 percent in 1958 to 77 percent by 1980.[43] The next two sections describe attempts to unbundle these two basic dimensions of strategy. (See Figure 6.)

Unbundling Industry Attractiveness

Thus far, we have made little mention of economists' contributions to thinking about competitive strategy. On the one hand, economic theory emphasizes the role of competitive forces in determining market outcomes. However, on the other hand, economists have often overlooked the importance of strategy because, since Adam Smith, they have traditionally focused on the case of perfect competition: an idealized situation in which large numbers of equally able competitors drive an industry's aggregate economic profits (i.e., profits in excess of the opportunity cost of the capital employed) down to zero. Under perfect competition, individual competitors are straitjacketed, in the sense of having a choice between producing efficiently and pricing at cost or shutting down.

Some economists did address the opposite case of perfect competition, namely pure monopoly, with Antoine Cournot providing the first

[43] William G. Shepherd, "Causes of Increased Competition in the U.S. Economy, 1939–1980," *Review of Economics and Statistics* (Nov. 1982): 619.

definitive analysis—as well as analysis of oligopoly under specific assumptions—in 1838.[44] Work on monopoly yielded some useful insights, such as the expectation of an inverse relation between the profitability of a monopolized industry and the price elasticity of the demand it faced—an insight that has remained central in modern marketing. Nevertheless, the assumption of monopoly obviously took things to the other, equally unfortunate, extreme by ruling out all directly competitive forces in the behavior of firms.

This state of affairs began to change at an applied level in the 1930s, as a number of economists, particularly those associated with the "Harvard school," began to argue that the *structure* of many industries might permit incumbent firms to earn positive economic profits over long periods of time.[45] Edward S. Mason argued that the structure of an industry would determine the conduct of buyers and sellers— their choices of critical decision variables—and, by implication, its performance along such dimensions as profitability, efficiency, and innovativeness.[46] Joe Bain, also of the Harvard Economics Department, advanced the research program of uncovering the general relation between industry structure and performance through empirical work focused on a limited number of structural variables—most notably, in two studies published in the 1950s. The first study found that the profitability of manufacturing industries in which the eight largest competitors accounted for more than 70 percent of sales was nearly twice that of industries with eight-firm concentration ratios of less than 70 percent.[47] The second study explained how, in certain industries, "established sellers can persistently raise their prices above a competitive level without attracting new firms to enter the industry."[48] Bain identified three basic barriers to entry: (1) an absolute cost advantage by an established firm (an enforceable patent, for instance); (2) a significant degree of product differentiation; and (3) economies of scale.

Bain's insights led to the rapid growth of a new subfield of economics, known as industrial organization, or "IO" for short, that explored the structural reasons why some industries were more profitable than others. By the mid-1970s, several hundred empirical studies in IO had

[44] Antoine A. Cournot, *Recherches sur les Principes Mathematiques de la Theorie des Richesses* (Paris, 1838), sects. 26, 27; and Jurg Niehans, *A History of Economic Theory* (Baltimore, 1990), 180–2.

[45] Economists associated with the Chicago School generally doubted the empirical importance of this possibility—except as an artifact of regulatory distortions.

[46] Mason's seminal work was "Price and Production Policies of Large-Scale Enterprise," *American Economic Review* (Mar. 1939): 61–4.

[47] Joe S. Bain, "Relation of Profit Rate to Industry Concentration: American Manufacturing, 1936–1940," *Quarterly Journal of Economics* (Aug. 1951): 293–324.

[48] Joe S. Bain, *Barriers to New Competition* (Cambridge, Mass., 1956), 3 n.

Industry	Return on Equity
Drugs	21.4
Printing and Publishing	15.5
Petroleum and Coal	13.1
Motor Vehicles and Equipment	11.6
Textile Mill Products	9.3
Iron and Steel	3.9

Figure 7. Differences in the Profitability of Selected Industries, 1971–1990. (Source: Anita M. McGahan, "Selected Profitability Data on U.S. Industries and Companies," Harvard Business School Publishing, No. 792-066 [1992].)

been carried out. While the relation between structural variables and performance turned out to be more complicated than had been suggested earlier,[49] these studies reinforced the idea that some industries are inherently much more profitable or "attractive" than others, as indicated below. (See Figure 7.)

Harvard Business School's Business Policy Group was aware of these insights from across the Charles River: excerpts from Bain's book on barriers to entry were even assigned as required readings for the business policy course in the early 1960s. But the immediate impact of IO on business strategy was limited. Although many problems can be discerned in retrospect, two seem to have been particularly important. First, IO economists focused on issues of public policy rather than business policy: they concerned themselves with the minimization rather than the maximization of "excess" profits. Second, the emphasis of Bain and his successors on using a limited list of structural variables to explain industry profitability shortchanged the richness of modern industrial competition ("conduct" within the IO paradigm).

Both of these problems with applying classical IO to business-strategic concerns about industry attractiveness were addressed by Michael Porter, a graduate of the Ph.D. program offered jointly by Harvard's Business School and its Economics Department. In 1974, Porter prepared a "Note on the Structural Analysis of Industries," which presented his first attempt to turn IO on its head by focusing on the business policy objective of profit maximization, rather than on the public policy objective of minimizing "excess" profits.[50] In 1980, he released his landmark book, *Competitive Strategy*, which owed much of its suc-

[49] See, for instance, Harvey J. Goldschmid, H. Michael Mann, and J. Fred Weston, eds., *Industrial Concentration: The New Learning* (Boston, 1974).

[50] Michael E. Porter, "Note on the Structural Analysis of Industries," Harvard Business School Teaching Note, no. 376-054 (1983).

cess to Porter's elaborate framework for the structural analysis of industry attractiveness. Figure 8 reproduces Porter's "five forces" approach to understanding the attractiveness of an industry environment for the "average" competitor within it. In developing this approach to strategy, Porter noted the trade-offs involved in using a "framework" rather than a more formal statistical "model." In his words, a framework "encompasses many variables and seeks to capture much of the complexity of actual competition. Frameworks identify the *relevant* variables and the questions that the user must answer in order to develop conclusions tailored to a particular industry and company" (emphasis added).[51] In academic terms, the drawback of frameworks such as the five forces is that they often range beyond the empirical evidence that is available. In practice, managers routinely have to consider much longer lists of variables than are embedded in the relatively simple quantitative models used by economists. In the case of the five forces, a survey of empirical literature in the late 1980s—more than a decade after Porter first developed his framework—revealed that only a few points were strongly supported by the empirical literature generated by the IO field.[52] (These points appear in bold print in Figure 8.) This does not mean that the other points are in conflict with IO research; rather, they reflect the experience of strategy practitioners, including Porter himself.

In managerial terms, one of the breakthroughs built into Porter's framework was that it emphasized "extended competition" for value rather than just competition between existing rivals. For this reason, and because it was easy to put into effect, the five-forces framework came to be used widely by managers and consultants. Subsequent years witnessed refinements and extensions, such as the rearrangement and incorporation of additional variables (e.g., import competition and multimarket contact) into the determinants of the intensity of five forces. The biggest conceptual advance, however, was one proposed in the mid-1990s by two strategists concerned with game theory, Adam Brandenburger and Barry Nalebuff, who argued that the process of creating value in the marketplace involved "four types of players—customers, suppliers, competitors, and complementors."[53] By a firm's "complementors," they meant other firms from which customers buy

---

[51] Michael E. Porter, "Toward a Dynamic Theory of Strategy," in Richard P. Rumelt, Dan E. Schendel, and David J. Teece, eds., *Fundamental Issues in Strategy* (Boston, 1994), 427–9.

[52] Richard Schmalensee, "Inter-Industry Studies of Structure and Performance," in Richard Schmalensee and R. D. Willig, eds., *Handbook of Industrial Organization*, vol. 2 (Amsterdam, 1989).

[53] Adam M. Brandenburger and Barry J. Nalebuff, *Co-opetition* (New York, 1996).

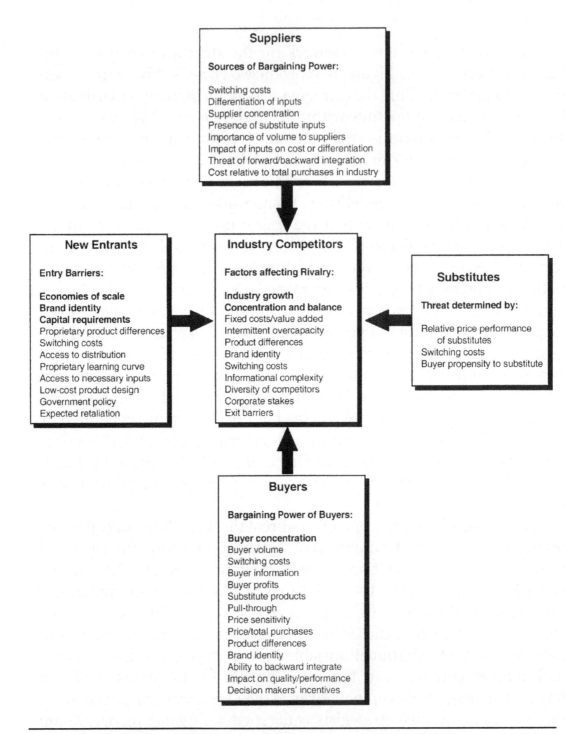

Figure 8. Porter's Five-Forces Framework for Industry Analysis.

complementary products and services, or to which suppliers sell complementary resources. As Brandenburger and Nalebuff pointed out, the practical importance of this group of players was evident in the amount of attention being paid in business to the subject of strategic alliances and partnerships. Their Value Net graphic depicted this more complete description of the business landscape—emphasizing, in particular, the equal roles played by competition and complementarity. (See Figure 9.)

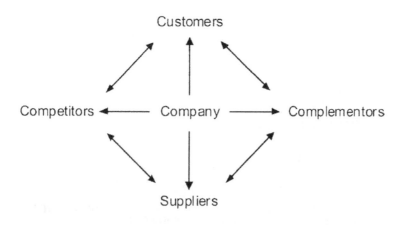

Figure 9. The Value Net. (Source: Adam M. Brandenburger and Barry J. Nalebuff, *Co-opetition* [New York, 1996], 17.)

Other strategists, however, argued that some very limiting assumptions were built into such frameworks. Thus, Kevin Coyne and Somu Subramanyam of McKinsey argued that the Porter framework made three tacit but crucial assumptions: First, that an industry consists of a set of unrelated buyers, sellers, substitutes, and competitors that interact at arm's length. Second, that wealth will accrue to players that are able to erect barriers against competitors and potential entrants, or, in other words, that the source of value is structural advantage. Third, that uncertainty is sufficiently low that you can accurately predict participants' behavior and choose a strategy accordingly.[54]

Unbundling Competitive Position

The second basic dimension of business strategy highlighted by Figure 6 is competitive position. While differences in the average profitability of industries can be large, as indicated in Figure 7, differences in profitability *within* industries can be even larger.[55] Indeed, in some cases firms in *unattractive* industries can significantly outperform the averages for more profitable industries, as indicated in Figure 10. In addition, one might argue that most businesses in most industry environments are better placed to try to alter their own competitive positions, rather than the overall attractiveness of the industry in which they operate. For both these reasons, competitive position has been of great interest to business strategists. (See Figure 10.)

[54] Kevin P. Coyne and Somu Subramanyam, "Bringing Discipline to Strategy," *McKinsey Quarterly* 4 (1996): 16.
[55] See, for instance, Richard P. Rumelt, "How Much Does Industry Matter?" *Strategic Management Journal* (March 1991): 167–85.

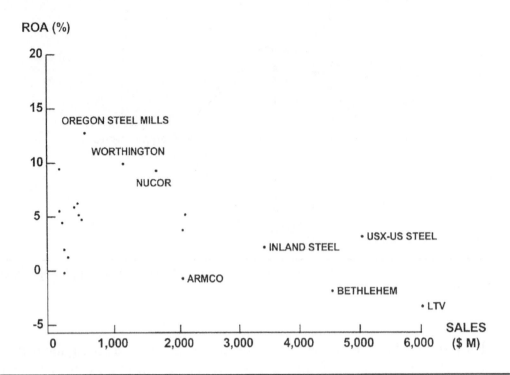

Figure 10. Profitability within the Steel Industry, 1973–1992. (Source: David Collis and Pankaj Ghemawat, "Industry Analysis: Understanding Industry Structure and Dynamics," in Liam Fahey and Robert M. Randall, *The Portable MBA in Strategy* [New York, 1994], 174.)

Traditional academic research has made a number of contributions to our understanding of positioning within industries, starting in the 1970s. The IO-based literature on strategic groups, initiated at Harvard by Michael Hunt's work on broad-line versus narrow-line strategies in the major home appliance industry, suggested that competitors within particular industries could be grouped in terms of their competitive strategies in ways that helped explain their interactions and relative profitability.[56] A stream of work at Purdue explored the heterogeneity of competitive positions, strategies, and performance in brewing and other industries with a combination of statistical analysis and qualitative case studies. More recently, several academic points of view about the sources of performance differences within industries have emerged — views that are explored more fully in the next section. However, it does seem accurate to say that the work that had the most impact on the strategic thinking of business about competitive positions in the late 1970s and the 1980s was more pragmatic than academic in its intent, with consultants once again playing a leading role.

[56] See Michael S. Hunt, "Competition in the Major Home Appliance Industry," DBA diss., Harvard University, 1972. A theoretical foundation for strategic groups was provided by Richard E. Caves and Michael E. Porter, "From Entry Barriers to Mobility Barriers," *Quarterly Journal of Economics* (Nov. 1977): 667–75.

Competitive Cost Analysis. With the rise of the experience curve in the 1960s, most strategists turned to some type of cost analysis as the basis for assessing competitive positions. The interest in competitive cost analysis survived the declining popularity of the experience curve in the 1970s but was reshaped by it in two important ways. First, more attention was paid to disaggregating businesses into their component activities or processes and to thinking about how costs in a particular activity might be shared across businesses. Second, strategists greatly enriched their menu of cost drivers to include more than just experience.

The disaggregation of businesses into their component activities seems to have been motivated, in part, by early attempts to "fix" the experience curve to deal with the rising real prices of many raw materials in the 1970s.[57] The proposed fix involved splitting costs into the costs of purchased materials and "cost added" (value added minus profit margins) and redefining the experience curve as applying only to the latter. The natural next step was to disaggregate a business's entire cost structure into activities whose costs might be expected to behave in interestingly different ways. As in the case of portfolio analysis, the idea of splitting businesses into component activities diffused quickly among consultants and their clients in the 1970s. A template for activity analysis that became especially prominent is reproduced in Figure 11.

Activity analysis also suggested a way of getting around the "free-standing" conception of individual businesses built into the concept of SBUs. One persistent problem in splitting diversified corporations into SBUs was that, with the exception of pure conglomerates, SBUs were often related in ways that meant they shared elements of their cost structure with each other. Consulting firms, particularly Bain and Strategic Planning Associates, both of whose founders had worked on a BCG study of Texas Instruments that was supposed to highlight the problem of shared costs, began to emphasize the development of what came to be called "field maps": matrices that identified shared costs at the level of individual activities that were linked across businesses, as illustrated below.[58]

The second important development in competitive cost analysis over the late 1970s and early 1980s involved enrichment of the menu of cost drivers considered by strategists. Scale effects, while officially lumped into the experience curve, had long been looked at independently in particular cases; even more specific treatment of the effects of scale was now forced by activity analysis that might indicate, for example, that advertising costs were driven by national scale, whereas distri-

---

[57] This is based on my experience working at BCG in the late 1970s.

[58] Walter Kiechel III, "The Decline of the Experience Curve," *Fortune* (5 Oct. 1981).

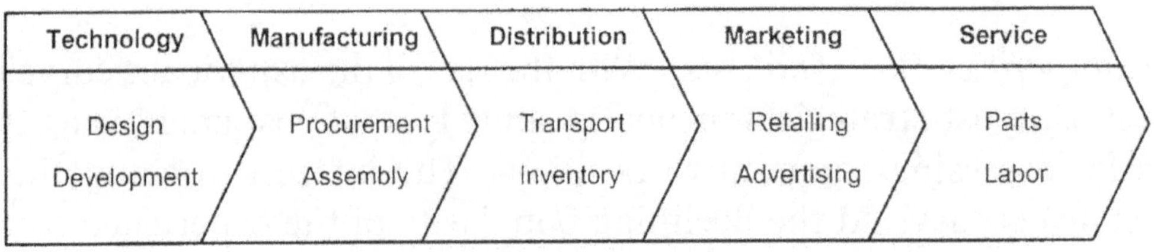

Technology	Manufacturing	Distribution	Marketing	Service
Design	Procurement	Transport	Retailing	Parts
Development	Assembly	Inventory	Advertising	Labor

Figure 11. McKinsey's Business System. (Source: Adapted from Carter F. Bales, P. C. Chatterjee, Donald J. Gogel, and Anupam P. Puri, "Competitive Cost Analysis," McKinsey staff paper [Jan. 1980], 6.)

bution costs were driven by local or regional scale. Field maps underscored the potential importance of economies (or diseconomies) of scope across businesses rather than scale within a business. The effects of capacity utilization on costs were dramatized by macroeconomic downturns in the wake of the two oil shocks. The globalization of competition in many industries highlighted the location of activities as a main driver of competitors' cost positions, and so on. Thus, an influential mid-1980s discussion of cost analysis enumerated ten distinct cost drivers.[59]

Customer Analysis. Increased sophistication in analyzing relative costs was accompanied by increased attention to customers in the process of analyzing competitive position. Customers had never been entirely invisible: even in the heyday of experience curve analysis, market segmentation had been an essential strategic tool—although it was sometimes used to gerrymander markets to "demonstrate" a positive link between share and cost advantage rather than for any analytic purpose. But, according to Walker Lewis, the founder of Strategic Planning Associates, "To those who defended in classic experience-curve strategy, about 80% of the businesses in the world were commodities."[60] This started to change in the 1970s.

Increased attention to customer analysis involved reconsideration of the idea that attaining low costs and offering customers low prices was always the best way to compete. More attention came to be paid to *differentiated* ways of competing that might let a business command a price premium by improving customers' performance or reducing their (other) costs. While (product) differentiation had always occupied center stage in marketing, the idea of looking at it in a cross-functional, competitive context that also accounted for relative costs apparently started to emerge in business strategy in the 1970s. Thus, a member of Harvard's Business Policy group recalls using the distinction between

[59] Michael E. Porter, *Competitive Advantage* (New York, 1985), ch. 3.
[60] Quoted in Kiechel, "The Decline of the Experience Curve."

cost and differentiation, which was implicit in two of the three sources of entry barriers identified by Joe Bain in the 1950s (see above), to organize classroom discussions in the early 1970s.[61] And McKinsey reportedly started to apply the distinction between cost and "value" to client studies later in that decade.[62] The first published accounts, in Michael Porter's book *Competitive Strategy* and in a *Harvard Business Review* article by William Hall, appeared in 1980.[63]

Both Hall and Porter argued that successful companies usually had to choose to compete either on the basis of low costs or by differentiating products through quality and performance characteristics. Porter also identified a focus option that cut across these two "generic strategies" and linked these strategic options to his work on industry analysis:

> In some industries, there are no opportunities for focus or differentiation—it's solely a cost game—and this is true in a number of bulk commodities. In other industries, cost is relatively unimportant because of buyer and product characteristics.[64]

Many other strategists agreed that, except in such special cases, the analysis of competitive position had to cover both relative cost and differentiation. There was continuing debate, however, about the proposition, explicitly put forth by Porter, that businesses "stuck in the middle" should be expected to perform less well than businesses that had targeted lower cost or more differentiated positions. Others saw optimal positioning as a choice from a continuum of trade-offs between cost and differentiation, rather than as a choice between two mutually exclusive (and extreme) generic strategies.

Porter's book, published in 1985, suggested analyzing cost and differentiation via the "value chain," a template that is reproduced in Figure 12. While Porter's value chain bore an obvious resemblance to McKinsey's business system, his discussion of it emphasized the importance of regrouping functions into the activities actually performed to produce, market, deliver, and support products, thinking about links between activities, and connecting the value chain to the determinants of competitive position in a specific way:

> Competitive advantage cannot be understood by looking at a firm as a whole. It stems from the many discrete activities a firm performs in designing, producing, marketing, delivering, and supporting its

---

[61] Interview with Hugo Uyterhoeven, 25 Apr. 1997.

[62] Interview with Fred Gluck, 18 Feb. 1997.

[63] Michael E. Porter, *Competitive Strategy* (New York, 1980), ch. 2; and William K. Hall, "Survival Strategies in a Hostile Environment," *Harvard Business Review* (Sept./Oct. 1980): 78–81.

[64] Porter, *Competitive Strategy*, 41–4.

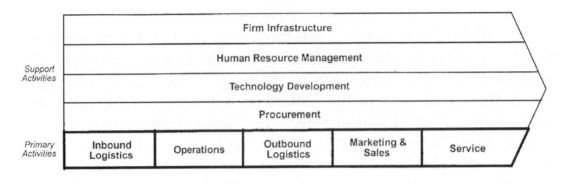

Figure 12. Porter's Value Chain. (Source: Michael E. Porter, *Competitive Advantage* [New York, 1985], 37.)

product. Each of these activities can contribute to a firm's relative cost position and create a basis for differentiation. . . . The value chain disaggregates a firm into its strategically relevant activities in order to understand the behavior of costs and the existing and potential sources of differentiation.[65]

Putting customer analysis and cost analysis together was promoted not only by disaggregating businesses into activities (or processes) but also by splitting customers into segments based on cost-to-serve as well as customer needs. Such "de-averaging" of customers was often said to expose situations in which 20 percent of a business's customers accounted for more than 80 percent, or even 100 percent, of its profits.[66] It also suggested new customer segmentation criteria. Thus, Bain & Company built a thriving "customer retention" practice, starting in the late 1980s, on the basis of the higher costs of capturing new customers as opposed to retaining existing ones.

Competitive Dynamics and History

The development of business systems, value chains, and similar templates naturally refocused attention on the problem of coordinating across a large number of choices linked in cross section that was highlighted, in a cross-functional context, in the original description of Harvard Business School's course on business policy. However, such attention tended to crowd out consideration of longitudinal links between choices, which was emphasized by Selznick's work on organizational commitments and distinctive competences and evident in Andrews's focus on the aspects of firm behavior that were "enduring and unchanging over relatively long periods of time."

[65] Porter, *Competitive Advantage*, 33, 37.
[66] Talk by Arnoldo Hax at MIT on 29 April 1997.

The need to return the time dimension to predominantly static ideas about competitive position was neatly illustrated by the techniques for "value-based strategic management" that began to be promoted by consulting firms like SPA and Marakon, among others, in the 1980s. The development and diffusion of value-based techniques, which connected positioning measures to shareholder value using spreadsheet models of discounted cash flows, was driven by increases in capital market pressures in the 1980s, particularly in the United States: merger and acquisition activity soared; hostile takeovers of even very large companies became far more common; many companies restructured to avoid them; levels of leverage generally increased; and there was creeping institutionalization of equity holdings.[67] Early value-based work focused on the spread between a company or division's rate of return and its cost of capital as the basis for "solving" the old corporate strategy problem of resource allocation across businesses. It quickly became clear, however, that estimated valuations were very sensitive to two other, more dynamic, drivers of value: the length of the time horizon over which positive spreads (competitive advantage) could be sustained on the assets in place, and the (profitable) reinvestment opportunities or growth options afforded by a strategy.[68] At the same time, analyses of business performance started to underscore the treacherousness of assuming that current profitability and growth could automatically be sustained. Thus, my analysis of 700 business units revealed that nine-tenths of the profitability differential between businesses that were initially above average and those that were initially below average vanished over a ten-year period.[69] (See Figure 13.)

The unsustainability of most competitive advantages was generally thought to reflect the "Red Queen" effect: the idea that as organizations struggled to adapt to competitive pressures, they would become stronger competitors, sending the overall level of competition spiraling upward and eliminating most, if not all, competitive advantages.[70] In the

[67] F. M. Scherer and David Ross, *Industrial Market Structure and Economic Performance* (Boston, 1990), ch. 5.

[68] Benjamin C. Esty, "Note on Value Drivers," Harvard Business School Teaching Note, no. 297-082 (1997).

[69] Pankaj Ghemawat, "Sustainable Advantage," *Harvard Business Review* (Sept./Oct. 1986): 53–8, and *Commitment* (New York, 1991), ch. 5.

[70] The first economic citation of the "Red Queen" effect is generally attributed to L. Van Valen. See L. Van Valen, "A New Evolutionary Law," *Evolutionary Theory* 1 (1973): 1–30. The literary reference is to Lewis Carroll's *Alice's Adventures in Wonderland* and *Through the Looking Glass* (New York, 1981; first published 1865–71), in which the Red Queen tells Alice: "*here*, you see, it takes all the running you can do, to keep in the same place. If you want to get somewhere else, you must run at least twice as fast . . ." (p. 127).

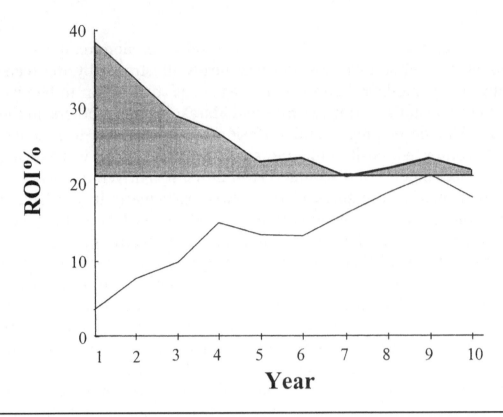

Figure 13. The Limits to Sustainability.

late 1980s and early 1990s, both academics and consultants started to wrestle with the dynamic question of how businesses might create *and* sustain competitive advantage in the presence of competitors who could not all be counted on to remain inert all the time.

From an academic perspective, many of the consultants' recommendations regarding dynamics amounted to no more, and no less, than the injunction to try to be smarter than the competition (for example, by focusing on customers' future needs while competitors remained focused on their current needs). The most thoughtful exception that had a truly dynamic orientation was work by George Stalk and others at BCG on time-based competition. In an article published in the *Harvard Business Review* in 1988, Stalk argued: "Today the leading edge of competition is the combination of fast response and increasing variety. Companies without these advantages are slipping into commodity-like competition, where customers buy mainly on price."[71] Stalk expanded on this argument in a book coauthored with Thomas Hout in 1990, according to which time-based competitors "[c]reate more information and share it more spontaneously. For the information technolo-

---

[71] George Stalk Jr., "Time—The Next Source of Competitive Advantage," *Harvard Business Review* (July/Aug. 1988).

gist, information is a fluid asset, a data stream. But to the manager of a business . . . information is fuzzy and takes many forms—knowing a customer's special needs, seeing where the market is heading . . ."[72]

Time-based competition quickly came to account for a substantial fraction of BCG's business. Eventually, however, its limitations also became apparent. In 1993, George Stalk and Alan Webber wrote that some Japanese companies had become so dedicated to shortening their product-development cycles that they had created a "strategic treadmill on which companies were caught, condemned to run faster and faster but always staying in the same place competitively."[73] In particular, Japanese electronics manufacturers had reached a remarkable level of efficiency, but it was an "efficiency that [did] not meet or create needs for any customer."[74]

For some, like Stalk himself, the lesson from this and similar episodes was that there were no sustainable advantages: "Strategy can never be a constant. . . . Strategy is and always has been a moving target."[75] However, others, primarily academics, continued to work in the 1990s on explanations of differences in performance that would continue to be useful even *after* they were widely grasped.[76] This academic work exploits, in different ways, the idea that history matters, that history affects both the opportunities available to competitors and the effectiveness with which competitors can exploit them. Such work can be seen as an attempt to add a historical or time dimension, involving stickiness and rigidities, to the two basic dimensions of early portfolio analytic grids: industry attractiveness and competitive position. The rest of this section briefly reviews four strands of academic inquiry that embodied new approaches to thinking about the time dimension.

Game Theory. Game theory is the mathematical study of interactions between players whose payoffs depend on each other's choices. A general theory of zero-sum games, in which one player's gain is exactly equal to other players' losses, was supplied by John von Neumann and Oskar Morgenstern in their pathbreaking book *The Theory of Games and Economic Behavior*.[77] There is no general theory of non-zero-sum games, which afford opportunities for cooperation as well as competi-

---

[72] Stalk and Hout, *Competing Against Time*, 179.

[73] George Stalk Jr. and Alan M. Webber, "Japan's Dark Side of Time," *Harvard Business Review* (July/Aug. 1993): 94.

[74] Ibid., 98–9.

[75] Ibid., 101–2.

[76] This test of stability is in the spirit of the game theorists, John von Neumann and Oskar Morgenstern. See their *Theory of Games and Economic Behavior* (Princeton, 1944).

[77] Ibid.

tion, but research in this area does supply a language and a set of logical tools for analyzing the outcome that is likely—the equilibrium point—given specific rules, payoff structures, and beliefs if players all behave "rationally."[78]

Economists trained in IO started to turn to game theory in the late 1970s as a way of studying competitor dynamics. Since the early 1980s, well over half of all the IO articles published in the leading economics journals have been concerned with some aspect of non-zero-sum game theory.[79] By the end of the 1980s alone, competition to invest in tangible and intangible assets, strategic control of information, horizontal mergers, network competition and product standardization, contracting, and numerous other settings in which interactive effects were apt to be important had all been modeled using game theory.[80] The effort continues.

Game-theory IO models tend, despite their diversity, to share an emphasis "on the *dynamics of strategic actions* and in particular on the role of *commitment*."[81] The emphasis on commitment or irreversibility grows out of game theory's focus on interactive effects. From this perspective, a strategic move is one that "purposefully limits your freedom of action. . . . It changes other players' expectations about your future responses, and you can turn this to your advantage. Others know that when you have the freedom to act, you also have the freedom to capitulate."[82]

The formalism of game theory is accompanied by several significant limitations: the sensitivity of the predictions of game-theory models to details, the limited number of variables considered in any one model, and assumptions of rationality that are often heroic, to name just a few.[83] Game theory's empirical base is also limited. The existing evidence suggests, nonetheless, that it merits attention in analyses of interactions between small numbers of firms. While game theory often formalizes preexisting intuitions, it can sometimes yield unanticipated, and even counterintuitive, predictions. Thus, game-theory modeling of

---

[78] There is also a branch of game theory that provides upper bounds on players' payoffs if freewheeling interactions between them are allowed. See Brandenburger and Nalebuff's *Co-opetition* for applications of this idea to business.

[79] Pankaj Ghemawat, *Games Businesses Play* (Cambridge, Mass., 1997), 3.

[80] For a late 1980s survey of game-theory IO, consult Carl Shapiro, "The Theory of Business Strategy," *RAND Journal of Economics* (Spring 1989): 125–37.

[81] Ibid., 127.

[82] Avinash K. Dixit and Barry J. Nalebuff, *Thinking Strategically* (New York, 1991), 120. Their logic is based on Thomas C. Schelling's pioneering book, *The Strategy of Conflict* (Cambridge, Mass., 1979; first published in 1960).

[83] For a detailed critique, see Richard P. Rumelt, Dan Schendel, and David J. Teece, "Strategic Management and Economics," *Strategic Management Journal* (Winter 1991): 5–29. For further discussion, see Ghemawat, *Games Businesses Play*, chap. 1.

shrinkage in, and exit from, declining industries yielded the prediction that, other things being equal, initial size should hurt survivability. This surprising prediction turns out to enjoy some empirical support![84]

The Resource-Based View of the Firm. The idea of looking at companies in terms of their resource endowments is an old one, but it was revived in the 1980s in an article by Birger Wernerfelt.[85] Wernerfelt noted: "The traditional concept of strategy [put forth by Kenneth Andrews in 1971] is phrased in terms of the resource position (strengths and weaknesses) of the firm, whereas most of our formal economic tools operate on the product market side."[86] While Wernerfelt also described resources and products as "two sides of the same coin," other adherents to what has come to be called the resource-based view (RBV) of the firm argue that superior product market positions rest on the ownership of scarce, firm-specific resources.

Resource-based theorists also seek to distinguish their perspective on sustained superior performance from that of IO economics by stressing the *intrinsic* inimitability of scarce, valuable resources for a variety of reasons: the ability to obtain a particular resource may be dependent on *unique, historical circumstances* that competitors cannot recreate; the link between the resources possessed by a firm and its sustained competitive advantage may be *causally ambiguous* or poorly understood; or the resource responsible for the advantage may be *socially complex* and therefore "beyond the ability of firms to systematically manage and influence" (e.g., corporate culture).[87] Game-theory IO, in contrast, has tended to focus on less extreme situations in which imitation of superior resources may be feasible but uneconomical (e.g., because of preemption).

Resource-based theorists therefore have traditionally tended to see firms as stuck with a few key resources, which they must deploy across product markets in ways that maximize total profits rather than profits in individual markets. This insight animated C. K. Prahalad and Gary Hamel's influential article, "The Core Competence of the Corporation,"

[84] For a discussion of the original models (by Ghemawat and Nalebuff) and the supporting empirical evidence, consult Ghemawat, *Games Businesses Play*, ch. 5.

[85] In the same year, Richard Rumelt also noted that the strategic firm "is characterized by a bundle of linked and idiosyncratic resources and resource conversion activities." See his chapter, "Towards a Strategic Theory of the Firm," in R. B. Lamb, ed., *Competitive Strategic Management* (Englewood Cliffs, N.J., 1984), 561.

[86] Birger Wernerfelt, "A Resource-based View of the Firm," *Strategic Management Journal* 5 (1984): 171. In addition to citing Andrews's 1971 book, *The Concept of Corporate Strategy*, Wernerfelt referred to the pioneering work of Edith Penrose, *The Theory of the Growth of the Firm* (Oxford, 1959).

[87] Jay B. Barney, "Firm Resources and Sustained Competitive Advantage," *Journal of Management* (March 1991): 107–11.

which attacked the SBU system of management for focusing on products rather than on underlying core competencies in a way that arguably bounded innovation, imprisoned resources, and led to a decline in investment: "In the short run, a company's competitiveness derives from the price/performance attributes of current products. . . . In the long run, competitiveness derives from the . . . core competencies that spawn unanticipated new products."[88]

To many resource-based theorists, the core competencies that Prahalad and Hamel celebrate are simply a neologism for the resources that the RBV has emphasized all along. Whether the same can be said about another, more distinct, line of research on dynamic capabilities that emerged in the 1990s is an open question.

Dynamic Capabilities. In the 1990s, a number of strategists have tried to extend the resource-based view by explaining how firm-specific capabilities to perform activities better than competitors can be built and redeployed over long periods of time. The dynamic-capabilities view of the firm differs from the RBV because capabilities are to be developed rather than taken as given, as described more fully in a pioneering article by David Teece, Gary Pisano, and Amy Shuen:

> If control over scarce resources is the source of economic profits, then it follows that issues such as skill acquisition and learning become fundamental strategic issues. It is this second dimension, encompassing skill acquisition, learning, and capability accumulation that . . . [we] refer to as "the dynamic capabilities approach." . . . Rents are viewed as not only resulting from uncertainty . . . but also from directed activities by firms which create differentiated capabilities, and from managerial efforts to strategically deploy these assets in coordinated ways.[89]

Taking dynamic capabilities also implies that one of the most strategic aspects of the firm is "the way things are done in the firm, or what might be referred to as its 'routines,' or patterns of current practice and learning."[90] As a result, "research in such areas as management of R&D, product and process development, manufacturing, and human resources tend to be quite relevant [to strategy]."[91] Research in these areas supplies some specific content to the idea that strategy execution is important.

[88] C. K. Prahalad and Gary Hamel, "The Core Competence of the Corporation," *Harvard Business Review* (May/June 1990): 81.

[89] David J. Teece, Gary Pisano, and Amy Shuen, "Dynamic Capabilities and Strategic Management," mimeo (June 1992): 12–13.

[90] David Teece and Gary Pisano, "The Dynamic Capabilities of Firms: An Introduction," *Industrial and Corporate Change* 3 (1994): 540–1. The idea of "routines" as a unit of analysis was pioneered by Richard R. Nelson and Sidney G. Winter, *An Evolutionary Theory of Economic Change* (Cambridge, Mass., 1982).

[91] Teece, Pisano, and Shuen, "Dynamic Capabilities and Strategic Management," 2.

The process of capability development is thought to have several interesting attributes. First, it is generally "path dependent." In other words, "a firm's previous investments and its repertoire of routines (its 'history') constrains its future behavior . . . because learning tends to be local." Second, capability development also tends to be subject to long time lags. And third, the "embeddedness" of capabilities in organizations can convert them into rigidities or sources of inertia—particularly when attempts are being made to create new, nontraditional capabilities.[92]

Commitment. A final, historically based approach to thinking about the dynamics of competition that is intimately related to the three discussed above focuses on commitment or irreversibility: the constraints imposed by past choices on present ones.[93] The managerial logic of focusing on decisions that involve significant levels of commitment has been articulated particularly well by a practicing manager:

> A decision to build the Edsel or Mustang (or locate your new factory in Orlando or Yakima) shouldn't be made hastily; nor without plenty of inputs. . . . [But there is] no point in taking three weeks to make a decision that can be made in three seconds—and corrected inexpensively later if wrong. The whole organization may be out of business while you oscillate between baby-blue or buffalo-brown coffee cups.[94]

Commitments to durable, firm-specific resources and capabilities that cannot easily be bought or sold account for the persistence observed in most strategies over time. Modern IO theory also flags such commitments as being responsible for the sustained profit differences among product market competitors: thought experiments as well as formal models indicate that, in the absence of the frictions implied by commitment, hit-and-run entry would lead to perfectly competitive (zero-profit) outcomes even without large numbers of competitors.[95] A final attraction of commitment as a way of organizing thinking about competitor dynamics is that it can be integrated with other modes of strategic analysis described earlier in this note, as indicated in Figure

[92] Dorothy Leonard-Barton, "Core Capabilities and Core Rigidities: A Paradox in Managing New Product Development," *Strategic Management Journal* (1992): 111–25.

[93] For a book-length discussion of commitments, see Pankaj Ghemawat, *Commitment* (New York, 1991). For connections to the other modes of dynamic analysis discussed in this section, see chs. 4 and 5 of Pankaj Ghemawat, *Strategy and the Business Landscape* (Reading, Mass., 1999).

[94] Robert Townsend, *Up the Organization* (New York, 1970).

[95] See, for instance, William J. Baumol, John C. Panzar, and Robert D. Willig, *Contestable Markets and the Theory of Industry Structure* (New York, 1982) for an analysis of the economic implications of zero commitment; and Richard E. Caves, "Economic Analysis and the Quest for Competitive Advantage," *American Economic Review* (May 1984): 127–32, for comments on the implications for business strategy.

Figure 14. Commitment and Strategy (Source: Adapted from Pankaj Ghemawat, "Resources and Strategy: An IO Perspective," Harvard Business School working paper [1991], 20, Fig. 3).

14. The ideas behind the figure are very simple. Traditional positioning concepts focus on optimizing the fit between product market activities on the right-hand side of the figure. The bold arrows running from left to right indicate that choices about which activities to perform, and how to perform them, are constrained by capabilities and resources that can be varied only in the long run and that are responsible for sustained profit differences between competitors. The two fainter arrows that feed back from right to left capture the ways in which the activities the organization performs and the resource commitments it makes affect its future opportunity set or capabilities. Finally, the bold arrow that runs from capabilities to resource commitments serves as a reminder that the terms on which an organization can commit resources depend, in part, on the capabilities it has built up.

Markets for Ideas at the Millennium[96]

A teleology was implicit in the discussion in the last three sections: starting in the 1970s, strategists first sought to probe the two basic dimensions of early portfolio-analytic grids, industry attractiveness and competitive position, and then to add a time or historical dimension to the analysis. Dynamic thinking along the lines discussed in the previous section and others (e.g., options thinking, systems dynamics, disruptive technologies and change management, to cite just four other areas of enquiry) has absorbed the bulk of academic strategists' attention in the last fifteen-plus years. But when one looks at the *practice* of strategy in the late 1990s, this simple narrative is complicated by an apparent profusion of tools and ideas about strategy in particular and management in general, many of which are quite ahistorical. Both points are illustrated by indexes of the influence of business ideas such as, for example, importance-weighted citation counts calculated by

[96] For a more extended discussion of the ideas in this postscript, see Pankaj Ghemawat, "Competition among Management Paradigms: An Economic Analysis," Harvard Business School Working Paper (2000).

Richard Pascale, admittedly with a significant subjective component, that are reproduced in Figure 15.[97] A complete enumeration, let alone discussion, of contemporary tools and ideas is beyond the scope of this essay, but a few broad points seem worth making about their recent profusion and turnover. Given the forward-looking nature of this discussion, it is inevitably more conjectural than the retrospectives in the previous sections.

Some of the profusion of ideas about strategy and management is probably to be celebrated. Thus, there are advantages to being able to choose from a large menu of ideas rather than from a small one, especially in complex environments where "one size doesn't fit all" (and especially when the fixed costs of idea development are low). Similarly, the rapid turnover of many ideas, which appears to have increased in recent years, can be explained in benign terms as well.[98] Thus, some argue that the world is changing rapidly, maybe faster than ever before; others, that the rapid peaking followed by a decline in attention to ideas may indicate that they have been successfully internalized rather than discredited; yet others, that at least some of the apparent turnover represents a rhetorical spur to action, rather than real change in the underlying ideas themselves.[99]

It seems difficult to maintain, however, that all the patterns evident in Figure 15 conform to monotonic ideals of progress. Consider, for example, what happened with business-process reengineering, the single most prominent entry as of 1995. Reengineering was popularized in the early 1990s by Michael Hammer and James Champy of the consulting firm CSC Index.[100] Hammer originally explained the idea in a 1990 article in the *Harvard Business Review*: "Rather than embedding outdated processes in silicon and software, we should obliterate them and start over. We should . . . use the power of modern information technol-

---

[97] For additional discussion of the methodology employed, consult Richard T. Pascale, *Managing on the Edge* (New York, 1990), 18–20.

[98] For some evidence that management ideas have become shorter-lived, see Paula P. Carson, Patricia A. Lanier, Kerry D. Carson, and Brandi N. Guidry, "Clearing a Path through the Management Fashion Jungle: Some Preliminary Trailblazing," *Academy of Management Journal* (December 2000).

[99] Richard D'Aveni, among many others, asserts unprecedented levels of environmental change in *Hypercompetition: Managing the Dynamics of Strategic Maneuvering* (New York, 1994). William Lee and Gary Skarke discuss apparently transient ideas that are permanently valuable in "Value-Added Fads: From Passing Fancy to Eternal Truths," *Journal of Management Consulting* (1996): 10–15. Robert G. Eccles and Nitin Nohria emphasize the rhetorical uses of changing the wrappers on a limited number of timeless truths about management in *Beyond the Hype: Rediscovering the Essence of Management* (Boston, 1992).

[100] See Michael Hammer and James Champy, *Reengineering the Corporation* (New York, 1993). See also John Micklethwait and Adrian Wooldridge, *The Witch Doctors* (New York, 1996). Micklethwait and Wooldridge devote a chapter to CSC Index.

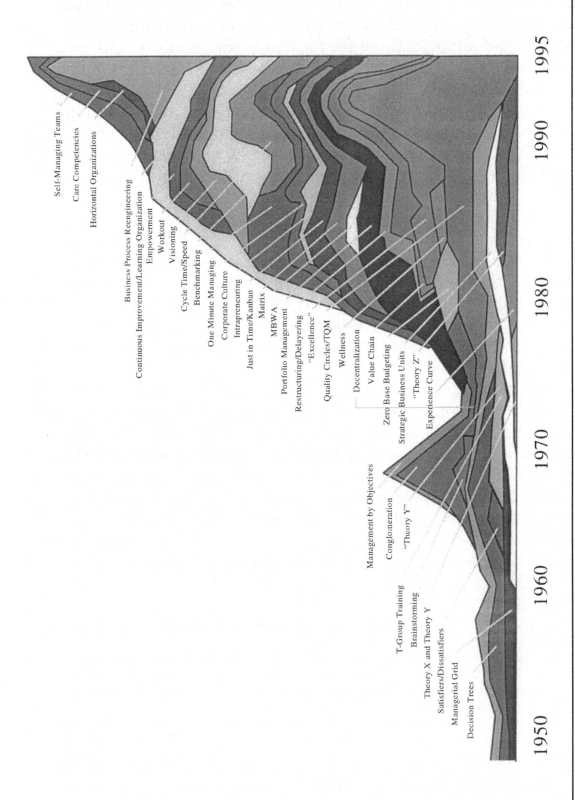

Figure 15. Ebbs, Flows, and Residual Impact of Business Fads, 1950–1995. (Source: Adapted from Richard T. Pascale, *Managing on the Edge* [New York, 1990], 18–20.)

ogy to radically redesign our business processes in order to achieve dramatic improvements in their performance."[101] Hammer and Champy's book, *Reengineering the Corporation*, which came out in 1993, sold nearly two million copies. Surveys in 1994 found that 78 percent of the Fortune 500 companies and 60 percent of a broader sample of 2,200 U.S. companies were engaged in some form of reengineering, on average with several projects apiece.[102] Consulting revenues from reengineering exploded to an estimated $2.5 billion by 1995.[103] After 1995, however, there was a bust: consulting revenues plummeted, by perhaps two-thirds over the next three years, as reengineering came to be seen as a euphemism for downsizing and as companies apparently shifted to placing more emphasis on growth (implying, incidentally, that there had been some excesses in their previous efforts to reengineer).

Much of the worry that the extent of profusion or turnover of ideas about management may be excessive from a social standpoint is linked to the observation that this is one of the few areas of intellectual enquiry in which it actually makes sense to talk about markets for ideas. Unlike, say, twenty-five or thirty years ago, truly large amounts of money are at stake, and are actively competed for, in the development of "blockbuster" ideas like reengineering—a process that increasingly seems to fit with the end state described by Schumpeter as the "routinization of innovation." Market-based theoretical models indicate that, on the supply side, private incentives to invest in developing new products are likely, in winner-take-all settings, to exceed social gains.[104] To the extent that market-based, commercial considerations increasingly influence the development of new ideas about management, they are a source of growing concern.

Concerns about supply-side salesmanship are exacerbated by the demand-side informational imperfections of markets for ideas, as opposed to more conventional products. Most fundamentally, the buyer of an idea is unable to judge how much information is worth until it is disclosed to him, but the seller has a difficult time repossessing the information in case the buyer decides, following disclosure, not to pay very much for it. Partial disclosure may avoid the total breakdown of market-based exchange in such situations but still leaves a residual in-

---

[101] Michael Hammer, "Reengineering Work: Don't Automate, Obliterate," *Harvard Business Review* (July/Aug. 1990): 104.

[102] Micklethwait and Wooldridge, *The Witch Doctors*, 29.

[103] See James O'Shea and Charles Madigan, *Dangerous Company: The Consulting Powerhouses and the Businesses They Save and Ruin* (New York, 1997).

[104] For a general discussion, see Robert H. Frank and Philip J. Cook, *The Winner-Take-All Society* (New York, 1995); for formal modeling and a discussion specific to the management idea business, see Ghemawat, "Competition among Management Paradigms."

formation asymmetry.[105] Performance contracting is sometimes proposed as an antidote to otherwise ineradicable informational problems of this sort, but its efficacy and use in the context of management ideas seem to be limited by noisy performance measurement. Instead, the market-based transfer of ideas to companies appears to be sustained by mechanisms such as reputation and observational learning. Based on microtheoretical analysis, these mechanisms may lead to "cascades" of ideas, in which companies that choose late optimally decide to ignore their own information and emulate the choices made earlier by other companies.[106] Such fadlike dynamics can also enhance the sales of products with broad, as opposed to niche, appeal.[107] And then there are contracting problems within, rather than between, firms that point in the same direction. In particular, models of principal-agent problems show that managers, in order to preserve or gain reputation when markets are imperfectly informed, may prefer either to "hide in the herd" so as not to be accountable or to "ride the herd" in order to prove quality.[108] The possible link to situations in which managers must decide which, if any, new ideas to adopt should be obvious. More broadly, demand-side considerations suggest some reasons to worry about patterns in the diffusion of new ideas as well as the incentives to develop them in the first place.

Whether such worries about the performance of markets for ideas actually make their effects felt in the real world of management is, ultimately, an empirical matter. Unfortunately, the informational imperfections noted above—and others, such as the difficulty of counting ideas—complicate systematic empirical analysis of product variety and turnover in management ideas. A shared basis for understanding the historical evolution of ideas, which I have attempted to provide in the specific context of competitive thinking about business strategy, is but a first step in unraveling such complications.

---

[105] See, for example, James J. Anton and Dennis A. Yao, "The Sale of Ideas: Strategic Disclosure, Property Rights, and Incomplete Contracts," unpublished working paper, Fuqua School of Business, Duke University (1998).

[106] See Sushil Bikhchandani, David Hirshleifer, and Ivo Welch, "Learning from the Behavior of Others: Conformity, Fads and Informational Cascades," *Journal of Economic Perspectives* (1998): 15–70.

[107] See Daniel L. McFadden and Kenneth E. Train, "Consumers' Evaluation of New Products: Learning from Self and Others," *Journal of Political Economy* (Aug. 1996): 683–703.

[108] These models derive some of their real-world appeal from the use of relative performance measures to evaluate managers. See Robert Gibbons and Kevin J. Murphy, "Relative Performance Evaluation of Chief Executive Officers," *Industrial and Labor Relations Review* (Feb. 1990): 30S–51S.

Academy of Management Executive, 2001, Vol. 15, No. 4

Are you sure you have a strategy?

Donald C. Hambrick and James W. Fredrickson

Executive Overview

After more than 30 years of hard thinking about strategy, consultants and scholars have provided an abundance of frameworks for analyzing strategic situations. Missing, however, has been any guidance as to what the product of these tools should be—or what actually constitutes a strategy. Strategy has become a catchall term used to mean whatever one wants it to mean. Executives now talk about their "service strategy," their "branding strategy," their "acquisition strategy," or whatever kind of strategy that is on their mind at a particular moment. But strategists—whether they are CEOs of established firms, division presidents, or entrepreneurs—must have a strategy, an integrated, overarching concept of how the business will achieve its objectives. If a business must have a single, unified strategy, then it must necessarily have parts. What are those parts? We present a framework for strategy design, arguing that a strategy has five elements, providing answers to five questions—arenas: where will we be active? vehicles: how will we get there? differentiators: how will we win in the marketplace? staging: what will be our speed and sequence of moves? economic logic: how will we obtain our returns? Our article develops and illustrates these domains of choice, particularly emphasizing how essential it is that they form a unified whole.

Consider these statements of strategy drawn from actual documents and announcements of several companies:

"Our strategy is to be the low-cost provider."

"We're pursuing a global strategy."

"The company's strategy is to integrate a set of regional acquisitions."

"Our strategy is to provide unrivaled customer service."

"Our strategic intent is to always be the first-mover."

"Our strategy is to move from defense to industrial applications."

What do these grand declarations have in common? Only that none of them is a strategy. They are strategic threads, mere elements of strategies.

But they are no more strategies than Dell Computer's strategy can be summed up as selling direct to customers, or than Hannibal's strategy was to use elephants to cross the Alps. And their use reflects an increasingly common syndrome—the catchall fragmentation of strategy.

After more than 30 years of hard thinking about strategy, consultants and scholars have provided executives with an abundance of frameworks for analyzing strategic situations. We now have five-forces analysis, core competencies, hypercompetition, the resource-based view of the firm, value chains, and a host of other helpful, often powerful, analytic tools.[1] Missing, however, has been any guidance as to what the product of these tools should be—or what actually constitutes a strategy. Indeed, the use of specific strategic tools tends to draw the strategist toward narrow, piecemeal conceptions of strategy that match the narrow scope of the tools themselves. For example, strategists who are drawn to Porter's five-forces analysis tend to think of strategy as a matter of selecting industries and segments within them. Executives who dwell on "co-opetition" or other game-theoretic frameworks see their world as a set of choices about dealing with adversaries and allies.

This problem of strategic fragmentation has worsened in recent years, as narrowly specialized academics and consultants have started plying their tools in the name of strategy. But strategy is not pricing. It is not capacity decisions. It is not setting R&D budgets. These are pieces of strategies, and they cannot be decided—or even considered—in isolation.

Imagine an aspiring painter who has been taught that colors and hues determine the beauty of a picture. But what can really be done with such advice? After all, magnificent pictures require far more than choosing colors: attention to shapes and figures, brush technique, and finishing processes. Most importantly, great paintings depend on artful combinations of *all* these elements. Some combinations are classic, tried-and-true; some are inventive and fresh; and many combinations—even for avant-garde art—spell trouble.

Strategy has become a catchall term used to mean whatever one wants it to mean. Business magazines now have regular sections devoted to strategy, typically discussing how featured firms are dealing with distinct issues, such as customer service, joint ventures, branding, or e-commerce. In turn, executives talk about their "service strategy," their "joint venture strategy," their "branding strategy," or whatever kind of strategy is on their minds at a particular moment.

Executives then communicate these strategic threads to their organizations in the mistaken belief that doing so will help managers make tough choices. But how does knowing that their firm is pursuing an "acquisition strategy" or a "first-mover strategy" help the vast majority of managers do their jobs or set priorities? How helpful is it to have new initiatives announced periodically with the word strategy tacked on? When executives call everything strategy, and end up with a collection of strategies, they create confusion and undermine their own credibility. They especially reveal that they don't really have an integrated conception of the business.

When executives call everything strategy, and end up with a collection of strategies, they create confusion and undermine their own credibility.

Many readers of works on the topic know that strategy is derived from the Greek *strategos*, or "the art of the general." But few have thought much about this important origin. For example, what is special about the general's job, compared with that of a field commander? The general is responsible for multiple units on multiple fronts and multiple battles over time. The general's challenge—and the value-added of generalship—is in orchestration and comprehensiveness. Great generals think about the whole. They have a strategy; it has pieces, or elements, but they form a coherent whole. Business generals, whether they are CEOs of established firms, division presidents, or entrepreneurs, must also have a strategy—a central, integrated, externally oriented concept of how the business will achieve its objectives. Without a strategy, time and resources are easily wasted on piecemeal, disparate activities; mid-level managers will fill the void with their own, often parochial, interpretations of what the business should be doing; and the result will be a potpourri of disjointed, feeble initiatives.

Examples abound of firms that have suffered because they lacked a coherent strategy. Once a towering force in retailing, Sears spent 10 sad years vacillating between an emphasis on hard goods and soft goods, venturing in and out of ill-chosen businesses, failing to differentiate itself in any of them, and never building a compelling economic logic. Similarly, the once-unassailable Xerox is engaged in an attempt to revive itself, amid criticism from its own executives that the company lacks a strategy. Says one: "I hear about asset sales, about refinancing, but I don't hear anyone saying convincingly, 'Here is your future.'"[2]

A strategy consists of an integrated set of choices, but it isn't a catchall for every important choice an executive faces. As Figure 1 portrays, the company's mission and objectives, for example, stand apart from, and guide, strategy. Thus we would not speak of the commitment of the *New York Times* to be America's newspaper of record as part of its strategy. GE's objective of being number one or number two in all its markets drives its strategy, but is not strategy itself. Nor would an objective of reaching a particular revenue or earnings target be part of a strategy.

Similarly, because strategy addresses how the business intends to engage its environment, choices about internal organizational arrangements are not part of strategy. So we should not speak of compensation policies, information systems, or training programs as being strategy. These are critically important choices, which should reinforce and support strategy; but they do not make up the strategy itself.[3] If everything important is thrown into the strategy bucket, then this essential concept quickly comes to mean nothing.

We do not mean to portray strategy development as a simple, linear process. Figure 1 leaves out

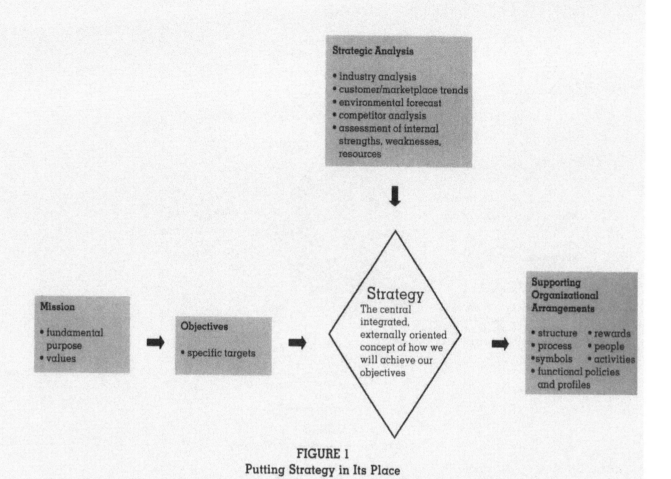

FIGURE 1
Putting Strategy in Its Place

feedback arrows and other indications that great strategists are iterative, loop thinkers.[4] The key is not in following a sequential process, but rather in achieving a robust, reinforced consistency among the elements of the strategy itself.

The Elements of Strategy

If a business must have a strategy, then the strategy must necessarily have parts. What are those parts? As Figure 2 portrays, a strategy has five elements, providing answers to five questions:

- Arenas: where will we be active?
- Vehicles: how will we get there?
- Differentiators: how will we win in the marketplace?
- Staging: what will be our speed and sequence of moves?
- Economic logic: how will we obtain our returns?

This article develops and illustrates these domains of choice, emphasizing how essential it is that they form a unified whole. Where others focus on the inputs to strategic thinking (the top box in Figure 1), we focus on the output—the composition and design of the strategy itself.

Arenas

The most fundamental choices strategists make are those of where, or in what arenas, the business will be active. This is akin to the question Peter Drucker posed decades ago: "What business will we be in?"[5] The answer, however, should not be one of broad generalities. For instance, "We will be the leader in information technology consulting" is more a vision or objective than part of a strategy. In articulating arenas, it is important to be as specific as possible about the product categories, market segments, geographic areas, and core technologies, as well as the value-adding stages (e.g., product design, manufacturing, selling, servicing, distribution) the business intends to take on.

For example, as a result of an in-depth analysis, a biotechnology company specified its arenas: the company intended to use T-cell receptor technology to develop both diagnostic and therapeutic products for battling a certain class of cancers; it chose to keep control of all research and product development activity, but to outsource manufacturing and a major part of the clinical testing process required for regulatory approvals. The company targeted the U.S. and major European markets as

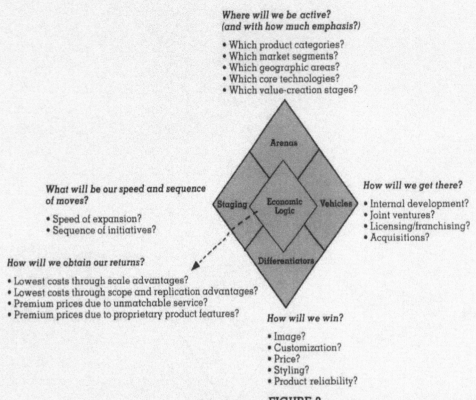

FIGURE 2
The Five Major Elements of Strategy

its geographic scope. The company's chosen arenas were highly specific, with products and markets even targeted by name. In other instances, especially in businesses with a wider array of products, market segments, or geographic scope, the strategy may instead reasonably specify the classes of, or criteria for, selected arenas—e.g., women's high-end fashion accessories, or countries with per-capita GDP over $5,000. But in all cases, the challenge is to be as specific as possible.

In choosing arenas, the strategist needs to indicate not only where the business will be active, but also how much emphasis will be placed on each. Some market segments, for instance, might be identified as centrally important, while others are deemed secondary. A strategy might reasonably be centered on one product category, with others—while necessary for defensive purposes or for offering customers a full line—being of distinctly less importance.

Vehicles

Beyond deciding on the arenas in which the business will be active, the strategist also needs to decide how to get there. Specifically, the means for attaining the needed presence in a particular product category, market segment, geographic area, or value-creation stage should be the result

of deliberate strategic choice. If we have decided to expand our product range, are we going to accomplish that by relying on organic, internal product development, or are there other vehicles—such as joint ventures or acquisitions—that offer a better means for achieving our broadened scope? If we are committed to international expansion, what should be our primary modes, or vehicles—greenfield startups, local acquisitions, licensing, or joint ventures? The executives of the biotechnology company noted earlier decided to rely on joint ventures to achieve their new presence in Europe, while committing to a series of tactical acquisitions for adding certain therapeutic products to complement their existing line of diagnostic products.

The means by which arenas are entered matters greatly. Therefore, selection of vehicles should not be an afterthought or viewed as a mere implementation detail. A decision to enter new product categories is rife with uncertainty. But that uncertainty may vary immensely depending on whether the entry is attempted by licensing other companies' technologies, where perhaps the firm has prior experience, or by acquisitions, where the company is a novice. Failure to explicitly consider and articulate the intended expansion vehicles can result in the hoped-for entry's being seriously delayed, unnecessarily costly, or totally stalled.

Failure to explicitly consider and articulate the intended expansion vehicles can result in the hoped-for entry's being seriously delayed, unnecessarily costly, or totally stalled.

There are steep learning curves associated with the use of alternative expansion modes. Research has found, for instance, that companies can develop highly advantageous, well-honed capabilities in making acquisitions or in managing joint ventures.[6] The company that uses various vehicles on an ad hoc or patchwork basis, without an overarching logic and programmatic approach, will be at a severe disadvantage compared with companies that have such coherence.

Differentiators

A strategy should specify not only where a firm will be active (arenas) and how it will get there (vehicles), but also how the firm will win in the marketplace—how it will get customers to come its way. In a competitive world, winning is the result of differentiators, and such edges don't just happen. Rather, they require executives to make up-front, conscious choices about which weapons will be assembled, honed, and deployed to beat competitors in the fight for customers, revenues, and profits. For example, Gillette uses its proprietary product and process technology to develop superior razor products, which the company further differentiates through a distinctive, aggressively advertised brand image. Goldman Sachs, the investment bank, provides customers unparalleled service by maintaining close relationships with client executives and coordinating the array of services it offers to each client. Southwest Airlines attracts and retains customers by offering the lowest possible fares and extraordinary on-time reliability.

Achieving a compelling marketplace advantage does not necessarily mean that the company has to be at the extreme on one differentiating dimension; rather, sometimes having the best combination of differentiators confers a tremendous marketplace advantage. This is the philosophy of Honda in automobiles. There are better cars than Hondas, and there are less expensive cars than Hondas; but many car buyers believe that there is no better value—quality for the price—than a Honda, a strategic position the company has worked hard to establish and reinforce.

Regardless of the intended differentiators—image, customization, price, product styling, after-sale services, or others—the critical issue for strategists is to make up-front, deliberate choices. Without that, two unfortunate outcomes loom. One is that, if top management doesn't attempt to create unique differentiation, none will occur. Again, differentiators don't just materialize; they are very hard to achieve. And firms without them lose.

The other negative outcome is that, without up-front, careful choices about differentiators, top management may seek to offer customers across-the-board superiority, trying simultaneously to outdistance competitors on too broad an array of differentiators—lower price, better service, superior styling, and so on. Such attempts are doomed, however, because of their inherent inconsistencies and extraordinary resource demands. In selecting differentiators, strategists should give explicit preference to those few forms of superiority that are mutually reinforcing (e.g., image and product styling), consistent with the firm's resources and capabilities, and, of course, highly valued in the arenas the company has targeted.

Staging

Choices of arenas, vehicles, and differentiators constitute what might be called the substance of a strategy—what executives plan to do. But this substance cries out for decisions on a fourth element—staging, or the speed and sequence of major moves to take in order to heighten the likelihood of success.[7] Most strategies do not call for equal, balanced initiatives on all fronts at all times. Instead, usually some initiatives must come first, followed only then by others, and then still others. In erecting a great building, foundations must be laid, followed by walls, and only then the roof.

Of course, in business strategy there is no universally superior sequence. Rather the strategist's judgment is required. Consider a printing equipment company that committed itself to broadening its product line and expanding internationally. The executives decided that the new products should be added first, in stage one, because the elite sales agents they planned to use for international expansion would not be able or willing to represent a narrow product line effectively. Even though the executives were anxious to expand geographically, if they had tried to do so without the more complete line in place, they would have wasted a great deal of time and money. The left half of Figure 3 shows their two-stage logic.

The executives of a regional title insurance company, as part of their new strategy, were committed

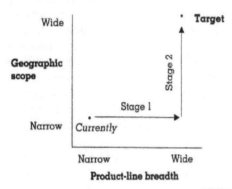
Printing equipment manufacturer with plans to expand internationally *and* broaden the product line

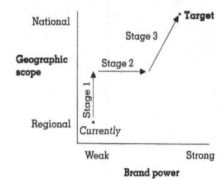
Regional title insurance company with plans to expand nationally by acquisition *and* build a superior, prestigious brand

FIGURE 3
Examples of Strategic Staging

to becoming national in scope through a series of acquisitions. For their differentiators, they planned to establish a prestigious brand backed by aggressive advertising and superb customer service. But the executives faced a chicken-and-egg problem: they couldn't make the acquisitions on favorable terms without the brand image in place; but with only their current limited geographic scope, they couldn't afford the quantity or quality of advertising needed to establish the brand. They decided on a three-stage plan (shown in the right half of Figure 3): 1) make selected acquisitions in adjacent regions, hence becoming a super-regional in size and scale; 2) invest moderately heavily in advertising and brand-building; 3) make acquisitions in additional regions on more favorable terms (because of the enhanced brand, a record of growth, and, they hoped, an appreciated stock price) while simultaneously continuing to push further in building the brand.

Decisions about staging can be driven by a number of factors. One, of course, is resources. Funding and staffing every envisioned initiative, at the needed levels, is generally not possible at the outset of a new strategic campaign. Urgency is a second factor affecting staging; some elements of a strategy may face brief windows of opportunity, requiring that they be pursued first and aggressively. A third factor is the achievement of credibility. Attaining certain thresholds—in specific arenas, differentiators, or vehicles—can be critically valuable for attracting resources and stakeholders that are needed for other parts of the strategy. A fourth factor is the pursuit of early wins. It may be far wiser to successfully tackle a part of the strategy that is relatively doable before attempting more challenging or unfamiliar initiatives. These are only some of the factors that might go into decisions about the speed and sequence of strategic initiatives. However, since the concept of staging has gone largely unexplored in the strategy literature, it is often given far too little attention by strategists themselves.

Economic logic

At the heart of a business strategy must be a clear idea of how profits will be generated—not just some profits, but profits above the firm's cost of capital.[8] It is not enough to vaguely count on having revenues that are above costs. Unless there's a compelling basis for it, customers and competitors won't let that happen. And it's not enough to generate a long list of reasons why customers will be eager to pay high prices for your products, along with a long list of reasons why your costs will be lower than your competitors'. That's a sure-fire route to strategic schizophrenia and mediocrity.

> *It is not enough to vaguely count on having revenues that are above costs. Unless there's a compelling basis for it, customers and competitors won't let that happen.*

The most successful strategies have a central economic logic that serves as the fulcrum for profit creation. In some cases, the economic key may be to obtain premium prices by offering customers a difficult-to-match product. For instance, the *New York Times* is able to charge readers a very high price (and strike highly favorable licensing arrangements with on-line information distributors) because of its exceptional journalistic quality; in addition, the *Times* is able to charge advertisers high prices because it delivers a large number of dedicated, affluent readers. ARAMARK, the highly profitable international food-service company, is able to obtain premium prices from corporate and institutional clients by offering a level of customized service and responsiveness that competitors cannot match. The company seeks out only those clients that want superior food service and are willing to pay for it. For example, once domestic airlines became less interested in distinguishing themselves through their in-flight meals, ARAMARK dropped that segment.

In some instances, the economic logic might reside on the cost side of the profit equation. ARAMARK—adding to its pricing leverage—uses its huge scale of operations and presence in multiple market segments (business, educational, healthcare, and correctional-system food service) to achieve a sizeable cost advantage in food purchases—an advantage that competitors cannot duplicate. GKN Sinter Metals, which has grown by acquisition to become the world's major powdered-metals company, benefits greatly from its scale in obtaining raw materials and in exploiting, in country after country, its leading-edge capabilities in metal-forming processes.

In these examples the economic logics are not fleeting or transitory. They are rooted in the firms' fundamental and relatively enduring capabilities. ARAMARK and the *New York Times* can charge premium prices because their offerings are superior in the eyes of their targeted customers, customers highly value that superiority, and competitors can't readily imitate the offerings. ARAMARK and GKN Sinter Metals have lower costs than their competitors because of systemic advantages of scale, experience, and know-how sharing. Granted, these leads may not last forever or be completely unassailable, but the economic logics that are at work at these companies account for their abilities to deliver strong year-in, year-out profits.

The Imperative of Strategic Comprehensiveness

By this point, it should be clear why a strategy needs to encompass all five elements—arenas, vehicles, differentiators, staging, and economic logic. First, all five are important enough to require intentionality. Surprisingly, most strategic plans emphasize one or two of the elements without giving any consideration to the others. Yet to develop a strategy without attention to all five leaves critical omissions.

Surprisingly, most strategic plans emphasize one or two of the elements without giving any consideration to the others.

Second, the five elements call not only for choice, but also for preparation and investment. All five require certain capabilities that cannot be generated spontaneously.

Third, all five elements must align with and support each other. When executives and academics think about alignment, they typically have in mind that internal organizational arrangements need to align with strategy (in tribute to the maxim that "structure follows strategy"[9]), but few pay much attention to the consistencies required among the elements of the strategy itself.

Finally, it is only after the specification of all five strategic elements that the strategist is in the best position to turn to designing all the other supporting activities—functional policies, organizational arrangements, operating programs, and processes—that are needed to reinforce the strategy. The five elements of the strategy diamond can be considered the hub or central nodes for designing a comprehensive, integrated activity system.[10]

Comprehensive Strategies at IKEA and Brake Products International

IKEA: Revolutionizing an industry

So far we have identified and discussed the five elements that make up a strategy and form our strategy diamond. But a strategy is more than simply choices on these five fronts: it is an integrated, mutually reinforcing set of choices—choices that form a coherent whole. To illustrate the importance of this coherence we will now discuss two examples of fully elaborated strategy diamonds. As a first illustration, consider the strategic intent of IKEA, the remarkably successful global furniture retailer. IKEA's strategy over the past 25 years has been highly coherent, with all five elements reinforcing each other.

The arenas in which IKEA operates are well defined: the company sells relatively inexpensive, contemporary, Scandinavian-style furniture and home furnishings. IKEA's target market is young, primarily white-collar customers. The geographic scope is worldwide, or at least all countries where socioeconomic and infrastructure conditions support the concept. IKEA is not only a retailer, but also maintains control of product design to ensure the integrity of its unique image and to accumulate unrivaled expertise in designing for efficient manufacturing. The company, however, does not manufacture, relying instead on a host of long-term suppliers who ensure efficient, geographically dispersed production.

IKEA is not only a retailer, but also maintains control of product design to ensure the integrity of its unique image and to accumulate unrivaled expertise in designing for efficient manufacturing.

As its primary vehicle for getting to its chosen arenas, IKEA engages in organic expansion, building its own wholly owned stores. IKEA has chosen not to make acquisitions of existing retailers, and it engages in very few joint ventures. This reflects top management's belief that the company needs to fully control local execution of its highly innovative retailing concept.

IKEA attracts customers and beats competitors by offering several important differentiators. First, its products are of very reliable quality but are low in price (generally 20 to 30 percent below the competition for comparable quality goods). Second, in contrast to the stressful, intimidating feeling that shoppers often encounter in conventional furniture stores, IKEA customers are treated to a fun, nonthreatening experience, where they are allowed to wander through a visually exciting store with only the help they request. And third, the company strives to make customer fulfillment immediate. Specifically, IKEA carries an extensive inventory at each store, which allows a customer to take the item home or have it delivered the same day. In contrast, conventional furniture retailers show floor models, but then require a 6- to 10-week wait for the delivery of each special-order item.

As for staging, or IKEA's speed and sequence of moves, once management realized that its approach would work in a variety of countries and cultures, the company committed itself to rapid international expansion, but only one region at a time. In general, the company's approach has been to use its limited resources to establish an early foothold by opening a single store in each targeted country. Each such entry is supported with aggressive public relations and advertising, in order to lay claim to the radically new retailing concept in that market. Later, IKEA comes back into each country and fills in with more stores.

The economic logic of IKEA rests primarily on scale economies and efficiencies of replication. Although the company doesn't sell absolutely identical products in all its geographic markets, IKEA has enough standardization that it can take great advantage of being the world's largest furniture retailer. Its costs from long-term suppliers are exceedingly low, and made even lower by IKEA's proprietary, easy-to-manufacture product designs.

In each region, IKEA has enough scale to achieve substantial distribution and promotional efficiencies. And each individual store is set up as a high-volume operation, allowing further economies in inventories, advertising, and staffing. IKEA's phased international expansion has allowed executives to benefit, in country after country, from what they have learned about site selection, store design, store openings, and ongoing operations. They are vigilant, astute learners, and they put that learning to great economic use.

Note how all of IKEA's actions (shown in Figure 4) fit together. For example, consider the strong alignment between its targeted arenas and its competitive differentiators. An emphasis on low price, fun, contemporary styling, and instant fulfillment is well suited to the company's focus on young, first-time furniture buyers. Or consider the logical fit between the company's differentiators and vehicles—providing a fun shopping experience and instant fulfillment requires very intricate local execution, which can be achieved far better through wholly owned stores than by using acquisitions, joint ventures, or franchises. These alignments, along with others, help account for IKEA's long string of years with double-digit sales growth, and current revenues of $8 billion.

The IKEA example allows us to illustrate the strategy diamond with a widely familiar business story. That example, however, is admittedly retrospective, looking backward to interpret the company's strategy according to the framework. But the real power and role of strategy, of course, is in looking forward. Based on a careful and complete analysis of a company's environment, marketplace, competitors, and internal capabilities, senior managers need to craft a strategic intent for their firm. The diamond is a useful framework for doing just that, as we will now illustrate with a business whose top executives set out to develop a new strategy that would allow them to break free from a spiral of mediocre profits and stagnant sales.

Brake Products International: Charting a new direction

The strategy diamond proved very useful when it was applied by the new executive team of Brake Products International (BPI), a disguised manufacturer of components used in braking and suspension systems for passenger cars and light trucks. In recent years, BPI had struggled as the worldwide auto industry consolidated. Its reaction had been a combination of disparate, half-hearted diversification initiatives, alternating with across-the-board

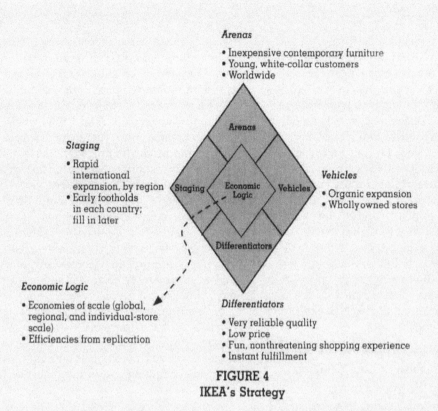

Arenas
- Inexpensive contemporary furniture
- Young, white-collar customers
- Worldwide

Staging
- Rapid international expansion, by region
- Early footholds in each country; fill in later

Vehicles
- Organic expansion
- Wholly owned stores

Economic Logic
- Economies of scale (global, regional, and individual-store scale)
- Efficiencies from replication

Differentiators
- Very reliable quality
- Low price
- Fun, nonthreatening shopping experience
- Instant fulfillment

FIGURE 4
IKEA's Strategy

expense cuts. The net result, predictably, was not good, and a new management team was brought in to try to revive performance. As part of this turnaround effort, BPI's new executives developed a new strategic intent by making critical decisions for each of the five elements—arenas, vehicles, differentiators, staging, and economic logic. We will not attempt to convey the analysis that gave rise to their choices, but rather (as with the IKEA example) will use BPI to illustrate the articulation of a comprehensive strategy.

For their targeted arenas, BPI executives committed to expanding beyond their current market scope of North American and European car plants by adding Asia, where global carmakers were rapidly expanding. They considered widening their product range to include additional auto components, but concluded that their unique design and manufacturing expertise was limited to brake and suspension components. They did decide, however, that they should apply their advanced capability in antilock-braking and electronic traction-control systems to develop braking products for off-road vehicles, including construction and farm equipment. As an additional commitment, executives decided to add a new service, systems integration, that would involve bundling BPI products with other related components, from other manufacturers, that form a complete suspension system, and then providing the carmakers with easy-to-han-

dle, preassembled systems modules. This initiative would allow the carmakers to reduce assembly costs significantly, as well as to deal with a single suspension-system supplier, with substantial logistics and inventory savings.

The management team identified three major vehicles for achieving BPI's presence in their selected arenas. First, they were committed to organic internal development of new generations of leading-edge braking systems, including those for off-road vehicles. To become the preferred suspension-system integrator for the major auto manufacturers, executives decided to enter into strategic alliances with the leading producers of other key suspension components. Finally, to serve carmakers that were expanding their operations in Asia, BPI planned to initiate equity joint ventures with brake companies in China, Korea, and Singapore. BPI would provide the technology and oversee the manufacturing of leading-edge, high-quality antilock brakes; the Asian partners would take the lead in marketing and government relations.

BPI's executives also committed to achieving and exploiting a small set of differentiators. The company was already a technology leader, particularly in antilock-braking systems and electronic traction-control systems. These proprietary technologies were seen as centrally important and would be further nurtured. Executives also believed they could establish a preeminent position as a systems integrator of entire suspension assemblies. However, achieving this advantage would require new types of manufacturing and logistics capabilities, as well as new skills in managing relationships with other component companies. This would include an extensive e-business capability that linked BPI with its suppliers and customers. And finally, as one of the few brakes/suspension companies with a manufacturing presence in North America and Europe—and now in Asia—BPI executives concluded that they had a potential advantage—what they referred to as "global reach"—that was well suited to the global consolidation of the automobile industry. If BPI did a better job of coordinating activities among its geographically dispersed operations, it could provide the one-stop, low-cost global purchasing that the industry giants increasingly sought.

If BPI did a better job of coordinating activities among its geographically dispersed operations, it could provide the one-stop, low-cost global purchasing that the industry giants increasingly sought.

BPI's executives approached decisions about staging very deliberately. They felt urgency on various fronts, but also realized that, after several years of lackluster performance, the firm lacked the resources and credibility to do everything all at once. As is often the case, decisions about staging were most important for those initiatives where the gaps between the status quo and the strategic intent were the greatest. For example, executives decided that, in order to provide a clear, early sign of continued commitment to the major global auto manufacturers, a critical first step was to establish the joint ventures with brake manufacturers in Asia. They felt just as much urgency to gain a first-mover advantage as a suspension-system integrator. Therefore, management committed to promptly establish alliances with a select group of manufacturers of other suspension components, and to experiment with one pilot customer. These two sets of initiatives constituted stage one of BPI's strategic intent. For stage two, the executives planned to launch the full versions of the systems-integration and global-reach concepts, complete with aggressive marketing. Also in this second stage, expansion into the off-road vehicle market would commence.

BPI's economic logic hinged on securing pre-

mium prices from its customers, by offering them at least three valuable, difficult-to-imitate benefits. First, BPI was the worldwide technology leader in braking systems; car companies would pay to get access to these products for their new high-end models. Second, BPI would allow global customers an economical single source for braking products; this would save customers considerable contract administration and quality-assurance costs—savings that they would be willing to share. And third, through its alliances with major suspension-component manufacturers, BPI would be able to deliver integrated-suspension-system kits to customers—again saving customers in purchasing costs, inventory costs, and even assembly costs, for which they would pay a premium.

BPI's turnaround was highly successful. The substance of the company's strategy (shown in Figure 5) was critically important in the turnaround, as was the concise strategy statement that was communicated throughout the firm. As the CEO stated:

> We've finally identified what we want to be, and what's important to us. Just as importantly, we've decided what we don't want to be, and have stopped wasting time and effort. Since we started talking about BPI in terms of arenas, vehicles, differentiators, staging, and economic logic, we have been able to get our top team on the same page. A whole host of decisions have logically fallen into place in support of our comprehensive strategic agenda.

Of Strategy, Better Strategy, and No Strategy

Our purpose in this article has been elemental—to identify what constitutes a strategy. This basic agenda is worthwhile because executives and scholars have lost track of what it means to engage in the art of the general. We particularly hope to counter the recent catchall fragmentation of the strategy concept, and to remind strategists that orchestrated holism is their charge.

But we do not want to be mistaken. We don't believe that it is sufficient to simply make these five sets of choices. No—a business needs not just a strategy, but a *sound* strategy. Some strategies are clearly far better than others. Fortunately, this is where the wealth of strategic-analysis tools that have been developed in the last 30 years becomes valuable. Such tools as industry analysis, technology cycles, value chains, and core competencies, among others,

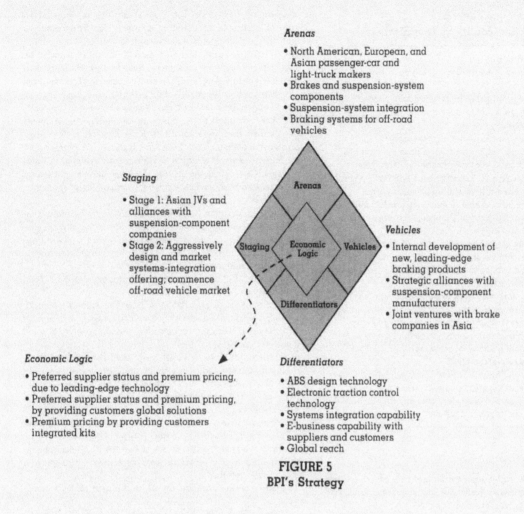

Arenas

- North American, European, and Asian passenger-car and light-truck makers
- Brakes and suspension-system components
- Suspension-system integration
- Braking systems for off-road vehicles

Staging

- Stage 1: Asian JVs and alliances with suspension-component companies
- Stage 2: Aggressively design and market systems-integration offering; commence off-road vehicle market

Vehicles

- Internal development of new, leading-edge braking products
- Strategic alliances with suspension-component manufacturers
- Joint ventures with brake companies in Asia

Economic Logic

- Preferred supplier status and premium pricing, due to leading-edge technology
- Preferred supplier status and premium pricing, by providing customers global solutions
- Premium pricing by providing customers integrated kits

Differentiators

- ABS design technology
- Electronic traction control technology
- Systems integration capability
- E-business capability with suppliers and customers
- Global reach

FIGURE 5
BPI's Strategy

are very helpful for improving the soundness of strategies. When we compare these tools and extract their most powerful central messages, several key criteria emerge to help executives test the quality of a proposed strategy. These criteria are presented in Table 1.[11] We strongly encourage executives to apply these tests throughout the strategy-design process and especially when a proposed strategy emerges.

There might be those who wonder whether strategy isn't a concept of yesteryear, whose time has come and gone. In an era of rapid, discontinuous environmental shifts, isn't the company that attempts to specify its future just flirting with disaster? Isn't it better to be flexible, fast-on-the-feet, ready to grab opportunities when the right ones come along?

Some of the skepticism about strategy stems from basic misconceptions. First, a strategy need not be static: it can evolve and be adjusted on an ongoing basis. Unexpected opportunities need not be ignored because they are outside the strategy. Second, a strategy doesn't require a business to become rigid. Some of the best strat-

egies for today's turbulent environment keep multiple options open and build in desirable flexibility—through alliances, outsourcing, leased assets, toehold investments in promising technologies, and numerous other means. A strategy can help to intentionally build in many forms of flexibility—if that's what is called for. Third, a strategy doesn't deal only with an unknowable, distant future. The appropriate lifespans of business strategies have become shorter in recent years. Strategy used to be equated with 5- or 10-year horizons, but today a horizon of two to three years is often more fitting. In any event, strategy does not deal as much with preordaining the future as it does with assessing current conditions and future likelihoods, then making the best decisions possible today.

Strategy is not primarily about planning. It is about intentional, informed, and integrated choices. The noted strategic thinkers Gary Hamel and C.K. Prahalad said: "[A company's] leadership cannot be planned for, but neither can it happen without a grand and well-considered aspiration."[12] We offer the strategy diamond as a way to craft and articulate a business aspiration.

Table 1
Testing the Quality of Your Strategy

Key Evaluation Criteria

1. **Does your strategy fit with what's going on in the environment?**
   Is there healthy profit potential where you're headed? Does your strategy align with the key success factors of your chosen environment?

2. **Does your strategy exploit your key resources?**
   With your particular mix of resources, does this strategy give you a good head start on competitors? Can you pursue this strategy more economically than competitors?

3. **Will your envisioned differentiators be sustainable?**
   Will competitors have difficulty matching you? If not, does your strategy explicitly include a ceaseless regimen of innovation and opportunity creation?

4. **Are the elements of your strategy internally consistent?**
   Have you made choices of arenas, vehicles, differentiators, and staging, and economic logic? Do they all fit and mutually reinforce each other?

5. **Do you have enough resources to pursue this strategy?**
   Do you have the money, managerial time and talent, and other capabilities to do all you envision? Are you sure you're not spreading your resources too thinly, only to be left with a collection of feeble positions?

6. **Is your strategy implementable?**
   Will your key constituencies allow you to pursue this strategy? Can your organization make it through the transition? Are you and your management team able and willing to lead the required changes?

Acknowledgments

We thank the following people for helpful suggestions: Ralph Biggadike, Warren Boeker, Kathy Harrigan, Paul Ingram, Xavier Martin, Atul Nerkar, and Jaeyong Song.

Endnotes

[1] Porter, M. E. 1980. *Competitive strategy.* New York: The Free Press, provides an in-depth discussion of the five-forces model. Hypercompetition is addressed in D'Aveni, R. A. 1994. *Hyper-competition.* New York: The Free Press. The resource-based view of the firm is discussed in Barney, J. 1991. Firm resources and sustained competitive advantage. *Journal of Management,* 17: 99–120. See Brandenburger, M., & Nalebuff, R. J. 1995. The right game: Use game theory to shape strategy. *Harvard Business Review,* July–August: 57–71, for a discussion of co-opetition.

[2] Bianco, A., & Moore, P. L. 2001. Downfall: The inside story of the management fiasco at Xerox. *BusinessWeek,* 5 March 2001.

[3] A widely applicable framework for strategy implementation is discussed in Galbraith, J. R., & Kazanjian, R. K. 1986. *Strategy implementation: Structure, systems and process,* 2nd ed. St. Paul: West Publishing. A similar tool is offered in Hambrick, D. C., & Cannella, A. 1989. Strategy implementation as substance and selling. *The Academy of Management Executive,* 3(4): 278–285.

[4] This observation has been made for years by many contributors, including Quinn, J. B. 1980. *Strategies for change: Logical incrementalism.* Homewood, IL: Richard D. Irwin Publishing; and Mintzberg, H. 1973. Strategy making in three modes. *California Management Review,* 15: 44–53.

[5] Drucker, P. 1954. *The practice of management.* New York: Harper & Row.

[6] Haleblian, J., & Finkelstein, S. 1999. The influence of organizational acquisition experience on acquisition performance: A behavioral learning perspective. *Administrative Science Quarterly,* 44: 29–56.

[7] Eisenhardt, K. M., & Brown, S. L. 1998. Time pacing: Competing in markets that won't stand still. *Harvard Business Review,* March–April: 59–69, discusses "time pacing" as a component of a process of contending with rapidly changing environments.

[8] The collapse of stock market valuations for Internet companies lacking in profits—or any prospect of profits—marked a return to economic reality. Profits above the firm's cost of capital are required in order to yield sustained or longer-term shareholder returns.

[9] Galbraith & Kazanjian, op. cit., and Hambrick & Cannella, op. cit.

[10] Porter, M. E. 1996. What is strategy? *Harvard Business Review,* November–December: 61–78.

[11] See Tilles, S. 1963. How to evaluate strategy. *Harvard Business Review,* July–August: 112–121, for a classic, but more limited, set of evaluative tests.

[12] See Hamel, G., & Prahalad, C. K. 1993. Strategy as stretch and leverage. *Harvard Business Review,* March–April: 84–91.

Donald C. Hambrick is the Samuel Bronfman Professor of Democratic Business Enterprise at the Graduate School of Business, Columbia University. He holds degrees from the University of Colorado (B.S.), Harvard University (MBA), and the Pennsylvania State University (Ph.D.). An active consultant and executive education instructor, he also served as president of the Academy of Management. Contact: dch2@columbia.edu.

James W. Fredrickson is a professor of strategic management and Chevron Oil Centennial Foundation Fellow in the McCombs School of Business of the University of Texas at Austin. He was previously on the faculties of Columbia University and the University of Pittsburgh, and holds a Ph.D. from the University of Washington. Contact: james.fredrickson@bus.utexas.edu.

How Competitive Forces Shape Strategy

Awareness of these forces can help a company stake out a position in its industry that is less vulnerable to attack

by Michael E. Porter

The essence of strategy formulation is coping with competition. Yet it is easy to view competition too narrowly and too pessimistically. While one sometimes hears executives complaining to the contrary, intense competition in an industry is neither coincidence nor bad luck.

Moreover, in the fight for market share, competition is not manifested only in the other players. Rather, competition in an industry is rooted in its underlying economics, and competitive forces exist that go well beyond the established combatants in a particular industry. Customers, suppliers, potential entrants, and substitute products are all competitors that may be more or less prominent or active depending on the industry.

The state of competition in an industry depends on five basic forces, which are diagrammed in the *Exhibit* on page 6. The collective strength of these forces determines the ultimate profit potential of an industry. It ranges from *intense* in industries like tires, metal cans, and steel, where no company earns spectacular returns on investment, to *mild* in industries like oil field services and equipment, soft drinks, and toiletries, where there is room for quite high returns.

In the economists' "perfectly competitive" industry, jockeying for position is unbridled and entry to the industry very easy. This kind of industry structure, of course, offers the worst prospect for long-run profitability. The weaker the forces collectively, however, the greater the opportunity for superior performance.

Mr. Porter is a specialist in industrial economics and business strategy. An associate professor of business administration at the Harvard Business School, he has created a course there entitled "Industry and Competitive Analysis." He sits on the boards of three companies and consults on strategy matters, and he has written many articles for economics journals and published two books. One of them, Interbrand Choice, Strategy and Bilateral Market Power *(Harvard University Press, 1976) is an out-growth of his doctoral thesis, for which he won the coveted Wells prize awarded by the Harvard economics department. He has recently completed two book manuscripts, one on competitive analysis in industry and the other (written with Michael Spence and Richard Caves) on competition in the open economy.*

Whatever their collective strength, the corporate strategist's goal is to find a position in the industry where his or her company can best defend itself against these forces or can influence them in its favor. The collective strength of the forces may be painfully apparent to all the antagonists; but to cope with them, the strategist must delve below the surface and analyze the sources of each. For example, what makes the industry vulnerable to entry, What determines the bargaining power of suppliers?

Knowledge of these underlying sources of competitive pressure provides the groundwork for a strategic agenda of action. They highlight the critical strengths and weaknesses of the company, animate the positioning of the company in its industry, clarify the areas where strategic changes may yield the greatest payoff, and highlight the places where industry trends promise to hold the greatest significance as either opportunities or threats. Understanding these sources also proves to be of help in considering areas for diversification.

Contending forces

The strongest competitive force or forces determine the profitability of an industry and so are of greatest importance in strategy formulation. For example, even a company with a strong position in an industry unthreatened by potential entrants will earn low returns if it faces a superior or a lower-cost substitute product—as the leading manufacturers of vacuum tubes and coffee percolators have learned to their sorrow. In such a situation, coping with the substitute product becomes the number one strategic priority.

Different forces take on prominence, of course, in shaping competition in each industry. In the ocean-going tanker industry the key force is probably the buyers (the major oil companies), while in tires it is powerful OEM buyers coupled with tough competitors. In the steel industry the key forces are foreign competitors and substitute materials.

Every industry has an underlying structure, or a set of fundamental economic and technical characteristics, that gives rise to these competitive forces. The strategist, wanting to position his or her company to cope best with its industry environment or to influence that environment in the company's favor, must learn what makes the environment tick.

This view of competition pertains equally to industries dealing in services and to those selling products. To avoid monotony in this article, I refer to both products and services as "products." The same general principles apply to all types of business.

A few characteristics are critical to the strength of each competitive force. I shall discuss them in this section.

Threat of entry

New entrants to an industry bring new capacity, the desire to gain market share, and often substantial resources. Companies diversifying through acquisition into the industry from other markets often leverage their resources to cause a shake-up, as Philip Morris did with Miller beer.

The seriousness of the threat of entry depends on the barriers present and on the reaction from existing competitors that entrants can expect. If barriers to entry are high and newcomers can expect sharp retaliation from the entrenched competitors, obviously the newcomers will not pose a serious threat of entering.

There are six major sources of barriers to entry:

1. *Economies of scale*—These economies deter entry by forcing the aspirant either to come in on a large scale or to accept a cost disadvantage. Scale economies in production, research, marketing, and service are probably the key barriers to entry in the mainframe computer industry, as Xerox and GE sadly discovered. Economies of scale can also act as hurdles in distribution, utilization of the sales force, financing, and nearly any other part of a business.

2. *Product differentiation*—Brand identification creates a barrier by forcing entrants to spend heavily to overcome customer loyalty. Advertising, customer service, being first in the industry, and product differences are among the factors fostering brand identification. It is perhaps the most important entry barrier in soft drinks, over-the-counter drugs, cosmetics, investment banking, and public accounting. To create high fences around their businesses, brewers couple brand identification with economies of scale in production, distribution, and marketing.

3. *Capital requirements*—The need to invest large financial resources in order to compete creates a barrier to entry, particularly if the capital is required for unrecoverable expenditures in up-front advertising or R&D. Capital is necessary not only for fixed facilities but also for customer credit, inventories, and absorbing start-up losses. While major corporations have the financial resources to invade almost any industry, the huge capital requirements in certain fields, such as computer manufacturing and mineral extraction, limit the pool of likely entrants.

4. *Cost disadvantages independent of size*—Entrenched companies may have cost advantages not

The Experience Curve as an Entry Barrier

In recent years, the experience curve has become widely discussed as a key element of industry structure. According to this concept, unit costs in many manufacturing industries (some dogmatic adherents say in *all* manufacturing industries) as well as in some service industries decline with "experience," or a particular company's cumulative volume of production. (The experience curve, which encompasses many factors, is a broader concept than the better known learning curve, which refers to the efficiency achieved over a period of time by workers through much repetition.)

The causes of the decline in unit costs are a combination of elements, including economies of scale, the learning curve for labor, and capital-labor substitution. The cost decline creates a barrier to entry because new competitors with no "experience" face higher costs than established ones, particularly the producer with the largest market share, and have difficulty catching up with the entrenched competitors.

Adherents of the experience curve concept stress the importance of achieving market leadership to maximize this barrier to entry, and they recommend aggressive action to achieve it, such as price cutting in anticipation of falling costs in order to build volume. For the combatant that cannot achieve a healthy market share, the prescription is usually, "Get out."

Is the experience curve an entry barrier on which strategies should be built? The answer is: not in every industry. In fact, in some industries, building a strategy on the experience curve can be potentially disastrous. That costs decline with experience in some industries is not news to corporate executives. The significance of the experience curve for strategy depends on what factors are causing the decline.

If costs are falling because a growing company can reap economies of scale through more efficient, automated facilities and vertical integration, then the cumulative volume of production is unimportant to its relative cost position. Here the lowest-cost producer is the one with the largest, most efficient facilities.

A new entrant may well be more efficient than the more experienced competitors; if it has built the newest plant, it will face no disadvantage in having to catch up. The strategic prescription, "You must have the largest, most efficient plant," is a lot different from, "You must produce the greatest cumulative output of the item to get your costs down."

Whether a drop in costs with cumulative (not absolute) volume erects an entry barrier also depends on the sources of the decline. If costs go down because of technical advances known generally in the industry or because of the development of improved equipment that can be copied or purchased from equipment suppliers, the experience curve is no entry barrier at all – in fact, new or less experienced competitors may actually enjoy a cost *advantage* over the leaders. Free of the legacy of heavy past investments, the newcomer or less experienced competitor can purchase or copy the newest and lowest-cost equipment and technology.

If, however, experience can be kept proprietary, the leaders will maintain a cost advantage. But new entrants may require less experience to reduce their costs than the leaders needed. All this suggests that the experience curve can be a shaky entry barrier on which to build a strategy.

While space does not permit a complete treatment here, I want to mention a few other crucial elements in determining the appropriateness of a strategy built on the entry barrier provided by the expenence curve:
□ The height of the barrier depends on how important costs are to competition compared with other areas like marketing, selling, and innovation.
□ The barrier can be nullified by product or process innovations leading to a substantially new technology and thereby creating an entirely new experience curve.* New entrants can leapfrog the industry leaders and alight on the new experience curve, to which those leaders may be poorly positioned to jump.
□ If more than one strong company is building its strategy on the experience curve, the consequences can be nearly fatal. By the time only one rival is left pursuing such a strategy, industry growth may have stopped and the prospects of reaping the spoils of victory long since evaporated.

*For an example drawn from the history of the automobile industry see William J. Abernathy and Kenneth Wayne, "The Limits of the Learning Curve," HBR September/October 1974, p.109.

available to potential rivals, no matter what their size and attainable economies of scale. These advantages can stem from the effects of the learning curve (and of its first cousin, the experience curve), proprietary technology, access to the best raw materials sources, assets purchased at preinflation prices, government subsidies, or favorable locations. Sometimes cost advantages are legally enforceable, as they are through patents. (For an analysis of the much-discussed experience curve as a barrier to entry, see the ruled insert above.)

5. *Access to distribution channels*—The newcomer on the block must, of course, secure distribution of its product or service. A new food product, for example, must displace others from the supermarket shelf via price breaks, promotions, intense

selling efforts, or some other means. The more limited the wholesale or retail channels are and the more that existing competitors have these tied up, obviously the tougher that entry into the industry will be. Sometimes this barrier is so high that, to surmount it, a new contestant must create its own distribution channels, as Timex did in the watch industry in the 1950s.

6. *Government policy*—The government can limit or even foreclose entry to industries with such controls as license requirements and limits on access to raw materials. Regulated industries like trucking, liquor retailing, and freight forwarding are noticeable examples; more subtle government restrictions operate in fields like ski-area development and coal mining. The government also can play a major indirect role by affecting entry barriers through controls such as air and water pollution standards and safety regulations.

The potential rival's expectations about the reaction of existing competitors also will influence its decision on whether to enter. The company is likely to have second thoughts if incumbents have previously lashed out at new entrants or if:

☐ The incumbents possess substantial resources to fight back, including excess cash and unused borrowing power, productive capacity, or clout with distribution channels and customers.

☐ The incumbents seem likely to cut prices because of a desire to keep market shares or because of industrywide excess capacity.

☐ Industry growth is slow, affecting its ability to absorb the new arrival and probably causing the financial performance of all the parties involved to decline.

Changing conditions

From a strategic standpoint there are two important additional points to note about the threat of entry.

First, it changes, of course, as these conditions change. The expiration of Polaroid's basic patents on instant photography, for instance, greatly reduced its absolute cost entry barrier built by proprietary technology. It is not surprising that Kodak plunged into the market. Product differentiation in printing has all but disappeared. Conversely, in the auto industry economies of scale increased enormously with post-World War II automation and vertical integration—virtually stopping successful new entry.

Second, strategic decisions involving a large segment of an industry can have a major impact on the conditions determining the threat of entry. For ex-

ample, the actions of many U.S. wine producers in the 1960s to step up product introductions, raise advertising levels, and expand distribution nationally surely strengthened the entry roadblocks by raising economies of scale and making access to distribution channels more difficult. Similarly, decisions by members of the recreational vehicle industry to vertically integrate in order to lower costs have greatly increased the economies of scale and raised the capital cost barriers.

Powerful suppliers & buyers

Suppliers can exert bargaining power on participants in an industry by raising prices or reducing the quality of purchased goods and services. Powerful suppliers can thereby squeeze profitability out of an industry unable to recover cost increases in its own prices. By raising their prices, soft drink concentrate producers have contributed to the erosion of profitability of bottling companies because the bottlers, facing intense competition from powdered mixes, fruit drinks, and other beverages, have limited freedom to raise *their* prices accordingly. Customers likewise can force down prices, demand higher quality or more service, and play competitors off against each other—all at the expense of industry profits.

The power of each important supplier or buyer group depends on a number of characteristics of its market situation and on the relative importance of its sales or purchases to the industry compared with its overall business.

A *supplier* group is powerful if:

☐ It is dominated by a few companies and is more concentrated than the industry it sells to.

☐ Its product is unique or at least differentiated, or if it has built up switching costs. Switching costs are fixed costs buyers face in changing suppliers. These arise because, among other things, a buyer's product specifications tie it to particular suppliers, it has invested heavily in specialized ancillary equipment or in reaming how to operate a supplier's equipment (as in computer software), or its production lines are connected to the supplier's manufacturing facilities (as in some manufacture of beverage containers).

☐ It is not obliged to contend with other products for sale to the industry. For instance, the competition between the steel companies and the aluminum companies to sell to the can industry checks the power of each supplier.

☐ It poses a credible threat of integrating forward into the industry's business. This provides a check against the industry's ability to improve the terms on which it purchases.

□ The industry is not an important customer of the supplier group. If the industry is an important customer, suppliers' fortunes will be closely tied to the industry, and they will want to protect the industry through reasonable pricing and assistance in activities like R&D and lobbying.

A *buyer* group is powerful if:

□ It is concentrated or purchases in large volumes. Large volume buyers are particularly potent forces if heavy fixed costs characterize the industry—as they do in metal containers, corn refining, and bulk chemicals, for example—which raise the stakes to keep capacity filled.

□ The products it purchases from the industry are standard or undifferentiated. The buyers, sure that they can always find alternative suppliers, may play one company against another, as they do in aluminum extrusion.

□ The products it purchases from the industry form a component of its product and represent a significant fraction of its cost. The buyers are likely to shop for a favorable price and purchase selectively. Where the product sold by the industry in question is a small fraction of buyers' costs, buyers are usually much less price sensitive.

□ It earns low profits, which create great incentive to lower its purchasing costs. Highly profitable buyers, however, are generally less price sensitive (that is, of course, if the item does not represent a large fraction of their costs).

□ The industry's product is unimportant to the quality of the buyers' products or services. Where the quality of the buyers' products is very much affected by the industry's product, buyers are generally less price sensitive. Industries in which this situation obtains include oil field equipment, where a malfunction can lead to large losses, and enclosures for electronic medical and test instruments, where the quality of the enclosure can influence the user's impression about the quality of the equipment inside.

□ The industry's product does not save the buyer money. Where the industry's product or service can pay for itself many times over, the buyer is rarely price sensitive; rather, he is interested in quality. This is true in services like investment banking and public accounting, where errors in judgment can be costly and embarrassing, and in businesses like the logging of oil wells, where an accurate survey can save thousands of dollars in drilling costs.

□ The buyers pose a credible threat of integrating backward to make the industry's product. The Big Three auto producers and major buyers of cars have often used the threat of self-manufacture as a bar-

Exhibit
Forces governing competition in an industry

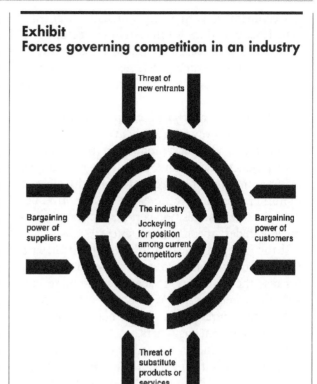

gaining lever. But sometimes an industry engenders a threat to buyers that its members may integrate forward.

Most of these sources of buyer power can be attributed to consumers as a group as well as to industrial and commercial buyers; only a modification of the frame of reference is necessary. Consumers tend to be more price sensitive if they are purchasing products that are undifferentiated, expensive relative to their incomes, and of a sort where quality is not particularly important.

The buying power of retailers is determined by the same rules, with one important addition. Retailers can gain significant bargaining power over manufacturers when they can influence consumers' purchasing decisions, as they do in audio components, jewelry, appliances, sporting goods, and other goods.

Strategic action

A company's choice of suppliers to buy from or buyer groups to sell to should be viewed as a crucial strategic decision. A company can improve its strategic posture by finding suppliers or buyers who possess the least power to influence it adversely.

Most common is the situation of a company being able to choose whom it will sell to—in other words, buyer selection. Rarely do all the buyer groups a company sells to enjoy equal power. Even if a company sells to a single industry, segments usually exist within that industry that exercise less power (and that are therefore less price sensitive) than others. For example, the replacement market for most products is less price sensitive than the overall market.

As a rule, a company can sell to powerful buyers and still come away with above-average profitability only if it is a low-cost producer in its industry or if its product enjoys some unusual, if not unique, features. In supplying large customers with electric motors, Emerson Electric earns high returns because its low cost position permits the company to meet or undercut competitors' prices.

If the company lacks a low cost position or a unique product, selling to everyone is self-defeating because the more sales it achieves, the more vulnerable it becomes. The company may have to muster the courage to turn away business and sell only to less potent customers.

Buyer selection has been a key to the success of National Can and Crown Cork & Seal. They focus on the segments of the can industry where they can create product differentiation, minimize the threat of backward integration, and otherwise mitigate the awesome power of their customers. Of course, some industries do not enjoy the luxury of selecting "good" buyers.

As the factors creating supplier and buyer power change with time or as a result of a company's strategic decisions, naturally the power of these groups rises or declines. In the ready-to-wear clothing industry, as the buyers (department stores and clothing stores) have become more concentrated and control has passed to large chains, the industry has come under increasing pressure and suffered falling margins. The industry has been unable to differentiate its product or engender switching costs that lock in its buyers enough to neutralize these trends.

Substitute products

By placing a ceiling on prices it can charge, substitute products or services limit the potential of an industry. Unless it can upgrade the quality of the product or differentiate it somehow (as via marketing), the industry will suffer in earnings and possibly in growth.

Manifestly, the more attractive the price-performance trade-off offered by substitute products, the firmer the lid placed on the industry's profit potential. Sugar producers confronted with the large-scale commercialization of high-fructose corn syrup, a sugar substitute, are learning this lesson today.

Substitutes not only limit profits in normal times; they also reduce the bonanza an industry can reap in boom times. In 1978 the producers of fiberglass insulation enjoyed unprecedented demand as a result of high energy costs and severe winter weather. But the industry's ability to raise prices was tempered by the plethora of insulation substitutes, including cellulose, rock wool, and styrofoam. These substitutes are bound to become an even stronger force once the current round of plant additions by fiberglass insulation producers has boosted capacity enough to meet demand (and then some).

Substitute products that deserve the most attention strategically are those that (a) are subject to trends improving their price-performance trade-off with the industry's product, or (b) are produced by industries earning high profits. Substitutes often come rapidly into play if some development increases competition in their industries and causes price reduction or performance improvement.

Jockeying for position

Rivalry among existing competitors takes the familiar form of jockeying for position—using tactics like price competition, product introduction, and advertising slugfests. Intense rivalry is related to the presence of a number of factors:

☐ Competitors are numerous or are roughly equal in size and power. In many U.S. industries in recent years foreign contenders, of course, have become part of the competitive picture.

☐ Industry growth is slow, precipitating fights for market share that involve expansion-minded members.

☐ The product or service lacks differentiation or switching costs, which lock in buyers and protect one combatant from raids on its customers by another.

☐ Fixed costs are high or the product is perishable, creating strong temptation to cut prices. Many basic materials businesses, like paper and aluminum, suffer from this problem when demand slackens.

☐ Capacity is normally augmented in large increments. Such additions, as in the chlorine and vinyl chloride businesses, disrupt the industry's supply-demand balance and often lead to periods of overcapacity and price cutting.

☐ Exit barriers are high. Exit barriers, like very specialized assets or management's loyalty to a particular business, keep companies competing even though they may be earning low or even negative returns on investment. Excess capacity remains functioning, and the profitability of the healthy competitors suffers as the sick ones hang on.[1] If the entire industry suffers from overcapacity, it may seek government help—particularly if foreign competition is present.

☐ The rivals are diverse in strategies, origins, and "personalities." They have different ideas about how to compete and continually run head-on into each other in the process.

As an industry matures, its growth rate changes, resulting in declining profits and (often) a shakeout. In the booming recreational vehicle industry of the early 1970s, nearly every producer did well; but slow growth since then has eliminated the high returns, except for the strongest members, not to mention many of the weaker companies. The same profit story has been played out in industry after industry—snowmobiles, aerosol packaging, and sports equipment are just a few examples.

An acquisition can introduce a very different personality to an industry, as has been the case with Black & Decker's takeover of McCullough, the producer of chain saws. Technological innovation can boost the level of fixed costs in the production process, as it did in the shift from batch to continuous-line photo finishing in the 1960s.

While a company must live with many of these factors—because they are built into industry economics—it may have some latitude for improving matters through strategic shifts. For example, it may try to raise buyers' switching costs or increase product differentiation. A focus on selling efforts in the fastest-growing segments of the industry or on market areas with the lowest fixed costs can reduce the impact of industry rivalry. If it is feasible, a company can try to avoid confrontation with competitors having high exit barriers and can thus sidestep involvement in bitter price cutting.

Formulation of strategy

Once having assessed the forces affecting competition in an industry and their underlying causes, the corporate strategist can identify the company's strengths and weaknesses. The crucial strengths and weaknesses from a strategic standpoint are the company's posture vis-à-vis the underlying causes of each force. Where does it stand against substitutes? Against the sources of enery barriers?

Then the strategist can devise a plan of action that may include (1) positioning the company so that its capabilities provide the best defense against the competitive force; and/or (2) influencing the balance of the forces through strategic moves, thereby improving the company's position; and/or (3) anticipating shifts in the factors underlying the

forces and responding to them, with the hope of exploiting change by choosing a strategy appropriate for the new competitive balance before opponents recognize it. I shall consider each strategic approach in turn.

Positioning the company

The first approach takes the structure of the industry as given and matches the company's strengths and weaknesses to it. Strategy can be viewed as building defenses against the competitive forces or as finding positions in the industry where the forces are weakest.

Knowledge of the company's capabilities and of the causes of the competitive forces will highlight the areas where the company should confront competition and where avoid it. If the company is a low-cost producer, it may choose to confront powerful buyers while it takes care to sell them only products not vulnerable to competition from substitutes.

The success of Dr Pepper in the soft drink industry illustrates the coupling of realistic knowledge of corporate strengths with sound industry analysis to yield a superior strategy. Coca-Cola and PepsiCola dominate Dr Pepper's industry, where many small concentrate producers compete for a piece of the action. Dr Pepper chose a strategy of avoiding the largest-selling drink segment, maintaining a narrow flavor line, forgoing the development of a captive bottler network, and marketing heavily. The company positioned itself so as to be least vulnerable to its competitive forces while it exploited its small size.

In the $11.5 billion soft drink industry, barriers to entry in the form of brand identification, large-scale marketing, and access to a bottler network are enormous. Rather than accept the formidable costs and scale economies in having its own bottler network—that is, following the lead of the Big Two and of Seven-Up—Dr Pepper took advantage of the different flavor of its drink to "piggyback" on Coke and Pepsi bottlers who wanted a full line to sell to customers. Dr Pepper coped with the power of these buyers through extraordinary service and other efforts to distinguish its treatment of them from that of Coke and Pepsi.

Many small companies in the soft drink business offer cola drinks that thrust them into head-to-head competition against the majors. Dr Pepper, however, maximized product differentiation by maintaining a narrow line of beverages built around an unusual flavor.

Finally, Dr Pepper met Coke and Pepsi with an advertising onslaught emphasizing the alleged uniqueness of its single flavor. This campaign built strong brand identification and great customer loyalty. Helping its efforts was the fact that Dr Pepper's formula involved lower raw materials cost, which gave the company an absolute cost advantage over its major competitors.

There are no economies of scale in soft drink concentrate production, so Dr Pepper could prosper despite its small share of the business (6%). Thus Dr Pepper confronted competition in marketing but avoided it in product line and in distribution. This artful positioning combined with good implementation has led to an enviable record in earnings and in the stock market.

Influencing the balance

When dealing with the forces that drive industry competition, a company can devise a strategy that takes the offensive. This posture is designed to do more than merely cope with the forces themselves; it is meant to alter their causes.

Innovations in marketing can raise brand identification or otherwise differentiate the product. Capital investments in large-scale facilities or vertical integration affect entry barriers. The balance of forces is partly a result of external factors and partly in the company's control.

Exploiting industry change

Industry evolution is important strategically because evolution, of course, brings with it changes in the sources of competition I have identified. In the familiar product life-cycle pattern, for example, growth rates change, product differentiation is said to decline as the business becomes more mature, and the companies tend to integrate vertically.

These trends are not so important in themselves; what is critical is whether they affect the sources of competition. Consider vertical integration. In the maturing minicomputer industry, extensive vertical integration, both in manufacturing and in software development, is taking place. This very significant trend is greatly raising economies of scale as well as the amount of capital necessary to compete in the industry. This in turn is raising barriers to entry and may drive some smaller competitors out of the industry once growth levels off.

Obviously, the trends carrying the highest priority from a strategic standpoint are those that affect the most important sources of competition in the industry and those that elevate new causes to the forefront. In contract aerosol packaging, for example, the trend toward less product differentiation is now dominant. It has increased buyers' power, lowered the barriers to entry, and intensified competi-

tion.

The framework for analyzing competition that I have described can also be used to predict the eventual profitability of an industry. In long-range planning the task is to examine each competitive force, forecast the magnitude of each underlying cause, and then construct a composite picture of the likely profit potential of the industry.

The outcome of such an exercise may differ a great deal from the existing industry structure. Today, for example, the solar heating business is populated by dozens and perhaps hundreds of companies, none with a major market position. Entry is easy, and competitors are battling to establish solar heating as a superior substitute for conventional methods.

The potential of this industry will depend largely on the shape of future barriers to entry, the improvement of the industry's position relative to substitutes, the ultimate intensity of competition, and the power captured by buyers and suppliers. These characteristics will in turn be influenced by such factors as the establishment of brand identities, significant economies of scale or experience curves in equipment manufacture wrought by technological change, the ultimate capital costs to compete, and the extent of overhead in production facilities.

The framework for analyzing industry competition has direct benefits in setting diversification strategy. It provides a road map for answering the extremely difficult question inherent in diversification decisions: "What is the potential of this business?" Combining the framework with judgment in its application, a company may be able to spot an industry with a good future before this good future is reflected in the prices of acquisition candidates.

Multifaceted rivalry

Corporate managers have directed a great deal of attention to defining their businesses as a crucial step in strategy formulation. Theodore Levitt, in his classic 1960 article in HBR, argued strongly for avoiding the myopia of narrow, product-oriented industry definition.[2] Numerous other authorities have also stressed the need to look beyond product to function in defining a business, beyond national boundaries to potential international competition, and beyond the ranks of one's competitors today to those that may become competitors tomorrow. As a result of these urgings, the proper definition of a company's industry or industries has become an endlessly debated subject.

One motive behind this debate is the desire to exploit new markets. Another, perhaps more important motive is the fear of overlooking latent sources of competition that someday may threaten the industry. Many managers concentrate so single-mindedly on their direct antagonists in the fight for market share that they fail to realize that they are also competing with their customers and their suppliers for bargaining power. Meanwhile, they also neglect to keep a wary eye out for new entrants to the contest or fail to recognize the subtle threat of substitute products.

The key to growth—even survival—is to stake out a position that is less vulnerable to attack from head-to-head opponents, whether established or new, and less vulnerable to erosion from the direction of buyers, suppliers, and substitute goods. Establishing such a position can take many forms—solidifying relationships with favorable customers, differentiating the product either substantively or psychologically through marketing, integrating forward or backward, establishing technological leadership.

---

[1] *For a more complete discussion of exit barriers and their implications for strategy, see my article, "Please Note Location of Nearest Exit,"* California Management Review, *Winter 1976, p. 21.*

[2] *Theodore Levitt, "Marketing Myopia," reprinted as an HBR Classic, September-October 1975, p. 26.*

Reprint 79208   To place an order, call 800-988-0886.

Strategy in the Digital Age

A little bit of history

The first programmable electronic computers emerged during World War 2, when they were used for code breaking and for ballistic calculations. Post war, their relevance for business became apparent, so that by the 1950s a first generation of computers was in use for data warehousing and routine processes such as payroll and billing. Since then, their growth both in power and in application has been exponential, so that Information Technology in organisations is now key to planning, controlling, scheduling, resource allocation and knowledge sharing.

The early Information Technology systems were applied to operations, dealing with organisations' day to day routine transactions. Developments in software, coupled with the advent of distributed computing as personal computers (PCs) arrived in the 1980s, led to the application of IT to databases for search , analysis and decision-making processes. The arrival of the Internet in the 1990s has enabled the use of IT as a truly strategic tool. These developments are traced in Figure 1 below.

Evolution of Organisational Applications of ICT

Based on Daft 2004

From Enterprise Platforms to Cloud Solutions ; changing how organisations perceive ICT from Capital Spend to a revenue item

Top
Strategy, plans
Non programmed

3 Strategic

Internal coordination	External Relationships
•Intranets	•EPOS, Extranets, EDI
•Enterprise Resource Planning	•Integrated Enterprise
•Knowledge Management	•E - Business

Mgmt Level

2 Decision making & Control
•Management Information systems
•Decision Support Systems
•Executive Information Systems
•Management Control systems
•Balanced Scorecard

Big Data :
Mobile telephony
Social networking
Smart Systems
???

1 Operations
•Transaction Processing Systems
•Data Warehousing

First Line
Operational,
Programmed

Low   System Complexity   High

1950's   1980s   2000....

Computer in the basement   Computers on peoples' desks   Computers in remote data centres ("the Cloud") & in peoples' hands, in the form of mobile device.

The Role of Information Technology in Organisations

An organisation's information technology comprises *hardware,* in the form of mainframe computers, cloud based resources, desktop PCs and mobile devices as well as *software* in the form of the various systems that store data and process them for effective management decision making and control. These systems include Knowledge Management, Decision Support, Executive Information, and Enterprise Resource Planning, a system that integrates all the various business processes across the entire organisation.

A commonly used classification divides Information Technology in organisations into two streams:

> **e-Business**, which is a broad concept, embracing any transaction over a digital network rather than in a physical setting. It includes the internal business processes of organisations, from data warehousing to data processing, data analysis, and the management of business processes, as well as organisations' communications linkages with employees, customers, suppliers and other key constituents. These applications are now migrating from corporate hard drives to "The Cloud", facilitated by high-capacity networks, low-cost computers and portable devices. This has the effect of reducing the cost and increasing the flexibility of data storage and data management, as companies can scale up as computing needs increase and then scale down again as demands decrease.

> **e–Commerce** is a more limited concept, referring to electronically mediated transactions between firms and their customers (Business to Customer) or other firms (Business to Business), not only buying and selling and other electronic financial transactions but also the exchange of all kinds of data between businesses, customers, and the public sector and citizens.

Old stagers, and new kids on the block

The digital revolution we have outlined above has created a host of new businesses – household names that didn't exist a decade ago. Organisations such as eBay, Facebook, LinkedIn, Expedia, Yahoo and many others would not exist without the Internet. Traditional music retailers like Tower and Virgin scrambled to invest in new channels as their customers migrated to music online. Amazon and Netflix are similar examples in book retailing and in TV viewing.

But the revolution has also transformed many other, more traditional organisations, not only in business but also in all sectors of the economy. Banks to utilities, civil service departments to Not-for-Profits and NGOs, all make extensive use of the Internet; indeed it is hard to imagine any organisation competing successfully in today's world without a presence on the Web.

The Competitive Challenge of Digital

While developments in IT, and especially the onset of the Internet ,have transformed all our lives and introduced new strategic challenges and opportunities for businesses, we should maintain a sense of proportion and understand that the Internet is essentially a *tool* – albeit a very powerful one – that greatly enhances connectivity. At its most basic it is a global network of interlinked computers, operating to standardised protocols, which enables data transfer between connected devices. The resulting data can be analysed, understood and exploited using the models for strategic analysis and diagnosis that are discussed in Theme 2 of our course.

For example, we can use Porter's 5 Forces model to gives an overview of the impact of the Internet on the competitive structure of industries:

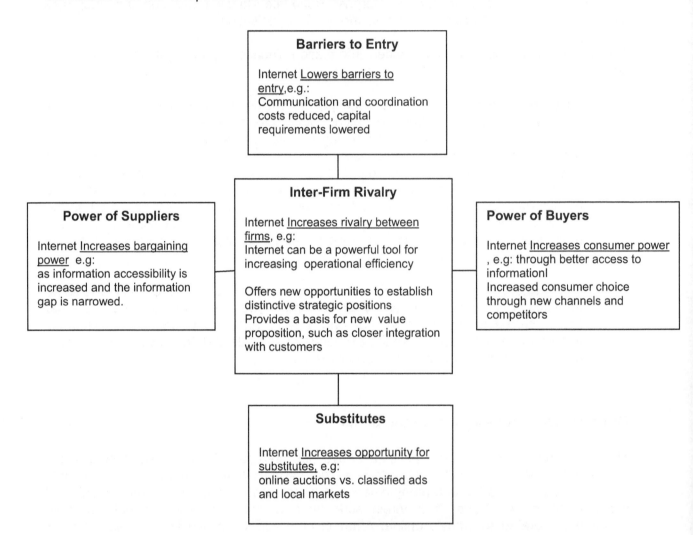

The role of the Navigator

When the Internet first emerged in the 1990s, a rush of new cyber-savvy businesses emerged in what has been described as a "land-grab", albeit in cyberspace as opposed to physical space (Evans & Wurster 1999). New technology entrepreneurs staked out claims as the traditional retailers struggled to understand the new landscape of e Commerce. In the rush to exploit the new medium, new on-line businesses were valued for their potential rather than actual performance, and inevitably this bubble burst in the dot.com crash of the late 1990s. But this proved a temporary set-back, and the on-line businesses quickly matured and prospered. This was a second generation of e Commerce, when the heady excitement of the land-grab gave way to a more competitive landscape, where traditional "bricks & mortar" businesses learned how to engage with the new technology, and the new entrants moved from claiming new territory to defending it. All the protagonists were focused on competitive advantage, and the strategies to achieve it.

In their seminal article mentioned above, Evans & Wurster reviewed these first two stages of the development of e Commerce. By 1999 when their article was published they were able to identify a new basis for competitiveness in the Internet age – Navigation, "the Battlefield on which Competitive Advantage will be Won or Lost"

Navigation – the new basis for competitive advantage
Navigation in business refers to the action of purchasers as they seek to make choices. In the world of physical commerce, navigation involves going to one or more shops to make a purchase, aided by advertising, branding and merchandising to help in making choices. At its simplest, when we browse in a shop, we are navigating. The shops can make navigation easier by creating suitable sections and displays in their stores. Manufacturers of consumer goods make navigation easier by developing quality brands that reduces our navigation costs because the brands are trusted. Stores can differentiate themselves by stocking only those ranges that appeal to its customers, in other words reduces their customers' navigation costs.

On the Internet, however "millions of people exchange massive amounts of information, directly, quickly and for free". In other words, Evans & Wurster argue, on-line businesses build competitive advantage by developing navigational tools that reduce customers search costs.

Richness v. Reach
Navigation, according to Evans & Wurster, has two key components – *richness* & *reach.* *Richness* is the depth and detail of information that a business can give a customer, as well as the depth and detail of information it collects about a customer. Rich product information can be very important for some consumers (e.g., hi-fi enthusiasts, a company purchasing specialised machinery).

Reach is about access and connection – how many customers can a business connect with and how many products can it offer to those customers. The retail superstore is a example of a business competing on reach – convenient locations and a broad selection of products).

Traditionally, these capabilities were traded off against one another: depending on the business context businesses would reduce the *richness of communication* in order to get a *wider reach*, and vice versa. The arrival of the Internet was a "game changer" in that it facilitated electronic commerce by many businesses that hitherto had never interacted with the ultimate consumer of their products. Thus, online, we can custom design and purchase a shirt; we can buy Parma ham direct from Italy as easily as a book from Amazon. With so many product suppliers populating cyberspace, there is now more information that anyone can deal with efficiently.

Out of this milieu pure navigators have emerged - businesses that help consumers make sense of information without being a party to the transaction. Obvious examples of these *cybermediaries* are Google, Pinterest, Tripadvisor and Quicken. Local example include Carzone.ie., the used car site used by most Irish dealers, or MyHome.ie. A pure navigation business can generate economic returns in a number of ways (i) through sale of advertising space on its site; (ii) through subscription from those profiled, (iii) through levying membership fees on users, and (iv) charging commission.

The Digital impact today and tomorrow

Evans & Wurster's paper was written 15 years ago. Their insights remain valid today, but there have been great changes in the scale and scope of information technologies, and their exponential development has continued to transform the effectiveness of business. Sophisticated IT systems now gather vast quantities of data and transform them into useful information for decision makers. In addition, new collaborative work systems allow teams to share information, collaborate electronically and access computer-based support data for group decision-making and problem-solving. In the future, the growth of RFID (radio frequency identification devices), or small microchips embedded in all objects might give birth to the so-called Internet of Things – when objects will communicate directly to other objects and organise their environment accordingly.

Perhaps the strongest force that is driving growth on the Internet today is the individual consumer, empowered by the growth of social networking, which is creating the most radical expansion in the field of IT since the development of the World Wide Web. Organisations are using blogs, wikis, peer-to-peer file-sharing and social networking for internal communications, sharing of ideas, customer relationship management, advertising and marketing; indeed there are a myriad of opportunities that organisations continue to explore.

It is against these exciting developments in IT that the two articles in this section should be read. They are not intended to give a comprehensive overview of the impact of IT in organisations, rather they exemplify some of the issues that the management community are addressing as the power and influence of technology continues on its inexorable growth.

The paper by Dewhurst & Willmott "Manager & Machine" tackles the issues of the evolving role of managers in an era when computers seem set to usurp traditional managerial roles in communication and decision-making. In reading this paper, you might reflect on its implications for Mintzberg's managerial roles, and on the knowledge workers as envisioned by Drucker.

The second reading "Strategic Principles for Competing in the Digital Age" by Hirt & Willmott sets out strategic challenges posed by this digital revolution; perhaps the key insight arising from this paper is the inevitable pace of change in the digital world, so that harnessing digital forces is "a journey not a destination, a relentless leadership experience ...."

Sources:

Daft, R.L. *"Organisation Theory & Design"* 8th ed. 2004

Evans, P. & T.S. Wurster, *"Getting Real about Virtual Commerce"* Harvard Business Review Nov/Dec 1999

John Quilliam
Trinity Business School
June 2015

SEPTEMBER 2014

McKinsey Quarterly

Manager and machine:
The new leadership equation

Martin Dewhurst and Paul Willmott

As artificial intelligence takes hold, what
will it take to be an effective executive?

In a 1967 *McKinsey Quarterly* article, "The manager and the
moron," Peter Drucker noted that "the computer makes no decisions;
it only carries out orders. It's a total moron, and therein lies its
strength. It forces us to think, to set the criteria. The stupider the
tool, the brighter the master has to be—and this is the dumbest
tool we have ever had."[1]

How things have changed. After years of promise and hype, machine
learning has at last hit the vertical part of the exponential curve.
Computers are replacing skilled practitioners in fields such as architecture, aviation, the law, medicine, and petroleum geology—
and changing the nature of work in a broad range of other jobs and
professions. Deep Knowledge Ventures, a Hong Kong venture-
capital firm, has gone so far as to appoint a decision-making algorithm
to its board of directors.

What would it take for algorithms to take over the C-suite? And
what will be senior leaders' most important contributions if they do?
Our answers to these admittedly speculative questions rest on our
work with senior leaders in a range of industries, particularly those
on the vanguard of the big data and advanced-analytics revolution.
We have also worked extensively alongside executives who have been
experimenting most actively with opening up their companies and

[1] Peter Drucker, "The manager and the moron," *McKinsey Quarterly*, 1967 Number 4,
mckinsey.com.

decision-making processes through crowdsourcing and social platforms within and across organizational boundaries.

Our argument is simple: the advances of brilliant machines will astound us, but they will transform the lives of senior executives only if managerial advances enable them to. There's still a great deal of work to be done to create data sets worthy of the most intelligent machines and their burgeoning decision-making potential. On top of that, there's a need for senior leaders to "let go" in ways that run counter to a century of organizational development.

If these two things happen—and they're likely to, for the simple reason that leading-edge organizations will seize competitive advantage and be imitated—the role of the senior leader will evolve. We'd suggest that, ironically enough, executives in the era of brilliant machines will be able to make the biggest difference through the human touch. By this we mean the questions they frame, their vigor in attacking exceptional circumstances highlighted by increasingly intelligent algorithms, and their ability to do things machines can't. That includes tolerating ambiguity and focusing on the "softer" side of management to engage the organization and build its capacity for self-renewal.

Missing links

The most impressive examples of machine learning substituting for human pattern recognition—such as the IBM supercomputer Watson's potential to predict oncological outcomes more accurately than physicians by reviewing, storing, and learning from reams of medical-journal articles—result from situations where inputs are of high quality. Contrast that with the state of affairs pervasive in many organizations that have access to big data and are taking a run at advanced analytics. The executives in these companies often find themselves beset by "polluted" or difficult-to-parse data, whose validity is subject to vigorous internal debates.

This isn't an article about big data per se—in recent *Quarterly* articles we've written extensively on what senior executives must do to address these issues—but we want to stress that "garbage in/ garbage out" applies as much to supercomputers as it did 50 years ago to the IBM System/360.[2] This management problem, which transcends CIOs and the IT organization, speaks to the need for a turbocharged data-analytics strategy, a new top-team mind-set, fresh talent approaches, and a concerted effort to break down information silos. These issues also transcend number crunching; as our colleagues have explained elsewhere, "weak signals" from social media and other sources also contain powerful insights and should be part of the data-creation process.[3]

The incentives for getting this right are large—early movers should be able to speed the quality and pace of decision making in a wide range of tactical and strategic areas, as we already see from the promising results of early big data and analytics efforts. Furthermore, early movers will probably gain new insights from their analysis of unstructured data, such as e-mail discussions between sales representatives or discussion threads in social media. Without behavioral shifts by senior leaders, though, their organizations won't realize the full power of the artificial intelligence at their fingertips. The challenge lies in part with the very notion that machine-learning insights are at the fingertips of senior executives.

That's certainly an appealing prospect: customized dashboards full of metadata describing and synthesizing deeper and more detailed operational, financial, and marketing information hold enormous power for the senior team. But these dashboards don't create themselves. Senior executives must find and set the software parameters needed to determine, for instance, which data gets prioritized and which gets flagged for escalation. It's no overstatement to say that these parameters determine the direction of the company—and the success of executives in guiding it there; for example, a bank can shift the mix between lending and deposit taking by changing prices. Machines may be able to adjust prices in real time, but executives must determine the target. Similarly, machines can monitor risks, but only after executives have determined the level of risk they're comfortable with.

[2] See Stefan Biesdorf, David Court, and Paul Willmott, "Big data: What's your plan?," *McKinsey Quarterly*, March 2013; and Brad Brown, David Court, and Paul Willmott, "Mobilizing your C-suite for big-data analytics," *McKinsey Quarterly*, November 2013, both available on mckinsey.com.

[3] See Martin Harrysson, Estelle Métayer, and Hugo Sarrazin, "The strength of 'weak signals,'" *McKinsey Quarterly*, February 2014, mckinsey.com.

Consider also the challenge posed by today's real-time sales data, which can be sliced by location, product, team, and channel. Previous generations of managers would probably have given their eyeteeth for that capability. Today's unaware executive risks drowning in minutiae, though. Some are already reacting by distancing themselves from technology—for instance, by employing layers of staffers to screen data, which gets turned into more easily digestible Power-Point slides. In so doing, however, executives risk getting a "filtered" view of reality that misses the power of the data available to them.

As artificial intelligence grows in power, the odds of sinking under the weight of even quite valuable insights grow as well. The answer isn't likely to be bureaucratizing information, but rather democratizing it: encouraging and expecting the organization to manage itself without bringing decisions upward. Business units and company-wide functions will of course continue reporting to the top team and CEO. But emboldened by sharper insights and pattern recognition from increasingly powerful computers, business units and functions will be able to make more and better decisions on their own. Reviewing the results of those decisions, and sharing the implications across the management team, will actually give managers lower down in the organization new sources of power vis-à-vis executives at the top. That will happen even as the CEO begins to morph, in part, into a "chief experimentation officer," who draws from acute observance of early signals to bolster a company's ability to experiment at scale, particularly in customer-facing industries.

We've already seen flashes of this development in companies that open up their strategy-development process to a broader range of internal and external participants. Companies such as 3M, Dutch insurer AEGON, Red Hat (the leading provider of Linux software), and defense contractor Rite-Solutions have found that the advantages include more insightful and actionable strategic plans, as well as greater buy-in from participants, since they helped to craft the plan in the first place.[4]

In a world where artificial intelligence supports all manner of day-to-day management decisions, the need to "let go" will be more

[4] See Arne Gast and Michele Zanini, "The social side of strategy," *McKinsey Quarterly*, May 2012, mckinsey.com.

significant and the discomfort for senior leaders higher. To some extent, we're describing a world where top executives' sources of comparative advantage are eroding because of technology and the manifested "brilliance of crowds." The contrast with the command-and-control era—when holding information close was a source of power, and information moved in one direction only, up the corporate hierarchy—could not be starker. Uncomfortable as this new world may be, the costs of the status quo are large and growing: information hoarders will slow the pace of their organizations and forsake the power of artificial intelligence while competitors exploit it.

The human edge

If senior leaders successfully fuel the insights of increasingly brilliant machines and devolve decision-making authority up and down the line, what will be left for top management to do?

Asking questions

A great deal, as it turns out—starting with asking good questions. Asking the right questions of the right people at the right times is a skill set computers lack and may never acquire. To be sure, the exponential advances of deep-learning algorithms mean that executive expertise, which typically runs deep in a particular domain or set of domains, is sometimes inferior to (or can get in the way of) insights generated by deep-learning algorithms, big data, and advanced analytics. In fact, there's a case for using an executive's domain expertise to frame the upfront questions that need asking and then turning the machines loose to answer those questions. That's a role for the people with an organization's strongest judgment: the senior leaders.

The importance of questions extends beyond steering machines, to interpreting their output. Recent history demonstrates the risk of relying on technology-based algorithmic insights without fully understanding how they drive decision making, for that makes it impossible to manage business and reputational risks (among others) properly. The potential for disaster is not small. The foremost cautionary tale, of course, comes from the banks prior to the 2008 financial crisis: C-suite executives and the managers one and two levels below them at major institutions did not fully understand how decisions were made in the "quant" areas of trading and asset management.

Algorithms and artificial intelligence may broaden this kind of analytical complexity beyond the financial world, to a whole new set of decision areas—again placing a premium on the tough questions senior leaders can ask. Penetrating this new world of analytical complexity is likely to be difficult, and an increasingly important role for senior executives may be establishing a set of small, often improvisatory, experiments to get a better handle on the implications of emerging insights and decision rules, as well as their own managerial styles.

Attacking exceptions

An increasingly important element of each leader's management tool kit is likely to be the ability to attack problematic "exceptions" vigorously. Smart machines should get better and better at telling managers when they have a problem. Early evidence of this development is coming in data-intensive areas, such as pricing or credit departments or call centers—and the same thing will probably happen in more strategic areas, ranging from competitive analysis to talent management, as information gets better and machines get smarter. Executives can therefore spend less time on day-to-day management issues, but when the exception report signals a difficulty, the ability to spring into action will help executives differentiate themselves and the health of their organizations.

Senior leaders will have to draw on a mixture of insight—examining exceptions to see if they require interventions, such as new credit limits for a big customer or an opportunity to start bundling a new service with an existing product—and inspiration, as leaders galvanize the organization to respond quickly and work in new ways. Exceptions may pave the way for innovation too, something we already see as leading-edge retailers and financial-services firms mine large sets of customer data.

Tolerating ambiguity

While algorithms and supercomputers are designed to seek answers, they are likely to be most definitive on relatively small questions. The bigger and broader the inquiry, the more likely that human synthesis will be central to problem solving, because machines, though they learn rapidly, provide many pieces without assembling the puzzle. That process of assembly and synthesis can be messy and slow, placing a fresh premium on the senior leaders' ability to tolerate ambiguity.

A straightforward example is the comfort digitally oriented executives are beginning to feel with a wide range of A/B testing to see what does and does not appeal to users or customers online. A/B testing is a small-scale version of the kind of experimentation that will increasingly hold sway as computers gain power, with fully fledged plans of action giving way to proof-of-concept (POC) ones, which make no claim to be either comprehensive or complete. POCs are a way to feel your way in uncertain terrain. Companies take an action, look at the result, and then push on to the next phase, step by step.

This necessary process will increasingly enable companies to proceed without knowing exactly where they're going. For executives, this will feel rather like stumbling along in the dark; reference points can be few. Many will struggle with the uncertainty this approach provokes and wrestle with the temptation to engineer an outcome before sufficient data emerge to allow an informed decision. The trick will be holding open a space for the emergence of new insights and using subtle interventions to keep the whole journey from going off the cliff. What's required, for executives, is the ability to remain in a state of unknowing while constantly filtering and evaluating the available information and its sources, tolerating tension and ambiguity, and delaying decisive action until clarity emerges. In such situations, the temptation to act quickly may provide a false sense of security and reassurance—but may also foreclose on potentially useful outcomes that would have emerged in the longer run.

Employing 'soft' skills

Humans have and will continue to have a strong comparative advantage when it comes to inspiring the troops, empathizing with customers, developing talent, and the like. Sometimes, machines will provide invaluable input, as Laszlo Bock at Google has famously shown in a wide range of human-resource data-analytics efforts. But translating this insight into messages that resonate with organizations will require a human touch. No computer will ever manage by walking around. And no effective executive will try to galvanize action by saying, "we're doing this because an algorithm told us to." Indeed, the contextualization of small-scale machine-made decisions is likely to become an important component of tomorrow's leadership tool kit. While this article isn't the place for a discourse on inspirational leadership, we're firmly convinced that simultaneous growth in the importance of softer management skills and technology savvy will boost the complexity and richness of the senior-executive role.

How different is tomorrow's effective leader from those of the past? In Peter Drucker's 1967 classic, *The Effective Executive*, he described a highly productive company president who "accomplished more in [one] monthly session than many other and equally able executives get done in a month of meetings." Yet this executive "had to resign himself to having at least half his time taken up by things of minor importance and dubious value . . . specific decisions on daily problems that should not have reached him but invariably did."[5] There should be less of dubious value coming across the senior executive's desk in the future. This will be liberating—but also raises the bar for the executive's ability to master the human dimensions that ultimately will provide the edge in the era of brilliant machines. ○

[5] Peter Drucker, *The Effective Executive: The Definitive Guide to Getting the Right Things Done*, New York, NY: Harper & Row, 1967.

Martin Dewhurst and **Paul Willmott** are directors in McKinsey's London office.

McKinsey Quarterly

MAY 2014

Strategic principles for competing in the digital age

Martin Hirt and Paul Willmott

Digitization is rewriting the rules of competition, with incumbent companies most at risk of being left behind. Here are six critical decisions CEOs must make to address the strategic challenge posed by the digital revolution.

The board of a large European insurer was pressing management for answers. A company known mostly for its online channel had begun to undercut premiums in a number of markets and was doing so without agents, building on its dazzling brand reputation online and using new technologies to engage buyers. Some of the insurer's senior managers were sure the threat would abate. Others pointed to serious downtrends in policy renewals among younger customers avidly using new web-based price-comparison tools. The board decided that the company needed to quicken its digital pace.

For many leaders, this story may sound familiar, harkening back to the scary days, 15 years ago, when they encountered the first wave of Internet competitors. Many incumbents responded effectively to these threats, some of which in any event dissipated with the dot-com crash. Today's challenge is different. Robust attackers are scaling up with incredible speed, inserting themselves artfully between you and your customers and zeroing in on lucrative value-chain segments.

The digital technologies underlying these competitive thrusts may not be new, but they are being used to new effect. Staggering amounts of information are accessible as never before—from proprietary big data to new public sources of open data. Analytical and processing capabilities have made similar leaps with algorithms scattering intelligence across digital networks, themselves often lodged in the cloud. Smart mobile devices make that information and computing power accessible to users around the world.

As these technologies gain momentum, they are profoundly changing the strategic context: altering the structure of competition, the conduct of business, and, ultimately, performance across industries. One banking CEO, for instance, says the industry is in the midst of a transition that occurs once every 100 years. To stay ahead of the unfolding trends and disruptions, leaders across industries will need to challenge their assumptions and pressure-test their strategies.

Opportunities and threats

Digitization often lowers entry barriers, causing long-established boundaries between sectors to tumble. At the same time, the "plug and play" nature of digital assets causes value chains to disaggregate, creating openings for focused, fast-moving competitors. New market entrants often scale up rapidly at lower cost than legacy players can, and returns may grow rapidly as more customers join the network.[1]

Digital capabilities increasingly will determine which companies create or lose value. Those shifts take place in the context of industry evolution, which isn't monolithic but can follow a well-worn path: new trends emerge and disruptive entrants appear, their products and services embraced by early adopters (exhibit). Advanced incumbents then begin to adjust to these changes, accelerating the rate of customer adoption until the industry's level of digitization—among companies but, perhaps more critically, among consumers as well—reaches a tipping point. Eventually, what was once radical is normal, and unprepared incumbents run the risk of becoming the next Blockbuster. Others, which have successfully built new capabilities (as Burberry did in retailing), become powerful digital players. (See the accompanying article, "The seven habits of highly effective digital enterprises," on mckinsey.com.) The opportunities for the leaders include:

- *Enhancing interactions among customers, suppliers, stakeholders, and employees.* For many transactions, consumers and businesses increasingly prefer digital channels, which make content universally accessible by mixing media (graphics and video, for example), tailoring messages for context (providing location or demographic information), and adding social connectivity (allowing communities to build around themes and needs, as well as ideas shared among friends). These channels lower the cost of transactions and record them transparently, which can help in resolving disputes.

- *Improving management decisions as algorithms crunch big data from social technologies or the Internet of Things.* Better decision making helps improve performance across business functions—for example, providing for finer marketing allocations (down to the level of individual consumers) or mitigating operational risks by sensing wear and tear on equipment.

- *Enabling new business or operating models, such as peer-to-peer product innovation or customer service.* China's Xiaomi crowdsources features of its new mobile phones rather than investing heavily in R&D, and Telstra crowdsources customer service, so that users support each other to resolve problems without charge. New business or operating models can also disintermediate existing customer–supplier relations—for example, when board-game developers or one-person shops manufacture products using 3-D printers and sell directly to Amazon.

[1] Almost 15 years ago, our colleague Marc Singer explored the early stages of these dynamics in a *McKinsey Quarterly* article he coauthored with McKinsey alumnus John Hagel, "Unbundling the corporation," June 2000, mckinsey.com.

Exhibit

How digitization transforms industries

The position of an industry on this curve depends on the degree to which companies and customers within it have embraced digitization. While conceptual, the curve shows how laggard incumbents have already disappeared from industries in which digital disruption began early, such as traditional media. In industries where digitization is less pervasive but more a gathering force, there is still time for incumbents to adapt and survive.

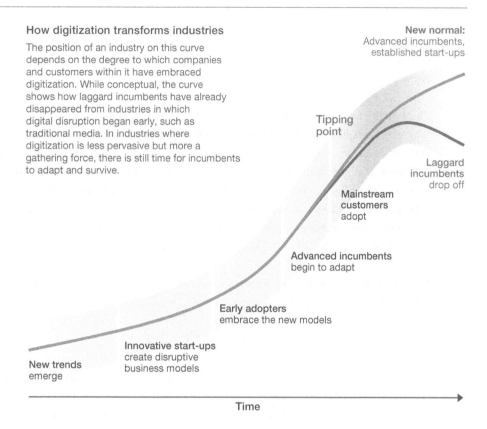

New normal:
Advanced incumbents,
established start-ups

Tipping
point

Laggard
incumbents
drop off

Mainstream
customers
adopt

Advanced incumbents
begin to adapt

Early adopters
embrace the new models

Innovative start-ups
create disruptive
business models

New trends
emerge

Time

The upshot is that digitization will change industry landscapes as it gives life to new sets of competitors. Some players may consider your capabilities a threat even before you have identified them as competitors. Indeed, the forces at work today will bring immediate challenges, opportunities—or both—to literally all digitally connected businesses.

Seven forces at work

Our research and experience with leading companies point to seven trends that could redefine competition.

1. New pressure on prices and margins

Digital technologies create near-perfect transparency, making it easy to compare prices, service levels, and product performance: consumers can switch among digital retailers, brands, and services with just a few clicks or finger swipes. This dynamic can commoditize products and services as consumers demand comparable features and simple interactions. Some banks, for instance, now find that simplifying products for easy purchase on mobile phones inadvertently contributes to a convergence between their offerings and those of competitors that are also pursuing mobile-friendly simplicity.

Third parties have jumped into this fray, disintermediating relationships between companies and their customers. The rise of price-comparison sites that aggregate information across vendors and allow consumers to compare prices and service offerings easily is a testament to this trend. In Europe, chain retailers, which traditionally dominate fast-moving consumer goods, have seen their revenues fall as customers flock to discounters after comparing prices even for staples like milk and bread. In South Korea, online aggregator OK Cashbag has inserted itself into the consumer's shopping behavior through a mobile app that pools product promotions and loyalty points for easy use across more than 50,000 merchants.

These dynamics create downward pressure on returns across consumer-facing industries, and the disruptive currents are now rippling out to B2B businesses.

2. Competitors emerge from unexpected places

Digital dynamics often undermine barriers to entry and long-standing sources of product differentiation. Web-based service providers in telecommunications or insurance, for example, can now tap markets without having to build distribution networks of offices and local agents. They can compete effectively by mining data on risks and on the incomes and preferences of customers.

At the same time, the expense of building brands online and the degree of consumer attention focused on a relatively small number of brands are redrawing battle lines in many markets. Singapore Post is investing in an e-commerce business that benefits from the company's logistics and warehousing backbone. Japanese web retailer Rakuten is using its network to offer financial services. Web powerhouses like Google and Twitter eagerly test industry boundaries through products such as Google Wallet and Twitter's retail offerings.

New competitors can often be smaller companies that will never reach scale but still do a lot of damage to incumbents. In the retailing industry, for instance, entrepreneurs are cherry-picking subcategories of products and severely undercutting pricing on small volumes, forcing bigger companies to do the same.

3. Winner-takes-all dynamics

Digital businesses reduce transaction and labor costs, increase returns to scale from aggregated data, and enjoy increases in the quality of digital talent and intellectual property as network effects kick in. The cost advantages can be significant: online retailers may generate three times the level of revenue per employee as even the top-performing discounters. Comparative advantage can materialize rapidly in these information-intensive models—not over the multiyear spans most companies expect.

Scale economies in data and talent often are decisive. In insurance, digital "natives" with large stores of consumer information may navigate risks better than traditional insurers do. Successful start-ups known for digital expertise and engineer-friendly cultures become magnets for the best digital talent, creating a virtuous cycle. These effects will accelerate consolidation in the industries where digital scale weighs most heavily, challenging more capital- and labor-intensive models. In our experience, banking, insurance, media, telecommunications, and travel are particularly vulnerable to these winner-takes-all market dynamics.

In France, for instance, the start-up Free has begun offering mobile service supported by a large and active digital community of "brand fans" and advocates. The company nurtures opinion-leader "alpha fans," who interact with the rest of the base on the Internet via blogs, social networks, and other channels, building a wave of buzz that quickly spreads across the digital world. Spending only modestly on traditional marketing, Free nonetheless has achieved high levels of customer satisfaction through its social-media efforts—and has gained substantial market share.[2]

4. Plug-and-play business models

As digital forces reduce transaction costs, value chains disaggregate. Third-party products and services—digital Lego blocks, in effect—can be quickly integrated into the gaps. Amazon, for instance, offers businesses logistics, online retail "storefronts," and IT services. For many businesses, it may not pay to build out those functions at competitive levels of performance, so they simply plug an existing offering into their value chains. In the United States, registered investment advisers have been the fastest-growing segment[3] of the investment-advisory business, for example. They are expanding so fast largely because they "insource" turnkey

[2] See Jacques Bughin, "Brand success in an era of digital Darwinism," *Journal of Brand Strategy*, 2014, Volume 2, Number 4, henrystewartpublications.com.
[3] By assets under management and other measures.

systems (including record keeping and operating infrastructure) purchased from Charles Schwab, Fidelity, and others that give them all the capabilities they need. With a license, individuals or small groups can be up and running their own firms.

In the travel industry, new portals are assembling entire trips: flights, hotels, and car rentals. The stand-alone offerings of third parties, sometimes from small companies or even individuals, plug into such portals. These packages are put together in real time, with dynamic pricing that depends on supply and demand. As more niche providers gain access to the new platforms, competition is intensifying.

5. Growing talent mismatches

Software replaces labor in digital businesses. We estimate, for instance, that of the 700 end-to-end processes in banks (opening an account or getting a car loan, for example), about half can be fully automated. Computers increasingly are performing complex tasks as well. "Brilliant machines," like IBM's Watson, are poised to take on the work of many call-center workers. Even knowledge-intensive areas, such as oncology diagnostics, are susceptible to challenge by machines: thanks to the ability to scan and store massive amounts of medical research and patients' MRI results, Watson diagnoses cancers with much higher levels of speed and accuracy than skilled physicians do. Digitization will encroach on a growing number of knowledge roles within companies as they automate many frontline and middle-management jobs based upon synthesizing information for C-level executives.

At the same time, companies are struggling to find the right talent in areas that can't be automated. Such areas include digital skills like those of artificial-intelligence programmers or data scientists and of people who lead digital strategies and think creatively about new business designs. A key challenge for senior managers will be sensitively reallocating the savings from automation to the talent needed to forge digital businesses. One global company, for example, is simultaneously planning to cut more than 10,000 employees (some through digital economies) while adding 3,000 to its digital business. Moves like these, writ large, could have significant social repercussions, elevating the opportunities and challenges associated with digital advances to a public-policy issue, not just a strategic-business one.

6. Converging global supply and demand

Digital technologies know no borders, and the customer's demand for a unified experience is raising pressure on global companies to standardize offerings. In the B2C domain, for example, many US consumers are accustomed to e-shopping in the United Kingdom for new fashions (see sidebar, "How digitization is reshaping global flows"). They have come to expect payment systems that work across borders, global distribution, and a uniform customer experience.

How digitization is reshaping global flows

Jacques Bughin, James Manyika, and Olivia Nottebohm

As the spread of the Internet and digital technologies reshapes the competitive landscape of industries, it is also revolutionizing the traditional flows of goods, services, finance, and people. All this is happening at breakneck pace (exhibit), as we showed in a recent report, *Global flows in a digital age: How trade, finance, people, and data connect the world economy.* The pace will only accelerate as global Internet traffic, which has expanded 18-fold since 2005, surges an additional 8-fold by 2025.

Digitization transforms global flows by vastly reducing marginal production and distribution costs in three ways. The first is the creation of purely digital goods, in both the B2B and B2C realms. The volume of digital consumer goods, from music to movies, transported and reproduced around the globe continues to soar. Apps that allow consumers to purchase virtual goods and digital services on mobile devices have become a significant industry. For businesses, digitization is transforming even physical flows of people into virtual flows, enabling remote work through tools for global collaboration. In some manufacturing sectors, it is now possible to ship a digital design file for 3-D printing and then make the product where it will be consumed instead of producing centrally and shipping the physical goods.

Second, digitization enhances the value of physical flows by the use of "digital wrappers" that pack information around goods as they traverse global value chains. Online reviews or customer ratings, for example, help consumers decide whether to purchase products. Increasingly common digital tags and sensors connected by wireless communications can identify objects and collect information about transactions, the location of a product, and when it is used. Such wrappers greatly improve processes ranging from payment systems to supply-chain management. Imagine Apple trying to assemble the iPod, with 451 parts from many different countries, without digital tracking and supply-chain-management tools.

Finally, digitization is creating online platforms that bring efficiency and speed to production and cross-border exchanges. Proliferating e-commerce platforms allow greater and faster flows of goods and services to new markets and help smaller players participate in expanding global trade. New online markets in information flows facilitate innovation through crowdsourcing, while other platforms let designers upload product designs, use 3-D printers to create physical items, and manage logistics and payments.

Jacques Bughin is a director in McKinsey's Brussels office; **James Manyika** is a director in the San Francisco office and a director of the McKinsey Global Institute; **Olivia Nottebohm** is a principal in the Silicon Valley office.

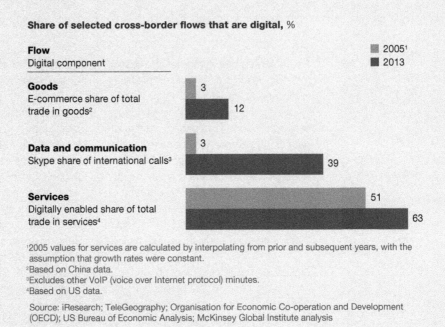

Exhibit

The digital component of global flows is growing quickly.

Share of selected cross-border flows that are digital, %

| Flow
Digital component | | 2005[1]
2013 |

Goods
E-commerce share of total trade in goods[2]
- 3
- 12

Data and communication
Skype share of international calls[3]
- 3
- 39

Services
Digitally enabled share of total trade in services[4]
- 51
- 63

[1]2005 values for services are calculated by interpolating from prior and subsequent years, with the assumption that growth rates were constant.
[2]Based on China data.
[3]Excludes other VoIP (voice over Internet protocol) minutes.
[4]Based on US data.

Source: iResearch; TeleGeography; Organisation for Economic Co-operation and Development (OECD); US Bureau of Economic Analysis; McKinsey Global Institute analysis

In B2B markets from banking to telecommunications, corporate purchasers are raising pressure on their suppliers to offer services that are standardized across borders, integrate with other offerings, and can be plugged into the purchasing companies' global business processes easily. One global bank has aligned its offerings with the borderless strategies of its major customers by creating a single website, across 20 countries, that integrates what had been an array of separate national or product touch points. A US technology company has given each of its larger customers a customized global portal that allows it to get better insights into their requirements, while giving them an integrated view of global prices and the availability of components.

7. Relentlessly evolving business models—at higher velocity

Digitization isn't a one-stop journey. A case in point is music, where the model has shifted from selling tapes and CDs (and then MP3s) to subscription models, like Spotify's. In transportation, digitization (a combination of mobile apps, sensors in cars, and data in the cloud) has propagated a powerful nonownership model best exemplified by Zipcar, whose service members pay to use vehicles by the hour or day. Google's ongoing tests of autonomous vehicles indicate even more radical possibilities to shift value. As the digital model expands, auto manufacturers will need to adapt to the swelling demand of car buyers for more automated, safer features. Related businesses, such as trucking and insurance, will be affected, too, as automation lowers the cost of transportation (driverless convoys) and "crash-less" cars rewrite the existing risk profiles of drivers.

Managing the strategic challenges: Six big decisions

Rethinking strategy in the face of these forces involves difficult decisions and trade-offs. Here are six of the thorniest.

Decision 1: Buy or sell businesses in your portfolio?

The growth and profitability of some businesses become less attractive in a digital world, and the capabilities needed to compete change as well. Consequently, the portfolio of businesses within a company may have to be altered if it is to achieve its desired financial profile or to assemble needed talent and systems.

Tesco has made a number of significant digital acquisitions over a two-year span to take on digital competition in consumer electronics. Beauty-product and fragrance retailer Sephora recently acquired Scentsa, a specialist in digital technologies that improve the in-store shopping experience. (Scentsa touch screens access product videos, link to databases on skin care and fragrance types, and make product recommendations.) Sephora officials said they bought the company to keep its technology out of competitors' reach and to help develop in-store products more rapidly.[4]

Companies that lack sufficient scale or expect a significant digital downside should consider divesting businesses. Some insurers, for instance, may find themselves outmatched by digital players that can fine-tune risks. In media, DMGT doubled down on an investment in their digital consumer businesses, while making tough structural decisions on their legacy print assets, including the divestment of local publications and increases in their national cover price. Home Depot continues to shift its investment strategy away from new stores to massive new warehouses that serve growing online sales. This year it bought Blinds.com, adding to a string of website acquisitions.[5]

[4] See Jason Del Rey, "In-store tech is so hot right now: Sephora acquires fragrance software startup Scentsa," *All Things D*, August 7, 2013, allthingsd.com.
[5] See Shelly Banjo, "Home Depot lumbers into e-commerce," *Wall Street Journal*, April 26, 2014, online.wsj.com.

Decision 2: Lead your customers or follow them?

Incumbents too have opportunities for launching disruptive strategies. One European real-estate brokerage group, with a large, exclusively controlled share of the listings market, decided to act before digital rivals moved into its space. It set up a web-based platform open to all brokers (many of them competitors) and has now become the leading national marketplace, with a growing share. In other situations, the right decision may be to forego digital moves—particularly in industries with high barriers to entry, regulatory complexities, and patents that protect profit streams.

Between these extremes lies the all-too-common reality that digital efforts risk cannibalizing products and services and could erode margins. Yet inaction is equally risky. In-house data on existing buyers can help incumbents with large customer bases develop insights (for example, in pricing and channel management) that are keener than those of small attackers. Brand advantages too can help traditional players outflank digital newbies.

Decision 3: Cooperate or compete with new attackers?

A large incumbent in an industry that's undergoing digital disruption can feel like a whale attacked by piranhas. While in the past, there may have been one or two new entrants entering your space, there may be dozens now—each causing pain, with none individually fatal. PayPal, for example, is taking slices of payment businesses, and Amazon is eating into small-business lending. Companies can neutralize attacks by rapidly building copycat propositions or even acquiring attackers. However, it's not feasible to defend all fronts simultaneously, so cooperation with some attackers can make more sense than competing.

Santander, for instance, recently went into partnership with start-up Funding Circle. The bank recognized that a segment of its customer base wanted access to peer-to-peer lending and in effect acknowledged that it would be costly to build a world-class offering from scratch. A group of UK banks formed a consortium to build a mobile-payment utility (Paym) to defend against technology companies entering their markets. British high-end grocer Waitrose collaborated with start-up Ocado to establish a digital channel and home distribution before eventually creating its own digital offering.

Digital technologies themselves are opening pathways to collaborative forms of innovation. Capital One launched Capital One Labs, opening its software interfaces to multiple third parties, which can defend a range of spaces along their value chains by accessing Capital One's risk- and credit-assessment capabilities without expending their own capital.

Decision 4: Diversify or double down on digital initiatives?

As digital opportunities and challenges proliferate, deciding where to place new bets is a growing headache for leaders. Diversification reduces risks, so many companies are tempted to let a thousand flowers bloom. But often these small initiatives, however innovative, don't get enough funding to endure or are easily replicated by competitors. One answer is to think like a private-equity fund, seeding multiple initiatives but being disciplined enough to kill off those that don't quickly gain momentum and to bankroll those with genuinely disruptive potential. Since 2010, Merck's Global Health Innovation Fund, with $500 million under management, has invested in more than 20 start-ups with positions in health informatics, personalized medicine, and other areas—and it continues to search for new prospects. Other companies, such as BMW and Deutsche Telekom, have set up units to finance digital start-ups.

The alternative is to double down in one area, which may be the right strategy in industries with massive value at stake. A European bank refocused its digital investments on 12 customer decision journeys,[6] such as buying a house, that account for less than 5 percent of its processes but nearly half of its cost base. A leading global pharmaceutical company has made significant investments in digital initiatives, pooling data with health insurers to improve rates of adherence to drug regimes. It is also using data to identify the right patients for clinical trials and thus to develop drugs more quickly, while investing in programs that encourage patients to use monitors and wearable devices to track treatment outcomes. Nordstrom has invested heavily to give its customers multichannel experiences. It focused initially on developing first-class shipping and inventory-management facilities and then extended its investments to mobile-shopping apps, kiosks, and capabilities for managing customer relationships across channels.

Decision 5: Keep digital businesses separate or integrate them with current nondigital ones?

[6] See David Court, Dave Elzinga, Susan Mulder, and Ole Jørgen Vetvik, "The consumer decision journey," *McKinsey Quarterly*, June 2009, mckinsey.com; and Alex Rawson, Ewan Duncan, and Conor Jones, "The truth about customer experience," *Harvard Business Review*, September 2013, hbr.org.

Integrating digital operations directly into physical businesses can create additional value—for example, by providing multichannel capabilities for customers or by helping companies share infrastructure, such as supply-chain networks. However, it can be hard to attract and retain digital talent in a traditional culture, and turf wars between the leaders of the digital and the main business are commonplace. Moreover, different businesses may have clashing views on, say, how to design and implement a multichannel strategy.

One global bank addressed such tensions by creating a groupwide center of excellence populated by digital specialists who advise business units and help them build tools. The digital teams will be integrated with the units eventually, but not until the teams reach critical mass and notch a number of successes. The UK department-store chain John Lewis bought additional digital capabilities with its acquisition of the UK division of Buy.com,[7] in 2001, ultimately combining it with the core business. Wal-Mart Stores established its digital business away from corporate headquarters to allow a new culture and new skills to grow. Hybrid approaches involving both stand-alone and well-integrated digital organizations are possible, of course, for companies with diverse business portfolios.

Decision 6: Delegate or own the digital agenda?

Advancing the digital agenda takes lots of senior-management time and attention. Customer behavior and competitive situations are evolving quickly, and an effective digital strategy calls for extensive cross-functional orchestration that may require CEO involvement. One global company, for example, attempted to digitize its processes to compete with a new entrant. The R&D function responsible for product design had little knowledge of how to create offerings that could be distributed effectively over digital channels. Meanwhile, a business unit under pricing pressure was leaning heavily on functional specialists for an outsize investment to redesign the back office. Eventually, the CEO stepped in and ordered a new approach, which organized the digitization effort around the decision journeys of clients.

Faced with the need to sort through functional and regional issues related to digitization, some companies are creating a new role: chief digital officer (or the equivalent), a common way to introduce outside talent with a digital mind-set to provide a focus for the digital agenda. Walgreens, a well-performing US pharmacy and retail chain, hired its president of digital and chief marketing officer (who reports directly to the CEO) from a top technology company six years ago. Her efforts have included leading the acquisition of drugstore.com, which still operates as a pure play. The acquisition upped Walgreens' skill set, and drugstore.com increasingly shares its digital infrastructure with the company's existing site: walgreens.com.

Relying on chief digital officers to drive the digital agenda carries some risk of balkanization. Some of them, lacking a CEO's strategic breadth and depth, may sacrifice the big picture for a narrower focus—say, on marketing or social media. Others may serve as divisional heads, taking full P&L responsibility for businesses that have embarked on robust digital strategies but lacking the influence or authority to get support for execution from the functional units.

[7] Buy.com was later acquired by Rakuten in July 2010.

Alternatively, CEOs can choose to "own" and direct the digital agenda personally, top down. That may be necessary if digitization is a top-three agenda item for a company or group, if digital businesses need substantial resources from the organization as a whole, or if pursuing new digital priorities requires navigating political minefields in business units or functions.

●   ●   ●

Regardless of the organizational or leadership model a CEO and board choose, it's important to keep in mind that digitization is a moving target. The emergent nature of digital forces means that harnessing them is a journey, not a destination—a relentless leadership experience and a rare opportunity to reposition companies for a new era of competition and growth. ▢

The authors would like to acknowledge the contributions of 'Tunde Olanrewaju and Meng Wei Tan to this article.

Martin Hirt is a director in McKinsey's Taipei office, and **Paul Willmott** is a director in the London office.

The Irish Dairy Board - Case Study

by Olivia Kinch

The Irish Dairy Board - Preparing the Pasture

The EU milk quota regime, which has fuelled growth in the Irish dairy industry since 1984, will be abolished in 2015. The predicted impact this regulatory reform will have on co-operatives such as The Irish Dairy Board (IDB) is momentous. This case explores how the IDB is preparing for the post-2015 era, through the imposition of a business transformation strategy. This strategy is motivated by the IDB's vision of creating "sustainable routes to market" whilst maintaining its grass root focus of providing the optimum level of return for the Irish farmer.

● ● ● ●

'By 2020, we hope to be the world's leading dairy manufacturing company. From 2012 - 2015 we will have invested €200 million across new product development, brand growth, capital expenditure and merger and acquisition activity to achieve our vision of securing sustainable routes to market' – Jeanne Kelly [i].

The year 2010 was a pivotal point in the success story of IDB when it arrived at a strategic crossroad. IDB's options were either to continue on a path of familiarity or reshape the business. IDB's proven success factors of the past would be rendered futile in the dramatically changed post-2015 dairy

Milk Quotas

Milk quotas were introduced in 1984 within the EU with the aim of controlling rising milk production. This quota system is set to be abolished in 2015. According to the Irish Government's Food Harvest 2020 Report, the abolition of milk quotas will result in a 50% increase in output by 2020. IDB is focused on positioning itself to avail of the subsequent growth opportunities that will arise from this regulatory reform.

industry. The IDB AGM of 2010 proved to be its single most important meeting of the last 50 years. The only item on the agenda - the

Irish Dairy Board

abolition of milk quotas. How will IDB prepare for this historic event?

The Establishment of the IDB

The tale of IDB emerges from the proud farming heritage of Ireland. With two thirds of the nation's land being used for agriculture, the natural environment itself provides a significant business opportunity. IDB is a dairy co-operative owned by dairy processors and companies with a direct link to the Irish dairy farmer. Paddy Smith, Minister for Agriculture in 1961, established IDB with a vision of securing the highest return for the Irish dairy farmer. Originally a semi-state organisation by the name of Bord Bainne (Milk Board) [ii], IDB replaced the Butter Marketing Committee following the approval of The Dairy Produce Marketing Act passed by the Oireachtas on 7th May 1961.

IDB emerged in a period where Irish butter was largely denied access into the European Economic Community's (EEC) market and was also subject to import quotas in the UK. Seeking economies of scale and further recognition, IDB centralised the overseas marketing of Irish dairy products. Ireland joined the EEC in 1973 and IDB thus became a limited co-operative, seeking to increase its presence in Continental Europe, beginning by introducing Kerrygold into Germany [iii].

Today, IDB provides scale and scope economies, logistics and distribution expertise, therefore, reducing cost duplication of Irish dairy processors[iv]. Headquartered in Dublin, the IDB boasts over 3,100 employees and has a global footprint in over 90 countries (Appendix 2), positioning itself as one of the oldest and most profitable multinational companies in the Irish market. With annualized sales of over €2 billion, the IDB has attained recognition as Ireland's largest dairy exporter, accounting for 60% of Irish dairy exports[v].

Industry Moo-vements

In recent years, the dairy industry has benefited from strong growth with turnover growing by 1.5% in 2012 to reach €1058.2 million[vi]. IDB's main causes for concern are the changes in the external environment. An inability to thrive in an EU without quotas

iD Irish Dairy Board

will be the very demise of IDB. The dairy industry has become oligopolistic (Appendix 1) in nature with further consolidations resulting in shared dominance between the "Big Four" processor-exporters. These top players consist of Kerry Group plc who lead the market with a 21.7% share, followed by Glanbia plc with 13.4% of the market and The Dairygold Co-operative. As they compete alongside IDB, profitable returns appear widely achievable with demand for dairy products remaining constant[vii].

The instability of the dairy industry is exemplified by the reliance on uncertain agricultural factors, such as weather conditions. Ireland suffered from a particularly wet summer in 2012, resulting in difficult cattle grazing conditions. Consequently, reduced grass growth led to an increased risk of crop disease. On an ongoing basis, IDB faces production challenges beyond its control. Increased awareness of this allows the use of financial instruments to hedge against these risks. IDB, for example, makes use of forward contracts to manage its exposure to foreign exchange risk.

Arguably an additional industrial "force" that heavily influences dairy operations in Ireland is regulation at global, European and domestic level. European level intervention takes the form of policies such as the Common Agricultural Policy (CAP- Appendix 1). Furthermore, global involvement is through Global Trade Policies. The preparation for growth in an era unrestricted by milk quotas is underway, however IDB remains apprehensive. There are fears that the expected increase in milk prices may create a "quota bubble"(Appendix 1) at the expense of dairy farmers, where companies such as IDB can expand their production and take advantage of rising milk prices in the near future. A further consideration is that initially, supply will exceed demand and tumbling prices will require security measures within IDB. With a stated focus on high return for the farmer, relationship management is central to the continued support of the co-operative network as it faces these uncertain fluctuations.

The Irish dairy industry is accredited with being the most sustainable in the world and it

ID Irish Dairy Board

Awards and Accreditations

✓ International Innovation award in ecommerce, 2009.

✓ Irish Exporters Association Exporter of the Year, 2010.

✓ "Best International Marketing" award at the All Ireland Marketing Awards, 2010 for Kerrygold Extra in Germany.

✓ Awarded 2010 Food and Drink Category Winner, Lighter softer butter, by Grocer Magazine.

✓ Product of the Year in Germany, 2011 with Kerrygold Extra.

is imperative that these efforts continue. IDB's status as "the most carbon efficient milk producer in the EU" is one result of Ireland's temperate climate providing abundant rainfall[viii].

In 2012, Bord Bia launched "Origin Green" which focuses on sustainable development in the food and drink industry; IDB was the first dairy company to achieve Origin Green status.

Efficiency, which may be fuelled by both innovation and operational excellence in the Irish dairy industry, is essential as it serves as an engine for economic growth. The industry has been described as the "jewel in the crown" of Ireland's economic recovery and is continually evolving in an attempt to capitalize on Ireland's favourable natural environment for dairy farming[ix].

The Structural Composition of IDB

Following a re-organisation in 2006 to "meet evolving needs of the marketplace" [x], IDB exports dairy products globally through 3 distinct business divisions; Consumer Foods Division, Dairy Trading & Ingredients, and DPI Specialty Foods. Turnover in each of these divisions is fairly balanced (Exhibit 2) with a skewness of 7% attributed to the Consumer Foods Division, largely due to the Kerrygold brand and its annual sales of 350 million packets [.]

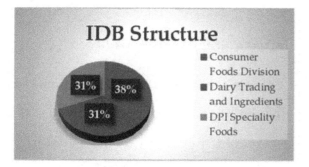

Irish Dairy Board

IDB Structure

- Consumer Foods Division
- Dairy Trading and Ingredients
- DPI Speciality Foods

31% 38% 31%

Exhibit 2- Source: (Annual Report 2012)x

The Consumer Foods Division involves the selling and marketing of a diversified portfolio of brands such as Kerrygold, Pilgrims Choice, MU, Dubliner and Beo (comprising of a variety of butters, cheeses, cow's milk and milk products). Dairy trading and ingredients are concerned with the procurement and the subsequent sale of dairy products to end users. Acquisitions have led to export market expansion within this division - the Thiel Cheese & Ingredients in Wisconsin in 2011 and The Cheese Warehouse in the UK in 2012. Lastly, DPI Specialty Foods division operates as the third largest Irish specialty distributor and logistics company in the US. Its core focus is facilitating geographic expansion for IDB by offering a range of specialty foods distributed to both local and national food retailers [x]. The US distribution environment is classified by cut throat competition as the US consumers' primary concern is value. Consequently, this sector remains a difficult one to operate in. However, in 2012, current CEO Kevin Lane made the call to restructure this division in order to tackle the issues presented by the price-sensitive US market.

IDB's Vision

'The IDB will become a leading global dairy organization, rewarding our customers, consumers and shareholders by delivering value through; Superior Customer Service; Customized Innovation; World Class Brands; An International Market Presence; and Outstanding People.'

(IDB website ,2014)[xi]

The Dawning of a New Era

2010 brought a new strategic vision for IDB and a leader to implement it, Kevin Lane. As it stands, IDB are in a very strong position to make this vision a reality. IDB has an ever increasing foothold in the global dairy

iD *Irish Dairy Board*

industry, and, 'cash in the bank' to further exploit the opportunities presented by the abolition of milk quotas. 17,000 Irish dairy farmers plan to double their milk production between 2015 and 2020 [i].

KEVIN LANE

Appointed as CEO to IDB in 2010. Studied sales and marketing in University of Limerick and then went on to work with Kerry Group. His experience with Kerry Group spans 22 years working in numerous positions and diversified geographical areas including the UK, US, Mexico and Canada. Before joining IDB, he was employed as Global President and Chief Executive of Kerry Group's Flavours division. Lane has been the driving force and leader of the business transformation strategy since joining IDB.

(IDB website, 2014) xi

Business Transformation Strategy

With the hope of achieving their vision, IDB introduced a business transformation strategy in 2010 (Appendix 3). Strategic success was reliant on commitment and enthusiasm. In recognising that this decade will be a transformational growth period for IDB, this strategy has the goal of repositioning IDB in the hope of securing and maximizing long-term gains post – 2015.

Value Added Growth
When a Brand Strikes Gold

Adding value in IDB can be achieved by strengthening its core brands like Kerrygold. Regarded as the foundation of the co-operative and "Ireland's only truly internationally known food brand" [xi], it is available in 50 international markets, holding a top 3 brand position in 27 of these. Despite being a premium butter brand, Kerrygold continually maintains and gains market share in its key export markets, Germany and the US. In 2012, IDB launched Kerrygold UHT milk in China as part of its brand expansion strategy, through partnering with a distribution company, Algrow Trading. This allowed the further global development of the Kerrygold brand. Today, the brand retails at half a billion Euro. Interestingly, IDB is solely responsible for the export of Kerrygold which is lucrative for the group as it begins to explore new markets [i]. Brand strength translates into value added,

Irish Dairy Board

and it is strong brands, like Kerrygold, that will secure the future of IDB.

Creating Brand Value – The Story of Kerrygold

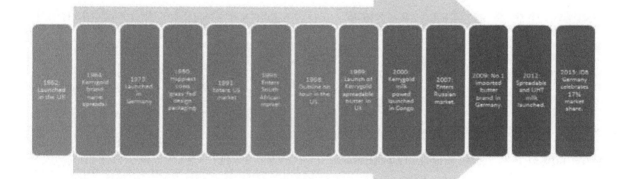

Innovation at the Heart of Success

IDB's group turnover exceeded €2.03billion in 2012, up 2% year on year. This success was aided significantly by the R&D capabilities gained by growing through acquisitions and consolidation. 2010 marked a turning point for capabilities development and innovation for IDB. IDB recognised the potential for growth by gaining greater consumer insight which allows for tailored products in response to consumer profiles. IDB's reaction was an increase in marketing spend and new product development. IDB appointed Fergal McGarry as Global Marketing and Innovation Director in 2012, demonstrating its

iD Irish Dairy Board

determination to establish a successful product mix and innovative ingredients solutions in order to create added value. "We are continuing to leverage our strength in product innovation having experienced a lot of growth around branded innovation" says McGarry[xii].

In relation to new product development, IDB has endeavoured to continually introduce "fresh" product ideas to the market. In 2011, 40 new products were introduced and a significant contribution arose from the acquisition of Thiel Cheese Ingredients in the US. This added new technology, innovation and product applications. In excess of 50 new products hit the market in 2012, among the

new product ranges were MU in the UK and Beo in Sub Saharan Africa. The dairy industry is not a fast moving arena for innovation, therefore incremental advances, such as range extensions, are favourable for IDB.

The approach to innovation is two-fold. Firstly, IDB is continuing to develop new products for its core markets. Secondly, IDB is changing existing products in order to suit its consumers in new and emerging markets.

IDB and Teagasc, Ireland's agriculture and food development programme, have undertaken a Collaborative Cheese Development Programme since 2010. In 2011, this partnership was formalised by the creation of the IDB Dairy Innovation Centre at the

FERGAL MC GARRY

Fergal Mc Garry was appointed Director of Global Marketing and Innovation at IDB in April 2012 for the purpose of increasing innovation activities and facilitating emerging market growth. Mc Garry has gained experience through serving as the Business Unit Director of Europe, Middle East and Africa (EMEA) for Johnson & Johnson where he had been working since 2005. Examples of other senior roles include Managing Director of Ireland and Commercial Director of Nordics. Prior to this he worked for AIB in Dublin and Warner Lambert in Canada. His education is comprised of a BBS degree from Trinity College Dublin and M.Sc. in Business Administration from York University, Canada.

Irish Dairy Board

Teagasc Food Centre, Moorepark, Co. Cork. IDB has gained the "intellectual knowledge" and "technical product expertise" of the Teagasc Research Centre and a technological advancement with the pilot scale, test equipment and manufacturing capacity of Moorepark Technology Ltd. This synergistic relationship has afforded IDB an insight into scientific advances in Irish institutes in exchange for 50 years of experience and routes to market. Kevin Lane states, "The collaboration is one important pillar of the IDB's innovation strategy. We are also developing our internal capabilities and working directly with our members in other specific areas" [xiii]. The Innovation Centre saw some successes in 2012 with the launch of Yogurt Ice Cream at Gulfood, the world's biggest food and hospitality show and the creation of a new powder blend for a customer in Sri Lanka.

In the same year (2012), a €12.7m capital investment was commissioned to replace the IDB's existing Adam's Food Ingredients facility in Leek, Strattfordshire, England with a new 65,000 square foot innovation focused plant. This R&D investment was the final stage in a UK capital development programme of €70m. The innovation centre is focused on developing customised dairy ingredient solutions for the UK and other export markets.

Fergal McGarry undoubtedly has had a positive effect on innovation output. In a 2012 report, IDB cited "building internal NPD capability across IDB group" as a key component of its approach. The group won 6 awards for innovation in the same year. 2012 saw an additional 40% increase in marketing, advertising and promotional spend, with an increased focus on digital media (AR 2012). Recognising the importance of innovation for growth strategy implementation, new product commercialisations continued into 2013 and the product innovation pipeline remains promising.

Irish Dairy Board

Market Expansion
The Strategic Use of Acquisitions

"We see a huge opportunity for branded Irish premium dairy products. Our strategic focus now is all around building new routes to market and further developing those markets that have been the cornerstone to date – the UK, the US and Germany." (Fergal McGarry)

Growth through acquisitions has been the chosen method of expansion to ready the company for 2015 onwards. IDB has acquired food ingredients businesses all over the world, positioning itself to sell Irish dairy produce to food manufacturers in over 90 countries. One such move was the Cheese Warehouse (TCW) acquisition in 2012 which has given IDB an "increased presence in the UK food sector" (AR, 2012). The acquisition of Adams Food Ingredients, a "leading powder specialist blending company", allows the Dairy Trading & Ingredients division access to new market opportunities, and a wider product scope than that of its traditional dairy output.

This increase in international presence has been aided by one of IDB's key strategic capabilities, market selection. Throughout its history IDB has focused on high-growth international markets, from West Germany in the 1970's to, more recently, the Middle East. Recognising the high-growth potential of the MENA region, IDB announced a €20million investment in Saudi Arabia in 2013. In order for an acquisition to be completed, it must make clear strategic sense. The target firm must align with IDB in terms of resources and the subsequent ability to exploit these.

The Cheese Warehouse
The strategic acquisition of TCW took place in 2012 to further strengthen the IDB's growing base in the UK market. TCW both strengthens and compliments IDB's existing cheese business through an increased presence in the UK foodservice; particularly in the growing food manufacturing sector. Lane stated that the acquisition continues the board's long term strategy of creating sustainable routes to market.

Irish Dairy Board

Management have an exceptionally disciplined approach to assess whether or not the target firm is suitable for IDB. Firstly, they must address the issue of price. IDB have a very strict due diligence process in place in order to analyse the price of a target firm. The cost of TCW acquisition was deemed a 'good' price by IDB as it has helped to advance the IDB's goals as well as fitting with its overall strategy. The transaction presented new and significant growth opportunities for IDB in the UK. This is increasingly important in light of the removal of milk quotas in 2015.

'As a result of the acquisition, there was a 9.5% increase in turnover in this particular sector' - Kevin Lane [x].

The UK – Growing with Ireland's lead trading partner

IDB's relationship with the UK continues to be strengthened and reinforced through continuous expansion and growth in the UK dairy industry. Last November, IDB's wholly owned subsidiary, Adams Foods, entered into a long term strategic partnership with First Milk, a UK dairy co-operative. This agreement was seen as 'adding a crucial element to the portfolio on the journey to becoming a complete and added value long term supplier to the critically important UK Market' – Kevin Lane, speaking in November 2013 [xi]. The partnership will reinforce Adams Foods position as one of the leading suppliers of Irish and British cheese in the UK. Additionally, it will establish a fully integrated supply chain for hard cheese across the UK food sector through harnessing complementary resources, skills and resources of both companies [xi].

IDB in the Saudi Sands
Emerging Market Growth

The diversity and dynamism in many emerging markets resists a "one size fits all" strategic approach. However, by targeting clusters within these economies, companies can seize significant growth opportunities. This is precisely what IDB is trying to achieve with its recent €20m investment in Saudi Arabia.

In October 2013, IDB announced a €20 million investment in Saudi Arabia. The investment included the acquisition of a 75% interest in a

iD Irish Dairy Board

dairy importer, sales and distribution business, Al Wazeen Trading. Additionally, this investment involves the development of a new state-of-the-art cheese manufacturing plant at the Al Wazeen Trading facility in Riyadh, the Saudi capital. This investment is an important component of milk quota abolishment preparations. It will provide a central hub to access the important dairy growth markets in the Middle East and North African regions.

The dairy raw material is coming from Ireland and will be manufactured locally. The IDB has researched the market extensively to understand consumer profiles in this particular market. In doing so, IDB is in a position to tailor its offering to suit local consumer needs and tastes.

Commenting on the investment, Kevin Lane states that it is a 'tremendous opportunity' of 'crucial importance' because IDB recognises as a business that it must 'move away from the core existing markets and develop new markets in growing regions where there will be a lot of demand in the future' [xiv].

As the battle for the wallet of the emerging market consumer shifts into higher gear, IDB recognises that thinking about growth at granular level will give it a better chance of success in these markets.

The IDB of 2014 – What Next?

"The future will be about growth" states Kevin Lane, Director Global Marketing and Innovation, IDB [x]. Debt levels increased substantially from 2009 – 2011 (Appendix 4). The most significant rise in debt levels occurred in 2010, due to once-off investments in an Enterprise Resource Planning system and the rollout of a new lean-manufacturing programme, with the aim of reducing costs in the future. With non-current liabilities at a

Why Saudi Arabia?

Dairy is a traditional part of the Middle Eastern diet with a consumption of around 1.2M tonnes in 2011	Due to its naturally dry climate, the Middle East is a milk-deficient region with majority of dairy consumption consisting of imported products	Due to location and free trade agreements, the EU is a leading supplier of dairy products into the Middle East	Total Irish Food and Drink exports to the Middle East in 2011 were valued at €250. Saudi Arabia is the largest regional market for Irish dairy exports accounting for €70M

Irish Dairy Board

peak of €80m, IDB implemented a "new financing model" the following year which decreased its long-term debt by over 80% to just €14m.

2012 saw IDB become virtually free of long-term debt and reduced its total debt by over €120m. This massive reduction in IDB's total debt was its lowest level since 2009, while its operating leverage fell once more below the 50% mark. According to CEO Kevin Lane, this "positions the Group very well for the future growth anticipated" [x].

During the same period, IDB consistently added to its revenue reserves, reaching €378m in 2012[x] from €358m in 2009 [xv]. This increase provides easier access to funds, allowing IDB to make investments at a lower cost. Together with its improved liquidity, as shown by the reduced debt levels, IDB is now in a strong position to capitalise on future opportunities and continue its growth into the future

IDB is well-established in developed markets like North America and the EU. Only 10% of IDB turnover in 2012 was from sales outside these regions. With an estimated 1 billion new consumers in emerging markets by 2020 due to population rises, there is significant room for revenue growth and possible new routes to market for IDB (Exhibit 3).

Exhibit 3.

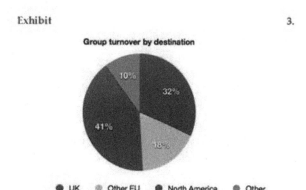

Group turnover by destination

- UK
- Other EU
- North America
- Other

Source: (Lane, 2011) v

The IDB's business transformation strategy has proved successful to date. The structural changes since 2010 have allowed IDB increase its foothold in key markets such as the UK, Germany and US, facilitating in-market expansion. The IDB's vision of becoming the world's leading multinational dairy company to compete with the likes of Fonterra and Alta will only be achieved through creating sustainable routes to market.

The intensity of rivalry in the global dairy industry will increase dramatically with the abolition of milk quotas in 2015. Have IDB

iD Irish Dairy Board

prepared enough to secure a leading industry position? With IDB's growth strategy becoming increasingly focused on emerging markets, is acquisition really the best way for the organisation to grow?

Appendix 1 – Glossary

1. **Oligopolistic** - An industry with few sellers and whose actions have detrimental effects on subsequent prices of competitors.

2. **Common Agricultural Policy (CAP)** - Implemented by the EU which controls agricultural subsidies.

3. **"Quota Bubble"**- Dramatic increase in prices of dairy products due to phenomenal demand. This will have consequences for dairy farmers in the long-run.

Appendix 2 – IDB Export Map

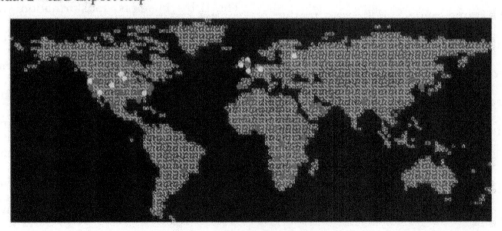

○ *I DB Key Subsidiaries*

● *Sales & Business Development Teams*

Irish Dairy Board

Appendix 3 – IDB's Business Transformation Strategy

Operational Excellence	Value Added Growth	Market Expansion
• Drive for excellence • Focus on cost efficiencies/lean manufacturing • Integration of manufacturing facilities	• Develop more innovative products • Increase marketing spend and investment in our brands and technologies • Significant in-market investment	• Focus on growing new customers • Growth in our core geographies • Accelerate growth in new markets – Russia, Middle East, Africa, China.

Appendix 4 – IDB's Financial Outline

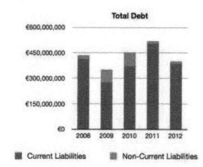
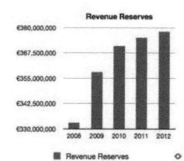
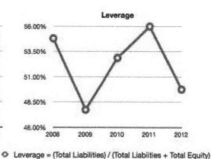

---

[i] Jeanne Kelly, Corporate Communications at Irish Dairy Board (2014). Phone interview 20 February 2014.

[ii] Irish Dairy Board, Food & Drink Export Ireland, IEA (2014)
http://www.exportfoodanddrink.org/index.php/membership/member-profiles/183-irish-dairy-board [Accessed February 10]

[iii] Irish Exporters Association, (2013) The IEA teams up with the Irish Farmers Association to stress the importance of Europe to the Agri-food sector.
http://www.irishexporters.ie/section/TheIEAteamsupwiththeIrishFarmersAssociationtostresstheimportanceofEurope totheAgrifoodsector [Accessed February 5].

[iv] Food and Drink Export Ireland (2014) Irish Dairy Board.
http://www.exportfoodanddrink.org/index.php/membership/member-profiles/183-irish-dairy-board [Accessed February 7]

[v] Lane, K., (2011) Making Profitable Expansion Happen. "The Role of IDB".

[vi] Food and Drink Industry Ireland, Ibec (2014) http://www.fdii.ie/Sectors/FDII/FDII.nsf/vPages/Dairy-industry-overview?OpenDocument [Accessed February 12]

[vii] Irish Dairy Board Co-Operative Limited (2013) Company profile, Marketline.

[viii] IDB Annual Report (2012) pp. 21 http://www.idb.ie/financial/annual-reports [Accessed February 5]

[x] IDB Annual Report (2012) Company profile http://www.idb.ie/financial/annual-reports [Accessed February 5]

[xi] IDB website (2014) http://www.idb.ie/ [Accessed February 5]

[xii] Business & Leadership (2013) Irish Dairy Board - a growing presence on the ground. http://www.businessandleadership.com/exporting/item/43199-irish-dairy-board-a-growi [Accessed Fenruary 15]

[xiii] Teagasc, Agriculture and Food Development Authority. (2011). IDB and Teagasc Team up to Establish New Dairy Innovation Centre. http://www.teagasc.ie/news/2011/201107-04.asp [Accesses February 18]

[xiv] RTE News Radio Source (2013) http://www.rte.ie/news/business/2013/1030/483544-irish-dairy-board/ [Accessed February 10]

[xv] IDB Annual Report (2009) http://www.idb.ie/financial/annual-reports [Accessed February 5]

References

Bord Bainne , **Irish Dairy Board, The Irish Dairy Board Cooperative Ltd**
http://www.bordbia.ie/eventsnews/events/FlavourOfTheFuturePofiles/Irish%20Dairy%20Board.pdf [Accessed **February 10]**

Strategic Management Theory and Practice

March 6 2014

"THANKS... PENNEYS"

Ailbhe Ryan | Chloe Monson | Jill Watkins | Emma Mooney | Jenny Molyneaux

This case study explores Penneys decision to compete in the US market and considers, in light of the company's past experiences, whether or not this strategic choice is sustainable, acceptable and feasible.

Penneys is an essential part of the Irish experience. This much loved Irish institution revolutionised Irish fashion shopping to such an extent that their name has become the automatic response to a compliment. With expansion set in its sights this billion pound organisation is set to have the whole world saying "Thanks... Penneys". Or will they?

No Longer Ireland's Little Secret

Having won the gratitude of shoppers in the UK, Germany, Spain, Portugal, France, Belgium, Austria, Italy and the Netherlands, Penneys are looking to please American customers with their 'cheap chic' clothing.

The first Penneys store opened its doors on Dublin's Mary Street in the summer of 1969. After a chance encounter with Garfield 'Garry' Weston, one of the family owners of Associated British Foods (ABF), Arthur Ryan was poached from Dunnes Stores to set up a discount clothing chain. Within a year, four more stores had been opened in Dublin and in 1973 locations were added in the UK under the moniker Primark; the change of name was made in order to avoid legal problems with the US firm JC Penny.

Since then, Primark has established further locations in the UK and across Europe, successfully establishing themselves as a leader in the fast fashion industry. Their style credentials were confirmed when one of their low cost jackets graced the pages of Vogue. Such is the enthusiasm for their products that more people showed up for their Oxford Street opening than for Topshop's well promoted Kate Moss collection, with the model herself standing in the window. Similarly, each new store opening is met by throngs of people. Today Primark boasts 278 stores and employs 54,000 people across the EU.

The secret of Primark's success can be largely attributed to the low cost of their up-to-the-minute fashion clothing. Much of Primark's products are imitations of top designer lines (a feature of many legal disputes). Their low-cost model means they refuse to spend on advertising, celebrity endorsements, or an online sales platform. They do not even play music in their stores in their efforts to keep costs down. They also recycle all cardboard shipping cartons into their famous brown paper bags and recycle 23 million coat hangers a year; these initiatives are good for the environment and the bottom line. The retailer relies on word of mouth and their 'big bag' policy to promote the brand. They have also recently launched 'Primania', an online forum which allows customers to show off their Primark style. The site receives over 300,000 visits a week, providing the brand with another low cost method of reaching its customers. Primark have a highly efficient supply chain, including a policy of buying large volumes of each garment directly from factories in low-cost economies, particularly in Asia.

> "Everyone would love them to go global, to do a H&M or Indexit. You cannot argue with the success they've had."
>
> Dirk Van Vlaanderen. Jeffries Analyst.[22]

Ryan's vision and work ethic has driven the business to monumental success, earning him the title of "Legendary Retailer,"[1] despite the fact that his fear of being kidnapped made him obsessively reclusive. In 2009, it was announced that Ryan was

Table 1. Primarks financials against those of their European and American competitors

2013	Primark	H&M	Inditex	Gap	New Look
Revenue	4,273	12,621,441	14,203,024	10,323,488	1,484
Operating profit	514	2,176,320	2,607,975	1,373,865	109.8
Income before tax	514	2,11,466	2,592,534	1,388,064	3.1
Net Income	514	1,683,880	2,022,567	818,309	3.4
Cash Flow	**	25	3,266,870	965,349	151.6
Total Assets	2,058,000	6,447,673	11,682,642	5,017,900	1,339.6
Shareholders Fund	**	4,442,000	7,879,742	1,957,550	329.8
Numbers of employees	54,000	116,000	128,300	135,000	**
Number of stores	278	2,936	6,340	1,492	803
Like for like sales growth	5%	0%	3%	2%	-0.7%

*Figures taken from a variety of sources and converted to sterling using Central Bank average 2013 rates
**Comparable figure unavailable

stepping down as Primark's Chief Executive to be replaced by Paul Marchant, who had previously been the organisation's chief operating officer. Ryan remains with Primark as chairman.

In 2014, backed by consistent growth in its existing locations, Marchant announced plans to open ten stores across large urban areas in the North East United States by 2016.

It's All About the Money

Arthur Ryan, when choosing fashion items for the store. admitted that "I only want to make money". The company's financials prove that they have done just that. From the outset, Primark's performance has been outstanding, underpinned by a "value retailing"[2] model of low gross margins and high volumes; known in the trade as "stack 'em high, sell 'em cheap". Within its first year of trading, Primark had generated a turnover of IR£1m[3]. Between then and the mid 1980s, sales grew to £86m from 44 stores in Ireland and the UK. Over the next decade, the number of stores increased by 50%, while sales grew at a considerably faster rate, rising by 240%.

In the face of recession, particularly considering their exposure to two of the worst hit economies of Ireland and Spain, Primark's business model proved resilient. Revenue grew year on year in the period since 2008. Its operating profits have also grown every year since 2011, an impressive result given its rate of expansion into prime urban retail locations.

During the recession, like-for-like sales grew at levels ranging from 3-7%, slightly better than their competitors. By 2009 it was noted that 1 in every 10 UK pounds spent on clothing was spent in Primark.[4] ABF attribute their growth to their buying strategies being closely attuned to customer demands and by updating their lines regularly. Their recent expansion policy has greatly contributed to this success by meeting new customer needs.

Primark's steady performance has brought it to the position where it is now estimated to have a market value of some £19bn, accounting for 80% of ABF's market share.[5]

Message found stitched into a dress purchased in Primark. Source: Newstalk[23]

Save Our Souls

Despite the glittering facade many believe Primark has a dark side. In the summer of 2014 distressing messages purporting to be from garment factory workers were found stitched into clothes in several stores in the UK. The messages read "degrading sweatshop conditions" and "forced to work exhausting hours".[6] The messages are likely to have been a hoax but they point to the underlying suspicions of many that there is no such thing as cheap clothing, it is merely that others pay through their forced labour.

In 2006 Primark joined the Ethical Trading Initiative (ETI) in response to receiving an extremely low score—3.5 out of 20—on the Ethical Index the previous year. The index ranked firms against criteria, such as how workers were treated along the supply chain. Primark scored lower than any other UK retailer and were excoriated for their poor business ethics.[7]

Only a few years later Primark was the target of a BBC undercover documentary that exposed the working conditions at factories in India that were contracted to manufacture clothing for the company. The documentary featured children sewing sequines on a top destined for the firms European stores, among other violations. The programme evoked public outrage that led to protests and boycotts. Primark denied knowledge of these practices and in their attempts to rectify the situation drew upon themselves even more criticism. By withdrawing contracts from the offending firms, thousands of workers were left without any employment. The firms troubles did not stop there.

A further report in 2008 produced by the UK charity War on Want condemned Primark for failing to improve conditions for Bangladeshi garment workers. Workers, they claimed, continued to work exhausting shifts for little pay. This was despite earlier claims by the retailer that supplier audits would prevent such practices occurring. [8]

The problems of poor working conditions were not only discovered in their foreign supply chain. A firm in Manchester that packaged knit-ware for Primark was found to be exploiting illegal immigrants, forcing them to work for less than half the minimum wage.[9] Again Primark was in the headlines for all the wrong reasons.

The worst was yet to come. On 24 April 2013 a building housing five garment factories, the Rana Plaza, in Bangladesh collapsed, killing 1,132 people and injuring more than 2,000. The unsafe building, packed with mostly female garment workers had been audited several times beforehand. Primark was one of the buyers and their clothing was found strewn among the bodies.

The Poster Boy for Child Labour

Primark has fought back. They claim that they have been unfairly made the "poster boy" for child labour and unethical working practices.[10] Their claims are not without foundation. The producers of the BBC Panorama documentary were forced to apologise to the company for using images of children testing beading on vests that were clearly not employees of the garment factory. However, the primary premise that unfair practices existed in supplier firms was not disputed.

More recent reports have also shown Primark in a better light. In 2011 Primark realised that improving the wellbeing of the predominantly female workforce in their supplier factories would increase productivity. They began a programme called HER which selects women to coach their colleagues on healthy practices. Primark was also the first, and for a significant period of time, the only company to provide immediate aid to the victims of the Rana Plaza disaster and their families. Not only did they provide short-term relief, they quickly agreed to discuss long-term compensation arrangements. Indeed, they were one of very few firms to meet with NGOs and government officials to discuss improvements for Bangladeshi workers in the aftermath of the disaster. Primark have also signed a legal accord agreeing to only using suppliers that comply with safety standards. While more could still be done they have been commended for their efforts. Ironically, because of their payment of compensation it is the Primark name that is constantly associated with the disaster in newspaper articles rather than the other firms involved.

Labour behind the Label is an NGO seeking to address low wages for garment workers in the developing world. They do this by encouraging large brands to insist on factory workers receiving a living wage. That is, one that will pay for the essentials in life, such as rent, food and medical treatment. In their 2014 report, Primark does not fair badly when compared to many familiar high-street names. The report remarks "for a company that has a lot to prove, when it says that it is not exploiting its workers by selling things so cheaply, more needs to be done".[11]

Yet the report also recognises the efforts they have made so far. Perhaps it is not Primark that should be in the spotlight but the entire garment industry. The assumption is often made that cheaper brands like Primark are culpable for poor practices but clothing from many higher cost brands are also made in the same environments for the same wages. Primark claim that 98% of their garments are made in the same factories as other, more expensive, high street stores.

**SAME T-SHIRT
SOLD IN**

PENNEYS
€7.50
Mid-market UK
Retailer
£44
Designer Label
£75

Source: The Independent [22]

Whose responsibility is it anyway?

The global apparel industry employ millions of people around the world. Design, branding and marketing, which generates higher value, has predominantly remained in developed countries, whereas manufacturing, which is considered less valuable, has moved in an almost wholesale fashion to low-cost economies. The industry is a "quintessential example of a buyer-driven production chain"[12] as there are power asymmetries between the buyer and supplier.

The shift of manufacturing to emerging economies was facilitated by the liberalisation of global trade regimes—for example the phasing out of the Multifibre Arrangement from the 1970s—allowed for increased exports and imports. Manufacturing in the garment industry is low capital and labour intensive. The availability of cheaper standardised labour in emerging economies enabled the rapid growth of the garment industry in regions of Asia such as Bangladesh.

The shift of production has provided impoverished nations with improved benefits to trade, GDP and employment. Such economies often have not had the infrastructure to provide citizens with opportunities for education or betterment. The garment industry enables these nations to exploit their low labour costs to their advantage. Indeed, a significant proportion of the population are employed in the industry, for example, over 90% in Cambodia.[13] While wages are low they are better than the money earned from other available jobs in those countries. Prospects for sustained economic growth are

> Responsibility to respect human rights "exists independently of States' abilities are/or unwillingness to fulfil their own human rights obligations, and does not diminish these obligations. And it exists over and above compliance with national laws and obligations protecting human rights"[29]

uncertain as they depend upon investor attributes and governmental policies and institutions. However, intensive competition between not only individual suppliers, but also nations, as they seek foreign investment from global brands, it is claimed, has resulted in a "race to the bottom".[14] For example, the extreme competition among Chinese and Mexican suppliers to supply the American apparel market meant that the purchasing power of Mexican workers declined by 28% in the late 1990s as costs were pushed downwards.[15]

In a global industry that is worth over £3 trillion[16], many manufacturing workers earn no-more than £5 a day, often working in substandard conditions. Powerful brands can insist upon rationalisation to ensure manufactures are responsive to cost, quality and speed of delivery. Fast turnarounds complement low prices in the apparel industry and has become a feature of sub-contracting manufacturing. The challenges of meeting short turnaround times at low cost has resulted in long working hours and wages that are often too low to live upon. In addition, the prevalence of short-term contracts makes jobs insecure and workers vulnerable. These can make workers unwilling to report employer misconducts to monitoring groups. Therefore instead of manufacturing jobs acting as a means to exit poverty many have become trapped.

Voice for the Voiceless

NGOs have stepped in to act as a voice to this voiceless workforce. Since the early 1990s they did much to raise awareness of the precarious working conditions faced in low-wage economies. Their aim was to mobilize the customer to put pressure on global brands in order to change practices. There are many examples of their exposing of poor practices, as is witnessed in Primark's case. Their task is not an easy one. Activists for groups such as 'Global

March Against Child Labour' have been murdered as they attempted to expose unethical practices, which makes it difficult to expose international firms.[17] However, when they do manage to expose firms, they can then offer codes of practice and monitoring to firms so that they can be redeemed in their consumers sight. As a consequence of this partnership labour practices have seen some improvement. However, NGOs continue to agitate for further improvements.

Role of Governments

Global brands argue that they are doing their best to bring improvements and to do more would make them uncompetitive. Ultimately, they believe that it is the responsibility of governments, and local suppliers, to set appropriate labour policies. The fact that majority of the 100 global firms outsourcing work to the factories in Rana Plaza refused to take any responsibility is an example of this attitude. [18]However, the underlying threat that apparel businesses may relocate to other countries discourages governments from introducing improved standards. This is why the UN regard businesses as having a responsibility to respect human rights regardless of the legal environment. Yet

without a legal framework, intense competition makes it difficult for firms to act alone.

Primark claim that their "prices are a result of its business model, not cheap labour".[19] While their labour may not be cheaper than that used by others the whole industry appears to be built on cheap labour.

From Paris to Berlin

Primark's European expansion began in Madrid in May 2006. While Britian is considered one of the best shopping destinations in the world domestic growth has been difficult due to market saturation. [20] In 2014 Primark have grown that number to above 65 and are still actively adding to it. The expansion required investing in store locations and distribution depots. European consumers have flocked to their stores, Penneys seem to be meeting an unmet need as consumer's seek fashion within constrained budgets. This seemingly insatiable demand is shaping the sourcing and practices of the firm as they seek to win in a competitive marketplace. As Primark gained confidence the expansion programme acclerated. In 2012, Weston claimed that moving beyond Europe would be an act of hubris.[21] But having learned from their European endeavours, Primark believe they are now ready to go stateside.

Shipping Up To Boston

Primark is entering the world's most attractive market in style. It is taking over the iconic and protected Boston landmark, the former Felienes department store. The doors will open at the end of 2015 and the expectation is that it will create the same buzz with American consumers as it has done with Europeans. Primark are planning to take a small share of the $200bn US clothing market by opening 10 stores in the corridor between Boston and Baltimore. In this region there are strong cultural links to Britain and Ireland, and tastes are more European. The stores will be leased in areas where footfall is already high. Beginning with a capital investment of just under €250m[22], by the end of the current expansion they will have 0.5 million square feet of American retail space.[23]

Best on Price

Jose Luis Martinez de Larramendi was appointed to head the US expansion in 2014 having successfully increased the companies Spanish presence to 39 stores in eight years. A significant feat in the home of their competitor Indexit, the parent of Zara. Primark believe they have an advantage over their US competitors because their stock turns over six times a season compared to the US average of two times. Martinez de Larramendi holds that Primark's efficiency at every level should result in the best price in the market. Primark has conducted intensive price benchmarking against likely competitors as their price positioning sets them apart from other brands targeting young fashion lovers.

Challenges

The American market penetration will challenge Primark. According to a survey conducted by Barclays Bank, the US market is considered the most difficult foreign market to enter, with less than half of UK retailers believe they can achieve commercially.[24] At first Primark will supply the new market from existing suppliers in Asia, although they will need to develop new distribution channels quickly. In order to maintain the low cost model Primark will need to create a new supply chain nearer to this new market. The company are hoping to develop relationships with suppliers in Guatemala and Mexico. Building these relationships could take time. Central to that low-cost business model is keeping advertising costs to a minimum. This strategy may in fact, be a disadvantage in a marketplace where the brand is unknown. However, Boston is a university town, and so their social media, and word-of-mouth strategy may work effectively there. Primark's attempt to break into the US market comes on the back of British retail failures. Success has alluded a long list of high-street brands such as Marks and Spencer, Tesco, Sainsburys, Laura Ashley, HMV and WH Smith. There have been some successes however.

The British young fashion retailer Topshop has gained market share. But so too have Primark's other European competitors Zara and H&M. While their success should bolster Primark's chances, their presence does add to an already highly competitive market. There is a broad spectrum of competitors ranging from K-Mart, Walmart and Target at discount store end to Forever 21 at the fast-fashion end.

It is uncertain if the competencies that Primark have developed to create their European success will be transferable to the American market. Much of their success has hinged on their supply chain configuration and their knowledge of Asian suppliers. Developing knowledge about

low-cost South American suppliers will take time. There is also concern that Primark's success with their 'recession chic' will fade as the global economy recovers, thus threatening their Pan-European expansion plans. However, retail analysts seem unconcerned about these issues, "I would be extremely surprised if they didn't succeed in the US".[25]

Treasure Hunting in the US

Primark's low-cost offerings are in line with current American consumer demand. BCG Consumer Sentiment Barometer Spring 2011 shows that American consumers spending is trending towards seeking value for money and saving. Paradoxically, the report showed a growth in conscientious consumption and 'treasure hunting' a euphemism for seeking out low-cost goods.[26] Surveys have revealed that 42% of American's have penalised firms that engage in unethical behaviour.[27] Primark's CSR policies will need to be perceived as credible if they want to succeed in America. Only time will tell if Primark will conquer the US marketplace and if the desire for low-cost goods will continue into the future.

As Primark expands globally, with new customers and new suppliers, and as the global economy shows signs of recovery will the whole world be saying "Thanks... Penneys!"?

References

The material for this case has been drawn from a wide range of sources.

[1] Draper Magazine, (2010) 'Most Influential Man in High Street Fashion', online. Available at: http://www.drapersonline.com/people/people-moves/next-generation/drapers-next-generation-retail-is-in-the-blood/5047687.article Accessed 10/12/14

[2]ABF (2008) 'ABF Annual Report', online. Available at: http://www.abf.co.uk/investorrelations/reports Accessed: 13/11/14

[3] ABF 2008 [as 2].

[4] McDougall, D. (2008) 'The hidden face of Primark fashion', *The Guardian.* online. Available at: http://www.theguardian.com/world/2008/jun/22/india.humanrights Accessed: 15/12/14

[5] Daneshkhu, S. (2014) 'Primark sales leap as ABF dismisses any online operations', *The Financial Times.* Available at: http://www.ft.com/intl/cms/s/0/86e8438e-0849-11e4-9380-00144feab7de.html#axzz3SxV3kNEn Accessed: 4/10/14

[6] Dearden, L. (2014) 'Primark denies forced labour allegations as more 'cry for help' labels emerge', *The Independant.* online. Available at: Accessed: 25/09/14

[7] Lee, M.M.H. (2011) 'Reacting to bad publicity over sweat shop issue: the case of Primark'. *Journal of International Management.* online. Available at: https://journalofinternationalmanagement.wordpress.com/2011/05/16/reacting-to-bad-publicity-over-sweat-shop-issue-the-case-of-primark/ Accessed: 25/10/2014

[8] War on Want. (2008) 'Fashion victims II: How UK clothing retailers are keeping workers in poverty'. online. Available at: http://www.waronwant.org/campaigns/supermarkets/fashion-victims/inform/16360-fashion-victims-ii Accessed: 12/11/14

[9] Dhariwal , N. (2009) 'Primark linked to UK sweatshops' BBC News. Available at: http://news.bbc.co.uk/2/hi/uk/7824291.stm Accessed: 11/11/14

[10] Sweney, M. (2011) 'Primark legal chief claims BBC made firm 'poster boy of child labour', *The Guardian.* online. Available at: http://www.theguardian.com/media/2011/jun/16/bbc-primark-child-labour Accessed: 23/10/14

[11] Clean Clothes Campaign. (2014) 'Tailored Wages', *Clean Clothes.* online. Available at: http://www.cleanclothes.org/livingwage/tailoredwages/tailored-wage-report-pdf Accessed 19/12/14

[12]'Gereffi, G., and Frederick, S. (2010) 'The global apparel value chain, trade and the crisis : challenges and opportunities for developing countries, Volume 1', *The World Bank.* online. Available at: http://millenniumindicators.un.org/unsd/trade/s_geneva2011/refdocs/RDs/Apparel%20Industry%20and%20Crisis%20(Gereffi%20-%20Apr%202010).pdf Accessed: 21/11/14

[13] International Labour Office, 2005. 'Better Factories Cambodia, Facts and Figures', *ILO*

[13] Clean Clothes Campaign, 2014. [as 10].

[15] Hasmath, R. and Hsu, J. (2007) "Big Business, NGOs and Labour Standards in Developing Nations: A Critical Reflection", *Asian Journal of Social Policy 3(1): 1-16.*

[16] Martin, M. (2013) 'Creating Sustainable Apparel Value Chains', *Impact Economy.* online. Available at:

[17] McDougall, D. (2008) 'The hidden face of Primark fashion', *The Guardian.* online. Available at: http://www.theguardian.com/world/2008/jun/22/india.humanrights Accessed: 15/12/14

[18] Clean Clothes Campaign & International Labour Rights Forum. (2013) 'Still Waiting: Six months after history's deadliest apparel industry disaster, workers continue to fight for compensation', online. Available at: http://www.cleanclothes.org/resources/publications/still-waiting Accessed 5/12/14.

[19] Evens, P. (2014) 'U.K. 'Cheap Chic' Chain Prepares to Make an Entrance in U.S.' *The Wall Street Journal.* online. Available at: http://www.wsj.com/articles/u-k-s-primark-gears-up-to-make-an-entrance-in-u-s-1414083964 Accessed: 9/10/14

[20] Barclays. (2013) 'The Global High Street: Opportunities for Retail', online. Available at: http://www.barclayscorporate.com/content/dam/corppublic/corporate/Documents/research/the-global-high-street.pdf Accessed: 12/12/14

[21] Murray, C. (2012) 'UPDATE 2-Primark to continue European expansion', *Reuters.* online. Available at: http://www.reuters.com/article/2012/11/06/abfoods-primark-idUSL5E8M633A20121106 Accessed 12/12/14.

[22] Clarkson, A. (2014) 'Penneys sets its cap at the $200bn US clothing market', *The Independant.* online. Available at: http://www.independent.ie/business/irish/penneys-sets-its-cap-at-the-200bn-us-clothing-market-30460604.html Accessed: 12/11/14

[23] ABF (2014) 'ABF Annual Report 2014'. online. Available at: http://www.abf.co.uk/documents/pdfs/2014/2014_abf_annual_report_and_accounts.pdf Accessed: 15/11/14

[24] Barclays 2013. [as 20].

[25] Evans, P. (2014) [as 19].

[26] Boston Consulting Group. (2011) 'Consumer Sentiment 2011: 'Navigating the New Consumer Realities', Available at: http://www.bcg.com/documents/file79398.pdf Accessed: 12/1/15

[27] International Institute for Sustainable Development. (2015) 'Corporate Social Responsibility Monitor'. *International Institute for Sustainable Development.* online. Available at: https://www.iisd.org/business/issues/sr_csrm.aspx Accessed: 02/02/15

[28] Newstalk (2014) 'Penneys asks girl who found 'forced to work' label inside dress to return it', *Newstalk.* online. Available at: http://www.newstalk.com/Pennys-asks-girl-who-found-forced-to-work-label-inside-dress-to-return-it Accessed: 2/12/14

[29] United Nations (2011) 'Guiding Principals on Business and Human Rights Implementing the United Nations "Protecting, Respect and Remedy" Framework. *United Nations.*

Theme 3

Modes of Organising

MIT

Massachusetts
Institute of Technology

Spring 1999

Volume 40
Number 3

Jay B. Barney

How a Firm's Capabilities Affect Boundary Decisions

Reprint 40313

How a Firm's Capabilities Affect Boundary Decisions

Jay B. Barney

Under certain conditions, a firm's capabilities and those of its potential partners can influence boundary decisions.

Jay B. Barney is professor and Bank One chair of corporate strategy at Fisher College of Business, The Ohio State University.

In a world of corporate refocusing, downsizing, and outsourcing, a critical strategic decision that many senior managers make is determining their firm's boundary. "Which business activities should be brought within the boundary of the firm?" and "Which business activities should be outsourced?" are essential strategic questions in determining a firm's boundary. Firms that bring the wrong business activities within their boundaries risk losing strategic focus and becoming bloated and bureaucratic. Firms that fail to bring the right business activities within their boundaries risk losing their competitive advantages and becoming "hollow corporations."[1]

Fortunately, a well-developed approach exists for determining a firm's boundary. Called *transactions cost economics,* this approach specifies the conditions under which firms should manage a particular economic exchange within their organizational boundary as well as the conditions under which it should be outsourced.[2] Not only is this approach well developed, it is remarkably simple, and many of its predictions and prescriptions have received empirical support.[3] Indeed, in its most popular version, this approach requires managers to consider only a single characteristic of an economic exchange — the level of transaction-specific investment — in order to decide whether to include an exchange within a firm's boundary. To date, the simplest conclusion one can make about transactions cost economic analysis of firm boundaries is that it seems to work.

So, in the face of this well-developed, empirically robust approach, why try to develop some new ideas about the best way to determine a firm's boundary? When I explain transactions cost economics to practicing managers and help them implement it, they often ask: "What role do firm capabilities play in this approach to firm boundaries?" To their great surprise, the answer to this question is: "Very little." Transactions cost economics does not focus on the capabilities of a firm or on the capabilities of its potential partners when deciding which economic exchanges to include within a firm's boundary and which to outsource.

Managers are often mystified by this response. "After all," they argue, "isn't the reason we make boundary choices simply an effort to discover the best way to gain access to the capabilities we need to be successful? And aren't some firms simply better at doing some things than we are? Shouldn't these differences have an impact on whether to outsource a particular exchange?"

In transactions cost economics, governance is the mechanism through which a firm manages an economic exchange.

I agree with these managers — the capabilities possessed by a firm and by its potential partners often should have a significant impact on boundary decisions. This paper describes the conditions under which a firm's decisions about how to manage its business activities should be affected by its capabilities and those of its potential partners. When these conditions hold — conditions that I argue are particularly common in rapidly evolving high-technology industries — firms should make boundary decisions that differ significantly from what would be suggested by traditional transactions cost analyses.

I begin by briefly summarizing transactions cost economics as applied to a firm's boundary decisions. Then I discuss the conditions under which capability considerations should figure prominently in those

decisions. Finally, I discuss whether these conditions are common, and thus how frequently transactions cost logic must be augmented by the capability logic presented here. I suggest that these conditions are not ubiquitous, but occur more frequently in certain industries, including rapidly evolving high-technology industries.

Transactions Cost Analyses of Boundary Decisions

Three concepts aid in understanding transactions cost economics as applied to firm boundary decisions: governance, opportunism, and transaction-specific investment.

In transactions cost economics, governance is the mechanism through which a firm manages an economic exchange. These mechanisms can be grouped into three broad categories: market governance, intermediate governance, and hierarchical governance.

• Firms use *market governance* to manage an exchange when they interact with other firms at arm's length across a nameless, faceless market and rely primarily on market-determined prices to manage an exchange. For example, oil refineries use market governance to gain access to crude oil purchased on the spot market; electronics firms use market governance to obtain standardized electrical components from component distributors; and food processors use market governance when purchasing food from farmers and food brokers.

• Firms use *intermediate governance* when they use complex contracts and other forms of strategic alliances, including joint ventures, to manage an exchange. For example, retail firms use intermediate governance to obtain products by negotiating long-term supply contracts with suppliers, by establishing electronic data interchange linkages with those suppliers, and when those suppliers locate critical operations near a retail firm's headquarters. Firms use intermediate governance when partnering to form a joint venture and when they use complex franchise agreements to manage an exchange. In all these cases, more complex contractual forms of governance replace independent arm's-length market relations.

• Firms use *hierarchical governance* when they bring an exchange within their boundary. For example, a manufacturing firm uses hierarchical governance when it owns and operates a factory supplying the products that it sells. A retail firm uses hierarchical governance when it owns and operates its own stores. A diversified firm uses hierarchical governance when it operates a sales and distribution network that two or more of the businesses it owns use to sell and distribute their products. In these cases, the parties to an exchange are no longer independent. Rather, some third party ("the boss") has the right to direct actions and decision making.

According to transactions cost logic, firms can use governance to mitigate the threat of opportunism.

In choosing how to govern an exchange, a firm determines its boundary. All exchanges managed through market and intermediate forms of governance are outside the boundary of the firm, and all exchanges managed through hierarchical forms of governance are within the boundary of the firm. According to transactions cost economics, managers determining their firm's boundary must constantly ask themselves: "Given the attributes of this exchange, what is the most efficient way to govern it?"

Transactions cost economics suggests that two issues are relevant when answering this question: the cost of a governance mechanism and the threat of opportunism in an exchange. In general, the more elaborate the governance, the more costly the governance.[4] Thus, the cost of using market governance to manage an exchange is less than the cost of using intermediate governance to manage it. In turn, the cost of using intermediate governance to manage an exchange is less than the cost of using hierarchical governance. If minimizing the cost of governance were the only goal, managers would always choose nonhierarchical forms of governance over hierarchical forms of governance, and they would always narrowly draw the boundary of their firm.

However, managers also must consider the threat of opportunism in an exchange. *Opportunism* exists when a party to an exchange takes unfair advantage of other parties to that exchange. For example, if a firm promising high-quality supplies instead delivers low-quality goods, it is behaving opportunistically. If a firm is consistently late in delivering a promised

product or service or charges a price higher than originally promised, it is being opportunistic.

But when will firms in an exchange be tempted to behave opportunistically? Transactions cost economics suggests that when one party to an exchange has made a large *transaction-specific investment* in that exchange, other parties to that exchange have a strong incentive to behave opportunistically. A transaction-specific investment is any investment that is significantly more valuable in a particular exchange than in any alternative exchange. For example, suppose that an oil pipeline company has built a pipeline from an oil field to supply an oil refinery owned by a second firm. Presumably, this pipeline is valuable if it is used to pump crude oil to the refinery. What is its value if it does not pump crude oil? Assuming there are no other refineries that could be supplied by the pipeline, the value of the pipeline drops significantly if it is not supplying this one refinery. Thus, this pipeline is a transaction-specific investment, since its value in a particular transaction is much greater than its value in alternative transactions.

The threat of opportunism exists when one party to an exchange has made a transaction-specific investment, while others have not made such an investment. Continuing with the pipeline example, suppose the refinery has alternative supplies of crude oil. If the refinery is not receiving crude oil through the pipeline, its value remains almost unchanged. The firm owning the refinery has not made a transaction-specific investment. In this setting, the refinery could demand that the pipeline company reduce the price of its crude oil, increase the quality of the crude it is delivering, or share in some upgrade expenses in the refinery. The pipeline company would have few alternatives but to do what the refinery asked. Because the pipeline firm made a transaction-specific investment and the refining firm did not make such an investment, the refining company could behave opportunistically.

According to transactions cost logic, firms can use governance to mitigate the threat of opportunism. In general, the more elaborate the governance mechanism, the more effective it will be in reducing the threat of opportunism created by transaction-specific investment. Thus, when high levels of transaction-specific investment characterize exchanges, the high cost of hierarchical governance is offset by its ability to reduce the threat of opportunism. When moderate levels of transaction-specific investment characterize exchanges, intermediate governance can reduce the threat of opportunism without the extra cost of hierarchical governance. Exchanges characterized by low levels of transaction-specific investment are not prone to opportunism, so firms should opt for the least costly form of governance available — market governance.

Firm capabilities do not play a significant role in traditional transactions cost analyses of boundaries.

Notice that in this entire discussion, never once do questions about the relative capabilities of a firm and its exchange partners arise. Firm capabilities simply do not play a significant role in traditional transactions cost analyses of firm boundaries.

Capability Considerations in Boundary Decisions

Now, suppose a firm finds that it does not possess all the capabilities it needs to be successful. In this setting, a firm has three ways it can gain access to the capabilities it needs.

• It can cooperate with firms that already possess the capabilities it needs. Here, a firm uses market or intermediate governance to gain access to these capabilities.

• It can try to develop these capabilities on its own. This is an example of using hierarchical governance to gain access to these capabilities.

• It can try to acquire another firm that already possesses these capabilities. This is another form of using hierarchical governance to gain access to capabilities.

Transactions cost logic suggests that the choice among these alternatives should depend on the level of transaction-specific investment required to gain access to the capabilities a firm needs. If required transaction-specific investment is high, then market and intermediate governance approaches to gain access to these capabilities should be abandoned in favor of hierarchical forms of governance. In this setting, firms should either develop the necessary capa-

bilities on their own, or they should acquire another firm that already possesses these capabilities.

But, what if these hierarchical approaches to gaining access to capabilities are themselves costly? In this setting, the decision about how to gain access to the capabilities that the firm needs does not depend only on the required level of specific investment, but also on the cost of developing these capabilities and on the cost of acquiring another firm that already possesses them. Indeed, when the costs of hierarchical governance are high, a firm might want to choose nonhierarchical approaches to gain access to needed capabilities even if there are significant transaction-specific investments — and thus significant threats of opportunism — associated with this approach.

Consider a firm that needs a distribution network in a foreign country in order to grow its business in that country. Suppose that such a distribution network already exists, but that another firm owns it. Using this other firm's distribution network may require high levels of transaction-specific investment, which could lead to opportunism in the future. This suggests that, other things being equal, this firm would prefer not to use the other firm's network to grow its business. However, other things are not always equal. If the cost to this firm of building a new distribution network in this foreign country is high and if it is not possible to acquire the firm that owns this distribution network,[5] then cooperating with this firm through intermediate or market governance to access the distribution network may be preferred over any alternatives. Opportunism stemming from transaction-specific investment is simply part of the cost of gaining access to capabilities that are too costly to obtain in alternative ways.[6]

Thus, for capabilities to play a significant role in determining a firm's boundary, it must be costly for a firm to create these capabilities on its own, and it must be costly for a firm to acquire another firm that already possesses these capabilities.

Creating Capabilities

There are numerous reasons why it might be costly for a firm to create a particular capability on its own.[7] Four important reasons are:

• The ability to create a capability in a cost-effective way may depend on unique historical conditions that no longer exist.

- The creation of a capability may be "path dependent."
- A capability may be socially complex.
- The actions that a firm would need to take to create a capability may not be fully known.

Historical Context. Sometimes a firm's ability to create capabilities in a cost-effective way depends on being in the "right place at the right time." Years later or under different circumstances, recreating certain opportunities may be impossible.

Caterpillar, for example, was able to create at low cost a worldwide service and support network for its heavy construction equipment business because it was the major supplier of this equipment to Allied forces during World War II. The Allies agreed to subsidize the creation of this service and support network because it was essential for the war effort and no similar firm had this type of network.

Being the only heavy construction equipment firm with such a network in place, Catepillar had an enormous competitive advantage immediately after the war. Moreover, for competing firms to create this same kind of network at the same low cost as Caterpillar, the unique conditions that had existed for Caterpillar during World War II would have had to be recreated. Obviously, this was not possible. Now, even though international overnight air freight services have rendered Caterpillar's traditional service and support network less important than at the end of World War II, the firm continues to enjoy the competitive head start it received by being in the "right place at the right time" in history.[8]

Path Dependence. Sometimes to create a particular capability, a firm must go through a long, difficult learning process. When no way to short-circuit this learning process exists, it is said to be *path dependent*. While other firms may want to create path-dependent capabilities for themselves, they must first go through the experiences that make it possible to develop those capabilities. This can be a time-consuming process that greatly increases the cost of creating a capability.

Consider, for example, the capability that some Japanese firms have to work cooperatively with their suppliers. Many U.S. manufacturers have coveted these capabilities to gain access to the low-cost, high-quality supplies that seem to be available to at least

some Japanese firms. However, quick creation of these capabilities among many U.S. manufacturers has been elusive. This difficulty is understandable when it is recognized that many Japanese firms have been working with the same network of suppliers for over 500 years. The experience that develops over 500 years is costly to create in a short period of time.[9]

Social Complexity. Sometimes it will be costly for a firm to create a particular capability because that capability is socially complex in nature. Examples of these socially complex firm capabilities include a firm's culture, its reputation among customers and suppliers, its trustworthiness, and so forth. These kinds of capabilities can enable a firm to pursue valuable business and corporate strategies. Firms without these capabilities may find it difficult to conceive of, let alone implement, these same strategies.

Socially complex capabilities are generally beyond the ability of managers to change in the short term.

However, even though the value of these capabilities may be known, it may still be difficult for a firm without them to create them. Socially complex capabilities are generally beyond the ability of managers to change in the short term. Rather, they evolve and change slowly over time.

Consider, for example, the economic performance of the "visionary" firms identified by Collins and Porras.[10] These well-known firms — including General Electric, Hewlett-Packard, Johnson & Johnson, Merck, Sony, Wal-Mart, and Disney — are organized around unique visions of their roles in the economy, their responsibilities to their customers and suppliers, and their commitment to their employees. These socially complex visions have profoundly affected the decisions made by these firms and the strategies they have pursued. Moreover, these firms have provided much higher returns to shareholders than competitors that do not have such socially complex visions.[11] Despite the well-documented success of these firms over many decades, many of their competitors have been unable to create their own unique visions and generate the same level of economic performance. When capabilities are socially complex — as the visions of these high-performing firms are — it can be difficult to create them.

Possessing invisible assets can enable a firm to create certain kinds of capabilities.

Causal Ambiguity. Finally, sometimes it is not clear which actions a firm should take to create a particular capability. When the relationship between actions a firm takes and the capabilities it creates is causally ambiguous, it can be difficult to create a particular set of capabilities.

Causal ambiguity about how to create capabilities exists whenever there are multiple competing hypotheses about how to create those capabilities and when these hypotheses cannot be tested. These conditions are particularly likely when the sources of a firm's capabilities are taken-for-granted, unspoken, and tacit attributes of a firm. Such organizational attributes have been described as "invisible assets."[12]

Possessing invisible assets can enable a firm to create certain kinds of capabilities. However, when the assets needed to create capabilities are invisible, it can be difficult for firms seeking to create these capabilities to know what they should do to create them. As long as multiple competing hypotheses about what a firm needs to do to create particular capabilities exist, a condition of causal ambiguity prevails, and firms cannot be sure what they must do to create them. Not knowing what to do to create a set of capabilities increases the difficulty of creating them.

Acquiring Capabilities

If firms cannot create capabilities on their own, they can still use hierarchical governance to gain access to those capabilities by acquiring other firms that already possess them. However, sometimes it can be costly to use acquisitions to gain access to capabilities. This can happen for at least five reasons:[13]

• There may be legal constraints on an acquisition.
• An acquisition may reduce the value of the capabilities that are held in the acquired firm.
• An acquisition can be costly to reverse if it turns out not to be valuable.
• There may be substantial "unwanted baggage" inextricably bound with the desired capabilities in the acquired firm.
• Leveraging acquired capabilities throughout an acquiring firm can be costly.

Legal Constraints on Acquisitions. Efforts to acquire a firm for its capabilities can be foiled by antitrust and local ownership restrictions.

For example, several years ago, Microsoft wanted to purchase Intuit, which had developed and marketed the most successful home accounting software on the market — Quicken. Undoubtedly, this acquisition would have benefited Microsoft, assuming it could have negotiated a reasonable price. Microsoft would have gained access to Intuit's programming capability, its installed base of users, and its reputation in the home accounting software market. However, this acquisition did not pass antitrust scrutiny, and Microsoft had to find another approach for entering this market.[14]

For political reasons, nations can restrict foreign ownership of domestic firms, making it illegal for a nondomestic firm to acquire a domestic firm. If a domestic firm possesses capabilities that a nondomestic firm needs and a nondomestic firm is unable to develop these capabilities on its own, it will have to find some alternative to acquisition to gain access to those capabilities.

Effect on the Value of Capabilities. Sometimes the acquisition of a firm can reduce the value of the capabilities that are being sought. Consider, for example, Publicis, the French advertising agency. One of this firm's greatest assets was its long-term contracts with several large French companies, many of which were at least partially owned by the French government. These clients strongly preferred working with a French advertising agency. If, during the consolidation of the international advertising industry in the late 1980s and early 1990s, Publicis had been acquired by, say, a U.S. advertising agency, the very thing that the U.S. agency may have been trying to purchase — Publicis' relationship with large French companies — would have been jeopardized. In this context, a firm interested in gaining access to Publicis' capabilities would have to find an alternative to acquisition, since the act of acquiring Publicis would have reduced the value of the capabilities being sought. Ultimately, Publicis entered into a strategic alliance with Foote, Cone & Belding, rather than be acquired.[15]

Strategic Flexibility and Uncertainty. Under conditions of high market uncertainty, a firm may not know what capabilities are needed for long-term success. In this situation, it has a strong incentive to maintain its flexibility, so it can move quickly to develop the required capabilities after uncertainty is resolved.

In an uncertain environment, acquiring another firm to gain access to its capabilities is a less flexible governance choice than, say, using intermediate or market governance to gain access to those capabilities. One firm may acquire another only to discover that the capabilities it was seeking are not valuable. As a result, this firm may have to sell the newly acquired firm. On the other hand, if a firm had used intermediate or market governance to gain access to these capabilities, the cost of withdrawing from that form of governance would have been much lower than the cost of selling an acquisition.

Under conditions of high uncertainty, firms prefer to gain access to another firm's capabilities through strategic alliances.

Indeed, empirical research strongly suggests that, under conditions of high uncertainty, firms prefer to gain access to another firm's capabilities through strategic alliances (as forms of intermediate governance) rather than through acquisitions.[16] Only after this uncertainty is resolved do firms use acquisitions to gain access to capabilities.

Unwanted "Baggage" and Diffused Capabilities.
Firms are bundles of capabilities that are often difficult to disentangle from each other. Rarely are desired capabilities conveniently located in a single division or group. Rather, they are often spread globally across multiple individuals, divisions, and groups. Such diffused capabilities cannot be easily extracted from their operating environments. In this setting, to gain access to a particular capability possessed by another firm through an acquisition, that entire firm may have to be acquired.

Whenever an entire firm is acquired, both desirable and undesirable capabilities are acquired. In principle, the problem of acquiring unwanted capability "baggage" can be solved by spinning off those parts of the acquired firm that are not important to the acquiring firm. However, when a firm's capabilities are diffused throughout its organization, it may be impossible to separate the desirable from the undesir-

able, the core from the baggage. In this setting, acquiring the baggage to access important capabilities significantly increases the cost of acquisition.

Leveraging Acquired Capabilities. Even if none of these other problems exists, acquiring another firm to gain access to its capabilities can still be costly. This is because it is often difficult to leverage the acquired capabilities across the relevant parts of the acquiring firm's operations.

Research indicates that most acquisitions fail.[17] By far the most important reason for this failure is the inability of acquiring firms to take full advantage of newly acquired capabilities. Integration difficulties stem from differences in culture, systems, approach, and so forth. Such differences raise the cost of using acquisitions to gain access to capabilities.

Bringing Capabilities into Boundary Decisions

Thus, when the cost of using hierarchical governance to gain access to capabilities is high, a firm may prefer using nonhierarchical governance for this purpose, even if the threat of opportunism is real. Opportunism is simply part of the cost of gaining access to the special capabilities controlled by another firm that cannot be developed internally or accessed through acquisition in a cost-effective way.[18] A firm seeking capabilities it needs for success must weigh the cost of any opportunism that might arise through gaining access to these capabilities via nonhierarchical means against the cost of gaining access to these capabilities through hierarchical forms of governance. Under-standing the conditions under which capabilities are costly to gain access to through hierarchical governance thus becomes an important determinant of a firm's boundary choices.

Prevalence of These Exchange Conditions

At this point, a careful reader is probably asking: "So what?" This discussion is only relevant if the conditions under which it is costly to use hierarchical governance to gain access to capabilities actually exist in some industries. If these conditions are rare, the issues raised here are managerially irrelevant. However, I believe that these conditions are not uncommon. In fact, in rapidly evolving high-technology industries they are quite common. Examples of such industries include biotechnology, microelectronics, and certain sectors of computer software.

Costliness of Creating Capabilities

Capabilities in these industries are often costly to create. History matters in these industries, and technology trajectories of different firms are highly path dependent. For example, biotechnology firms that want to manufacture on a large scale must almost certainly first learn how to manufacture in small batches. Firms that want to write complex software must have, first, the ability to write software modules within these complex programs and, second, the ability to continuously integrate these modules to create their software products. There is no known way to short-circuit these path-dependent capability development processes.[19]

Firms in these industries also rely on socially complex capabilities to pursue strategic objectives. Research in the pharmaceutical industry, for example, suggests that some firms are highly skilled at integrating product development efforts across multiple scientific disciplines, whereas other firms are less skilled in this way.[20] These socially complex capabilities are costly for firms to create on their own.

Finally, given the uncertainty in these industries, there can be causal ambiguity about how to develop capabilities that are critical to success. Often, this is due to the underdeveloped scientific knowledge that underpins these industries. For example, biotechnology firms often have difficulty replicating their own successful manufacturing efforts, let alone providing guidance to other firms on how to develop manufacturing capabilities.[21] This lack of scientific knowledge, together with the thousands of small decisions that make up some of the core processes in these industries, leads to high levels of causal ambiguity. When firms cannot know definitively what they should do to build capabilities, internal development can be costly.

Costliness of Acquiring Capabilities

Even if a firm finds that it is costly to develop the capabilities it needs on its own, it could still use hier-

archical governance to gain access to these capabilities by acquiring a firm that already possesses them. However, the cost of such acquisitions in rapidly evolving high-technology industries can also be high. Over and above any legal, ownership, and asset value constraints on acquisitions, uncertainty about the future puts a premium on maintaining flexibility in these industries. Acquisitions in high-technology industries constrain a firm's options in a costly-to-reverse way, suggesting that nonhierarchical forms of governance as a way to gain access to capabilities are preferred.[22]

Moreover, given the rapidly changing technical needs of firms in these industries, it is not unusual for capabilities to be required by a firm for limited activities, for short time periods, or for highly specialized purposes.[23] It is unlikely that an acquiring firm will be able to integrate an acquired firm's capabilities rapidly enough to address these kinds of episodic needs. And even if this integration occurs, after the acquiring firm no longer needs these capabilities, they become costly unwanted baggage.

Conclusion

All this suggests that firms in rapidly evolving high-technology industries will often prefer to gain access to capabilities through nonhierarchical forms of governance, despite the threat of opportunism that such a decision may entail. Because it can be costly for these firms to develop capabilities on their own and costly to acquire another firm that already possesses these capabilities, using market or intermediate forms of governance becomes a more attractive alternative. The cost of using hierarchical governance to acquire capabilities must be compared with the cost of using nonhierarchical governance to gain access to capabilities. While the threat of opportunism stemming from transaction-specific investment is an important consideration in making this boundary decision, it is certainly not the only consideration. Stated differently, the attributes of the capabilities a firm is trying to gain access to can have an important impact on the firm's boundary choices.

References

■ 1. The concept of a "hollow corporation" was first introduced in:
N. Jones, "The Hollow Corporation," *Business Week,* 3 March 1986, pp. 56-59; and
M. Postin, "The Hollow Corporation," *Executive Excellence,* volume 5, May 1988, pp. 11-12.

■ 2. The foundations of transactions cost economics were outlined in:
Ronald Coase, "The Nature of the Firm," *Economica,* volume 4, 1937, pp. 386-405.
However, these ideas remained somewhat undeveloped until the work of Oliver Williamson, beginning in the 1960s. Williamson's work is summarized in two books:

O. Williamson, *Markets and Hierarchies: Analysis and Anti-Trust Implications* (New York: Free Press, 1975); and
O. Williamson, *The Economic Institutions of Capitalism* (New York: Free Press, 1985).
■ 3. Empirical tests of transactions cost economics are reviewed in:
J. Barney and W. Hesterly, "Organizational

Economics: Understanding the Relationship between Organizations and Economic Analysis," in S. Clegg, C. Hardy, and W. Nord, eds., *Handbook of Organization Theory* (London: Sage, 1996), pp. 115-147; and
J. Mahoney, "The Choice of Organizational Form: Vertical Financial Ownership versus Other Methods of Vertical Integration," *Strategic Management Journal*, volume 13, November 1992, pp. 559-584. Some of the secondary predictions of transactions cost economics and especially those that deal with the role of uncertainty in determining a firm's boundaries do not receive as consistent support as its primary predictions. Also, many transactions cost predictions do not seem to hold as consistently in high-technology industries. These empirical limitations of transactions cost thinking are important for subsequent sections of this paper.

■ 4. Direct costs, indirect costs, and opportunity costs are relevant in determining the cost of a governance mechanism for a firm.

■ 5. Perhaps, for example, this foreign firm may be owned by the government.

■ 6. More formally, firms will choose nonhierarchical governance when the value of an exchange is greater than the cost of opportunism stemming from transaction-specific investment and when the cost of opportunism from transaction-specific investment is less than the cost of using hierarchical governance.

■ 7. This discussion draws heavily on the resource-based view of the firm. This theory was first outlined in:
B. Wernerfelt, "A Resource-Based View of the Firm," *Strategic Management Journal*, volume 5, April-June 1984, pp. 171-180;
R. Rumelt, "Toward a Strategic Theory of the Firm," in R. Lamb, ed., *Competitive Strategic Management* (Englewood Cliffs, New Jersey: Prentice-Hall, 1984), pp. 556-570; and
J. Barney, "Strategic Factor Markets: Expectations, Luck, and Business Strategy," *Management Science*, volume 32, October 1986, pp. 1512-1514.
The reasons why some capabilities are costly to create are discussed in:

I. Dierickx and K. Cool, "Asset Stock Accumulation and Sustainability of Competitive Advantage," *Management Science*, volume 35, December 1989, pp. 1504-1511; and
J. Barney, "Firm Resources and Sustained Competitive Advantage," *Journal of Management*, volume 17, January 1991, pp. 99-120.

■ 8. Caterpillar's unique history is discussed in:
M.J. Rukstad and J. Horn, "Caterpillar and the Construction Equipment Industry in 1988" (Boston: Harvard Business School, Case 9-389-097, 1989).

■ 9. These supply relationships and the value they create for Japanese firms are discussed in:
J. Dyer and W. Ouchi, "Japanese Style Partnerships: Giving Companies a Competitive Edge," *Sloan Management Review*, volume 35, Fall 1993, pp. 51-63.

■ 10. See J.C. Collins and J. Porras, *Built to Last* (New York: HarperCollins, 1994).

■ 11. Collins and Porras estimate that $1 invested in their sample of eighteen "visionary firms" in 1926 would have been worth $6,536 in 1995, while $1 invested in a matched sample of firms competing during the same time in the same industries would have been worth $415. See:
Ibid., p. 3.

■ 12. The term "invisible assets" was introduced in:
H. Itami, *Mobilizing Invisible Assets* (Cambridge, Massachusetts: Harvard University Press, 1987).

■ 13. Many of the reasons why the cost of acquiring a firm to gain access to its capabilities can rise are discussed in:
B. Kogut, "Joint Ventures: Theoretical and Empirical Perspectives," *Strategic Management Journal*, volume 9, August 1988, pp. 319-332;
J.F. Hennart, "A Transaction Cost Theory of Equity Joint Ventures," *Strategic Management Journal*, volume 9, August 1988, pp. 361-374; and
B. Kogut, "Joint Ventures and the Option to Expand and Acquire," *Management Science*, volume 37, January 1991, pp. 19-33.

■ 14. For a discussion of the specific antitrust issues in the Intuit-Microsoft case, see:
"Will Regulators Get Tough on M&A," *Mergers and Acquisitions*, volume 31, July-August 1996, pp. 42-51.

■ 15. The Publicis and Foote, Cone & Belding alliance is described in:
R.M. Kanter, "FCB and Publicis (A): Forming the Alliance" (Boston: Harvard Business School, Case 9-393-099, 1993).

■ 16. Kogut (1991).

■ 17. M. Porter, "From Competitive Advantage to Corporate Strategy," *Harvard Business Review*, volume 67, May-June 1987, pp. 43-59.

■ 18. Of course, firms will want to minimize the threat of opportunism in this situation. This suggests that they will prefer some form of intermediate governance (i.e., a strategic alliance) over market forms of governance to access capabilities that they cannot develop internally and cannot access through an acquisition.

■ 19. The path-dependent nature of manufacturing in biotechnology is described in:
G. Pisano, "Nucleon, Inc." (Boston: Harvard Business School, Case 9-692-041, 1991).
The path-dependent nature of software development is described in:
J.D. Blackburn, G. Hoedemakear, and L.N. Van Wassenhove,"Concurrent Software Engineering: Prospects and Pitfalls," *IEEE Transactions on Engineering Management*, volume 43, May 1996, pp. 179-188.

■ 20. See R. Henderson and I. Cockburn, "Measuring Competence: Exploring Firm Effects in Pharmaceutical Research," *Strategic Management Journal*, volume 15, Winter 1994 (special issue), pp. 63-84.

■ 21. Pisano (1991).

■ 22. Kogut (1991).

■ 23. For a discussion of these time dynamics in rapidly evolving high-technology industries, see:
K. Eisenhardt and S. Brown, "Time Pacing: Competing in Markets That Won't Stand Still," *Harvard Business Review*, volume 76, March-April 1998, pp. 59-69.

Reprint 40313

*Management practices
that work well in one
phase may bring on
a crisis in another.*

EVOLUTION AND REVOLUTION AS ORGANIZATIONS GROW

BY LARRY E. GREINER

K EY EXECUTIVES of a retail store chain hold on to an organizational structure long after it has served its purpose because the structure is the source of their power. The company eventually goes into bankruptcy.

A large bank disciplines a "rebellious" manager who is blamed for current control problems, when the underlying causes are centralized procedures that are holding back expansion into new markets. Many young managers subsequently leave the bank, competition moves in, and profits decline.

This article originally appeared in the July–August 1972 issue of HBR. For the article's republication as a Classic, the author has removed some outdated material from the opening sections. He has also written a commentary, "Revolution Is Still Inevitable," to update his observations.

The problems at these companies are rooted more in past decisions than in present events or market dynamics. Yet management, in its haste to grow, often overlooks such critical developmental questions as, Where has our organization been? Where is it now? and What do the answers to these questions mean for where it is going? Instead, management fixes its gaze outward on the environment and toward the future, as if more precise market projections will provide the organization with a new identity.

In stressing the force of history on an organization, I have drawn from the legacies of European psychologists who argue that the behavior of individuals is determined primarily by past events and experiences, rather than by what lies ahead. Extending that thesis to problems of

---

Larry E. Greiner *is a professor of management and organization at the University of Southern California's Marshall School of Business in Los Angeles.*

organizational development, we can identify a series of developmental phases through which companies tend to pass as they grow. Each phase begins with a period of evolution, with steady growth and stability, and ends with a revolutionary period of substantial organizational turmoil and change – for instance, when centralized practices eventually lead to demands for decentralization. The resolution of each revolutionary period determines whether or not a company will move forward into its next stage of evolutionary growth.

A Model of How Organizations Develop

To date, research on organizational development has been largely empirical, and scholars have not attempted to create a model of the overall process. When we analyze the research, however, five key dimensions emerge: an organization's age and size, its stages of evolution and revolution, and the growth rate of its industry. The graph "How Companies Grow" shows how these elements interact to shape an organization's development.

Age of the Organization. The most obvious and essential dimension for any model of development is the life span of an organization (represented on the graph as the horizontal axis). History shows that the same organizational practices are not maintained throughout a long life span. This demonstrates a most basic

Managerial problems and practices are rooted in time. They do not last throughout the life of an organization.

point: management problems and principles are rooted in time. The concept of decentralization, for example, can describe corporate practices at one period but can lose its descriptive power at another.

The passage of time also contributes to the institutionalization of managerial attitudes. As these attitudes become rigid and eventually

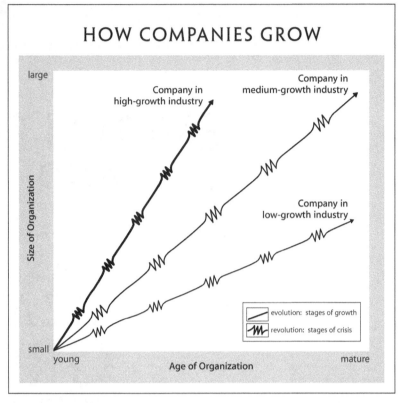

HOW COMPANIES GROW

large — Company in high-growth industry

Company in medium-growth industry

Size of Organization

Company in low-growth industry

evolution: stages of growth
revolution: stages of crisis

small

young — Age of Organization — mature

outdated, the behavior of employees becomes not only more predictable but also more difficult to change.

Size of the Organization. This dimension is depicted on the chart as the vertical axis. A company's problems and solutions tend to change markedly as the number of its employees and its sales volume increase. Problems of coordination and communication magnify, new functions emerge, levels in the management hierarchy multiply, and jobs become more interrelated. Thus, time is not the only determinant of structure; in fact, organizations that do not become larger can retain many of the same management issues and practices over long periods.

Stages of Evolution. As organizations age and grow, another phenomenon emerges: prolonged growth that we can term the *evolutionary period.* Most growing organizations do not expand for two years and then contract for one; rather, those that survive a crisis usually enjoy four to eight years of continuous growth

without a major economic setback or severe internal disruption. The term *evolution* seems appropriate for describing these quiet periods because only modest adjustments appear to be necessary for maintaining growth under the same overall pattern of management.

Stages of Revolution. Smooth evolution is not inevitable or indefinitely sustainable; it cannot be assumed that organizational growth is linear. *Fortune*'s "500" list, for example, has had considerable turnover during the last 50 years. In fact, evidence from numerous case histories reveals periods of substantial turbulence interspersed between smoother periods of evolution.

We can term the turbulent times *periods of revolution* because they typically exhibit a serious upheaval of management practices. Traditional management practices that were appropriate for a smaller size and earlier time no longer work and are brought under scrutiny by frustrated top-level managers and disillusioned lower-level managers. During such periods of crisis, a number of companies fall short. Those that are unable to abandon past practices and effect major organizational changes are likely either to fold or to level off in their growth rates.

The critical task for management in each revolutionary period is to find a new set of organizational practices that will become the basis for managing the next period of evolutionary growth. Interestingly enough, those new practices eventually sow the seeds of their own decay and lead to another period of revolution. Managers therefore experience the irony of seeing a major solution in one period become a major problem in a later period.

Growth Rate of the Industry. The speed at which an organization experiences phases of evolution and revolution is closely related to the market environment of its industry. For example, a company in a rapidly expanding market will have to add employees quickly; hence, the need for new organizational structures to accommodate large staff increases is accelerated. Whereas evolutionary periods tend to be relatively short in fast-growing industries, much longer evolutionary periods occur in mature or slow-growing industries.

Evolution can also be prolonged, and revolutions delayed, when profits come easily. For instance, companies that make grievous errors in a prosperous industry can still look good on their profit-and-loss statements; thus, they can buy time before a crisis forces changes in management practices. The aerospace industry in its highly profitable infancy is an example. Yet revolutionary periods still occur, as one did in aerospace when profit opportunities began to dry up. By contrast, when the market environment is poor, revolutions seem to be much more severe and difficult to resolve.

Phases of Growth

With the foregoing framework in mind, we can now examine in depth the five specific phases of evolution and revolution. As shown in the graph "The Five Phases of Growth," each evolutionary period is charac-

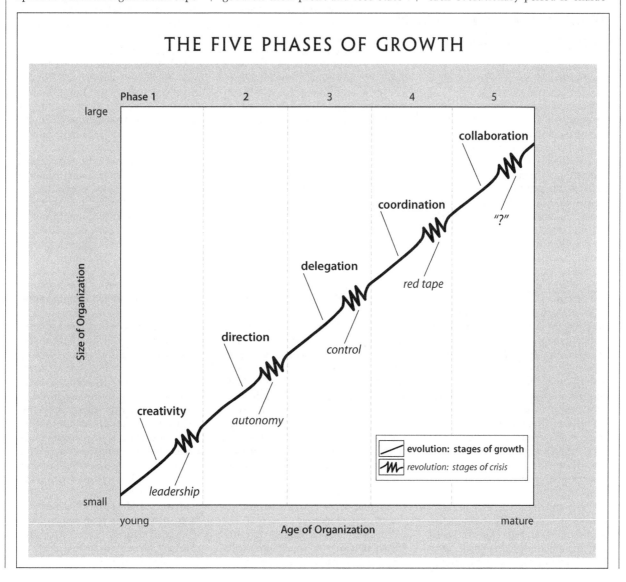

THE FIVE PHASES OF GROWTH

| evolution: stages of growth |
| revolution: stages of crisis |

terized by the dominant management style used to achieve growth; each revolutionary period is characterized by the dominant management problem that must be solved before growth can continue. The pattern presented in the chart seems to be typical for companies in industries with moderate growth over a long period; companies in faster-growing industries tend to experience all five phases more rapidly, whereas those in slower-growing in-

Creative activities are essential for a company to get off the ground. But as the company grows, those very activities become the problem.

dustries encounter only two or three phases over many years.

It is important to note that each phase is at once a result of the previous phase and a cause for the next phase. For example, the evolutionary management style in Phase 3 is delegation, which grows out of and becomes the solution to demands for greater autonomy in the preceding Phase 2 revolution. The style of delegation used in Phase 3, however, eventually provokes a revolutionary crisis that is characterized by attempts to regain control over the diversity created through increased delegation.

For each phase, managers are limited in what they can do if growth is to occur. For example, a company experiencing an autonomy crisis in Phase 2 cannot return to directive management for a solution; it must adopt a new style – delegation – in order to move forward.

Phase 1: Creativity. In the birth stage of an organization, the emphasis is on creating both a product and a market. The following are the characteristics of the period of creative evolution:

■ The founders of the company are usually technically or entrepreneurially oriented, and they generally disdain management activities; their physical and mental energies are ab-

sorbed entirely by making and selling a new product.

■ Communication among employees is frequent and informal.

■ Long hours of work are rewarded by modest salaries and the promise of ownership benefits.

■ Decisions and motivation are highly sensitive to marketplace feedback; management acts as customers react.

All the foregoing individualistic and creative activities are essential for a company to get off the ground. But as the company grows, those very activities become the problem. Larger production runs require knowledge about the efficiencies of manufacturing. Increased numbers of employees cannot be managed exclusively through informal communication, and new employees are not motivated by an intense dedication to the product or organization. Additional capital must be secured, and new accounting procedures are needed for financial control. The company's founders find themselves burdened with unwanted management responsibilities. They long for the "good old days" and try to act as they did in the past. Conflicts among harried leaders emerge and grow more intense.

At this point, a *crisis of leadership* occurs, which is the onset of the first revolution. Who will lead the company out of confusion and solve the managerial problems confronting it? Obviously, a strong manager is needed – one who has the necessary knowledge and skills to introduce new business techniques. But finding that manager is easier said than done. The founders often resist stepping aside, even though they are probably temperamentally unsuited to the job. So here is the first critical choice in an organization's development: to locate and install a strong business manager who is acceptable to the founders and who can pull the organization together.

Phase 2: Direction. Those companies that survive the first phase by installing a capable business manager

usually embark on a period of sustained growth under able, directive leadership. Here are the characteristics of this evolutionary period:

■ A functional organizational structure is introduced to separate manufacturing from marketing activities, and job assignments become increasingly specialized.

■ Accounting systems for inventory and purchasing are introduced.

■ Incentives, budgets, and work standards are adopted.

■ Communication becomes more formal and impersonal as a hierarchy of titles and positions grows.

■ The new manager and his or her key supervisors assume most of the responsibility for instituting direction; lower-level supervisors are treated more as functional specialists than as autonomous decision-making managers.

Although the new directive techniques channel employees' energy more efficiently into growth, they eventually become inappropriate for controlling a more diverse and complex organization. Lower-level employees find themselves restricted by a cumbersome and centralized hierarchy. They have come to possess more direct knowledge about markets and machinery than do their leaders at the top; consequently, they feel torn between following procedures and taking initiative on their own.

Thus, the second revolution emerges from a *crisis of autonomy*. The solution adopted by most companies is to move toward more delegation. Yet it is difficult for top-level managers who previously were successful at being directive to give up responsibility to lower-level managers. Moreover, the lower-level managers are not accustomed to making decisions for themselves. As a result, numerous companies founder during this revolutionary period by adhering to centralized methods, while lower-level employees become disenchanted and leave the organization.

Phase 3: Delegation. The next era of growth evolves from the successful application of a decentralized organizational structure. It exhibits these characteristics:

- Much greater responsibility is given to the managers of plants and market territories.
- Profit centers and bonuses are used to motivate employees.
- Top-level executives at headquarters limit themselves to managing by exception based on periodic reports from the field.
- Management often concentrates on acquiring outside enterprises that can be lined up with other decentralized units.
- Communication from the top is infrequent and usually occurs by correspondence, telephone, or brief visits to field locations.

The delegation phase allows companies to expand by means of the heightened motivation of managers at lower levels. Managers in decentralized organizations, who have greater authority and incentives, are able to penetrate larger markets, respond faster to customers, and develop new products.

A serious problem eventually emerges, however, as top-level executives sense that they are losing control over a highly diversified field operation. Autonomous field managers prefer to run their own shows without coordinating plans, money, technology, and personnel with the rest of the organization. Freedom breeds a parochial attitude.

Soon, the organization falls into a *crisis of control*. The Phase 3 revolu-

The delegation phase brings a new period of growth, but freedom eventually breeds a parochial attitude.

tion is under way when top management seeks to regain control over the company as a whole. Some top-management teams attempt a return to centralized management, which usually fails because of the organization's newly vast scope of operations. Those companies that move ahead find a new solution in the use of special coordination techniques.

Phase 4: Coordination. The evolutionary period of the coordination phase is characterized by the use of formal systems for achieving greater coordination and by top-level executives taking responsibility for the initiation and administration of these new systems. For example:

- Decentralized units are merged into product groups.
- Formal planning procedures are established and intensively reviewed.
- Numerous staff members are hired and located at headquarters to initiate companywide programs of control and review for line managers.
- Capital expenditures are carefully weighed and parceled out across the organization.
- Each product group is treated as an investment center where return on invested capital is an important criterion used in allocating funds.
- Certain technical functions, such as data processing, are centralized at headquarters, while daily operating decisions remain decentralized.
- Stock options and companywide profit sharing are used to encourage employees to identify with the organization as a whole.

All these new coordination systems prove useful for achieving growth through the more efficient allocation of a company's limited resources. The systems prompt field managers to look beyond the needs of their local units. Although these managers still have a great deal of decision-making responsibility, they learn to justify their actions more carefully to a watchdog audience at headquarters.

A lack of confidence, however, gradually builds between line and staff, and between headquarters and the field. The many systems and programs introduced begin to exceed their usefulness. A *red-tape crisis* is in full swing. Line managers, for example, increasingly resent direction from those who are not familiar with local conditions. And staff people, for their part, complain about uncooperative and uninformed line managers. Together, both groups criticize the bureaucratic system that has evolved. Procedures take precedence over problem solving, and in-

novation dims. In short, the organization has become too large and complex to be managed through formal programs and rigid systems. The Phase 4 revolution is under way.

Phase 5: Collaboration. The last observable phase emphasizes strong interpersonal collaboration in an attempt to overcome the red-tape crisis. Where Phase 4 was managed through formal systems and procedures, Phase 5 emphasizes spontaneity in management action through teams and the skillful confrontation of interpersonal differences. Social control and self-discipline replace formal control. This transition is especially difficult for the experts who created the coordination systems as well as for the line managers who relied on formal methods for answers.

The Phase 5 evolution, then, builds around a more flexible and behavioral approach to management. Here are its characteristics:

- The focus is on solving problems quickly through team action.
- Teams are combined across functions to handle specific tasks.
- Staff experts at headquarters are reduced in number, reassigned, and combined into interdisciplinary teams that consult with, not direct, field units.
- A matrix-type structure is frequently used to assemble the right teams for the appropriate problems.
- Formal control systems are simplified and combined into single multipurpose systems.
- Conferences of key managers are held frequently to focus on major problems.
- Educational programs are used to train managers in behavioral skills for achieving better teamwork and conflict resolution.
- Real-time information systems are integrated into daily decision-making processes.
- Economic rewards are geared more to team performance than to individual achievement.
- Experimenting with new practices is encouraged throughout the organization.

What will be the revolution in response to this stage of evolution? Many large U.S. companies are now in the Phase 5 evolutionary stage, so the answer is critical. Although there is little clear evidence regarding the outcome, I imagine that the revolution arising from the "?" crisis will center around the psychological saturation of employees who grow emotionally and physically exhausted from the intensity of teamwork and the heavy pressure for innovative solutions.

My hunch is that the Phase 5 revolution will be solved through new structures and programs that allow employees to periodically rest, reflect, and revitalize themselves. We may even see companies with dual organizational structures: a *habit structure* for getting the daily work done and a *reflective structure* for stimulating new perspective and personal enrichment. Employees could move back and forth between the two structures as their energies dissipate and are refueled.

One European organization has implemented just such a structure. Five reflective groups have been established outside the company's usual structure for the purpose of continuously evaluating five task activities basic to the organization. The groups report directly to the managing director, although their findings are made public throughout the organization. Membership in each group includes all levels and functions in the company, and employees are rotated through the groups every six months.

Other concrete examples now in practice include providing sabbaticals for employees, moving managers in and out of hot-spot jobs, establishing a four-day workweek, ensuring job security, building phys-

REVOLUTION IS STILL INEVITABLE

I wrote the first draft of this article while I was felled by a bad leg during a ski vacation in Switzerland. At the time, the business world was buzzing with numerous faddish techniques. Perhaps it was the size and height of the mountains that made me feel that there were deeper and more powerful forces at work in organizations.

Four basic points still seem valid about the model. First, we continue to observe major phases of development in the life of growing companies, lasting anywhere from 3 to 15 years each. Although scholars debate the precise length and nature of these phases, everyone agrees that each phase contains its own unique structure, systems, and leadership. The growth rate of the industry seems to determine the phases' length.

Second, transitions between developmental phases still do not occur naturally or smoothly, regardless of the strength of top management. All organizations appear to experience revolutionary difficulty and upheaval, and many of these organizations falter, plateau, fail, or get acquired rather than grow further. IBM before Lou Gerstner and General Electric before Jack Welch both suffered badly at the end of the fourth phase of coor-

dination, when sophisticated management systems evolved into rigid bureaucracies.

Third, the logic of paradox underlying the model continues to ring true, although it often haunts and confuses the managerial psyche. Managers have difficulty in understanding that an organizational solution introduced by them personally in one phase eventually sows the seeds of revolution.

Fourth, the greatest resistance to change appears at the top because revolution often means that units under each senior executive will be eliminated or transformed. That is why we so often see new chief executives recruited from the outside and why senior managers frequently leave companies. Executives depart not because they are "bad" managers but because they just don't fit with where the company needs to go.

As for the differences that I have observed since the article's original publication, there is obviously much more "death" in the life of organizations today. Few organizations make it through all the phases of growth. If they don't fail, as most do in the initial phase of creativity and entrepreneurship, they often get acquired by companies that are in a later phase.

The phases are not as cleanly marked off as I depicted them. The vestiges of one phase remain as new approaches are introduced. Such overlaps are most notable in the case of the first-phase entrepreneur hanging on when professional management is added in the second phase of direction.

There are also miniphases within each evolutionary stage. The delegation phase, for example, does not typically begin with the complete decentralization of the entire organization into multiple product units, as the article implies. Usually one product group is launched, and then others are added over time. Also, as delegation – or *decentralization*, as I now prefer to call this phase – advances, senior managers at the corporate office are not as hands-off as I depicted them. The addition of multiple product or geographic units over time requires a sophisticated level of involvement by senior management to review strategies, evaluate results, and communicate the organization's values – but not to micromanage the units under them.

I would change some of the things I said about the fifth phase of collaboration. My original description of this phase suggests that the entire organization is

ical facilities for relaxation during the workday, making jobs more interchangeable, creating an extra team on the assembly line so that one team is always off for reeducation, and switching to longer vacations and more flexible work hours.

The Chinese practice of requiring executives to spend time periodically on lower-level jobs may also be worth a nonideological evaluation. For too long, U.S. management has assumed that career progress should be equated with an upward path toward title, salary, and power. Could

it be that some vice presidents of marketing might just long for, and even benefit from, temporary duty in field sales?

Implications of History

Let me now summarize some important implications for practicing managers. The main features of this discussion are depicted in the table "Organizational Practices in the Five Phases of Growth," which shows the specific management actions that characterize each growth phase. These actions are also the

solutions that ended each preceding revolutionary period.

In one sense, I hope that many readers will react to my model by seeing it as obvious and natural for depicting the growth of an organization. To me, this type of reaction is a useful test of the model's validity.

But at a more reflective level, I imagine some of these reactions come more from hindsight than from foresight. Experienced managers who have been through a developmental sequence can identify that sequence now, but how did they

turned into a matrix of teams. I now see the matrix as confined largely to senior management, where the heads of geographic areas, product lines, and functional disciplines collaborate as a team in order to ensure that their decisions are coordinated and implemented across global markets. The most significant change in this phase occurs when the previously bureaucratic Phase 4 control-oriented staff and systems are replaced by a smaller number of consulting staff experts who help facilitate, rather than control, decisions.

My speculation that "psychological saturation" is the crisis ending Phase 5 now seems wrong. Instead, I think the crisis is one of realizing that there is no internal solution, such as new products, for stimulating further growth. Rather, the organization begins to look outside for partners or for opportunities to sell itself to a bigger company.

A sixth phase may be evolving in which growth depends on the design of extra-organizational solutions, such as creating a holding company or a network organization composed of alliances and cross-ownership. GE may have developed a similar model in which a periphery of companies is built around a core "money" company

or bank (GE Capital) that attracts capital, earns high returns, and feeds the growth of other units.

I doubt that the advancement of information technology has made much of a difference in the basic aspects of the model. Information technology appears useful as a tool that evolves in different forms to fit each phase. For example, the Phase 2 functional organizational structure requires data that reflect revenue and cost centers, whereas Phase 3 decentralization needs data that measure profit center performance.

I wrote the article mainly about industrial and consumer goods companies, not about knowledge organizations or service businesses, which had yet to come into prominence. After recently studying a number of consulting, law, and investment firms, our research team found that those organizations also experience evolution and revolution as they grow.

In the first, entrepreneurial phase, the professional service firm pursues and tests a variety of market paths. The phase ends with the partners arguing about whether or not to stay together to concentrate on one partner's vision for the future. In the second phase, the firm focuses on one major service and

eventually finds itself with a debate among the partners about whether to continue focusing on the current practice or to open another office or add additional services. A third phase of geographic or service expansion typically ends with a struggle over ownership: how much equity are the original partners willing to share with the younger partners who led the expansion and brought in new clients? The fourth phase involves institutionalizing the firm's name, reputation, and its standard way of operating, and ends in a crisis of cultural conformity in the face of which the firm must restore innovation and flexibility.

Finally, as a strong caveat, I always remind myself and others that the "ev and rev" model depicted in this article provides only a simple outline of the broad challenges facing a management concerned with growth. It is not a cookie-cutter solution or panacea. The rate of growth, the effective resolution of revolutions, and the performance of the company within phases still depend on the fundamentals of good management: skillful leadership, a winning strategy, the heightened motivation of employees, and a deep concern for customers.

ORGANIZATIONAL PRACTICES
IN THE FIVE PHASES OF GROWTH

CATEGORY	PHASE 1	PHASE 2	PHASE 3	PHASE 4	PHASE 5
Management Focus	Make and sell	Efficiency of operations	Expansion of market	Consolidation of organization	Problem solving and innovation
Organizational Structure	Informal	Centralized and functional	Decentralized and geographical	Line staff and product groups	Matrix of teams
Top-Management Style	Individualistic and entrepreneurial	Directive	Delegative	Watchdog	Participative
Control System	Market results	Standards and cost centers	Reports and profit centers	Plans and investment centers	Mutual goal setting
Management Reward Emphasis	Ownership	Salary and merit increases	Individual bonus	Profit sharing and stock options	Team bonus

react when in the midst of a stage of evolution or revolution? They can probably recall the limits of their own developmental understanding at that time. Perhaps they resisted desirable changes or were even swept emotionally into a revolution without being able to propose constructive solutions. So let me offer some explicit guidelines for managers of growing organizations to keep in mind.

Know where you are in the developmental sequence. Every organization and its component parts are at different stages of development. The task of top management is to be aware of the stages; otherwise, it may not recognize when the time for change has come, or it may act to impose the wrong solution.

Leaders at the top should be ready to work with the flow of the tide rather than against it; yet they should be cautious because it is tempting to skip phases out of impatience. Each phase produces certain strengths and learning experiences in the organization that will be essential for success in subsequent phases. A child prodigy, for example, may be able to read like a teenager,

but he cannot behave like one until he matures through a sequence of experiences.

I also doubt that managers can or should act to avoid revolutions. Rather, these periods of tension provide the pressure, ideas, and awareness that afford a platform for change and the introduction of new practices.

Recognize the limited range of solutions. In each revolutionary stage, it becomes evident that the stage can come to a close only by means of certain specific solutions; moreover, these solutions are different from those that were applied to the problems of the preceding revolution. Too often, it is tempting to choose solutions that were tried before but that actually make it impossible for the new phase of growth to evolve.

Management must be prepared to dismantle current structures before the revolutionary stage becomes too turbulent. Top-level managers, realizing that their own managerial styles are no longer appropriate, may

even have to take themselves out of leadership positions. A good Phase 2 manager facing Phase 3 might be wise to find a position at another Phase 2 organization that better fits his or her talents, either outside the company or with one of its newer subsidiaries.

Finally, evolution is not an automatic affair; it is a contest for survival. To move ahead, companies must consciously introduce planned

Too often, it is tempting to choose solutions that were tried before but that actually make it impossible for the new phase to emerge.

structures that not only solve a current crisis but also fit the next phase of growth. That requires considerable self-awareness on the part of top management as well as great interpersonal skills in persuading other managers that change is needed.

Realize that solutions breed new problems. Managers often fail to recognize that organizational solutions create problems for the future, such as when a decision to delegate eventually causes a problem of control. Actions in the past determine much of what will happen to a company in the future.

An awareness of this effect should help managers evaluate company problems with a historical understanding instead of pinning the blame on a current development. Better yet, it should place managers in a position to predict problems and thereby to prepare solutions and coping strategies before a revolution gets out of hand.

Top management that is aware of the problems ahead could well decide not to expand the organization.

Managers may, for instance, prefer to retain the informal practices of a small company, knowing that this way of life is inherent in the organization's limited size, not in their congenial personalities. If they choose to grow, they may actually grow themselves out of a job and a way of life they enjoy.

And what about very large organizations? Can they find new solutions for continued evolution? Or are they reaching a stage when the government will act to break them up because they are too large?

Clearly, there is still much to learn about processes of development in organizations. The phases outlined here are merely five in number and are still only approximations. Researchers are just beginning to study the specific developmental problems of structure, control, rewards, and management style in different industries and in a variety of cultures.

One should not, however, wait for conclusive evidence before educating managers to think and act from a developmental perspective. The critical dimension of time has been missing for too long from our management theories and practices. The intriguing paradox is that by learning more about history, we may do a better job in the future.   ⊖

Reprint 98308

To place an order, call 1-800-988-0886.

Organization Design:
Fashion or Fit?

by Henry Mintzberg

Harvard Business Review

Reprint 81106

JANUARY–FEBRUARY 1981

Organization Design: Fashion or Fit?

by Henry Mintzberg

- A conglomerate takes over a small manufacturer and tries to impose budgets, plans, organizational charts, and untold systems on it. The result: declining sales and product innovation—and near bankruptcy—until the division managers buy back the company and promptly turn it around.
- Consultants make constant offers to introduce the latest management techniques. Years ago LRP and OD were in style, later, QWL and ZBB.
- A government sends in its analysts to rationalize, standardize, and formalize citywide school systems, hospitals, and welfare agencies. The results are devastating.

These incidents suggest that a great many problems in organizational design stem from the assumption that organizations are all alike: mere collections of component parts to which elements of structure can be added and deleted at will, a sort of organizational bazaar.

The opposite assumption is that effective organizations achieve a coherence among their component parts, that they do not change one element without considering the consequences to all of the others. Spans of control, degrees of job enlargement, forms of decentralization, planning systems, and matrix structure should not be picked and chosen at random. Rather, they should be selected according to internally consistent groupings. And these groupings should be consistent with the situation of the organization—its age and size, the conditions of the industry in which it operates, and its production technol-

ogy. In essence, like all phenomena from atoms to stars, the characteristics of organizations fall into natural clusters, or *configurations*. When these char-

Why has it taken the automobile industry so long to adapt to the cry for smaller cars? Why does a film production group leave its conglomerate company to start on its own? Why do so many public hospitals and universities wither under government controls? These questions can be answered in many ways, with lots of reasons. But one reason common to them all, the author of this article would say, is that some element in the organization's design was ill suited to the task. Large machine bureaucracies are perfect for efficient mass production but not for adapting quickly to new situations. Film production divisions rely on flexible structures in order to innovate, which is difficult to achieve in a conglomerate that controls operations with the bottom line. Finally, public hospitals and universities require a form of professional control incompatible with the technocratic standards governments tend to impose. The author of this article has found that many organizations fall close to one of five natural "configurations," each a combinaton of certain elements of structure and situation. When managers and organizational designers try to mix and match the elements of different ones, they may emerge with a misfit that, like an ill-cut piece of clothing, won't wear very well. The key to organizational design, then, is consistency and coherence.

Mr. Mintzberg is professor in the faculty of management at McGill University. This is third HBR article; his first, "The Manager's Job: Folklore and Fact," won the McKinsey Award in 1975. The current article is adapted from his most recent book, The Structuring of Organizations *(Prentice-Hall, 1979).*

EXHIBIT 1
The Five Basic Parts of the Organization

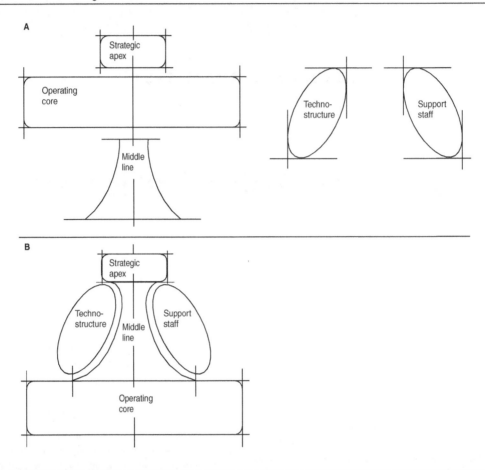

acteristics are mismatched—when the wrong ones are put together—the organization does not function effectively, does not achieve a natural harmony. If managers are to design effective organizations, they need to pay attention to the fit.

If we look at the enormous amount of research on organizational structuring in light of this idea, a lot of the confusion falls away and a striking convergence is revealed. Specifically, five clear configurations emerge that are distinct in their structures, in the situations in which they are found, and even in the periods of history in which they first developed. They are the simple structure, machine bureaucracy, professional bureaucracy, divisionalized form, and adhocracy. In this article I describe these configurations and consider the messages they contain for managers.

DERIVING THE CONFIGURATIONS

In order to describe and distinguish the five configurations, I designed an adaptable picture of five com-

ponent parts (see part A, *Exhibit 1*). An organization begins with a person who has an idea. This person forms the *strategic apex*, or top management. He or she hires people to do the basic work of the organization, in what can be called the *operating core*. As the organization grows, it acquires intermediate managers between the chief executive and the workers. These managers form the *middle line*. The organization may also find that it needs two kinds of staff personnel. First are the analysts who design systems concerned with the formal planning and control of the work; they form the *technostructure*. Second is the *support staff*, providing indirect services to the rest of the organization—everything from the cafeteria and the mail room to the public relations department and the legal counsel.

These five parts together make the whole organization (see part B, *Exhibit 1*). Not all organizations need all of these parts. Some use few and are simple, others combine all in rather complex ways. The central purpose of structure is to coordinate the work divided in a variety of ways; how that coordination is

EXHIBIT 2
The Five Configurations

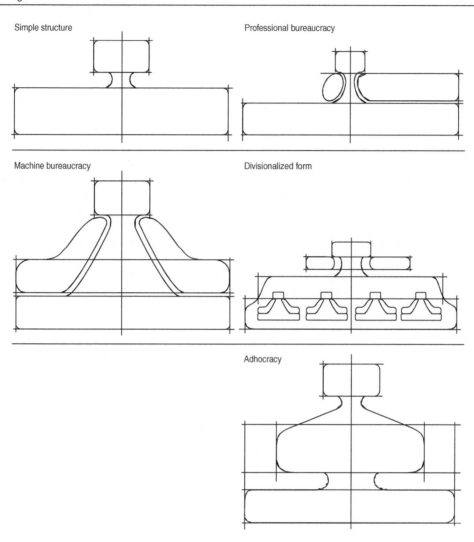

Simple structure

Professional bureaucracy

Machine bureaucracy

Divisionalized form

Adhocracy

---

achieved—by whom and with what—dictates what the organization will look like (see *Exhibit 2*):

- In the simplest case, coordination is achieved at the strategic apex by *direct supervision*—the chief executive officer gives the orders. The configuration called *simple structure* emerges, with a minimum of staff and middle line.
- When coordination depends on the *standardization of work*, an organization's entire administrative structure—especially its technostructure, which designs the standards—needs to be elaborated. This gives rise to the configuration called *machine bureaucracy*.
- When, instead, coordination is through the *standardization of skills* of its employees, the

organization needs highly trained professionals in its operating core and considerable support staff to back them up. Neither its technostructure nor its middle line is very elaborate. The resulting configuration is called *professional bureaucracy*.

- Organizations will sometimes be divided into parallel operating units, allowing autonomy to the middle-line managers of each, with coordination achieved through the *standardization of outputs* (including performance) of these units. The configuration called the *divisionalized form* emerges.
- Finally, the most complex organizations engage sophisticated specialists, especially in their support staffs, and require them to combine their

efforts in project teams coordinated by *mutual adjustment*. This results in the *adhocracy* configuration, in which line and staff as well as a number of other distinctions tend to break down.

I shall describe each of these five configurations in terms of structure and situation. But first let me list the elements of structure, which are described in more detail in the Appendix. These include the following:

- Specialization of tasks
- Formalization of procedures (job descriptions, rules, and so forth)
- Formal training and indoctrination required for the job
- Grouping of units (notably by function performed or market served)
- Size of each of the units (that is, the span of control of its manager)
- Action planning and performance control systems
- Liaison devices, such as task forces, integrating managers, and matrix structure
- Delegation of power down the chain of authority (called *vertical decentralization*).
- Delegation of power out from that chain of authority to non-managers (called *horizontal decentralization*).

Also included in the *Appendix*, together with their impact on these elements of structure, are the situational factors—namely, the age and size of the organization, its technical system of production, and various characteristics of its environment (e.g., how stable or complex it is) and of its power system (e.g., how tightly it is controlled externally.)

Our job now is to see how all of these elements cluster into the five configurations. I describe each in the sections that follow and summarize these descriptions in *Exhibit 3*, where all the elements are displayed in relation to the configurations. In the discussions of each configuration, it should become more evident how all of its elements of structure and situation form themselves into a tightly knit, highly cohesive package. No one element determines the others; rather, all are locked together to form an integrated system.

Simple Structure

The name tells all, and *Exhibit 2* shows all. The structure is simple—not much more than one large unit consisting of one or a few top managers and a group of operators who do the basic work. The most common simple structure is, of course, the classic entrepreneurial company.

What characterizes this configuration above all is what is missing. Little of its behavior is standardized or formalized, and minimal use is made of planning, training, or the liaison devices. The absence of standardization means that the organization has little need for staff analysts. Few middle-line managers are hired because so much of the coordination is achieved at the strategic apex by direct supervision. That is where the real power in this configuration lies. Even the support staff is minimized to keep the structure lean and flexible— simple structures would rather buy than make.

The organization must be flexible because it operates in a dynamic environment, often by choice because that is the one place it can outmaneuver the bureaucracies. And that environment must be simple, as must the organization's system of production, so that the chief executive can retain highly centralized control. In turn, centralized control makes the simple structure ideal for rapid, flexible innovation, at least of the simple kind. With the right chief executive, the organization can turn on a dime and run circles around the slower-moving bureaucracies. That is why so much innovation comes not from the giant mass producers but from small entrepreneurial companies. But where complex forms of innovation are required, the simple structure falters because of its centralization. As we shall see, that kind of innovation requires another configuration, one that engages highly trained specialists and gives them considerable power.

Simple structures are often young and small, in part because aging and growth encourage them to bureaucratize but also because their vulnerability causes many of them to fail. They never get a chance to grow old and large. One heart attack can wipe them out—as can a chief executive so obsessed with innovation that he or she forgets about the operations, or vice versa. The corporate landscape is littered with the wrecks of entrepreneurial companies whose leaders encouraged growth and mass production yet could never accept the transition to bureaucratic forms of structure that these changes required.

Yet some simple structures have managed to grow very large under the tight control of clever, autocratic leaders, the most famous example being the Ford Motor Co. in the later years of its founder.

Almost all organizations begin their lives as simple structures, granting their founding chief executives considerable latitude to set them up. And most revert to simple structure—no matter how large or what other configuration normally fits their needs—when they face extreme pressure or hostility in their environment. In other words, systems and procedures are suspended as power reverts to the chief executive to give him or her a chance to set things right.

EXHIBIT 3
Dimensions of the Five Configurations

	SIMPLE STRUCTURE	MACHINE BUREAUCRACY	PROFESSIONAL BUREAUCRACY	DIVISIONAL-IZED FORM	ADHOCRACY
Key Means of Coordination	Direct supervision	Standardization of work	Standardization of skills	Standardization of outputs	Mutual adjustment
Key Part of Organization	Strategic apex	Technostructure	Operating core	Middle line	Support staff (with operating core in operating adhocracy)
STRUCTURAL ELEMENTS					
Specialization of Jobs	Little specialization	*Much horizontal and vertical specialization*	*Much horizontal specialization*	Some horizontal and vertical specialization (between divisions and headquarters)	*Much horizontal specialization*
Training and Indoctrination	Little training and indoctrination	Little training and indoctrination	*Much training and indoctrination*	Some training and indoctrination (of division managers)	Much training
Formalization of Behavior— Bureaucratic/ Organic	*Little formalization— organic*	*Much formalization— bureaucratic*	*Little formalization— bureaucratic*	Much formalization (within divisions)— bureaucratic	*Little formalization— organic*
Grouping	Usually functional	*Usually functional*	Functional and market	*Market*	Functional and market
Unit Size	Wide	Wide at bottom, narrow elsewhere	Wide at bottom, narrow elsewhere	Wide at top	Narrow throughout
Planning and Control Systems	Little planning and control	Action planning	Little planning and control	*Much performance control*	Limited action planning (esp. in administrative adhocracy)
Liaison Devices	Few liaison devices	Few liaison devices	Liaison devices in administration	Few liaison devices	*Many liaison devices throughout*
Decentralization	*Centralization*	*Limited horizontal decentralization*	*Horizontal and vertical decentralization*	Limited vertical decentralization	*Selective decentralization*
SITUATIONAL ELEMENTS					
Age and Size	Typically young and small	Typically old and large	Varies	Typically old and very large	Typically young (operating adhocracy
Technical System	Simple, not regulating	Regulating but not automated, not very complex	Not regulating or complex	Divisible, otherwise like machine bureaucracy	Very complex, often automated (in administrative adhocracy), not regulating or complex (in operating adhocracy)

EXHIBIT 3
Dimensions of the Five Configurations (Continued)

	SIMPLE STRUCTURE	MACHINE BUREAUCRACY	PROFESSIONAL BUREAUCRACY	DIVISIONAL-IZED FORM	ADHOCRACY
Environment	Simple and dynamic; sometimes hostile	Simple and stable	Complex and stable	Relatively simple and stable; diversified markets (esp. products and services)	Complex and dynamic; sometimes disparate (in administrative adhocracy)
Power	Chief executive control; often owner managed; not fashionable	Technocratic and external control; not fashionable	Professional operator control; fashionable	Middle-line control; fashionable (esp. in industry)	Expert control; very fashionable

Note: Italic type in columns 2–6 indicates key design parameters.

The heyday of the simple structure probably occurred during the period of the great American trusts, late in the nineteenth century. Although today less in fashion and to many a relic of more autocratic times, the simple structure remains a widespread and necessary configuration—for building up most new organizations and for operating those in simple, dynamic environments and those facing extreme, hostile pressures.

Machine Bureaucracy

Just as the simple structure is prevalent in pre-Industrial Revolution industries such as agriculture, the machine bureaucracy is the offspring of industrialization, with its emphasis on the standardization of work for coordination and its resulting low-skilled, highly specialized jobs. *Exhibit 2* shows that, in contrast to simple structure, the machine bureaucracy elaborates its administration. First, it requires many analysts to design and maintain its systems of standardization— notably those that formalize its behaviors and plan its actions. And by virtue of the organization's dependence on these systems, these analysts gain a degree of informal power, which results in a certain amount of horizontal decentralization.

A large hierarchy emerges in the middle line to oversee the specialized work of the operating core and to keep the lid on conflicts that inevitably result from the rigid departmentalization, as well as from the alienation that often goes with routine, circumscribed jobs. That middle-line hierarchy is usually structured on a functional basis all the way up to the top, where the real power of coordination lies. In other words, machine bureaucracy tends to be centralized in the vertical sense—formal power is concentrated at the top.

And why the large support staff shown in *Exhibit 2*? Because machine bureaucracies depend on stability to function (change interrupts the smooth functioning of the system), they tend not only to seek out stable environments in which to function but also to stabilize the environments they find themselves in. One way they do this is to envelop within their structures all of the support services possible, ones that simple structures prefer to buy. For the same reason they also tend to integrate vertically—to become their own suppliers and customers. And that of course causes many machine bureaucracies to grow very large. So we see the two-sided effect of size here: size drives the organization to bureaucratize ("We do that every day; let's standardize it!"), but bureaucracy also encourages the organization to grow larger. Aging also encourages this configuration; the organization standardizes its work because "we've done that before."

To enable the top managers to maintain centralized control, both the environment and the production system of the machine bureaucracy must be fairly simple. In fact, machine bureaucracies fit most naturally with mass production, where the products, processes, and distribution systems are usually rationalized and thus easy to comprehend. And so machine bureaucracy is most common among large, mature mass-production companies, such as automobile manufacturers, as well as the largest of the established providers of mass services, such as insurance companies and railroads. Thus McDonald's is a classic example of this configuration—achieving enormous success in its simple industry through meticulous standardization.

Because external controls encourage bureaucratization and centralization, this configuration is often assumed by organizations that are tightly controlled from the outside. That is why government agencies, which are subject to many such controls, tend to be driven toward the machine bureaucracy structure regardless of their other conditions.

The problems of the machine bureaucracy are legendary—dull and repetitive work, alienated employees, obsession with control (of markets as well as workers), massive size, and inadaptability. These are machines suited to specific purposes, not to adapting to new ones. For all of these reasons, the machine bureaucracy is no longer fashionable. Bureaucracy has become a dirty word. Yet this is the configuration that gets the products out cheaply and efficiently. And here too there can be a sense of harmony, as in the Swiss railroad system whose trains depart as the second hand sweeps past the twelve.

In a society consumed by its appetite for mass-produced goods, dependent on consistency in so many spheres (how else to deliver millions of pieces of mail every day?) and unable to automate a great many of its routine jobs, machine bureaucracy remains indispensable—and probably the most prevalent of the five configurations today.

Professional Bureaucracy

This bureaucratic configuration relies on the standardization of skills rather than work processes or outputs for its coordination and so emerges as dramatically different from the machine bureaucracy. It is the structure hospitals, universities, and accounting firms tend most often to favor. Most important, because it relies for its operating tasks on trained professionals—skilled people who must be given considerable control over their own work—the organization surrenders a good deal of its power not only to the professionals themselves but also to the associations and institutions that select and train them in the first place. As a result, the structure emerges as very decentralized; power over many decisions, both operating and strategic, flows all the way down the hierarchy to the professionals of the operating core. For them this is the most democratic structure of all.

Because the operating procedures, although complex, are rather standardized—taking out appendixes in a hospital, teaching the American Motors case in a business school, doing an audit in an accounting firm—each professional can work independently of his or her colleagues, with the assurance that much of the necessary coordination will be effected automatically through standardization of skills. Thus a colleague of mine observed a five-hour open heart

operation in which the surgeon and anesthesiologist never exchanged a single word!

As can be seen in *Exhibit 2*, above the operating core we find a unique structure. Since the main standardization occurs as a result of training that takes place outside the professional bureaucracy, a technostructure is hardly needed. And because the professionals work independently, the size of operating units can be very large, and so few first-line managers are needed. (I work in a business school where 55 professors report directly to one dean.) Yet even those few managers, and those above them, do little direct supervision; much of their time is spent linking their units to the broader environment, notably to ensure adequate financing. Thus to become a top manager in a consulting firm is to become a salesperson.

On the other hand, the support staff is typically very large in order to back up the high-priced professionals. But that staff does a very different kind of work—much of it the simple and routine jobs that the professionals shed. As a result, parallel hierarchies emerge in the professional bureaucracy—one democratic with bottom-up power for the professionals, a second autocratic with top-down control for the support staff.

Professional bureaucracy is most effective for organizations that find themselves in stable yet complex environments. Complexity requires that decision-making power be decentralized to highly trained individuals, and stability enables these individuals to apply standardized skills and so to work with a good deal of autonomy. To further ensure that autonomy, the production system must be neither highly regulating, complex, nor automated. Surgeons use their scalpels and editors their pencils; both must be sharp but are otherwise simple instruments that allow their users considerable freedom in performing their complex work.

Standardization is the great strength as well as the great weakness of professional bureaucracy. That is what enables the professionals to perfect their skills and so achieve great efficiency and effectiveness. But that same standardization raises problems of adaptability. This is not a structure to innovate but one to perfect what is already known. Thus, so long as the environment is stable, the professional bureaucracy does its job well. It identifies the needs of its clients and offers a set of standardized programs to serve them. In other words, pigeonholing is its great forte; change messes up the pigeonholes. New needs arise that fall between or across the slots, and the standard programs no longer apply. Another configuration is required.

Professional bureaucracy, a product of the middle years of this century, is a highly fashionable structure today for two reasons. First, it is very democratic, at least for its professional workers. And second, it offers them considerable autonomy, freeing the professionals even from the need to coordinate closely with each other. To release themselves from the close control of administrators and analysts, not to mention their own colleagues, many people today seek to have themselves declared "professional"—and thereby turn their organizations into professional bureaucracies.

Divisionalized Form

Like the professional bureaucracy, the divisionalized form is not so much an integrated organization as a set of rather independent entities joined together by a loose administrative overlay. But whereas those entities of the professional bureaucracy are individuals—professionals in the operating core—in the divisionalized form they are units in the middle line, called divisions.

The divisionalized form differs from the other four configurations in one central respect: it is not a complete but a partial structure, superimposed on others. Those others are in the divisions, each of which is driven toward machine bureaucracy.

An organization divisionalizes for one reason above all—because its product lines are diversified. (And that tends to happen most often in the largest and most mature organizations, those that have run out of opportunities or become stalled in their traditional markets.) Such diversification encourages the organization to create a market-based unit, or division, for each distinct product line (as indicated in *Exhibit 2*) and to grant considerable autonomy to each division to run its own business.

That autonomy notwithstanding, divisionalization does *not* amount to decentralization, although the terms are often equated with each other. Decentralization is an expression of the dispersal of decision-making power in an organization. Divisionalization refers to a structure of semiautonomous market-based units. A divisionalized structure in which the managers at the heads of these units retain the lion's share of the power is far more centralized than many functional structures where large numbers of specialists get involved in the making of important decisions.

In fact, the most famous example of divisionalization involved centralization. Alfred Sloan adopted the divisionalized form at General Motors to reduce the power of the different units, to integrate the holding company William Durant had put together. That kind of centralization appears to have continued to the point where the automotive units in some ways seem closer to functional marketing departments than true divisions.[1]

But how does top management maintain a semblance of control over the divisions? Some direct supervision is used—headquarters managers visit the divisions periodically and authorize some of their more important decisions. But too much of that interferes with the necessary autonomy of the divisions. So headquarters relies on performance control systems or, in other words, on the standardization of outputs. It leaves the operating details to the divisions and exercises control by measuring their performance periodically. And to design these control systems, headquarters creates a small technostructure. It also establishes a small central support staff to provide certain services common to the divisions (such as legal counsel and external relations).

This performance control system has an interesting effect on the internal structure of the division. First, the division is treated as a single integrated entity with one consistent, standardized, and quantifiable set of goals. Those goals tend to get translated down the line into more and more specific subgoals and, eventually, work standards. In other words, they encourage the bureaucratization of structure. And second, headquarters tends to impose its standards through the managers of the divisions, whom it holds responsible for divisional performance. That tends to result in centralization within the divisions. And centralization coupled with bureaucratization gives machine bureaucracy. That is the structure that works best in the divisions.

Simple structures and adhocracies make poor divisions because they abhor standards—they operate in dynamic environments where standards of any kind are difficult to establish. (This might partly explain why Alan Ladd, Jr. felt he had to leave the film division of Twentieth-Century Fox.[2]) And professional bureaucracies are not logically treated as integrated entities, nor can their goals be easily quantified. (How does one measure cure in a psychiatric ward or knowledge generated in a university?)

This conclusion is, of course, consistent with the earlier argument that external control (in this case, from headquarters) pushes an organization toward machine bureaucracy. The point is invariably illustrated when a conglomerate takes over an entrepreneurial company and imposes a lot of bureaucratic systems and standards on its simple structure.

The divisionalized form was created to solve the problem of adaptability in machine bureaucracy. By overlaying another level of administration that could add and subtract divisions, the organization found a way to adapt itself to new conditions and to spread its risk. But there is another side to these arguments. Some evidence suggests that the control systems of these structures discourage risk taking and innovation, that the division head who must justify his or her performance every month is not free to experiment the way the independent entrepreneur is.[3]

Moreover, to spread risk is to spread the consequences of that risk; a disaster in one division can pull down the entire organization. Indeed, the fear of this is what elicits the direct control of major new investments, which is what often discourages ambitious innovation. Finally, the divisionalized form does not solve the problem of adaptability of machine bureaucracy, it merely deflects it. When a division goes sour, all that headquarters seems able to do is change the management (as an independent board of directors would do) or divest it. From society's point of view, the problem remains.

Finally, from a social perspective, the divisionalized form raises a number of serious issues. By enabling organizations to grow very large, it leads to the concentration of a great deal of economic power in a few hands. And there is some evidence that it sometimes encourages that power to be used irresponsibly. By emphasizing the measurement of performance as its means of control, a bias arises in favor of those divisional goals that can be operationalized, which usually means the economic ones, not the social ones. That the division is driven by such measures to be socially unresponsive would not seem inappropriate—for the business of the corporation is, after all, economic.

The problem is that in big businesses (where the divisionalized form is prevalent) every strategic decision has social as well as economic consequences. When the screws of the performance control system are turned tight, the division managers, in order to achieve the results expected of them, are driven to ignore the social consequences of their decisions. At that point, *un*responsive behavior becomes *ir*responsible.[4]

The divisionalized structure has become very fashionable in the past few decades, having spread in pure or modified form through most of the *Fortune* "500" in a series of waves and then into European companies.[5] It has also become fashionable in the nonbusiness sector in the guise of "multiversities," large hospital systems, unions, and government itself. And yet it seems fundamentally ill suited to these sectors for two reasons.

First, the success of the divisionalized form depends on goals that can be measured. But outside the business sector, goals are often social in nature and nonquantifiable. The result of performance control, then, is an inappropriate displacement of social goals by economic ones.

Second, the divisions often require structures other than machine bureaucracy. The professionals in the multiversities, for example, often balk at the technocratic controls and the top-down decision making

that tends to accompany external control of their campuses. In other words, the divisionalized form can be a misfit just as can any of the other configurations.

Adhocracy

None of the structures discussed so far suits the industries of our age—industries such as aerospace, petrochemicals, think-tank consulting, and filmmaking. These organizations need above all to innovate in complex ways. The bureaucratic structures are too inflexible, and the simple structure is too centralized. These industries require "project structures" that fuse experts drawn from different specialties into smoothly functioning creative teams. Hence they tend to favor our fifth configuration, adhocracy, a structure of interacting project teams.

Adhocracy is the most difficult of the five configurations to describe because it is both complex and nonstandardized. Indeed, adhocracy contradicts much of what we accept on faith in organizations—consistency in output, control by administrators, unity of command, strategy emanating from the top. It is a tremendously fluid structure, in which power is constantly shifting and coordination and control are by mutual adjustment through the informal communication and interaction of competent experts. Moreover, adhocracy is the newest of the five configurations, the one researchers have had the least chance to study. Yet it is emerging as a key structural configuration, one that deserves a good deal of consideration.

These comments notwithstanding, adhocracy is a no less coherent configuration than any of the others. Like the professional bureaucracy, adhocracy relies on trained and specialized experts to get the bulk of its work done. But in its case, the experts must work together to create new things instead of working apart to perfect established skills. Hence, for coordination adhocracy must rely extensively on mutual adjustment, which it encourages by the use of the liaison devices—integrating managers, task forces, and matrix structure.

In professional bureaucracy, the experts are concentrated in the operating core, where much of the power lies. But in adhocracy, they tend to be dispersed throughout the structure according to the decisions they make—in the operating core, middle line, technostructure, strategic apex, and especially support staff. Thus, whereas in each of the other configurations power is more or less concentrated, in adhocracy it is distributed unevenly. It flows, not according to authority or status but to wherever the experts needed for a particular decision happen to be found.

Managers abound in the adhocracy—functional managers, project managers, integrating managers.

This results in narrow "spans of control" by conventional measures. That is not a reflection of control but of the small size of the project teams. The managers of adhocracy do not control in the conventional sense of direct supervision; typically they are experts too who take their place alongside the others in the teams, concerned especially with linking the different teams together.

As can be seen in *Exhibit 2*, many of the distinctions of conventional structure disappear in the adhocracy. With power based on expertise instead of authority, the line/staff distinction evaporates. And with power distributed throughout the structure, the distinction between the strategic apex and the rest of the structure also blurs. In a project structure, strategy is not formulated from above and then implemented lower down; rather, it evolves by virtue of the multitude of decisions made for the projects themselves. In other words, the adhocracy is continually developing its strategy as it accepts and works out new projects, the creative results of which can never be predicted. And so everyone who gets involved in the project work—and in the adhocracy that can mean virtually everyone—becomes a strategy maker.

There are two basic types of adhocracy, operating and administrative. The *operating* adhocracy carries out innovative projects directly on behalf of its clients, usually under contract, as in a creative advertising agency, a think-tank consulting firm, a manufacturer of engineering prototypes. Professional bureaucracies work in some of these industries too, but with a different orientation. The operating adhocracy treats each client problem as a unique one to be solved in creative fashion; the professional bureaucracy pigeonholes it so that it can provide a standard skill.

For example, there are some consulting firms that tailor their solutions to the client's order and others that sell standard packages off the rack. When the latter fits, it proves much cheaper. When it does not, the money is wasted. In one case, the experts must cooperate with each other in organic structures to innovate; in the other, they can apply their standard skills autonomously in bureaucratic structures.

In the operating adhocracy, the operating and administrative work blend into a single effort. That is, the organization cannot easily separate the planning and design of the operating work—in other words, the project—from its actual execution. So another classic distinction disappears. As shown above the dotted lines in *Exhibit 2*, the organization emerges as an organic mass in which line managers, staff, and operating experts all work together on project teams in ever-shifting relationships.

The *administrative* adhocracy undertakes projects on its own behalf, as in a space agency or a producer of electronic components. NASA, for example, as described during the Apollo era by Margaret K. Chandler and Leonard R. Sayles, seems to be a perfect example of administrative adhocracy.[6] In this type of adhocracy, in contrast to the other, we find a sharp separation of the administrative from the operating work—the latter shown by the dotted lines in *Exhibit 2*. This results in a two-part structure. The administrative component carries out the innovative design work, combining line managers and staff experts in project teams. And the operating component, which puts the results into production, is separated or "truncated" so that its need for standardization will not interfere with the project work.

Sometimes the operations are contracted out altogether. Other times, they are set up in independent structures, as in the printing function in newspapers. And when the operations of an organization are highly automated, the same effect takes place naturally. The operations essentially run themselves, while the administrative component tends to adopt a project orientation concerned with change and innovation, with bringing new facilities on line. Note also the effects of automation— a reduction in the need for rules, since these are built right into the machinery, and a blurring of the line/staff distinction, since control becomes a question more of expertise than authority. What does it mean to supervise a machine? Thus the effect of automation is to reduce the degree of machine bureaucracy in the administration and to drive it toward administrative adhocracy.

Both kinds of adhocracy are commonly found in environments that are complex as well as dynamic. These are the two conditions that call for sophisticated innovation, which requires the cooperative efforts of many different kinds of experts. In the case of administrative adhocracy, the production system is also typically complex and, as noted, often automated. These production systems create the need for highly skilled support staffers, who must be given a good deal of power over technical decisions.

For its part, the operating adhocracy is often associated with young organizations. For one thing, with no standard products or services, organizations that use it tend to be highly vulnerable, and many of them disappear at an early age. For another, age drives these organizations toward bureaucracy, as the employees themselves age and tend to seek an escape from the instability of the structure and its environment. The innovative consulting firm converges on a few of its most successful projects, packages them into standard skills, and settles down to life as a professional bureaucracy; the manufacturer of prototypes hits on a hot product and becomes a machine bureaucracy to mass-produce it.

But not all adhocracies make such a transition.

Some endure as they are, continuing to innovate over long periods of time. We see this, for example, in studies of the National Film Board of Canada, famous since the 1940s for its creativity in both films and the techniques of filmmaking.

Finally, fashion is a factor associated with adhocracy. This is clearly the structure of our age, prevalent in almost every industry that has grown up since World War II (and none I can think of established before that time). Every characteristic of adhocracy is very much in vogue today—expertise, organic structure, project teams and task forces, diffused power, matrix structure, sophisticated and often automated production systems, youth, and dynamic, complex environments. Adhocracy is the only one of the five configurations that combines some sense of democracy with an absence of bureaucracy.

Yet, like all the others, this configuration too has its limitations. Adhocracy in some sense achieves its effectiveness through inefficiency. It is inundated with managers and costly liaison devices for communication; nothing ever seems to get done without everyone talking to everyone else. Ambiguity abounds, giving rise to all sorts of conflicts and political pressures. Adhocracy can do no ordinary thing well. But it is extraordinary at innovation.

CONFIGURATIONS AS A DIAGNOSTIC TOOL

What in fact are these configurations? Are they (1) abstract ideals, (2) real-life structures, one of which an organization had better use if it is to survive, or (3) building blocks for more complex structures? In some sense, the answer is a qualified yes in all three cases. These are certainly abstract ideals, simplifications of the complex world of structure. Yet the abstract ideal can come to life too. Every organization experiences the five pulls that underlie these configurations: the pull to centralize by the top management, the pull to formalize by the technostructure, the pull to professionalize by the operators, the pull to balkanize by the managers of the middle line, and the pull to collaborate by the support staff.

Where one pull dominates—where the conditions favor it above all—then the organization will tend to organize itself close to one of the configurations. I have cited examples of this throughout my discussion—the entrepreneurial company, the hamburger chain, the university, the conglomerate, the space agency.

But one pull does not always dominate; two may have to exist in balance. Symphony orchestras engage highly trained specialists who perfect their skills, as do the operators in professional bureaucracy. But

their efforts must be tightly coordinated hence, the reliance on the direct supervision of a leader—a conductor—as in simple structure. Thus a hybrid of the two configurations emerges that is eminently sensible for the symphony orchestra (even if it does generate a good deal of conflict between leader and operators).

Likewise, we have companies that are diversified around a central theme that creates linkages among their different product lines. As a result, they continually experience the pull to separate, as in the divisionalized form, and also integrate, as in machine bureaucracy or perhaps adhocracy. And what configuration should we impute to an IBM? Clearly, there is too much going on in many giant organizations to describe them as one configuration or another. But the framework of the five configurations can still help us to understand how their different parts are organized and fit together—or refuse to.

The point is that managers can improve their organizational designs by considering the different pulls their organizations experience and the configurations toward which they are drawn. In other words, this set of five configurations can serve as an effective tool in diagnosing the problems of organizational design, especially those of the *fit* among component parts. Let us consider four basic forms of misfit to show how managers can use the set of configurations as a diagnostic tool.

Are the Internal Elements Consistent?

Management that grabs at every structural innovation that comes along may be doing its organization great harm. It risks going off in all directions: yesterday long-range planning to pin managers down, today Outward Bound to open them up. Quality of working life programs as well as all those fashionable features of adhocracy—integrating managers, matrix structure, and the like—have exemplary aims: to create more satisfying work conditions and to increase the flexibility of the organization. But are they appropriate for a machine bureaucracy? Do enlarged jobs really fit with the requirements of the mass production of automobiles? Can the jobs ever be made large enough to really satisfy the workers—and the cost-conscious customers?

I believe that in the fashionable world of organizational design, fit remains an important characteristic. The *hautes structurières* of New York—the consulting firms that seek to bring the latest in structural fashion to their clients—would do well to pay a great deal more attention to that fit. Machine bureaucracy functions best when its reporting relationships are sharply defined and its operating core staffed with workers who prefer routine and stability. The nature of the work in this configuration—managerial as well as operating—is rooted in the reality of mass production, in the costs of manual labor compared with those of automated machines, and in the size and age of the organization.

Until we are prepared to change our whole way of living—for example, to pay more for handcrafted instead of mass-produced products and so to consume less—we would do better to spend our time trying not to convert our machine bureaucracies into something else but to ensure that they work effectively as the bureaucracies they are meant to be. Organizations, like individuals, can avoid identity crises by deciding what it is they wish to be and then pursuing it with a healthy obsession.

Are the External Controls Functional?

An organization may achieve its own internal consistency and then have it destroyed by the imposition of external controls. The typical effect of those controls is to drive the organization toward machine bureaucracy. In other words, it is the simple structures, professional bureaucracies, and adhocracies that suffer most from such controls. Two cases of this seem rampant in our society: one is the takeover of small, private companies by larger divisionalized ones, making bureaucracies of entrepreneurial ventures; the other is the tendency for governments to assume increasingly direct control of what used to be more independent organizations—public school systems, hospitals, universities, and social welfare agencies.

As organizations are taken over in these ways—brought into the hierarchies of other organizations—two things happen. They become centralized and formalized.[7] In other words, they are driven toward machine bureaucracy. Government administrators assume that just a little more formal control will bring this callous hospital or that weak school in line. Yet the cure—even when the symptoms are understood—is worse than the disease. The worst way to correct deficiencies in professional work is through control by technocratic standards. Professional bureaucracies cannot be managed like machines.

In the school system, such standards imposed from outside the classroom serve only to discourage the competent teachers, not to improve the weak ones. The performance of teachers—as that of all other professionals—depends primarily on their skills and training. Retraining or, more likely, replacing them is the basic means to improvement.

For almost a century now, the management literature—from time study through operations research to long-range planning—has promoted machine bureaucracy as the "one best way." That assumption is

false; it is one way among a number suited to only certain conditions.

Is There a Part That Does Not Fit?

Sometimes an organization's management, recognizing the need for internal consistency, hives off a part in need of special treatment—establishes it in a pocket off in a corner to be left alone. But the problem all too often is that it is not left alone. The research laboratory may be built out in the country, far from the managers and analysts who run the machine bureaucracy back home. But the distance is only physical.

Standards have a long administrative reach: it is difficult to corner off a small component and pretend that it will not be influenced by the rest. Each organization, not to mention each configuration, develops its own norms, traditions, beliefs—in other words, its own ideology. And that permeates every part of it. Unless there is a rough balance among opposing forces—as in the symphony orchestra—the prevailing ideology will tend to dominate. That is why adhocracies need especially tolerant controllers, just as machine bureaucracies must usually scale down their expectations for their research laboratories.

Is the Right Structure in the Wrong Situation?

Some organizations do indeed achieve and maintain an internal consistency. But then they find that it is designed for an environment the organization is no longer in. To have a nice, neat machine bureaucracy in a dynamic industry calling for constant innovation or, alternately, a flexible adhocracy in a stable industry calling for minimum cost makes no sense. Remember that these are configurations of situation as well as structure. Indeed, the very notion of configuration is that all the elements interact in a system. One element does not cause another; instead, all influence each other interactively. Structure is no more designed to fit the situation than situation is selected to fit the structure.

The way to deal with the right structure in the wrong environment may be to change the environment, not the structure. Often, in fact, it is far easier to shift industries or retreat to a suitable niche in an industry than to undo a cohesive structure. Thus the entrepreneur goes after a new, dynamic environment when the old one stabilizes and the bureaucracies begin to move in. When a situation changes suddenly—as it did for oil companies some years ago—a rapid change in situation or structure would seem to be mandatory. But what of a gradual change in situation? How should the organization adapt, for example, when its long-stable markets slowly become dynamic?

Essentially, the organization has two choices. It can

adapt continuously to the environment at the expense of internal consistency—that is steadily redesign its structure to maintain external fit. Or it can maintain internal consistency at the expense of a gradually worsening fit with its environment, at least until the fit becomes so bad that it must undergo sudden structural redesign to achieve a new internally consistent configuration. In other words, the choice is between evolution and revolution, between perpetual mild adaptation, which favors external fit over time, and infrequent major realignment, which favors internal consistency over time.

In his research on configuration, Danny Miller found that effective companies usually opt for revolution. Forced to decide whether to spend most of their time with a good external fit or with an established internal consistency, they choose consistency and put up with brief periods of severe disruption to realign the fit occasionally. It is better, apparently, to maintain at least partial configuration than none at all. Miller called this process, appropriately enough, a "quantum" theory of structural change.[8]

FIT OVER FASHION

To conclude, consistency, coherence, and fit—harmony—are critical factors in organization design, but they come at a price. An organization cannot be all things to all people. It should do what it does well and suffer the consequences. Be an efficient machine bureaucracy where that is appropriate and do not pretend to be highly adaptive. Or be an adaptive adhocracy and do not pretend to be highly efficient. Or create some new configuration to suit internal needs. The point is not really *which* configuration you have; it is *that* you achieve configuration.

1. *See* Leonard Wrigley, "Diversification and Divisional Autonomy," DBA thesis, Harvard Business School, 1970.

2. See "When Friends Run the Business," HBR July-August 1980, p. 87.

3. *See* Wrigley, "Diversification and Divisional Autonomy."

4. For a full discussion of the problems of implementing social goals in the divisionalized form, *see* Robert W. Ackerman, *The Social Challenge to Business* (Cambridge: Harvard University Press, 1975).

5. For a review of this trend, see Bruce R. Scott, "The Industrial State: Old Myths and New Realities," HBR March-April 1973, p. 133.

6. Margaret K. Chandler and Leonard Sayles, Managing Large Systems (New York: Harper & Row, 1971).

7. There is a good deal of evidence for this conclusion. See, for example, Yitzhak Samuel and Bilha F. Mannheim, "A Multidimensional Approach Toward a Typology of Bureaucracy," *Administrative Science Quarterly*, June 1970, p. 216; Edward A. Holdaway, John F. Newberry, David J. Hickson, and Peter Heron, "Dimensions of Organizations in Complex Societies: The Educational Sector," *Administrative Science Quarterly*, March 1975, p. 37; D. S. Pugh, D. J. Hickson, C. R. Hinnings, and C. Turner, "The Context of Organization Structures," *Administrative Science Quarterly*, March 1969, P. 91; Bernard C. Reimann, "On Dimensions of Bureaucratic Structure: An Empirical Reappraisal," *Administrative Science Quarterly*, December 1973, p. 462.

8. Danny Miller, *Revolution and Evolution: A Quantum View of Organizational Adaptation*, working paper, McGill University, 1980.

Appendix:
Elements of the configurations

Elements of structure

Job specialization refers to the number of tasks in a given job and the worker's control over these tasks. A job is horizontally specialized to the extent that it encompasses few narrowly defined tasks, vertically specialized to the extent that the worker lacks control of the tasks he or she performs. Unskilled jobs are typically highly specialized in both dimensions, while skilled or professional jobs are typically specialized horizontally but not vertically. Job enrichment refers to the enlargement of jobs in both the vertical and horizontal dimensions.

Behavior formalization refers to the standardization of work processes by imposition of operating instructions, job descriptions, rules, regulations, and the like. Structures that rely on standardization for coordination are generally referred to as bureaucratic, those that do not as organic.

Training and indoctrination refer to the use of formal instructional programs to establish and standardize in people the requisite skills, knowledge, and norms to do particular jobs. Training is a key design parameter in all work we call professional. Training and formalization are basically substitutes for achieving the standardization (in effect the bureaucratization) of behavior. In the one, the standards are internalized in formal training as skills or norms; in the other, they are imposed on the job as rules.

Unit grouping refers to the optional bases by which positions are grouped together into units and these units into higher-order units. Grouping encourages coordination by putting different jobs under common supervision, by requiring them to share common resources and achieve common measures of performance, and by facilitating mutual adjustment among them. The various bases for grouping - by work process, product, client, area, etc—can be reduced to two fundamentals: the function performed or the market served.

Unit size refers to the number of positions (or units) contained in a single unit. The equivalent term "span of control" is not used here because sometimes units are kept small despite an absence of close supervisory control. For example, when experts coordinate extensively by mutual adjustment, as in an engineering team in a space agency, they will form into small teams. In this case, unit size is small and span of control is low despite a relative absence of direct supervision. In contrast when work is highly standardized (because of either formalization or training), unit size can be very large because there is little need for direct supervision

One foreman can supervise dozens of assemblers because they work according to very tight instructions.

Planning and control systems are used to standardize outputs. They may be divided into two types—action planning systems, which specify the results of specific action before they are taken (for example, that holes should be drilled with diameters of three centimeters), and, performance control systems, which specify the results of whole ranges of actions after the fact (for example, that sales of a division should grow by 10% in a given year).

Liaison devices refer to a whole set of mechanisms used to encourage mutual adjustment within and among units. They range from liaison positions (such as the purchasing engineer who stands between purchasing and engineering); through task forces, standing committees that bring together members of many departments, and integrating managers (such as brand managers); and finally to fully developed matrix structures.

Vertical decentralization describes the extent to which decision making is delegated to managers down the middle line, while **horizontal decentralization** describes the extent to which non-managers (that is, people in the operating core, technostructure, and support staff) control decision processes. Moreover, decentralization may be selective, concerning only specific kinds of decisions, or parallel, concerning many kinds of decisions altogether. Five types of decentralization may be found: vertical and horizontal centralization, where all power rests at the strategic apex; limited horizontal decentralization (selective), where the strategic apex shares some power with the technostructure that standardizes everybody else's work; limited vertical decentralization (parallel); where managers of market-based units are delegated the power to control most of the decisions concerning their line units; vertical and horizontal decentralization, where most of the power rests in the operating core at the bottom of the structure; and selective vertical and horizontal decentralization, where the power over different decisions is dispersed widely in the organization - among managers, staff experts, and operators who work in groups at various levels in the hierarchy.

Elements of situation

The age and size of the organization affect particularly the extent to which its behavior is formalized and its administrative structure (technostructure and middle line) elaborated. As they age and grow, organizations appear to go through distinct structural transitions, much as insects metamorphose—for example, from simple organic to elaborated bureaucratic structure, from functional grouping to market-based grouping.

The **technical system** of the organization influences especially the operating core and those staff units most clearly associated with it. When the technical system of the organization regulates the work of the operating core - as it typically does in mass production - it has the effect of bureaucratizing the organization by virtue of the standards it imposes on lower-level workers. Alternately, when the technical system succeeds in automating the operating work (as in much process production) it reduces the need for external rules and regulations: the necessary rules are automatically incorporated into the machines enabling the structure to be organic. And when the technical system is complex as is often the case in process production, the organization must create a significant professional support staff to deal with it and then must decentralize selectively to that staff many of the decisions concerned with the technical system.

The **environment** of the organization can vary in its degree of complexity, in how static or dynamic it is, in the diversity of its markets and in the hostility it contains for the organization. The more complex the environment, the more difficulty central management has in comprehending it and the greater the need for decentralization. The more dynamic the environment, the greater the difficulty in standardizing work, outputs, or skills and so the less bureaucratic the structure. These relationships suggest four kinds of structures: two in stable environments (one simple, the other complex) lead-

ing, respectively, to a centralized and a decentralized bureaucracy; and two in dynamic environments(again, one simple the other complex) leading, respectively, to a centralized and a decentralized organic structure. Market diversity, as noted earlier, encourages the organization to set up market-based divisions (instead of functional departments) to deal with each, while extreme hostility in the environment drives the organization to centralize power temporarily - no matter what its normal structure to fight off the threat,

The **power** factors of the organization include external control, personal power needs, and fashion. The more an organization is controlled externally, the more centralized and bureaucratic it tends to become. This can be explained by the fact that the two most effective means to control an organization from the outside are to hold its most powerful decision maker, the chief executive officer, responsible for its actions and to impose clearly defined standards on it (performance targets or rules and regulations).

Moreover, because the externally controlled organization must be especially careful about its actions— often having to justify these to outsiders—it tends to formalize much of its behavior and insist that its chief executive authorize key decisions. A second factor, individual power needs (especially by the chief executive) tend to generate excessively centralized structures. And fashion has been shown to be a factor in organization design, the structure of the day often being favored even by organizations for which it is inappropriate.

Massachusetts
Institute of Technology

Winter 1991

Volume 32
Number 2

Henry Mintzberg | The Effective Organization: Forces and Forms

Reprint 3225

The Effective Organization: Forces and Forms

Henry Mintzberg   *McGill University*

FROM HIS FIRST BOOK, *The Nature of Managerial Work*, to his latest, *Mintzberg on Management*, Henry Mintzberg has been a provocative, influential voice in the general management discussion. This article develops his work on organizational structures, refining his theories to better explain how effective organizations manage the contradictory internal forces that can so easily tear them apart. There is no best way, he argues; organizations must build their own structures, using established forms or combining them. But while there is no blueprint for the effective organization, we can be aware of the dangers—when the force for efficiency, for instance, begins to suppress innovation, or when healthy internal competition deteriorates into petty politics. Managing an organization is like building with LEGOs, he writes, and the best structure is the one that balances forces most gracefully.

WHAT MAKES an organization effective? For a long time we thought we had the answer. Frederick Taylor told us about the "one best way" at the turn of the century, and organizations long pursued this holy grail. First it was Taylor's time and motion studies, later the participative management of the human relations people, in more recent years the wonders of strategic planning. It was as if every manager had to see the world through the same pair of glasses, although the fashion for lenses changed from time to time.

Then along came the so-called "contingency theorists," who argued that "it all depends." Effective organizations designed themselves to match their conditions. They used those time and motion studies for mass production, they used strategic planning under conditions of relative stability, and so forth. Trouble was, all this advice never came together: managers were made to feel like diners at a buffet table, urged to take a little bit of this and a little bit of that.

In a way, these two approaches to organizational effectiveness are reflected in the most popular management writings of today. I like to call them "Peterian" and "Porterian." Tom Peters and Robert

Waterman implore managers to "stick to their knitting" and to design their structures with "simultaneous loose-tight properties," among other best ways, while Michael Porter insists that they use competitive analysis to choose strategic positions that best match the characteristics of their industries.[1] To Porter, effectiveness resides in strategy, while to Peters it is the operations that count—executing any strategy with excellence.

While I agree that being effective depends on doing the right thing as well as doing things right, as Peter Drucker put it years ago, I believe we have to probe more deeply to find out what really makes an organization effective. We need to understand what gets it to a viable strategy in the first place, what makes it excellent once it's there, and how some organizations are able to sustain viability and excellence in the face of change.

Some years ago I thought I had another answer. I argued that effective organizations "got it all together." By choosing "configuration," they brought their various characteristics of structure, strategy, and context into natural co-alignment.[2] For example, some achieved integration as efficient machines, while others coalesced around product innovation. In a sense, these organizations played jigsaw puzzle, fitting all the pieces of their operations into one neat image.

Recently, however, I have begun to wonder about

Henry Mintzberg is Bronfman Professor of Management at McGill University. Permission granted by LEGO Overseas A/S, Billund Denmark, to use the copyrighted word LEGO.

configuration. There are certainly many effective organizations that seem to fit one image or another – IBM as that "big blue" machine, 3M as the product innovator. But some rather effective organizations do not, and even those that do sometimes confound things. How does that big blue machine come up with critical adaptations when it has to, and why does 3M have those tight financial controls? Thus I have begun to consider another view of organizational effectiveness, in which organizations do not slot themselves into established images so much as build their own unique solutions to problems. "Do your own thing" is its motto, LEGO its metaphor.

This article builds a framework around these two approaches. It proposes that the effective organization plays LEGO as well as jigsaw puzzle. The pieces of the game are the forces that organizations experience; the integrating images are the forms that organizations take. Together, they constitute a powerful framework by which to diagnose and deal with the problems organizations face. Below I introduce the forces, as the basic building blocks of all organizations. Then I shall outline the framework that is to follow.

A System of Forces

Much of what happens in organizations can, in my experience, be captured by the interplay of seven basic forces. I array five of these around the outside of a pentagon and put two in the middle, as shown in Figure 1. They are described below.

• First is the force for *direction*; this gives a sense of where the organization must go as an integrated entity. Without such direction – which today is apt to be called strategic vision, years ago grand strategy – the various activities of an organization cannot easily mesh to achieve common purpose.

• Next is the force for *efficiency*, which attempts to ensure a viable ratio of benefits gained to costs incurred. Without some concern for efficiency, all but the most protected of organizations must eventually falter. Efficiency generally means standardization and formalization; often it reduces to economy. In current practice, it focuses on rationalization and restructuring, among other things.

• Across from the force for efficiency is that for *proficiency* – for carrying out certain tasks with high levels of knowledge and skill. Without proficiency, the difficult work of organizations – whether surgery in the hospital or engineering in the

corporation – just could not get done.

• Below efficiency is the force for *concentration* – for particular units to concentrate their efforts on serving particular markets. Without such concentration, it becomes difficult to manage an organization that is diversified.

• At the bottom right is the force for *innovation*. Organizations need central direction and focused concentration, and they need efficiency and proficiency. But they also need to discover new things for their customers and themselves – to adapt and to learn.

• Finally, inside the pentagon are two forces I call catalytic: *cooperation* and *competition*. One describes the pulling together of ideology, the other the pulling apart of politics. By ideology, I mean more than just the culture of an organization, I mean the rich culture of norms, beliefs, and values that knit a disparate set of people into a harmonious, cooperative entity. By politics I mean behaviour that is technically not sanctioned or legitimate. It acts outside the bounds of legal authority and acknowledged expertise and therefore tends to be conflictive in nature. No serious organization is ever entirely free of politics, few perhaps of at least some vestiges of ideology.

This article's view of organizational effectiveness will be developed as follows. Taking these forces

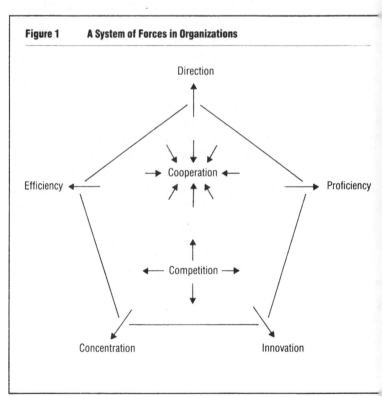

Figure 1   A System of Forces in Organizations

as fundamental and their interplay as key to understanding what goes on in organizations, I shall argue first that when one force dominates an organization, it is drawn toward a coherent, established form, described as *configuration*. That facilitates its management, but also raises the problem of *contamination*. When no single force dominates, the organization must instead function as a balanced *combination* of different forces, including periods of *conversion* from one form to another. But combination raises the problem of *cleavage*. Both contamination and cleavage require the management of *contradiction*, and here the catalytic forces, cooperation and competition, come into play. But these two forces are themselves contradictory, and so the effective organization must balance them as well. Put this all together and you get a fascinating game of jigsaw puzzle-cum-LEGO. This may seem complicated, but bear with me; reading about it here will prove a lot easier than managing it in practice. It may even help!

Configuration

Charles Darwin once wrote about "lumpers" as opposed to "splitters"— synthesizers who think in broad categories and prefer to slot things into well-established pigeonholes, as opposed to analyzers who tend to split things up finely.[3] In a way, of course, we are all lumpers: we all like neat envelopes into which we can put our confusing experiences.

It is ironic, therefore, that in the field of management we do not have established categories by which to distinguish different organizations. Imagine biology without some system of species to consider living things. Biologists might well end up, for example, debating the "one best dwelling" for all mammals — bears as well as beavers. Silly as this example may seem, that is what we do in management all the time.

Configuration refers to any form of organization that is consistent and highly integrated. In the spirit of the jigsaw puzzle, a configuration is an image whose pieces all fit neatly together.

A Portfolio of Forms

In principle, all kinds of configurations are possible. In practice, however, only a few seem to occur commonly.

Our pentagon contains seven forces. I believe that configuration occurs when any one of these forces dominates an organization, driving it to a corresponding form. That gives us seven basic forms, described below, five of which are shown at the nodes of the pentagon, in Figure 2.

• The *entrepreneurial* form tends to occur when the force for direction dominates an organization, so that the chief executive takes personal control of much of what goes on. This happens especially in startup and turnaround situations, both of which require the imposition of strong vision from the top; it also happens in small, owner-managed companies. As a result, there are few middle management and staff positions, or else they are relatively weak. As a turnaround example, when Jan Carlzon took over the airline SAS in the early 1980s, he established direct links with the operating employees, bypassing much of the established administration and dispensing with many of the standard control systems in order to impose his new vision.

• The *machine* form tends to appear when the force for efficiency becomes paramount; this typically occurs in mass production and mass service organizations (automobile companies, retail banks, etc.) and in ones with an overriding need for control (as in nuclear power plants and many government departments). Here, especially in the larger, more mature organization, middle management and staff functions are fully developed; they focus on regulating the work of the operating employees by imposing rules, regulations, and standards of various kinds.

• The *professional* form tends to arise when proficiency is the dominant force, as in hospitals, accounting practices, and engineering offices. What matters here is the drive to perfect existing skills and knowledge, rather than to invent new ones. This makes the professional organization a consummate pigeonholer: the hospital, for example, prefers to diagnose entering patients as quickly as possible so that it can get on with administering the most appropriate standardized treatment. This characteristic allows for the considerable autonomy found in these organizations: each professional works remarkably free of his or her colleagues, let alone of the managers ostensibly in charge.

• The *adhocracy* form develops in response to an overriding need for innovation. Again we have an organization of skilled experts. But here, because the organization exists to create novelty — such as the unique film or the new engineering prototype—the experts must combine their efforts in multidisciplinary project teams. Doing so requires a good deal of informal communication, with the result that the structure becomes fluid, sometimes called "intrapreneurial." Some adhocracy organizations, such as advertising agencies and think tank consulting firms, innovate directly on behalf of their clients. Others use project work to innovate for themselves, bringing their own new products or facilities on line—for example, some high-technology and chemical firms.

• The *diversified* form tends to arise when the force for concentration, particularly on distinct products and markets, overrides the others. Such organizations first diversify and then divisionalize. Each division is given relative autonomy, subject to the performance controls imposed by a small, central headquarters. The diversified form is, of course,

best known in the world of large, conglomerate corporations. But when governments speak of accountability, they have much the same structure in mind.

• The forces for cooperation and for competition can sometimes dominate, too, giving rise to forms I call the *ideological* and the *political*. Examples of both are readily available: the spirited Israeli kibbutz is ideological, and the conflictive regulatory agency in which infighting takes over is political. But I believe these forms are not all that common, at least compared with the others discussed above, and so our discussion will proceed from here mainly on the basis of five forms and seven forces, shown in Figure 2.[4]

Do these forms really exist in practice? In one sense, they do not. After all, they are just words on pieces of paper, caricatures that simplify a com-

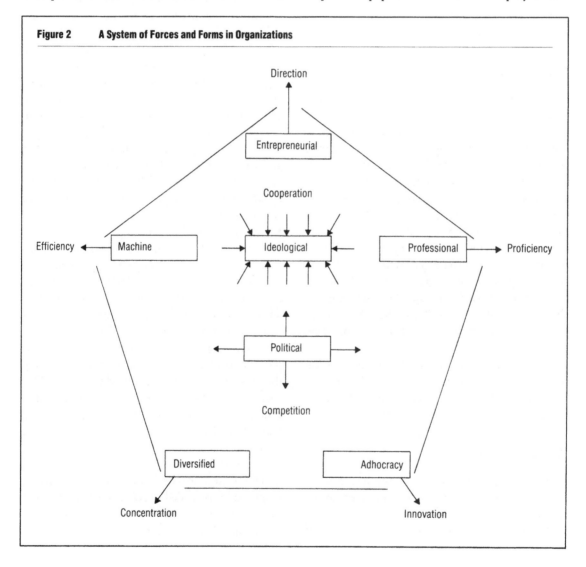

Figure 2   A System of Forces and Forms in Organizations

plex reality. No serious organization can be labeled a pure machine or a pure adhocracy. On the other hand, we can't carry reality around in our heads; we think in terms of simplifications, called theories or models, of which these forms are examples. We must, therefore, turn to a second question: whether the forms are *useful*. And again I shall answer, yes and no.

While no configuration ever matches a real organization perfectly, some do come remarkably close; examples include the highly regulated Swiss hotel and the free-wheeling Silicon Valley innovator. Just as species exist in nature in response to distinct ecological niches, so too do configurations evolve in human society. The hotel guest does not want surprises—no jack-in-the-box popping up when the pillow is lifted, thank you—just the predictability of that wake-up call at 8:00, not 8:07. But in that niche called advertising, the client that gets no surprises may well take its business elsewhere.

My basic point about configuration is simple: when the form fits, the organization may be well advised to wear it, at least for a time. With configuration, an organization achieves a sense of order, of integration. There is internal consistency, synergy among processes, fit with the external context. It is the organization without configuration, much like the individual without personality, that tends to suffer the identity crises.

Outsiders also appreciate configuration; it helps them to understand an organization. We walk into a McDonald's and know immediately what drives it, likewise a 3M. But more important is what configuration does for the managers: it makes the organization more manageable. With the course set, it is easier to steer, and also to deflect pressures that are peripheral. No configuration is perfect—the professional one, for example, tends to belittle its clients, while the machine one often alienates its workers—but there is something to be said for consistency. Closely controlled workers may not be happier than the autonomous ones of the professional organization, but they are certainly better off than ones confused by quality circles in the morning and time studies in the afternoon. Better to have the definition and discipline of configuration than to dissipate one's energies trying to be all things to all people.

Moreover, much of what we know about organizations in practice applies to specific configurations. There may not be any one best way, but

there are certainly preferred ways in particular contexts—for example, time studies in machine organizations and matrix structures in adhocracies.

Thus, configuration seems to be effective for classification, for comprehension, for diagnosis, and for design. But only so long as everything holds still. Introduce the dynamics of evolutionary change and, sooner or later, configuration becomes ineffective.

Contamination by Configuration

In harmony, consistency, and fit lies configuration's great strength—and also its debilitating weakness. Experience shows that the dominant force sometimes dominates to the point of undermining all the others. For example, the quest for efficiency in a machine organization can almost totally suppress the capacity for innovation, while in an adhocracy the need for some modicum of efficiency often gets suppressed. I call this phenomenon *contamination*, although we might just as easily rephrase Lord Acton's dictum: among the forces of organizations, too, power tends to corrupt and absolute power corrupts absolutely. For example, the story of medical care in the United States could well be described as the contamination of efficiency by proficiency. No one can deny the primacy of proficiency—who would go to a hospital that favors efficiency?—but few people would defend the extent to which it has been allowed to dominate.

Machine organizations recognize this problem when they locate their research and development facilities far from the head office so that their capacity for innovation will not be contaminated by the technocratic staff. Unfortunately, while lead may block X-rays, there is no known medium to shield the effects of a dominant culture. (The controller drops by, just to have a look: "What, no shoes? Can't they be creative dressed properly?") Of course, the opposite case is also well known. Just ask its members, "Who's the most miserable person in an adhocracy?" as I do in workshops with them. The inevitable reply is a brief silence followed by a few smiles, then growing laughter as everyone turns to some poor person cowering in the corner. Of course, it's the controller. Controllers may wear shoes, but that hardly helps them keep the lid on all the madness.

"Contamination" is another way of saying that a configuration is not merely a structure, not even merely a power system: each is a culture in its own right. Of course, contamination may seem like a small price to pay for being coherently organized. True enough. Until things go out of control.

Configuration out of Control

A configuration is geared not only to a general context but also to specific conditions—for example, a particular leader in an entrepreneurial organization, or a particular product and market in a machine one. Thus, when the need arises for change, the dominating force may act to hold the organization in place. Then other forces must come into play. But because of contamination, the other forces may well be too weak. And so the organization goes out of control. For example, a machine organization in need of a new strategy may find neither the direction of an entrepreneurial leader nor the innovation of intrapreneurial subordinates. And so its internal consistency is perpetuated while it falls increasingly out of touch with its context.

In addition, each configuration is capable of driving itself out of control. That is to say, each contains the seeds of its own destruction. These reside in its dominating force and come into play through the effects of contamination. With too much proficiency in a professional organization, unconstrained by efficiency and direction, the professionals become overindulged (as in many of today's universities, not to mention medicine); with too much technocratic regulation in a machine organization, free of the force for innovation, an obsession with control arises (as in far too much contemporary industry and government).

My colleagues, Danny Miller and Manfred Kets de Vries, have published an interesting book about *The Neurotic Organization*.[5] They discuss organizations that become dramatic, paranoid, schizoid, compulsive, and depressive. In each case, a system that may once have been healthy has run out of control. Very roughly, I believe these five organizational neuroses correspond to what tends to happen to each of the five forms. The entrepreneurial organization tends to go out of control by becoming dramatic, as its leader, free of the other forces, takes the system off on a personal ego trip. The machine organization seems predisposed to compulsion once its analysts and their technocratic controls take over. Those who have worked in universities and hospitals understand the collective paranoid tendencies of professionals, especially when free of the constraining forces of adminis-

tration and innovation. I need not dwell on the depressive effects of obsession with the "bottom line" in the diversified organization; the impact on morale and innovation are now widely appreciated. As for the adhocracy organization, its problem is that, while it must continually innovate, it must also exploit the benefits of that innovation. One requires divergent thinking, the other convergent. Other forces help balance that tension; without them, the organization can easily become schizoid.

In effect, each form goes over the edge in its own particular way, so that behaviours that were once functional become dysfunctional when pursued to excess. Alongside excellence go the "perils of excellence."[6] This is easily seen on our pentagon. Remove all the arrows but one at any node, and the organization, no longer anchored, flies off in that direction.

Containment of Configuration

Thus I conclude that truly effective organizations do not exist in pure form. What keeps a configuration effective is not only the dominance of a single force but also the constraining effects of other forces. I call this *containment*. For example, people inclined to break the rules may feel hard pressed in the machine organization. But without some of them, the organization may be unable to deal with unexpected problems. Similarly, administration may not be powerful in the professional organization, but if it is allowed to atrophy, anarchy inevitably results. Thus, to manage configuration effectively is to exploit one form but also to reconcile different forces. But how does the effective organization deal with this contradiction?

Combination

Configuration is a good thing when you can have it. Unfortunately, some organizations all of the time, and all organizations some of the time, *cannot*. They must instead balance competing forces.

Consider the symphony orchestra. Proficiency is clearly a critical force, but so too is direction: such an organization is not conceivable without highly skilled players as well as leadership from a strong conductor. The Russians apparently tried a leaderless orchestra shortly after the revolution, but soon gave it up.

I shall use the word *combination* for the organization that balances different forces. In effect, it does not make it near any one node of the pentagon but instead finds its place somewhere inside.

How common are combinations as compared with configurations? To some extent the answer lies in the eyes of the beholder: what looks like a relatively pure form to one person (a lumper) may look like a combination of forces to another (a splitter). Still, it is interesting to consider how organizations appear to intelligent observers. For several years now, we have sent McGill MBA students out to study organizations in the Montreal area, having first exposed them to, among other things, a book of mine on the five forms of structure. At year end, I have circulated a questionnaire asking them to categorize the organization as one of the forms, a combination of two or more, or neither. In just over half the cases—sixty-six out of one hundred and twenty-three—the students felt that a single form fit best. They identified twenty-five entrepreneurial, thirteen machine, eleven diversified, nine adhocracy, and eight professional organizations. All the rest were labeled combinations—seventeen different ones in all. Diversified machines were the most common (nine), followed by innovative professionals (eight), entrepreneurial professionals (six), and entrepreneurial machines (five).[7]

Kinds of Combinations

Combinations themselves may take a variety of forms. They may balance just two forces or several; these forces may meet directly or indirectly; and the balance may be steady over time or oscillate back and forth.

When only two of the five forces meet in rough balance, the organization might be described as a *hybrid*. This is the case with the symphony orchestra, which can be found somewhere along the line between the entrepreneurial and professional forms. Organizations can, of course, combine several forces in rough balance as well.

Consider Apple Computers. It seems to have developed under its founder, Steve Jobs, largely as an adhocracy organization that emphasized new product development. The next CEO, John Sculley, apparently felt the need to temper that innovation; he paid more attention to efficiency in production and distribution. When I presented this framework at an executive program a couple of years ago, an employee of Apple Canada saw other things going on in his operation: he added an en-

trepreneurial form in sales due to a dynamic leader, professional forms in marketing and training to reflect the skills there, and another adhocracy form in a new venture unit. Organizations that experience such multiple combinations are, of course, the ones that must really play LEGO.

Then there is the question of how the different forces interact with each other. In some cases, they confront each other directly; in others, they can be separated over time or place. The combination in the symphony orchestra must be close and pervasive—leadership and professional skill meet regularly, face-to-face. In organizations like Apple, however, where different units favor different forces, they can act somewhat independently. And some organizations are lucky enough to buffer the effects of the different forces; in newspapers, the more professional editorial function simply hands over its camera-ready copy to the machinelike plant for production, and there is little need for interaction.

Finally, contrasting with the combinations maintained continuously are those that achieve balance in a dynamic equilibrium over time. In other words, power oscillates between the competing forces. Richard Cyert and James March wrote some years ago about the "sequential attention to goals" in organizations, where conflicting needs are attended to each in their own turn.[8] For example, a period of innovation to emphasize new product development might be followed by one of consolidation to rationalize product lines. (Might Apple Computers simply be in one of these cycles, the innovation of Jobs having been replaced by the consolidation of Sculley? Or will Sculley himself be able to get the organization to balance these two forces?)

Cleavage in Combinations

Necessary as it may sometimes be, all is not rosy in the world of combination. If configuration encourages contamination, which can drive the organization out of control, then combination encourages *cleavage*, which can have much the same effect. Instead of one force dominating, two or more forces confront each other and eventually paralyze the organization.

In effect, a natural fault line exists between any two opposing forces. Pushed to the limit, fissures begin to open up. In fact, Fellini made a film with exactly this theme. Called "Orchestra Rehearsal," it is about musicians who revolt against their conductor, and so bring on complete anarchy, followed by paralysis. Only then are they prepared to cooperate with their leader, because only then do they realize he is necessary to perform effectively. But one need not turn to allegories to find examples of cleavage. It occurs in most combinations—for example, in the classic battles between the R&D people, who promote new product innovation, and the production people, who want to stabilize manufacturing for operating efficiency. Cleavage can, of course, be avoided when the different forces are naturally buffered, as in the newspaper example. But few combination organizations are so fortunate.

I have discussed combination as if it is unavoidable in certain organizations, but implied that configuration is advantageous where possible, because it is more easily managed. But in reality, combination of one kind or another is necessary in every organization. The nodes of the pentagon, where the pure configurations lie, are only imaginary ideals. Indeed, any organization that reaches one is probably on its way out of control. It is the inside of the pentagon that has the space; that is where the effective organization must find its place. Some may fall close to one of the nodes, as configuration, *more or less*, while others may sit between nodes as combinations. But ultimately, configuration and combination are not so very different: one represents a tilt in favor of one force over others, the other more of a balance between forces. The question thus becomes again: how does the effective organization deal with the contradiction?

Conversion

So far our discussion has suggested that an organization finds its place in the pentagon and then stays there, more or less. But, in fact, few organizations get the chance to spend their entire lives in one place: their needs change, and they must undergo *conversion* from one configuration or combination to another.

Any number of external changes can cause such a conversion. An adhocracy organization may chance upon a great invention and settle down in machine form to exploit it. Or the stable market of a machine organization may suddenly become subject to so much change that it has to become innovative. Some conversions are, of course, temporary; the machine organization in trouble, for example, becomes entrepreneurial for a time to al-

low a forceful leader to impose new direction (so-called turnaround). This seems to describe Chrysler's experience when Iacocca arrived, as well as SAS's when Carlzon took over.

Cycles of Conversion

Of particular interest here is another type of conversion, which is somewhat predictable in nature because it is driven by forces intrinsic to the organization. Earlier I discussed the seeds of destruction contained in each configuration. Sometimes they destroy the organization, but sometimes they destroy only the configuration and drive the organization toward a more viable form. For example, the entrepreneurial form is inherently vulnerable, dependent as it is on a single leader. It may work well for the young organization, but with aging and growth the need for direction may be displaced by the need for efficiency. Then conversion to the machine form becomes necessary—the power of one leader must be replaced by that of numerous administrators.

The implication is that organizations often go through stages as they develop—if they develop—possibly sequenced into life cycles. In fact, I have placed the forces and forms on the pentagon to reflect the most common of these, with the simple, earlier stages near the top and the more complex ones lower down.

What appears to be the most common life cycle, especially in business, occurs around the left side of the figure. Organizations generally begin in the entrepreneurial form, because startup requires clear direction and attracts strong leaders. As these organizations grow, many settle into the machine form to exploit increasingly established markets. But with greater growth, established markets can become saturated, which often drives the successful organization to diversify its markets and then divisionalize its structure, taking it finally to the bottom left of the pentagon.

Those organizations highly dependent on expertise, however, will instead go down the right side of the pentagon, using the professional form if their services are more standardized and the adhocracy form if they are more innovative. (Some adhocracies eventually settle down by converting to the professional form, where they can exploit certain of the skills they have developed; this happens often in the consulting business, for example.)

Ideology is shown above politics on the pentagon because it tends to be associated with the earlier stages of an organization's life, politics with the later ones. Any organization can, of course, have a strong culture, just as any can become politicized. But ideologies develop rather more easily in young organizations, especially with charismatic leadership in the entrepreneurial stage, whereas it is extremely difficult to build a strong and lasting culture in a mature organization. Politics, in contrast, typically spreads as the energy of a youthful organization dissipates and its activities become more diffuse. Moreover, ideologies tend to dissipate over time, as norms rigidify into procedures and beliefs become rules; then political activity tends to rise in its place. Typically, the old and spent organizations are the most politicized; indeed, it is often their political conflict that finally kills them.

Cleavage in Conversion

Conversions may be necessary, but that does not make them easy. Some do occur quickly, because a change is long overdue, much as a supersaturated liquid, below the freezing point, solidifies the moment it is disturbed. But most conversions require periods of prolonged and agonizing transition. Two sides battle, usually an old guard committed to the status quo and young "upstarts" in favor of the change. As Apple Computer grew large, for example, a John Sculley intent on settling it down confronted a Steve Jobs who wished to maintain its freewheeling style of innovation.

The organization in transition becomes, of course, a form of combination, and it has the same problem of cleavage. Given that the challenge is to the very base of its power, however, there can be no recourse to higher authority to reconcile the conflict. Once again, then, the question arises: how does the effective organization deal with the contradiction?

Contradiction

The question of how to manage contradiction has concluded each section of this article. I believe the answer lies in the two forces in the middle of the pentagon. Organizations that have to reconcile contradictory forces, especially in dealing with change, often turn to the cooperative force of ideology or the competitive force of politics. Indeed, I believe that these two forces themselves represent a con-

tradiction that must be managed if an organization is not to run out of control.

I have placed these two forces in the middle of the pentagon for a particular reason. While it is true that each can dominate an organization, and so draw it toward a distinct form (referred to earlier as ideological and political), I believe that these forces more commonly act differently from the other five. While the other forces tend to infiltrate parts of the organization, and so isolate them, these tend instead to *infuse* the entire organization. Thus I refer to them as *catalytic*, noting that one tends to be centripetal, drawing behavior inward toward a common core, and the other centrifugal, driving behavior away from any central tendency. I shall argue that both can promote change and also prevent it, and that either way the organization is sometimes rendered more effective, sometimes less.

Cooperation through Ideology

Ideology represents the force for cooperation in an organization, for collegiality and consensus. People pull together for the common good—"we" are in this together.

I use the word ideology here to describe a rich culture in an organization, the uniqueness and attractiveness of which binds the members tightly to it. They commit themselves personally to the organization and identify with its needs.

Such an ideology can infuse any form of organization. It is often found in the entrepreneurial form, because, as already noted, organizational ideologies are usually created by charismatic leaders. But after such leaders move on, these ideologies can sustain themselves in other forms too. Thus we have the ideological machine that is McDonald's and perhaps an ideological adhocracy built by Messrs. Hewlett and Packard. And one study some years ago described colleges such as Swarthmore and Antioch as "distinctive," in other words professional forms infused with powerful ideologies.[9]

Ideology encourages the members of an organization to look inward—to take their lead from the organization's own vision, instead of looking outward to what comparable organizations are doing. (Of course, when ideology is strong, there are no comparable organizations!) A good example of this is Hewlett-Packard's "next bench syndrome": the product designer receives his or her stimulus for innovation, not from the aggregations of marketing research reports, but from the needs of a particular colleague at the next bench.

This looking inward is represented on the pentagon by the direction of the arrows of cooperation. They form a circle facing inward, as if to shield the organization from outside influences. Ideology above all draws people to work together to take the organization where all of them believe it must go. In this sense, ideology should be thought of as the spirit of an organization, the life force that infuses the skeleton of its formal structure.

Thus the existence of an ideology would seem to render any particular configuration more effective. People get fired up to pursue efficiency, or proficiency, or whatever else drives the organization. When this happens to a machine organization—as in a McDonald's, which is very responsive to its customers and very sensitive to its employees—I like to call it a "snappy machine." Bureaucratic machines are not supposed to be snappy, but ideology changes the nature of their quest for efficiency. This, of course, is the central message of the Peters and Waterman book, *In Search of Excellence*: effectiveness is achieved, not by opportunism, not even by clever strategic positioning, but by a management that knows exactly what it must do ("sticks to its knitting") and then does it with the fervor of religious missionaries ("hands on, value driven.")[10]

There seems to be another important implication: ideology helps an organization to manage contradiction and so to deal with change. The different forces no longer need conflict in quite the same way. Infused with the common ideology, units used to opposing each other can instead pull together, reducing contamination and cleavage and so facilitating adaptation.

I have always wondered why it is that IBM could come up with the important change when it had to, much like McDonald's, so machinelike, yet rather creative in its advertising and new product development. Likewise, if 3M and Hewlett-Packard really do conform largely to the adhocracy model, why do they have such tight control systems? I suspect we have the answer here. Their strong cultures enable these organizations to reconcile forces that work against each other in ordinary organizations. People develop a grudging respect for one another: when it matters, they cooperate for the common good. "Old Joe, over there, that nut in R&D: we production guys sometimes wonder about him. But we know this place could never function without him." Likewise in the great symphony orchestra, the musicians respect their conductor, without whom they know they could never produce beautiful music.

Such organizations can more easily reconcile opposing forces because what matters to their people is the organization itself, not any of its particular parts. If you believe in IBM more than marketing finesse or technical virtuosity per se, then when things really matter you will suspend your departmental rivalries to enable IBM to adapt.

In *Competitive Strategy*, Michael Porter warns about getting "stuck in the middle" between a strategy of "cost leadership" and one of "differentiation" (one representing the force for efficiency, the other representing quality and innovation).[11] How, then, has Toyota been able to produce such high-quality automobiles at such reasonable cost? Why didn't Toyota get stuck in the middle?

I believe that Porter's admonition stems from the view, prevalent in U.S. management circles throughout this century and reflected equally in my discussion of configuration, that if an organization favors one particular force, then others must suffer. If the efficiency experts have the upper hand, then quality gets slighted; if the designers get their way, productive efficiency must lag; and so on. This may be true so long as an organization is managed as a collection of different parts—a portfolio of products and functions. But when the spirit of ideology infuses the structure, an organization takes on an integrated life of its own, and contradictions get reconciled.

Thanks to Frederick Taylor and Henry Ford, workers on U.S. assembly lines have long had good reason to consider themselves mere cogs in their bureaucratic machines. Each had a job to do and was not to think about anything else—including quality and innovation. Indeed, even at the highest levels, this separation of functions has had its effect: critics of General Motors continue to bemoan the product development consequences of having had all those financial people in the chief executive's chair. But at Toyota, one has the impression that each individual is made to feel like an embodiment of the entire system—that no matter what job one does, it helps to make Toyota great. Isn't that why the assembly workers are allowed to shut down the line? Each one is treated as a person capable of making decisions for the good of Toyota. Thus the only thing that gets stuck in the middle at Toyota is the conventional management thinking of the West!

So far I have discussed the reconciliation of contradictions between different people and units. But even more powerful can be the effect of reconciling these forces within individuals themselves. Where ideology is strong, not just the researchers are responsible for innovation, nor the accountants for efficiency; everyone internalizes the different forces in carrying out his or her own job. In metaphorical terms, it is easy to change hats if they are all emblazoned with the same insignia.

Limits to Cooperation

Overall, then, ideology sounds like a wonderful thing. But all is not rosy in the world of culture, either. For one thing, ideologies are difficult to build, especially in established organizations, and difficult to sustain once built. For another thing, established ideologies can sometimes get in the way of organizational effectiveness.

The impression left by a good deal of current writing and consulting notwithstanding, ideology is not there for the taking, to be plucked off the tree of management technology like any other piece of fashionable fruit. As Karl Weick has argued, "A corporation doesn't *have* a culture. A corporation *is* a culture. That's why they're so horribly difficult to change."[12] The fact is that there are no five easy steps to a better culture. At best, those steps lay down a thin veneer of impressions that wash off in the first political storm; at worst, they destroy whatever good remains in the prevailing culture. Effective ideologies are built slowly and patiently by committed leaders who establish compelling missions for their organizations, nurture them carefully, and care deeply about the people who make them work.

But even after an ideology is established, the time can come — and usually does eventually — when its effect is to render the organization ineffective, sometimes to the point of destroying it. This is suggested by Weick's comment that ideologies are "so horribly difficult to change."

I argued above that ideology promotes change by allowing an organization to reconcile contradictory forces. Now I should like to argue exactly the opposite case. Ideology discourages change by forcing everyone to work within the same set of beliefs. In other words, strong cultures are immutable: they may promote change within their own boundaries, but they themselves are not to be changed. Receiving "the word" enables people to ask every question but one: the word itself must never be questioned.

I can explain this by introducing two views of strategy, one as position, the other as perspective.[13] In one case, the organization looks down to specific product-market positions (as depicted in Michael Porter's work), in the other it looks up to a general philosophy of functioning (as in Peter Drucker's earlier writings about the "concept of a business"). I like to ask people in my management seminars whether Egg McMuffin was a strategic change for McDonald's. Some argue yes, of course, because it brought the firm into the breakfast market. Others dismiss this as a variation in product line — pure McDonald's, just different ingredients in a new package. Their disagreement concerns not the change at McDonald's so much as their implicit definition of strategy. To the former, strategy is position (the breakfast market), to the latter it is perspective (the McDonald's way). The important point here is that change of position *within* perspective is easy to accomplish (the McDonald's way, but now for breakfast), whereas change of perspective (a new way, that is, a new ideology) is extremely difficult. (Anyone for McDuckling a l'Orange?) The very ideology that makes an organization so adaptive within its own niche undermines efforts to move it to a different niche.

Thus, when change of a fundamental nature must be made — in strategy, structure, form, whatever — the ideology that may for so long have been the key to the organization's effectiveness suddenly becomes its central problem. Ideology becomes a force for the status quo; indeed, because those who perceive the need for change are forced to challenge it, the ideology begins to breed politics!

To understand this negative effect of ideology, take another look at Figure 2. All those arrows face inward. The halo they form may protect the organization, but at the possible expense of isolating it from the outside world. In other words, ideology can cause the other forces to atrophy: direction comes to be interpreted in terms of an outmoded system of beliefs, forcing efficiency, proficiency, and innovation into ever-narrower corners. As the other arrows of the figure disappear, those of ideology close in on the organization, causing it to *implode*. That is how the organization dominated by the force of ideology goes out of control. It isolates itself and eventually dies. We have no need for the extreme example of a Jonestown to appreciate this negative consequence of ideology. We all know organizations with strong cultures that, like that proverbial bird, flew in ever-diminishing circles until they disappeared up their own rear ends.

Competition through Politics

If the centripetal force of ideology, ostensibly so constructive, turns out to have a negative consequence, then perhaps the centrifugal force of politics, ostensibly so destructive, has a positive one.

Politics represents the force for competition within an organization—for conflict and confrontation. People pull apart for their own needs. "They" get in "our" way.

Politics can infuse any of the configurations or combinations, exacerbating contamination and cleavage. Indeed, both problems were characterized as intrinsically conflictive in the first place; the presence of politics for other reasons simply enhances them. The people behind the dominant force in a configuration—say, the accountants in a machine organization, or the experts in a professional one—lord their power over everyone else, while those behind each of the opposing forces in a hybrid relish any opportunity to do battle with each other to gain advantage. Thus, in contrast to a machinelike Toyota pulling together is the Chrysler Iaccoca first encountered, pulling apart; the ideology of an innovative Hewlett-Packard stands in contrast to the politics of a NASA during the Challenger tragedy. For every college that is distinctive, there are others that are destructive.

Politics is generally a parochial force in organizations, encouraging people to pursue their own ends. Infusing the parts of an organization with the competitive force of politics thus reinforces their tendency to fly off in different directions. At the limit, the organization dominated by politics goes out of control by *exploding*. Nothing remains at the core—no central direction, no integrating ideology, and, therefore, no directed effort at efficiency or proficiency or innovation.

In this respect, politics may be a more natural force than ideology. That is to say, organizations left alone seem to pull apart rather more easily than they pull together. Getting human beings to cooperate seems to require continual effort on the part of a dedicated management.

Benefits of Competition

But we cannot dismiss politics as merely divisive. Politics' constructive role in organizations is suggested by the very problems of ideology. If pulling together discourages people from addressing fundamental change, then pulling apart may be the only way to ensure that they do.

Most organizations have a deeply rooted status quo, reinforced especially by the forces of efficiency, proficiency, and ideology, all designed to promote development *within an established perspective*. Thus, to achieve fundamental change in an organization, especially one that has achieved configuration and, moreover, is infused with ideology, the established forces must be challenged, and that means politics. In the absence of entrepreneurial or intrapreneurial capabilities, and sometimes despite them, politics may be the only force capable of stimulating the change. The organization must, in other words, pull apart before it can pull together again. It appears to be inevitable that a great deal of the most significant change is driven, not by managerial insight or specialized expertise or ideological commitment, let alone the procedures of planning, but by political challenge.

I conclude that both politics and ideology can promote organizational effectiveness as well as undermine it. Ideology infused into an organization can be a force for revitalization, energizing the system and making its people more responsive. But that same ideology can also hinder fundamental change. Likewise, politics often impedes necessary change and wastes valuable resources. But political challenge may also be the only means to promote really fundamental change. Thus there remains one last contradiction to reconcile, that between ideology and politics themselves.

Combining Cooperation and Competition

The two catalytic forces of ideology and politics are themselves contradictory forces that have to be reconciled if an organization is to remain truly effective in the long run. Pulling together ideologically infuses life into an organization; pulling apart politically challenges the status quo; only by encouraging both can an organization sustain its viability. The centripetal force of ideology must contain and in turn be contained by the centrifugal force of politics. That is how an organization can keep itself from imploding or exploding—from isolating itself, on the one hand, and going off in all directions, on the other. Moreover, maintaining a balance between these two forces—in their own form of combination—can discourage the other forces from going out of control. Ideology helps secondary forces to contain a dominant one; politics encourages them to challenge it. All of this is somewhat reminiscent of that old children's game (with extended rules!): paper (ideology) covers scissors (politics) and can also help cover rocks (the force for efficiency), while scissors cut paper and can even wedge rocks out of their resting places.

Let me turn one last time to the arrows of the pentagon. Imagine first the diverging arrows of competition contained within the converging circle of cooperation. Issues are debated and people are challenged, but only within the existing culture. The two achieve an equilibrium, as in the case of the Talmudic scholars who fight furiously with each other over the interpretation of every word in their ancient books, yet close ranks to present a united front to the outside world. Is that not the very behavior we find in some of our most effective business corporations, IBM among others? Or reverse the relationship and put the arrows pulling apart outside those of the halo pulling together. Outside challenges keep a culture from closing in on itself.

Thus, I believe that only through achieving some kind of balance of these two catalytic forces can an organization maintain its effectiveness. That balance need not, however, be steady state. Quite the contrary. It should constitute a dynamic equilibrium over time, to avoid constant tension between ideology and politics. Most of the time, the cooperative pulling together of ideology, contained by a healthy internal competition, is to be preferred, so that the organization can vigorously pursue its established strategic perspective. But occasionally, when fundamental change becomes necessary, the organization has to be able to pull apart through the competitive force of politics. That seems to be the best combination of these two forces.

Conclusion

What is it, then, that makes an organization effective? Of course, were the answer easy—and easily applied—all organizations would be equally effective. Clearly, to be effective means to do the right thing and to do it right—to be both "Porterian"

and "Peterian." But I have argued that there is more to organizational effectiveness than this, that the answer must also lie in managing the consistency of form as well as the contradiction of forces. Organizations need focus, but they also need balance. The prescriptions of this article perhaps reduce to the following.

Attain configuration if you can. Getting everything together into a known form, if it all fits, more or less, is not a bad way to organize. One force can dominate just so long as you attend to the other forces, too, to avoid contamination. Otherwise, build a combination if you must, or if you can benefit from the balance of forces. But then be careful about cleavage. And whichever it is, watch out for the occasional need for conversion, during which you must also be careful of cleavage. No matter what, you will still have to manage contradiction. Thus it is critical that you infuse your organization with the cooperative force of ideology, to make it excellent. But beware of that force going out of control, too. Encourage healthy competition, occasionally even outright politics, to ensure needed adaptation. Just be sure to balance ideology and politics in their own dynamic equilibrium.

Of course, this may sound like my own "best way." But it is not a simple way, nor should it encourage conformity. Playing jigsaw puzzle and LEGO with the same pieces is no easy matter. But that is what effective organizations seem to do. ∎

References

1

See T.S. Peters and R.H. Waterman, *In Search of Excellence* (New York: Harper and Row, 1982); and
M.E. Porter, *Competitive Strategy: Techniques for Analyzing Industries and Competitors* (New York: The Free Press, 1980).

2

See H. Mintzberg, *The Structuring of Organizations* (Englewood Cliffs, New Jersey: Prentice-Hall, 1979) and *Mintzberg on Management* (New York: The Free Press, 1989). See also: D. Miller and H. Mintzberg, "The Case for Configuration," in *Organizations: A Quantum View*, eds. D. Miller and P.H. Friesen (Englewood Cliffs, New Jersey: Prentice-Hall, 1984).

3

C. Darwin, *The Life and Letters of Charles Darwin*, ed. F. Darwin (London: John Murray, 1887), p. 105.

4

The first five forms were described in some detail, under slightly different labels, in Mintzberg (1979). The last two forms were developed in:

H. Mintzberg, *Power In and Around Organizations* (Englewood Cliffs, New Jersey: Prentice-Hall, 1983).

5

D. Miller and M. Kets de Vries, *The Neurotic Organization* (San Francisco: Jossey-Bass, 1984). See also:

D. Miller and M. Kets de Vries, *Unstable at the Top* (New York: New American Library, 1987).

6

See D. Miller, *The Icarus Paradox* (New York: Harper & Row, 1990).

7

One might think that the high incidence of entrepreneurial forms reflects the students' bias toward studying small organizations, but I think not. Many more small organizations exist, in business and elsewhere, than large ones, and they are usually entrepreneurial. I would expect the larger ones to be predominantly machine in form in any western society. As for the incidence of combinations, I believe that the diversified and adhocracy forms are the most difficult to sustain (the former is a conglomerate with no links between the divisions, the latter is a very loose and free-wheeling structure), and so

these should be most common in hybrid combinations. Also, some of the combinations reflect common transitions in organizations, especially from the entrepreneurial to the machine form.

8

R.M. Cyert and J.G. March, *A Behavioral Theory of the Firm* (Englewood Cliffs, New Jersey: Prentice-Hall, 1963).

9

B.R. Clark, *The Distinctive College* (Chicago: Aldine, 1970).

10

Peters and Waterman (1982).

11

Porter (1980).

12

Quoted in W. Kiechel III, "Sniping at Strategic Planning (Interview with Himself)," *Planning Review*, May 1984, p. 11.

13

See H. Mintzberg, "Five Ps for Strategy," *California Management Review*, Fall 1987, pp. 11–24.

Reprint 3225

A new form of organization—delayered, downsized, and operating through a network of market-sensitive business units—is changing the global business terrain. What does the growth of these new "network organizations" mean for the training and selection of tomorrow's managers?

Managing 21st Century Network Organizations

CHARLES C. SNOW   **RAYMOND E. MILES**

HENRY J. COLEMAN, JR.

What began, quietly, more than a decade ago, has become a revolution. In industry after industry, multilevel hierarchies have given way to clusters of business units coordinated by market mechanisms rather than by layers of middle-management planners and schedulers.

These market-guided entities are now commonly called "network organizations," and their displacement of centrally managed hierarchies has been relentless, though hardly painless—particularly to the million or so managers whose positions have been abolished. Our descriptions of emerging network structures in the late 1970s helped identify this organizational form. Since then, awareness and acceptance have spread rapidly throughout the business community, and recent authors have heralded the network as the organizational form of the future.

The widespread changeover is producing a new agenda for both managers and scholars. To this point, there is growing agreement about the basic characteristics of the network organization, the forces that have shaped it, and some of the arenas for which the network organization appears to be ideally suited, and in which it has achieved major success. What is much less clear, however, is how networks are designed and operated, and where their future applications lie. Most troublesome, perhaps, is the question of how the managers of tomorrow's network organizations should be selected and trained.

In this article, we first review the progress of the network form and the factors affecting its deployment across the developed and newly industrializing countries of the world. Next, we discuss the major varieties of the network organization, describing and illustrating three specific types of networks: stable, dynamic, and internal. Finally, we identify three managerial roles (architect, lead operator, and caretaker) critical to the success of every network, and we speculate on how managers may be educated to carry out these roles.

Charles C. Snow is professor of business administration in The Smeal College of Business Administration at The Pennsylvania State University, where he teaches courses in competitive strategy and organizational design. He received his B.S. from San Diego State University and his Ph.D. from the University of California, Berkeley. He has written many books and articles on strategic management and is an active lecturer in executive education programs. He has been a Visiting Scholar at Dartmouth College (The Amos Tuck School) and a Presidential Fellow at the American Graduate School of International Management. He serves on the board of directors of a health care firm that specializes in radiation therapy.

NETWORK STRUCTURES— CAUSES AND EFFECTS

The large, vertically integrated companies that dominated the U.S. economy during the first three quarters of this century arose to serve a growing domestic market for efficiently produced goods. These companies then used their advantages of scale and experience to expand into overseas markets served by less efficient or war-damaged competitors.

Then, during the 1980s in particular, markets around the world changed dramatically, as did the technologies available to serve those markets. Today, competitive pressures demand both efficiency *and* effectiveness. Firms must adapt with increasing speed to market pressures and competitors' innovations, simultaneously controlling and even lowering product or service costs.

Confronted by these demands, the large enterprises designed for the business environment of the 1950s and 1960s—firms that typically sought scale economies through central planning and control mechanisms—understandably faltered. The declining effectiveness of traditionally organized firms produced a new business equation. Instead of advocating resource accumulation and control, this equation linked competitive success to doing fewer things better, with less. Specifically, managers who want their companies to be strong competitors in the 21st century are urged to:

• Search globally for opportunities and resources.

• Maximize returns on all the assets dedicated to a business—whether owned by the managers' firm or by other firms.

• Perform only those functions for which the company has, or can develop, expert skill.

• Outsource those activities that can be performed quicker, more effectively, or at lower cost, by others.

Not surprisingly, firms following these prescriptions frequently find themselves organizing into networks. One firm in the network may research and design a product, another may engineer and manufacture it, a third may handle distribution, and so on. (See Exhibit 1.) When numerous designers, producers, and distributors interact, they bring competitive forces to bear on each element of the product or service value chain, and market factors heavily influence resource-allocation decisions. By using a network structure, a firm can operate an ongoing business both efficiently and innovatively, focusing on those things it does well and contracting with other firms for the remaining resources. Alternatively, it can enter new businesses with minimal financial exposure and at an optimal size, given its unique competencies.

Exhibit 2 summarizes both the competitive realities facing today's firms and the organizational imperatives these realities produce. The benefits of the network structure in meeting these imperatives, as well as some of the possible costs associated with networks, are discussed below.

Globalization and Technological Change

Globalization today is a compelling reality, with at least 70 to 85 percent of the U.S. economy feeling the impact of foreign competition. In growing strength and numbers, foreign competitors reduce profit margins on low-end goods to the barest minimum, and they innovate across high-end products and services at ever-increasing rates.

Moreover, foreign competitors are technologically sophisticated. Around the world, technology is changing at a faster rate than ever before. Perhaps more important, technological innovations are transferring from one industry to another and across international borders at increasing speed. Firms thus find it difficult to build barriers of either technology or location around their businesses.

As a response to increasing globalization and the ease of technology transfer, many U.S. firms are focusing on only those things they do especially well, outsourcing a growing roster of goods and services and ridding themselves of minimally productive assets. Such delayered companies are not only less costly to operate, they are also more agile. By

Raymond E. Miles is the Trefethen Professor of Organizational Behavior in the Walter A. Haas School of Business, the University of California at Berkeley, where he served as dean from 1983 to 1990. For the past ten years, Professor Miles' research and writing have focused on the interaction of organizational strategy, structure, and managerial processes. The conceptual framework and organizational typology emerging from this research (done in conjunction with Professor Charles C. Snow and others) are broadly used and have stimulated a continuing research stream.

Professor Miles' most recent work focuses on advanced forms of organizational design at the corporate and plant level, including dynamic network structures, alternative mechanisms for resource allocation and coordination in complex structures, contingency models of strategic human resources management, and work system designs that use surplus human capabilities. In line with his continuing interest in industrial relations, he is studying the impact of management theory and organization design on the fundamental structure and philosophy of the U.S. industrial relations system.

Henry J. Coleman, Jr., is dean of the School of Administration and Management at Columbia Pacific University in San Rafael, California. He holds a Ph.D. in business administration from the University of California, Berkeley. He has contributed to the book, *Organizational Strategy, Structure, and Process* (McGraw-Hill, 1978) and to the *Academy of Management Review*. His consulting work has been in the areas of strategic management and organizational behavior with a variety of organizations in the private sector. He has served on the business faculties at California Polytechnic State University (San Luis Obispo, CA), Holy Names College (Oakland, CA), and National University, San Diego.

limiting operations and performing them expertly, firms require less planning and coordination, and they can accelerate product and service innovations to keep pace with marketplace changes.

For these smaller, more adaptive companies, the global economy contains not only an increasing number of competitors but also more candidates for outsourcing and partnering relationships. Indeed, alliances of various kinds have given rise to the "stateless" corporation in which people, assets, and transactions move freely across international borders. As the world economy continues to concentrate into three regional centers (Europe, North America, and the Pacific Rim), companies scramble for presence in each of these huge markets—something most cannot do single-handedly.

Thus, whether the objective is to extend distribution reach, increase manufacturing efficiency and adaptability, add design capability, or whatever, the global economy is full of opportunities for networking. Of course, the opportunities available to one firm are probably equally accessible to others, raising concern that the outsourcing firm may not find a manufacturer, supplier, distributor, or designer when one is needed. Further, there are oft-expressed concerns about quality assurance in geographically far-flung networks and worries that extensive outsourcing will increase the likelihood of innovative products being copied (and improved) as technological competence spreads.

Deregulation

Changing regulatory processes in the U.S. and abroad are a corollary of more sophisticated global competition. Financial deregulation, in particular, has caused an explosion of international profit-seeking activity. For example, the development of overseas capital markets has vaulted formerly minor functions, such as cash management, into the strategic limelight. Many U.S. companies now sweep excess cash from their accounts every afternoon and deposit the funds in overnight money market accounts somewhere in the world.

EXHIBIT 1
NETWORK ORGANIZATION STRUCTURE

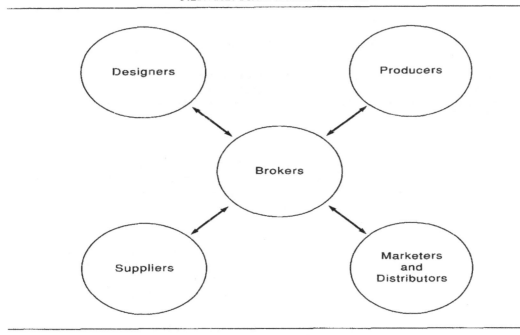

Frequently, firms find the rules of the game being rewritten after they have placed their bets. Cross-national differences and changes in tax laws, investment credits, and currency exchange rates force companies to constantly re-evaluate how they report profits and invest excess cash.

Essentially, deregulation unleashes entrepreneurial behavior, which in turn raises the level of competition. Often deregulation creates new outsourcing opportunities—as seen, for example, in the increased privatization of public corporations and agencies in many countries. Most important, deregulation reduces margins, and this requires companies to maximize returns on all assets—those they control as well as those their vendors and partners control.

Work Force Demographics

Changes in the composition of the U.S. work force are also driving companies to abandon the old business equation. Our work force is becoming older, and its growth is slowing. Seventy-five percent of the people who will be in the work force in the year 2000 are already working. As the work force matures, human resource costs will rise, in part because older employees draw more heavily on their companies' health-care and pension benefits. Because older workers are less inclined to move or to be retrained, flexibility and mobility for this segment of the work force will decline. Rising costs and decreasing flexibility are stimulating U.S. companies to search globally for new human resources and to develop empowerment schemes that generate greater returns from their current stock of human capital. Increasingly, so-called minorities will become a larger majority. Women already form a sizable and growing segment of the work force. Immigration from non-English-speaking countries will likely continue (and perhaps expand), adding to training requirements at a time when U.S. public education is in a troubled state.

Given these demographic trends, the network structure and its operating mechanisms offer some distinct advantages. First, as older workers and some women with small children seek shorter working hours, firms al-

EXHIBIT 2
ORGANIZATIONAL RESPONSES TO THE NEW BUSINESS ENVIRONMENT

The New Competitive Reality

Driving Forces

Globalization
  Strong new players at every stage of the
    value chain (upstream and downstream)
  Competition has reduced all margins—no
    slack left in most economic systems

Technological Change and Technology Transfer
  Shorter product life cycles
  Lower barriers to entry
  Economies of scope as well as scale

Interactive Forces

Deregulation
  Legal and policy changes produce
    uncertainty and increase competition
  Public services are being privatized

Changing Workforce Demographics
  Domestic workforce is becoming more mature,
    diverse, and less well trained and educated
  Global workforce is becoming more mobile

Facilitating Forces
  CAD/CAM and other manufacturing advances
  Faster, lower cost communications and
    computer technologies
  More social and political freedom

Organizational Imperatives

Product and Service Demands
  Focus on distinctive competence
  Reduce costs and accelerate innovation
  Hold only productive assets
  Reduce overall cycle time

Managerial Requirements
  Build smaller, better trained permanent
    workforces
  Develop and use links to part-time and
    temporary human resources
  Develop and use links to global
    technological resources

---

ready skilled in outsourcing will invent new means of accommodating these employees' requests for part-time and telecommuting work. Second, firms retain as small a permanent work force as possible, turning more frequently to consulting firms and other resources for temporary employees. Third, more and more firms will allow their employees to make their services available to other firms on a contractual basis.

Although the network form allows for a smaller permanent work force, it requires that work force to be highly trained. In fact, it is the ability of the various network components to apply their expertise to a wide range of related activities that provides the overall network with agility and cost effi-

ciency. For their permanent employees, network firms must be prepared to make large and continuing investments in training and development. Most employees in these companies will need to know how to perform numerous operations, and demonstrate an in-depth understanding of the firm's technologies.

Communications and Computer Technologies

Network organizations cannot operate effectively unless member firms have the ability to communicate quickly, accurately, and over great distances. Advances in fiber optics, satellite communications, and facsimile machines have made it much easier for managers to communicate within international network organizations. In addition, microcomputers now offer managers and employees all the computational capacity they need, 24 hours a day. And the micros can follow their users wherever they go. Moreover, the cost of data transmission has been declining consistently since the early 1970s, and the decline shows no signs of slowing down. In short, information-processing capacity and geographic distance are no longer major constraints in designing an organization.

Even more important in the long run, computers are changing the traditional concept of product design and production. Today's computer-aided product engineer can quickly produce a multitude of designs or modifications, each complete with parts and components specifications. To evaluate the design of smaller components, an engineer can use stereo lithography, a computer-aided design/laser hookup that "grows" a prototype in a vat, thus achieving a first stage of "desktop manufacturing." Moreover, computer-controlled, general-purpose plant equipment can manufacture directly from computer-stored specifications. Thus, a single manufacturing site can serve several product designers, using their instructions to guide expensive, but usually fully loaded, equipment. Organizationally speaking, we are at the point where capital investments in complex general-purpose machinery can provide a manufacturing component with the ability to serve numerous partners in a network arrangement.

To summarize, globalization and technological change, coupled with deregulation and changing work force demographics, have created a new competitive reality. Taken together, these forces are placing heavy demands on firms to be simultaneously effi-

cient and adáptive. Global competition and deregulation have squeezed most of the slack out of the U.S. economy, and firms can afford to hold only fully employed, flexible resources. Fortunately, however, network structures permit both high utilization and flexibility. Relying on computer-aided communications, product design, and manufacturing, companies can now forge sophisticated linkages—quickly.

TYPES OF NETWORK ORGANIZATIONS

As firms turned to some form of network organization to meet competitive challenges, three types of structures became prominent: internal, stable, and dynamic. Though similar in purpose, each type is distinctly suited to a particular competitive environment. (See Exhibit 3.)

Internal Network

An internal network typically arises to capture entrepreneurial and market benefits without having the company engage in much outsourcing. The internal-network firm owns most or all of the assets associated with a particular business. Managers who control these assets are encouraged (if not required) to expose them to the discipline of the market. The basic logic of the internal network is that if internal units have to operate with prices set by the market (instead of artificial transfer prices), then they will constantly seek innovations that improve their performance.

The General Motors' components business provides a good example of an internal network.[1] Through a series of reorganizations and consolidations (mostly in the 1980s), GM reduced the number of its components divisions to eight. Each of the eight divisions pursues its

---

[1] *The General Motors and BMW examples used in this article to illustrate internal and stable networks, respectively, were drawn from Charles Sabel, Horst Kern, and Gary Herrigel, "Collaborative Manufacturing: New Supplier Relations in the Automobile Industry and the Redefinition of the Industrial Corporation" (Working Paper, Massachusetts Institute of Technology, 1989).*

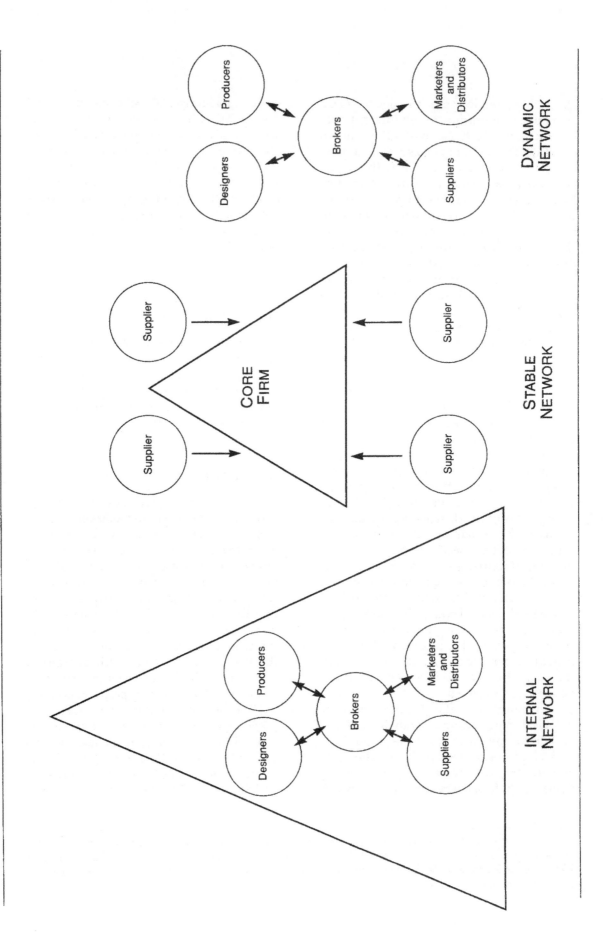

EXHIBIT 3
COMMON NETWORK TYPES

own specialty; together, they create what has been called a "specialization consortium."

Turning GM's formerly rigid and inefficient components divisions into a group of coordinated and flexible subcontractors required two major actions. First, the parent corporation established clear performance measures for each of the divisions so that their behavior could be legitimately compared to that of external suppliers. Usually, this meant converting each components facility into a business unit that was encouraged to sell its products on the open market. Second, each division was assigned (or retained) an area of expertise related to a particular automotive system or subassembly. Each division was to be *the* expert at providing its product and to cooperate with other divisions in the consortium whenever appropriate.

To cite a specific example, the AC-Rochester Division was formed in 1988 by merging the former AC Spark Plugs Division and the Rochester Products Division. The combined division specializes in products that govern the flow of air and fluids into and out of the automobile (filters, fuel and exhaust systems, and so forth). The division is organized into several business units, each a specialist, just as AC-Rochester itself is a specialist within the consortium of components divisions. The various business units of AC-Rochester sell their products to GM, of course, but they also sell to Mitsubishi Motors (Japan), Daewoo (Korea), Opel (Europe), and other manufacturers.

If this organizational arrangement were to be extended throughout General Motors, then the parent corporation would eventually evolve toward the brokering function shown in Exhibit 1. That is, corporate headquarters would become a holding company that maintained an interest in a broad array of specialization consortia, each of which possessed the ability to compete favorably in international markets. It would seek, through subsidies, taxes, loans, and investments, to keep the "internal economy" healthy, focused, and renewing.

Multinational resource-based companies also gravitate toward internal networks. For example, an international oil company would likely find it too costly to hold resources for exploration, extraction, refining, and distribution in every country in which it operates. Nor is deployment from a central location very practical. No matter where its resources were concentrated, the firm could not allocate them quickly and efficiently with a central planning mechanism. Instead, an internal network is constructed. For the network to operate properly, each of its nodes must interact regularly with outsiders—trading, buying, or selling products and raw materials to other firms in order to bring real prices to bear on internal transactions. Thus, inside the company, clusters of business units, grouped by region and product category, can be seen buying and selling from one another as well as from outside firms.

A well-conceived internal network can reduce resource redundancy and decrease response time to market opportunities. Such a network achieves total resource utilization. But there are pitfalls. Internal networks may sometimes fall victim to corporate politics. Instead of exchanging goods or services at verifiable market prices, divisions transfer goods at administered prices that do not reflect external realities—and bad decisions result.

Stable Network

The stable network typically employs partial outsourcing and is a way of injecting flexibility into the overall value chain. In the stable network, assets are owned by several firms, but dedicated to a particular business. Often, a set of vendors is nestled around a large "core" firm, either providing inputs to the firm or distributing its outputs. (Again, see Exhibit 3.)

BMW, for example, is organized as a stable network. In principle, any part of a BMW is a candidate for outsourcing, and somewhere between 55 and 75 percent of total production costs at BMW come from outsourced parts. As at GM, various internal BMW operating units are obligated to prove their competence according to market standards. Beyond this, however, BMW keeps pace with developments in a variety of relevant product and process technologies through its own subsidiaries, and by partnering with other firms. Three subsidiaries concentrate on technologically advanced forms of automobile development and production: BMW Motor Sports Group, Advanced Engineering Group, and the Motorcycle Group. Each of these subsidiaries, especially Motor Sports and Advanced Engineering, focuses on extending the boundaries of knowledge related to automobile engineering and design. The basic objective of these research groups is to understand enough about a particular technology to know who among potential outside vendors would be the best provider. Further, BMW engages in joint ventures and uses its own venture capital fund to participate financially in the operations of other firms. Currently, four areas are closely monitored: new product materials, new production technologies (e.g., with Cecigram in France), electronics (with Leowe Opta), and basic research in several related fields.

Thus, we can see different forms of network operating within the same industry. In its components business, GM is almost entirely an internal network, whereas BMW relies to a greater extent on outsourcing and partnering.

A stable network spreads asset ownership and risk across independent firms. In bad times, however, the "parent" firm may have to protect the health of smaller "family members." The benefits of stability are the dependability of supply or distribution, as well as close cooperation on scheduling and quality requirements. The "costs" of stability are mutual dependence and some loss of flexibility.

Dynamic Network

In faster-paced or discontinuous competitive environments, some firms have pushed the network form to the apparent limits of its capabilities. Businesses such as fashion, toys, publishing, motion pictures, and biotechnology may require or allow firms to outsource extensively. (See Exhibit 3.) In such circumstances, the lead firm identifies and assembles assets owned largely (or entirely) by other companies. Lead firms typically rely on a core skill such as manufacturing (e.g., Motorola), R&D/design (e.g., Reebok), design/assembly (e.g., Dell Computer), or, in some cases, pure brokering.

An example of a broker-led dynamic network is Lewis Galoob Toys. Only a hundred or so employees run the entire operation. Independent inventors and entertainment companies conceive most of Galoob's products, while outside specialists do most of the design and engineering. Galoob contracts for manufacturing and packaging with a dozen or so vendors in Hong Kong, and they, in turn, pass on the most labor-intensive work to factories in China. When the toys arrive in the U.S., Galoob distributes through commissioned manufacturers' representatives. Galoob does not even collect its accounts. It sells its receivables to Commercial Credit Corporation, a factoring company that also sets Galoob's credit policy. In short, Galoob is the chief broker among all of these independent specialists.

Dynamic networks can provide both specialization and flexibility. Each network node practices its particular expertise, and, if brokers are able to package resources quickly, the company achieves maximum responsiveness. However, dynamic networks run the risk of quality variation across firms, of needed expertise being temporarily unavailable, and of possible exploitation of proprietary knowledge or technology. The dynamic network operates best in competitive situations where there are myriad players, each guided by market pressures to be reliable and to stay at the leading edge of its specialty. The dynamic network is also appropriate in settings where design and production cycles are short enough to prevent knockoffs or where proprietary rights can be protected by law or by outsourcing only standard parts and assemblies.

THE BROKER'S ROLE

In hierarchically organized firms, the fundamental role of management is to plan, organize, and control resources that are held inhouse. In many network firms, however,

EXHIBIT 4
A VALUE CHAIN GRID OF FIRMS AND THREE OPERATING NETWORKS

EXHIBIT 4
A VALUE CHAIN GRID OF FIRMS AND THREE OPERATING NETWORKS

Manufacturers and Components Suppliers → Designers and Assemblers → Distributors → Marketers and Retailers

Row 1: A — A — A — A

Row 2: B — B — C D E — F G H

Row 3: I J K — L M N — O — O

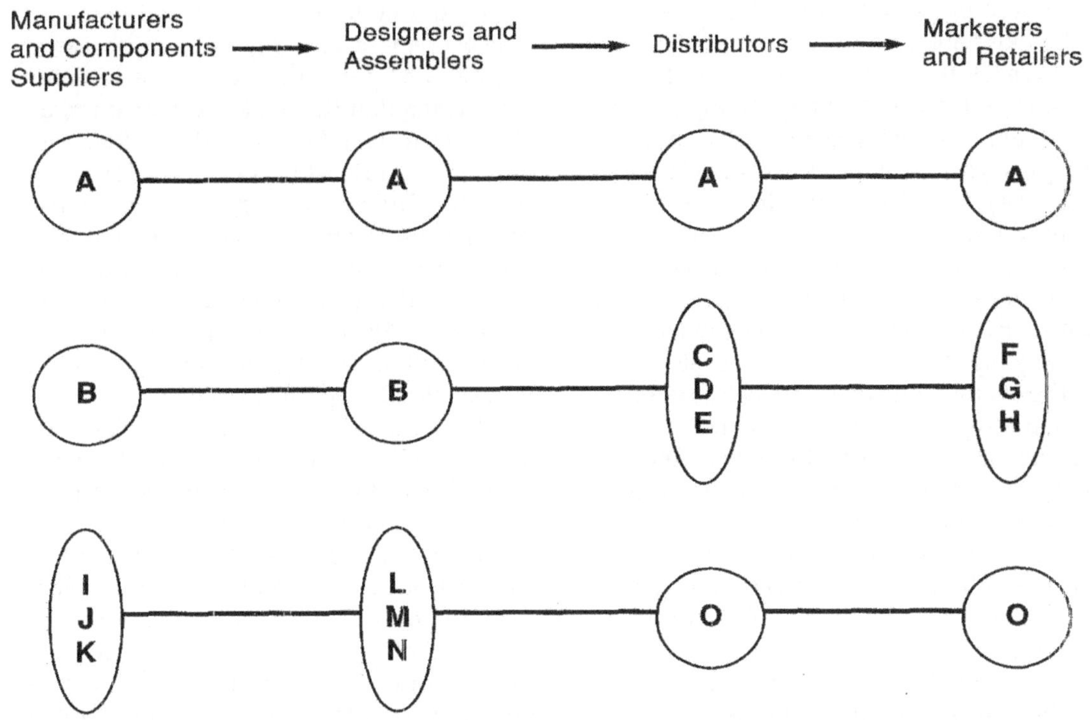

certain key managers operate *across* rather than *within* hierarchies, creating and assembling resources controlled by outside parties. These managers, therefore, can be thought of as brokers. Three broker roles are especially important to the success of network organizations: architect, lead operator, and caretaker.

Architect

Managers who act as architects facilitate the emergence of specific operating networks. Entrepreneurial behavior of this sort has been going on for centuries. For example, beginning in the 13th century, some early network architects fueled the rapid growth of the European cottage textile industry by designing a "putting out" system that organized an army of rural workers who spun thread and wove cloth in their homes. The architects of this system financed the network by providing workers with raw materials to be paid for when the finished

goods were delivered. In some cases, brokers also supplied product designs and special equipment suitable for cottage production.

A network architect seldom has a clear or complete vision of all the specific operating networks that may ultimately emerge from his or her efforts. Frequently, the architect has in mind only a vague concept of the product and of the value chain required to offer it. This business concept is then brought into clearer focus as the broker seeks out firms with desirable expertise, takes an equity position in a firm to coax it into the value chain, helps create new groups that are needed in specialized support roles, and so on.

In designing an internal network, it may be relatively easy to identify the appropriate organizational units for each stage of the value chain. In the early years at General Motors, for example, Alfred Sloan envisioned an internal network of automotive suppliers, assemblers, producers, and distributors that could be assembled from among the various firms that William Durant had acquired. The internal network that GM uses today is the modern-day result of a similar process.

In both stable and dynamic networks, the architect's role is likely to be more complicated, because the resources that must be organized are not contained entirely within the firm. The managers who designed BMW's stable network, for example, had to identify several outside firms who would be suitable partners for long-term R&D relationships. When partners and relationships change frequently, as in dynamic networks, certain managers must devote ongoing effort to the architect's role.

The overall result of the architect's efforts can be portrayed as a grid of firms and value-chain elements, such as that shown in Exhibit 4. A grid can be developed entirely within an industry, or it can cut across established industry boundaries. The critical factor is that all firms recognize that they are part of the grid and are at least minimally committed to supporting it. Under these conditions, a number of specific operating networks may emerge.

The personal computer business, for example, is organized in large part around three types of operating networks. One type, perhaps best represented by Tandy Corporation (Radio Shack) offers a product that is mostly designed, manufactured, and sold in-house. Thus, Tandy by itself performs all of the major functions along the value chain. A second network type, represented by Apple Computer, looks much like the Tandy network at the upstream (manufacturing) end, but it contains more distributors and retailers downstream. The third type of network, of which there are many examples, has as its center of gravity the distribution and retailing portion of the value chain. Here distributor-retailers buy off-the-shelf components from various manufacturers, then assemble and sell customized packages of computer hardware and software to specialized market segments.

Lead Operator

As the grid of firms clustered around a particular business evolves, emphasis shifts from design to decisions about operation. Managers who act primarily as lead operators take advantage of the groundwork laid by manager-architects (although the two roles may overlap considerably and may be played by the same person or group). Essentially, this means that the lead operator formally connects specific firms together into an operating network. At Galoob Toys, for example, a handful of key executives perform this role. They select from a known set of potential partners those individuals and firms needed to design, manufacture, and sell children's toys. The firm outsources virtually every operating activity, choosing to perform only the brokering role in-house.

The lead-operator role is often played by a firm positioned downstream in the value chain. Brokers in the lead firm rely on their negotiating and contracting skills to hook together firms into more-or-less permanent alliances. Nike, an R&D and marketing company, operates this way. However, the lead-operator role is not limited to downstream firms. For example, some large semiconductor manufacturers, such as Intel, have formed alliances with particular assemblers and distributors to promote the sale of new memory and operating chips. These firms advertise their new designs to potential end-users, and major exhibitions are staged to showcase the latest hardware and software developments.

Caretaker

Networks require continual enhancement if they are to operate smoothly and effectively. Thus, the process of network development is ongoing. Managers who focus on enhancement activity could be called caretakers. The caretaker role is multifaceted and may be just as important as the architect and lead-operator roles to the ultimate success of a network.

A caretaker may have to monitor a large number of relationships with respect to the specific operating network as well as to the larger grid of firms from which it came. In the operating network, this means sharing information among firms about how the network runs, as well as information on recent technological and marketing developments, schedules, and so on. Downstream firms in the value chain need to be kept abreast of new manufacturing capabilities, and upstream firms need an awareness and understanding of coming changes in the marketplace. Thus, the caretaker does more than help the network plan; managers who play this role also help the network learn.

With regard to the grid of potential network firms, the caretaker may engage in nurturing and disciplinary behavior. For example, a caretaker may notice that a particular firm appears to be falling behind technologically, or in some other way devaluing its usefulness to the grid. Appropriate actions could be taken to rectify the situation. An even more troublesome case occurs when a firm exploits its position in the grid—for example, by obtaining some short-run gain at the expense of its actual or potential partners. Here the caretaker's challenge is to point out the dysfunctional effects of such behavior on the overall system and teach the offending firm how to behave more appropriately for the common good.

IMPLICATIONS FOR BROKER SELECTION AND DEVELOPMENT

If, as seems likely, network organizations continue to spread, it is important to consider how managers with broker skills will be selected and developed. Positions labeled network architect, operator, or caretaker are not commonly found on organization charts, and no career paths are obvious. Nevertheless, it seems that many corporate experiences, and even some university courses, may be vehicles for developing needed skills. Some examples are discussed below.

Network Design

Many business experiences have characteristics related to network design. For example, in consumer packaged goods firms, product and brand managers learn to build informal networks among the various designers, producers, distributors, and marketers involved in the offering of their product. Similarly, project managers in matrix organizations develop network-building skills as they work across the functional boundaries of their firms and with outside contractors.

Network designers are essentially entrepreneurs, not only pulling together the skills and equipment needed to produce a new product or service, but also, on occasion, arranging the financing. Indeed, many of the network organizations found today in the personal computer, biotechnology, fashion, and entertainment businesses are the joint product of numerous entrepreneurs who originally created a piece of the overall value-chain grid.

However, in most corporations only a limited number of managers are individuals with direct entrepreneurial experience that can be drawn on as a resource. Therefore, firms like 3M and Texas Instruments practice "intrapreneuring"—rewarding their employees for turning ideas into prototype products or services, frequently with limited resources. In fact, one Swedish consulting firm (the Foresight Group) helps firms select and develop intrapreneurs. Interestingly, these consultants accept only volunteers, and they require them to work on their chosen projects while carrying out their regular duties (some limited financial support is also provided). Volunteers are encouraged to "scrounge" for needed resources—both inside and outside the organization. This process has developed many new products, complete with their own internal or external network already in place. The characteristics of intrapreneuring—individual initiative, cross-functional team building, resource acquisition, and so on—are very consistent with the development of successful networks.

Many business schools now offer courses or workshops in entrepreneurship, and most of these cover product and project management, intrapreneuring, and the writing of business plans. While coursework is not a direct substitute for hands-on experience, these courses, often relying on guest lecturers, give students opportunity to explore many aspects of network design and operation.

Network Operation

The task of putting a network into operation by linking all the value-chain components needed for a given product or service involves not only conceptual and organizational skills but also the skill to negotiate mutually beneficial returns for the contributions of all participants. Here one might look to purchasing or sales as a likely breeding ground for negotiations knowledge and skill. However, experience in such arenas as construction or engineering management may be even more relevant, in that the process of subcontracting is closely akin to network operation. "Partnering" is now common in the construction industry, a process whereby the various parties involved in a project meet in a team-building session to uncover mutual interests and to create the mechanisms and build the trust necessary for resolving the inevitable disputes and inequities.

Again, many business schools now offer courses in negotiation strategies and skills, with emphasis on collaboration and ethical behavior. Understanding the processes of (and the responsibilities involved in) collaborative negotiation is an essential characteristic of the lead operator. The quest is not for an airtight legal contract guaranteeing one's own rights, but for an objective, clearly understood relationship that protects all parties' interests.

Increasingly, as networks extend across international borders, both the network architect and lead operator will require extensive international knowledge and experience. Architects must keep abreast of available skills and resources around the world, and operators must understand how cross-cultural relationships are forged and maintained. It seems likely that courses exploring general international similarities and differences will be helpful, as will courses focused on specific skills, such as those involved in countertrade. Japanese companies are noted for both their ability to build lasting relationships and for their extensive programs for assuring that managers gain hands-on experience across their organizations and various operating regions. Few U.S. firms appear to be as dedicated to such cross-training and experience, and few are as adept at building effective internal and external relationships.

Network Caretaking

In some ways, the function of caretaking—maintaining and enhancing an existing network—is both the least understood and the most challenging of the three broker roles. One aspect of caretaking is simply taking care of one's self—for example, by being an active member of a trade association. A more important purpose of the caretaking function is to develop a sense of community among the members of a network. Networks operate effectively when member firms voluntarily behave as if they are all part of a broader organization sharing common objectives and rewards. This sense of community may be easier to instill in an internal network, where assets are held by a single firm, than in a dynamic network, where assets are spread across changeable combinations of designers, manufacturers, suppliers, and so on. Nevertheless, in either case, the network somehow must create an organization "culture" that transcends ownership and national borders.

Clearly, brokers involved in the task of nurturing networks will benefit from team-building skills. General Electric's Workout Program, for example, is designed in part to bring GE's managers, customers, and vendors together to form effective working relationships. Once more, business school courses may be helpful in this area, but theory lags practice. That is, courses in organization development and change contain many useful concepts, but most are oriented toward developing the single firm, not the set of firms that constitutes a network.

In sum, the job of broker, with its attendant roles of architect, lead operator, and caretaker, is unlikely to be filled by managers from any particular part of today's corporation. Individuals from product management, sales, and purchasing may possess some of the knowledge and skills required by the effective network broker. However, none of these functions appears to be the sole source of future brokers. Further, the broker's job is far too complex to lend itself to the use of any available selection instruments. Consequently, as is often the case, a manager's track record may be the best selection and placement device. In any case, however they are chosen, managers must be found for an increasing number of broker positions in the next century.

THE FUTURE

The forces currently pushing many American companies toward network forms of organization are likely to continue unabated. In fact, the recent emergence of Eastern Europe as a significant factor in the global economy will add to the turbulence currently found in many industries. New foreign producers will add to competitive pressures, and emerging foreign markets will offer opportunities for flexible first movers. In short, it is difficult to imagine any industry ever returning to a form of competition in which traditional pyramidical organizations can survive.

In the future, network organizations will emerge in a variety of circumstances. Dynamic networks, for example, will appear on the fringes of those mature industries that are in danger of stagnation. The ability of networks to generate new products with lower levels of investment will help to invigorate these industry segments. Also, dynamic networks will continue to operate in emerging industries where the pace of new product development and overall market demand cannot be accurately predicted. Alternatively, the efficiency-oriented stable network will become the dominant organizational form in mature, healthy industries. Lastly, an internal network will develop in situations where firms find it is difficult to create a new set of suppliers, but are unwilling to risk the poten-

tial inflexibility associated with wholly self-contained units.

Global competition in the 21st century will force every firm to become, at least to some extent, a network designer, operator, and caretaker. And as competition intensifies, companies will find themselves constantly subjecting virtually every internal asset to market tests in order to justify its ownership. However, the most successful firms will not only maximize the utilization of their assets, they will also learn how to market and deploy those assets to other firms. For example, firms will share or lease physical assets (e.g., more than one firm will use the same plant), their skilled staff groups (e.g., logistics units will sell services to other firms), and even their line work teams (e.g., autonomous work groups will be loaned on credit to other firms during slack periods).

Ultimately, every firm may have to decide whether it should create (or join) a cost-based or investment-based network. Eventually, cost-based global networks, which rely on inexpensive labor (or base plants in locales where there is minimal concern for ecological conditions, thus lowering environmental costs) will approach an equilibrium from which it will be difficult to extract further competitive advantages. Investment-driven networks, on the other hand, can be self-renewing. These networks will be constructed around those firms that are prepared to make continual capital expenditures—either for the most-advanced technology or for additional training and development of top-quality people.

If you wish to make photocopies or obtain reprints of this or other articles in ORGANIZATIONAL DYNAMICS, please refer to the special reprint service instructions on page 80.

NETWORK ORGANIZATIONS:
A BIBLIOGRAPHIC HISTORY

Beginning in the late 1950s and early 1960s, some management theorists advocated the democratization and decentralization of large companies in order to "humanize" the workplace. In the 1970s, these prescriptions changed to disaggregation and decoupling, advocated for economic reasons. When a number of American firms began to disaggregate by taking their manufacturing operations offshore, the network organization as we know it today was born.

In our early work, we discussed how market forces could be injected into traditional organization structures to make them more efficient and responsive (Raymond Miles and Charles Snow, *Organizational Strategy, Structure, and Process*, McGraw-Hill, 1978, Chapter 9). Subsequent publications extended market concepts to internal work teams (Raymond Miles and Howard Rosenberg, "The Human Resources Approach to Management: Second- Generation Issues," *Organizational Dynamics*, 1982), as well as to external groups, which we called "dynamic networks" (Raymond Miles and Charles Snow, "Fit, Failure, and the Hall of Fame," *California Management Review*, 1984). As network organizations became more plentiful in the 1980s, it was possible to describe them in more detail (Raymond Miles and Charles Snow, "Network Organizations: New Concepts for New Forms," *California Management Review*, 1986; Hans Thorelli, "Networks: Between Markets and Hierarchies," *Strategic Management Journal*, 1986).

The network form of organization gained wide visibility after it was the subject of a *Business Week* cover story in 1986 ("The Hollow Corporation," March 3, 1986). This story sparked a debate in the business press about the merits and drawbacks of networks (see, for example, a series of articles by Christopher Lorenz in *The Financial Times*).

By the end of the 1980s, network organiza-tions in their various forms were a fact of organizational life. A virtual explosion of books and articles explored—and generally endorsed—strategic alliances, value-adding partnerships, and other types of network structures. In general, network organizations were seen as a powerful tool for American and foreign firms to strengthen their positions in the global economy. Most notable among these writings were Peter Drucker, *The New Realities* (Harper & Row, 1989); William Halal, *The New Capitalism* (Wiley, 1986); Charles Handy, *The Age of Unreason* (Harvard Business School Press, 1990); Russell Johnston and Paul Lawrence, "Beyond Vertical Integration—the Rise of the Value-Adding Partnership," (*Harvard Business Review*, 1988); Rosabeth Kanter, *When Giants Learn to Dance* (Simon and Schuster, 1989); and Robert Reich, *The Work of Nations* (Knopf, 1991).

Finally, conceptual and empirical articles have recently begun to examine the strategic and managerial implications of the network structure. These include the impact of networks on (a) labor relations and human resources development (Raymond Miles, "Adapting to Technology and Competition: A New Industrial Relations System for the 21st Century," *California Management Review*, 1989); (b) financing strategies (John Kensinger and John Martin, "Financing Network Organizations," *Journal of Applied Corporate Finance*, 1991); (c) the delivery of public services (Michael Lawless and Rita Moore, "Interorganizational Systems in Public Service Delivery: A New Application of the Dynamic Network Framework," *Human Relations*, 1989); and (d) managerial processes (Charles Snow and James Thomas, "Building Networks: Broker Roles and Behaviors," in Peter Lorange, et al., Editors, *Strategic Processes: Designing for the 1990's*, Basil Blackwell, 1992).

Theme 4

Managing People

Knowledge-worker productivity: The biggest challenge
Peter F Drucker
California Management Review; Winter 1999; 41, 2; ABI/INFORM Global

Knowledge-Worker Productivity:

THE BIGGEST CHALLENGE

Peter F. Drucker

T he most important, and indeed the truly unique, contribution of management in the 20th century was the fifty-fold increase in the productivity of the *manual worker* in manufacturing. The most important contribution management needs to make in the 21st century is similarly to increase the productivity of *knowledge work* and *knowledge workers*. The most valuable assets of a 20th-century company was its *production equipment*. The most valuable asset of a 21st-century institution (whether business or non-business) will be its *knowledge workers* and their *productivity*.

The Productivity of the Manual Worker

First, we must take a look at where we are. It was only a little over a hundred years ago that for the first time an educated person actually *looked* at manual work and manual workers, and then began to study both. The Greek poet Hesiod (eighth century B.C.) and the Roman poet Virgil (700 years later) sang about the work of the farmer. Theirs are still among the finest poems in any language, but neither the work they sang about nor their farmers bear even the most remote resemblance to reality, nor were they meant to have any. Neither Hesiod nor Virgil ever held a sickle in their hands, ever herded sheep, or even looked at the people who did either. When Karl Marx, 1900 years after Virgil, came to write about manual work and manual workers, he too never looked at either, nor had he ever as much as touched a machine. The first man to do both—that is, to work as a manual worker and then to study manual work—was Frederick Winslow Taylor (1856-1915).

Throughout history there have been steady advances in what we today call "productivity" (the term itself is barely fifty years old). They were the result of new tools, new methods, and new technologies; they were advances in what the economist calls "capital." There were few advances throughout the ages in what the economist calls "labor"—that is, in the productivity of the worker. It was axiomatic throughout history that workers could produce more only by working harder or by working longer hours. The 19th-century economists disagreed about most things as much as economists do today. However, they all agreed—from David Ricardo through Karl Marx—that there are enormous differences in *skill* between workers, but there are none in respect to productivity other than between hard workers and lazy ones, or between physically strong workers and weak ones. Productivity did not exist. It still is an "extraneous factor" and not part of the equation in most contemporary economic theory (e.g., in Keynes, but also in that of the Austrian School).

In the decade after Taylor first looked at work and studied it, the productivity of the manual worker began its unprecedented rise. Since then, it has been going up steadily at the rate of 3% per annum compound—which means it has been risen fifty-fold since Taylor. On this achievement rest *all* of the economic and social gains of the 20th century. The productivity of the manual worker has created what we now call "developed" economies. Before Taylor, there was no such thing—all economies were equally "underdeveloped." An underdeveloped economy today—or even an "emerging" one—is one that has not, or at least has not yet, made the manual worker more productive.

The Principles of Manual-Work Productivity

Taylor's principles sound deceptively simple. The first step in making the manual worker more productive is to look at the task and to analyze its constituent motions. The next step is to record each motion, the physical effort it takes, and the time it takes. Then motions that are not needed can be eliminated; and whenever we have looked at manual work, we have found that a great many of the traditionally most-hallowed procedures turn out to be waste and do not add anything. Then, each of the motions that remain as essential to obtaining the finished product is set up so as to be done the simplest way, the easiest way, the way that puts the least physical and mental strain on the operator, and the way that requires the least time. Next, these motions are put together again into a "job" that is in a logical sequence. Finally, the tools needed to do the motions are redesigned. Whenever we have looked at any job—no matter for how many thousands of years it has been performed—we have found that the traditional tools are wrong for the task. This was the case, for instance, with the shovel used to carry sand in a foundry (the first task Taylor studied). It was the wrong shape, the wrong size, and had the wrong handle. We found this to be equally true of the surgeon's traditional tools. Taylor's principles sound obvious—effective methods always do. However, it took Taylor twenty years of experimentation to work them out.

Over these last hundred years, there have been countless further changes, revisions, and refinements. The name by which the methodology goes has also changed over the past century. Taylor himself first called his method "Task Analysis" or "Task Management." Twenty years later it was re-christened "Scientific Management." Another twenty years later, after the First World War, it came to be knows as "Industrial Engineering" in the U.S. and Japan, and as "Rationalization" in Germany.

To proclaim that one's method "rejects" Taylor or "replaces" him is almost standard "public relations." For what made Taylor and his method so powerful has also made it unpopular. What Taylor *saw* when he actually looked at work violated everything poets and philosophers had said about work from Hesiod and Virgil to Karl Marx. They all celebrated "skill." Taylor showed that in manual work there is no such thing. There are only simple, repetitive motions. What makes them more productive is *knowledge*, that is, the way the simple, unskilled motions are put together, organized, and executed. In fact, Taylor was the first person to apply knowledge to work.[1]

This also earned Taylor the undying enmity of the labor unions of his time, all of which were craft unions and based on the *mystique* of craft skill and their monopoly on it. Moreover, Taylor advocated—and this is still anathema to a labor union—that workers be paid according to their productivity—that is, for their output, rather than for their input (e.g., for hours worked). However, Taylor's definition of work as a series of operations also largely explains his rejection by the people who themselves do not do any manual work: the descendants of the poets and philosophers of old, the Literati and Intellectuals. Taylor destroyed the romance of work. Instead of a "noble skill," it becomes a series of simple motions.

Nevertheless, every method during these past hundred years that has had the slightest success in raising the productivity of manual workers—and with it their real wages—has been based on Taylor's principles, no matter how loudly his antagonists proclaimed their differences with Taylor. This is true of "work enlargement," "work enrichment," and "job rotation"—all of which use Taylor's methods to lessen the worker's fatigue and thereby increase the worker's productivity. It is also true of such extensions of Taylor's principles of task analysis and industrial engineering as Henry Ford's assembly line (developed after 1914, when Taylor himself was already sick, old, and retired). It is just as true of the Japanese "Quality Circle," "Continuous Improvement"(*Kaizen*), and "Just-In-Time Delivery."

The best example, however, is W. Edward Deming's "Total Quality Management." What Deming did—and what makes Total Quality Management effective—is to analyze and organize the job exactly the way Taylor did. However, he also added Quality Control (around 1940) that was based on a statistical theory that was only developed ten years after Taylor's death. Finally, in the 1970s, Deming substituted closed-circuit television and computer simulation for

Taylor's stopwatch and motion photos. Deming's Quality Control Analysts are the spitting image of Taylor's Efficiency Engineers and function the same way.

Whatever his limitations and shortcomings—and he had many—no other American, not even Henry Ford, has had anything like Taylor's impact. "Scientific Management" (and its successor "Industrial Engineering") is the one American philosophy that has swept the world—more so even than the Constitution and the Federalist Papers. In the past century, there has been only one worldwide philosophy that could compete with Taylor's: namely, Marxism. In the end, Taylor has triumphed over Marx.

During the First World War, Scientific Management swept through the U.S. together with Ford's Taylor-based assembly line. In the 1920s, Scientific Management swept through Western Europe and began to be adopted in Japan.

During the Second World War, both the German achievement and the American achievement were squarely based on applying Taylor's principles to Training. The German General Staff, after having lost the First World War, applied "Rationalization" (i.e., Taylor's Scientific Management) to the job of the soldier and to military training. This enabled Hitler to create a superb fighting machine in the six short years between his coming to power and 1939. In the U.S., the same principles were applied to the training of an industrial work force, first tentatively during the First World War and then, with full power, during the Second World War. This enabled the Americans to outproduce the Germans, even though a larger proportion of the U.S. than the German male population was in uniform and thus not in industrial production. Then, training-based Scientific Management gave the U.S. civilian work force more than twice—if not three times—the productivity of the workers in Hitler's Germany and in Hitler-dominated Europe. Scientific Management thus gave the U.S. the capacity to outnumber both Germans and Japanese on the battlefield and yet still outproduce both by several orders of magnitude.

Since 1950, economic development outside the Western World has largely been based on copying what the U.S. did in the Second World War, i.e., on applying Scientific Management to making the manual worker more productive. All earlier economic development had been based on technological innovation—first in France in the 18th century, then in Great Britain from 1760 until 1850, and finally in the new economic Great Powers, Germany and the U.S., in the second half of the 19th century. The non-Western countries that developed after the Second World War, beginning with Japan, eschewed technological innovation. Instead, they imported the training that the U.S. had developed during the Second World War based on Taylor's principles and they used it to make highly productive, almost overnight, a still largely unskilled and pre-industrial work force. (In Japan, for instance, almost two-thirds of the working population were still, in 1950, living on the land and unskilled in any work except cultivating rice). However, while highly productive, this new work force was still—for a decade or more—paid pre-industrial wages so that these countries—first Japan, then Korea, then Taiwan and Singapore—could produce the same manufactured products as the developed countries, but at a fraction of their labor costs.

The Future of Manual-Worker Productivity

Taylor's approach was designed for manual work in *manufacturing*, and at first applied only to it. Nevertheless, even within these traditional limitations, Taylor's approach still has enormous scope. It is still going to be the organizing principle in countries in which manual work, and especially manual work in manufacturing, is the growth sector of the society and economy—that is, "Third World" countries with very large and still growing numbers of young people with little education and little skill.

However, there is equal—or even greater—opportunity in the *developed* countries to organize non-manufacturing production (i.e., production work in services) on the production principles now being developed in manufacturing —and that means applying Industrial Engineering to the job and work of the individual service worker. There is equally a tremendous amount of knowledge work—including work requiring highly advanced and thoroughly theoretical knowledge—that includes *manual* operations. The productivity of these operations also requires Industrial Engineering.

Still, in developed countries, the central challenge is no longer to make manual work more productive—after all, we know how to do it. The central challenge will be to make knowledge workers more productive. Knowledge workers are rapidly becoming the largest single group in the work force of every developed country. They may already compose two-fifths of the U.S. work force —and a still smaller but rapidly growing proportion of the work force of all other developed countries. It is on their productivity, above all, that the future prosperity—and indeed the future survival—of the developed economies will increasingly depend.

What We Know About Knowledge-Worker Productivity

Work on the productivity of the knowledge worker has barely begun. In terms of actual work on knowledge-worker productivity, we will be in the year 2000 roughly where we were in the year 1900 in terms of the productivity of the manual worker. Nevertheless, we already know infinitely more about the productivity of the knowledge worker than we did then about that of the manual worker. We even know a good many of the answers. We also know the challenges to which we do not yet know the answers, and on which we need to go to work.

Six major factors determine knowledge-worker productivity.

- Knowledge-worker productivity demands that we ask the question: *"What is the task?"*

- It demands that we impose the responsibility for their productivity on the individual knowledge workers themselves. Knowledge Workers *have* to manage themselves. They have to have *autonomy.*

- Continuing innovation has to be part of the work, the task and the responsibility of knowledge workers.

- Knowledge work requires continuous learning on the part of the knowledge worker, but equally continuous teaching on the part of the knowledge worker.

- Productivity of the knowledge worker is not—at least not primarily—a matter of the *quantity* of output. *Quality* is at least as important.

- Finally, knowledge-worker productivity requires that the knowledge worker is both seen and treated as an "asset" rather than a "cost." It requires that knowledge workers *want* to work for the organization in preference to all other opportunities.

Each of these requirements (except perhaps the last one) is almost the exact opposite of what is needed to increase the productivity of the manual worker. In manual work, of course, quality also matters. However, lack of quality is a restraint. There has to be a certain minimum quality standard. The achievement of Total Quality Management—that is, of the application of 20th century Statistical Theory to manual work—is the ability to cut (though not entirely to eliminate) production that falls below this minimum standard.

In most knowledge work, quality is not a minimum and a restraint. Quality is the essence of the output. In judging the performance of a teacher, we do not ask how many students there can be in his or her class. We ask how many students learn anything—and that's a quality question. In appraising the performance of a medical laboratory, the question of how many tests it can run through its machines is quite secondary to the question of how many tests results are valid and reliable. This is true even for the work of the file clerk.

Productivity of knowledge work therefore has to aim first at obtaining quality—and not minimum quality but optimum if not maximum quality. Only then can one ask: "What is the volume, the quantity of work?" This not only means that we approach the task of making more productive the knowledge worker from the quality of the work rather than the quantity, it also means that we will have to learn to define quality.

What Is the Task?

The crucial question in knowledge-worker productivity is: *What is the task?* It is also the one most at odds with manual-worker productivity. In manual work, the key question is always: *How should the work be done?* In manual work, the task is always given. None of the people who work on manual-worker productivity ever asked: "What is the manual worker supposed to do?" Their only question was: "How does the manual worker best do the job?" This was just as true of Frederick W. Taylor's Scientific Management as it was true of the people at Sears Roebuck or the Ford Motor Company who first designed the assembly line, and as it is true of W. Edward Deming's Total Quality Control.

Again, in knowledge work the key question is: What is the task? One reason for this is that knowledge work, unlike manual work, does not program the worker. The worker on the automobile assembly line who puts on a wheel is programmed by the simultaneous arrival of the car's chassis on one line and the wheel on the other line. The farmer who plows a field in preparation for planting does not climb out of his tractor to take a telephone call, to attend a meeting, or to write a memo. *What* is to be done is always obvious in manual work.

However, in knowledge work the task does not program the worker. A major crisis in a hospital, such as when a patient suddenly goes into coma, does of course control the nurse's task and programs her; but otherwise, it is largely the nurse's decision whether to spend time at the patient bed or whether to spend time filling out papers. Engineers are constantly being pulled off their task by having to write a report or rewrite it, by being asked to attend a meeting, and so on. The job of the salesperson in the department store is to serve the customer and to provide the merchandise the customer is interested in or should become interested in. Instead, the salesperson spends an enormous amount of time on paperwork, on checking whether merchandise is in stock, on checking when and how it can be delivered, and so on—all things that take salespeople away from the customer and do not add anything to their productivity in doing what salespeople are being paid for, which is to sell and to satisfy the customer.

The first requirement in tackling knowledge work is to find out what the task is so as to make it possible to concentrate knowledge workers on the task and to eliminate everything else—at least as far as it can possibly be eliminated. This requires that the knowledge workers themselves define what the task is or should be—and only the knowledge workers themselves can do that. Work on knowledge-worker productivity therefore begins with asking the knowledge workers themselves: *What is your task? What should it be? What should you be expected to contribute?* and *What hampers you in doing your task and should be eliminated?*

Knowledge workers themselves almost always have thought through these questions and can answer them. Still, it then usually takes time and hard work to restructure their jobs so that they can actually make the contribution they are already being paid for. However, asking the questions and taking action on the answers usually doubles or triples knowledge-worker productivity, and quite fast.

Nurses in a major hospital were asked these questions. They were sharply divided as to what their task was, with one group saying "patient care" and another saying "satisfying the physicians." However, they were in complete agreement on the things that made them unproductive. They called them "chores" —paperwork, arranging flowers, answering the phone calls of patients' relatives, answering the patients' bells, and so on. All—or nearly all—of these could be turned over to a non-nurse floor clerk, paid a fraction of a nurse's pay. The productivity of the nurses on the floor immediately more than doubled, as measured by the time nurses spent at the patients' beds. Patient satisfaction more than doubled and turnover of nurses (which had been catastrophically high) almost disappeared—all within four months.

Once the task has been defined, the next requirements can be tackled, and they will be tackled by the knowledge workers themselves. These requirements are:

- Knowledge workers' *responsibility* for their own contribution. It is the knowledge worker's decision what he or she should be held accountable for in terms of quality and quantity with respect to time and with respect to cost. Knowledge workers have to have autonomy and that entails responsibility.
- Continuous innovation *has to be built into the knowledge worker's job.*
- *Continuous learning* and *continuous teaching* have to be built into the job.

One central requirement of knowledge-worker productivity remains. We have to answer the question: What is quality? In some knowledge work—and especially in some work requiring a high degree of knowledge—we already measure quality. Surgeons, for example, are routinely measured, especially by their colleagues, by their success rates in difficult and dangerous procedures (e.g., by the survival rates of their open-heart surgical patients or the full recovery rates of their orthopedic-surgery patients). By and large, we mainly have judgments rather than measures regarding the quality of a great deal of knowledge work. The main trouble is, however, not the difficulty of measuring quality. It is the difficulty—and more particularly the sharp disagreements—in defining what the task is and what it should be.

The best example of this is the American school system. As every one knows, public schools in the American inner city have become disaster areas. Next to them—in the same location and serving the same kind of children—are private (mostly Christian) schools in which the kids behave well and learn well. There is endless speculation to explain these enormous quality differences. A major reason is surely that the two kinds of school define their tasks differently. The typical public school defines its task as "helping the underprivileged," while the typical private school (and especially the Parochial Schools of the Catholic Church) define their task as "enabling those who want to learn, to learn." One therefore is governed by its scholastic failures, the other one by its scholastic successes.

Similarly, the research departments at two major pharmaceutical companies have totally different results because they define their tasks differently. One sees its task as not having failures, that is, in working steadily on fairly minor but predictable improvements in existing products and for established markets. The other one defines its task as producing "breakthroughs" and therefore courts risks. Both are considered fairly successful—by themselves, by their own top managements, and by outside analysts. Yet each operates quite differently and quite differently defines its own productivity and that of its research scientists.

To define quality in knowledge work and to convert the definition into knowledge-worker productivity is thus to a large extent a matter of defining the task. It requires the difficult, risk-taking, and always controversial definition as to what "results" are for a given enterprise and a given activity. We therefore actually *know* how to do it. Nevertheless, the question is a completely new one for most organizations and also for most knowledge workers. To answer it *requires* controversy, *requires* dissent.

The Knowledge Worker as Capital Asset

In no other area is the difference greater between manual-worker productivity and knowledge-worker productivity than in their respective *economics*. Economic theory and most business practice sees manual workers as a *cost*. To be productive, knowledge workers must be considered a *capital asset*. Costs need to be controlled and reduced. Assets need to be made to grow.

To be sure, in managing manual workers we learned fairly early that high turnover (i.e., losing workers) is very costly. The Ford Motor Company, as is well known, increased the pay of skilled workers from eighty cents a day to $5.00 a day on January 1, 1914. It did so because its turnover had been so excessive as to make its labor costs prohibitively high; it had to hire 60,000 people a year to keep 10,000. Even so, everybody (including Henry Ford himself, who had at first been bitterly opposed to this increase) was convinced that the higher wages would greatly reduce the company's profits. Instead, in the very first year, profits almost doubled. Paid $5.00 a day, practically no workers left—in fact, the Ford Motor Company soon had a waiting list.

However, short of the costs of turnover, rehiring, retraining, and so on, the manual worker is still being seen as a cost. This is true even in Japan, despite the emphasis on lifetime employment and on building a "loyal," permanent work force. The management of people at work, based on millennia of work being almost totally manual work, still assumes that with few exceptions (e.g., highly skilled people) one manual worker is like any other manual worker.

This is definitely not true for knowledge work. Employees who do manual work do not own the means of production. They may, and often do, have a lot of valuable experience, but that experience is valuable only at the place where they work. It is not portable. Knowledge workers, however, *own* the means of production. That knowledge between their ears is a totally portable and enormous capital asset. Because knowledge workers own their means of production, they are mobile. It may not be true for most of them that the organization needs them more than they need the organization. For most of them it is a symbiotic relationship in which they need each other in equal measure. It is not true, as it was for the manual worker in modern industry, that they need the job much more than the job needs them.

Management's job is to preserve the assets of the institution in its care. What does this mean when the knowledge of the individual knowledge worker becomes an asset—and, in more and more cases, the *main* asset—of an institution? What does this mean for personnel policy? What is needed to attract and to hold the highest producing knowledge workers? What is needed to increase their productivity and to convert their increased productivity into performance capacity for the organization?

The Technologists

A very large number of knowledge workers do both knowledge work *and* manual work. I call them "technologists." This group includes people who apply knowledge of the highest order.

Surgeons preparing for an operation to correct a brain aneurysm before it produces a lethal brain hemorrhage, spend hours in diagnosis *before* they cut —and that requires specialized knowledge of the highest order. Again, during the surgery, an unexpected complication may occur which calls for theoretical knowledge and judgment, both of the very highest order. However, the surgery itself is manual work—and manual work consisting of repetitive, manual operations in which the emphasis is on speed, accuracy, and uniformity. These operations are studied, organized, learned, and practiced exactly like any manual work—that is, by the same methods Taylor first developed for factory work.

The technologist group also contains large numbers of people in whose work knowledge is relatively subordinate—though it is always crucial. The file clerk's job—and that of the clerk's computer-operator successor—requires a knowledge of the alphabet that no experience can teach. This knowledge is a small part of an otherwise manual task, but it is its foundation and is absolutely crucial.

Technologists may be the single biggest group of knowledge workers. They may also be the fastest-growing group. They include the great majority of health-care workers: lab-technicians; rehabilitation technicians; technicians in imaging such as X-ray, ultrasound, magnetic-resonance imaging; and so on. They include dentists and all dental-support people. They include automobile mechanics and all kinds of repair and installation people. In fact, the technologist may be the true successor to the 19th and 20th century skilled workers.

Technologists are also the one group in which developed countries can have a true and long-lasting competitive advantage. When it comes to truly high knowledge, no country can any longer have much of a lead the way 19th century Germany had through its University. Among theoretical physicists, mathematicians, economic theorists, and the like, there is no "nationality." Any country can, at fairly low cost, train a substantial number of high-knowledge people. India, for instance, despite her poverty, has been training fairly large numbers of first-rate physicians and first-rate computer programers. Similarly, there is no "nationality" in respect to the productivity of manual labor. Training based on Scientific Management has made all countries capable of attaining —overnight—the manual-worker productivity of the most advanced country, industry, or company. Only by educating technologists can the developed countries still have a meaningful and lasting competitive edge.

The U.S. is so far the only country that has developed this advantage through its unique nationwide systems of community colleges. The community college was actually *designed* (beginning in the 1920s) to educate technologists who have *both* the needed theoretical knowledge *and* the manual skill. On this, I am convinced, rests both the still huge productivity advantage of the American economy and the (so far unique) American ability to create, almost overnight, new and different industries.

Currently, nothing quite like the American Community College exists in any other nation. The famous Japanese school system produces either people prepared only for manual work or people prepared only for knowledge work. Not until the year 2003 is the first Japanese institution devoted to train technologists supposed to get started. The even more famous German apprenticeship system (started in the 1830s) was one of the main factors in Germany's becoming the world's leading manufacturer. However, it focused—and still focuses— primarily on manual skills and slights theoretical knowledge. It is thus in danger of becoming rapidly obsolete.

Other developed countries should be expected to catch up with the U.S. fairly fast. "Emerging" or "Third World" countries are, however, likely to be decades behind—in part because educating technologists is expensive, in part because in these countries people of knowledge still look down with disdain, if not with contempt, on working with one's hands. "That's what we have servants for" is still their prevailing attitude. However, in developed countries—and again foremost in the U.S.—more and more manual workers are going to be technologists. To increase knowledge-worker productivity, increasing the productivity of technologists deserves to be given high priority.

The job was actually done more than seventy years ago by the American Telephone Company (AT&T) for its technologists, the people who install, maintain, and replace telephones. By the early 1920s, the technologists working outside the telephone office and at the customer's location had become a major cost center—and at the same time a major cause of customer unhappiness and dissatisfaction. It took about five years or so (from 1920 until 1925) for AT&T—which had by that time acquired a near monopoly on providing telephone service in the United States and in parts of Canada—to realize that the task was not installing, maintaining, repairing, and replacing telephones and telephone connections. *The task was to create a satisfied customer*. Once they realized this, it became fairly easy to organize the job. It meant, first, that the technicians themselves had to define what "satisfaction" meant. The results were standards that established that every order for a new telephone or an additional telephone connection would have to be satisfied within 48 hours, and that every request for repair would have to be satisfied the same day if made before noon, or by noon the following day. Then it became clear that the individual service people—in those days all men, of course—would have to be active participants in such decisions as whether to have one person installing and replacing telephones and another one maintaining and repairing them or whether the same people had to be able to do all jobs (which in the end turned out to be the right answer). Then these people had to be taught a very substantial amount of theoretical knowledge—and in those days few of them had more than six years of schooling. They had to understand how a telephone works. They had to understand how a switchboard works. They had to understand how the telephone system works. These people were not qualified engineers nor skilled craftsmen, but they had to know enough electronics to diagnose unexpected problems and be able to cope with them. Then they were trained in the repetitive manual operation or in the "one right way" (that is, through the methods of Scientific Management) and *they* made the decisions (e.g., where and how to connect the individual telephone to the system and what particular kind of telephone and service would be the most suitable for a given home or a given office). They had to become salesmen in addition to being servicemen.

Finally, the telephone company faced the problem how to define *quality*. The technologist had to work by himself. He could not be supervised. He, therefore, had to define quality, and he had to deliver it. It took another several years before that was answered. At first the telephone company thought that this meant a sample check, which had supervisors go out and look at a sample (maybe every 20th or 30th job done by an individual service person) and check it for quality. This very soon turned out to be the wrong way of doing the job, annoying servicemen and customers alike. Then the telephone company defined quality as "no complaints"—and they soon found out that only extremely unhappy customers complained. It then had to redefine quality as "positive customer satisfaction." In the end, this then meant that the serviceman himself controlled quality (e.g., by calling up a week or ten days after he had done a job and asking the customer whether the work was satisfactory and whether there was anything more the technician could possibly do to give the customer the best possible and most satisfactory service).

I have intentionally gone into considerable detail in describing this early example because it exemplifies the three elements for making the worker who is both a knowledge worker and a manual worker both effective and productive.

- First, there is the answer to the question "What is the task?"—the key question in making every knowledge worker more productive. As the example of the Bell System shows, this is not an obvious answer. As the Bell System people learned, the only people who knew the answer to this were the technologists themselves. In fact, until they asked the technologists, they floundered. However, as soon as the technologists were asked, the answer came back loud and clear: "a satisfied customer."

- Then, the technologists had to take full responsibility for giving customer satisfaction, that is, for delivering quality. This showed what *formal knowledge* the technologist needed. Only then could the *manual* part of the job be organized for manual-worker productivity.

- Above all, this example shows that technologists have to be treated as *knowledge workers*. No matter how important the manual part of their work—and it may take as much time as it did in the case of the AT&T installers—the focus has to be on making the technologist knowledgeable, responsible, and productive as a knowledge worker.

Knowledge Work as a System

Productivity of the knowledge worker will almost always require that the *work itself* be restructured and be made part of a *system*. One example is servicing expensive equipment, such as huge and expensive earth-moving machines. Traditionally, this had been seen as distinct and separate from the job of making and selling the machines. However, when the U.S. Caterpillar Company, the world's largest producer of such equipment, asked "What are we getting paid for?" the answer was "We are not getting paid for machinery. We are getting paid for what the machinery does at the customer's place of business. That means keeping the equipment running, since even one hour during which the equipment is out of operation may cost the customer far more than the equipment itself." In other words, the answer to "What is our business?" was "Service." This then led to a total restructuring of operations all the way back to the factory in order that the customer could be guaranteed continuing operations and immediate repairs or replacements. The service representative, usually a technologist, has become the true "decision maker."

As another example, a group of about 25 orthopedic surgeons in a Midwestern U.S. city, have organized themselves as a "system" to: produce the highest quality work; make optimal use of the limited and expensive resources of operating and recovery rooms; make optimal use of the supporting knowledge people such as anesthesiologists or surgical nurses; build continuous learning and continuous innovation into the work of the entire group and of every member thereof; and, finally, minimize costs. Each of the surgeons retains full control of his or her practice. He or she is fully responsible for obtaining and treating the individual patient. Traditionally, surgeons schedules surgeries early in the morning. Hence, operating rooms and recovery rooms are standing empty most of the time. The group now schedules the use of operating and recovery rooms for the entire group so that this scarce and extremely expensive resource is utilized ten hours a day. The group, as a group, decides on the standardization of tools and equipment so as to obtain the highest quality at the lowest cost. Finally, the group has also built quality control into its system. Every three months three surgeons are designated to scrutinize every operation done by each of the members—the diagnosis, the surgery, the after-treatment. They then sit down with the individual surgeons and discuss their performance. They suggest where there is need for improvement and they also may recommend that a certain surgeon be asked to leave the group when his or her work is not satisfactory. Each year, the quality standards that these supervising committees apply are discussed with the whole group and are raised, often substantially. As a result, this group now does almost four times as much work as it did before. It has cut the costs by 50%, half of it by cutting back on the waste of operating and recovery rooms and half by standardizing tools and equipment. In such measurable areas as success rates in knee or shoulder replacements and in recovery after sports injuries, it has greatly improved its results.

What to do about knowledge-worker productivity is thus largely known. So is *how* to do it.

How to Begin?

Making knowledge workers more productive requires changes in basic attitude, whereas making the manual worker more productive only required telling the worker how to do the job. Furthermore, making knowledge workers more productive requires changes in attitude not only on the part of the individual knowledge worker, but on the part of the whole organization. It therefore has to be "piloted," as any major change should be. The first step is to find an area in the organization where there is a group of knowledge workers who are receptive. (The orthopedic surgeons, for instance, first had their new ideas tried out by four physicians who had long argued for radical changes.) The next step is to work consistently, patiently, and for a considerable length of time with this small group. The first attempts, even if greeted with great enthusiasm, will almost certainly run into all kinds of unexpected problems. It is only after the productivity of this small group of knowledge workers has been substantially increased that the new ways of doing the work can be extended to a larger area, if not to the entire organization. At this point, the main problems will be known, such as where resistance can be expected (e.g., from middle management) or what changes in task, organization, measurements, or attitudes are needed for full effectiveness. To bypass the pilot stage—and there is always pressure to do so—only means that the mistakes become public while the successes stay hidden. It only means discrediting the entire enterprise. If properly piloted, a great deal can be done to improve knowledge-worker productivity.

Knowledge-worker productivity is the biggest of the 21st-century management challenges. In the developed countries, it is their first *survival requirement*. In no other way can the developed countries hope to maintain themselves, let alone maintain their leadership and their standards of living. In the 20th century, this leadership very largely depended on making the manual worker more productive. Any country, any industry, any business can do that today using the methods that the developed countries have worked out and put into practice in the 120 years since Frederick Winslow Taylor first looked at manual work. Anybody today, any place, can apply those policies to training, the organization of work, and the productivity of workers—even if they are barely literate, if not illiterate, and totally unskilled.

Above all, the supply of young people available for manual work will be rapidly shrinking in the developed countries—in the West and in Japan very fast, in the U.S. somewhat more slowly—whereas the supply of such people will still grow fast in the emerging and developing countries for at least another thirty or forty years. The only possible advantage developed countries can hope to have is in the supply of people prepared, educated, and trained for knowledge work. There, for another fifty years, the developed countries can expect to have substantial advantages, both in quality and in quantity. Whether this advantage will translate into performance depends on the ability of the developed countries —and of every industry in it, of every company in it, of every institution in it— to raise the productivity of the knowledge worker and to raise it as fast as the developed countries have raised the productivity of the manual worker in the last hundred years.

The countries and the industries that have emerged as the leaders in the last hundred years in the world are the countries and the industries that have led in raising the productivity of the manual worker—the U.S. first, Japan and Germany second. Fifty years from now, if not much sooner, leadership in the world economy will have moved to the countries and to the industries that have most systematically and most successfully raised knowledge-worker productivity.

The Governance of the Corporation

What does the emergence of the knowledge worker and of knowledge-worker productivity mean for the *governance of the corporation*? What does it mean for the future and structure of the economic system?

In the last ten or fifteen years, pension funds and other institutional investors became the main share owners of the equity capital of publicly owned companies in all developed countries. In the U.S., this has triggered a furious debate on the governance of corporations. With the emergence of pension funds and mutual funds as the owners of publicly owned companies, power has shifted to these new owners. Similar shifts in both the definition of the purpose of economic organizations (such as the business corporation) and their governance can be expected to occur in all developed countries.

Within a fairly short period of time, we will face the problem of the governance of corporations again. We will have to redefine the purpose of the employing organization and of its management as *both* satisfying the legal owners (such as shareholders) and satisfying the owners of the human capital that gives the organization its wealth-producing power—that is, satisfying the knowledge workers. Increasingly, the ability of organizations—and not only of businesses—to survive will come to depend on their "comparative advantage" in making the knowledge worker more productive. The ability to attract and hold the best of the knowledge workers is the first and most fundamental precondition.

However, can this be *measured* or is it purely an "intangible"? This will surely be a central problem for management, for investors, and for capital markets. What does "capitalism" mean when knowledge governs rather than money? And what do "free markets" mean when knowledge workers—and no one else can "own" knowledge—are the true assets? Knowledge workers can neither be bought nor be sold. They do not come with a merger or an acquisition. In fact, although they are the greatest "value," they have no "market value"—that means, of course, that they are not an "asset" in any sense of the term.

These questions go far beyond the scope of this article. However, it is certain that the emergence as *key questions* of the knowledge worker and of the knowledge-worker's productivity will, within a few decades, bring about fundamental changes in the very structure and nature of the economic system.

Notes

1. For work in the oldest knowledge profession—that is, in Medicine—Taylor's close contemporary William Osler (1849-1919) did what Taylor did and at the same time in his 1892 book *The Principles and Practice of Medicine* (arguably the best textbook since Euclid's *Geometry* in the third century B.C.). Osler's work has rightly been called the application of Scientific Management to Medical Diagnosis. Like Taylor, Osler preached that there is no "skill," there is only *method*.

Harvard Business Review

www.hbr.org

What makes the difference between a team that performs and one that doesn't?

The Discipline of Teams

by Jon R. Katzenbach and Douglas K. Smith

What makes the difference between a team that performs and one that doesn't?

BEST OF HBR 1993

The Discipline of Teams

by Jon R. Katzenbach and Douglas K. Smith

It won't surprise anyone to find an article on teams by Jon Katzenbach and Douglas Smith figuring into an issue devoted to high performance. While Peter Drucker may have been the first to point out that a team-based organization can be highly effective, Katzenbach and Smith's work made it possible for companies to implement the idea.

In this groundbreaking 1993 article, the authors say that if managers want to make better decisions about teams, they must be clear about what a team is. They define a team as "a small number of people with complementary skills who are committed to a common purpose, set of performance goals, and approach for which they hold themselves mutually accountable." That definition lays down the discipline that teams must share to be effective.

Katzenbach and Smith discuss the four elements—common commitment and purpose, performance goals, complementary skills, and mutual accountability—that make teams function. They also classify teams into three varieties—teams that recommend things, teams that make or do things, and teams that run things—and describe how each type faces different challenges.

Early in the 1980s, Bill Greenwood and a small band of rebel railroaders took on most of the top management of Burlington Northern and created a multibillion-dollar business in "piggybacking" rail services despite widespread resistance, even resentment, within the company. The Medical Products Group at Hewlett-Packard owes most of its leading performance to the remarkable efforts of Dean Morton, Lew Platt, Ben Holmes, Dick Alberding, and a handful of their colleagues who revitalized a health care business that most others had written off. At Knight Ridder, Jim Batten's "customer obsession" vision took root at the *Tallahassee Democrat* when 14 frontline enthusiasts turned a charter to eliminate errors into a mission of major change and took the entire paper along with them.

Such are the stories and the work of teams—real teams that perform, not amorphous groups that we call teams because we think that the label is motivating and energizing. The difference between teams that perform and other groups that don't is a subject to which most of us pay far too little attention. Part of the problem is that "team" is a word and concept so familiar to everyone. (See the exhibit "Not All Groups Are Teams: How to Tell the Difference.")

Or at least that's what we thought when we set out to do research for our book *The Wisdom of Teams* (HarperBusiness, 1993). We wanted to discover what differentiates various levels of team performance, where and how teams work best, and what top management can do to enhance their effectiveness. We talked with hundreds of people on more than 50 different teams in 30 companies and beyond, from Motorola and Hewlett-Packard to Operation Desert Storm and the Girl Scouts.

We found that there is a basic discipline that makes teams work. We also found that teams and good performance are inseparable: You cannot have one without the other. But people use the word "team" so loosely that it gets in the way of learning and applying the discipline that leads to good performance. For managers to make better decisions about whether, when, or how to encourage and use teams, it is important to be more precise about what a team is and what it isn't.

Most executives advocate teamwork. And they should. Teamwork represents a set of values that encourage listening and responding constructively to views expressed by others, giving others the benefit of the doubt, providing support, and recognizing the interests and achievements of others. Such values help teams perform, and they also promote individual performance as well as the performance of an entire organization. But teamwork values by themselves are not exclusive to teams, nor are they enough to ensure team performance. (See the sidebar "Building Team Performance.")

Nor is a team just any group working together. Committees, councils, and task forces are not necessarily teams. Groups do not become teams simply because that is what someone calls them. The entire workforce of any large and complex organization is *never* a team, but think about how often that platitude is offered up.

To understand how teams deliver extra performance, we must distinguish between teams and other forms of working groups. That distinction turns on performance results. A working group's performance is a function of what its members do as individuals. A team's perfor-

mance includes both individual results and what we call "collective work products." A collective work product is what two or more members must work on together, such as interviews, surveys, or experiments. Whatever it is, a collective work product reflects the joint, real contribution of team members.

Working groups are both prevalent and effective in large organizations where individual accountability is most important. The best working groups come together to share information, perspectives, and insights; to make decisions that help each person do his or her job better; and to reinforce individual performance standards. But the focus is always on individual goals and accountabilities. Working-group members don't take responsibility for results other than their own. Nor do they try to develop incremental performance contributions requiring the combined work of two or more members.

Teams differ fundamentally from working groups because they require both individual and mutual accountability. Teams rely on more than group discussion, debate, and decision, on more than sharing information and best-practice performance standards. Teams produce discrete work products through the joint contributions of their members. This is what makes possible performance levels greater than the sum of all the individual bests of team members. Simply stated, a team is more than the sum of its parts.

The first step in developing a disciplined approach to team management is to think about teams as discrete units of performance and not just as positive sets of values. Having observed and worked with scores of teams in action, both successes and failures, we offer the following. Think of it as a working definition or, better still, an essential discipline that real teams share: *A team is a small number of people with complementary skills who are committed to a common purpose, set of performance goals, and approach for which they hold themselves mutually accountable.*

The essence of a team is common commitment. Without it, groups perform as individuals; with it, they become a powerful unit of collective performance. This kind of commitment requires a purpose in which team members can believe. Whether the purpose is to "transform the contributions of suppliers into the satisfaction of customers," to "make our com-

Jon R. Katzenbach is a founder and senior partner of Katzenbach Partners, a strategic and organizational consulting firm, and a former director of McKinsey & Company. His most recent book is *Why Pride Matters More Than Money: The Power of the World's Greatest Motivational Force* (Crown Business, 2003). **Douglas K. Smith** is an organizational consultant and a former partner at McKinsey & Company. His most recent book is *On Value and Values: Thinking Differently About We in an Age of Me* (Financial Times Prentice Hall, 2004).

pany one we can be proud of again," or to "prove that all children can learn," credible team purposes have an element related to winning, being first, revolutionizing, or being on the cutting edge.

Teams develop direction, momentum, and commitment by working to shape a meaningful purpose. Building ownership and commitment to team purpose, however, is not incompatible with taking initial direction from outside the team. The often-asserted assumption that a team cannot "own" its purpose unless management leaves it alone actually confuses more potential teams than it helps. In fact, it is the exceptional case—for example, entrepreneurial situations—when a team creates a purpose entirely on its own.

Most successful teams shape their purposes in response to a demand or opportunity put in their path, usually by higher management. This helps teams get started by broadly framing the company's performance expectation. Management is responsible for clarifying the charter, rationale, and performance challenge for the team, but management must also leave enough flexibility for the team to develop commitment around its own spin on that purpose, set of specific goals, timing, and approach.

The best teams invest a tremendous amount of time and effort exploring, shaping, and agreeing on a purpose that belongs to them both collectively and individually. This "purposing" activity continues throughout the life of the team. By contrast, failed teams rarely develop a common purpose. For whatever reason—an insufficient focus on performance, lack of effort, poor leadership—they do not coalesce around a challenging aspiration.

The best teams also translate their common purpose into specific performance goals, such as reducing the reject rate from suppliers by 50% or increasing the math scores of graduates from 40% to 95%. Indeed, if a team fails to establish specific performance goals or if those goals do not relate directly to the team's overall purpose, team members become confused, pull apart, and revert to mediocre performance. By contrast, when purposes and goals build on one another and are combined with team commitment, they become a powerful engine of performance.

Transforming broad directives into specific and measurable performance goals is the surest first step for a team trying to shape a purpose meaningful to its members. Specific goals, such as getting a new product to market in less than half the normal time, responding to all customers within 24 hours, or achieving a zero-defect rate while simultaneously cutting costs by 40%, all provide firm footholds for teams. There are several reasons:

• Specific team-performance goals help define a set of work products that are different both from an organization-wide mission and from individual job objectives. As a result, such work products require the collective effort of team members to make something specific happen that, in and of itself, adds real value to results. By contrast, simply gathering from time to time to make decisions will not sustain team performance.

• The specificity of performance objectives facilitates clear communication and constructive conflict within the team. When a plant-level team, for example, sets a goal of reducing average machine changeover time to two hours, the clarity of the goal forces the team to concentrate on what it would take either to achieve or to reconsider the goal. When such goals are clear, discussions can focus on how to pursue them or whether to change them; when goals are ambiguous or nonexistent, such discussions are much less productive.

• The attainability of specific goals helps teams maintain their focus on getting results. A product-development team at Eli Lilly's Peripheral Systems Division set definite yardsticks for the market introduction of an ultrasonic probe to help doctors locate deep veins and arteries.

Not All Groups Are Teams: How to Tell the Difference

Working Group
- Strong, clearly focused leader
- Individual accountability
- The group's purpose is the same as the broader organizational mission
- Individual work products
- Runs efficient meetings
- Measures its effectiveness indirectly by its influence on others (such as financial performance of the business)
- Discusses, decides, and delegates

Team
- Shared leadership roles
- Individual and mutual accountability
- Specific team purpose that the team itself delivers
- Collective work products
- Encourages open-ended discussion and active problem-solving meetings
- Measures performance directly by assessing collective work products
- Discusses, decides, and does real work together

Building Team Performance

Although there is no guaranteed how-to recipe for building team performance, we observed a number of approaches shared by many successful teams.

Establish urgency, demanding performance standards, and direction. All team members need to believe the team has urgent and worthwhile purposes, and they want to know what the expectations are. Indeed, the more urgent and meaningful the rationale, the more likely it is that the team will live up to its performance potential, as was the case for a customer-service team that was told that further growth for the entire company would be impossible without major improvements in that area. Teams work best in a compelling context. That is why companies with strong performance ethics usually form teams readily.

Select members for skill and skill potential, not personality. No team succeeds without all the skills needed to meet its purpose and performance goals. Yet most teams figure out the skills they will need after they are formed. The wise manager will choose people for their existing skills and their potential to improve existing skills and learn new ones.

Pay particular attention to first meetings and actions. Initial impressions always mean a great deal. When potential teams first gather, everyone monitors the signals given by others to confirm, suspend, or dispel assumptions and concerns. They pay particular attention to those in authority: the team leader and any executives who set up, oversee, or otherwise influence the team. And, as always, what such leaders do is more important than what they say. If a senior executive leaves the team kickoff to take a phone call ten minutes after the session has begun and he never returns, people get the message.

Set some clear rules of behavior. All effective teams develop rules of conduct at the outset to help them achieve their purpose and performance goals. The most critical initial rules pertain to attendance (for example, "no interruptions to take phone calls"), discussion ("no sacred cows"), confidentiality ("the only things to leave this room are what we agree on"), analytic approach ("facts are friendly"), end-product orientation ("everyone gets assignments and does them"), constructive confrontation ("no finger pointing"), and, often the most important, contributions ("everyone does real work").

Set and seize upon a few immediate performance-oriented tasks and goals. Most effective teams trace their advancement to key performance-oriented events. Such events can be set in motion by immediately establishing a few challenging goals that can be reached early on. There is no such thing as a real team without performance results, so the sooner such results occur, the sooner the team congeals.

Challenge the group regularly with fresh facts and information. New information causes a team to redefine and enrich its understanding of the performance challenge, thereby helping the team shape a common purpose, set clearer goals, and improve its common approach. A plant quality improvement team knew the cost of poor quality was high, but it wasn't until they researched the different types of defects and put a price tag on each one that they knew where to go next. Conversely, teams err when

they assume that all the information needed exists in the collective experience and knowledge of their members.

Spend lots of time together. Common sense tells us that team members must spend a lot of time together, scheduled and unscheduled, especially in the beginning. Indeed, creative insights as well as personal bonding require impromptu and casual interactions just as much as analyzing spreadsheets and interviewing customers. Busy executives and managers too often intentionally minimize the time they spend together. The successful teams we've observed all gave themselves the time to learn to be a team. This time need not always be spent together physically; electronic, fax, and phone time can also count as time spent together.

Exploit the power of positive feedback, recognition, and reward. Positive reinforcement works as well in a team context as elsewhere. Giving out "gold stars" helps shape new behaviors critical to team performance. If people in the group, for example, are alert to a shy person's initial efforts to speak up and contribute, they can give the honest positive reinforcement that encourages continued contributions. There are many ways to recognize and reward team performance beyond direct compensation, from having a senior executive speak directly to the team about the urgency of its mission to using awards to recognize contributions. Ultimately, however, the satisfaction shared by a team in its own performance becomes the most cherished reward.

The probe had to have an audible signal through a specified depth of tissue, be capable of being manufactured at a rate of 100 per day, and have a unit cost less than a preestablished amount. Because the team could measure its progress against each of these specific objectives, the team knew throughout the development process where it stood. Either it had achieved its goals or not.

• As Outward Bound and other team-building programs illustrate, specific objectives have a leveling effect conducive to team behavior. When a small group of people challenge themselves to get over a wall or to reduce cycle time by 50%, their respective titles, perks, and other stripes fade into the background. The teams that succeed evaluate what and how each individual can best contribute to the team's goal and, more important, do so in terms of the performance objective itself rather than a person's status or personality.

• Specific goals allow a team to achieve small wins as it pursues its broader purpose. These small wins are invaluable to building commitment and overcoming the inevitable obstacles that get in the way of a long-term purpose. For example, the Knight Ridder team mentioned at the outset turned a narrow goal to eliminate errors into a compelling customer service purpose.

• Performance goals are compelling. They are symbols of accomplishment that motivate and energize. They challenge the people on a team to commit themselves, as a team, to make a difference. Drama, urgency, and a healthy fear of failure combine to drive teams that have their collective eye on an attainable, but challenging, goal. Nobody but the team can make it happen. It's their challenge.

The combination of purpose and specific goals is essential to performance. Each depends on the other to remain relevant and vital. Clear performance goals help a team keep track of progress and hold itself accountable; the broader, even nobler, aspirations in a team's purpose supply both meaning and emotional energy.

Virtually all effective teams we have met, read or heard about, or been members of have ranged between two and 25 people. For example, the Burlington Northern piggybacking team had seven members, and the Knight Ridder newspaper team had 14. The majority of them have numbered less than ten. Small size

is admittedly more of a pragmatic guide than an absolute necessity for success. A large number of people, say 50 or more, can theoretically become a team. But groups of such size are more likely to break into subteams rather than function as a single unit.

Why? Large numbers of people have trouble interacting constructively as a group, much less doing real work together. Ten people are far more likely than 50 to work through their individual, functional, and hierarchical differences toward a common plan and to hold themselves jointly accountable for the results.

Large groups also face logistical issues, such as finding enough physical space and time to meet. And they confront more complex constraints, like crowd or herd behaviors, which prevent the intense sharing of viewpoints needed to build a team. As a result, when they try to develop a common purpose, they usually produce only superficial "missions" and well-meaning intentions that cannot be translated into concrete objectives. They tend fairly quickly to reach a point when meetings become a chore, a clear sign that most of the people in the group are uncertain why they have gathered, beyond some notion of getting along better. Anyone who has been through one of these exercises understands how frustrating it can be. This kind of failure tends to foster cynicism, which gets in the way of future team efforts.

In addition to finding the right size, teams must develop the right mix of skills; that is, each of the complementary skills necessary to do the team's job. As obvious as it sounds, it is a common failing in potential teams. Skill requirements fall into three fairly self-evident categories.

Technical or Functional Expertise. It would make little sense for a group of doctors to litigate an employment discrimination case in a court of law. Yet teams of doctors and lawyers often try medical malpractice or personal injury cases. Similarly, product development groups that include only marketers or engineers are less likely to succeed than those with the complementary skills of both.

Problem-Solving and Decision-Making Skills. Teams must be able to identify the problems and opportunities they face, evaluate the options they have for moving forward, and then make necessary trade-offs and decisions about how to proceed. Most teams need

People use the word "team" so loosely that it gets in the way of learning and applying the discipline that leads to good performance.

some members with these skills to begin with, although many will develop them best on the job.

Interpersonal Skills. Common understanding and purpose cannot arise without effective communication and constructive conflict, which in turn depend on interpersonal skills. These skills include risk taking, helpful criticism, objectivity, active listening, giving the benefit of the doubt, and recognizing the interests and achievements of others.

Obviously, a team cannot get started without some minimum complement of skills, especially technical and functional ones. Still, think about how often you've been part of a team whose members were chosen primarily on the basis of personal compatibility or formal position in the organization, and in which the skill mix of its members wasn't given much thought.

It is equally common to overemphasize skills in team selection. Yet in all the successful teams we've encountered, not one had all the needed skills at the outset. The Burlington Northern team, for example, initially had no members who were skilled marketers despite the fact that their performance challenge was a marketing one. In fact, we discovered that teams are powerful vehicles for developing the skills needed to meet the team's performance challenge. Accordingly, team member selection ought to ride as much on skill potential as on skills already proven.

Effective teams develop strong commitment to a common approach; that is, to how they will work together to accomplish their purpose. Team members must agree on who will do particular jobs, how schedules will be set and adhered to, what skills need to be developed, how continuing membership in the team is to be earned, and how the group will make and modify decisions. This element of commitment is as important to team performance as the team's commitment to its purpose and goals.

Agreeing on the specifics of work and how they fit together to integrate individual skills and advance team performance lies at the heart of shaping a common approach. It is perhaps self-evident that an approach that delegates all the real work to a few members (or staff outsiders) and thus relies on reviews and meetings for its only "work together" aspects, cannot sustain a real team. Every member of a successful team does equivalent amounts of real work; all members, including the team leader, contribute in concrete ways to the team's work product. This is a very important element of the emotional logic that drives team performance.

When individuals approach a team situation, especially in a business setting, each has preexisting job assignments as well as strengths and weaknesses reflecting a variety of talents, backgrounds, personalities, and prejudices. Only through the mutual discovery and understanding of how to apply all its human resources to a common purpose can a team develop and agree on the best approach to achieve its goals. At the heart of such long and, at times, difficult interactions lies a commitment-building process in which the team candidly explores who is best suited to each task as well as how individual roles will come together. In effect, the team establishes a social contract among members that relates to their purpose and guides and obligates how they must work together.

No group ever becomes a team until it can hold itself accountable as a team. Like common purpose and approach, mutual accountability is a stiff test. Think, for example, about the subtle but critical difference between "the boss holds me accountable" and "we hold ourselves accountable." The first case can lead to the second, but without the second, there can be no team.

Companies like Hewlett-Packard and Motorola have an ingrained performance ethic that enables teams to form organically whenever there is a clear performance challenge requiring collective rather than individual effort. In these companies, the factor of mutual accountability is commonplace. "Being in the boat together" is how their performance game is played.

At its core, team accountability is about the sincere promises we make to ourselves and others, promises that underpin two critical aspects of effective teams: commitment and trust. Most of us enter a potential team situation cautiously because ingrained individualism and experience discourage us from putting our fates in the hands of others or accepting responsibility for others. Teams do not succeed by ignoring or wishing away such behavior.

Mutual accountability cannot be coerced any more than people can be made to trust one another. But when a team shares a common purpose, goals, and approach, mutual accountability grows as a natural counterpart. Accountability arises from and reinforces the time, energy, and action invested in figuring out what the team is trying to accomplish and how best to get it done.

When people work together toward a common objective, trust and commitment follow. Consequently, teams enjoying a strong common purpose and approach inevitably hold themselves responsible, both as individuals and as a team, for the team's performance. This sense of mutual accountability also produces the rich rewards of mutual achievement in which all members share. What we heard over and over from members of effective teams is that they found the experience energizing and motivating in ways that their "normal" jobs never could match.

On the other hand, groups established primarily for the sake of becoming a team or for job enhancement, communication, organizational effectiveness, or excellence rarely become effective teams, as demonstrated by the bad feelings left in many companies after experimenting with quality circles that never translated "quality" into specific goals. Only when appropriate performance goals are set does the process of discussing the goals and the approaches to them give team members a clearer and clearer choice: They can disagree with a goal and the path that the team selects and, in effect, opt out, or they can pitch in and become accountable with and to their teammates.

The discipline of teams we've outlined is critical to the success of all teams. Yet it is also useful to go one step further. Most teams can be classified in one of three ways: teams that recommend things, teams that make or do things, and teams that run things. In our experience, each type faces a characteristic set of challenges.

Teams That Recommend Things. These teams include task forces; project groups; and audit, quality, or safety groups asked to study and solve particular problems. Teams that recommend things almost always have predetermined completion dates. Two critical issues are unique to such teams: getting off to a fast and constructive start and dealing with the ultimate handoff that's required to get recommendations implemented.

The key to the first issue lies in the clarity of the team's charter and the composition of its membership. In addition to wanting to know why and how their efforts are important, task forces need a clear definition of whom management expects to participate and the time commitment required. Management can help by ensuring that the team includes people with the skills and influence necessary for crafting practical recommendations that will carry weight throughout the organization. Moreover, management can help the team get the necessary cooperation by opening doors and dealing with political obstacles.

Missing the handoff is almost always the problem that stymies teams that recommend things. To avoid this, the transfer of responsibility for recommendations to those who must implement them demands top management's time and attention. The more top managers assume that recommendations will "just happen," the less likely it is that they will. The more involvement task force members have in implementing their recommendations, the more likely they are to get implemented.

To the extent that people outside the task force will have to carry the ball, it is critical to involve them in the process early and often, certainly well before recommendations are finalized. Such involvement may take many forms, including participating in interviews, helping with analyses, contributing and critiquing ideas, and conducting experiments and trials. At a minimum, anyone responsible for implementation should receive a briefing on the task force's purpose, approach, and objectives at the beginning of the effort as well as regular reviews of progress.

Teams That Make or Do Things. These teams include people at or near the front lines who are responsible for doing the basic manufacturing, development, operations, marketing, sales, service, and other value-adding activities of a business. With some exceptions, such as new-product development or process design teams, teams that make or do things tend to have no set completion dates because their activities are ongoing.

In deciding where team performance might have the greatest impact, top management should concentrate on what we call the company's "critical delivery points"—that is, places in the organization where the cost and value of the company's products and services are most directly determined. Such critical delivery points might include where accounts get managed, customer service performed, products designed, and productivity determined. If performance at critical delivery points depends on combining multiple skills, perspectives, and judgments in real time, then the team option is the smartest one.

When an organization does require a significant number of teams at these points, the sheer challenge of maximizing the performance of so many groups will demand a carefully constructed and performance-focused set of management processes. The issue here for top management is how to build the necessary systems and process supports without falling into the trap of appearing to promote teams for their own sake.

The imperative here, returning to our earlier discussion of the basic discipline of teams, is a relentless focus on performance. If management fails to pay persistent attention to the link between teams and performance, the organization becomes convinced that "this year, we are doing 'teams'." Top management can help by instituting processes like pay schemes and training for teams responsive to their real time needs, but more than anything else, top management must make clear and compelling demands on the teams themselves and then pay constant attention to their progress with respect to both team basics and performance results. This means focusing on specific teams and specific performance challenges. Otherwise "performance," like "team," will become a cliché.

Teams That Run Things. Despite the fact that many leaders refer to the group reporting to them as a team, few groups really are. And groups that become real teams seldom think of themselves as a team because they are so focused on performance results. Yet the opportunity for such teams includes groups from the top of the enterprise down through the divisional or functional level. Whether it is in charge of thousands of people or just a handful, as long as the group oversees some business, ongoing program, or significant functional activity, it is a team that runs things.

The main issue these teams face is determining whether a real team approach is the right one. Many groups that run things can be more effective as working groups than as teams. The key judgment is whether the sum of individual bests will suffice for the performance challenge at hand or whether the group must deliver substantial incremental performance requiring real joint work products. Although the team option promises greater performance, it also brings more risk, and managers must be brutally honest in assessing the trade-offs.

Members may have to overcome a natural reluctance to trust their fate to others. The price of faking the team approach is high: At best, members get diverted from their individual goals, costs outweigh benefits, and people resent the imposition on their time and priorities. At worst, serious animosities develop that undercut even the potential personal bests of the working-group approach.

Working groups present fewer risks. Effective working groups need little time to shape their purpose, since the leader usually establishes it. Meetings are run against well-prioritized agendas. And decisions are implemented through specific individual assignments and accountabilities. Most of the time, therefore, if performance aspirations can be met through individuals doing their respective jobs well, the working-group approach is more comfortable, less risky, and less disruptive than trying for more elusive team performance levels. Indeed, if there is no performance need for the team approach, efforts spent to improve the effectiveness of the working group make much more sense than floundering around trying to become a team.

Having said that, we believe the extra level of performance teams can achieve is becoming critical for a growing number of companies, especially as they move through major changes during which company performance depends on broad-based behavioral change. When top management uses teams to run things, it should make sure the team succeeds in identifying specific purposes and goals.

This is a second major issue for teams that run things. Too often, such teams confuse the broad mission of the total organization with the specific purpose of their small group at the top. The discipline of teams tells us that for a real team to form, there must be a team purpose that is distinctive and specific to the small group and that requires its members to roll up their sleeves and accomplish something beyond individual end products. If a group of managers looks only at the economic performance of the part of the organization it runs to assess overall effectiveness, the group will not have any team performance goals of its own.

While the basic discipline of teams does not differ for them, teams at the top are certainly the most difficult. The complexities of long-term challenges, heavy demands on executive time, and the deep-seated individualism of senior people conspire against teams at the top. At the same time, teams at the top are the most powerful. At first we thought such teams were nearly impossible. That is because we were looking at the teams as defined by the formal organizational structure; that is, the leader and all his or her direct reports equals the team. Then we discovered that real teams at the top were often smaller and less formalized: Whitehead and Weinberg at Goldman Sachs; Hewlett and Packard at HP; Krasnoff, Pall, and Hardy at Pall Corporation; Kendall, Pearson, and Calloway at Pepsi; Haas and Haas at Levi Strauss; Batten and Ridder at Knight Ridder. They were mostly twos and threes, with an occasional fourth.

Nonetheless, real teams at the top of large, complex organizations are still few and far between. Far too many groups at the top of large corporations needlessly constrain themselves from achieving real team levels of performance because they assume that all direct reports must be on the team, that team goals must be identical to corporate goals, that the team members' positions rather than skills determine their respective roles, that a team must be a team all the time, and that the team leader is above doing real work.

As understandable as these assumptions may be, most of them are unwarranted. They do not apply to the teams at the top we have observed, and when replaced with more realistic and flexible assumptions that permit the team discipline to be applied, real team performance at the top can and does occur. More-over, as more and more companies are confronted with the need to manage major change across their organizations, we will see more real teams at the top.

We believe that teams will become the primary unit of performance in high-performance organizations. But that does not mean that teams will crowd out individual opportunity or formal hierarchy and process. Rather, teams will enhance existing structures without replacing them. A team opportunity exists anywhere hierarchy or organizational boundaries inhibit the skills and perspectives needed for optimal results. Thus, new-product innovation requires preserving functional excellence through structure while eradicating functional bias through teams. And frontline productivity requires preserving direction and guidance through hierarchy while drawing on energy and flexibility through self-managing teams.

We are convinced that every company faces specific performance challenges for which teams are the most practical and powerful vehicle at top management's disposal. The critical role for senior managers, therefore, is to worry about company performance and the kinds of teams that can deliver it. This means top management must recognize a team's unique potential to deliver results, deploy teams strategically when they are the best tool for the job, and foster the basic discipline of teams that will make them effective. By doing so, top management creates the kind of environment that enables team as well as individual and organizational performance.

Reprint R0507P
Harvard Business Review OnPoint 4428
To order, see the next page
or call 800-988-0886 or 617-783-7500
or go to www.hbr.org

Every company faces specific performance challenges for which teams are the most practical and powerful vehicle at top management's disposal.

Further Reading

This article is also available in an enhanced *Harvard Business Review* OnPoint edition, (Product no. 4428), which includes a summary of its key points and company examples to help you put the ideas to work. The OnPoint edition also includes the following suggestions for further reading:

How Management Teams Can Have a Good Fight
Kathleen M. Eisenhardt, Jean L. Kahwajy, and L. J. Bourgeois III
Harvard Business Review
July–August 1997
Product no. 536X

How the Right Measures Help Teams Excel
Christopher Meyer
Harvard Business Review
May–June 1994
Product no. 94305

Team Talk: The Power of Language in Team Dynamics
Anne Donnellon
Harvard Business School Press
1996
Product no. 619X

Harvard Business Review ♛

To Order

For reprints, *Harvard Business Review* OnPoint orders, and subscriptions to *Harvard Business Review:*
Call 800-988-0886 or 617-783-7500.
Go to www.hbr.org

For customized and quantity orders of reprints and *Harvard Business Review* OnPoint products:
Call Rich Gravelin at
617-783-7626,
or e-mail him at
rgravelin@hbsp.harvard.edu

Harvard Business Review

www.hbrreprints.org

BEST OF HBR 1998

IQ and technical skills are important, but emotional intelligence is the sine qua non of leadership.

What Makes a Leader?

by Daniel Goleman

Included with this full-text *Harvard Business Review* article:

BEST OF HBR 1998

What Makes a Leader?

The Idea in Brief

Asked to define the ideal leader, many would emphasize traits such as intelligence, toughness, determination, and vision. Often left off the list are softer, more personal qualities—but recent studies indicate that they are also essential. Although a certain degree of analytical and technical skill is a minimum requirement for success, what is called "emotional intelligence" may be the key attribute that distinguishes outstanding performers from those who are merely adequate. For example, in a 1996 study of a global food and beverage company, where senior managers had a certain critical mass of emotional intelligence, their divisions outperformed yearly earnings goals by 20%. Division leaders without that critical mass underperformed by almost the same amount.

The Idea in Practice

There are five components to emotional intelligence: self-awareness, self-regulation, motivation, empathy, and social skill. All five traits sound desirable to just about everyone. But organizations too often implicitly discourage their people from developing them.

SELF-MANAGEMENT SKILLS

1. Self-awareness. Emotional intelligence begins with this trait. People with a high degree of self-awareness know their weaknesses and aren't afraid to talk about them. Someone who understands that he works poorly under tight deadlines, for example, will work hard to plan his time carefully, and will let his colleagues know why. Many executives looking for potential leaders mistake such candor for "wimpiness."

2. Self-regulation. This attribute flows from self-awareness, but runs in a different direction. People with this trait are able to control their impulses or even channel them for good purposes.

3. Motivation. A passion for achievement for its own sake—not simply the ability to respond to whatever incentives a company offers—is the kind of motivation that is essential for leadership.

THE ABILITY TO RELATE TO OTHERS

4. Empathy. In addition to self-management skills, emotional intelligence requires a facility for dealing with others. And that starts with empathy—taking into account the feelings of others when making decisions—as opposed to taking on everyone's troubles.

▶ Example:
Consider two division chiefs at a company forced to make layoffs. One manager gave a hard-hitting speech emphasizing the number of people who would be fired. The other manager, while not hiding the bad news, took into account his people's anxieties. He promised to keep them informed

and to treat everyone fairly. Many executives would have refrained from such a show of consideration, lest they appear to lack toughness. But the tough manager demoralized his talented people—most of whom ended up leaving his division entirely.

5. Social skill. All the preceding traits culminate in this fifth one: the ability to build rapport with others, to get them to cooperate, to move them in a direction you desire. Managers who simply try to be sociable—while lacking the other components of emotional intelligence—are likely to fail. Social skill, by contrast, is friendliness with a purpose.

CAN YOU BOOST YOUR EMOTIONAL INTELLIGENCE?

Absolutely—but not with traditional training programs that target the rational part of the brain. Extended practice, feedback from colleagues, and your own enthusiasm for making the change are essential to becoming an effective leader.

IQ and technical skills are important, but emotional intelligence is the sine qua non of leadership.

BEST OF HBR 1998

What Makes a Leader?

by Daniel Goleman

It was Daniel Goleman who first brought the term "emotional intelligence" to a wide audience with his 1995 book of that name, and it was Goleman who first applied the concept to business with his 1998 HBR article, reprinted here. In his research at nearly 200 large, global companies, Goleman found that while the qualities traditionally associated with leadership—such as intelligence, toughness, determination, and vision—are required for success, they are insufficient. Truly effective leaders are also distinguished by a high degree of emotional intelligence, which includes self-awareness, self-regulation, motivation, empathy, and social skill.

These qualities may sound "soft" and unbusinesslike, but Goleman found direct ties between emotional intelligence and measurable business results. While emotional intelligence's relevance to business has continued to spark debate over the past six years, Goleman's article remains the definitive reference on the subject, with a description of each component of emotional intelligence and a detailed discussion of how to recognize it in potential leaders, how

and why it connects to performance, and how it can be learned.

Every businessperson knows a story about a highly intelligent, highly skilled executive who was promoted into a leadership position only to fail at the job. And they also know a story about someone with solid—but not extraordinary—intellectual abilities and technical skills who was promoted into a similar position and then soared.

Such anecdotes support the widespread belief that identifying individuals with the "right stuff" to be leaders is more art than science. After all, the personal styles of superb leaders vary: Some leaders are subdued and analytical; others shout their manifestos from the mountaintops. And just as important, different situations call for different types of leadership. Most mergers need a sensitive negotiator at the helm, whereas many turnarounds require a more forceful authority.

I have found, however, that the most effective leaders are alike in one crucial way: They all have a high degree of what has come to be known as *emotional intelligence*. It's not that IQ and technical skills are irrelevant. They do matter, but mainly as "threshold capabilities"; that is, they are the entry-level requirements for executive positions. But my research, along with other recent studies, clearly shows that emotional intelligence is the sine qua non of leadership. Without it, a person can have the best training in the world, an incisive, analytical mind, and an endless supply of smart ideas, but he still won't make a great leader.

In the course of the past year, my colleagues and I have focused on how emotional intelligence operates at work. We have examined the relationship between emotional intelligence and effective performance, especially in leaders. And we have observed how emotional intelligence shows itself on the job. How can you tell if someone has high emotional intelligence, for example, and how can you recognize it in yourself? In the following pages, we'll explore these questions, taking each of the components of emotional intelligence—self-awareness, self-regulation, motivation, empathy, and social skill—in turn.

Evaluating Emotional Intelligence

Most large companies today have employed trained psychologists to develop what are known as "competency models" to aid them in identifying, training, and promoting likely stars in the leadership firmament. The psychologists have also developed such models for lower-level positions. And in recent years, I have analyzed competency models from 188 companies, most of which were large and global and included the likes of Lucent Technologies, British Airways, and Credit Suisse.

In carrying out this work, my objective was to determine which personal capabilities drove outstanding performance within these organizations, and to what degree they did so. I grouped capabilities into three categories: purely technical skills like accounting and business planning; cognitive abilities like analytical reasoning; and competencies demonstrating emotional intelligence, such as the ability to work with others and effectiveness in leading change.

To create some of the competency models, psychologists asked senior managers at the companies to identify the capabilities that typified the organization's most outstanding leaders. To create other models, the psychologists used

objective criteria, such as a division's profitability, to differentiate the star performers at senior levels within their organizations from the average ones. Those individuals were then extensively interviewed and tested, and their capabilities were compared. This process resulted in the creation of lists of ingredients for highly effective leaders. The lists ranged in length from seven to 15 items and included such ingredients as initiative and strategic vision.

When I analyzed all this data, I found dramatic results. To be sure, intellect was a driver of outstanding performance. Cognitive skills such as big-picture thinking and long-term vision were particularly important. But when I calculated the ratio of technical skills, IQ, and emotional intelligence as ingredients of excellent performance, emotional intelligence proved to be twice as important as the others for jobs at all levels.

Moreover, my analysis showed that emotional intelligence played an increasingly important role at the highest levels of the company, where differences in technical skills are of negligible importance. In other words, the higher the rank of a person considered to be a star performer, the more emotional intelligence capabilities showed up as the reason for his or her effectiveness. When I compared star performers with average ones in senior leadership positions, nearly 90% of the difference in their profiles was attributable to emotional intelligence factors rather than cognitive abilities.

Other researchers have confirmed that emotional intelligence not only distinguishes outstanding leaders but can also be linked to strong performance. The findings of the late David McClelland, the renowned researcher in human and organizational behavior, are a good example. In a 1996 study of a global food and beverage company, McClelland found that when senior managers had a critical mass of emotional intelligence capabilities, their divisions outperformed yearly earnings goals by 20%. Meanwhile, division leaders without that critical mass underperformed by almost the same amount. McClelland's findings, interestingly, held as true in the company's U.S. divisions as in its divisions in Asia and Europe.

In short, the numbers are beginning to tell us a persuasive story about the link between a company's success and the emotional intelligence of its leaders. And just as important, research is also demonstrating that people can, if

Daniel Goleman is the author of *Emotional Intelligence* (Bantam, 1995) and a coauthor of *Primal Leadership: Realizing the Power of Emotional Intelligence* (Harvard Business School, 2002). He is the cochairman of the Consortium for Research on Emotional Intelligence in Organizations, which is based at Rutgers University's Graduate School of Applied and Professional Psychology in Piscataway, New Jersey. He can be reached at Daniel.Goleman@verizon.net.

they take the right approach, develop their emotional intelligence. (See the sidebar "Can Emotional Intelligence Be Learned?")

Self-Awareness

Self-awareness is the first component of emotional intelligence—which makes sense when one considers that the Delphic oracle gave the advice to "know thyself" thousands of years ago. Self-awareness means having a deep understanding of one's emotions, strengths, weaknesses, needs, and drives. People with strong self-awareness are neither overly critical nor unrealistically hopeful. Rather, they are honest—with themselves and with others.

People who have a high degree of self-awareness recognize how their feelings affect them, other people, and their job performance. Thus, a self-aware person who knows that tight deadlines bring out the worst in him plans his time carefully and gets his work done well in advance. Another person with high self-awareness will be able to work with a demanding client. She will understand the client's impact on her moods and the deeper reasons for her frustra-

tion. "Their trivial demands take us away from the real work that needs to be done," she might explain. And she will go one step further and turn her anger into something constructive.

Self-awareness extends to a person's understanding of his or her values and goals. Someone who is highly self-aware knows where he is headed and why; so, for example, he will be able to be firm in turning down a job offer that is tempting financially but does not fit with his principles or long-term goals. A person who lacks self-awareness is apt to make decisions that bring on inner turmoil by treading on buried values. "The money looked good so I signed on," someone might say two years into a job, "but the work means so little to me that I'm constantly bored." The decisions of self-aware people mesh with their values; consequently, they often find work to be energizing.

How can one recognize self-awareness? First and foremost, it shows itself as candor and an ability to assess oneself realistically. People with high self-awareness are able to speak accurately and openly—although not necessarily effusively or confessionally—about their emo-

The Five Components of Emotional Intelligence at Work

	Definition	Hallmarks
Self-Awareness	the ability to recognize and understand your moods, emotions, and drives, as well as their effect on others	self-confidence realistic self-assessment self-deprecating sense of humor
Self-Regulation	the ability to control or redirect disruptive impulses and moods the propensity to suspend judgment – to think before acting	trustworthiness and integrity comfort with ambiguity openness to change
Motivation	a passion to work for reasons that go beyond money or status a propensity to pursue goals with energy and persistence	strong drive to achieve optimism, even in the face of failure organizational commitment
Empathy	the ability to understand the emotional makeup of other people skill in treating people according to their emotional reactions	expertise in building and retaining talent cross-cultural sensitivity service to clients and customers
Social Skill	proficiency in managing relationships and building networks an ability to find common ground and build rapport	effectiveness in leading change persuasiveness expertise in building and leading teams

tions and the impact they have on their work. For instance, one manager I know of was skeptical about a new personal-shopper service that her company, a major department-store chain, was about to introduce. Without prompting from her team or her boss, she offered them an explanation: "It's hard for me to get behind the rollout of this service," she admitted, "because I really wanted to run the project, but I wasn't selected. Bear with me while I deal with that." The manager did indeed examine her feelings;

a week later, she was supporting the project fully.

Such self-knowledge often shows itself in the hiring process. Ask a candidate to describe a time he got carried away by his feelings and did something he later regretted. Self-aware candidates will be frank in admitting to failure—and will often tell their tales with a smile. One of the hallmarks of self-awareness is a self-deprecating sense of humor.

Self-awareness can also be identified during performance reviews. Self-aware people know—

Can Emotional Intelligence Be Learned?

For ages, people have debated if leaders are born or made. So too goes the debate about emotional intelligence. Are people born with certain levels of empathy, for example, or do they acquire empathy as a result of life's experiences? The answer is both. Scientific inquiry strongly suggests that there is a genetic component to emotional intelligence. Psychological and developmental research indicates that nurture plays a role as well. How much of each perhaps will never be known, but research and practice clearly demonstrate that emotional intelligence can be learned.

One thing is certain: Emotional intelligence increases with age. There is an old-fashioned word for the phenomenon: maturity. Yet even with maturity, some people still need training to enhance their emotional intelligence. Unfortunately, far too many training programs that intend to build leadership skills—including emotional intelligence—are a waste of time and money. The problem is simple: They focus on the wrong part of the brain.

Emotional intelligence is born largely in the neurotransmitters of the brain's limbic system, which governs feelings, impulses, and drives. Research indicates that the limbic system learns best through motivation, extended practice, and feedback. Compare this with the kind of learning that goes on in the neocortex, which governs analytical and technical ability. The neocortex grasps concepts and logic. It is the part of the brain that figures out how to use a computer or make a sales call by reading a book. Not surprisingly—but mistakenly—it is also the part of the brain targeted by most training programs aimed at enhancing emotional intelligence. When such programs take, in effect, a neocortical approach, my research

with the Consortium for Research on Emotional Intelligence in Organizations has shown they can even have a *negative* impact on people's job performance.

To enhance emotional intelligence, organizations must refocus their training to include the limbic system. They must help people break old behavioral habits and establish new ones. That not only takes much more time than conventional training programs, it also requires an individualized approach.

Imagine an executive who is thought to be low on empathy by her colleagues. Part of that deficit shows itself as an inability to listen; she interrupts people and doesn't pay close attention to what they're saying. To fix the problem, the executive needs to be motivated to change, and then she needs practice and feedback from others in the company. A colleague or coach could be tapped to let the executive know when she has been observed failing to listen. She would then have to replay the incident and give a better response; that is, demonstrate her ability to absorb what others are saying. And the executive could be directed to observe certain executives who listen well and to mimic their behavior.

With persistence and practice, such a process can lead to lasting results. I know one Wall Street executive who sought to improve his empathy—specifically his ability to read people's reactions and see their perspectives. Before beginning his quest, the executive's subordinates were terrified of working with him. People even went so far as to hide bad news from him. Naturally, he was shocked when finally confronted with these facts. He went home and told his family—but they only confirmed what he had heard at work. When their

opinions on any given subject did not mesh with his, they, too, were frightened of him.

Enlisting the help of a coach, the executive went to work to heighten his empathy through practice and feedback. His first step was to take a vacation to a foreign country where he did not speak the language. While there, he monitored his reactions to the unfamiliar and his openness to people who were different from him. When he returned home, humbled by his week abroad, the executive asked his coach to shadow him for parts of the day, several times a week, to critique how he treated people with new or different perspectives. At the same time, he consciously used on-the-job interactions as opportunities to practice "hearing" ideas that differed from his. Finally, the executive had himself videotaped in meetings and asked those who worked for and with him to critique his ability to acknowledge and understand the feelings of others. It took several months, but the executive's emotional intelligence did ultimately rise, and the improvement was reflected in his overall performance on the job.

It's important to emphasize that building one's emotional intelligence cannot—will not—happen without sincere desire and concerted effort. A brief seminar won't help; nor can one buy a how-to manual. It is much harder to learn to empathize—to internalize empathy as a natural response to people—than it is to become adept at regression analysis. But it can be done. "Nothing great was ever achieved without enthusiasm," wrote Ralph Waldo Emerson. If your goal is to become a real leader, these words can serve as a guidepost in your efforts to develop high emotional intelligence.

and are comfortable talking about—their limitations and strengths, and they often demonstrate a thirst for constructive criticism. By contrast, people with low self-awareness interpret the message that they need to improve as a threat or a sign of failure.

Self-aware people can also be recognized by their self-confidence. They have a firm grasp of their capabilities and are less likely to set themselves up to fail by, for example, overstretching on assignments. They know, too, when to ask for help. And the risks they take on the job are calculated. They won't ask for a challenge that they know they can't handle alone. They'll play to their strengths.

Consider the actions of a midlevel employee who was invited to sit in on a strategy meeting with her company's top executives. Although she was the most junior person in the room, she did not sit there quietly, listening in awe-struck or fearful silence. She knew she had a head for clear logic and the skill to present ideas persuasively, and she offered cogent suggestions about the company's strategy. At the same time, her self-awareness stopped her from wandering into territory where she knew she was weak.

Despite the value of having self-aware people in the workplace, my research indicates that senior executives don't often give self-awareness the credit it deserves when they look for potential leaders. Many executives mistake candor about feelings for "wimpiness" and fail to give due respect to employees who openly acknowledge their shortcomings. Such people are too readily dismissed as "not tough enough" to lead others.

In fact, the opposite is true. In the first place, people generally admire and respect candor. Furthermore, leaders are constantly required to make judgment calls that require a candid assessment of capabilities—their own and those of others. Do we have the management expertise to acquire a competitor? Can we launch a new product within six months? People who assess themselves honestly—that is, self-aware people—are well suited to do the same for the organizations they run.

Self-Regulation

Biological impulses drive our emotions. We cannot do away with them—but we can do much to manage them. Self-regulation, which is like an ongoing inner conversation, is the component of emotional intelligence that frees us from being prisoners of our feelings. People engaged in such a conversation feel bad moods and emotional impulses just as everyone else does, but they find ways to control them and even to channel them in useful ways.

Imagine an executive who has just watched a team of his employees present a botched analysis to the company's board of directors. In the gloom that follows, the executive might find himself tempted to pound on the table in anger or kick over a chair. He could leap up and scream at the group. Or he might maintain a grim silence, glaring at everyone before stalking off.

But if he had a gift for self-regulation, he would choose a different approach. He would pick his words carefully, acknowledging the team's poor performance without rushing to any hasty judgment. He would then step back to consider the reasons for the failure. Are they personal—a lack of effort? Are there any mitigating factors? What was his role in the debacle? After considering these questions, he would call the team together, lay out the incident's consequences, and offer his feelings about it. He would then present his analysis of the problem and a well-considered solution.

Why does self-regulation matter so much for leaders? First of all, people who are in control of their feelings and impulses—that is, people who are reasonable—are able to create an environment of trust and fairness. In such an environment, politics and infighting are sharply reduced and productivity is high. Talented people flock to the organization and aren't tempted to leave. And self-regulation has a trickle-down effect. No one wants to be known as a hothead when the boss is known for her calm approach. Fewer bad moods at the top mean fewer throughout the organization.

Second, self-regulation is important for competitive reasons. Everyone knows that business today is rife with ambiguity and change. Companies merge and break apart regularly. Technology transforms work at a dizzying pace. People who have mastered their emotions are able to roll with the changes. When a new program is announced, they don't panic; instead, they are able to suspend judgment, seek out information, and listen to the executives as they explain the new program. As the initiative moves forward, these people are able to move with it.

Sometimes they even lead the way. Consider the case of a manager at a large manufacturing company. Like her colleagues, she had used a certain software program for five years. The program drove how she collected and reported data and how she thought about the company's strategy. One day, senior executives announced that a new program was to be installed that would radically change how information was gathered and assessed within the organization. While many people in the company complained bitterly about how disruptive the change would be, the manager mulled over the reasons for the new program and was convinced of its potential to improve performance. She eagerly attended training sessions—some of her colleagues refused to do so—and was eventually promoted to run several divisions, in part because she used the new technology so effectively.

I want to push the importance of self-regulation to leadership even further and make the case that it enhances integrity, which is not only a personal virtue but also an organizational strength. Many of the bad things that happen in companies are a function of impulsive behavior. People rarely plan to exaggerate profits, pad expense accounts, dip into the till, or abuse power for selfish ends. Instead, an opportunity presents itself, and people with low impulse control just say yes.

By contrast, consider the behavior of the senior executive at a large food company. The executive was scrupulously honest in his negotiations with local distributors. He would routinely lay out his cost structure in detail, thereby giving the distributors a realistic understanding of the company's pricing. This approach meant the executive couldn't always drive a hard bargain. Now, on occasion, he felt the urge to increase profits by withholding information about the company's costs. But he challenged that impulse—he saw that it made more sense in the long run to counteract it. His emotional self-regulation paid off in strong, lasting relationships with distributors that benefited the company more than any short-term financial gains would have.

The signs of emotional self-regulation, therefore, are easy to see: a propensity for reflection and thoughtfulness; comfort with ambiguity and change; and integrity—an ability to say no to impulsive urges.

Like self-awareness, self-regulation often does not get its due. People who can master their emotions are sometimes seen as cold fish—

their considered responses are taken as a lack of passion. People with fiery temperaments are frequently thought of as "classic" leaders—their outbursts are considered hallmarks of charisma and power. But when such people make it to the top, their impulsiveness often works against them. In my research, extreme displays of negative emotion have never emerged as a driver of good leadership.

Motivation

If there is one trait that virtually all effective leaders have, it is motivation. They are driven to achieve beyond expectations—their own and everyone else's. The key word here is *achieve*. Plenty of people are motivated by external factors, such as a big salary or the status that comes from having an impressive title or being part of a prestigious company. By contrast, those with leadership potential are motivated by a deeply embedded desire to achieve for the sake of achievement.

If you are looking for leaders, how can you identify people who are motivated by the drive to achieve rather than by external rewards? The first sign is a passion for the work itself—such people seek out creative challenges, love to learn, and take great pride in a job well done. They also display an unflagging energy to do things better. People with such energy often seem restless with the status quo. They are persistent with their questions about why things are done one way rather than another; they are eager to explore new approaches to their work.

A cosmetics company manager, for example, was frustrated that he had to wait two weeks to get sales results from people in the field. He finally tracked down an automated phone system that would beep each of his salespeople at 5 pm every day. An automated message then prompted them to punch in their numbers—how many calls and sales they had made that day. The system shortened the feedback time on sales results from weeks to hours.

That story illustrates two other common traits of people who are driven to achieve. They are forever raising the performance bar, and they like to keep score. Take the performance bar first. During performance reviews, people with high levels of motivation might ask to be "stretched" by their superiors. Of course, an employee who combines self-awareness with internal motivation will recognize her limits—but she won't settle for objectives that seem too easy to fulfill.

And it follows naturally that people who are driven to do better also want a way of tracking progress—their own, their team's, and their company's. Whereas people with low achievement motivation are often fuzzy about results, those with high achievement motivation often keep score by tracking such hard measures as profitability or market share. I know of a money manager who starts and ends his day on the Internet, gauging the performance of his stock fund against four industry-set benchmarks.

Interestingly, people with high motivation remain optimistic even when the score is against them. In such cases, self-regulation combines with achievement motivation to overcome the frustration and depression that come after a setback or failure. Take the case of an another portfolio manager at a large investment company. After several successful years, her fund tumbled for three consecutive quarters, leading three large institutional clients to shift their business elsewhere.

Some executives would have blamed the nosedive on circumstances outside their control; others might have seen the setback as evidence of personal failure. This portfolio manager, however, saw an opportunity to prove she could lead a turnaround. Two years later, when she was promoted to a very senior level in the company, she described the experience as "the best thing that ever happened to me; I learned so much from it."

Executives trying to recognize high levels of achievement motivation in their people can look for one last piece of evidence: commitment to the organization. When people love their jobs for the work itself, they often feel committed to the organizations that make that work possible. Committed employees are likely to stay with an organization even when they are pursued by headhunters waving money.

It's not difficult to understand how and why a motivation to achieve translates into strong leadership. If you set the performance bar high for yourself, you will do the same for the organization when you are in a position to do so. Likewise, a drive to surpass goals and an interest in keeping score can be contagious. Leaders with these traits can often build a team of managers around them with the same traits. And of course, optimism and organizational commitment are fundamental to leadership—just try to imagine running a company without them.

Empathy

Of all the dimensions of emotional intelligence, empathy is the most easily recognized. We have all felt the empathy of a sensitive teacher or friend; we have all been struck by its absence in an unfeeling coach or boss. But when it comes to business, we rarely hear people praised, let alone rewarded, for their empathy. The very word seems unbusinesslike, out of place amid the tough realities of the marketplace.

But empathy doesn't mean a kind of "I'm OK, you're OK" mushiness. For a leader, that is, it doesn't mean adopting other people's emotions as one's own and trying to please everybody. That would be a nightmare—it would make action impossible. Rather, empathy means thoughtfully considering employees' feelings—along with other factors—in the process of making intelligent decisions.

For an example of empathy in action, consider what happened when two giant brokerage companies merged, creating redundant jobs in all their divisions. One division manager called his people together and gave a gloomy speech that emphasized the number of people who would soon be fired. The manager of another division gave his people a different kind of speech. He was up-front about his own worry and confusion, and he promised to keep people informed and to treat everyone fairly.

The difference between these two managers was empathy. The first manager was too worried about his own fate to consider the feelings of his anxiety-stricken colleagues. The second knew intuitively what his people were feeling, and he acknowledged their fears with his words. Is it any surprise that the first manager saw his division sink as many demoralized people, especially the most talented, departed? By contrast, the second manager continued to be a strong leader, his best people stayed, and his division remained as productive as ever.

Empathy is particularly important today as a component of leadership for at least three reasons: the increasing use of teams; the rapid pace of globalization; and the growing need to retain talent.

Consider the challenge of leading a team. As anyone who has ever been a part of one can attest, teams are cauldrons of bubbling emotions. They are often charged with reaching a consensus—which is hard enough with two people and much more difficult as the numbers increase. Even in groups with as few as four or five members, alliances form and clashing agendas get set. A team's leader must be able to sense and understand the viewpoints of everyone around the table.

That's exactly what a marketing manager at a large information technology company was able to do when she was appointed to lead a troubled team. The group was in turmoil, overloaded by work and missing deadlines. Tensions were high among the members. Tinkering with procedures was not enough to bring the group together and make it an effective part of the company.

So the manager took several steps. In a series of one-on-one sessions, she took the time to listen to everyone in the group—what was frustrating them, how they rated their colleagues, whether they felt they had been ignored. And then she directed the team in a way that brought it together: She encouraged people to speak more openly about their frustrations, and she helped people raise constructive complaints during meetings. In short, her empathy allowed her to understand her team's emotional makeup. The result was not just heightened collaboration among members but also added business, as the team was called on for help by a wider range of internal clients.

Globalization is another reason for the rising importance of empathy for business leaders. Cross-cultural dialogue can easily lead to miscues and misunderstandings. Empathy is an antidote. People who have it are attuned to subtleties in body language; they can hear the message beneath the words being spoken. Beyond that, they have a deep understanding of both the existence and the importance of cultural and ethnic differences.

Consider the case of an American consultant whose team had just pitched a project to a potential Japanese client. In its dealings with Americans, the team was accustomed to being bombarded with questions after such a proposal, but this time it was greeted with a long silence. Other members of the team, taking the silence as disapproval, were ready to pack and leave. The lead consultant gestured them to stop. Although he was not particularly familiar with Japanese culture, he read the client's face and posture and sensed not rejection but interest—even deep consideration. He was right: When the client finally spoke, it was to give the consulting firm the job.

Finally, empathy plays a key role in the re-

tention of talent, particularly in today's information economy. Leaders have always needed empathy to develop and keep good people, but today the stakes are higher. When good people leave, they take the company's knowledge with them.

That's where coaching and mentoring come in. It has repeatedly been shown that coaching and mentoring pay off not just in better performance but also in increased job satisfaction and decreased turnover. But what makes coaching and mentoring work best is the nature of the relationship. Outstanding coaches and mentors get inside the heads of the people they are helping. They sense how to give effective feedback. They know when to push for better performance and when to hold back. In the way they motivate their protégés, they demonstrate empathy in action.

In what is probably sounding like a refrain, let me repeat that empathy doesn't get much respect in business. People wonder how leaders can make hard decisions if they are "feeling" for all the people who will be affected. But leaders with empathy do more than sympathize with people around them: They use their knowledge to improve their companies in subtle but important ways.

Social Skill

The first three components of emotional intelligence are self-management skills. The last two, empathy and social skill, concern a person's ability to manage relationships with others. As a component of emotional intelligence, social skill is not as simple as it sounds. It's not just a matter of friendliness, although people with high levels of social skill are rarely mean-spirited. Social skill, rather, is friendliness with a purpose: moving people in the direction you desire, whether that's agreement on a new marketing strategy or enthusiasm about a new product.

Socially skilled people tend to have a wide circle of acquaintances, and they have a knack for finding common ground with people of all kinds—a knack for building rapport. That doesn't mean they socialize continually; it means they work according to the assumption that nothing important gets done alone. Such people have a network in place when the time for action comes.

Social skill is the culmination of the other dimensions of emotional intelligence. People tend to be very effective at managing relationships when they can understand and control their own emotions and can empathize with the feelings of others. Even motivation contributes to social skill. Remember that people who are driven to achieve tend to be optimistic, even in the face of setbacks or failure. When people are upbeat, their "glow" is cast upon conversations and other social encounters. They are popular, and for good reason.

Because it is the outcome of the other dimensions of emotional intelligence, social skill is recognizable on the job in many ways that will by now sound familiar. Socially skilled people, for instance, are adept at managing teams—that's their empathy at work. Likewise, they are expert persuaders—a manifestation of self-awareness, self-regulation, and empathy combined. Given those skills, good persuaders know when to make an emotional plea, for instance, and when an appeal to reason will work better. And motivation, when publicly visible, makes such people excellent collaborators; their passion for the work spreads to others, and they are driven to find solutions.

But sometimes social skill shows itself in ways the other emotional intelligence components do not. For instance, socially skilled people may at times appear not to be working while at work. They seem to be idly schmoozing—chatting in the hallways with colleagues or joking around with people who are not even connected to their "real" jobs. Socially skilled people, however, don't think it makes sense to arbitrarily limit the scope of their relationships. They build bonds widely because they know that in these fluid times, they may need help someday from people they are just getting to know today.

For example, consider the case of an executive in the strategy department of a global computer manufacturer. By 1993, he was convinced that the company's future lay with the Internet. Over the course of the next year, he found kindred spirits and used his social skill to stitch together a virtual community that cut across levels, divisions, and nations. He then used this de facto team to put up a corporate Web site, among the first by a major company. And, on his own initiative, with no budget or formal status, he signed up the company to participate in an annual Internet industry convention. Calling on his allies and persuading various divisions to donate funds, he recruited more than 50 people from a dozen different units to represent the company at the convention.

Management took notice: Within a year of the conference, the executive's team formed the basis for the company's first Internet division, and he was formally put in charge of it. To get there, the executive had ignored conventional boundaries, forging and maintaining connections with people in every corner of the organization.

Is social skill considered a key leadership capability in most companies? The answer is yes, especially when compared with the other components of emotional intelligence. People seem to know intuitively that leaders need to manage relationships effectively; no leader is an island. After all, the leader's task is to get work done through other people, and social skill makes that possible. A leader who cannot express her empathy may as well not have it at all. And a leader's motivation will be useless if he cannot communicate his passion to the organization. Social skill allows leaders to put their emotional intelligence to work.

It would be foolish to assert that good-old-fashioned IQ and technical ability are not important ingredients in strong leadership. But the recipe would not be complete without emotional intelligence. It was once thought that the components of emotional intelligence were "nice to have" in business leaders. But now we know that, for the sake of performance, these are ingredients that leaders "need to have."

It is fortunate, then, that emotional intelligence can be learned. The process is not easy. It takes time and, most of all, commitment. But the benefits that come from having a well-developed emotional intelligence, both for the individual and for the organization, make it worth the effort.

Reprint R0401H
To order, see the next page
or call 800-988-0886 or 617-783-7500
or go to www.hbrreprints.org

BEST OF HBR 1998

What Makes a Leader?

Further Reading

ARTICLES

The Manager's Job: Folklore and Fact
by Henry Mintzberg
Harvard Business Review
March–April 1990
Product no. 90210

Whereas Goleman emphasizes emotional intelligence, Mintzberg focuses on specific skills. In this HBR Classic, Mintzberg uses his and other research to debunk myths about the manager's role. Managerial work involves interpersonal roles, informational roles, and decisional roles, he notes. These in turn require the ability to develop peer relationships, carry out negotiations, motivate subordinates, resolve conflicts, establish information networks and disseminate information, make decisions with little or ambiguous information, and allocate resources. Good self-management skills are characteristic of most leaders; outstanding leaders also have the ability to empathize with others and to use social skills to advance an agenda.

The Work of Leadership
by Ronald A. Heifetz and Donald L. Laurie
Harvard Business Review
January–February 1997
Product no. 97106

Successfully leading an organization through an adaptive challenge calls for leaders with a high degree of emotional intelligence. But Heifetz and Laurie focus on the requirements of adaptive work, not on emotional maturity. The principles for leading adaptive work include: "getting on the balcony," forming a picture of the entire pattern of activity; identifying the key challenge; regulating distress; maintaining disciplined attention; giving the work back to the people; and protecting voices of leadership from below.

The Ways Chief Executive Officers Lead
by Charles M. Farkas and Suzy Wetlaufer
Harvard Business Review
May–June 1996
Product no. 96303

CEOs inspire a variety of sentiments ranging from awe to wrath, but there's little debate over CEOs' importance in the business world. The authors conducted 160 interviews with executives around the world. Instead of finding 160 different approaches, they found five, each with a singular focus: strategy, people, expertise, controls, or change. The five components of emotional intelligence, singly or in combination, have a great effect on how each focus is expressed in an organization.

BOOK

John P. Kotter on What Leaders Really Do
by John P. Kotter
Harvard Business School Press
1999
Product no. 8974

In this collection of six articles, Kotter shares his observations on the nature of leadership gained over the past 30 years. Without leadership that can deal successfully with today's increasingly fast-moving and competitive business environment, he warns, organizations will slow down, stagnate, and lose their way. He presents his views on the current state of leadership through ten observations and revisits his now famous eight-step process for organizational transformation. In contrast to Goleman's article on emotional intelligence, which is about leadership qualities, Kotter's work focuses on action: What does a leader do to lead? And how will leadership need to be different in the future?

Harvard Business Review ⟨shield⟩

To Order

For *Harvard Business Review* reprints and subscriptions, call 800-988-0886 or 617-783-7500. Go to www.hbrreprints.org

For customized and quantity orders of *Harvard Business Review* article reprints, call 617-783-7626, or e-mail customizations@hbsp.harvard.edu

Harvard Business Review ⬡

www.hbr.org

BEST OF HBR 2001

What catapults a company from merely good to truly great? A five-year research project searched for the answer to that question, and its discoveries ought to change the way we think about leadership.

Level 5 Leadership
The Triumph of Humility and Fierce Resolve

by Jim Collins

What catapults a company from merely good to truly great? A five-year research project searched for the answer to that question, and its discoveries ought to change the way we think about leadership.

BEST OF HBR 2001

Level 5 Leadership
The Triumph of Humility and Fierce Resolve

by Jim Collins

If there's one management expert who is synonymous with the term "high-performance organization," it is Jim Collins, who has spent the past 20 years trying to understand how some companies are able to sustain superlative performance.

It may seem surprising that of the seven factors Collins identified as essential to take a company from good to great, he chose to focus on leadership in this 2001 piece. However, even a casual rereading of the article will convince you that he was right to do so.

Collins argues that the key ingredient that allows a company to become great is having a Level 5 leader: an executive in whom genuine personal humility blends with intense professional will. To learn that such CEOs exist still comes as a pleasant shock. But while the idea may sound counterintuitive today, it was downright heretical when Collins first wrote about it—the corporate scandals in the United States hadn't broken out, and almost everyone believed that CEOs should be charismatic, larger-than-life figures. Collins was the first to blow that belief out of the water.

In 1971, a seemingly ordinary man named Darwin E. Smith was named chief executive of Kimberly-Clark, a stodgy old paper company whose stock had fallen 36% behind the general market during the previous 20 years. Smith, the company's mild-mannered in-house lawyer, wasn't so sure the board had made the right choice—a feeling that was reinforced when a Kimberly-Clark director pulled him aside and reminded him that he lacked some of the qualifications for the position. But CEO he was, and CEO he remained for 20 years.

What a 20 years it was. In that period, Smith created a stunning transformation at Kimberly-Clark, turning it into the leading consumer paper products company in the world. Under his stewardship, the company beat its rivals Scott Paper and Procter & Gamble. And in doing so, Kimberly-Clark generated cumulative stock returns that were 4.1 times greater than those of the general market, outperforming venerable companies such as Hewlett-Packard, 3M, Coca-Cola, and General Electric.

Smith's turnaround of Kimberly-Clark is one the best examples in the twentieth century of a leader taking a company from merely good to truly great. And yet few people—even ardent students of business history—have heard of Darwin Smith. He probably would have liked it that way. Smith is a classic example of a Level 5 leader—an individual who blends extreme personal humility with intense professional will. According to our five-year research study, executives who possess this paradoxical combination of traits are catalysts for the statistically rare event of transforming a good company into a great one. (The research is described in the sidebar "One Question, Five Years, 11 Companies.")

"Level 5" refers to the highest level in a hierarchy of executive capabilities that we identified during our research. Leaders at the other four levels in the hierarchy can produce high degrees of success but not enough to elevate companies from mediocrity to sustained excellence. (For more details about this concept, see the exhibit "The Level 5 Hierarchy.") And while Level 5 leadership is not the only requirement for transforming a good company into a great one—other factors include getting the right people on the bus (and the wrong people off the bus) and creating a culture of discipline—our research shows it to be essential. Good-to-great transformations don't happen without Level 5 leaders at the helm. They just don't.

Not What You Would Expect

Our discovery of Level 5 leadership is counterintuitive. Indeed, it is countercultural. People generally assume that transforming companies from good to great requires larger-than-life leaders—big personalities like Lee Iacocca, Al Dunlap, Jack Welch, and Stanley Gault, who make headlines and become celebrities.

Compared with those CEOs, Darwin Smith seems to have come from Mars. Shy, unpretentious, even awkward, Smith shunned attention. When a journalist asked him to describe his management style, Smith just stared back at the scribe from the other side of his thick black-rimmed glasses. He was dressed unfashionably, like a farm boy wearing his first J.C. Penney suit. Finally, after a long and uncomfortable silence, he said, "Eccentric." Needless to say, the *Wall Street Journal* did not publish a splashy feature on Darwin Smith.

But if you were to consider Smith soft or meek, you would be terribly mistaken. His lack of pretense was coupled with a fierce, even stoic, resolve toward life. Smith grew up on an Indiana farm and put himself through night school at Indiana University by working the day shift at International Harvester. One day, he lost a finger on the job. The story goes that he went to class that evening and returned to work the very next day. Eventually, this poor but determined Indiana farm boy earned admission to Harvard Law School.

He showed the same iron will when he was at the helm of Kimberly-Clark. Indeed, two months after Smith became CEO, doctors diagnosed him with nose and throat cancer and told him he had less than a year to live. He duly informed the board of his illness but said he had no plans to die anytime soon. Smith held to his demanding work schedule while commuting weekly from Wisconsin to Houston for radiation therapy. He lived 25 more years, 20 of them as CEO.

Smith's ferocious resolve was crucial to the rebuilding of Kimberly-Clark, especially when he made the most dramatic decision in the company's history: selling the mills.

To explain: Shortly after he took over, Smith and his team had concluded that the company's traditional core business—coated paper—was doomed to mediocrity. Its economics were bad and the competition weak. But, they reasoned, if Kimberly-Clark were thrust into the fire of the consumer paper products business, better economics and world-class competition like Procter & Gamble would force it to achieve greatness or perish.

And so, like the general who burned the boats upon landing on enemy soil, leaving his troops to succeed or die, Smith announced that Kimberly-Clark would sell its mills—even the namesake mill in Kimberly, Wisconsin. All proceeds would be thrown into the consumer business, with investments in brands like Huggies diapers and Kleenex tissues. The business media called the move stupid, and Wall Street analysts downgraded the stock. But Smith never wavered. Twenty-five years later, Kimberly-Clark owned Scott Paper and beat Procter & Gamble in six of eight product categories. In retirement, Smith reflected on his exceptional performance, saying simply, "I never stopped trying to become qualified for the job."

Jim Collins operates a management research laboratory in Boulder, Colorado. He is a coauthor with Jerry I. Porras of *Built to Last: Successful Habits of Visionary Companies* (HarperBusiness, 2002). The ideas in this article appeared in his book *Good to Great: Why Some Companies Make the Leap…and Others Don't* (HarperBusiness, 2001).

One Question, Five Years, 11 Companies

The Level 5 discovery derives from a research project that began in 1996, when my research teams and I set out to answer one question: Can a good company become a great company and, if so, how? Most great companies grew up with superb parents—people like George Merck, David Packard, and Walt Disney—who instilled greatness early on. But what about the vast majority of companies that wake up partway through life and realize that they're good but not great?

To answer that question, we looked for companies that had shifted from good performance to great performance—and sustained it. We identified comparison companies that had failed to make that sustained shift. We then studied the contrast between the two groups to discover common variables that distinguished those who made and sustained a shift from those who could have but didn't.

More precisely, we searched for a specific pattern: cumulative stock returns at or below the general stock market for 15 years, punctuated by a transition point, then cumulative returns at least three times the market over the next 15 years. (See the accompanying exhibit.) We used data from the University of Chicago Center for Research in Security Prices and adjusted for stock splits and all dividends reinvested. The shift had to be distinct from the industry; if the whole industry showed the same shift, we'd drop the company. We began with 1,435 companies that appeared on the *Fortune* 500 from 1965 to 1995; we found 11 good-to-great examples. That's not a sample; that's the total number that jumped all our hurdles and passed into the study.

Those that made the cut averaged cumulative stock returns 6.9 times the general stock market for the 15 years after the point of transition. To put that in perspective, General Electric under Jack Welch outperformed the general stock market by 2.8:1 during his tenure from 1986 to 2000. One dollar invested in a mutual fund of the good-to-great companies in 1965 grew to $470 by 2000 compared with $56 in the general stock market. These are remarkable numbers, made all the more so by the fact that they came from previously unremarkable companies.

For each good-to-great example, we selected the best direct comparison, based on similarity of business, size, age, customers, and performance leading up to the transition. We also constructed a set of six "unsustained" comparisons (companies that showed a short-lived shift but then fell off) to address the question of sustainability. To be conservative, we consistently picked comparison companies that, if anything, were in better shape than the good-to-great companies were in the years just before the transition.

With 22 research associates working in groups of four to six at a time from 1996 to 2000, our study involved a wide range of both qualitative and quantitative analyses. On the qualitative front, we collected nearly 6,000 articles, conducted 87 interviews with key executives, analyzed companies' internal strategy documents, and culled through analysts' reports. On the quantitative front, we ran financial metrics, examined executive compensation, compared patterns of management turnover, quantified company layoffs and restructurings, and calculated the effect of acquisitions and divestitures on companies' stocks. We then synthesized the results to identify the drivers of good-to-great transformations. One was Level 5 leadership. (The others are described in the sidebar "Not by Level 5 Alone.")

Since only 11 companies qualified as good-to-great, a research finding had to meet a stiff standard before we would deem it significant. Every component in the final framework showed up in all 11 good-to-great companies during the transition era, regardless of industry (from steel to banking), transition decade (from the 1950s to the 1990s), circumstances (from plodding along to dire crisis), or size (from tens of millions to tens of billions). Additionally, every component had to show up in less than 30% of the comparison companies during the relevant years. Level 5 easily made it into the framework as one of the strongest, most consistent contrasts between the good-to-great and the comparison companies.

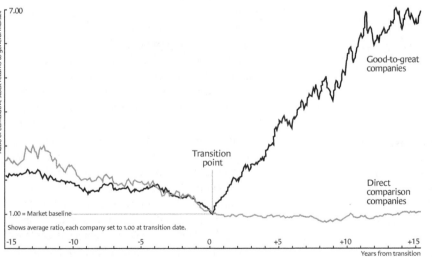

Not What We Expected, Either

We'll look in depth at Level 5 leadership, but first let's set an important context for our findings. We were not looking for Level 5 or anything like it. Our original question was, Can a good company become a great one and, if so, how? In fact, I gave the research teams explicit instructions to downplay the role of top executives in their analyses of this question so we wouldn't slip into the simplistic "credit the leader" or "blame the leader" thinking that is so common today.

But Level 5 found us. Over the course of the study, research teams kept saying, "We can't ignore the top executives even if we want to. There is something consistently unusual about them." I would push back, arguing, "The comparison companies also had leaders. So what's

different here?" Back and forth the debate raged. Finally, as should always be the case, the data won. The executives at companies that went from good to great and sustained that performance for 15 years or more were all cut from the same cloth—one remarkably different from that which produced the executives at the comparison companies in our study. It didn't matter whether the company was in crisis or steady state, consumer or industrial, offering services or products. It didn't matter when the transition took place or how big the company. The successful organizations all had a Level 5 leader at the time of transition.

Furthermore, the absence of Level 5 leadership showed up consistently across the comparison companies. The point: Level 5 is an empirical finding, not an ideological one. And that's important to note, given how much the Level 5 finding contradicts not only conventional wisdom but much of management theory to date. (For more about our findings on good-to-great transformations, see the sidebar "Not by Level 5 Alone.")

The Level 5 Hierarchy

The Level 5 leader sits on top of a hierarchy of capabilities and is, according to our research, a necessary requirement for transforming an organization from good to great. But what lies beneath? Four other layers, each one appropriate in its own right but none with the power of Level 5. Individuals do not need to proceed sequentially through each level of the hierarchy to reach the top, but to be a full-fledged Level 5 requires the capabilities of all the lower levels, plus the special characteristics of Level 5.

Level 5
Executive
Builds enduring greatness through a paradoxical combination of personal humility plus professional will.

Level 4
Effective Leader
Catalyzes commitment to and vigorous pursuit of a clear and compelling vision; stimulates the group to high performance standards.

Level 3
Competent Manager
Organizes people and resources toward the effective and efficient pursuit of predetermined objectives.

Level 2
Contributing Team Member
Contributes to the achievement of group objectives; works effectively with others in a group setting.

Level 1
Highly Capable Individual
Makes productive contributions through talent, knowledge, skills, and good work habits.

Humility + Will = Level 5

Level 5 leaders are a study in duality: modest and willful, shy and fearless. To grasp this concept, consider Abraham Lincoln, who never let his ego get in the way of his ambition to create an enduring great nation. Author Henry Adams called him "a quiet, peaceful, shy figure." But those who thought Lincoln's understated manner signaled weakness in the man found themselves terribly mistaken—to the scale of 250,000 Confederate and 360,000 Union lives, including Lincoln's own.

It might be a stretch to compare the 11 Level 5 CEOs in our research to Lincoln, but they did display the same kind of duality. Take Colman M. Mockler, CEO of Gillette from 1975 to 1991. Mockler, who faced down three takeover attempts, was a reserved, gracious man with a gentle, almost patrician manner. Despite epic battles with raiders—he took on Ronald Perelman twice and the former Coniston Partners once—he never lost his shy, courteous style. At the height of crisis, he maintained a calm business-as-usual demeanor, dispensing first with ongoing business before turning to the takeover.

And yet, those who mistook Mockler's outward modesty as a sign of inner weakness were beaten in the end. In one proxy battle, Mockler and other senior executives called thousands of investors, one by one, to win their votes. Mockler simply would not give in. He chose to fight for the future greatness of Gillette even though he could have pocketed millions by flipping his stock.

Consider the consequences had Mockler capitulated. If a share flipper had accepted the full 44% price premium offered by Perelman and then invested those shares in the general market for ten years, he still would have come out 64% behind a shareholder who stayed with Mockler and Gillette. If Mockler had given up the fight, it's likely that none of us would be shaving with Sensor, Lady Sensor, or the Mach III—and hundreds of millions of people would have a more painful battle with daily stubble.

Sadly, Mockler never had the chance to enjoy the full fruits of his efforts. In January 1991, Gillette received an advance copy of *Forbes*. The cover featured an artist's rendition of the publicity-shy Mockler standing on a mountaintop, holding a giant razor above his head in a triumphant pose. Walking back to his office just minutes after seeing this public acknowledgment of his 16 years of struggle, Mockler crumpled to the floor and died of a massive heart attack.

Even if Mockler had known he would die in office, he could not have changed his approach. His placid persona hid an inner inten-

Not by Level 5 Alone

Level 5 leadership is an essential factor for taking a company from good to great, but it's not the only one. Our research uncovered multiple factors that deliver companies to greatness. And it is the combined package—Level 5 plus these other drivers—that takes companies beyond unremarkable. There is a symbiotic relationship between Level 5 and the rest of our findings: Level 5 enables implementation of the other findings, and practicing the other findings may help you get to Level 5. We've already talked about who Level 5 leaders are; the rest of our findings describe what they do. Here is a brief look at some of the other key findings.

First Who
We expected that good-to-great leaders would start with the vision and strategy. Instead, they attended to people first, strategy second. They got the right people on the bus, moved the wrong people off, ushered the right people to the right seats—and then they figured out where to drive it.

Stockdale Paradox
This finding is named after Admiral James Stockdale, winner of the Medal of Honor, who survived seven years in a Vietcong POW camp by hanging on to two contradictory beliefs:

His life couldn't be worse at the moment, and his life would someday be better than ever. Like Stockdale, people at the good-to-great companies in our research confronted the most brutal facts of their current reality, yet simultaneously maintained absolute faith that they would prevail in the end. And they held both disciplines—faith and facts—at the same time, all the time.

Buildup-Breakthrough Flywheel
Good-to-great transformations do not happen overnight or in one big leap. Rather, the process resembles relentlessly pushing a gi-ant, heavy flywheel in one direction. At first, pushing it gets the flywheel to turn once. With consistent effort, it goes two turns, then five, then ten, building increasing momentum until—bang!—the wheel hits the breakthrough point, and the momentum really kicks in. Our comparison companies never sustained the kind of breakthrough momentum that the good-to-great companies did; instead, they lurched back and forth with radical change programs, reactionary moves, and restructurings.

The Hedgehog Concept
In a famous essay, philosopher and scholar Isaiah Berlin described two approaches to thought and life using a simple parable: The fox knows a little about many things, but the hedgehog knows only one big thing very well. The fox is complex; the hedgehog simple. And the hedgehog wins. Our research shows that breakthroughs require a simple, hedgehog-like understanding of three intersecting circles: what a company can be the best in the world at, how its economics work best, and what best ignites the passions of its people. Breakthroughs happen when you get the hedgehog concept and become systematic and consis-tent with it, eliminating virtually anything that does not fit in the three circles.

Technology Accelerators
The good-to-great companies had a paradoxical relationship with technology. On the one hand, they assiduously avoided jumping on new technology bandwagons. On the other, they were pioneers in the application of carefully selected technologies, making bold, farsighted investments in those that directly linked to their hedgehog concept. Like turbochargers, these technology accelerators create an explosion in flywheel momentum.

A Culture of Discipline
When you look across the good-to-great transformations, they consistently display three forms of discipline: disciplined people, disciplined thought, and disciplined action. When you have disciplined people, you don't need hierarchy. When you have disciplined thought, you don't need bureaucracy. When you have disciplined action, you don't need excessive controls. When you combine a culture of discipline with an ethic of entrepreneurship, you get the magical alchemy of great performance.

sity, a dedication to making anything he touched the best—not just because of what he would get but because he couldn't imagine doing it any other way. Mockler could not give up the company to those who would destroy it, any more than Lincoln would risk losing the chance to build an enduring great nation.

A Compelling Modesty

The Mockler story illustrates the modesty typical of Level 5 leaders. (For a summary of Level 5 traits, see the exhibit "The Yin and Yang of Level 5.") Indeed, throughout our interviews with such executives, we were struck by the way they talked about themselves—or rather, didn't talk about themselves. They'd go on and on about the company and the contributions of other executives, but they would instinctively deflect discussion about their own role. When pressed to talk about themselves, they'd say things like, "I hope I'm not sounding like a big shot," or "I don't think I can take much credit for what happened. We were blessed with marvelous people." One Level 5 leader even asserted, "There are a lot of people in this company who could do my job better than I do."

By contrast, consider the courtship of personal celebrity by the comparison CEOs. Scott Paper, the comparison company to Kimberly-Clark, hired Al Dunlap as CEO—a man who would tell anyone who would listen (and many who would have preferred not to) about his accomplishments. After 19 months atop Scott Pa-

per, Dunlap said in *BusinessWeek,* "The Scott story will go down in the annals of American business history as one of the most successful, quickest turnarounds ever. It makes other turnarounds pale by comparison." He personally accrued $100 million for 603 days of work at Scott Paper—about $165,000 per day—largely by slashing the workforce, halving the R&D budget, and putting the company on growth steroids in preparation for sale. After selling off the company and pocketing his quick millions, Dunlap wrote an autobiography in which he boastfully dubbed himself "Rambo in pinstripes." It's hard to imagine Darwin Smith thinking, "Hey, that Rambo character reminds me of me," let alone stating it publicly.

Granted, the Scott Paper story is one of the more dramatic in our study, but it's not an isolated case. In more than two-thirds of the comparison companies, we noted the presence of a gargantuan ego that contributed to the demise or continued mediocrity of the company. We found this pattern particularly strong in the unsustained comparison companies—the companies that would show a shift in performance under a talented yet egocentric Level 4 leader, only to decline in later years.

Lee Iacocca, for example, saved Chrysler from the brink of catastrophe, performing one of the most celebrated (and deservedly so) turnarounds in U.S. business history. The automaker's stock rose 2.9 times higher than the general market about halfway through his tenure. But then Iacocca diverted his attention to transforming himself. He appeared regularly on talk shows like the *Today Show* and *Larry King Live,* starred in more than 80 commercials, entertained the idea of running for president of the United States, and promoted his autobiography, which sold 7 million copies worldwide. Iacocca's personal stock soared, but Chrysler's stock fell 31% below the market in the second half of his tenure.

And once Iacocca had accumulated all the fame and perks, he found it difficult to leave center stage. He postponed his retirement so many times that Chrysler's insiders began to joke that Iacocca stood for "I Am Chairman of Chrysler Corporation Always." When he finally retired, he demanded that the board continue to provide a private jet and stock options. Later, he joined forces with noted takeover artist Kirk Kerkorian to launch a hostile bid for

The Yin and Yang of Level 5

Personal Humility

Demonstrates a compelling modesty, shunning public adulation; never boastful.

Acts with quiet, calm determination; relies principally on inspired standards, not inspiring charisma, to motivate.

Channels ambition into the company, not the self; sets up successors for even more greatness in the next generation.

Looks in the mirror, not out the window, to apportion responsibility for poor results, never blaming other people, external factors, or bad luck.

Professional Will

Creates superb results, a clear catalyst in the transition from good to great.

Demonstrates an unwavering resolve to do whatever must be done to produce the best long-term results, no matter how difficult.

Sets the standard of building an enduring great company; will settle for nothing less.

Looks out the window, not in the mirror, to apportion credit for the success of the company—to other people, external factors, and good luck.

Chrysler. (It failed.) Iacocca did make one final brilliant decision: He picked a modest yet determined man—perhaps even a Level 5—as his successor. Bob Eaton rescued Chrysler from its second near-death crisis in a decade and set the foundation for a more enduring corporate transition.

An Unwavering Resolve

Besides extreme humility, Level 5 leaders also display tremendous professional will. When George Cain became CEO of Abbott Laboratories, it was a drowsy, family-controlled business sitting at the bottom quartile of the pharmaceutical industry, living off its cash cow, erythromycin. Cain was a typical Level 5 leader in his lack of pretense; he didn't have the kind of inspiring personality that would galvanize the company. But he had something much more powerful: inspired standards. He could not stand mediocrity in any form and was utterly intolerant of anyone who would accept the idea that good is good enough. For the next 14 years, he relentlessly imposed his will for greatness on Abbott Labs.

Among Cain's first tasks was to destroy one of the root causes of Abbott's middling performance: nepotism. By systematically rebuilding both the board and the executive team with the best people he could find, Cain made his statement. Family ties no longer mattered. If you couldn't become the best executive in the industry within your span of responsibility, you would lose your paycheck.

Such near-ruthless rebuilding might be expected from an outsider brought in to turn the company around, but Cain was an 18-year insider—and a part of the family, the son of a previous president. Holiday gatherings were probably tense for a few years in the Cain clan—"Sorry I had to fire you. Want another slice of turkey?"—but in the end, family members were pleased with the performance of their stock. Cain had set in motion a profitable growth machine. From its transition in 1974 to 2000, Abbott created shareholder returns that beat the market 4.5:1, outperforming industry superstars Merck and Pfizer by a factor of two.

Another good example of iron-willed Level 5 leadership comes from Charles R. "Cork" Walgreen III, who transformed dowdy Walgreens into a company that outperformed the stock market 16:1 from its transition in 1975 to 2000. After years of dialogue and debate within his executive team about what to do with Walgreens' food-service operations, this CEO sensed the team had finally reached a watershed: The company's brightest future lay in convenient drugstores, not in food service. Dan Jorndt, who succeeded Walgreen in 1988, describes what happened next:

> Cork said at one of our planning committee meetings, "Okay, now I am going to draw the line in the sand. We are going to be out of the restaurant business completely in five years." At the time we had more than 500 restaurants. You could have heard a pin drop. He said, "I want to let everybody know the clock is ticking." Six months later we were at our next planning committee meeting and someone mentioned just in passing that we had only five years to be out of the restaurant business. Cork was not a real vociferous fellow. He sort of tapped on the table and said, "Listen, you now have four and a half years. I said you had five years six months ago. Now you've got four and a half years." Well, that next day things really clicked into gear for winding down our restaurant business. Cork never wavered. He never doubted. He never second-guessed.

Like Darwin Smith selling the mills at Kimberly-Clark, Cork Walgreen required stoic resolve to make his decisions. Food service was not the largest part of the business, although it did add substantial profits to the bottom line. The real problem was more emotional than financial. Walgreens had, after all, invented the malted milk shake, and food service had been a long-standing family tradition dating back to Cork's grandfather. Not only that, some food-service outlets were even named after the CEO—for example, a restaurant chain named Corky's. But no matter; if Walgreen had to fly in the face of family tradition in order to refocus on the one arena in which Walgreens could be the best in the world—convenient drugstores—and terminate everything else that would not produce great results, then Cork would do it. Quietly, doggedly, simply.

One final, yet compelling, note on our findings about Level 5: Because Level 5 leaders have ambition not for themselves but for their companies, they routinely select superb successors. Level 5 leaders want to see their companies become even more successful in the next generation and are comfortable with the idea that most people won't even know that the roots of that success trace back to them. As one

Good-to-great transformations don't happen without Level 5 leaders at the helm. They just don't.

Level 5 CEO said, "I want to look from my porch, see the company as one of the great companies in the world someday, and be able to say, 'I used to work there.' " By contrast, Level 4 leaders often fail to set up the company for enduring success. After all, what better testament to your own personal greatness than that the place falls apart after you leave?

In more than three-quarters of the comparison companies, we found executives who set up their successors for failure, chose weak successors, or both. Consider the case of Rubbermaid, which grew from obscurity to become one of *Fortune*'s most admired companies—and then, just as quickly, disintegrated into such sorry shape that it had to be acquired by Newell.

The architect of this remarkable story was a charismatic and brilliant leader named Stanley C. Gault, whose name became synonymous in the late 1980s with Rubbermaid's success. Across the 312 articles collected by our research team about the company, Gault comes through as a hard-driving, egocentric executive. In one article, he responds to the accusation of being a tyrant with the statement, "Yes, but I'm a sincere tyrant." In another, drawn directly from his own comments on leading change, the word "I" appears 44 times, while the word "we" appears 16 times. Of course, Gault had every reason to be proud of his executive success: Rubbermaid generated 40 consecutive quarters of earnings growth under his leadership—an impressive performance, to be sure, and one that deserves respect.

But Gault did not leave behind a company that would be great without him. His chosen successor lasted a year on the job and the next in line faced a management team so shallow that he had to temporarily shoulder four jobs while scrambling to identify a new number-two executive. Gault's successors struggled not only with a management void but also with strategic voids that would eventually bring the company to its knees.

Of course, you might say—as one *Fortune* article did—that the fact that Rubbermaid fell apart after Gault left proves his greatness as a leader. Gault was a tremendous Level 4 leader, perhaps one of the best in the last 50 years. But he was not at Level 5, and that is one crucial reason why Rubbermaid went from good to great for a brief, shining moment and then just as quickly went from great to irrelevant.

The Window and the Mirror

As part of our research, we interviewed Alan L. Wurtzel, the Level 5 leader responsible for turning Circuit City from a ramshackle company on the edge of bankruptcy into one of America's most successful electronics retailers. In the 15 years after its transition date in 1982, Circuit City outperformed the market 18.5:1.

We asked Wurtzel to list the top five factors in his company's transformation, ranked by importance. His number one factor? Luck. "We were in a great industry, with the wind at our backs," he said. But wait a minute, we retorted, Silo—your comparison company—was in the same industry, with the same wind and bigger sails. The conversation went back and forth, with Wurtzel refusing to take much credit for the transition, preferring to attribute it largely to just being in the right place at the right time. Later, when we asked him to discuss the factors that would sustain a good-to-great transformation, he said, "The first thing that comes to mind is luck. I was lucky to find the right successor."

Luck. What an odd factor to talk about. Yet the Level 5 leaders we identified invoked it frequently. We asked an executive at steel company Nucor why it had such a remarkable track record for making good decisions. His response? "I guess we were just lucky." Joseph F. Cullman III, the Level 5 CEO of Philip Morris, flat out refused to take credit for his company's success, citing his good fortune to have great colleagues, successors, and predecessors. Even the book he wrote about his career—which he penned at the urging of his colleagues and which he never intended to distribute widely outside the company—had the unusual title *I'm a Lucky Guy*.

At first, we were puzzled by the Level 5 leaders' emphasis on good luck. After all, there is no evidence that the companies that had progressed from good to great were blessed with more good luck (or more bad luck, for that matter) than the comparison companies. But then we began to notice an interesting pattern in the executives at the comparison companies: They often blamed their situations on bad luck, bemoaning the difficulties of the environment they faced.

Compare Bethlehem Steel and Nucor, for example. Both steel companies operated with products that are hard to differentiate, and both faced a competitive challenge from cheap imported steel. Both companies paid significantly higher wages than most of their foreign competitors. And yet executives at the two companies held completely different views of the same environment.

Bethlehem Steel's CEO summed up the company's problems in 1983 by blaming the imports: "Our first, second, and third problems are imports." Meanwhile, Ken Iverson and his crew at Nucor saw the imports as a blessing: "Aren't we lucky; steel is heavy, and they have to ship it all the way across the ocean, giving us a huge advantage." Indeed, Iverson saw the first, second, and third problems facing the U.S. steel industry not in imports but in management. He even went so far as to speak out publicly against government protection against imports, telling a gathering of stunned steel executives in 1977 that the real problems facing the industry lay in the fact that management had failed to keep pace with technology.

The emphasis on luck turns out to be part of a broader pattern that we have come to call "the window and the mirror." Level 5 leaders, inherently humble, look out the window to apportion credit—even undue credit—to factors outside themselves. If they can't find a specific person or event to give credit to, they credit good luck. At the same time, they look in the mirror to assign responsibility, never citing bad luck or external factors when things go poorly. Conversely, the comparison executives frequently looked out the window for factors to blame but preened in the mirror to credit themselves when things went well.

The funny thing about the window-and-mirror concept is that it does not reflect reality. According to our research, the Level 5 leaders were responsible for their companies' transformations. But they would never admit that. We can't climb inside their heads and assess whether they deeply believed what they saw through the window and in the mirror. But it doesn't really matter, because they acted as if they believed it, and they acted with such consistency that it produced exceptional results.

Born or Bred?

Not long ago, I shared the Level 5 finding with a gathering of senior executives. A woman who had recently become chief executive of her company raised her hand. "I believe what you've told us about Level 5 leadership," she said, "but I'm disturbed because I know I'm not there yet, and maybe I never will be. Part of the reason I got this job is because of my strong ego. Are you telling me that I can't make my company great if I'm not Level 5?"

"Let me return to the data," I responded. "Of 1,435 companies that appeared on the *Fortune* 500 since 1965, only 11 made it into our study. In those 11, all of them had Level 5 leaders in key positions, including the CEO role, at the pivotal time of transition. Now, to reiterate, we're not saying that Level 5 is the only element required for the move from good to great, but it appears to be essential."

She sat there, quiet for a moment, and you could guess what many people in the room were thinking. Finally, she raised her hand again. "Can you learn to become Level 5?" I still do not know the answer to that question. Our research, frankly, did not delve into how Level 5 leaders come to be, nor did we attempt to explain or codify the nature of their emotional lives. We speculated on the unique psychology of Level 5 leaders. Were they "guilty" of displacement—shifting their own raw ambition onto something other than themselves? Were they sublimating their egos for dark and complex reasons rooted in childhood trauma? Who knows? And perhaps more important, do the psychological roots of Level 5 leadership matter any more than do the roots of charisma or intelligence? The question remains: Can Level 5 be developed?

My preliminary hypothesis is that there are two categories of people: those who don't have the Level 5 seed within them and those who do. The first category consists of people who could never in a million years bring themselves to subjugate their own needs to the greater ambition of something larger and more lasting than themselves. For those people, work will always be first and foremost about what they get—the fame, fortune, power, adulation, and so on. Work will never be about what they build, create, and contribute. The great irony is that the animus and personal ambition that often drives people to become a Level 4 leader stands at odds with the humility required to rise to Level 5.

When you combine that irony with the fact that boards of directors frequently operate under the false belief that a larger-than-life, egocentric leader is required to make a company great, you can quickly see why Level 5 leaders rarely appear at the top of our institu-

The great irony is that the animus and personal ambition that often drives people to become a Level 4 leader stands at odds with the humility required to rise to Level 5.

We keep putting people in positions of power who lack the seed to become a Level 5 leader, and that is one major reason why there are so few companies that make a sustained and verifiable shift from good to great.

tions. We keep putting people in positions of power who lack the seed to become a Level 5 leader, and that is one major reason why there are so few companies that make a sustained and verifiable shift from good to great.

The second category consists of people who could evolve to Level 5; the capability resides within them, perhaps buried or ignored or simply nascent. Under the right circumstances—with self-reflection, a mentor, loving parents, a significant life experience, or other factors—the seed can begin to develop. Some of the Level 5 leaders in our study had significant life experiences that might have sparked development of the seed. Darwin Smith fully blossomed as a Level 5 after his near-death experience with cancer. Joe Cullman was profoundly affected by his World War II experiences, particularly the last-minute change of orders that took him off a doomed ship on which he surely would have died; he considered the next 60-odd years a great gift. A strong religious belief or conversion might also nurture the seed. Colman Mockler, for example, converted to evangelical Christianity while getting his MBA at Harvard, and later, according to the book *Cutting Edge* by Gordon McKibben, he became a prime mover in a group of Boston business executives that met frequently over breakfast to discuss the carryover of religious values to corporate life.

We would love to be able to give you a list of steps for getting to Level 5—other than contracting cancer, going through a religious conversion, or getting different parents—but we have no solid research data that would support a credible list. Our research exposed Level 5 as a key component inside the black box of what it takes to shift a company from good to great. Yet inside that black box is another—the inner development of a person to Level 5 leadership. We could speculate on what that inner box

might hold, but it would mostly be just that: speculation.

In short, Level 5 is a very satisfying idea, a truthful idea, a powerful idea, and, to make the move from good to great, very likely an essential idea. But to provide "ten steps to Level 5 leadership" would trivialize the concept.

My best advice, based on the research, is to practice the other good-to-great disciplines that we discovered. Since we found a tight symbiotic relationship between each of the other findings and Level 5, we suspect that conscientiously trying to lead using the other disciplines can help you move in the right direction. There is no guarantee that doing so will turn executives into full-fledged Level 5 leaders, but it gives them a tangible place to begin, especially if they have the seed within.

We cannot say for sure what percentage of people have the seed within, nor how many of those can nurture it enough to become Level 5. Even those of us on the research team who identified Level 5 do not know whether we will succeed in evolving to its heights. And yet all of us who worked on the finding have been inspired by the idea of trying to move toward Level 5. Darwin Smith, Colman Mockler, Alan Wurtzel, and all the other Level 5 leaders we learned about have become role models for us. Whether or not we make it to Level 5, it is worth trying. For like all basic truths about what is best in human beings, when we catch a glimpse of that truth, we know that our own lives and all that we touch will be the better for making the effort to get there.

Reprint R0507M
Harvard Business Review OnPoint 5831
To order, see the next page
or call 800-988-0886 or 617-783-7500
or go to www.hbr.org

Harvard Business Review OnPoint articles enhance the full-text article with a summary of its key points and a selection of its company examples to help you quickly absorb and apply the concepts. *Harvard Business Review* OnPoint collections include three OnPoint articles and an overview comparing the various perspectives on a specific topic.

Further Reading

Level 5 Leadership is also part of the *Harvard Business Review* OnPoint collection **What Great Leaders Do,** Product no. 1479, which includes these additional articles:

What Great Managers Do
Marcus Buckingham
Harvard Business Review
July 2005
Product no. 1487

Moments of Greatness: Entering the Fundamental State of Leadership
Robert E. Quinn
Harvard Business Review
July 2005
Product no. 1460

Harvard Business Review

To Order

For reprints, *Harvard Business Review* OnPoint orders, and subscriptions to *Harvard Business Review:*
Call 800-988-0886 or 617-783-7500.
Go to www.hbr.org

For customized and quantity orders of reprints and *Harvard Business Review* OnPoint products:
Call Rich Gravelin at
617-783-7626,
or e-mail him at
rgravelin@hbsp.harvard.edu

With workers defining their own job standards, quality and productivity at the Fremont plant went from worst to best.

Time-and-Motion Regained

by Paul S. Adler

Standardization is the death of creativity.

Time-and-motion regimentation prevents continuous improvement.

Hierarchy suffocates learning.

U.S. manufacturing is in the throes of revolution, and assumptions like these are becoming the new conventional wisdom about work. This new gospel sets up Frederick Winslow Taylor and his time-and-motion studies as the villain. It asserts that quality, productivity, and learning depend on management's ability to free workers from the coercive constraints of bureaucracy. It insists that detailed standards, implemented with great discipline in a hierarchical organization, will inevitably alienate employees, poison labor relations, stifle initiative and innovation, and hobble an organization's capacity to change and to learn.

But what if, as I believe, this new creed is wrong? What if bureaucracy can actually be designed to encourage innovation and commitment? What if standardization, properly understood and practiced, should prove itself a wellspring of continuous learning and motivation?

In Fremont, California, a GM-Toyota joint venture called New United Motor Manufacturing Inc., NUMMI, for short, has succeeded in employing an innovative form of Taylor's time-and-motion regimentation on the factory floor not only to create world-class productivity and quality but also to increase worker motivation and satisfaction. What's more, NUMMI's intensely Taylorist procedures appear to encourage rather than discourage organizational learning and, therefore, continuous improvement.

This outcome seems surprising because for decades our attitudes toward work have been shaped by a chain of reasoning that has led us to expect (and guaranteed that we would get) a vicious circle of escalating managerial coercion and employee recalcitrance. The reasoning runs something like this:

☐ When tasks are routine and repetitive, efficiency and quality require standardized work procedures.

☐ High levels of standardization rob jobs of their intrinsic interest, reducing motivation and creativity.

Paul S. Adler is associate professor at the University of Southern California School of Business Administration. He has recently edited two collections of essays: Technology and the Future of Work *and* Usability: Turning Technologies into Tools. *This article is based on a two-year study of the New United Motor Manufacturing Inc. plant in Fremont, California.*

☐ Demotivating work leads to dysfunctional employee behavior such as absenteeism, high turnover, poor attention to quality, strikes, even sabotage.

☐ Counterproductive behavior by the work force requires more authoritarian management, more hierarchical layers, and even higher levels of standardization.

In short, Taylorism leads inevitably to workforce discontent and union belligerence, which in turn lead inevitably to higher levels of bureaucratic excess. The organization of work comes to build on the dehumanizing logic of coercion and reluctant compliance. Meanwhile, quality, profits, and job satisfaction all suffer.

NUMMI's experience flies directly in the face of this thinking. That's because the second step in this chain of reasoning is false. Formal work standards developed by industrial engineers and imposed on workers *are* alienating. But procedures that are designed by the workers themselves in a continuous, successful effort to improve productivity, quality, skills, and understanding can humanize even the most disciplined forms of bureaucracy. Moreover, NUMMI shows that hierarchy can provide support and expertise instead of a mere command structure.

What the NUMMI experiment shows is that hierarchy and standardization, with all their known advantages for efficiency, need not build on the logic of coercion. They can build instead on the logic of learning, a logic that motivates workers and taps their potential contribution to continuous improvement.

In practice, NUMMI's "learning bureaucracy" achieves three ends. First, it serves management by improving overall quality and productivity. Second, it serves workers by involving them in the design and control of their own work, increasing their motivation and job satisfaction, and altering the balance of power between labor and management. Third, it serves the interests of the entire organization – management and the work force – by creating a formal system to encourage learning, to capture and communicate innovation, and to institutionalize continuous improvement.

The Worst Plant in the World

NUMMI is housed in what was once the General Motors assembly plant in Fremont, California, 35 miles southeast of San Francisco, which opened in 1963 and manufactured GM trucks and the Chevy Malibu and Century. At the old GM-Fremont plant, work was organized along traditional Taylorist lines, with more than 80 industrial engineers establishing assembly-line norms that management then did its best to impose on the work force, with the predictable results.

Over the years, GM-Fremont came to be what one manager called "the worst plant in the world."

> ## GM-Fremont had low productivity, abysmal quality, drug and alcohol abuse, and absenteeism over 20%.

Productivity was among the lowest of any GM plant, quality was abysmal, and drug and alcohol abuse were rampant both on and off the job. Absenteeism was so high that the plant employed 20% more workers than it needed just to ensure an adequate labor force on any given day. The United Auto Workers local earned a national reputation for militancy; from 1963 to 1982, wildcat strikes and sickouts closed the plant four times. The backlog of unresolved grievances often exceeded 5,000.

GM-Fremont reached its peak employment of 6,800 hourly workers in 1978. Numbers then declined steadily to a little over 3,000 when GM finally closed the plant in February 1982.

Discussions between GM and Toyota about a possible joint venture began that same year. In February 1983, the two companies reached an agreement in principle to produce a version of the Toyota Corolla, renamed the Nova, at the Fremont plant, using Toyota's production system. GM would be responsible for marketing and sales; Toyota would take on product design, engineering, and daily operations. The new entity, NUMMI, would manufacture and assemble the car. Beginning in 1986, the plant also made Corolla FXs. In 1988, both the Nova and the FX were phased out, and Fremont began building Corollas, Geo Prizms, and, as of late 1991, Toyota trucks.

The two companies' objectives were complementary. GM wanted to learn about Toyota's production system. It also obtained a high-quality subcompact for its Chevrolet division at a time when GM's market share was rapidly eroding. Toyota wanted to help defuse the trade issue by building cars in the United States. To do this, it needed to learn about U.S. suppliers.

Toyota later claimed it had also wanted "to gain experience with American union labor," but at first Toyota wanted nothing to do with the UAW. As it happened, there was no alternative. GM offered them no other facility, and the UAW had de facto control of Fremont. Moreover, GM was afraid of a union backlash at other plants if it tried to set up the joint venture as a nonunion shop.

In September 1983, NUMMI and the union signed a letter of intent recognizing the UAW as sole bargaining agent for the NUMMI labor force, specifying prevailing auto-industry wages and benefits, and stipulating that a majority of the work force would be hired from among the workers laid off from GM-Fremont. In return, the UAW agreed to support the implementation of a new production system and to negotiate a new contract.

NUMMI was formally organized in February 1984. Toyota contributed $100 million in capital, and GM supplied the Fremont plant. Hiring began in May. Every applicant went through three days of production simulations, written examinations, discussions, and interviews. Managers and union officials jointly evaluated applicants for the hourly jobs: team leader and team member. The union also played a role in selecting managers, except for the 16 who came directly from GM and a group of about 30 Toyota managers and production coordinators who came from Japan. The CEO, Tatsuo Toyoda, brought with him the prestige of the company's founding family.

Over the following 20 months, NUMMI hired 2,200 hourly workers – 85% from the old GM-Fremont plant, among them the old union hierarchy. (Almost none of GM-Fremont's salaried employees

---

> The NUMMI production system not only made people work harder, it made them work smarter as well.

---

was rehired. In any case, many had long since moved to other GM plants.) Since GM-Fremont had done little hiring for several years before it closed, the average age of the new work force was 41. Most had high school educations. About 26% were Hispanic, 20% black, and 15% female.

The first group of 450 team leaders and the entire NUMMI management team attended a three-week training program at the Toyota plant in Japan – Takaoka – on which NUMMI was modeled. These people then helped to set up the new plant and train workers.

The NUMMI production system required people to work harder than they had at GM-Fremont. Jobs at the old plant occupied an experienced worker

about 45 seconds out of 60. NUMMI's norm is closer to 57 seconds out of 60. And because workers have to meet much higher quality and efficiency standards, they have to work not only harder but smarter as well.

By the end of 1986, NUMMI's productivity was higher than that of any other GM facility and more than twice that of its predecessor, GM-Fremont. In fact, NUMMI's productivity was nearly as high as Takaoka's, even though its workers were, on average, ten years older and much less experienced with the Toyota production system. Quality, as rated by internal GM audits, customer surveys, and *Consumer Reports* was much higher than at any other GM plant and, again, almost as high as Takaoka's.

Equally important, absenteeism has dropped from between 20% and 25% at the old GM-Fremont plant to a steady 3% to 4% at NUMMI; substance abuse is a minimal problem; and participation in the suggestion program has risen steadily from 26% in 1986 to 92% in 1991. When GM-Fremont closed its doors, it had more than 2,000 grievances outstanding. As of the end of 1991, some 700 grievances had been filed at NUMMI altogether over the course of eight years. The overall proportion of employees describing themselves as "satisfied" or "very satisfied" has risen progressively to more than 90%.

In 1990, Toyota announced that it would invest $350 million in an additional assembly line to build a Toyota truck for the U.S. market. So NUMMI hired 650 hourly workers on top of the 3,100 – plus 400 salaried personnel – already employed. The first trucks rolled off the line in August 1991.

Fear, Selection, Socialization

NUMMI's remarkable turnaround poses an obvious question: How is it possible to convert a plant from worst to best quality and from dismal to superlative productivity over the course of a few months? The most obvious answers are not entirely satisfying.

For example, fear. The GM-Fremont plant closed in 1982, and the people rehired by NUMMI didn't go back to work until 1984. Two years of unemployment can produce a great deal of cooperation. In fact, some NUMMI workers believe management makes deliberate use of the specter of another plant closure as a veiled threat to keep people in line. But the chairman of the union bargaining committee points out that while the old plant's closure obviously made workers more receptive to NUMMI's

Voices from the Factory Floor: Excerpts from Interviews with

Team Leader

I'll never forget when I was first hired by GM many years ago. The personnel manager who hired us got the...workers who were starting that day into a room and explained: "You new employees have been hired in the same way we requisition sandpaper. We'll put you back on the street whenever you aren't needed any more." How in the hell can you expect to foster a loyal and productive work force when you start out hearing stuff like that? At NUMMI, the message when we came aboard was "Welcome to the family."

Team Leader

Once you start working as a real team, you're not just work acquaintances anymore. When you really have confidence in your co-workers, you trust them, you're proud of what you can do together, then you become loyal to them. That's what keeps the absenteeism rate so low here. When I wake up in the morning, I know there's no one out there to replace me if I'm feeling sick or hung over or whatever....At NUMMI, I know my team needs me.

Team Leader

The average worker is definitely busier at NUMMI than he was at Fremont. That's the point of the NUMMI production system and the way it ties together standardized work, no inventories, and no quality defects. The work teams at NUMMI aren't like the autonomous teams you read about in other plants. Here we're not autonomous, because we're all tied together really tightly. But it's not like we're just getting squeezed to work harder, because it's the workers who are making the whole thing work – we're the ones that make the standardized work and the *kaizen* suggestions. We run the plant – and if it's not running right, we stop it. At GM-Fremont, we ran only our own little jobs. We'd work really fast to build up a stock cushion so we could take a break for a few minutes to smoke a cigarette or chat with a buddy. That kind of "hurry up and wait" game made work really tiring. There was material and finished parts all over the place, and half of it was defective anyway. Being consistently busy without being hassled and without being overworked takes a lot of the pain out of the job. You work harder at NUMMI, but I swear it, you go home at the end of the day feeling less tired – and feeling a hell of a lot better about yourself!

Team Member

In our standardized work training, our teachers told us we should approach our fellow team members and suggest ways to improve their jobs. Hell, do you see me trying that with a team member who's six-foot-four and weighs 250 pounds? You'd be picking me up off the floor if I tried that....Standardized work is a joke as far as I can see. We're supposed to go to management and tell them when we have extra seconds to spare. Why would I do that when all that will happen is that they'll take my spare seconds away and work me even harder than before? I'd rather just do the job the way I'm already comfortable with. I'm no fool.

Department Manager

Our assumption at NUMMI is that people come to work to do a fair day's work. There are exceptions, and you would be foolish to ignore them. But 90% of people, if you give them a chance to work smarter and improve their jobs, and if they find that by doing that they have created free time for themselves, will spontaneously look for new things to do. I've got hundreds of examples. I don't think that people work harder at NUMMI than in other plants. Not physically anyway. But the mental challenge is much greater.

Team Leader

I don't think industrial engineers are dumb. They're just ignorant. Anyone can watch someone else doing a job and come up with improvement suggestions that sound good....And it's even easier to come up with the ideal procedure if you don't even bother to watch the worker at work, but just do it from your office, on paper. Almost anything can look good that way. Even when we do our own analysis in our teams, some of the silliest ideas can slip through before we actually try them out.

There's a lot of things that enter into a good job design....The person actually doing the job is the only one who can see all factors. And in the United States, engineers have never had to work on the floor – not

new approach, a return to old coercive management methods would have produced a rapid return to old antagonistic work-force behavior patterns.

A second possibility is that management weeded out troublemakers in the rehiring process. But in fact NUMMI rehired the entire union hierarchy and many well-known militants. In general, very few applicants were screened out. The union even won a second chance for some who failed drug tests the first time around.

A third answer is that NUMMI made use of a comprehensive socialization process during hiring to instill a new set of values in the new work force. Certainly, NUMMI did its best to shape and alter the attitudes of both workers and managers. For example, the company tried to undercut the custom-

Managers, Workers, and Union Officials

like in Japan. So they don't know what they don't know....Today *we* drive the process, and if we need help, the engineer is there the next day to work on it with us.

UAW Official

One thing I really like about the Toyota style is that they'll put in a machine to save you from bending down. The Toyota philosophy is that the worker should use the machine and not vice versa....It would be fine if the robots worked perfectly – and the engineers always seem to imagine that they will. But they don't, so the worker ends up being used by the machine. At NUMMI, we just put in a robot for installing the spare tire – that really helps the worker, because it was always a hell of a tiring job. It took awhile, and we had to raise it in the safety meetings and argue about it. And they came through. That would never happen at GM-Fremont – you never saw automation simply to help the worker.

UAW Official

In the future we're going to need union leaders with more technical and management knowledge. We're much more involved now in deciding how the plant operates. That stretches our capabilities. Management is coming to us asking for our input....The old approach was much simpler – "You make the damned decision, and I'll grieve it if I want." Now we need to understand how the production system works, to take the time to analyze things, to formulate much more detailed proposals. This system really allows us to take as much power as we know what to do with.

UAW Official

Now when I try to explain [NUMMI] to old UAW buddies from other plants...they figure that I'm forced to say all this stuff because they shut our plant down and I had no choice. They figure going along with the team concept and all the rest was just the price we had to pay to get our jobs back. I explain to them that the plant is cleaner, it's safer, we've got more say on important issues, and we have a real opportunity to build our strength as a union. I explain to them that our members can broaden their understanding of the man-

ufacturing system and build their self-esteem, and that the training we've gotten in manufacturing, problem solving, quality, and so on can help them reach their full potential and get more out of their lives. I explain to them that in a system like this, workers have got a chance to make a real contribution to society – we don't have to let managers do all the thinking. But these guys just don't see it. Maybe it's because they haven't personally experienced the way NUMMI works. Whatever the reason, they just see it all as weakening the union. Someone like Irving Bluestone probably understands what we're doing. He had the idea a long time ago: if the worker has the right to vote for the president of the United States, he ought to have the right to participate in decisions on the shop floor.

Team Member

In the old days, we had to worry about management playing its games, and the union was there to defend us. But now, with the union taking on its new role, it's not as simple as before, and we have to worry about both the management games and the union games. I don't want the type of union muscle we used to have. You could get away with almost anything in the old plant, because the union would get you off the hook. It was really crazy. But it wasn't productive.

Team Leader

There are people here who will tell you they hate this place. All I say is: actions speak louder than words. If people were disgruntled, there's no way that we'd be building the highest quality vehicle. You wouldn't have a plant that's this clean. You would still have the drug problems we had before. You would still have all the yelling and screaming. You can't force all that. And try this: go into any of the bathrooms, and you'll see there's no graffiti. If people have a problem with their manager, they don't have to tell him on the bathroom wall. They can tell him to his face. And the boss's first words will be: "Why?" Something's happened here at NUMMI. When I was at GM, I remember a few years ago I got an award from my foreman for coming to work for a full 40 hours in one week. A certificate! At NUMMI, I've had perfect attendance for two years.

ary we-they divisions between workers and management by eliminating special parking and eating facilities for managers and by introducing an identical dress code – uniforms – for everyone. Management also devoted a great deal of attention to each individual hire and welcomed each personally to the company that was going to build "the finest vehicles in America."

However much these three factors – fear of unemployment, selection, and socialization – may have contributed to the final outcome, they do not adequately explain NUMMI's continuing success or its ability to let workers draw improved motivation and greater satisfaction from a system that places them in a more regimented and bureaucratic environment and makes them work harder and faster. The most critical piece of that explanation lies in the production system itself and in the policies and practices that buttress it.

The NUMMI Production System

The idea of a production *system* is itself something of a novelty in many U.S. manufacturing plants. All factories have production techniques, procedures, and policies, but these usually comprise not so much a system as an ad hoc accumulation of responses to changing and often contradictory business and design demands. NUMMI's production system is a finely tuned, superbly integrated whole, refined by Toyota over decades of manufacturing experience.

The basic techniques are familiar at least in name. The assembly line is a just-in-time operation that does away with work-in-progress and makes quality assurance the responsibility of each work station. The application of *kaizen*, or continuous improvement, includes an extraordinarily active suggestion program, constant refinement of procedures, and the designation of special kaizen teams to study individual suggestions or carry out specific improvement projects. Every machine and process is designed to detect malfunctions, missing parts, and improper assemblies automatically. Every job is carefully analyzed to achieve maximum efficiency and quality. Job rotation is standard; workers are cross-trained in all team assignments and then allowed to shift from one task to another. Planned production leveling eliminates variation in daily and weekly schedules.

This system is essentially the same one Toyota uses in Japan, the same one many American manufacturers are now beginning to adopt. But NUMMI's approach is distinctive in two respects: first,

> The NUMMI approach has two distinctive features: a commitment to the social context of work and a focus on standardization.

its strong commitment to the social context in which work is performed, and, second, its intense focus on standardized work.

In terms of social context, NUMMI seeks to build an atmosphere of trust and common purpose.

NUMMI maintains exceptional consistency in its strategies and principles, it carefully builds consensus around important decisions, and it has programs ensuring adequate communication of results and other essential information.

The basic structural unit is the production team, of which NUMMI has approximately 350, each consisting of five to seven people and a leader. The idea is that small teams encourage participative decision making and team bonding. Four teams comprise a group, led by a group leader who represents the first layer of management.

Above and beyond the production teams, the bigger team is everyone – all the workers, team leaders, managers, engineers, and staff in the plant as well as NUMMI's suppliers. Toyota leadership wants workers to understand that the company is not the property of management but of everyone together. In NUMMI's view, the primary purpose and responsibility of the management hierarchy is to support the production teams with problem-solving expertise.

The most substantive expression of this big-team strategy is the no-layoff policy spelled out in NUMMI's collective-bargaining agreement with the union. Recognizing that "job security is essential to an employee's well being," NUMMI agrees "that it will not lay off employees unless compelled to do so by severe economic conditions that threaten the long-term viability of the Company." NUMMI agrees to take such drastic measures as reducing management salaries and assigning previously subcontracted work to bargaining unit employees before resorting to layoffs.

Management sees the no-layoff policy as a critical support for its overall production strategy not only because it reinforces the team culture, but also because it eliminates workers' fear that they are jeopardizing jobs every time they come up with an idea to improve efficiency.

Workers came to trust this no-layoff commitment when in 1988 poor sales of the Nova brought capacity utilization down to around 60%. Workers no longer needed on the assembly line were not laid off but instead assigned to kaizen teams and sent to training classes.

Another important support for NUMMI's team concept is its radically simplified job classification system. Where GM-Fremont had 18 skilled trades classifications, NUMMI has two. Where GM-Fremont had 80 hourly pay rates, at NUMMI all production workers get the same hourly rate – currently $17.85 – regardless of their jobs, except that team leaders get an extra 60 cents. There are no seniority-, performance-, or merit-based bonuses.

Important as money is, equity is more important still in reducing tensions and resentments.

The second distinctive feature of NUMMI's system is standardization. Typically, American companies approach team empowerment by allowing teams considerable autonomy in how they accomplish tasks. NUMMI, in contrast, is obsessive about standardized work procedures. It sees what one NUMMI manager has called "the intelligent interpretation and application of Taylor's time-and-motion studies" as the principal key to its success. The reference to Taylor may be jarring, but it fits.

Standardized Work...

At GM-Fremont, industrial engineers did all time-and-motion analysis and formal job design, and workers tended to view them with resentment or contempt. The problem, as one union official described it, was that management assumed a "divine right" to design jobs however it saw fit. Industrial engineers with no direct experience of the work beyond capsule observation would shut themselves in a room, ponder various potentials of the human body, time the result, and promulgate a task design. Or so it seemed to workers, whom no one ever consulted despite their intimate familiarity with the specific difficulties of the work in question.

Normally, when an industrial engineer presented one of these pedantically designed jobs to a supervisor, the supervisor would politely accept it, then promptly discard it in favor of the more traditional kick-ass-and-take-names technique. The worker, in turn, usually ignored both engineer and foreman and did the job however he or she was able – except, of course, when one of them was looking. If an industrial engineer was actually "observing" – stopwatch and clipboard in hand – standard practice was to slow down and make the work look harder. The entire charade was part of an ongoing game of coercion and avoidance. Multiply this scenario by two shifts and thousands of workers, and the result is anything *but* the rational production of a high-quality car.

At NUMMI, in radical contrast to GM-Fremont, team members themselves hold the stopwatch. They learn the techniques of work analysis, description, and improvement. This change in the design and implementation of standardized work has far-reaching implications for worker motivation and self-esteem, for the balance of power between workers and management, and for the capacity of the company to innovate, learn, and remember.

The job design process itself is relatively simple. Team members begin by timing one another with stopwatches, looking for the safest, most efficient way to do each task at a sustainable pace. They pick the best performance, break it down into its fundamental parts, then explore ways of improving each element. The team then takes the resulting analyses, compares them with those of the other shift at the same work station, and writes the detailed specifications that become the standard work definition for everyone on both teams.

Taking part in the group's analytical and descriptive work involves every team member in a commitment to perform each task identically. In one sense, therefore, standardized work is simply a means of reducing variability in task performance, which may seem a relatively trivial achievement. In fact, however, reduced variability leads to a whole series of interconnected improvements:
☐ Safety improves and injuries decline because workers get a chance to examine all the possible sources of strain and danger systematically.
☐ Quality standards rise because workers have identified the most effective procedure for each job.
☐ Inventory control grows easier, and inventory carrying costs go down because the process flows more smoothly.
☐ Job rotation becomes much more efficient and equitable, which makes absences less troublesome.
☐ Flexibility improves because all workers are now industrial engineers and can work in parallel to respond rapidly to changing demands. For example, NUMMI can convert to a new line speed in four to six weeks, a process that might easily have taken six months to a year at GM-Fremont, with its engineers frantically recalculating thousands of tasks

> If orders decline, NUMMI can slow the production line to produce fewer cars. In the same situation, GM-Fremont had to lay off an entire shift.

and trying to force the new standards on workers. In fact, GM-Fremont never even attempted anything as demanding as a line-speed change. If orders declined, GM-Fremont had to lay off an entire shift. NUMMI's new capacity to alter line speed means, among other things, that the plant can accommodate a drop in orders by slowing production.
☐ Standardized work also has the overall benefit of giving control of each job to the people who know it

best. It empowers the work force. Not surprisingly, NUMMI discovered that workers bought into the process quite readily. As one manager put it, "They understood the technique because it had been done *to* them for years, and they liked the idea because now they had a chance to do it for themselves."

...and Continuous Improvement

Yet by far the most striking advantage of standardized work is that it gives continuous improvement a specific base to build on. As one manager put it, "You can't improve a process you don't understand." In this sense, standardization is the essential precondition for learning.

Indeed, standardization is not only a vehicle and a precondition for improvement but also a direct stimulus. Once workers have studied and refined their work procedures, problems with materials and equipment quickly rise to the surface. Moreover, since each worker is now an expert, each work station is now an inspection station – and a center of innovation.

At GM-Fremont, worker suggestions were apt to meet a brick wall of indifference. At NUMMI, engineers and managers are meant to function as a support system rather than an authority system. When a team can't solve a problem on its own, it can seek and get help. When a worker proposes complex innovation, engineers are available to help assess the suggestion and design its implementation.

The difference between traditional Taylorism and the learning-oriented NUMMI version resembles the difference between computer software designed to be "idiot-proof" and the kinds of computer systems that are meant to leverage and enhance their users' capabilities. The first "de-skills" the operator's task to an extent that virtually eliminates the possibility of error, but it also eliminates the operator's ability to respond to unpredictable events, to use the system in novel ways or adapt it to new applications. The idiot-proof system may be easy to use, but it is also static and boring. Leveraging systems make demands on the operator. They take time to learn and require thought and skill to use, but they are immensely flexible, responsive, and satisfying once mastered.

The difference goes deeper yet. At GM-Fremont – where work procedures were designed to be idiot-proof – the relationship between production system and worker was adversarial. Standards and hierarchy were there to coerce effort from reluctant workers. If the system functioned as expected and the

operator was sufficiently tractable and unimaginative, the two together could turn out a fair product. There was little the operator could improve on, however, and the role of the system was utterly rigid until it broke down, whereupon everything stopped until a specialist arrived.

At NUMMI, the relationship of workers to the production system is cooperative and dynamic. Instead of circumventing user intelligence and initiative, the production system is designed to realize as much as possible of the latent collaborative potential between the workers and the system.

Suggestion programs illustrate the two approaches to organizational technology design. At many companies, suggestion programs are idiot-proof and opaque. They are designed primarily to screen out dumb ideas, and the basic review criteria, the identity of the judges, the status of proposals, and the reasons for rejection are all a black box as far as the workers are concerned. Predictably, a lot of these programs sputter along or die out altogether.

At NUMMI, the program is designed to encourage a growing flow of suggestions and to help workers see and understand criteria, evaluators, process, status, and results. Like a computer system designed to leverage rather than de-skill, the program helps employees form a mental model of the program's inner workings. Not surprisingly, workers made more than 10,000 suggestions in 1991, of which more than 80% were implemented.

In systems that de-skill and idiot-proof, technology controls, indeed dominates, workers. In systems designed for what experts call usability, the operator both learns from and "teaches" the technology. Using learned analytical tools, their own experience, and the expertise of leaders and engineers, workers create a consensual standard that they teach to the system by writing job descriptions. The system then teaches these standards back to workers, who, then, by further analysis, consultation, and consensus, make additional improvements. Continual reiteration of this disciplined process of analysis, standardization, re-analysis, refinement, and restandardization creates an intensely structured system of continuous improvement. And the salient characteristic of this bureaucracy is learning, not coercion.

This learning orientation captures the imagination. People no one had ever asked to solve a problem, workers who never finished high school, men and women who had spent 20 years or more in the auto industry without a single day of off-the-job training found themselves suddenly caught up in the statistical analysis of equipment downtime, putting together Pareto charts. One worker reported that he did literally a hundred graphs before he got one right.

A woman on the safety committee in the body shop described how she applied kaizen techniques to her kitchen at home after a fire on her stove. She analyzed the kitchen layout, installed a fire extinguisher, and relocated her pot tops so she could use them to smother flames. In short, she subjected herself and her home work space to the formal problem-solving procedures she had learned at the NUMMI plant.

The paradoxical feature such stories have in common is their enthusiasm for a form of disciplined behavior that both theory and past practice seem to rule out. This paradox grows from our failure to distinguish between what Taylorist, bureaucratic production systems *can* be and what, regrettably, they have usually been.

The Psychology of Work

The chain of reasoning by which disciplined standardization leads inescapably to coercion, resentment, resistance, and further coercion seems to turn Taylorism and bureaucracy into what sociologist Max Weber called an iron cage. Taylorism and bureaucracy may have a devastating effect on innovation and motivation, the reasoning goes, but their technical efficiency and their power to enforce compliance seem to be the perfect tools for dealing with employees assumed to be recalcitrant. Taylor himself at least occasionally endorsed this coercive view of work. Italics bristling, he once

wrote, "It is only through the *enforced* standardization of methods, *enforced* adoption of the best implements and working conditions, and *enforced* cooperation that this faster work can be assured. And the duty of enforcing the adoption of standards and of enforcing this cooperation rests with the *management* alone."

Against this background, it is hardly surprising that most managers and academics, at least in the West, have come to believe that Taylorism and bureaucracy will inevitably alienate workers and squander their human potential. But the psychological assumption underlying this expectation is that workers are incapable of delayed gratification. Managers seem to believe that performance will improve only as work comes more and more to resemble free play – our model of an intrinsically motivating activity. Indeed, it is an an elementary axiom of economics that work is something that workers will always avoid.

NUMMI demonstrates the error of imputing infantile psychology to workers. Interviews with NUMMI team members suggest, in fact, that this whole historical accumulation of assumptions obscures three sources of adult motivation that the NUMMI production system successfully taps into:

First, the desire for excellence.

Second, a mature sense of realism.

Third, the positive response to respect and trust.

The first of these – the desire to do a good job, the instinct for workmanship – comes up again and again in conversations with workers. The NUMMI production system and the training that went with it increased both the real competence of workers and their feelings of competence. Workers talk a lot

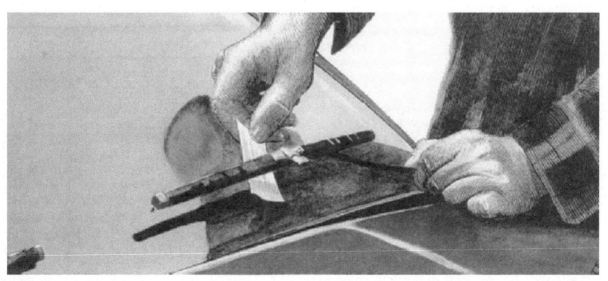

Workers once ashamed of their products are now inclined to let car owners know that they "helped build this one."

about expertise, pride, and self-esteem. One UAW official named "building a quality product" as one of the strategic goals that the union found most compelling at NUMMI. Perhaps the most striking story about pride in all the interviews came from a team leader:

> Before, when I saw a Chevy truck, I'd chuckle to myself and think, "You deserve that piece of crap if you were stupid enough to buy one." I was ashamed to say that I worked at the Fremont plant. But when I was down at the Monterey Aquarium a few weekends ago, I left my business card – the grunts even have business cards – on the windshield of a parked Nova with a note that said, "I helped build this one." I never felt pride in my job before.

The second element of motivation is a mature sense of realism – in this case, the understanding that unless NUMMI constantly improves its performance, competitors will take its market and its workers' jobs. A useful psychological theory cannot assume that workers are so captive to the pleasure principle that their only source of motivation is the immediate pleasure of intrinsically meaningful work. The evidence suggests that at least some of the workers at NUMMI are powerfully motivated by the simple recognition that international competition now forces them to "earn their money the old-fashioned way."

Other things being equal, work that is intrinsically motivating – as opposed to mundane and routine – is better than work that isn't. But workers at NUMMI recognize that other things are *not* equal, and they are realistic in their recognition of having had an unlucky draw in terms of education and opportunity. They see automobile assembly as work

> ## Some workers take powerful motivation from the knowledge that they have to "earn their money the old-fashioned way."

that can never have much instrinsic value, but they understand that their own motivation levels can nevertheless vary from strongly negative, at GM-Fremont, to strongly positive, at NUMMI.

"What we have here is not some workers' utopia," said one NUMMI worker. "Working on an assembly line in an automobile factory is still a lousy job....We want to continue to minimize the negative parts of the job by utilizing the new system." Even though this work lacks the kind of intrinsic interest that would bring a worker in on a free Sunday, for example, the difference between the levels of motivation at NUMMI and at GM-Fremont spells the difference between world-class and worst-in-class.

The third explanation of increased motivation is the respect and trust that management shows workers in NUMMI's ongoing operations. For example, when the plant first began operations, the new NUMMI managers responded quickly to requests from workers and union representatives for items like new gloves and floor mats, which surprised workers used to seeing requests like these turn into battles over management prerogative.

After a few months of getting everything they asked for, workers and union representatives started trying to think of ways to reciprocate. Eventually, they decided that chrome water fountains were unnecessary and told management they'd found some plastic ones for half the price. A few weeks later, management upped the ante one more time by giving work teams their own accounts so they could order supplies for team members without prior approval from management. This kind of behavior led workers to conclude that they did indeed share common goals with management.

Power and Empowerment

The NUMMI production system confronts us with a set of formalized procedures that seem designed not primarily as instruments of domination but as elements of productive technique that all participants recognize as tools in their own collective interest. Management *and* labor support the NUMMI system. In fact, the first and overwhelming fact to emerge from interviews is that no one at NUMMI wants to go back to the old GM-Fremont days. Whatever their criticisms and whatever their positions, everyone feels that NUMMI is a far superior work environment.

NUMMI's no-layoff policy, management efforts to build an atmosphere of trust and respect, the NUMMI production system – especially the stimulus of its learning orientation – all help to explain this attitude. Beyond these formal policies, however, there are two more factors that help explain NUMMI's success with workers. The first of these, as we've seen, is the psychology of work. The final piece of the puzzle has to do with power.

There are two kinds of power to consider: hierarchical power within the organization and the power balance between labor and management. NUMMI takes a distinctive approach to both.

In terms of hierarchical layers, NUMMI is a fairly typical U.S. manufacturing plant, and in this sense, as well as in work-flow procedures, it is a very bureaucratic organization. NUMMI's structure is not flat. It has several well-populated layers of middle management. But consistent with the idea of turning the technologies of coercion into tools for learning, the function of hierarchy at NUMMI is not control but support.

Decisions at NUMMI are made by broad vertical and horizontal consensus. At first glance, decision making appears to be somewhat *more* centralized than at most U.S. factories, but this is because consensus-based decision making draws higher and lower layers into a dialogue, not because higher levels wield greater unilateral control. Both ends of the hierarchical spectrum are drawn into more decision-making discussions than either would experience in a conventional organization.

The contrast with the popular approaches to empowerment is striking. At one U.S. telecommunications company, the model organization today is a plant of 90 workers in self-managed teams, all reporting to a single plant manager. The company's old model included a heavy layer of middle management whose key function was to command and control, so it is easy to understand the inspiring effect of the new approach. But at NUMMI, middle management layers are layers of expertise, not of rights to command, and if middle managers have authority, it is the authority of experience, mastery, and the capacity to coach.

As for the second aspect of power, many observers have assumed that the intense discipline of Toyota-style operations requires complete management control over workers and elimination of independent work-force and union power. But at NUMMI, the power of workers and the union local is still considerable. In some ways, their power has actually increased. In fact, it may be that the NUMMI model has succeeded only *because* of this high level of worker and union power.

What makes the NUMMI production system so enormously effective is its ability to make production problems immediately visible and to mobilize the power of teamwork. Implemented with trust and respect, both these features of the system create real empowerment. Wielded autocratically, they would have the opposite effect. Visible control could easily turn into ubiquitous surveillance. Teamwork could become a means of mobilizing peer pressure. A healthy level of challenge could degenerate into stress and anxiety.

The NUMMI production system thus gives managers enormous potential control over workers. With this potential power ready at hand, and under pressure to improve business performance, there is a real danger that the relationship will sooner or later slide back into the old coercive pattern.

But such a slide would have an immediate and substantial negative impact on business performance, because labor would respond in kind. An alienated work force wipes out the very foundation

> The new system gives workers great positive power to improve production and great negative power to disrupt it.

of continuous improvement and dries up the flow of worker suggestions that fuel it. And the lack of inventory buffers means that disaffected workers could easily bring the whole just-in-time production system to a grinding halt. Alongside workers' positive power to improve quality and efficiency, the system also gives workers an enormous negative power to disrupt production.

In other words, NUMMI's production system increases the power both of management over workers and of workers over management.

A system this highly charged needs a robust governance process in which the voices of management and labor can be clearly heard and effectively harmonized on high-level policy issues as well as on work-team operating issues. The union gives workers this voice.

When, for example, workers felt frustrated by what they saw as favoritism in management's selection of team leaders, the union largely eliminated the problem by negotiating a joint union-management selection process based on objective tests and performance criteria.

As one UAW official put it, "The key to NUMMI's success is that management gave up some of its power, some of its traditional prerogatives. If managers want to motivate workers to contribute and to learn, they have to give up some of their power. If managers want workers to trust them, we need to be 50-50 in making the decision. Don't just make the decision and say, 'Trust me.'"

Union leaders and top management confer regularly on- and off-site to consider a broad range of policy issues that go far beyond the traditional scope of collective bargaining. The union local has embraced the NUMMI concept and its goals. But its ability and willingness to act as a vehicle for worker concerns adds greatly to the long-term effectiveness of the organization.

NUMMI's ability to sustain its productivity, quality, and improvement record now depends on workers' motivation, which rests, in turn, on the perception and reality of influence, control, and equitable treatment. It is in management's own interest that any abuse of management prerogatives should meet with swift and certain penalties. The contribution of labor's positive power depends on the reality of its negative power.

In this way, the union not only serves workers' special interests, it also serves the larger strategic goals of the business by effectively depriving management of absolute domain and helping to maintain management discipline.

Empowerment is a powerful and increasingly popular approach to reinvigorating moribund organizations. The NUMMI case points up two of empowerment's potential pitfalls and suggests ways of overcoming them.

First, worker empowerment degenerates into exploitation if changes at the first level of management are not continuously reinforced by changes throughout the management hierarchy. Strong employee voice is needed to ensure that shop-floor concerns are heard at all levels of management. Without it, workers' new power is little more than the power to make more money for management.

Second, worker empowerment degenerates into abandonment if work teams fail to get the right tools, training in their use, and support in their implementation. Standardized work, extensive training in problem solving, a responsive management hierarchy, and supportive specialist functions are key success factors for empowerment strategies.

Taylorist time-and-motion discipline and formal bureaucratic structures are essential for efficiency and quality in routine operations. But these principles of organizational design need not lead to rigidity and alienation. NUMMI points the way beyond Taylor-as-villain to the design of a truly learning-oriented bureaucracy.

Reprint 93101

Theme 5

Managing Organisations Today

The Social Responsibility of Business is to Increase its Profits

by Milton Friedman

When I hear businessmen speak eloquently about the "social responsibilities of business in a free-enterprise system," I am reminded of the wonderful line about the Frenchman who discovered at the age of 70 that he had been speaking prose all his life. The businessmen believe that they are defending free enterprise when they declaim that business is not concerned "merely" with profit but also with promoting desirable "social" ends; that business has a "social conscience" and takes seriously its responsibilities for providing employment, eliminating discrimination, avoiding pollution and whatever else may be the catchwords of the contemporary crop of reformers. In fact they are–or would be if they or anyone else took them seriously–preaching pure and unadulterated socialism. Businessmen who talk this way are unwitting puppets of the intellectual forces that have been undermining the basis of a free society these past decades.

The discussions of the "social responsibilities of business" are notable for their analytical looseness and lack of rigor. What does it mean to say that "business" has responsibilities? Only people can have responsibilities. A corporation is an artificial person and in this sense may have artificial responsibilities, but "business" as a whole cannot be said to have responsibilities, even in this vague sense. The first step toward clarity in examining the doctrine of the social responsibility of business is to ask precisely what it implies for whom.

Presumably, the individuals who are to be responsible are businessmen, which means individual proprietors or corporate executives. Most of the discussion of social responsibility is directed at corporations, so in what follows I shall mostly neglect the individual proprietors and speak of corporate executives.

In a free-enterprise, private-property system, a corporate executive is an employee of the owners of the business. He has direct responsibility to his employers. That responsibility is to conduct the business in accordance with their desires, which generally will be to make as much money as possible while conforming to the basic rules of the society, both those embodied in law and those embodied in ethical custom. Of course, in some cases his employers may have a different objective. A group of persons might establish a corporation for an eleemosynary purpose–for example, a hospital or a school. The manager of such a corporation will not have money profit as his objective but the rendering of certain services.

In either case, the key point is that, in his capacity as a corporate executive, the manager is the agent of the individuals who own the corporation or establish the eleemosynary institution, and his primary responsibility is to them.

Needless to say, this does not mean that it is easy to judge how well he is performing his task. But at least the criterion of performance is straightforward, and the persons among whom a voluntary contractual arrangement exists are clearly defined.

Of course, the corporate executive is also a person in his own right. As a person, he may have many other responsibilities that he recognizes or assumes voluntarily–to his family, his conscience, his feelings of charity, his church, his clubs, his city, his country. He ma}. feel impelled by these responsibilities to devote part of his income to causes he regards as worthy, to refuse to work for particular corporations, even to leave his job, for example, to join his country's armed forces. Ifwe wish, we may refer to some of these responsibilities as "social responsibilities." But in these respects he is acting as a principal, not an agent; he is spending his own money or time or energy, not the money of his employers or the time or energy he has contracted to devote to their purposes. If these are "social responsibilities," they are the social responsibilities of individuals, not of business.

What does it mean to say that the corporate executive has a "social responsibility" in his capacity as businessman? If this statement is not pure rhetoric, it must mean that he is to act in some way that is not in the interest of his employers. For example, that he is to refrain from increasing the price of the product in order to contribute to the social objective of preventing inflation, even though a price in crease would be in the best interests of the corporation. Or that he is to make expenditures on reducing pollution beyond the amount that is in the best interests of the corporation or that is required by law in order to contribute to the social objective of improving the environment. Or that, at the expense of corporate profits, he is to hire "hardcore" un-employed instead of better qualified available workmen to contribute to the social objective of reducing poverty.

In each of these cases, the corporate executive would be spending someone else's money for a general social interest. Insofar as his actions in accord with his "social responsibility" reduce returns to stockholders, he is spending their money. Insofar as his actions raise the price to customers, he is spending the customers' money. Insofar as his actions lower the wages of some employees, he is spending their money.

The stockholders or the customers or the employees could separately spend their own money on the particular action if they wished to do so. The executive is exercising a distinct "social responsibility," rather than serving as an agent of the stockholders or the customers or the employees, only if he spends the money in a different way than they would have spent it.

But if he does this, he is in effect imposing taxes, on the one hand, and deciding how the tax proceeds shall be spent, on the other.

This process raises political questions on two levels: principle and consequences. On the level of political principle, the imposition of taxes and the expenditure of tax proceeds are governmental functions. We have established elaborate constitutional, parliamentary and judicial provisions to control these functions, to assure that taxes are imposed so far as possible in accordance with the preferences and desires of the public–after all, "taxation without representation" was one of the battle cries of the American Revolution. We have a system of checks and balances to separate the legislative function of imposing taxes and enacting expenditures from the executive function of collecting taxes and administering expenditure programs and from the judicial function of mediating disputes and interpreting the law.

Here the businessman—self-selected or appointed directly or indirectly by stockholders—is to be simultaneously legislator, executive and, jurist. He is to decide whom to tax by how much and for what purpose, and he is to spend the proceeds—all this guided only by general exhortations from on high to restrain inflation, improve the environment, fight poverty and so on and on.

The whole justification for permitting the corporate executive to be selected by the stockholders is that the executive is an agent serving the interests of his principal. This justification disappears when the corporate executive imposes taxes and spends the proceeds for "social" purposes. He becomes in effect a public employee, a civil servant, even though he remains in name an employee of a private enterprise. On grounds of political principle, it is intolerable that such civil servants—insofar as their actions in the name of social responsibility are real and not just window-dressing—should be selected as they are now. If they are to be civil servants, then they must be elected through a political process. If they are to impose taxes and make expenditures to foster "social" objectives, then political machinery must be set up to make the assessment of taxes and to determine through a political process the objectives to be served.

This is the basic reason why the doctrine of "social responsibility" involves the acceptance of the socialist view that political mechanisms, not market mechanisms, are the appropriate way to determine the allocation of scarce resources to alternative uses.

On the grounds of consequences, can the corporate executive in fact discharge his alleged "social responsibilities?" On the other hand, suppose he could get away with spending the stockholders' or customers' or employees' money. How is he to know how to spend it? He is told that he must contribute to fighting inflation. How is he to know what action of his will contribute to that end? He is presumably an expert in running his company—in producing a product or selling it or financing it. But nothing about his selection makes him an expert on inflation. Will his hold ing down the price of his product reduce inflationary pressure? Or, by leaving more spending power in the hands of his customers, simply divert it elsewhere? Or, by forcing him to produce less because of the lower price, will it simply contribute to shortages? Even if he could answer these questions, how much cost is he justified in imposing on his stockholders, customers and employees for this social purpose? What is his appropriate share and what is the appropriate share of others?

And, whether he wants to or not, can he get away with spending his stockholders', customers' or employees' money? Will not the stockholders fire him? (Either the present ones or those who take over when his actions in the name of social responsibility have reduced the corporation's profits and the price of its stock.) His customers and his employees can desert him for other producers and employers less scrupulous in exercising their social responsibilities.

This facet of "social responsibility" doc trine is brought into sharp relief when the doctrine is used to justify wage restraint by trade unions. The conflict of interest is naked and clear when union officials are asked to subordinate the interest of their members to some more general purpose. If the union officials try to enforce wage restraint, the consequence is likely to be wildcat strikes, rank-and-file revolts and the emergence of strong competitors for their jobs. We thus have the ironic phenomenon that union leaders–at least in the U.S.–have objected to Government interference with the market far more consistently and courageously than have business leaders.

The difficulty of exercising "social responsibility" illustrates, of course, the great virtue of private competitive enterprise–it forces people to be responsible for their own actions and makes it difficult for them to "exploit" other people for either selfish or unselfish purposes. They can do good–but only at their own expense.

Many a reader who has followed the argument this far may be tempted to remonstrate that it is all well and good to speak of Government's having the responsibility to impose taxes and determine expenditures for such "social" purposes as controlling pollution or training the hard-core unemployed, but that the problems are too urgent to wait on the slow course of political processes, that the exercise of social responsibility by businessmen is a quicker and surer way to solve pressing current problems.

Aside from the question of fact–I share Adam Smith's skepticism about the benefits that can be expected from "those who affected to trade for the public good"–this argument must be rejected on grounds of principle. What it amounts to is an assertion that those who favor the taxes and expenditures in question have failed to persuade a majority of their fellow citizens to be of like mind and that they are seeking to attain by undemocratic procedures what they cannot attain by democratic procedures. In a free society, it is hard for "evil" people to do "evil," especially since one man's good is another's evil.

I have, for simplicity, concentrated on the special case of the corporate executive, except only for the brief digression on trade unions. But precisely the same argument applies to the newer phenomenon of calling upon stockholders to require corporations to exercise social responsibility (the recent G.M crusade for example). In most of these cases, what is in effect involved is some stockholders trying to get other stockholders (or customers or employees) to contribute against their will to "social" causes favored by the activists. Insofar as they succeed, they are again imposing taxes and spending the proceeds.

The situation of the individual proprietor is somewhat different. If he acts to reduce the returns of his enterprise in order to exercise his "social responsibility," he is spending his own money, not someone else's. If he wishes to spend his money on such purposes, that is his right, and I cannot see that there is any objection to his doing so. In the process, he, too, may impose costs on employees and customers. However, because he is far less likely than a large corporation or union to have monopolistic power, any such side effects will tend to be minor.

Of course, in practice the doctrine of social responsibility is frequently a cloak for actions that are justified on other grounds rather than a reason for those actions.

To illustrate, it may well be in the long run interest of a corporation that is a major employer in a small community to devote resources to providing amenities to that community or to improving its government. That may make it easier to attract desirable employees, it may reduce the wage bill or lessen losses from pilferage and sabotage or have other worthwhile effects. Or it may be that, given the laws about the deductibility of corporate charitable contributions, the stockholders can contribute more to charities they favor by having the corporation make the gift than by doing it themselves, since they can in that way contribute an amount that would otherwise have been paid as corporate taxes.

In each of these–and many similar–cases, there is a strong temptation to rationalize these actions as an exercise of "social responsibility." In the present climate of opinion, with its wide spread aversion to "capitalism," "profits," the "soulless corporation" and so on, this is one way for a corporation to generate goodwill as a by-product of expenditures that are entirely justified in its own self-interest.

It would be inconsistent of me to call on corporate executives to refrain from this hyp-ocritical window-dressing because it harms the foundations of a free society. That would be to call on them to exercise a "social responsibility"! If our institutions, and the attitudes of the public make it in their self-interest to cloak their actions in this way, I cannot summon much indignation to denounce them. At the same time, I can express admiration for those individual proprietors or owners of closely held corporations or stockholders of more broadly held corporations who disdain such tactics as approaching fraud.

Whether blameworthy or not, the use of the cloak of social responsibility, and the nonsense spoken in its name by influential and prestigious businessmen, does clearly harm the foundations of a free society. I have been impressed time and again by the schizophrenic character of many businessmen. They are capable of being extremely farsighted and clearheaded in matters that are internal to their businesses. They are incredibly shortsighted and muddleheaded in matters that are outside their businesses but affect the possible survival of business in general. This shortsightedness is strikingly exemplified in the calls from many businessmen for wage and price guidelines or controls or income policies. There is nothing that could do more in a brief period to destroy a market system and replace it by a centrally controlled system than effective governmental control of prices and wages.

The shortsightedness is also exemplified in speeches by businessmen on social responsibility. This may gain them kudos in the short run. But it helps to strengthen the already too prevalent view that the pursuit of profits is wicked and immoral and must be curbed and controlled by external forces. Once this view is adopted, the external forces that curb the market will not be the social consciences, however highly developed, of the pontificating executives; it will be the iron fist of Government bureaucrats. Here, as with price and wage controls, businessmen seem to me to reveal a suicidal impulse.

The political principle that underlies the market mechanism is unanimity. In an ideal free market resting on private property, no individual can coerce any other, all cooperation is voluntary, all parties to such cooperation benefit or they need not participate. There are no values, no "social" responsibilities in any sense other than the shared values and responsibilities of individuals. Society is a collection of individuals and of the various groups they voluntarily form.

The political principle that underlies the political mechanism is conformity. The indi-vidual must serve a more general social interest–whether that be determined by a church or a dictator or a majority. The individual may have a vote and say in what is to be done, but if he is overruled, he must conform. It is appropriate for some to require others to contribute to a general social purpose whether they wish to or not.

Unfortunately, unanimity is not always feasible. There are some respects in which conformity appears unavoidable, so I do not see how one can avoid the use of the political mechanism altogether.

But the doctrine of "social responsibility" taken seriously would extend the scope of the political mechanism to every human activity. It does not differ in philosophy from the most explicitly collectivist doctrine. It differs only by professing to believe that collectivist ends can be attained without collectivist means. That is why, in my book *Capitalism and Freedom*, I have called it a "fundamentally subversive doctrine" in a free society, and have said that in such a society, "there is one and only one social responsibility of business–to use it resources and engage in activities designed to increase its profits so long as it stays within the rules of the game, which is to say, engages in open and free competition without deception or fraud."

In the wake of recent corporate scandals, it is again time to ask ourselves the most fundamental of questions.

What's a Business For?

by Charles Handy

C OULD CAPITALISTS ACTUALLY bring down capitalism? A writer for the *New York Times* asked that question earlier this year, as the accounting scandals involving big U.S. companies piled up. No, he concluded, probably not. A few rotten apples would not contaminate the whole orchard, the markets would eventually sort the good from the bad, and, in due time, the world would go on much as before.

Not everyone is so complacent. Markets rely on rules and laws, but those rules and laws in turn depend on truth and trust. Conceal truth or erode trust, and the game becomes so unreliable that no one will want to play. The markets will empty and share prices will collapse, as ordinary people find other places to put their money – into their houses, maybe, or under their beds. The great virtue of capitalism – that it provides a way for the savings of society to be used for the creation of wealth – will have been eroded. So we will be left to rely increasingly on governments for the creation of our wealth, something that they have always been conspicuously bad at doing.

Such extreme scenarios might have seemed laughable a few years ago, when the triumph of American-style capitalism appeared self-evident, but no one should be laughing now. In the recent scandals, truth seemed too easily sacrificed to expediency and to the need, as the companies saw it, to reassure the markets that profits were on target. John May, a stock analyst for a U.S. investor service, pointed out that the pro forma earnings announcements by the top 100 NASDAQ companies in the first nine months of 2001 overstated actual audited profits by $100 billion. Even the audited accounts, it now seems, often made things appear better than they really were.

Trust, too, is fragile. Like a piece of china, once cracked it is never quite the same. And people's trust in business, and those who lead it, is today cracking. To many, it seems that executives no longer run their companies for the benefit of consumers, or even of their shareholders and employees, but for their personal ambition and financial gain. A Gallup poll conducted early this year found that 90% of Americans felt that people running corporations could not be trusted to look after the interests of their employees, and only 18% thought

your balance sheet and share price than relying on organic growth and, for those at the top, can be much more interesting. The fact that most mergers and acquisitions do not, in the end, add value has not discouraged many executives from trying.

One result of the obsession with share price is an inevitable shortening of horizons. Paul Kennedy is not alone in believing that companies are mortgaging

that business takes care of itself before it cares for others only fuels the latent distrust.

Europeans continue to look at America with a mix of envy and trepidation. They admire the dynamism, the entrepreneurial energy, and the insistence on everyone's right to chart his or her own life. But they worry now, as they watch their own stock markets follow Wall Street downhill, that the flaws in the American model of capitalism are contagious.

> Few business leaders, thankfully, have been guilty of deliberate fraud or wickedness. All they've been doing is playing the game according to the new rules.

that corporations looked after their shareholders a great deal. Forty-three percent, in fact, believed that senior executives were only in it for themselves. In Britain, that figure, according to another poll, was 95%.

What has gone wrong? It is tempting to blame the people at the top. Keynes once wrote, "Capitalism is the astounding belief that the most wickedest of men will do the most wickedest of things for the greatest good of everyone." Keynes was exaggerating. Personal greed, insufficient scrutiny of corporate affairs, an insensitivity or an indifference to public opinion: Those charges could be leveled against some business leaders, but few, thankfully, have been guilty of deliberate fraud or wickedness. All they've been doing is playing the game according to the new rules.

In the current Anglo-American version of stock market capitalism, the criterion of success is shareholder value, as expressed by a company's share price. There are many ways of influencing share price, of which increasing productivity and long-term profitability is only one. Cutting or postponing expenditures that are geared to the future rather than the present will increase profits immediately even if it imperils them over the long term. Buying and selling businesses is another favored strategy. It is a far quicker way to boost

their futures in return for a higher stock price in the present, but he may be optimistic in sensing the end of the obsession with shareholder value.

The stock option, that new favorite child of stock market capitalism, must also shoulder a large part of the blame. Whereas in 1980 only about 2% of executive pay in the United States was tied to stock options, it is now thought to be more than 60%. Executives, not unnaturally, want to realize their options as soon as they can, rather than relying on the actions of their successors. The stock option has also acquired a new popularity in Europe, as more and more companies go public. To many Europeans, however, hugely undervalued stock options seem like just another way of allowing executives to steal from their companies and their shareholders.

Europeans raise their eyebrows, sometimes in jealousy but more often in outrage, at the levels of executive remuneration under stock market capitalism. Reports that CEOs in America earn more than 400 times the wages of their lowest-paid workers make a mockery of Plato's ideal, in what was, admittedly, a smaller and simpler world, that no person should be worth more than four times another. Why, some wonder, should business executives be rewarded so much better financially than those who serve society in all the other professions? The suspicion, right or wrong,

The American disease is not just a matter of dubious personal ethics or of some rogue companies fudging the odd billion. The country's whole business culture may have become distorted. This was the culture that enraptured America for a generation, a culture underpinned by a doctrine that proclaimed the market king, always gave priority to the shareholder, and believed that business was the key engine of progress and thus should take precedence in policy decisions. It was a heady doctrine that simplified life with its dogma of the bottom line, and during the Thatcher years it infected Britain. It certainly revived the entrepreneurial spirit in that country, but it also contributed to a decline in civic society and to an erosion of the attention and money paid to the nonbusiness sectors of health, education, and transport – a neglect whose effects haunt the current British government.

Continental Europe was always less enthralled by the American model. Stock market capitalism had no place for many of the things that Europeans take for granted as the benefits of citizenship – free health care and quality education for all, housing for the disadvantaged, and a guarantee of reasonable living standards in old age, sickness,

Charles Handy writes on business and management from London. His last article for HBR was "Tocqueville Revisited: The Meaning of American Prosperity" (January 2001). His most recent book is The Elephant and the Flea: Reflections of a Reluctant Capitalist *(Harvard Business School Press, 2002).*

or unemployment. Nevertheless, the accusations from across the Atlantic of a lack of dynamism in Europe, of sclerotic economies bogged down in regulations, and of lackluster management began to hurt, and even on the Continent the American way of business started to take hold. Now, after a series of Europe's own examples of skulduggery at the top and a couple of high-profile corporate collapses due to overambitious acquisition policies, many on the Continent wonder if they've drifted too far toward stock market capitalism.

We can now see, with hindsight, that in the boom years of the 1990s America had often been creating value where none existed, bidding up the market capitalizations of companies to 64 times earnings, or more. And that's far from the country's only problem. The level of indebtedness of U.S. consumers may well be unsustainable, along with the country's debts to foreigners. Add to this the erosion of confidence in the balance sheets and boards of directors of some of the largest U.S. corporations, and the whole system of channeling the savings of citizens into fruitful investments begins to look questionable. That is the contagion that Europe fears.

Capitalist fundamentalism may have lost its sheen, but the urgent need now is to retain the energy produced by the old model while remedying its flaws. Better and tougher regulation would help, as would a clearer separation of auditing from consulting. Corporate governance will now surely be taken more seriously by all concerned, with responsibilities more clearly defined, penalties spelled out, and watchdogs appointed. But these will be plasters on an open sore. They will not cure the disease that lies at the core of the business culture.

We cannot escape the fundamental question, Whom and what is a business for? The answer once seemed clear, but no longer. The terms of business have changed. Ownership has been replaced by investment, and a company's assets are increasingly found in its people,

not in its buildings and machinery. In light of this transformation, we need to rethink our assumptions about the purpose of business. And as we do so, we need to ask whether there are things that American business can learn from Europe, just as there have been valuable lessons that the Europeans have absorbed from the dynamism of the Americans.

Both sides of the Atlantic would agree that there is, first, a clear and important need to meet the expectations of a company's theoretical owners: the shareholders. It would, however, be more accurate to call most of them investors, perhaps even gamblers. They have none of the pride or responsibility of ownership and are, if truth be told, only there for the money. Nevertheless, if management fails to meet their financial hopes, the share price will fall, exposing the company to unwanted predators and making it more difficult to raise new finance. But to turn shareholders' needs into a purpose is to be guilty of a logical confusion, to mistake a necessary condition for a sufficient one. We need to eat to live; food is a necessary condition of life. But if we lived mainly to eat, making food a sufficient or sole purpose of life, we would become gross. The purpose of a business, in other words, is not to make a profit, full stop. It is to make a profit so that the business can do something more or better. That "something" becomes the real justification for the business. Owners know this. Investors needn't care.

To many this will sound like quibbling with words. Not so. It is a moral issue. To mistake the means for the end is to be turned in on oneself, which Saint Augustine called one of the greatest sins. Deep down, the suspicions about capitalism are rooted in a feeling that its instruments, the corporations, are immoral in that they have no purpose other than themselves. To make this assumption may be to do many companies a great injustice, but they have let themselves down through their own rhetoric and behavior. It is salutary to ask about any organization, "If it did not exist, would we invent it?" "Only if it

could do something better or more useful than anyone else" would have to be the answer, and profit would be the means to that larger end.

The idea that those who provide the finance are a company's rightful owners, rather than just its financiers, dates from the early days of business, when the financier was genuinely the owner and usually the chief executive as well. A second and related hangover from earlier times is the idea that a company is a piece of property, subject to the laws of property and ownership. This was true two centuries ago, when corporate law originated and a company consisted of a set of physical assets. Now that the value of a company resides largely in its intellectual property, in its brands and patents and in the skills and experience of its workforce, it seems unreal to treat these things as the property of financiers, to be disposed of as they wish. This may still be the law, but it hardly seems like justice. Surely, those who carry this intellectual property within them, who contribute their time and talents rather than their money, should have some rights, some say in the future of what they also think of as "their" company?

It gets worse. The employees of a company are treated, by the law and the accounts, as the property of the owners and are recorded as costs, not assets. This is demeaning, at the very least. Costs are things to be minimized, assets things to be cherished and grown. The language and the measures of business need to be reversed. A good business is a community with a purpose, and a community is not something to be "owned." A community has members, and those members have certain rights, including the right to vote or express their views on major issues. It is ironic that those countries that boast most stridently about their democratic principles derive their wealth from institutions that are defiantly undemocratic, in which all serious power is held by outsiders and power inside is wielded by a dictatorship or, at best, an oligarchy.

Corporate law in both America and

Britain is out of date. It no longer fits the reality of business in the knowledge economy. Perhaps it didn't even fit business in the industrial era. In 1944 Lord Eustace Percy, in Britain, said this: "Here is the most urgent challenge to political invention ever offered to statesman or jurist. The human association which in fact produces and distributes wealth, the association of workmen, managers, technicians, and directors, is not an association recognized by law. The association which the law does recognize – the association of shareholders, creditors and directors – is incapable of production or distribution and is not expected by the law to perform these functions. We have to give law to the real association and to withdraw meaningless privileges from the imaginary one." Almost 60 years later, the European management writer Arie de Geus argued that companies die because their managers focus on the economic activity of producing goods and services and forget that their organization's true nature is that of a community of people. Nothing, it seems, has changed.

The countries of mainland Europe, however, have always regarded the corporation as a community whose members have legal rights, including, in Germany for instance, the right of the employees to have half, minus one, of the seats on the supervisory board as well as numerous safeguards against dismissal without due cause and an array of statutory benefits. These rights certainly limit the flexibility of management, but they help cultivate a sense of community, generating the feeling of security that makes innovation and experimentation possible and the loyalty and commitment that can see a company through bad times. Shareholders are seen as trustees of the wealth inherited from the past. Their duty is to preserve and, if possible, increase that wealth so that it can be passed on to future generations.

Such an approach is easier for companies on the Continent. Their more closed systems of ownership and greater reliance on long-term bank finance shield them from predators and short-term profit pressures. In most cases, a company's equity capital is concentrated in the hands of other companies, banks, or family networks, with private shareholders owning only a small percentage. Pension funds, too, are neither as large nor as powerful as they are in America and Britain, mainly because European companies keep pensions under their own control, using the funds as working capital. Ownership and governance structures differ from country to country, but in general it can be said that the cult of equity is not as prominent in mainland Europe. As a result, hostile takeovers are difficult and rare, and companies can pay greater heed to the long term and to the needs of constituents other than shareholders.

Countries are shaped by their histories. The Anglo-Saxon nations could not adopt any of the European models even if they wished to. Both cultures, however, need to restore confidence in the wealth-creating possibilities of capitalism and in its instruments, the corporations. In both cultures some things need to change. More honesty and reality in the reporting of results would help, for a start. But when so many of a company's assets are now invisible, and therefore uncountable, and when the webs of alliances, joint ventures, and subcontracting partnerships are so complex, it will never be possible to present a simple financial picture of a major business or to find one number that sums it all up. America's new requirement that chief executives and chief financial officers attest to the truth of their companies' financial statements may concentrate their minds wonderfully, but they can hardly be expected to double-check the work of their accountants and auditors.

If, however, this new requirement pushes accountability for truth telling down the line, some good may result. If a company takes seriously the idea of itself as a wealth-creating community, with members rather than employees, then it will only be sensible for members to validate the results of their work before presenting them to the financiers, who might, in turn, have greater trust in the accuracy of those statements. And if the cult of the stock option wanes with the decline of the stock market and companies decide to reward their key people with a share of the profits instead, then those members will be even more likely to take a keen interest in the truth of the numbers. It seems only fair that dividends be paid to those who contribute their skills as well as to those who have contributed their money. Most of the latter, after all, have not in fact paid any money to the company itself but only to the shares' previous owners.

It may be only a matter of time before such changes come to pass. Already, people whose personal assets are highly valued – bankers, brokers, film actors, sports stars, and the like – make a share of profits, or a bonus, a condition of their employment. Others, such as authors, get all their remuneration from a share of the income stream. This form of performance-related pay, in which the contribution of a single member or group

> The urgent need now is to retain the energy produced by the old model while remedying its flaws.

can be identified, seems bound to grow along with the bargaining power of key talent. We should not ignore the examples of organizations, such as sports teams and publishing houses, whose success has always been tied to the talents of individuals and who, over the years or even the centuries, have had to work out how best to share both the risks and the rewards of innovative work. In the growing world of talent businesses, employees will be increasingly unwilling to sell the fruits of their intellectual assets for an annual salary.

A few small European corporations already distribute a fixed proportion of after-tax profits to the workforce, and these payments become a very tangible expression of members' rights. As the practice spreads, it will make sense to discuss strategies and plans in broad outline with representatives of the members so that they can share in the responsibility for their future earnings. Democracy, of sorts, will have crept in through the pay packet, bringing with it, one hopes, more understanding, more commitment, and more contribution.

Such changes in compensation may help remedy capitalism's democracy deficit, but they won't repair the image of business in the wider community. They might, in fact, be seen as spreading the cult of selfishness a little wider. Two more things need to happen to cure capitalism's current disease – and there are signs that these changes are already under way.

The ancient Hippocratic oath that many doctors swear on graduation includes an injunction to do no harm. Today's anti-globalization protesters claim that global businesses not only do harm, but that the harm outweighs the good. If those charges are to be rebutted, and if business is to restore its reputation as the friend, not the enemy, of progress around the world, then the leaders of those companies need to bind themselves with an equivalent oath. Doing no harm goes beyond meeting the legal requirements regarding the environment, conditions of employment, community relations, and ethics. The law always lags behind best practice. Business needs to take the lead in areas such as environmental and social sustainability instead of forever letting itself be pushed onto the defensive.

John Browne, CEO of BP, the oil giant, is one person who is prepared to do some of the necessary advocacy. In a public lecture broadcast on BBC radio in 2000, he said that the business community is not in opposition to sustainable development but is in fact essential to delivering sustainability, because only business can produce the technological innovations and deliver the means for genuine progress on this front. And busi-

ness needs a sustainable planet for its own survival, for few companies are short-term entities; they want to do business again and again, over decades. Many other business leaders now agree with Browne, and they are beginning

> It seems only fair that dividends be paid to those who contribute their skills as well as to those who have contributed their money.

to shape their actions to fit their words. Some are even finding that there is money to be made from creating the products and services that sustainability requires.

Unfortunately, the majority of companies still see such concepts as sustainability and social responsibility as pursuits that only the rich can afford. For them, the business of business is business and should remain so. If society wants to put more constraints on the way business operates, they argue, it can pass more laws and enforce more regulations. Such a minimalist and legalistic approach leaves business looking like the potential despoiler who must be reined in. And given the legal time lag, the reins may always seem too loose.

In the knowledge economy, sustainability must extend to the human as well as the environmental level. Many people have seen their ability to balance work with the rest of their lives deteriorate steadily, as they fall victim to the stresses of the long-hours culture. An executive life, some worry, is becoming unsustainable in social terms. We are in danger of populating companies with the modern equivalent of monks, people who forgo all else for the sake of their calling. If the contemporary business, with its foundation of human assets, is to survive, it will have to find better ways to protect people from the demands of the jobs it gives them.

Neglecting the environment may drive away customers, but neglecting people's lives may drive away key members of the workforce. Here, again, it would help for companies to see themselves as communities whose members have individual needs as well as individual skills and talents. They are not anonymous human resources.

The European example – with its five-to seven-week annual holidays, legally mandated parental leaves for fathers and mothers together, growing use of sabbaticals for senior executives, and working weeks of fewer than 40 hours – helps promote the idea that long work is not necessarily good work, and that the organization serves its own interests when it protects the overzealous from themselves. Many French companies were surprised that productivity increased when their last government required them to restrict the working week to 35 hours on average (a requirement being repealed by the current government). Europe's approach is one manifestation of the concept of the organization as community. The growing practice of customizing workers' contracts and development plans is another.

More corporate democracy and better corporate behavior will go a long way to improve the current business culture in the eyes of the public, but unless these changes are accompanied by a new vision of the purpose of business, they will be seen as mere palliatives. It is time to raise our sights above the purely pragmatic. Article 14, section 2 of the German constitution states, "Property imposes duties. Its use should also serve the public weal." There is no such clause in the United States Constitution, but the sentiment is echoed in some companies' philosophies. Dave Packard once said, "I think many people assume, wrongly, that a company exists simply to make money. While this is an important result of a company's existence, we have to go deeper and find the real reasons for our being. As we investigate this, we inevitably come to the conclusion that a group of people get together and exist as an institution that we call a company so that they are able to accomplish something collectively that they could not accomplish separately – they make a contribution to society, a phrase which sounds trite but is fundamental."

The contribution ethic has always been a strong motivating force. To survive, even to prosper, is not enough. We hanker to leave a footprint in the sands of time, and if we can do that with the help and companionship of others, so

by the need to provide adequate returns to those who risk their money and their careers, but it is, in itself, a noble cause. We should make more of it. We should, as charitable organizations do, measure success in terms of outcomes for others as well as for ourselves.

George W. Merck, the son of the pharmaceutical company's founder, always insisted that medicine was for the patients, not for the profits. In 1987, in keeping with this core value, his successors

neglected market in the billions of poor in the developing world. Companies like Unilever and Citicorp are beginning to adapt their technologies to enter this market. Unilever can now deliver ice cream in India for just two cents a portion because it has rethought the technology of refrigeration. Citicorp can now provide financial services to people, also in India, who have only $25 to invest, again through rethinking technology. In both cases the companies make money, but the driving force is the need to serve neglected consumers. Profit often comes from progress.

There are more such stories of enlightened business in both American and European companies, but they remain the minority. Until and unless they become the norm, capitalism will continue to be seen as the rich man's game, serving mainly itself and its agents. High-minded talent may start to shun it and customers desert it. Worse, democratic pressures may force governments to shackle corporations, limiting their independence and regulating the smallest details of their operations. And we shall all be the losers. ◘

> We should, as charitable organizations do, measure success in terms of outcomes for others as well as for ourselves.

much the better. We need to associate with a cause in order to give purpose to our lives. The pursuit of a cause does not have to be the prerogative of charities and the not-for-profit sector. Nor does a mission to improve the world make business into a social agency.

By creating new products, spreading technology and raising productivity, enhancing quality and improving service, business has always been the active agent of progress. It helps make the good things of life available and affordable to ever more people. This process is driven by competition and spurred on

decided to give away a drug called Mectizan, which cures river blindness, an affliction in a number of developing countries. The shareholders were probably not consulted, but had they been, many would have been proud to be associated with such a gesture.

Business cannot always afford to be so generous to so many people, but doing good does not necessarily rule out making a reasonable profit. You can, for example, make money by serving the poor as well as the rich. As C.K. Prahalad and Allen Hammond recently pointed out in this magazine, there is a huge

Reprint RO212C

To place an order, call 1-800-988-0886.

HBR.ORG

JANUARY–FEBRUARY 2011
REPRINT R1101C

Harvard Business Review

THE BIG IDEA

Creating Shared Value

How to reinvent capitalism—and unleash a wave of innovation and growth *by Michael E. Porter and Mark R. Kramer*

The Big Idea

Capitalism is under siege.... Diminished
to set policies that sap economic growth....
The purpose of the corporation must be

CREATING SH

trust in business is causing political leaders

Business is caught in a vicious circle....

redefined around

ARED VALUE

How to reinvent capitalism—and unleash a wave of innovation and growth *by Michael E. Porter and Mark R. Kramer*

THE CAPITALIST SYSTEM is under siege. In recent years business increasingly has been viewed as a major cause of social, environmental, and economic problems. Companies are widely perceived to be prospering at the expense of the broader community.

Even worse, the more business has begun to embrace corporate responsibility, the more it has been blamed for society's failures. The legitimacy of business has fallen to levels not seen in recent history. This diminished trust in business leads political leaders to set policies that undermine competitiveness and sap economic growth. Business is caught in a vicious circle.

A big part of the problem lies with companies themselves, which remain trapped in an outdated approach to value creation that has emerged over the past few decades. They continue to view value creation narrowly, optimizing short-term financial performance in a bubble while missing the most important customer needs and ignoring the broader influences that determine their longer-term success. How else could companies overlook the well-being of their customers, the depletion of natural resources vital to their businesses, the viability of key suppliers, or the economic distress of the communities in which they produce and sell? How else could companies think that simply shifting activities to locations with ever lower wages was a sustainable "solution" to competitive challenges? Government and civil society have often exacerbated the problem by attempting to address social weaknesses at the expense of business. The presumed trade-offs between economic efficiency and social progress have been institutionalized in decades of policy choices.

Companies must take the lead in bringing business and society back together. The recognition is there among sophisticated business and thought leaders, and promising elements of a new model are emerging. Yet we still lack an overall framework for guiding these efforts, and most companies remain stuck in a "social responsibility" mind-set in which societal issues are at the periphery, not the core.

The solution lies in the principle of shared value, which involves creating economic value in a way that *also* creates value for society by addressing its needs and challenges. Businesses must reconnect company success with social progress. Shared value is not social responsibility, philanthropy, or even sustainability, but a new way to achieve economic success. It is not on the margin of what companies do but at the center. We believe that it can give rise to the next major transformation of business thinking.

A growing number of companies known for their hard-nosed approach to business—such as GE, Google, IBM, Intel, Johnson & Johnson, Nestlé, Unilever, and Wal-Mart—have already embarked on important efforts to create shared value by reconceiving the intersection between society and corporate performance. Yet our recognition of the transformative power of shared value is still in its genesis. Realizing it will require leaders and managers to develop new skills and knowledge—such as a far deeper appreciation of societal needs, a greater understanding of the true bases of company productivity, and the ability to collaborate across profit/nonprofit boundaries. And government must learn how to regulate in ways that enable shared value rather than work against it.

Capitalism is an unparalleled vehicle for meeting human needs, improving efficiency, creating jobs, and building wealth. But a narrow conception of capitalism has prevented business from harnessing its full potential to meet society's broader challenges. The opportunities have been there all along but have been overlooked. Businesses acting as businesses, not as charitable donors, are the most powerful force for addressing the pressing issues we face. The moment for a new conception of capitalism is now; society's needs are large and growing, while customers, employees, and a new generation of young people are asking business to step up.

The purpose of the corporation must be redefined as creating shared value, not just profit per se. This will drive the next wave of innovation and productivity growth in the global economy. It will also reshape capitalism and its relationship to society. Perhaps most important of all, learning how to create shared value is our best chance to legitimize business again.

Moving Beyond Trade-Offs

Business and society have been pitted against each other for too long. That is in part because economists have legitimized the idea that to provide societal benefits, companies must temper their economic success. In neoclassical thinking, a requirement for social improvement—such as safety or hiring the disabled—imposes a constraint on the corporation. Adding a constraint to a firm that is already maximiz-

Idea in Brief

The concept of shared value—which focuses on the connections between societal and economic progress—has the power to unleash the next wave of global growth.

An increasing number of companies known for their hard-nosed approach to business—such as Google, IBM, Intel, Johnson & Johnson, Nestlé, Unilever, and Wal-Mart—have begun to embark on important shared value initiatives. But our understanding of the potential of shared value is just beginning.

There are three key ways that companies can create shared value opportunities:
- By reconceiving products and markets
- By redefining productivity in the value chain
- By enabling local cluster development

Every firm should look at decisions and opportunities through the lens of shared value. This will lead to new approaches that generate greater innovation and growth for companies—and also greater benefits for society.

Societal needs, not just conventional economic needs, define markets, and social harms can create internal costs for firms.

ing profits, says the theory, will inevitably raise costs and reduce those profits.

A related concept, with the same conclusion, is the notion of externalities. Externalities arise when firms create social costs that they do not have to bear, such as pollution. Thus, society must impose taxes, regulations, and penalties so that firms "internalize" these externalities—a belief influencing many government policy decisions.

This perspective has also shaped the strategies of firms themselves, which have largely excluded social and environmental considerations from their economic thinking. Firms have taken the broader context in which they do business as a given and resisted regulatory standards as invariably contrary to their interests. Solving social problems has been ceded to governments and to NGOs. Corporate responsibility programs—a reaction to external pressure—have emerged largely to improve firms' reputations and are treated as a necessary expense. Anything more is seen by many as an irresponsible use of shareholders' money. Governments, for their part, have often regulated in a way that makes shared value more difficult to achieve. Implicitly, each side has assumed that the other is an obstacle to pursuing its goals and acted accordingly.

The concept of shared value, in contrast, recognizes that societal needs, not just conventional economic needs, define markets. It also recognizes that social harms or weaknesses frequently create *internal* costs for firms—such as wasted energy or raw materials, costly accidents, and the need for remedial training to compensate for inadequa-cies in education. And addressing societal harms and constraints does not necessarily raise costs for firms, because they can innovate through using new technologies, operating methods, and management approaches—and as a result, increase their productivity and expand their markets.

Shared value, then, is not about personal values. Nor is it about "sharing" the value already created by firms—a redistribution approach. Instead, it is about expanding the total pool of economic and social value. A good example of this difference in perspective is the fair trade movement in purchasing. Fair trade aims to increase the proportion of revenue that goes to poor farmers by paying them higher prices for the same crops. Though this may be a noble sentiment, fair trade is mostly about redistribution rather than expanding the overall amount of value created. A shared value perspective, instead, focuses on improving growing techniques and strengthening the local cluster of supporting suppliers and other institutions in order to increase farmers' efficiency, yields, product quality, and sustainability. This leads to a bigger pie of revenue and profits that benefits both farmers and the companies that buy from them. Early studies of cocoa farmers in the Côte d'Ivoire, for instance, suggest that while fair trade can increase farmers' incomes by 10% to 20%, shared value investments can raise their incomes by more than 300%. Initial investment and time may be required to implement new procurement practices and develop the supporting cluster, but the return will be greater economic value and broader strategic benefits for all participants.

The Roots of Shared Value

At a very basic level, the competitiveness of a company and the health of the communities around it are closely intertwined. A business needs a successful community, not only to create demand for its products but also to provide critical public assets and a supportive environment. A community needs successful businesses to provide jobs and wealth creation opportunities for its citizens. This interdependence means that public policies that undermine the productivity and competitiveness of businesses are self-defeating, especially in a global economy where facilities and jobs can easily move elsewhere. NGOs and governments have not always appreciated this connection.

In the old, narrow view of capitalism, business contributes to society by making a profit, which supports employment, wages, purchases, investments, and taxes. Conducting business as usual is sufficient social benefit. A firm is largely a self-contained entity, and social or community issues fall outside its proper scope. (This is the argument advanced persuasively by Milton Friedman in his critique of the whole notion of corporate social responsibility.)

WHAT IS "SHARED VALUE"?

The concept of shared value can be defined as policies and operating practices that enhance the competitiveness of a company while simultaneously advancing the economic and social conditions in the communities in which it operates. Shared value creation focuses on identifying and expanding the connections between societal and economic progress.

The concept rests on the premise that both economic and social progress must be addressed using value principles. Value is defined as benefits relative to costs, not just benefits alone. Value creation is an idea that has long been recognized in business, where profit is revenues earned from customers minus the costs incurred. However, businesses have rarely approached societal issues from a value perspective but have treated them as peripheral matters. This has obscured the connections between economic and social concerns.

In the social sector, thinking in value terms is even less common. Social organizations and government entities often see success solely in terms of the benefits achieved or the money expended. As governments and NGOs begin to think more in value terms, their interest in collaborating with business will inevitably grow.

This perspective has permeated management thinking for the past two decades. Firms focused on enticing consumers to buy more and more of their products. Facing growing competition and shorter-term performance pressures from shareholders, managers resorted to waves of restructuring, personnel reductions, and relocation to lower-cost regions, while leveraging balance sheets to return capital to investors. The results were often commoditization, price competition, little true innovation, slow organic growth, and no clear competitive advantage.

In this kind of competition, the communities in which companies operate perceive little benefit even as profits rise. Instead, they perceive that profits come at their expense, an impression that has become even stronger in the current economic recovery, in which rising earnings have done little to offset high unemployment, local business distress, and severe pressures on community services.

It was not always this way. The best companies once took on a broad range of roles in meeting the needs of workers, communities, and supporting businesses. As other social institutions appeared on the scene, however, these roles fell away or were delegated. Shortening investor time horizons began to narrow thinking about appropriate investments. As the vertically integrated firm gave way to greater reliance on outside vendors, outsourcing and offshoring weakened the connection between firms and their communities. As firms moved disparate activities to more and more locations, they often lost touch with any location. Indeed, many companies no longer recognize a home—but see themselves as "global" companies.

These transformations drove major progress in economic efficiency. However, something profoundly important was lost in the process, as more-fundamental opportunities for value creation were missed. The scope of strategic thinking contracted.

Strategy theory holds that to be successful, a company must create a distinctive value proposition that meets the needs of a chosen set of customers. The firm gains competitive advantage from how it configures the value chain, or the set of activities involved in creating, producing, selling, delivering, and supporting its products or services. For decades businesspeople have studied positioning and the best ways to design activities and integrate them. However, companies have overlooked opportunities to meet fundamental societal needs and misunderstood how societal harms and weaknesses affect value chains. Our field of vision has simply been too narrow.

In understanding the business environment, managers have focused most of their attention on the industry, or the particular business in which the firm competes. This is because industry structure has a decisive impact on a firm's profitability. What has been missed, however, is the profound effect that location can have on productivity and innovation. Companies have failed to grasp the importance of the broader business environment surrounding their major operations.

How Shared Value Is Created

Companies can create economic value by creating societal value. There are three distinct ways to do this: by reconceiving products and markets, redefining productivity in the value chain, and building supportive industry clusters at the company's locations. Each of these is part of the virtuous circle of shared value; improving value in one area gives rise to opportunities in the others.

The concept of shared value resets the boundaries of capitalism. By better connecting companies' success with societal improvement, it opens up many ways to serve new needs, gain efficiency, create differentiation, and expand markets.

The ability to create shared value applies equally to advanced economies and developing countries, though the specific opportunities will differ. The opportunities will also differ markedly across industries and companies—but every company has them. And their range and scope is far broader than has been recognized. *[The idea of shared value was initially explored in a December 2006 HBR article by Michael E. Porter and Mark R. Kramer, "Strategy and Society: The Link Between Competitive Advantage and Corporate Social Responsibility."]*

Reconceiving Products and Markets

Society's needs are huge—health, better housing, improved nutrition, help for the aging, greater financial security, less environmental damage. Arguably, they are the greatest unmet needs in the global economy. In business we have spent decades learning how to parse and manufacture demand while missing the most important demand of all. Too many companies have lost sight of that most basic of questions: Is our product good for our customers? Or for our customers' customers?

In advanced economies, demand for products and services that meet societal needs is rapidly growing. Food companies that traditionally concentrated on taste and quantity to drive more and more consumption are refocusing on the fundamental need for better nutrition. Intel and IBM are both devising ways to help utilities harness digital intelligence in order to economize on power usage. Wells Fargo has developed a line of products and tools that help customers budget, manage credit, and pay down debt. Sales of GE's Ecomagination products reached $18 billion in 2009—the size of a *Fortune* 150 company. GE now predicts that revenues of Ecomagination products will grow at twice the rate of total company revenues over the next five years.

In these and many other ways, whole new avenues for innovation open up, and shared value is created. Society's gains are even greater, because businesses will often be far more effective than governments and nonprofits are at marketing that motivates customers to embrace products and services that create societal benefits, like healthier food or environmentally friendly products.

BLURRING THE PROFIT/NONPROFIT BOUNDARY

The concept of shared value blurs the line between for-profit and nonprofit organizations. New kinds of hybrid enterprises are rapidly appearing. For example, WaterHealth International, a fast-growing for-profit, uses innovative water purification techniques to distribute clean water at minimal cost to more than one million people in rural India, Ghana, and the Philippines. Its investors include not only the socially focused Acumen Fund and the International Finance Corporation of the World Bank but also Dow Chemical's venture fund. Revolution Foods, a four-year-old venture-capital-backed U.S. start-up, provides 60,000 fresh, healthful, and nutritious meals to students daily—and does so at a higher gross margin than traditional competitors. Waste Concern, a hybrid profit/nonprofit enterprise started in Bangladesh 15 years ago, has built the capacity to convert 700 tons of trash, collected daily from neighborhood slums, into organic fertilizer, thereby increasing crop yields and reducing CO_2 emissions. Seeded with capital from the Lions Club and the United Nations Development Programme, the company improves health conditions while earning a substantial gross margin through fertilizer sales and carbon credits.

The blurring of the boundary between successful for-profits and nonprofits is one of the strong signs that creating shared value is possible.

THE CONNECTION BETWEEN COMPETITIVE ADVANTAGE AND SOCIAL ISSUES

There are numerous ways in which addressing societal concerns can yield productivity benefits to a firm. Consider, for example, what happens when a firm invests in a wellness program. Society benefits because employees and their families become healthier, and the firm minimizes employee absences and lost productivity. The graphic below depicts some areas where the connections are strongest.

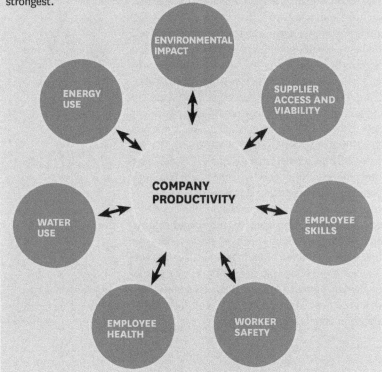

are helping the poor save money securely and transforming the ability of small farmers to produce and market their crops. In Kenya, Vodafone's M-PESA mobile banking service signed up 10 million customers in three years; the funds it handles now represent 11% of that country's GDP. In India, Thomson Reuters has developed a promising monthly service for farmers who earn an average of $2,000 a year. For a fee of $5 a quarter, it provides weather and crop-pricing information and agricultural advice. The service reaches an estimated 2 million farmers, and early research indicates that it has helped increase the incomes of more than 60% of them—in some cases even tripling incomes. As capitalism begins to work in poorer communities, new opportunities for economic development and social progress increase exponentially.

For a company, the starting point for creating this kind of shared value is to identify all the societal needs, benefits, and harms that are or could be embodied in the firm's products. The opportunities are not static; they change constantly as technology evolves, economies develop, and societal priorities shift. An ongoing exploration of societal needs will lead companies to discover new opportunities for differentiation and repositioning in traditional markets, and to recognize the potential of new markets they previously overlooked.

Meeting needs in underserved markets often requires redesigned products or different distribution methods. These requirements can trigger fundamental innovations that also have application in traditional markets. Microfinance, for example, was invented to serve unmet financing needs in developing countries. Now it is growing rapidly in the United States, where it is filling an important gap that was unrecognized.

Redefining Productivity In the Value Chain

A company's value chain inevitably affects—and is affected by—numerous societal issues, such as natural resource and water use, health and safety, working conditions, and equal treatment in the workplace. Opportunities to create shared value arise because societal problems can create economic costs in the firm's value chain. Many so-called externalities actually inflict internal costs on the firm, even in the absence of regulation or resource taxes. Excess packaging of products and greenhouse gases

Equal or greater opportunities arise from serving disadvantaged communities and developing countries. Though societal needs are even more pressing there, these communities have not been recognized as viable markets. Today attention is riveted on India, China, and increasingly, Brazil, which offer firms the prospect of reaching billions of new customers at the bottom of the pyramid—a notion persuasively articulated by C.K. Prahalad. Yet these countries have always had huge needs, as do many developing countries.

Similar opportunities await in nontraditional communities in advanced countries. We have learned, for example, that poor urban areas are America's most underserved market; their substantial concentrated purchasing power has often been overlooked. (See the research of the Initiative for a Competitive Inner City, at icic.org.)

The societal benefits of providing appropriate products to lower-income and disadvantaged consumers can be profound, while the profits for companies can be substantial. For example, low-priced cell phones that provide mobile banking services

By reducing its packaging and cutting 100 million miles from the delivery routes of its trucks, Wal-Mart lowered carbon emissions and saved $200 million in costs.

are not just costly to the environment but costly to the business. Wal-Mart, for example, was able to address both issues by reducing its packaging and rerouting its trucks to cut 100 million miles from its delivery routes in 2009, saving $200 million even as it shipped more products. Innovation in disposing of plastic used in stores has saved millions in lower disposal costs to landfills.

The new thinking reveals that the congruence between societal progress and productivity in the value chain is far greater than traditionally believed (see the exhibit "The Connection Between Competitive Advantage and Social Issues"). The synergy increases when firms approach societal issues from a shared value perspective and invent new ways of operating to address them. So far, however, few companies have reaped the full productivity benefits in areas such as health, safety, environmental performance, and employee retention and capability.

But there are unmistakable signs of change. Efforts to minimize pollution were once thought to inevitably increase business costs—and to occur only because of regulation and taxes. Today there is a growing consensus that major improvements in environmental performance can often be achieved with better technology at nominal incremental cost and can even yield net cost savings through enhanced resource utilization, process efficiency, and quality.

In each of the areas in the exhibit, a deeper understanding of productivity and a growing awareness of the fallacy of short-term cost reductions (which often actually lower productivity or make it unsustainable) are giving rise to new approaches. The following are some of the most important ways in which shared value thinking is transforming the value chain, which are not independent but often mutually reinforcing. Efforts in these and other areas are still works in process, whose implications will be felt for years to come.

Energy use and logistics. The use of energy throughout the value chain is being reexamined, whether it be in processes, transportation, buildings, supply chains, distribution channels, or support ser-

vices. Triggered by energy price spikes and a new awareness of opportunities for energy efficiency, this reexamination was under way even before carbon emissions became a global focus. The result has been striking improvements in energy utilization through better technology, recycling, cogeneration, and numerous other practices—all of which create shared value.

We are learning that shipping is expensive, not just because of energy costs and emissions but because it adds time, complexity, inventory costs, and management costs. Logistical systems are beginning to be redesigned to reduce shipping distances, streamline handling, improve vehicle routing, and the like. All of these steps create shared value. The British retailer Marks & Spencer's ambitious overhaul of its supply chain, for example, which involves steps as simple as stopping the purchase of supplies from one hemisphere to ship to another, is expected to save the retailer £175 million annually by fiscal 2016, while hugely reducing carbon emissions. In the process of reexamining logistics, thinking about outsourcing and location will also be revised (as we will discuss below).

Resource use. Heightened environmental awareness and advances in technology are catalyzing new approaches in areas such as utilization of water, raw materials, and packaging, as well as expanding recycling and reuse. The opportunities apply to all resources, not just those that have been identified by environmentalists. Better resource utilization—enabled by improving technology—will permeate all parts of the value chain and will spread to suppliers and channels. Landfills will fill more slowly.

For example, Coca-Cola has already reduced its worldwide water consumption by 9% from a 2004 baseline—nearly halfway to its goal of a 20% reduction by 2012. Dow Chemical managed to reduce consumption of fresh water at its largest production site by one billion gallons—enough water to supply nearly 40,000 people in the U.S. for a year—resulting in savings of $4 million. The demand for water-saving technology has allowed India's Jain Irrigation, a leading global manufacturer of complete drip irrigation systems for water conservation, to achieve a 41% compound annual growth rate in revenue over the past five years.

Procurement. The traditional playbook calls for companies to commoditize and exert maximum bargaining power on suppliers to drive down prices—even when purchasing from small businesses or subsistence-level farmers. More recently, firms have been rapidly outsourcing to suppliers in lower-wage locations.

Today some companies are beginning to understand that marginalized suppliers cannot remain productive or sustain, much less improve, their quality. By increasing access to inputs, sharing technology, and providing financing, companies can improve supplier quality and productivity while ensuring access to growing volume. Improving productivity will often trump lower prices. As suppliers get stronger, their environmental impact often falls dramatically, which further improves their efficiency. Shared value is created.

A good example of such new procurement thinking can be found at Nespresso, one of Nestlé's fastest-growing divisions, which has enjoyed annual growth of 30% since 2000. Nespresso combines a sophisticated espresso machine with single-cup aluminum capsules containing ground coffees from around the world. Offering quality and convenience, Nespresso has expanded the market for premium coffee.

THE ROLE OF SOCIAL ENTREPRENEURS

Businesses are not the only players in finding profitable solutions to social problems. A whole generation of social entrepreneurs is pioneering new product concepts that meet social needs using viable business models. Because they are not locked into narrow traditional business thinking, social entrepreneurs are often well ahead of established corporations in discovering these opportunities. Social enterprises that create shared value can scale up far more rapidly than purely social programs, which often suffer from an inability to grow and become self-sustaining.

Real social entrepreneurship should be measured by its ability to create shared value, not just social benefit.

Obtaining a reliable supply of specialized coffees is extremely challenging, however. Most coffees are grown by small farmers in impoverished rural areas of Africa and Latin America, who are trapped in a cycle of low productivity, poor quality, and environmental degradation that limits production volume. To address these issues, Nestlé redesigned procurement. It worked intensively with its growers, providing advice on farming practices, guaranteeing bank loans, and helping secure inputs such as plant stock, pesticides, and fertilizers. Nestlé established local facilities to measure the quality of the coffee at the point of purchase, which allowed it to pay a premium for better beans directly to the growers and thus improve their incentives. Greater yield per hectare and higher production quality increased growers' incomes, and the environmental impact of farms shrank. Meanwhile, Nestlé's reliable supply of good coffee grew significantly. Shared value was created.

Embedded in the Nestlé example is a far broader insight, which is the advantage of buying from capable local suppliers. Outsourcing to other locations and countries creates transaction costs and inefficiencies that can offset lower wage and input costs. Capable local suppliers help firms avoid these costs and can reduce cycle time, increase flexibility, foster faster learning, and enable innovation. Buying local includes not only local companies but also local units of national or international companies. When firms buy locally, their suppliers can get stronger, increase their profits, hire more people, and pay better wages—all of which will benefit other businesses in the community. Shared value is created.

Distribution. Companies are beginning to re-examine distribution practices from a shared value perspective. As iTunes, Kindle, and Google Scholar (which offers texts of scholarly literature online) demonstrate, profitable new distribution models can also dramatically reduce paper and plastic usage. Similarly, microfinance has created a cost-efficient new model of distributing financial services to small businesses.

Opportunities for new distribution models can be even greater in nontraditional markets. For example, Hindustan Unilever is creating a new direct-to-home distribution system, run by underprivileged female entrepreneurs, in Indian villages of fewer than 2,000 people. Unilever provides microcredit and training and now has more than 45,000 entrepreneurs covering some 100,000 villages

By investing in employee wellness programs, Johnson & Johnson has saved $250 million on health care costs.

across 15 Indian states. Project Shakti, as this distribution system is called, benefits communities not only by giving women skills that often double their household income but also by reducing the spread of communicable diseases through increased access to hygiene products. This is a good example of how the unique ability of business to market to hard-to-reach consumers can benefit society by getting life-altering products into the hands of people that need them. Project Shakti now accounts for 5% of Unilever's total revenues in India and has extended the company's reach into rural areas and built its brand in media-dark regions, creating major economic value for the company.

Employee productivity. The focus on holding down wage levels, reducing benefits, and offshoring is beginning to give way to an awareness of the positive effects that a living wage, safety, wellness, training, and opportunities for advancement for employees have on productivity. Many companies, for example, traditionally sought to minimize the cost of "expensive" employee health care coverage or even eliminate health coverage altogether. Today leading companies have learned that because of lost workdays and diminished employee productivity, poor health costs them more than health benefits do. Take Johnson & Johnson. By helping employees stop smoking (a two-thirds reduction in the past 15 years) and implementing numerous other wellness programs, the company has saved $250 million on health care costs, a return of $2.71 for every dollar spent on wellness from 2002 to 2008. Moreover, Johnson & Johnson has benefited from a more present and productive workforce. If labor unions focused more on shared value, too, these kinds of employee approaches would spread even faster.

Location. Business thinking has embraced the myth that location no longer matters, because logistics are inexpensive, information flows rapidly, and markets are global. The cheaper the location, then, the better. Concern about the local communities in which a company operates has faded.

That oversimplified thinking is now being challenged, partly by the rising costs of energy and car-

bon emissions but also by a greater recognition of the productivity cost of highly dispersed production systems and the hidden costs of distant procurement discussed earlier. Wal-Mart, for example, is increasingly sourcing produce for its food sections from local farms near its warehouses. It has discovered that the savings on transportation costs and the ability to restock in smaller quantities more than offset the lower prices of industrial farms farther away. Nestlé is establishing smaller plants closer to its markets and stepping up efforts to maximize the use of locally available materials.

The calculus of locating activities in developing countries is also changing. Olam International, a leading cashew producer, traditionally shipped its nuts from Africa to Asia for processing at facilities staffed by productive Asian workers. But by opening local processing plants and training workers in Tanzania, Mozambique, Nigeria, and Côte d'Ivoire, Olam has cut processing and shipping costs by as much as 25%—not to mention, greatly reduced carbon emissions. In making this move, Olam also built preferred relationships with local farmers. And it has provided direct employment to 17,000 people—95% of whom are women—and indirect employment to an equal number of people, in rural areas where jobs otherwise were not available.

These trends may well lead companies to remake their value chains by moving some activities closer to home and having fewer major production locations. Until now, many companies have thought that being global meant moving production to locations with the lowest labor costs and designing their supply chains to achieve the most immediate impact on expenses. In reality, the strongest international competitors will often be those that can establish deeper roots in important communities. Companies that can embrace this new locational thinking will create shared value.

AS THESE examples illustrate, reimagining value chains from the perspective of shared value will offer significant new ways to innovate and unlock new economic value that most businesses have missed.

Enabling Local Cluster Development

No company is self-contained. The success of every company is affected by the supporting companies and infrastructure around it. Productivity and innovation are strongly influenced by "clusters," or geographic concentrations of firms, related businesses, suppliers, service providers, and logistical infrastructure in a particular field—such as IT in Silicon Valley, cut flowers in Kenya, and diamond cutting in Surat, India.

Clusters include not only businesses but institutions such as academic programs, trade associations, and standards organizations. They also draw on the broader public assets in the surrounding community, such as schools and universities, clean water, fair-competition laws, quality standards, and market transparency.

Clusters are prominent in all successful and growing regional economies and play a crucial role in driving productivity, innovation, and competitiveness. Capable local suppliers foster greater logistical efficiency and ease of collaboration, as we have discussed. Stronger local capabilities in such areas as training, transportation services, and related industries also boost productivity. Without a supporting cluster, conversely, productivity suffers.

Deficiencies in the framework conditions surrounding the cluster also create internal costs for firms. Poor public education imposes productivity and remedial-training costs. Poor transportation infrastructure drives up the costs of logistics. Gender or racial discrimination reduces the pool of capable employees. Poverty limits the demand for products and leads to environmental degradation, unhealthy workers, and high security costs. As companies have increasingly become disconnected from their communities, however, their influence in solving these problems has waned even as their costs have grown.

Firms create shared value by building clusters to improve company productivity while addressing gaps or failures in the framework conditions surrounding the cluster. Efforts to develop or attract capable suppliers, for example, enable the procurement benefits we discussed earlier. A focus on clusters and location has been all but absent in management thinking. Cluster thinking has also been

Creating Shared Value: Implications for Government and

While our focus here is primarily on companies, the principles of shared value apply equally to governments and nonprofit organizations.

Governments and NGOs will be most effective if they think in value terms—considering benefits relative to costs—and focus on the results achieved rather than the funds and effort expended. Activists have tended to approach social improvement from an ideological or absolutist perspective, as if social benefits should be pursued at any cost. Governments and NGOs often assume that trade-offs between economic and social benefits are inevitable, exacerbating these trade-offs through their approaches. For example, much environmental regulation still takes the form of command-and-control mandates and enforcement actions designed to embarrass and punish companies.

Regulators would accomplish much more by focusing on measuring environmental performance and introducing standards, phase-in periods, and support for technology that would promote innovation, improve the environment, and increase competitiveness simultaneously.

The principle of shared value creation cuts across the traditional divide between the responsibilities of business and those of government or civil society. From society's perspective, it does not matter what types of organizations created the value. What matters is that benefits are delivered by those organizations—or combinations of organizations—that are best positioned to achieve the most impact for the least cost. Finding ways to boost productivity is equally valuable whether in the service of commercial or societal objectives. In short, the principle of value creation should guide the use of resources across all areas of societal concern.

Fortunately, a new type of NGO has emerged that understands the importance of productivity and value creation. Such organizations have often had a remarkable impact. One example is TechnoServe, which has partnered with both regional and global corporations to promote the development of competitive agricultural clusters in more than 30 countries. Root Capital accomplishes a similar objective by providing financing to farmers and businesses that are too large for microfinance but too small for normal bank financing. Since 2000, Root Capital has lent more than $200 million to 282 businesses,

missing in many economic development initiatives, which have failed because they involved isolated interventions and overlooked critical complementary investments.

A key aspect of cluster building in developing and developed countries alike is the formation of open and transparent markets. In inefficient or monopolized markets where workers are exploited, where suppliers do not receive fair prices, and where price transparency is lacking, productivity suffers. Enabling fair and open markets, which is often best done in conjunction with partners, can allow a company to secure reliable supplies and give suppliers better incentives for quality and efficiency while also substantially improving the incomes and purchasing power of local citizens. A positive cycle of economic and social development results.

When a firm builds clusters in its key locations, it also amplifies the connection between its success and its communities' success. A firm's growth has multiplier effects, as jobs are created in supporting industries, new companies are seeded, and demand for ancillary services rises. A company's efforts to improve framework conditions for the cluster spill over to other participants and the local economy. Workforce development initiatives, for example, increase the supply of skilled employees for many other firms as well.

At Nespresso, Nestlé also worked to build clusters, which made its new procurement practices far more effective. It set out to build agricultural, technical, financial, and logistical firms and capabilities in each coffee region, to further support efficiency and high-quality local production. Nestlé led efforts to increase access to essential agricultural inputs such as plant stock, fertilizers, and irrigation equipment; strengthen regional farmer co-ops by helping them finance shared wet-milling facilities for producing higher-quality beans; and support an extension program to advise all farmers on growing techniques. It also worked in partnership with the Rainforest Alliance, a leading international NGO, to teach farmers more-sustainable practices that make production volumes more reliable. In the process, Nestlé's productivity improved.

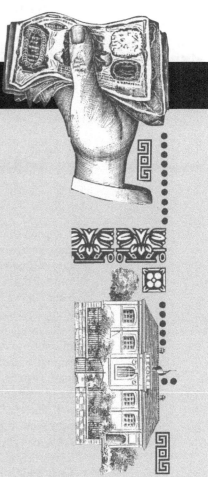

Civil Society

through which it has reached 400,000 farmers and artisans. It has financed the cultivation of 1.4 million acres of organic agriculture in Latin America and Africa. Root Capital regularly works with corporations, utilizing future purchase orders as collateral for its loans to farmers and helping to strengthen corporate supply chains and improve the quality of purchased inputs.

Some private foundations have begun to see the power of working with businesses to create shared value. The Bill & Melinda Gates Foundation, for example, has formed partnerships with leading global corporations to foster agricultural clusters in developing countries. The foundation carefully focuses on commodities where climate and soil conditions give a particular region a true competitive advantage. The partnerships bring in NGOs like TechnoServe and Root Capital,

as well as government officials, to work on precompetitive issues that improve the cluster and upgrade the value chain for all participants. This approach recognizes that helping small farmers increase their yields will not create any lasting benefits unless there are ready buyers for their crops, other enterprises that can process the crops once they are harvested, and a local cluster that includes efficient logistical infrastructure, input availability, and the like. The active engagement of corporations is essential to mobilizing these elements.

Forward-thinking foundations can also serve as honest brokers and allay fears by mitigating power imbalances between small local enterprises, NGOs, governments, and companies. Such efforts will require a new assumption that shared value can come only as a result of effective collaboration among all parties.

Government Regulation and Shared Value

The right kind of government regulation can encourage companies to pursue shared value; the wrong kind works against it and even makes trade-offs between economic and social goals inevitable.

Regulation is necessary for well-functioning markets, something that became abundantly clear during the recent financial crisis. However, the ways in which regulations are designed and implemented determine whether they benefit society or work against it.

Regulations that enhance shared value set goals and stimulate innovation. They highlight a societal objective and create a level playing field to encourage companies to invest in shared value rather than maximize short-term profit. Such regulations have a number of characteristics:

First, they set clear and measurable social goals, whether they involve energy use, health matters, or safety. Where appropriate, they set prices for resources (such as water) that reflect true costs. Second,

they set performance standards but do not prescribe the methods to achieve them—those are left to companies. Third, they define phase-in periods for meeting standards, which reflect the investment or new-product cycle in the industry. Phase-in periods give companies time to develop and introduce new products and processes in a way consistent with the economics of their business. Fourth, they put in place universal measurement and performance-reporting systems, with government investing in infrastructure for collecting reliable benchmarking data (such as nutritional deficiencies in each community). This motivates and enables continual improvement beyond current targets. Finally, appropriate regulations require efficient and timely reporting of results, which can then be audited by the government as necessary, rather than impose

detailed and expensive compliance processes on everyone.

Regulation that discourages shared value looks very different. It forces compliance with particular practices, rather than focusing on measurable social improvement. It mandates a particular approach to meeting a standard—blocking innovation and almost always inflicting cost on companies. When governments fall into the trap of this sort of regulation, they undermine the very progress that they seek while triggering fierce resistance from business that slows progress further and blocks shared value that would improve competitiveness.

To be sure, companies locked into the old mind-set will resist even well-constructed regulation. As shared value principles become more widely accepted, however, business and government will become more aligned on regulation in many areas. Companies will come to understand that the right kind of regulation can actually foster economic value creation.

Finally, regulation will be needed to limit the pursuit of exploitative, unfair, or deceptive practices in which companies benefit at the expense of society. Strict antitrust policy, for example, is essential to ensure that the benefits of company success flow to customers, suppliers, and workers.

A good example of a company working to improve framework conditions in its cluster is Yara, the world's largest mineral fertilizer company. Yara realized that the lack of logistical infrastructure in many parts of Africa was preventing farmers from gaining efficient access to fertilizers and other essential agricultural inputs, and from transporting their crops efficiently to market. Yara is tackling this problem through a $60 million investment in a program to improve ports and roads, which is designed to create agricultural growth corridors in Mozambique and Tanzania. The company is working on this initiative with local governments and support from the Norwegian government. In Mozambique alone, the corridor is expected to benefit more than 200,000 small farmers and create 350,000 new jobs. The im-

provements will help Yara grow its business but will support the whole agricultural cluster, creating huge multiplier effects.

The benefits of cluster building apply not only in emerging economies but also in advanced countries. North Carolina's Research Triangle is a notable example of public and private collaboration that has created shared value by developing clusters in such areas as information technology and life sciences. That region, which has benefited from continued investment from both the private sector and local government, has experienced huge growth in employment, incomes, and company performance, and has fared better than most during the downturn.

To support cluster development in the communities in which they operate, companies need to identify gaps and deficiencies in areas such as logistics, suppliers, distribution channels, training, market organization, and educational institutions. Then the task is to focus on the weaknesses that represent the greatest constraints to the company's own productivity and growth, and distinguish those areas that the company is best equipped to influence directly from those in which collaboration is more cost-effective. Here is where the shared value opportunities will be greatest. Initiatives that address cluster weaknesses that constrain companies will be much more effective than community-focused corporate social responsibility programs, which often have

ternal influences on corporate success. It highlights the immense human needs to be met, the large new markets to serve, and the internal costs of social and community deficits—as well as the competitive advantages available from addressing them. Until recently, companies have simply not approached their businesses this way.

Creating shared value will be more effective and far more sustainable than the majority of today's corporate efforts in the social arena. Companies will make real strides on the environment, for example, when they treat it as a productivity driver rather than a feel-good response to external pressure. Or consider

Not all profit is equal. Profits involving a social purpose represent a higher form of capitalism, one that creates a positive cycle of company and community prosperity.

limited impact because they take on too many areas without focusing on value.

But efforts to enhance infrastructure and institutions in a region often require collective action, as the Nestlé, Yara, and Research Triangle examples show. Companies should try to enlist partners to share the cost, win support, and assemble the right skills. The most successful cluster development programs are ones that involve collaboration within the private sector, as well as trade associations, government agencies, and NGOs.

Creating Shared Value in Practice

Not all profit is equal—an idea that has been lost in the narrow, short-term focus of financial markets and in much management thinking. Profits involving a social purpose represent a higher form of capitalism—one that will enable society to advance more rapidly while allowing companies to grow even more. The result is a positive cycle of company and community prosperity, which leads to profits that endure.

Creating shared value presumes compliance with the law and ethical standards, as well as mitigating any harm caused by the business, but goes far beyond that. The opportunity to create economic value through creating societal value will be one of the most powerful forces driving growth in the global economy. This thinking represents a new way of understanding customers, productivity, and the ex-

access to housing. A shared value approach would have led financial services companies to create innovative products that prudently increased access to home ownership. This was recognized by the Mexican construction company Urbi, which pioneered a mortgage-financing "rent-to-own" plan. Major U.S. banks, in contrast, promoted unsustainable financing vehicles that turned out to be socially and economically devastating, while claiming they were socially responsible because they had charitable contribution programs.

Inevitably, the most fertile opportunities for creating shared value will be closely related to a company's particular business, and in areas most important to the business. Here a company can benefit the most economically and hence sustain its commitment over time. Here is also where a company brings the most resources to bear, and where its scale and market presence equip it to have a meaningful impact on a societal problem.

Ironically, many of the shared value pioneers have been those with more-limited resources—social entrepreneurs and companies in developing countries. These outsiders have been able to see the opportunities more clearly. In the process, the distinction between for-profits and nonprofits is blurring.

Shared value is defining a whole new set of best practices that all companies must embrace. It will also become an integral part of strategy. The essence of strategy is choosing a unique positioning and a distinctive value chain to deliver on it. Shared value opens up many new needs to meet, new products to offer, new customers to serve, and new ways to configure the value chain. And the competitive advantages that arise from creating shared value will often be more sustainable than conventional cost and quality improvements. The cycle of imitation and zero-sum competition can be broken.

The opportunities to create shared value are widespread and growing. Not every company will have them in every area, but our experience has been that companies discover more and more opportunities over time as their line operating units grasp this concept. It has taken a decade, but GE's Ecomagination initiative, for example, is now producing a stream of fast-growing products and services across the company.

A shared value lens can be applied to every major company decision. Could our product design incorporate greater social benefits? Are we serving all the communities that would benefit from our products? Do our processes and logistical approaches maximize efficiencies in energy and water use? Could our new plant be constructed in a way that achieves greater community impact? How are gaps in our cluster holding back our efficiency and speed of innovation? How could we enhance our community a a business location? If sites are comparable economically, at which one will the local community benefit the most? If a company can improve societal conditions, it will often improve business conditions and thereby trigger positive feedback loops.

The three avenues for creating shared value are mutually reinforcing. Enhancing the cluster, for example, will enable more local procurement and less dispersed supply chains. New products and services that meet social needs or serve overlooked markets will require new value chain choices in areas such as production, marketing, and distribution. And new value chain configurations will create demand for equipment and technology that save energy, conserve resources, and support employees.

Creating shared value will require concrete and tailored metrics for each business unit in each of the three areas. While some companies have begun to track various social impacts, few have yet tied them to their economic interests at the business level.

Shared value creation will involve new and heightened forms of collaboration. While some shared value opportunities are possible for a company to seize on its own, others will benefit from insights, skills, and resources that cut across profit nonprofit and private/public boundaries. Here companies will be less successful if they attempt to tackle societal problems on their own, especially those involving cluster development. Major competitors may also need to work together on precompetitive framework conditions, something that has not been common in reputation-driven CSR initiatives. Successful collaboration will be data driven, clearly linked to defined outcomes, well connected to the goals of all stakeholders, and tracked with clear metrics.

Governments and NGOs can enable and reinforce shared value or work against it. (For more on this

HOW SHARED VALUE DIFFERS FROM CORPORATE SOCIAL RESPONSIBILITY

Creating shared value (CSV) should supersede corporate social responsibility (CSR) in guiding the investments of companies in their communities. CSR programs focus mostly on reputation and have only a limited connection to the business, making them hard to justify and maintain over the long run. In contrast, CSV is integral to a company's profitability and competitive position. It leverages the unique resources and expertise of the company to create economic value by creating social value.

CSR → CSV

CSR	CSV
Value: doing good	Value: economic and societal benefits relative to cost
Citizenship, philanthropy, sustainability	Joint company and community value creation
Discretionary or in response to external pressure	Integral to competing
Separate from profit maximization	Integral to profit maximization
Agenda is determined by external reporting and personal preferences	Agenda is company specific and internally generated
Impact limited by corporate footprint and CSR budget	Realigns the entire company budget
Example: Fair trade purchasing	Example: Transforming procurement to increase quality and yield

In both cases, compliance with laws and ethical standards and reducing harm from corporate activities are assumed.

topic, see the sidebar "Government Regulation and Shared Value.")

The Next Evolution in Capitalism

Shared value holds the key to unlocking the next wave of business innovation and growth. It will also reconnect company success and community success in ways that have been lost in an age of narrow management approaches, short-term thinking, and deepening divides among society's institutions.

Shared value focuses companies on the right kind of profits—profits that create societal benefits rather than diminish them. Capital markets will undoubtedly continue to pressure companies to generate short-term profits, and some companies will surely continue to reap profits at the expense of societal needs. But such profits will often prove to be short-lived, and far greater opportunities will be missed.

The moment for an expanded view of value creation has come. A host of factors, such as the growing social awareness of employees and citizens and the increased scarcity of natural resources, will drive unprecedented opportunities to create shared value.

We need a more sophisticated form of capitalism, one imbued with a social purpose. But that purpose should arise not out of charity but out of a deeper understanding of competition and economic value creation. This next evolution in the capitalist model recognizes new and better ways to develop products, serve markets, and build productive enterprises.

Creating shared value represents a broader conception of Adam Smith's invisible hand. It opens the doors of the pin factory to a wider set of influences. It is not philanthropy but self-interested behavior to create economic value by creating societal value. If all companies individually pursued shared value connected to their particular businesses, society's overall interests would be served. And companies would acquire legitimacy in the eyes of the communities in which they operated, which would allow democracy to work as governments set policies that fostered and supported business. Survival of the fittest would still prevail, but market competition would benefit society in ways we have lost.

Creating shared value represents a new approach to managing that cuts across disciplines. Because of the traditional divide between economic concerns and social ones, people in the public and private sectors have often followed very different educational and career paths. As a result, few managers have the understanding of social and environmental issues required to move beyond today's CSR approaches, and few social sector leaders have the managerial training and entrepreneurial mind-set needed to design and implement shared value models. Most business schools still teach the narrow view of capitalism, even though more and more of their graduates hunger for a greater sense of purpose and a growing number are drawn to social entrepreneurship. The results have been missed opportunity and public cynicism.

Business school curricula will need to broaden in a number of areas. For example, the efficient use and stewardship of all forms of resources will define the next-generation thinking on value chains. Customer behavior and marketing courses will have to move beyond persuasion and demand creation to the study of deeper human needs and how to serve nontraditional customer groups. Clusters, and the broader locational influences on company productivity and innovation, will form a new core discipline in business schools; economic development will no longer be left only to public policy and economics departments. Business and government courses will examine the economic impact of societal factors on enterprises, moving beyond the effects of regulation and macroeconomics. And finance will need to rethink how capital markets can actually support true value creation in companies—their fundamental purpose—not just benefit financial market participants.

There is nothing soft about the concept of shared value. These proposed changes in business school curricula are not qualitative and do not depart from economic value creation. Instead, they represent the next stage in our understanding of markets, competition, and business management.

NOT ALL societal problems can be solved through shared value solutions. But shared value offers corporations the opportunity to utilize their skills, resources, and management capability to lead social progress in ways that even the best-intentioned governmental and social sector organizations can rarely match. In the process, businesses can earn the respect of society again. ▄

HBR Reprint R1101C

Michael E. Porter is the Bishop William Lawrence University Professor at Harvard University. He is a frequent contributor to *Harvard Business Review* and a six-time McKinsey Award winner. **Mark R. Kramer** cofounded FSG, a global social impact consulting firm, with Professor Porter and is its managing director. He is also a senior fellow of the CSR initiative at Harvard's Kennedy School of Government.

E X C H A N G E

How Can Organizations Be Competitive but Dare to Care?

by Andrew Delios

Executive Overview

The issue of social responsibility, manifested as an organization's caring efforts for its employees and the environment, has considerable importance in business practice and research. Although there is a ground-swell of interest supporting organizations that dare to care, the bounds of what it means to care, especially the organizational implications of caring, have yet to be established. In this exchange, I argue that it is certainly within the responsibility of an organization's leaders to develop socially responsible practices, but the nature of industry and the institutional environments in which organizations exist jeopardize the competitiveness of organizations that implement such practices. Further, globalization amplifies the economic risks to the organizations that dare to care. Organizational leaders thus need to proactively change the nature of their competitive environment to one more supportive of social responsibility. Organizational leaders can do so through their influence on policy makers and other organizations that shape the formal and informal norms of business practices across world regions.

Many people believe that organizations have the imperative to care for society. Others take the approach of Ahlstrom (2010) in this issue, who argues that organizations are charged solely with the task of providing jobs for their employees. Ahlstrom argues that if organizations provide a good working environment, employees will generate innovations that can lead to growth. Economic growth leads to wealth creation, which presumably spreads benefits throughout society, thereby leading to improved welfare for all. Yet there is an important limiting assumption to this argument. Ahlstrom implicitly assumes that the sole economic environment in which a firm is enmeshed is the one related to its internal organization.

This assumption, that organizations are tasked only with providing jobs for their employees, has its roots in classic works in management. In the early part of the 20th century, for example, Barnard (1938) wrote that a firm is an efficient means of organizing activities that are too large in scope for an individual to do efficiently by himself. Organizations are, therefore, economic entities that perform a set of functions more effectively in a hierarchy than through market-mediated transactions between firms (Williamson, 1975). Hence, the relationship between employees and the organization should be entirely transactional and nothing more.

In this view, the organization is but a nexus of contracts between the individuals in the firm (Jensen & Meckling, 1976). From this perspective, one can argue that given a set of appropriate incentives, organizational structures, and task definitions, an organization will fulfill its fundamental task of providing jobs and in so doing,

---

I thank Garry Bruton, Joep Cornelissen, Jane Lu, and Steve Floyd for helpful comments and Yu Shu for excellent and timely research assistance.

* **Andrew Delios** (andrew@nus.edu.sg) is Professor at the National University of Singapore.

be socially responsible by contributing to wealth creation. Yet this argument, and by extension Ahlstrom's, is missing two important points. It ignores the external environmental forces on an organization and it ignores the fact that organizations are social entities, populated by real communities of people. As such, an economics-based view on markets and organizations is an incomplete and undersocialized one (Granovetter, 1985).

More specifically, Ahlstrom's argument ignores the fundamental fact that wealth creation does not equate to equitable wealth distribution. Economic growth can lead to wealth creation, but informal and formal norms in a society dictate how that wealth is distributed. Ahlstrom's argument misses the point that wealth distribution from organizations to society is a function of bargaining between stakeholders, and it is related to the incentives and stresses placed on an organization by the structure of the industry in which it operates.

In addition, Ahlstrom's argument ignores the fact that organizations are a dominant social institution enmeshed in broad industry and institutional environments. Beyond providing economic opportunities for their employees and contributing to the general welfare of society through wealth creation, organizations are also social entities and, some might argue, among the dominant institutions in many countries worldwide. It follows that organizations are a focal point for an employee's life, extending far beyond the exchange of labor for pay. As such, organizations have a responsibility to their stakeholders, particularly their employees, that extends beyond the provision of a fair day's wages for a fair day's work.

This responsibility is often reflected in calls for organizations to be more socially responsible to both their internal and external stakeholders, which fundamentally relates to questions about how wealth that is created in an organization is distributed to society. Although such calls are laudable and planted in solid ethical ground, an organization's leaders, however enlightened and empathetic, must be responsive to the competitive forces emanating from their industry and institutional environments. An organization's leaders cannot ignore the competitive imperatives that underlie an organization's ability to continue to exist. Developments in the world economy through the 1990s and 2000s have heightened levels of competition to the detriment of the very social benefits, through equitable wealth distribution, that can be provided by an organization to its employees. Organizations have tended to be passive as heightened competition has eroded social benefits. At the same time, organizations have been quite active in lobbying and influencing policy makers to improve the economic largesse, garnered through tax holidays or other fiscal incentives, that can be received when investing in a particular market.

My contention is that organizational leaders need to shift the direction of their activism if they truly want to create and sustain socially responsible and caring organizations. Through their interactions with national-level policy makers, influential individuals, and not-for-profit organizations, business leaders need to be deeply and proactively concerned with creating an environment of formal and informal norms that promotes a harmonization in cross-national standards for levels of social responsibility. Rather than being effective arbitragers of markets, if an organization's leaders truly aspire to clear rhetorical hurdles to caring, they will seek to reduce cross-national differences in formal and informal standards of corporate responsibility such that organizations can implement initiatives to care without being competitively disadvantaged.

Before we turn to the arguments underlying this contention about how an organization's leaders can be challenged to care more, it is important to consider briefly a bit of the history of how points of view on caring in the organization-employee relationship have advanced over time.

From Pig Iron to Silicon

Now one of the very first requirements for a man who is fit to handle pig iron as a regular occupation is that he shall be so stupid and so phlegmatic that he more nearly resembles in his mental make-up the ox than any other type (Taylor, 1911, p. 59).

Our perspectives on organizations have evolved considerably from their century-old roots. In his famous treatise on the principles of management, Taylor (1911) espoused a systemized, scientific, and efficient approach to management. In this approach to organization, managers were overseers, charged with keeping workers focused on their jobs and reducing incidences of soldiering (workers colluding to avoid work), to lay the foundations for the pursuit of productivity gains through systemization and the creation of organization memory on routine tasks.

The task of frontline managers, or foremen, was to create a highly transactional environment, indeed even more transactional than could be found in an organizational economist's dream world. Foremen created a work environment in which tasks were clearly defined and circumscribed; the organizations provided the resources for the successful completion of the task, and there was high pay for successful work but low pay in the event of failure.

From these hundred-year-old roots sprouted organizations that have become much less transactional in their approaches to their relationships with employees, both in terms of the relationship between work and reward and in the definition of work. A high percentage of organizations in the 21st century are not places to slave one's labor, where managers practice efficiency and control techniques without regard for the human nature of the tasks. Instead, the organization-employee relationship has become much more complex. Further, an organization is often the central institution in its employees' lives. Organizations are social communities, and one of the dominant institutions for social contact in today's world. A purely transactional perspective on organizations, in which we just focus on the work that individuals do in an organization and the awarding of appropriate compensation for this work, creates an eidolon that falls short of the reality of the complete guise of an organization.

These statements in and of themselves are not profound. What is profound is the creation of organizational environments that recognize, foster, and support humane values that empathize with and support employees. Organizations that leverage their centrality in their employees' lives can build a strong sense of attachment that reinforces the economic and hierarchical ties that bind employees to the organization (Ouchi, 1980). This attachment increases an organization's control over an individual, but not in the way Taylor yearned for. Instead, attachment is positive and social; it leads to an alignment of purpose and activities (Alvesson & Lindkvist, 1993; Wilkins & Ouchi, 1983), which can be an important precursor to the reciprocal gains that come from an organization's investments in its relationships with its employees. Attachment yields control, but can also lead to inspired efforts and involvement by employees, such that organizations that aspire to provide a positive, caring work environment will not be pariahs for doing so, but can be paragons of competitiveness (Bolino, Turnley, & Bloodgood, 2002; Leana & Van Buren, 1999).

Unlike in Taylor's world, where informal groups of employees in organizations were regarded as dysfunctional, organizational theorists now recognize the substantial benefits and competitive advantages that community can create for an organization. Inter-firm and intra-firm networks of employees help to generate alignment in organizations through the generation of similar attitudes and the process of imitation. Networks provide key actors in an organization with access to resources that they require to undertake activities that can help generate competitive advantages (Brass, Galaskiewicz, Greve, & Tsai, 2004). Networks founded on trust, interaction, and sharing can also lead to greater innovative output (Tsai & Ghoshal, 1998).

Without going into too much depth in intra-organizational research on the social and networked communities that can comprise an organization, the point should be clear that organizations are much more than transactional entities. An organization is a social entity that can provide value beyond the nexus of contracts that constitute the explicit, legal relationship between the corporate entity and the individual. This value can be to the individual as well as to the organization, and such value that is yielded to the organization becomes a strong part of the justification for why organizations can and should dare to care. It is not simply altruism. It is not simply an exercise of moral and ethical beliefs. Instead, organizations that foster a sense of community and promote attachment and a strong acculturation of employees to the organization have opportunities to make competitive gains. Such a perspective is often attached to anecdotes on the success of enlightened organizations such as Google.

Pragmatist or Pollyanna

An oft-cited exemplar of a highly desirable employment environment that exhibits great care for its employees is Google. Google's offices, whether they are in the United States or Switzerland, are filled with computers and much more—slides, firehouse poles, hammocks, and game rooms. The company provides free breakfasts, lunches, and dinners and multiple places, such as in-house libraries, where employees can meet and relax (BBC, 2008). The point of this environment is to stimulate creativity, interaction, and innovation in employees—the foundations for Google's competitive advantage in its search engine and other related businesses.

Without a doubt, such an environment will foster positive attitudes in employees, enhance organizational attachment, and even perhaps stimulate innovation. Whether measured on innovation, growth, market share, or financial market performance dimensions, Google is a very successful company. This raises an interesting, important question: Does Google's dominant market position provide it with the resource slack to engage in these organizational experiments in caring, or have these organizational features in fact led to its competitive advantage in its markets? This further raises the question of endogeneity: Do profitable organizations care more or do caring organizations profit more? A related question concerns whether organizations that have less of a competitive lead on their ever-evolving and ambitious competitors can engage in similar initiatives.

Some of the answers to these questions can be found in recent management research on organizations. Research suggests that organizations can gain competitive advantages by establishing pro-

actively positive policies toward their employees (Grant, Dutton, & Russo, 2008). For example, organizations can heighten competitive advantages, via employee performance, when they invest in their employees, when they offer job security, and when they care for their employees beyond the simple contractual terms of attachment (Tsui, Pearce, Porter, & Tripoli, 1997). Much of this research has the laudable goal of demonstrating how practices that promote caring for employees—such as more benefits, training opportunities, health insurance, and more flexibility through the provision of sick days or other means of not attending work on a daily basis—can lead to better organizational performance (Pfeffer, 2010). Although this research has focused on the U.S. context, related research in other geographic settings, such as China, has also demonstrated a similar positive organizational outcome of supportive and caring management practices (Jiang, Baker, & Frazier, 2009).

Even though doing more for employees, or doing more for the environment, might plausibly lead to better organizational performance (Harter, Schmidt, & Hayes, 2002), there are two related considerations. First, there is the question of how the gains, or increased rents, are divided among the various stakeholders in the organization. Organizations need to ensure that such organizational gains do not just translate into an increase in the rents obtained by the organization's shareholders, such as is likely to occur when the owners of the organization are more transactional than relational, or highly engaged with other stakeholders (David, O'Brien, Yoshikawa, & Delios, 2010). Second, the gains need to be balanced against the increases that will be incurred in the organization's cost structure. Socially oriented initiatives will lead to an increase in an organization's cost structure (Ambec & Lanoie, 2008). Whether these costs can be offset by organizational improvements or whether the costs jeopardize the organization's competitiveness is a question fundamental to the reification and creation of caring organizations.

The increased cost structure is not a relevant question if a similar perspective is shared by all organizations about what their responsibilities are to their employees. In such a harmonious situation, we would routinely find organizations undertaking such socially positive actions. Despite the groundswell of support for organizations to adopt a series of internal or external social outcomes or goals as part of their strategy (Rynes, Bartunek, Dutton, & Margolis, 2010), this backing tends to be rooted in one corner of our rather large and diverse world.

Even if we can see the moral and ethical legitimacy of developing caring organizations, the core fact remains that organizations must be sensitive to the cost of such initiatives, as organizations cannot escape their economic imperative. An organization must be competitive in its markets, but the rules and approaches governing the nature of competition across markets worldwide can vary in very stark ways. When an organization's leaders consider instituting practices that heighten that organization's level of responsibility to and care for employees and external constituents, substantial challenges to the implementation of such a perspective can arise when we have different perspectives on the nature of employee-organization and environment-environment relationships across organizations. Such variance is most pronounced when organizations are engaged in international competition.

The Dickens It Is

When the business historians turn to writing about the exploits of organizations in the 1990s and 2000s, a dominant story will be founded in the spirit of capitalism and entrepreneurism that emerged in these two decades in two of the southern provinces of China—Fujian and Guangdong. From the crumbles of central planning arose a tremendous number of vibrant, but temporary, corporations. Entrepreneurs built organizations that survived and thrived in the short term, with their profits being the nourishment for the seeds of ideas for the growth of new short-lived organizations.

The competitive foundation that fed the growth of these limited-term companies was entirely cost based. Entrepreneurs sought to put together the pieces of companies that manufactured lighters, assorted toys, small clothing components,

and other forms of minimal-capital, labor-intensive manufacturing with but one thought in mind: minimize cost to be competitive and profitable (Golley, 2002). Factories were bare-bones and entirely minimalist, while labor conditions and wage structures were the realization of the Lincoln Electric dream on a grand, and sometimes detestable, scale.

Within this environment of no-holds-barred capitalism, labor was an important cog—and a costable one, at least on a per-piece-of-production basis. The environment was entirely transaction based. Any compensation earned by an employee was based on his or her output. Companies needed this form of relationship with their employees, as more often than not, contracts with buyer firms were temporary in nature, with competitors waiting to secure the next production contract via a lower bid. In this Williamsonian world, workers represented a soft spot. There was little scope for collective action on the parts of the employees in these enterprises, leading to a continuation of low wages, risk of delayed or non-payment of wages, and even default of wages given notice of resignation (Tsui, 2010). Compensation for illness or industrial accidents was almost nonexistent, and even when paid was insultingly low to the value of one's limbs.

These conditions existed across organizations in the south of China, often regardless of whether the company controlling the factory was locally owned or foreign-owned. Conditions such as these persisted until China passed a new labor law in 2008 that improved the rights of mainland workers, along such essential lines as the introduction of a minimum wage and basic benefits for blue-collar workers (Wang, Appelbaum, Degiuli, & Lichtenstein, 2009). Yet the introduction of this labor law exacerbated the increased cost structure that was becoming part of China's business environment through the 2000s, where factors of production such as labor and land had already begun to erode the cost competitiveness of the region.

As a consequence, enterprises began to leave China, and they were not replaced. In Guangdong alone, 3,500 of nearly 5,000 toy-exporting businesses withdrew from the market in 2008 (Roberts, 2010). The prospect of this form of business returning is unlikely, as other low-cost environments have beckoned. The cost of daring to care, following the institution of a legal and regulatory framework that better protected the rights of workers, even in very basic ways, was the loss of those very same enterprises that drove the unprecedented economic development of the south of China. Part of the reason for this is rooted in the foundations that led to the growth of this region: Conditions governing and regulating the employment and compensation of skilled and unskilled workers vary worldwide. This variance will factor into the decision making of astute executives who are seeking to be competitive in industries that are global and who face substantial cost pressures to be competitive. Daring to provide benefits beyond those dictated by local norms, be they legal or social, jeopardizes the competitiveness and sustainability of the organization, making the tenet a fundamental one: It is challenging to care when the organization no longer exists.

If Scott Had Gone North With a Porter

The epilogue to this China story is that it is not about China. It is about industries and institutions. The pressures exerted on organizations in China are a consequence of a globalization trend that has seen increases in cost-based competition, the disintegration of value chains, a greater prevalence of offshoring and outsourcing activities, and the dominance of larger buyers over dispersed, small, and numerous supplier firms that compete for short-term contracts in offshored locations such as China (Contractor, Kumar, Kundu, & Pedersen, 2010). The pressure on supplier firms in China to be low cost, and increasingly so, is tremendous. There is no differentiation in this commoditized manufacturing, and the loyalty from a buyer to a particular supplier is too weak to withstand the pressure of a higher cost structure.

If these suppliers dared to care, the consequence would be that organizations that cared more would be competitively disadvantaged in the short term, and likely liquidated in the medium term. Given this industry structure, cost-based competition prevails. Organizations do not have the slack or latitude to entertain the thought of

creating libraries, lunches, or leisure for their employees. Further, the institutional environment, as reflected in the regulations and legal frameworks that defined the key parameters of the employee-organization relationship, permitted, until recently, such conditions to exist and persist.

Indeed, the continued emergence of globalization across more and more regions of the world creates pressures in other countries akin to what we have seen in China in the 1990s and 2000s. Managers in multinational firms struggle to contend with pressures to compete and with the multiple formal and informal institutional standards that pervade the markets in which they have operations, be they subsidiary, export, or outsourced activities (Meyer, Mudambi, & Narula, 2010). The pressures are faced by multinational firms competing in multiple business environments, with substantial variance in their institutions. The pressures are also faced by firms competing in business environments, such as emerging and transition economies, where the institutional and competitive norms have been evolving rapidly.

Much of the development we have seen in business environments in the 1990s and 2000s has been a shift toward privatization and the emergence of market environments. Such a transition has occurred at various rates in the countries of central and eastern Europe, in numerous Asian economies, and in South American countries (Wright, Filatotchev, Hoskisson, & Peng, 2005). The transition has changed the competitive conditions faced by organizations in these business environments, which has often redefined the nature of the employee-organization relationship. The experience of Escorts Limited provides a good example of this point.

Escorts, Airplanes, and iPhones

Escorts Limited had been operating in India for several decades, as a manufacturer of bi-wheelers (scooters and motorcycles), construction equipment, tractors, and other related products, when liberalization reforms hit the Indian economy in 1991 (Anand & Delios, 1994). The shift from the pre-1990s licensed-Raj regime in India to a more open and competitive business environment post-1990s placed strains on the operations of many long-standing, traditional companies in India, such as Escorts Limited. Pre-1991, Escorts Limited had enjoyed a monopoly or duopoly position in many of its markets. Its organization was vast and redundant in many of its divisions and operations, and its employee practices were munificent. Employee compensation was not overly high, but similar to many other organizations Escorts Limited had a highly paternalistic relationship with its employees. Further, employees had little to no concern about being laid off or fired. Employment was effectively for life.

Post-1991, with the emergence of new domestic and international competitors in India and the establishment of competition along price, quality, and product innovation dimensions, Escorts Limited faced pressures not only to be more innovative and efficient, but also to reduce redundancies and streamline the organization. The organization necessarily became less munificent as a response, and there was a greater focus on employee training, output, and productivity. Escorts Limited did not become a draconian organization, such as depicted in the example on organizations in southern China, but changes in the competitive environment did mean that the nature of the relationship between the organization and its employees became more transactional and less secure for the employees.

Other long-standing organizations in India faced a similar set of pressures from the opening up of the country's markets to competition. Yet, in many instances, perhaps particularly where an organization maintained a position of market dominance, it continued to operate in the pre-1990s paternalistic and caring mode. By 2010, such companies had become paragons for organizational theorists (Cappelli, Singh, Singh, & Useem, 2010).

Titan Industries is one such company. Founded in 1984, Titan is primarily a manufacturer of watches. It is jointly owned by the Tata Group and an investment arm of the state government of Tamil Nadu. Titan has held a position of market dominance in India's watch industry almost since its foundation. Its paternalistic organizational culture still very much typifies the structure of many

of the companies founded in preliberalization India: Labor conditions are stable, pressure on the factory floor is low, wages are reasonable albeit not tremendously high, and turnover is low.

Organizations in emerging and transition economies are not the only ones facing pressures to change. Consider, for example, deregulation in developed economies such as the United States and the United Kingdom. In many instances, as deregulation has progressed, organizations that were once bastions of employee benefits have become bereft of the bonuses that bolstered employees' lives. To be competitive in liberated and deregulated environments, organizations have been forced to seek reductions in employee benefits. The postal industry in many developed countries, for example, has faced increased cost pressures with the deregulation of the industry and technology changes that created new means of communication and new competitors to carry mail, documents, and parcels. National postal organizations have been forced to seek cost reductions through contractual concessions from employees and their unions. The result? Not surprisingly, labor relations have deteriorated, and the incidence of strikes has increased. Similarly, foreign competition increased in the auto industry in North America from the 1980s to the 2000s, leading to a worsening of labor relations, as major automakers renegotiated the terms of benefits and compensation for employees. These renegotiations were sought to lower cost structures so that the North American automakers could be competitive with the new entrants.

The airline industry, which has also undergone waves of deregulation and internationalization, is yet another example. Airlines were once a preferred employer; mechanics, in-flight staff, customer service representatives, and pilots were each party to a substantial set of benefits in the pre-deregulation days of protected markets and protected routes. Yet, with deregulation has come a greater sophistication in the nature of competition—more competition, greater differentiation, and the emergence of low-cost competitors. As incumbent national carriers had less insulation from competition because of the changes in the regulations governing competition in the industry, national legacy carriers tried to reduce employee benefits and compensation. The rounds of negotiation with unions were never easy. Labor relations worsened, employee dissatisfaction increased, and new contract offers were often met by strike action.

A dramatic example of what can happen when the nature of the organization-employee relationship changes can be found in Sabena Belgian World Airlines. In the 1990s, after the European airline industry was deregulated, Sabena faced endless rounds of often contentious and potentially violent strike action (Crossan & Pierce, 1994a) as management sought to gain more from employees and heighten productivity while more effectively controlling costs (Crossan & Pierce, 1994b). In 2001, Sabena went out of business after 78 years of operations, as it was unable to negotiate and strategize its way to competitiveness in the new deregulated airline environment in Europe. These conditions in the airline industry in Europe have persisted through the 2000s, as evidenced by the British Airways strikes in 2010 (Werdigier, 2010).

The challenge for an organization is how to be socially responsive and realistically commit to enhancing employee welfare, given intense competitive conditions. In industries exposed to such competitive pressures, there is little slack for an organization to engage in initiatives that yield a greater share of the organization's rents to its employees. Markets, shareholders, and bankers are single-mindedly focused on profits, and are notoriously impatient.

Take the case of Foxconn in Shenzhen, China. In 2010, Foxconn was the largest manufacturer of electronics and computer components for major computer and electronics brands, such as Dell, Hewlett-Packard, and Apple. Unlike the original labor-intensive manufacturers that once populated southern China, Foxconn was a sophisticated, high value-added manufacturer that made components for new and innovative products such as the iPhone and the iPad. The company had 800,000 employees, 400,000 of whom worked in its complex in Shenzhen. To be productive and efficient, and to continue to receive manufacturing contracts, Foxconn had substantial rigidities

in its hierarchical management. Management compelled employees to undertake fast, accurate assembly that often entailed mandated overtime. The pressures on employees were substantial, leading to at least 10 suicides and three attempted suicides (*China Post*, 2010).

Foxconn's response to the suicides and external criticisms about its working environment was to implement a 30% pay hike on its basic salary of US$130 per month. When Foxconn announced this pay hike on June 1, 2010, its parent company, Hon Hai Precision Industry, a major listed company in Taiwan, saw its share price fall by 4.02%, with anticipation that it could drop another 8%. Clearly, the market did not foresee that the pay raise would be met by decreased turnover and heightened product quality and productivity to the extent required to offset the increase of US$310 million in operating costs created by the pay raise. Interestingly, the leaders in dumping Hon Hai's stock were foreign institutional investors.

Even if efforts to enhance the employee environment could lead to greater commitment and attachment to the organization and better employee and organizational performance, such benefits might be realized too late to be usefully pursued. Given the emerging competitive exigencies found in developed and emerging economies, even when an organization's leaders are predisposed to caring, such efforts might not be realizable on a sustainable level. Fundamentally, M. E. Porter trumps E. H. Porter. Organizations cannot escape the discipline of a competitive market. Caring efforts, however noble, remain as much a dream as a reality.

Enter the Keystone Kops

If industries worldwide are moving toward heightened levels of competition through greater internationalization and the emergence of new domestic competition, then the prospects for an organization to have the slack to dare to care are not particularly high.

For some organizations, such as Google, profound competitive advantages can provide the resource slack to care. Other organizations might actually become more competitively advantaged by caring, through a variety of mediating mechanisms such as increased organizational attachment, greater retention rates, better employee communication, and innovation creation and adoption. Such cases, however, are the organizational outliers to the competitive dictates of the industry and institutional environments in which all organizations are situated.

The reality is that the vast majority of organizations are subject to the Darwinian forces of the market, where strength is defined by efficiency and effectiveness and the creation of margins that can feed the next generation of products and competition. Managers in organizations can dare to care only as much as allowed by their advantages, by the level of competition, or by the institutional forces governing the formal and informal norms of business. Even if management educators can create programs that encourage managers to care, or even if such predispositions are inherent and need only to be awakened, the influence of competitive markets still has to be overcome.

If markets can be made noncompetitive, such as by the implementation of protectionist measures, then organizations will have the slack to be able to care. But in this case, the treatment is worse than the cure. The fallacies in the logic of protectionism, restraint of trade, and barriers to trade are well accepted (Bhagwati, 2004). Protectionist regulations reduce the pace of wealth creation and limit the amount of goods and services available to the population at large.

As protectionism is not the solution, then organizations need to turn to the manipulation of the rules of the game—namely the informal and formal regulations and practices that define the nature of competition in an environment. Elected officials or policy makers in a country or region develop the formal laws and regulations that govern the competitive environment. The formal regulations in an environment can either facilitate or constrain organizations from pursuing actions that are not commensurate with a broad social good by better serving the needs of employees and external stakeholders. In some business environments, such legislation that governs the rules of the game has been enacted through the promulgation of laws that protect the rights of workers (minimum age and wage laws), the environment (EPA regulations in the U.S.), and consumers (anti-monopoly regulation).

Aside from the formal legal and regulatory environment, informal norms can also influence the types of practices pursued by organizations. For example, cultural norms can exert social pressures that determine whether a given business practice will be commonly pursued by organizations (March & Olsen, 1989). Informal norms are often characterized along normative, regulative, and cognitive dimensions (Scott, 2001), with these norms providing legitimacy for the pursuit of specific actions by organizations. Such legitimization can lead to the widespread adoption of various organizational actions (Edelman & Suchman, 1997), such as ones that increase an organization's level of social responsibility.

Although formal and informal regulations and norms can promote common business practices in a country, the power to create such norms, especially formal ones, resides in the policy-making environment. Policy makers (e.g., federal or national governments) enact policies that can harmonize the competitive environment, but such harmonization is restricted to the borders of the nation in which the policies have been enacted.

Consequently, institutional environments, and the formal and informal norms of business, vary across countries. Further, it is unlikely that dispersed national governments will independently act in concert to harmonize domestic policies and regulations, as the process of regulatory diffusion is a complex one (Levi Faur & Jordana, 2005). In fact, the opposite will be true, as governments compete to lure organizations to their domestic markets with a mix of fiscal and regulatory incentives. Further, policy makers will act in their own best interests and in the interests of the population that provides them with their power. Seldom is the logic of the calculus of policy makers benevolently oriented toward a wider social good in which independent states become aligned on regulations that guide the social conduct of organizations.

Even though the power to create socially oriented regulations and laws does exist in the hands of the public officials who have political power, it is possible for organizations to exert influence on the preferences of these policy makers (Henisz & Delios, 2001). Organizations are not powerless to influence the direction of change in the policy environments in which they operate. Given a true motivation to care, leaders in organizations can work with policy makers to harmonize competitive practices across the various institutional environments in which they operate. That said, such an approach involves a fundamental change in the ways in which business leaders seek to interact with policy makers. Rather than influencing, leveraging, or arbitraging differences in institutional environments to create competitive advantages (Henisz & Delios, 2002), organizations can take an active role in influencing international efforts to develop regulations that enable organizations to adopt a social caring agenda, without sacrificing competitiveness. This statement is consistent with the point that organizations can act as a means by which regulatory standards can be spread across national borders (Christmann, 2004; Terlaak, 2007).

This kind of organizational effort could supplement the tactics that are traditionally used to humanize and harmonize working regulations internationally. Nongovernmental organizations (NGOs), such as the International Labor Organization (ILO), have played an important role in propagating socially just organizational practices. Multilateral organizations such as the ILO have become the international standard bearers for caring in organizations. Of course these organizations set voluntary standards, employing neither carrot nor stick to foster caring. Instead, they appeal to moral suasion, influence the preferences of national-level policy makers, and provide information and education about the types and consequences of desirable and undesirable organizational practices. For-profit organizations could well play a critical role in this process of influence and the development of socially oriented formal and informal norms.

To the Organization and Beyond

National governments, and the policy makers embedded therein, have and will continue to have the central authority to shape and define the formal and informal norms of business prac-

tices in a given institutional environment. With globalization, however, there is an increased need for organizations to become more active as agents of positive change in the business environments in which they operate. Instead of being tacit or explicit supporters of a regulatory devolution that supports open markets and a more open playing field for the pursuit of unjust, unfair, and sometimes unsavory business practices, organizations need to catalyze and foster the institution of an international set of regulations that create powerful social and regulatory bounds for the definition and enforcement of business practices that are socially responsible. Multilateral organizations and other powerful NGOs can also help shape the policies that are enacted, but NGOs will be more effective at shaping the decisions that national-level policy makers enact when such efforts are bolstered by the strong and genuine support of the organizations whose behavior and actions will be regulated by such policies.

Such efforts will entail more direct action than rhetoric directed at improving the social responsibility of an organization, to either its employees or external stakeholders. Efforts need to extend beyond using social responsibility initiatives as a public relations vehicle to foster reputational and economic gains. Genuine interest in an organization's leaders and managers to improve the social and ethical responsibility of its business practices need to be manifest as attempts to change the competitive realities that hamper the practical effectiveness of such efforts.

It is time for organizational leaders to recognize the gravity of their position as the heads of one of the dominant institutions in today's world. True, it is challenging enough to manage the internal operations of an organization well, but the responsibilities of an organization's leaders extend to shaping the business environments in which they operate. An organization's leaders need to be attuned to the development of caring initiatives within their own organizations, but more important, they need to be active agents to counter the industrial and regulatory forces that make such caring potentially foolhardy when faced with the constraints imposed by global competition.

References

Ahlstrom, D. (2010). Innovation and growth: How business contributes to society. *Academy of Management Perspectives*, 24(3), 10–23.

Alvesson, M., & Lindkvist, L. (1993). Transaction costs, clans and corporate culture. *Journal of Management Studies*, 30, 427–452.

Ambec, S., & Lanoie, P. (2008). Does it pay to be green? A systematic overview. *Academy of Management Perspectives*, 22(4), 45–62.

Anand, J., & Delios, A. (1995). *Escorts Limited: 1993* (Case Study, No. 995M009). London, Ontario, Canada: Ivey Publishing.

Barnard, C. (1938). *The function of the executive*. Cambridge, MA: Harvard University Press.

BBC. (2008, March 13). Sliding into work at Google HQ. *BBC Online*. Retrieved May 24, 2010, from http://news.bbc.co.uk/2/hi/technology/7292600.stm

Bhagwati, J. (2004). *In defense of globalization*. New York: Oxford University Press.

Bolino, M. C., Turnley, W. H., & Bloodgood, J. M. (2002). Citizenship behavior and the creation of social capital in organizations. *Academy of Management Review*, 27(4), 505–522.

Brass, D. J., Galaskiewicz, J., Greve, H. R., & Tsai, W. P. (2004). Taking stock of networks and organizations: A multilevel perspective. *Academy of Management Journal*, 47(6), 795–817.

Cappelli, P., Singh, H., Singh, J., & Useem, M. (2010). The India way: Lessons for the U.S. *Academy of Management Perspectives*, 24(2), 6–24.

The China Post. (2010, June 3). Hon Hai shares plunge on Foxconn pay hike.

Christmann, P. (2004). Multinational companies and the natural environment: Determinants of global environmental policy standardization. *Academy of Management Journal*, 47(5), 747–760.

Contractor, F. J., Kumar, V., Kundu, S. K., & Pedersen, T. (in press). Reconceptualizing the firm in a world of outsourcing and offshoring: The organizational and geographical relocation of high-value company functions. *Journal of Management Studies*.

Crossan, M. M., & Pierce, B. (1994a). *Sabena Belgian World Airlines (A)* (Case Study, No. 9A94M003). London, Ontario, Canada: Ivey Publishing.

Crossan, M. M., & Pierce, B. (1994b). *Sabena Belgian World Airlines Strike* (Case Study, No. 9A94M005). London, Ontario, Canada: Ivey Publishing.

David, P., O'Brien, J. P., Yoshikawa, T., & Delios, A. (in press). Do shareholders or stakeholders appropriate the rents from corporate diversification? The influence of ownership structure. *Academy of Management Journal*.

Edelman, L. B., & Suchman, M. C. (1997). The legal environments of organizations. *Annual Review of Sociology*, 23(1), 479–515.

Golley, J. (2002). Regional patterns of industrial development during China's economic transition. *Economics of Transition*, 10(3), 761–801.

Granovetter, M. (1985). Economic action and social structure: The problem of embeddedness. *The American Journal of Sociology*, 91(3), 481–510.

Grant, A. M., Dutton, J. E., & Russo, B. D. (2008). Giving commitment: Employee support programs and the prosocial sensemaking process. *Academy of Management Journal*, 51(5), 898–918.

Harter, J. K., Schmidt, F. L., & Hayes, T. L. (2002). Business-unit-level relationship between employee satisfaction, employee engagement, and business outcomes: A meta-analysis. *Journal of Applied Psychology*, 87(2), 268–279.

Henisz, W. J., & Delios. A. (2001). Uncertainty, imitation and plant location: Japanese multinational corporations, 1990–96. *Administrative Science Quarterly*, 46(3), 443–475.

Henisz, W. J., & Delios. A. (2002). Learning about the institutional environment. In P. Ingram & B. Silverman (Eds.), *The new institutionalism in strategic management* (Volume 19, pp. 337–370). Bingley, UK: Emerald Group Publishing Limited.

Jensen, M. C., & Meckling, W. H. (1976). Theory of the firm: Managerial behavior, agency costs and ownership structure. *Journal of Financial Economics*, 3, 305–360.

Jiang, B., Baker, R. C., & Frazier, G. V. (2009). An analysis of job dissatisfaction and turnover to reduce global supply chain risk: Evidence from China. *Journal of Operations Management*, 27(2), 169–184.

Leana, C. R., & Van Buren, H. J. (1999). Organizational social capital and employment practices. *Academy of Management Review*, 24(3), 538–555.

Levi-Faur, D., & Jordana, J. (2005). Regulatory capitalism: Policy irritants and convergent divergence. *The Annals of the American Academy of Political Science*, 598, 191–197.

March, J. G., & Olsen, J. P. (1989). *Rediscovering institutions: The organizational basis of politics*. New York: Free Press.

Meyer, K. E., Mudambi, R., & Narula, R. (in press). Multinational enterprises and local contexts: The opportunities and challenges of multiple-embeddedness. *Journal of Management Studies*.

Ouchi, W. G. (1980). Markets, bureaucracies, and clans. *Administrative Science Quarterly*, 25, 129–141.

Pfeffer, J. (2010). Building sustainable organizations: The human factor. *Academy of Management Perspectives*, 24(1), 34–45.

Roberts, D. (2010, May 13). Why factories are leaving China. *Business Week Online*. Retrieved May 13, 2010, from http://www.businessweek.com/magazine/content/10_21/b4179011091633.htm

Rynes, S., Bartunek, J., Dutton, J., & Margolis, J. (2010). Call for papers: Academy of Management Review special topic forum: Understanding and creating caring and compassionate organizations. *Academy of Management Review*, 35(2), 334–336.

Scott, R. (2001). *Institutions and organizations*. Thousand Oaks, CA: Sage.

Taylor, F. (1911). *Principles of scientific management*. New York and London: Harper & Brothers.

Terlaak, A. (2007). Order without law? The role of certified management standards in shaping socially desired firm behaviors. *Academy of Management Review, 32*(3), 968–985.

Tsai, W. P., & Ghoshal, S. (1998). Social capital and value creation: The role of intrafirm networks. *Academy of Management Journal, 41*(4), 464–476.

Tsui, A. S., Pearce, J. L., Porter, L. W., & Tripoli, A. M. (1997). Alternative approaches to the employee-organization relationship: Does investment in employees pay off? *Academy of Management Journal, 40*(5), 1089–1121.

Tsui, E. (2010, March 19). Guangdong raises its minimum wage amid China inflation fears. *Financial Times Online.* Retrieved March 19, 2010, from http://www.ftchinese.com/story/001031820/en

Wang, H., Appelbaum, R. P., Degiuli, F., & Lichtenstein, N. (2009). China's new labor contract law: Is China moving towards increased power for workers? *Third World Quarterly, 30*(3), 485–501.

Werdigier, J. (2010, March 19). British Airways strike begins, threatening a weak economy. *The New York Times.* Retrieved March 19, 2010, from http://www.nytimes.com/2010/03/20/business/20air.html

Wilkins, A. L., & Ouchi, W. G. (1983). Efficient cultures: Exploring the relationship between culture and organizational performance. *Administrative Science Quarterly, 28*(3), 468–481.

Williamson, O. E. (1975). *Markets and hierarchies: Analysis and antitrust implications.* New York: Free Press.

Wright, M., Filatotchev, I., Hoskisson, R. E., & Peng, M. W. (2005). Strategy research in emerging economies: Challenging the conventional wisdom. *Journal of Management Studies, 42*(1), 1–33.

www.hbr.org

Growing Green
Three Smart Paths to Developing Sustainable Products

by Gregory Unruh and Richard Ettenson

Included with this full-text *Harvard Business Review* article:

Growing Green

Three Smart Paths to Developing Sustainable Products

Idea in Brief

Green growth is at the top of many leaders' agendas, but the way forward is rarely clear. Here are three broad product strategies that can align your green goals with your capabilities.

An *accentuate* strategy involves highlighting existing green attributes in your company's portfolio. An alternative is to *acquire* a green brand. If you have substantial product-development skills and assets, you can *architect* new offerings—build them from scratch. Which strategy is best depends on how "greenable" your portfolio is and how advanced your green product development capabilities are.

For any of these paths, understanding customers' expectations and competitors' capabilities, and aligning offerings and messaging to prevent charges of green-washing, are essential to success.

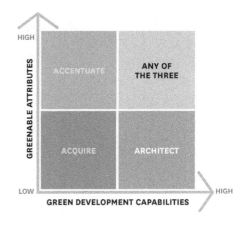

Growing Green
Three Smart Paths to Developing Sustainable Products

by Gregory Unruh and Richard Ettenson

Soon after its launch, in 1987, Clorox's Brita water filter seized a leadership position among pitcher filtration systems, and by 2002 it controlled 70% of the market. But over the next five years, as the market contracted, Brita's share declined. Management's patience with the brand soon wore thin, and in May 2007 Clorox CEO Don Knauss told shareholders that Brita had two years to improve or it would be sold off. "When I got on board," Knauss remembers, "the question was, How quickly can we sell this thing?" Then came a remarkable turn: Brita recovered its momentum within months, achieving double-digit growth and leading the brand back with a vengeance.

How did its managers do it? By going green, as we'll detail below.

That strategy wouldn't have been obvious 10 years ago. But thanks to aggressive leadership by some of the world's biggest companies—Wal-Mart, GE, and DuPont among them—green growth has risen to the top of the agenda for many businesses. From 2007 to 2009 eco-friendly product launches in-

creased by more than 500%. A recent IBM survey found that two-thirds of executives see sustainability as a revenue driver, and half of them expect green initiatives to confer competitive advantage. This dramatic shift in corporate mind-set and practices over the past decade reflects a growing awareness that environmental responsibility can be a platform for both growth and differentiation.

Nonetheless, the best approach to achieving green growth isn't always clear. This article is for executives who believe that developing green products makes sense for their organization and need to determine the best path forward. We will introduce and describe three broad strategies—*accentuate*, *acquire*, and *architect*—that companies can use to align their green goals with their capabilities. These strategies emerged from 10 in-depth case studies of consumer product and industrial companies that were moving into the green space; we validated the studies in discussions with dozens of senior and midlevel sustainability executives. The framework now plays a central role in the core executive MBA course offerings in sustainable business strategy and in the executive education programs at Thunderbird School of Global Management.

As we'll see, green product development brings with it unique cultural, operational, and execution challenges.

Path #1: Accentuate

An accentuate strategy involves playing up existing or latent green attributes in your current portfolio. Of the three strategies, it's the most straightforward to craft and implement and thus is a good place to start.

Some companies find it easy to accentuate. For example, Church & Dwight's Arm & Hammer baking soda has attributes that were just waiting to be leveraged. As green competitors emerged, and as customers demanded more environmentally friendly choices, Arm & Hammer's managers emphasized its green credentials, positioning the brand as "the #1 environmentally sensible alternative for cleaning and deodorizing" and "committed to the environment since 1846."

Other companies may have to work harder than Church & Dwight did, but they can still harvest low-hanging green fruit. Consider how Brita repositioned its water filters. A decade ago Brita's sales were siphoned off by the rising popularity of bottled water, which exploded into a billion-dollar business. But water bottlers attracted loud critics such as the World Wide Fund for Nature and Corporate Accountability International, which condemned them for clogging landfills with plastic and deceptively advertising their product as better tasting and healthier than tap water.

Brita's managers were quick to see an opportunity. Company research showed that replacing bottled water with Brita systems could potentially keep millions of bottles a year out of landfills. To capitalize on this benefit, the managers pursued an integrated cross-media communications strategy to tout Brita's green attributes, educate consumers about bottle waste, and encourage a switch to greener alternatives. As part of this strategy, the company launched FilterForGood, a website that invites visitors to pledge that they will reduce plastic waste by switching to reusable bottles. A device on the site graphically updates the tally of bottles saved. Brita's managers ensured that the media picked up on FilterForGood—for ex-

ample, by arranging a partnership with NBC's television show *The Biggest Loser*. Within a year the company's water pitcher sales jumped a robust 23%, compared with just 2% for the category overall.

Brita's impressive success came in part because it did not overreach in its sustainability claims. Companies that decide to pursue an accentuate strategy would be wise to follow its lead. Activists and environmental experts will not hesitate to point out greenwashing or other undesirable corporate behavior when they see it. Consider the experience of Arm & Hammer. Promoting the environmentally friendly attributes of the product was easy, but the company overlooked a major liability: It used animal testing. Activists took to the blogosphere and called on customers to switch to the cruelty-free and equally green Bob's Red Mill baking soda. Although such complaints won't necessarily reach or resonate with all your customers, anticipating and heading off criticism will strengthen your overall greening efforts. Transparency in claims and authenticity in execution are important elements in the long-term success of any green strategy.

The broader your brand portfolio, of course, the more exposed you may be to activist and consumer backlash. Most companies lack a green heritage; their products were developed before sustainability was a concern. So they must carefully gauge how the rest of their portfolio will look by comparison with the accentuated product. Touting the green attributes of some products inevitably prompts the response "Great! But what about the rest of your offerings?" A big gulf between your green and nongreen products can undermine your legitimate sustainability claims.

Consider BP's troubled "Beyond Petroleum" rebranding effort. The company's Helios logo and the prominent solar panels on its service stations could not hide the fact that more than 90% of its revenues came from oil. *Fortune* highlighted the disparity when it wrote, "Here's a novel advertising strategy—pitch your least important product and ignore your most important one." To avoid negative commentary like this, make sure your strategy aligns with customers' perceptions.

Brita did that well. Its managers were careful in their initial communications not to claim that their brand was a "green product" made by a "green company." They recognized that

Gregory Unruh (gregoryunruh.com) is a professor and the director of the Lincoln Center at Thunderbird School of Global Management and the author of *Earth, Inc.* (Harvard Business Press, 2010). **Richard Ettenson** (richard .ettenson@thunderbird.edu) is an associate professor and a Thelma H. Kieckhefer research fellow in global brand marketing at Thunderbird.

Brita filter cartridges had to be replaced every few months and were not being recycled. Because the FilterForGood campaign was predicated on eliminating that kind of waste, the managers realized that they needed a recycling solution for the cartridges. They forged an approach in collaboration with Preserve, which manufactures products using recycled plastic, and with Whole Foods Market to provide a solution that was simple for customers and highly visible.

"The filter recycling program builds on the success of Brita's FilterForGood campaign," the company announced—and went on to share credit with its customers: "Now Brita users are making another positive impact by recycling Brita pitcher filters." By accentuating the product's green attributes and eliminating or mitigating its nongreen elements, Brita enhanced the credibility of its sustainability efforts.

Path #2: Acquire

If your portfolio has no obvious candidates for accentuation, a good alternative is to buy someone else's green brand. Many high-profile green acquisitions have been made since 2000, including The Body Shop by L'Oréal, Ben & Jerry's by Unilever, and Tom's of Maine by Colgate-Palmolive. In such deals the buyer's channel and distribution capabilities are often expected to substantially broaden the green brand's customer base. Within a year after Unilever acquired Ben & Jerry's, for example, sales had increased by 70% and Ben & Jerry's had displaced Häagen Dazs as the leading premium ice cream brand.

The prospect of such robust growth is of course appealing, but managers who seek another company's green assets should be mindful of two considerations: Culture clash and strategic fit. Any merger or acquisition can stumble when company cultures collide. In green acquisitions that have idealistic, iconoclastic founders and countercultural workforces, the problem is exacerbated. Consider Groupe Danone's takeover of Stonyfield Farm. When shareholders forced Stonyfield's founder, Gary Hirshberg, to sell, he spent two years compiling a list of conditions—including rules about worker protection and environmental restrictions on business operations—to ensure that the company's social mission would be preserved. It took another two years to close the deal. By contrast, Unilever got

around some but not all of the "founder challenges" at Ben & Jerry's by completing what was in effect a hostile buyout of the brand. This approach caused many activists to cry foul and deprived Unilever of the wholehearted support of the ice cream maker's founders. Ben Cohen said, "Most of what had been the soul of Ben & Jerry's is not gonna be around anymore."

All acquisitions present myriad management challenges, so the problems of integrating an idiosyncratic green business may not seem like a big deal. But scrutiny by the green community may undermine the otherwise solid business benefits of the acquisition. Even if product sales go well, sharp questions will most likely arise about the new parent's green credentials. If the acquisition goes badly and sales tumble, not only is the value of the new asset diminished but—potentially even more damaging—the acquirer risks being accused of deliberately destroying a green competitor. Coke faced such criticism after it bought Planet Java coffee drinks and Mad River Traders teas and juices and then phased them out two years later.

An acquiring company's actions may have an adverse effect on the carefully crafted brand image of the acquisition. For example, when Danone's agreement with Stonyfield about employee protection ended, Danone sent out pink slips and met with hostile reactions in the press. Such criticism may have limited impact on the bottom line, but it can diminish the credibility of a company's green efforts.

Successful green brands are attractive targets because they have loyal customer bases and because they come with specialized knowledge about eco-friendly innovation and manufacturing, sustainable supply chain management, and green market development. Bill Morrissey, the vice president of environmental sustainability for Clorox, told us that Clorox had not only growth but also knowledge transfer in mind when it acquired Burt's Bees, which had two decades of leadership in the green product space.

Path #3: Architect

For companies with a history of innovation and substantial new-product-development assets, architecting green offerings—building them from scratch—becomes a possibility. Although architecting can be slower and more

Best Practices: Who Accentuates Well?

Supply chain: Nike requires that its leather suppliers not source from clear-cut Amazon forests.

Manufacturing: Frito-Lay installed solar panels on its SunChips factory.

Product: CSX markets rail as the most environmentally friendly option for moving freight.

Packaging: Sara Lee's modified packaging for Hillshire Farm has resulted in 900 fewer truck trips a year.

Marketing communications: Stihl points out that its trimmers and blowers have emission levels lower than those required by the EPA.

costly than accentuating or acquiring, it may be the best strategy for some companies, because it forces them to build valuable competencies. Toyota took this route when it developed the Prius. Although the company is currently addressing a raft of quality problems, the lessons of its architect strategy still stand. The Prius was not the first hybrid introduced in the U.S. market (the Honda Insight was), but it now dominates the fast-growing market for more-fuel-efficient cars. Toyota's bold move to create a green brand has paid handsome dividends. The Prius towers over the Insight, its closest competitor, in market share. Its dominance has so distracted consumers from rival brands that some Honda dealers complain of customers who walk into their showrooms and request a test-drive in the "Honda Prius." Toyota has also successfully transferred its hybrid expertise and green know-how to other brands in its portfolio. In 2005 the company became the first to establish green credentials in the luxury-car space when it produced a hybrid version of the Lexus. Over time, Toyota's luxury competitors were forced to follow suit. Mercedes-Benz and BMW recently introduced hybrid models to meet growing consumer demand and to establish their green credentials and capabilities, and Audi and Porsche will soon do the same.

Clorox, too, in developing its Green Works cleaning products, shows how companies with limited green expertise but substantial product development capabilities can architect a green brand. Green Works has received a lot of press, but the details of Clorox's strategy—which we studied from inside the company—are less well known. The line of household cleaners emerged from a small skunkworks in the Clorox Technical Center led by a handful of independent and dedicated scientists. In less than a year company researchers established the benchmark definition and best practices for a "natural" cleaning product and proceeded to design a line of offerings that would deliver the efficacy customers demand. The big surprise came when the marketing team shopped the original five Green Works products (glass, surface, all-purpose, bathroom, and toilet-bowl cleaners) to major distributors, including Wal-Mart and Safeway. According to a Green Works manager, "The realistic part of our expectations was 'Hey, if we get three or four SKUs, we'll be pretty happy.'" To the team's delight, Wal-Mart wanted all five. Distributors across the board asked for the entire Green Works line and requested that the brand be extended into other categories.

The development of Green Works induced Clorox to accumulate a range of new competencies, including specialized knowledge about eco-conscious consumers' preferences and expertise in the supply chain for natural-product sourcing and procurement. Through its deepened relationships with Wal-Mart and other distributors, Clorox quickly doubled the size of the "green clean" market. Even niche brands such as Seventh Generation and Method benefited from its market development.

Making Green Growth Happen

With an understanding of the three paths to green growth, managers can begin to craft a strategy that suits their objectives and their business context. They should begin by evaluating each option: Is it feasible? Is it desirable? How would it be implemented?

Feasibility. In this step companies take stock of their assets along two dimensions: greenable attributes of their existing products and brands, and organizational green product and brand development capabilities. The first requires a careful review of opportunities to promote brands' green benefits. Of course, each product will have its own category-specific attributes, ranging from recyclability to energy efficiency to reduced toxicity. The Global Reporting Initiative's list of more than 70 sustainability performance indicators, at www.gri.com, is an excellent resource for managers. It can help them to identify less obvious green features and benefits that are suited to an accentuate approach or to frame strategies and gauge capabilities required for an architect approach.

The second dimension involves appraising the company's green resources and capabilities. This may include a broad review of the processes and priorities for innovation and new-product development, supply chain management, the coordination of and collaboration among distributors, and even partnerships with environmental organizations.

Desirability. In this step, managers assess the strategic fit of each option with the company's objectives and the resources they can bring to bear on the green initiative. They need to consider speed to market and the investments, reputation, and competencies that

Best Practices: Who Acquires Well?

Negotiations: Colgate approached Tom's of Maine with trust and respect, viewing the deal as a partnership rather than a takeover.

Company independence: Unilever agreed to keep Ben & Jerry's separate from its U.S. ice cream business, with an independent board of directors.

Internal communications: Tom's of Maine assured employees that the acquisition would help Colgate innovate around sustainability principles.

External communications: A joint press release from Danone and Stonyfield highlighted the benefits "to both companies of two-way knowledge and talent transfer.

Analyzing Growth Options

To evaluate the fit of a given green product strategy, ask the following questions:

Accentuate

First steps What's our strategic goal?

- To leverage latent assets?
- Revitalize existing brands?
- Broaden appeal to green customers?
- Gain green credibility?

Are there potential green brands in our portfolio?

Do we have the resources and capabilities needed for this initiative?

Your portfolio How will this initiative affect the positioning of and resources for our existing brands?

Should our greened brand be a stand-alone or a strategic brand that puts a green halo on the business as a whole?

Your customers Which consumers in the category are looking for greener products?

Does our candidate brand have "permission" to enter the green space?

Can we enhance the value of green in the category?

Your competitors Are our competitors greening their existing products?

Can we differentiate our brand?

How can we exploit our competitors' green weaknesses?

How can we capture a "share of voice" in the category?

Red flags Do we have environmental skeletons in our current portfolio or business model?

Will our green claims be credible—or are we vulnerable to accusations of "greenwashing"?

Acquire

First steps What's our strategic goal?

- To capture customers?
- Bring in new green capabilities?
- Broaden access to mainstream customers?
- Gain green credibility?

Which companies would make attractive green acquisitions?

Do we have the resources and capabilities needed for this initiative?

Your portfolio How will this initiative affect the positioning of and resources for our existing brands?

Will the initiative provide new abilities that can be applied to other brands?

Should our acquired brand be a stand-alone or a strategic brand that puts a green halo on the business as a whole?

Your customers Can we sell the green brand to our current customers?

Will acquired customers view us as a credible steward of the brand?

Your competitors Is this the prototypical brand in the green niche?

How can we exploit our competitors' green weaknesses?

How can we prevent competitors from poaching our newly acquired customers?

Can we add green attributes to the new brand or emphasize existing attributes to increase competitiveness?

Red flags Do we have environmental skeletons in our current portfolio or business model?

Will our green claims be credible—or are we vulnerable to accusations of "greenwashing"?

Does the proposed acquisition have an iconic founder, a countercultural workforce, or some other aspect that might create culture clash?

Can we preserve the integrity—"the magic"—of the acquired brand?

Architect

First steps What's our strategic goal?

- To create new green solutions?
- Develop unique competencies?
- Respond to new market needs?
- Gain green credibility?

Will an independent business unit be required?

Do we have the resources and capabilities needed for this initiative?

Your portfolio How will this initiative affect the positioning of and resources for our existing brands?

Will the initiative provide new abilities that can be applied to other brands?

What will be the relationship between the parent and the new line?

Your customers What innovations are consumers looking for in a greener alternative?

Does our parent brand have "permission" to enter the green space?

Will this initiative require us to develop a new brand?

Will we need to educate and develop the market and bring new customers into the category?

Your competitors Are we creating a new green category?

Can we differentiate our brand?

How can we exploit our competitors' green weaknesses?

Does the category already have entrenched competitors?

Red flags Do we have environmental skeletons in our current portfolio or business model?

Will our green claims be credible—or are we vulnerable to accusations of "greenwashing"?

Best Practices: Who Architects Well?

New-product development: Toyota directed its engineers to develop a new fuel-efficient and environmentally friendly vehicle within three years.

New production methods: Patagonia created a line of products using a closed-loop production system it calls EcoCircle.

Skunkworks: Clorox provided the resources for a separate Green Works business unit.

the initiative will require. For example, an acquire strategy will deliver high speed to market for a company setting out with low green credentials and low to medium green capabilities—but it involves significant investment. A company choosing an architect strategy must have high green capabilities and medium to high green credentials—and be prepared for a low speed to market. Companies unwilling or unable to allocate major resources for green initiatives will find accentuation the most attractive way to enter green markets. For others, green growth may be part of an enterprisewide sustainability initiative to retool operations, shift the culture, and, ultimately, reposition the organization.

Implementation. This third step involves acting on all the factors that affect successful execution. As outlined in the exhibit "Analyzing Growth Options," companies must align their green strategy with their existing product portfolio and devote or develop the re-

sources and capabilities needed to achieve their strategic goals. They must ensure that the strategy satisfies customers' expectations and, when possible, takes advantage of competitors' green weaknesses. Finally, they must address "red flag" issues that could undermine implementation.

Whatever path you choose—accentuate, acquire, or architect—activists, customers, and the public won't see your green initiatives as independent of your other activities and offerings. Rather, they will view your efforts as part of the organization's overall approach. That means the companies that ultimately succeed in growing green will be distinguished by their commitment to corporatewide sustainability as well as the performance of their green products.

Reprint R1006G
To order, call 800-988-0886 or 617-783-7500 or go to www.hbr.org

To Order

For *Harvard Business Review* reprints and subscriptions, call 800-988-0886 or 617-783-7500. Go to www.hbr.org

For customized and quantity orders of *Harvard Business Review* article reprints, call 617-783-7626, or e-mail customizations@hbsp.harvard.edu

Harvard Business Review

www.hbr.org

U.S. and Canada
800-988-0886
617-783-7500
617-783-7555 fax